Lynn Picknett and Clive Prince are writers, researchers and lecturers on the paranormal, the occult and historical and religious mysteries. Since 1989 they have worked together on the research which produced *Turin Shroud: In Whose Image?*, which revealed Leonardo's secret membership of an extensive heretical brotherhood as well as his connection with the world's most renowned fake.

The authors live in London.

D0035832

THE TEMPLAR REVELATION

SECRET GUARDIANS OF THE TRUE IDENTITY OF CHRIST

Lynn Picknett
and Clive Prince

CORGI BOOKS

THE TEMPLAR REVELATION
A CORGI BOOK : 0 552 14330 8

Originally published in Great Britain by Bantam Press,
a division of Transworld Publishers

PRINTING HISTORY
Bantam Press edition published 1997
Corgi edition published 1998

9 10 8

Set in 10/11pt Century Old Style by
Phoenix Typesetting, Ilkley, West Yorkshire.

Corgi Books are published by Transworld Publishers,
61–63 Uxbridge Road, London W5 5SA,
a division of The Random House Group Ltd,
in Australia by Random House Australia (Pty) Ltd,
20 Alfred Street, Milsons Point, Sydney, NSW 2061, Australia,
in New Zealand by Random House New Zealand Ltd,
18 Poland Road, Glenfield, Auckland 10, New Zealand
and in South Africa by Random House (Pty) Ltd,
Endulini, 5a Jubilee Road, Parktown 2193, South Africa.

Printed and bound in Great Britain by
Cox & Wyman Ltd, Reading, Berkshire.

*For those we love most, both in time
and beyond . . .*

Acknowledgements

This book would not have been possible without the help and support of a great many people, but, due to the controversial nature of our conclusions, we must point out that those listed below do not necessarily share our opinions.

We would like to thank:

Keith Prince, for his meticulous research, both in the library and in the field, on our behalf, for his incisive and often highly unorthodox thoughts on the subject – and for literally risking life and limb for this project.

Craig Oakley, for unfailing support, enthusiasm and help with our research.

Filip Coppens, for enthusiastically directing us to, and supplying us with, much invaluable research material.

Lavinia Trevor, our agent, for smoothing the way for this book and keeping the pressure off us.

Jim Cochrane, our editor at Bantam Press, for his informed and constructive comments – and for keeping the pressure *on* us. And thanks too, to his colleagues Kate Melhuish, Sheila Corr and Martin Macrae.

Lucien Morgan, for really making us think about this book!

The material on Rennes-le-Château in chapters Eight and Nine owes a great debt to information supplied by, and discussions with, many people:

In the UK, to members of the Rennes-le-Château Research group, especially John and Joy Millar, Gay Roberts, Howard Barkway, Jonothon Boulter, Marke Pawson, and Guy Patton. Thanks to Guy also for help with our research into the Knights Templar.

In France, particular thanks are due to Alain Féral, Sonia Moreu, Antoine and Claire Captier, Jean-Luc and Louise Robin,

Celia Brooke, Marcel Captier and Elizabeth van Buren. (And also to Monique and Michel Marrot at La Pomme Bleue at Rennes-le-Château, whose meals often made our day.) We would also like to acknowledge our debt to the late Jos Bertaulet and his research into Notre-Dame de Marceille. Thanks to his widow Suzanne and sons Christian and Diederick for their hospitality.

John Stephenson and Anita Forsythe, for looking after us at Ferran, enlivening our trips to the Languedoc and sharing their local knowledge with us. Thanks too for their wonderful hospitality and entertainment, and for lending us Gold.

Peter Humber for allowing us to use his house in the Languedoc during our first research trip, and for his *very* relaxed reaction to what we nearly did to it . . . and thanks too, to the villagers of Ferran and the Fire Department of Montréal for coming to our aid on that fateful 17 January 1995. And also for Peter's late-lamented Café Fou in Boundary Road, which seemed fated to be our refuge, somehow.

Robert Howells, for many highly enjoyable after-hours discussions into all matters esoteric, and for the benefit of his wide-ranging knowledge.

André Douzet, for generously sharing the results of his exhaustive research into French mysteries.

Niven Sinclair, for his great generosity and fascinating insights into Rosslyn Chapel and the Knights Templar.

Jane Lyle, for sharing her extensive knowledge about sacred sexuality with us, and – as always – for laughter, encouragement and practical support.

Steve Wilson, for his help with the Mandaeans, for giving us a platform at 'Talking Stick' and for an entertaining and memorable train journey.

Karine Esparseil López, for her help with French translations, support and much-valued friendship.

Thanks also to the following for their help in various ways, either by supplying us with much-needed information or simply with their support and encouragement:

Nicole Dawe and Charles Bywaters and and their respective

daughters, Laura Dawe and Kathryn and Jennifer Bywaters; Trevor Poots; Andy Collins; Dominique Hyde; Lionel Beer and his TEMS group; Steve Moore of *Fortean Times*; Bob and Veronica Cowley of RILKO; Georges Keiss; Yuri Stoyanov; Benoist Rivière; Henri Buthion; Jean-Pierre Aptel; André Galaup; Louis Vazart; Gino Sandri; Manfred Cassirer; Alun Harris; John Spencer; Steve Pear; Olivia Robertson of the Fellowship of Isis; Caroline Wise; Gareth Medway; Tony Pritchett; Mick and Lorraine Jones; Mark Bennett; Dave Smith and Natalie Hac; Loren McLaughlin; David N. Corona; Dr Richard Wiseman; Sylvia Patton; Barry and Fiona Johnstone; Sarah Litvinoff; Vida Adamoli; Helen Scott; Michèle Kaczynski; Mary Saxe-Falstein; Sally 'Morgana' Morgan; Will Fowler; Sheila and Eric Taylor; Samuel López; James Dew; Nic Davis; Lisa Bailey; David Bell; I-N. And to the staff of the British Library Reading Rooms and the Westminster Reference Library.

Thanks to the joint emergency services of Limoux and Carcassonne for rescuing Keith Prince – and to our anonymous friend who telephoned for help from Notre-Dame de Marceille.

THE TEMPLAR
REVELATION

Contents

Introduction   15

Part One: The Threads of Heresy   19

1: The Secret Code of Leonardo da Vinci   21

2: Into the Underworld   43

3: In the Footsteps of the Magdalene   73

4: Heartland of Heresy   108

5: Guardians of the Grail   134

6: The Templar Legacy   162

7: Sex: The Ultimate Sacrament   198

8: 'This is a Terrible Place'   239

9: A Curious Treasure   265

10: Divining the Underground Stream   291

Part Two: The Web of Truth   297

11: Gospel Untruths   299

12: The Woman Whom Jesus Kissed   323

13: Son of the Goddess   349

14: John Christ   400

15: Followers of the King of Light   427

16: The Great Heresy   444

17: Out of Egypt   463

Appendix 1   Continental Occult Freemasonry   481

Appendix II   Rennes-le-Château and the 'Tomb
of God'   485
Notes and References   490
Select Bibliography   534
Index   547

Introduction

Leonardo da Vinci started the quest that led to this book. It was our research into that fascinating but elusive Renaissance genius and his part in faking the Turin Shroud that developed into a much wider and more involving investigation into the 'heresies' that had secretly driven his ambitions. We had to find out what he was part of, what he knew and believed, and why he had employed certain codes and symbols in the work he left for posterity. So – although we are aware that this is a mixed blessing – we have Leonardo to thank for the discoveries that have become this book.

It seemed strange at first to find ourselves drawn into the complex and often murky world of secret societies and heterodox beliefs. After all, Leonardo is commonly supposed to have been an atheist and a rationalist. But we were to find that he was no such thing. Very soon, in any case, we had left him behind and found ourselves alone with some profoundly disturbing implications. What had started as a modest enquiry into some interesting but hardly world-shattering cults had become an investigation into the very roots and beliefs of Christianity itself.

It was essentially a journey through time and space: first forward from Leonardo to the present day, then backwards beyond the Renaissance, through the Middle Ages to first-century Palestine, to the scene set by the words and deeds of our three main protagonists – John the Baptist, Mary Magdalene and Jesus. Along the way we had to pause and examine many groups and secret organizations with a totally new and objective eye: the Freemasons, the Knights Templar, the Cathars, the Priory of Sion, the Essenes and the cult of Isis and Osiris.

Of course these subjects have been discussed in many other

recent books, notably *The Holy Blood and the Holy Grail* by Michael Baigent, Richard Leigh and Henry Lincoln – which was originally a particular inspiration to both of us – *The Sign and the Seal* by Graham Hancock, *The Temple and the Lodge* by Baigent and Leigh, and most recently, *The Hiram Key* by Christopher Knight and Robert Lomas. We owe a debt of gratitude to all these writers for the light they have shed on our shared areas of investigation, but we believe that all of them have failed to find the essential key to the heart of these mysteries.

This is hardly surprising. Our entire culture is based on certain assumptions about the past, and in particular about Christianity and the character and motives of its founder. But if those assumptions are *wrong*, then the conclusions based on them will stop very short of the truth, or will at least present a distorted picture of the facts.

When we first confronted the disturbing conclusions that we set out in this book we had to believe we were mistaken. But there came a point when we had to make a decision: should we carry on with our investigation and make our conclusions public, or forget we had ever made those crucial discoveries? We decided to go ahead; after all, this book seems to follow on naturally from those listed above as if its time has truly come.

In tracing the beliefs held by thousands of 'heretics' over the centuries we have uncovered a remarkably consistent picture. Underneath the traditions of many apparently disparate groups there lie the same – or very similar – secrets. At first we thought that these societies were secret out of mere custom, or perhaps affectation – but now we understand why they needed to keep their knowledge away from the authorities, and especially from the Church. The main question, however, is not what they believed, but whether or not those beliefs were based on anything substantial. For if they were, and if the heretical underground really did hold the missing key to Christianity, then what we are left with is a truly revolutionary scenario.

This book traces our eight-year quest into largely uncharted territory, for although others have made maps for us to follow, they stopped short of where we had to go.

Lynn Picknett
Clive Prince
St John's Wood
London
    22 July 1996

PART ONE

THE THREADS OF HERESY

CHAPTER ONE

The Secret Code of Leonardo da Vinci

It is one of the most famous – and enduring – works of art in the world. Leonardo da Vinci's fresco *The Last Supper* is the one surviving piece of the original church of Santa Maria delle Grazie near Milan, being on the only wall that remained standing after Allied bombing reduced the rest of the building to rubble in the Second World War. Although many other admired artists such as Ghirlandaio and Nicolas Poussin – even such an idiosyncratic painter as Salvador Dali – have also given the world their version of this significant biblical scene, it is Leonardo's which has, for some reason, captured the imagination more than most. Versions of it are seen everywhere, encompassing both ends of the spectrum of taste, from the sublime to the ridiculous.

Some images may be so familiar that they are never truly examined, and although they lie openly before the viewer's gaze and invite closer scrutiny, at their most profound and meaningful level they actually remain totally closed books. So it is with Leonardo's *Last Supper* – and, unbelievably enough, with almost all of his other remaining works.

It was the work of Leonardo (1452–1519) – that tortured genius of Renaissance Italy – that was to draw us on to a path that led to discoveries so breathtaking in their implications that at first it seemed impossible: impossible that generations of academics had simply not observed what leapt to our startled notice – and impossible that such explosive information had lain patiently waiting all this time for writers like us from outside the mainstream of historical or religious research to discover.

So, to begin our story proper we have to return to Leonardo's

Last Supper and look at it with new eyes. This is not the time to view it in the context of the familiar art-historical assumptions. This is the moment when it is appropriate to see it as a complete newcomer to this most familiar of scenes would see it, to let the scales of preconception fall from one's eyes and, perhaps for the first time, really look at it.

The central figure is, of course, that of Jesus, whom Leonardo referred to as 'the Redeemer' in his notes for the work. (Even so, the reader is warned against making any of the obvious assumptions here.) He looks contemplatively downwards and slightly to his left, hands outstretched on the table before him as if presenting some gift to the viewer. As this is the Last Supper at which, so the New Testament tells us, Jesus initiated the sacrament of the bread and wine, urging his followers to partake of them as his 'flesh' and 'blood', one might reasonably expect some chalice or cup of wine to be set before him, to be encompassed by that gesture. After all, for Christians this meal came immediately before Jesus' 'Passion' in the garden of Gethsemane when he fervently prayed that 'this cup pass from me . . .' – another allusion to the wine/blood imagery – and also before his death by crucifixion when his holy blood was spilled on behalf of all mankind. Yet there is no wine in front of Jesus (and a mere token amount on the whole table). Could it be that those spread hands are making what, according to the artists, is essentially an empty gesture?

In the light of the missing wine, perhaps it is also no accident that of all the bread on the table very little is actually broken. As Jesus himself identified the bread with his own body which was to be broken in the supreme sacrifice, is some subtle message being conveyed about the true nature of Jesus' suffering?

This, however, is merely the tip of the iceberg of the unorthodoxy depicted in this painting. In the biblical account it is the young St John – known as 'the Beloved' – who was physically so close to Jesus on this occasion as to be leaning 'on his bosom'. Yet Leonardo's representation of this young person does not, as required by the biblical 'stage directions', so recline, but instead leans exaggeratedly away from the Redeemer, head almost coquettishly tilted to the right. Even where this one character is concerned this is by no means all, for newcomers to the painting might be forgiven for harbouring curious uncertainties about the so-called St John. For while it is true that the artist's own predilections tended to represent the epitome of male beauty as somewhat effeminate, *surely this is a woman we are looking at.* Everything about 'him' is startlingly feminine. Aged and weathered though the fresco may be, one can still make out the tiny, graceful hands, the pretty, elfin features, the distinctly female bosom and the gold necklace. This woman, for surely it is such, is also wearing garments that mark her out as being special. They are the mirror image of the Redeemer's: where one wears a blue robe and a red cloak, the other wears a red robe and a blue cloak in the identical style. No-one else at the table wears clothes that mirror those of Jesus in this way. But then no-one else at the table is a woman.

Central to the overall composition is the shape that Jesus and this woman make together – a giant, spreadeagled 'M', almost as if they were literally joined at the hip but had suffered a falling out, or even grown apart. To our knowledge no academic has referred to this feminine character as anything other than 'St John', and the 'M' shape has also passed them by. Leonardo was, we have discovered in our researches, an excellent psychologist who amused himself by presenting the patrons who had given him standard religious commissions with highly unorthodox images, knowing that people will view the most startling heresy with equanimity because they usually only see what they expect to see. If you are commissioned to paint a standard Christian scene and present the public with something that looks superficially like it, they will never question its dubious symbolism. Yet Leonardo must have hoped that perhaps others who shared his unusual interpretation of the New Testament message would recognize his version, or that someone, somewhere, some objective observer, would one day seize on the image of this mysterious woman linked with the letter 'M' and ask the obvious questions. Who was this 'M' and why was she so important? Why would Leonardo risk his reputation – even his life in those days of the flaming pyre – to include her in this crucial Christian scene?

Whoever she is, her own fate appears to be less than secure, for a hand cuts across her gracefully bent neck in what seems to be a threatening gesture. The Redeemer, too, is menaced by an upright forefinger positively thrust into his face with obvious vehemence. Both Jesus and 'M' appear totally oblivious to these threats, each apparently lost in the world of their own thoughts, each in their own way serene and composed. But it is as if secret symbols are being employed, not only to warn Jesus and his female companion of their separate fates, but also to instruct (or perhaps remind) the observer of some information which it would otherwise be dangerous to make public. Is Leonardo using this painting to convey some private belief which it would have been little short of insane to share with a wider audience in any obvious fashion? And could it be that this belief might have a message for many more than his immediate circle, perhaps even for us today?

Let us look further at this astonishing work. To the observer's right of the fresco a tall bearded man bends almost double to speak to the last disciple at the table. In doing so he has turned his back completely on the Redeemer. It is this disciple – St Thaddeus or St Jude – whose model is acknowledged to be Leonardo himself. Nothing that Renaissance painters ever depicted was accidental or included merely to be pretty, and this particular exemplar of the time and the profession was known to be a stickler for the visual *double entendre*. (His preoccupation with using the right model for the various disciples can be detected in his wry suggestion that the irritating Prior of the Santa Maria Monastery himself sit for the character of Judas!) So why did Leonardo paint himself looking so obviously away from Jesus?

There is more. An anomalous hand points a dagger at a disciple's stomach one person away from 'M'. By no stretch of the imagination could the hand belong to anyone sitting at that table because it is physically impossible for those near by to have twisted round to get the dagger in that position. However, what is truly amazing about this disembodied hand is not so much that it exists, but that in all our reading about Leonardo we have come across only a couple of references to it, and they show a curious reluctance to find anything unusual about it. Like the St John who is really a woman, nothing could be more obvious – and more bizarre – once it is pointed out, yet usually it is completely blanked out by the observer's eye and mind simply because it is so extraordinary and so outrageous.

We have often heard it said that Leonardo was a pious Christian whose religious paintings reflected the depth of his faith. As we have seen so far, at least one of them includes highly dubious imagery in terms of Christian orthodoxy, and our further research, as we shall see, reveals that nothing could be further from the truth than the idea that Leonardo was a true believer – a believer, that is, in any accepted, or acceptable, form of Christianity. Already, the curious and anomalous features in just one of his works seem to indicate that he was trying to tell us of another layer of meaning in that familiar biblical scene, of another world of belief beyond the accepted outline of the image frozen on that fifteenth-century mural near Milan.

Whatever those heterodox inclusions may mean, they were, it cannot be stressed too much, totally at variance with orthodox Christianity. This itself is hardly news to many of today's materialist/rationalists, for to them Leonardo was the first real scientist, a man who had no time for superstitions or religion in any form, who was the very antithesis of the mystic or the occultist. Yet they, too, have failed to see what is plainly set out before their eyes. To paint the Last Supper without significant amounts of wine is like painting the critical moment of a coronation without the crown: it either misses the point completely or is making quite another one, to the extent that it marks the painter out as nothing less than an out and out heretic, someone who did possess religious beliefs, but

25

ones which were at odds, perhaps even at war, with those of Christian orthodoxy. And Leonardo's other works, we have discovered, underline his own specific heretical obsessions through carefully applied and consistent imagery, something that would not happen if the artist were an atheist merely engaged in earning his living. These uncalled for inclusions and symbols are also much, much more than the sceptic's satirical response to such a commission – they are not just the equivalent of sticking a red nose on St Peter, for example. What we are looking at in the *Last Supper* and his other works is the secret code of Leonardo da Vinci, which we believe has a startling relevance to the world today.

It may be argued that whatever Leonardo did or did not believe, this was merely the foible of one man, and a notoriously odd man at that, one whose story was one of endless paradoxes. He might have been a loner, but he was also the life and soul of the party; he despised fortune-tellers, but his accounts listed monies paid to astrologers; he was a vegetarian and caring animal-lover but his tenderness rarely extended to humankind; he obsessively dissected corpses and watched executions with an anatomist's eye; he was both a profound thinker and a master of riddles, conjuring tricks and hoaxes. Given such a complex outlook, it is perhaps only to be expected that his personal views on religion and philosophy were unusual, even quirky. For that reason alone, it may be tempting to dismiss his heretical beliefs as irrelevant to today. While it is generally admitted that Leonardo was hugely gifted, the modern tendency to arrogant 'epochism' seeks to undermine his achievements. After all, when he was in his prime, even the technique of printing was a novelty. What could one lone inventor of such a primitive time possibly have to offer a world that is endlessly informed by surfing the Net, and which can, in a matter of seconds, communicate through the telephone or the fax machine with people on continents that had not even been discovered in his day?

There are two answers to that. The first is that Leonardo was not, to use a paradox, a run-of-the-mill genius. Whereas most people know that he designed flying machines and primitive military tanks, some of his inventions were so unlikely for his day that those of a more whimsical turn of mind have even suggested that he might have actually had visions of the future. His designs for a bicycle, for example, only came to light in the late 1960s[1]. Unlike the painfully protracted trial-and-error stages in the development of the early Victorian bicycle, however, *the da Vinci roadracer had two wheels of equal size and a chain and gear mechanism.* But even more fascinating than the actual design, is the question of what possible reason he could have had for inventing a bike in the first place. For man has always wanted to fly like the birds, but having a driving desire to pedal along less than perfect roads precariously balanced on two wheels is completely mystifying (and does not, unlike flying, figure in any classic fable). Leonardo also predicted the telephone, among many other futuristic claims to fame.

If Leonardo was even more of a genius than the history books allow, there is still the question as to what possible knowledge he could have had that would impinge in any meaningful or widespread way five centuries after he lived. While it might be argued that the teachings of a first-century rabbi might be expected to have even less relevance to our time and place, it is also true that some ideas are universal and eternal, and that the truth, if it can be found or defined, is never essentially undermined by the passage of the centuries.

It was not, however, either Leonardo's philosophy (whether overt or covert) or his art which first attracted both of us to him. It was his most paradoxical work, one that is both incredibly famous and at the same time least known, which drew us into our intensive Leonardo research. As described in detail in our last book[2], we discovered that it was the Maestro who had faked the Turin Shroud, which had long been believed to have been miraculously imprinted with Jesus' image at the time of his death. In 1988, carbon dating tests proved it to all but a handful of desperate believers to be an artefact of late medieval or early Renaissance times, but to us it remained a truly remarkable image – to say the least. Uppermost in our minds was the question of the identity of the hoaxer, for whoever had created this amazing 'relic' had to be a genius.

The Turin Shroud, as all the literature – both for and against its authenticity – recognizes, behaves like a photograph. It exhibits a curious 'negative effect', which means that it looks like a vague scorchmark to the naked eye but can be seen in fine detail in photographic negative. Because no known painting or brassrubbing behaves in this way, the negative effect has been taken by the 'Shroudies' (believers that it is truly the Shroud of Jesus) to be proof of the miraculous qualities of the image. However, we discovered that the image on the Turin Shroud behaves like a photograph *because that is precisely what it is*.

Incredible though it may seem at first, the Turin Shroud is a photograph. We, together with Keith Prince, reconstructed what we believed the original technique to be and in doing so became the first people ever to replicate all the hitherto un-explained characteristics of the Turin Shroud[3]. And, despite the Shroudies' claims that it was impossible, we did so using extremely basic equipment. We used a camera obscura (a pinhole camera), chemically coated cloth, treated with materials readily available in the fifteenth century, and large doses of light. However, the subject of our experimental photo-graph was a plaster bust of a girl, which was disappointingly lightyears away in status from the original model. For although the face on the Shroud was not, as had been widely claimed, that of Jesus, it was in fact the face of the hoaxer himself. In brief, *the Turin Shroud is, among many other things, a five-hundred-year-old photograph of none other than Leonardo da Vinci*.

Despite some curious claims to the contrary[4], this cannot have been the work of a pious Christian believer. The Turin Shroud, seen in photographic negative, apparently shows the broken and bleeding body of Jesus. It must be remembered that this is no ordinary blood, for to Christians it is not only literally divine: it is also the vehicle through which the world can be redeemed. To our minds, one simply cannot fake that blood and be considered a believer – nor could one have even the least respect for the person of Jesus and replace his image with that of oneself. Leonardo did both of these things, with meticulous care and even, one suspects, a certain relish. Of course he knew that, as the supposed image of Jesus – for no-one would realize it was the Florentine artist himself[5] – the Shroud would be prayed over by a sizeable number of pilgrims even during his own lifetime. For all we know he actually hovered in the shadows and watched them do it – it would have been in keeping with what we know of his character. But did he also guess just how many pilgrims would be crossing themselves in front of his image over the centuries? Did he imagine that one day intelligent people would actually be converted to Catholicism simply by looking into that beautiful, tortured face? And could he possibly have foreseen that the West's cultural image of what Jesus looked like would come largely from the image on the Turin Shroud? Did he realize that one day millions of people the world over would be worshipping the image of a fifteenth-century homosexual heretic in the place of their beloved God, that *Leonardo da Vinci was literally to become the image of Jesus Christ?*

The Shroud was, we believe, *very nearly* the most outrageous – and successful – joke ever played on history. But, although it has fooled millions, it is more than a hymn to the art of the tasteless hoax. We believe that Leonardo used the opportunity to create the ultimate Christian relic as a vehicle for two things: an innovative technique and an encoded heretical belief. The technique of primitive photography was – as events were to show[6] – highly dangerous to make public in that paranoid and superstitious era. But it no doubt amused Leonardo to make sure that this prototype was looked after by the very priests he despised. Of course it could be that this ironic priestly guardianship was purely coincidental, merely a fateful twist in an already remarkable story, but to us it smacks of Leonardo's passion for total control, which can be seen here to reach far beyond the grave.

The Turin Shroud, fake and work of genius though it is, also carries certain symbols that underline Leonardo's own particular obsessions, as seen in his other, more generally accepted, works. For example, there is at the base of Shroudman's neck a distinct demarcation line. When the image as a whole is turned into a 'contour map', using the most sophisticated computer technology, we can see that the line marks the lower end of the head image at the front, while there is, as it were, a sea of unimaged, flat darkness immediately under it until the image begins again at the upper chest[7]. We believe there are two reasons for this. One is purely practical, for the front image is a composite, the body being that of a genuinely crucified man and the face being Leonardo's own, so that line perhaps of necessity indicates the 'join' of the two images. However, this hoaxer was no mean workman, and it would have been relatively easy to obscure or fudge that tell-tale demarcation line. But what if Leonardo, in fact, actually had no desire to get rid of it? What if he left it there deliberately in order to make a point 'for those with eyes to see'?

What possible heresy can the Turin Shroud carry, even in code? Surely there is a limit to the symbols one can hide in a simple, stark image of a naked crucified man – and one that has been analyzed by many top scientists using state-of-the-art equipment? While we will be returning to this theme in due course, let us merely hint for now that these questions may be answered by looking afresh at two main aspects of the image. The first concerns the abundance of blood which appears to be running freshly down Jesus' arms – and which may appear, superficially, to contradict the symbolic lack of wine on the table of the *Last Supper*, but which in fact reinforces that particular point. The second concerns the obvious demarcation line between head and body, as if Leonardo were drawing our attention to a beheading... As far as we know, Jesus was not beheaded and the image is a composite, so we are being asked to consider the images of two separate characters who were nevertheless closely linked in some way. But even so, why should someone who was beheaded be set 'over' one who was crucified?

As will be seen, this clue of the severed head on the Turin Shroud is merely a reinforcement of symbols in many of Leonardo's other works. We have noted how the anomalous young woman, 'M', in his *Last Supper*, is apparently being menaced by a hand slicing across her delicate neck, and how Jesus himself is being threatened by an upright finger thrust into his face, apparently as a warning – or perhaps a reminder, or both. In Leonardo's works this upright forefinger is always, in every case, a direct reference to John the Baptist.

This saint, the alleged forerunner of Jesus, who told the world to 'behold the Lamb of God', whose sandals he was not worthy to unlatch, was of supreme importance to Leonardo, if only to judge from his omnipresence in the artist's surviving works. This obsession itself is curious for one who is so widely deemed by modern rationalists to have had no time for religion. A man to whom all the characters and traditions of Christianity were as nothing would hardly have devoted so much time and energy to one particular saint as he did to John the Baptist. Time and time again it is this John who dominates Leonardo's life, both at a conscious level in his works and at a synchronistic level in the coincidences that surrounded him. It is almost as if the Baptist followed him around. For example, his beloved city of Florence itself is dedicated to that saint, as is the cathedral in Turin wherein Leonardo's fake Holy Shroud lies in state. His last painting, which, with the *Mona Lisa*, stood unclaimed in the chamber of his dying hours, was of John the Baptist, and his only surviving piece of sculpture (executed together with Giovan Francesco Rustici, a known occultist) also depicted the Baptist. It now stands above the entrance to the baptistry in Florence, high above the heads of the tourists and, unfortunately, providing fair game for the irreverent flocks of pigeons.

That upright forefinger – what we call the 'John gesture' – was featured in Raphael's *The School of Athens* (1509). There we see the venerable character of Plato exhibiting this sign, but in the circumstances it is not quite such a mysterious

31

allusion as one might suspect. In fact, the model for Plato was none other than Leonardo himself, obviously making a gesture that was not only characteristic of him in some way, but also profoundly significant to him (and presumably also to Raphael and others of their circle).

In case it is thought that we are making too much of what we term 'the John gesture', let us look at other examples of it in Leonardo's work.

It figures in several of his paintings and, as we have said, always carries the same significance. In his unfinished *Adoration of the Magi* (which was begun in 1481) an anonymous bystander makes this gesture close to a mound of earth out of which grows a carob tree. Most observers would hardly notice this, for their eyes would inevitably be drawn to what they would believe the whole point of the picture to be – as the title suggests, the worshipping of the Holy Family by the 'wise men', or Magi. The beautiful and dreamy Virgin, with the infant Jesus on her knee, is portrayed as an insipid and colourless character. The Magi kneel, presenting her with their gifts for the child, while in the background a crowd mills around, apparently also worshipping the mother and child. But, like the *Last Supper*, this is only superficially a Christian painting and repays closer scrutiny.

The worshippers in the foreground are hardly examples of health and beauty. Gaunt almost to the point of being corpse-like, their outstretched hands appear not so much to be raised in wonderment but more as if they are clawing in a nightmarish fashion at the couple. The Magi present their gifts – but only two of the legendary three. Frankincense and myrrh are being offered, but no gold. To those of Leonardo's day, gold meant not only immediate wealth, but was also a symbol of kingship – and here it is being withheld from Jesus.

If one looks behind the Virgin and the Magi there appears to be a second group of worshippers. These are much healthier and more normal-looking – but if one follows their eyelines it is obvious that they are not looking at the Virgin and child at all, but seem instead to be revering the roots of the carob tree, at which one man is making the 'John gesture'. And the carob tree is traditionally associated with – John the Baptist[8] . . .

Down to the bottom right-hand corner of the painting a young man turns deliberately away from the Holy Family. It is generally accepted that this is Leonardo himself, but the somewhat weak argument that is often used to explain this aversion – that the artist felt himself unworthy to face them – will scarcely stand up. For Leonardo is widely known to have been no lover of the Church. Besides, in the character of St Thaddeus or St Jude in the *Last Supper* he is also pointedly turned away from the Redeemer, thus underlining some extreme emotional response to the central figures in the Christian story. And as Leonardo was hardly the epitome of either piety or humility, this reaction is unlikely to have been inspired by a sense of inferiority or obsequiousness.

Turning to Leonardo's beautiful and haunting cartoon for the *Virgin and Child with St Anne* (1501), which graces London's National Gallery, again there are elements that should – but rarely do – disturb the observer with their subversive implications. The drawing shows the Virgin and child together with St Anne (Mary's mother) and John the Baptist as a child. The infant Jesus is apparently blessing his cousin John, who gazes upwards reflectively, while St Anne peers intently into her daughter's oblivious face from close quarters – and is making the 'John gesture' with a curiously large and masculine hand. However, this upraised forefinger rises immediately over the tiny hand of Jesus which is giving the blessing, as if overshadowing it both literally and metaphorically. And although the Virgin appears to be seated in an extremely uncomfortable way – almost 'sidesaddle', in fact – it is the baby Jesus whose positioning is particularly odd. The Virgin holds him as if she has just thrust him forward to make his blessing, as if she has brought him into the picture simply to do so but can only hold him there with difficulty. Meanwhile, John rests casually against St Anne's knee as if unconcerned at the honour he is being given. Could it be that the Virgin's own mother is

33

reminding her of something secret connected with John?

According to the accompanying notice in the National Gallery, some art experts, puzzled by the youthfulness of St Anne and the anomalous presence of John the Baptist, have speculated that the painting actually depicted Mary and her cousin Elisabeth – *John's mother*. This seems plausible, and if correct, reinforces the point.

This apparent reversal of the usual roles of Jesus and John can also be seen on one of the two versions of Leonardo's *Virgin of the Rocks*. Art historians have never satisfactorily explained why there should be two, but one is currently exhibited in the National Gallery in London, and the other – to us by far the more interesting – is in the Louvre in Paris.

The original commission was from an organization known as the Confraternity of the Immaculate Conception, and was for a single painting to be the centrepiece of a triptych for the altar of their chapel in the church of San Francesco Grand in Milan[9]. (The other two paintings for the triptych were to be by other artists.) The contract, dated 25 April 1483, still exists, and sheds interesting light on the expected work – and on what the members of the confraternity actually received. In it they carefully specified the shape and dimensions of the painting they wanted – a necessity, for the frame for the triptych already existed. Oddly, both of Leonardo's finished versions meet these specifications, although why he did two of them is unknown. We may, however, hazard a guess about these divergent interpretations which has little to do with perfectionism and more with an awareness of their explosive potential.

The contract also specified the theme of the painting. It was to portray an event not found in the Gospels but long present in Christian legend. This was the story of how, during the flight into Egypt, Joseph, Mary and the baby Jesus had sheltered in a desert cave, where they met the infant John the Baptist, who was protected by the archangel Uriel. The point of this legend is that it allowed an escape from one of the more obvious and embarrassing questions raised by the Gospel

34

story of Jesus' baptism. Why should a supposedly sinless Jesus require baptism at all, given that the ritual is a symbolic gesture of having one's sins washed away and of one's commitment to future godliness? Why should the Son of God himself have submitted to what was clearly an act of authority on the part of the Baptist?

This legend tells how, at this remarkably fortuitous meeting of the two holy infants, Jesus conferred on his cousin John the authority to baptize him when they were both adults. For several reasons this seems to us to be a most ironic commission for the confraternity to give Leonardo, but equally one might suspect that he would have delighted in receiving it – and in making the interpretation, at least in one of the versions, very much his own.

In the style of the day, the members of the confraternity had specified a lavish and ornate painting, complete with lashings of gold leaf and a flurry of cherubs and ghostly Old Testament prophets to fill out the space. What they got in the end was quite different, to such an extent that relations between them and the artist became acrimonious, culminating in a lawsuit that dragged on for more than twenty years.

Leonardo chose to represent the scene as realistically as possible, with no extraneous characters – there were to be no fat cherubs or shadowy prophets of doom for him. In fact, the *dramatis personae* have been perhaps excessively whittled down, for although this scene supposedly depicts the flight into Egypt of the Holy Family, Joseph does not appear in it at all.

The Louvre version, which was the earlier, shows a blue-robed Virgin with a protective arm around one child, the other infant being grouped with Uriel. Curiously, the two children are identical, but odder still, it is the child with the angel who is blessing the other, and Mary's child who is kneeling in subservience. This has led art historians to assume that, for some reason, Leonardo chose to pose the child John with Mary. After all, there are no labels with which to identify the individuals, and surely the child who has the authority to bless must be Jesus.

There are, however, other ways to interpret this picture, ways that not only suggest strong subliminal and highly unorthodox messages, but also reinforce the codes used in Leonardo's other works. Perhaps the similarity of the two children here suggests that Leonardo was deliberately fudging their identity for his own purposes. And, while Mary is protectively embracing the child generally accepted as being John with her left hand, her right is stretched out above the head of 'Jesus' in what seems to be a gesture of downright hostility. This is what Serge Bramly, in his recent biography of Leonardo, describes as 'reminiscent of an eagle's talons'[10]. Uriel is pointing across to Mary's child, but is also, significantly, looking enigmatically out at the observer – that is, resolutely away from the Virgin and child. While it may be easier and more acceptable to interpret this gesture as an indication of the one who is to be the Messiah, there are other possible meanings.

What if the child with Mary, in the Louvre version of *The Virgin of the Rocks*, *is* Jesus – as one might logically expect – and the youngster with Uriel is John? Remember that in this case it is John who is blessing Jesus, with the latter submitting to his authority. Uriel, as John's special protector, is avoiding even looking at Jesus. And Mary, protecting her son, is casting a threatening hand high above the head of the baby John. Several inches directly below her outstretched palm the pointing hand of Uriel cuts straight across, as if the two gestures are encompassing some cryptic clue. It is as if Leonardo is indicating that some object, some significant – but invisible – thing ought to fill the space between them. In the context it is by no means fanciful to understand that Mary's outstretched fingers are meant to look as if they were placed on the crown of an invisible head, while Uriel's pointing forefinger cuts across the space precisely where the neck would be. This phantom head floats just above the child who is with Uriel . . . So this child *is* effectively labelled after all, for which of the two of them was to die by beheading? And if this is truly John the Baptist, it is he who is shown to be giving the blessing, to be the superior one.

Yet when we turn to the much later National Gallery version, we find that all the elements needed to make these heretical deductions are missing – but those elements only. The two children are quite different in appearance, and the one with Mary bears the traditional long-stemmed cross of the Baptist (although it is true that this may have been added by a later artist). Here Mary's right hand is still outstretched above the other child, but this time there is no suggestion of a threat. Uriel no longer points, nor looks away from the scene. It is as if Leonardo is inviting us to 'spot the difference' – daring us to draw our own conclusions from the anomalous details.

This kind of examination of Leonardo's work reveals a plethora of provocative and disturbing undercurrents. There does seem to be a repetition, using several ingenious subliminal symbols and signals, of the John the Baptist theme. Time and time again he, and images denoting him, are elevated above the figure of Jesus – even, if we are right, in the symbols that are cunningly laid on the Turin Shroud itself.

There is something driven about this insistence, not least in the very intricacy of the images that Leonardo used, and indeed, in the risk he took in presenting even such clever and subliminal heresy to the world. Perhaps, as we have already hinted, the reason he finished so little of his work was not so much that he was a perfectionist, but more that he was only too aware of what might happen to him if anyone of note saw through the thin layer of orthodoxy to the outright 'blasphemy' that lay just under the surface. Perhaps even the intellectual and physical giant that was Leonardo was a little wary of falling foul of the authorities – once was quite enough for him[11].

However, there was surely no need for him to put his head on the block by working such heretical messages into his paintings unless he had a passionate belief in them. As we have already seen, far from being the atheistic materialist so beloved of many moderns, Leonardo was deeply, seriously committed to a system of belief that ran totally counter to what was then, and still is now, mainstream Christianity. It was what many would choose to call the 'occult'.

To most people today that is a word that has immediate, and less than positive, connotations. It is taken to mean black magic, or the cavortings of depraved charlatans – or both. In fact, the word 'occult' simply means 'hidden' and is commonly used in astronomy, such as in the description of one heavenly body 'occulting', or eclipsing, another. Where Leonardo was concerned, one might agree that while there were indeed elements in his life and beliefs that smacked of sinister rites and magical practices, it is also true that what he sought was, above and beyond anything else, knowledge. Most of what he sought had, however, been effectively 'occulted' by society – and by one omnipresent and powerful organization in particular. Throughout most of Europe at that time the Church frowned upon any scientific experimentation and took drastic steps to silence those who made their unorthodox or particularly individual views public.

However, Florence – where Leonardo was born and brought up, and at whose court his career really began – was a flourishing centre for a new wave of knowledge. This, astonishingly enough, was due entirely to this city being a haven for large numbers of influential occultists and magicians. Leonardo's first patrons, the de Medici family who ruled Florence, actively encouraged occult scholarship and even sponsored researchers to look for, and translate, specific lost manuscripts.

· This fascination with the arcane was not the Renaissance equivalent of today's newspaper horoscopes. Although there were inevitably areas of investigation that would seem to us naive or downright superstitious, there were also many more which represented a serious attempt to understand the universe and man's place within it. The magician, however, sought to go a little further, and discover how to control the forces of nature. Seen in this light, perhaps it is not so remarkable that Leonardo of all people was, as we believe, an active participant in the occult culture of his time and place. And the distinguished historian Dame Frances Yates has even suggested that the whole key to Leonardo's far-ranging genius might have lain in contemporary ideas of magic[12].

The details of the precise philosophies so prevalent in this Florentine occult movement can be found in our previous book[13], but briefly, the lynchpin of all the groups of the day was hermeticism, which takes its name from Hermes Trismegistus, the great, if legendary, Egyptian magus whose books presented a coherent magical system. By far the most important part of hermetic thinking was the idea that man was in some way literally divine – a concept that was in itself so threatening to the Church's hold on the hearts and minds of its flock as to be deemed anathema.

Hermetic principles were certainly demonstrated in Leonardo's life and work, but at first glance there would seem to be a glaring discrepancy between these sophisticated philosophical and cosmological ideas and heretical notions which nevertheless upheld the importance of biblical figures. (We must stress that the heterodox beliefs of Leonardo and his circle were not merely the result of a reaction against a corrupt and credulous Church. As history has shown, there was indeed a strong, and certainly not undercover, reaction to the Church of Rome – the whole Protestant movement. But had Leonardo been alive today we would not find him worshipping in *that* kind of church either.)

However, there is a great deal of evidence that hermeticists could also be outright heretics. Giordano Bruno (1548–1600), the fanatical preacher of hermeticism, proclaimed that his beliefs came from an ancient Egyptian religion that preceded Christianity – and which eclipsed it in importance[14].

Part of this flourishing occult world – but still too wary of the Church's disapproval to be anything other than an underground movement – were the alchemists. Again they are a group which suffers from a modern preconception. Today they are derided as fools who wasted their lives trying vainly to turn base metal into gold; in fact this image was a useful smokescreen for the serious alchemists who were more concerned with proper scientific experimentation – but also with personal transformation and its implicit total control of one's own fate. Again, it is not difficult to see that someone as hungry for knowledge as Leonardo would be part of that movement, perhaps even a prime mover in it. While there is no direct evidence for his involvement, he was known to consort with committed occultists of all shades, and our own research into his faking of the Turin Shroud suggests strongly that the image was the direct result of his own 'alchemical' experiments. (In fact we have come to the conclusion that photography itself was once one of the great alchemical secrets[15].)

Put simply: it is highly unlikely that Leonardo would have been unfamiliar with any system of knowledge that was available in his day, but at the same time, given the risks involved in being openly part of them, it is equally unlikely that he would commit any evidence of this to paper. Yet, as we have seen, the symbols and images he repeatedly used in his so-called Christian paintings were hardly those which, had they realized their true nature, would have been appreciated by the Church authorities.

Even so, a fascination with hermeticism might seem, superficially at least, to be almost at the opposite end of the scale to a preoccupation with John the Baptist – and the putative significance of the woman 'M'. In fact, it was this discrepancy which puzzled us to such an extent that we delved further. Of course it could be argued that what all this endless raising of forefingers means is that one Renaissance genius was obsessed with John the Baptist. But was it possible that a deeper significance lay behind Leonardo's own personal belief? Was the message that can be read into his paintings in some way actually *true*?

Certainly the Maestro has long been acknowledged in occult circles as being the possessor of secret knowledge. When we began researching his part in the Turin Shroud we came across many rumours among such people to the effect not only that he had a hand in its creation, but also that he was a known magus of some renown. There is even a nineteenth-century Parisian poster advertising the Salon of the Rose + Cross – a meeting-place for artistically minded occultists – that depicts Leonardo as Keeper of the Holy Grail (which in such circles can be taken to be shorthand for Keeper of the Mysteries). Again, rumours and artistic licence do not in themselves add up to much, but, taken together with all the indications listed above, they certainly whetted our appetite to know more about the unknown Leonardo.

So far we had isolated the major strand of what appeared to be Leonardo's obsession: John the Baptist. While it was only natural that he would receive commissions to paint or sculpt that saint while living in Florence – a place that was dedicated to John – it is a fact that, when left to himself, Leonardo chose to do so. After all, the last painting he was to work on before his death in 1519 – which was not commissioned by anyone, but painted for his own reasons – was of John the Baptist. Perhaps he wanted the image to look at as he lay dying. And even when he had been paid to paint an orthodox Christian scene, he always, if he could get away with it, emphasized the role of the Baptist in it.

As we have seen, his images of John are elaborately concocted to convey a specific message, even if it is grasped imperfectly and subliminally. John is certainly depicted as important – but then he *was* the forerunner, herald and blood relative of Jesus, so it is only natural that his role should be recognized in this way. Yet Leonardo is not telling us that the Baptist was, like everyone else, inferior to Jesus. In his *Virgin of the Rocks* the angel is, arguably, pointing to *John*, who is blessing Jesus and not vice versa. In the *Adoration of the Magi* the healthy, normal-looking people are worshipping the elevated roots of the carob tree – John's tree – and not the colourless Virgin and child. And the 'John gesture', that upraised right-hand forefinger, is thrust into Jesus' face at the *Last Supper* in what is clearly no loving or supportive manner;

41

at the very least, it seems to be saying in a bluntly threatening manner, 'Remember John'. And that least known of Leonardo's works, the Shroud of Turin, bears the same kind of symbolism, with its image of an apparently severed head being placed 'over' a classically crucified body. The overwhelming evidence is that, to Leonardo at least, John the Baptist was actually superior to Jesus.

All this might make Leonardo appear to have been a voice crying in the wilderness. After all, many great minds have been eccentric, to say the least. Perhaps this was yet another area of his life in which he stood outside the conventions of his day, unappreciated and alone. But we were also aware, even at the outset of our research in the late 1980s, that evidence – albeit of a highly controversial nature – had emerged in recent years that linked him with a sinister and powerful secret society. This group, which allegedly existed many centuries before Leonardo, involved some of the most influential individuals and families in European history, and – according to some sources – it still exists today. Not only, it is said, were members of the aristocracy prime movers in this organization, but also some of today's most eminent figures in political and economic life keep it alive for their own particular aims.

If we had fondly imagined in those early days that we would be spending our time in art galleries decoding Renaissance paintings we could hardly have been further from the truth.

CHAPTER TWO

Into the Underworld

Our research into the 'unknown Leonardo' was to become a long and incredibly involved quest – more, one might say, of an initiation than a simple journey from A to B. Along the way we were to find ourselves in many blind alleys, and to become enmeshed in the underworld of those connected with secret societies who delight not only in playing sinister games but also in being the agents of misinformation and confusion. We often found ourselves bemusedly wondering just how simple research into the life and work of Leonardo da Vinci could possibly have led us into a world that we had not believed existed outside one of the more impenetrable movies of the great French surrealist Jean Cocteau such as his *Orphée,* with its depiction of an Underworld reached by magically walking through mirrors.

In fact it was that very exponent of the bizarre – Cocteau – who was to provide yet more clues not only about Leonardo's own beliefs, but also about the existence of a continuing underground tradition that had the same preoccupations. We were to discover that Cocteau (1889–1963) does seem to have been involved in this secret society – the evidence for which will be discussed below. But first let us analyse the most immediate sort of evidence – that of one's own eyes.

Surprisingly close to the bright lights and clamour of London's Leicester Square is the church of Notre-Dame de France. Located in Leicester Place, virtually next door to a fashionably popular 'adult' ice-cream parlour, it is notoriously difficult to find, because its facade hardly announces itself with the flamboyance that one has come to associate with large Catholic churches. One can walk past it without a second glance, and certainly without realizing just how significantly its decor differs from that of most other Christian churches.

Originally built in 1865 on a site with associations with the Knights Templar, Notre-Dame de France was almost totally destroyed by Nazi bombs in the Blitz, and rebuilt in the late 1950s. Once past its modest exterior, the visitor finds him or herself in a large, high, airy hall that at first may seem typical of modern Catholic design. Almost bereft of the garish statuary that over-adorns many older buildings, it nevertheless contains small plaques depicting the Stations of the Cross, a high altar beneath a large tapestry of a young blonde Virgin surrounded by adoring animals – which, although somewhat reminiscent of one of Disney's more cutesy scenes, is still within what constitutes an acceptable depiction of the youthful Mary – and a few plaster saints presiding over side chapels. But to the visitor's left side, as he or she looks towards the main altar, there is a small chapel that has no cult statue, but nevertheless has very much its own cult following. Visitors come to admire and take photographs of its unusual mural, which was the work of Jean Cocteau, who finished it in 1960, and the church is proud to sell postcards of its very own, and rightly famous, work of art. But, just as in the case of Leonardo's so-called 'Christian' paintings, this fresco, when meticulously scrutinized, reveals considerably less than orthodox symbolism. And the comparison with Leonardo's work is no accident. Even given the gap of some 500 years, could it nevertheless be said that he and Cocteau were somehow collaborating across the centuries?

Before we turn our attention to Cocteau's curiosity, let us look at the church of Notre-Dame de France in general. Although not unique, it is certainly unusual for a Catholic church to be round, and here its shape is actually emphasized in several details. For example, there is a striking, dome-shaped skylight decorated with a design of concentric rings, which it may not be too fanciful to interpret as some kind of spider's web. And the walls, both inside and out, bear the repeated motif of alternate equal-armed crosses – and yet more circles.

The post-war church, new though it might be, rose up proudly incorporating a stone slab which had been taken from Chartres Cathedral, that jewel in the crown of Gothic architecture – and, as we were to discover, a focus for those groups whose religious beliefs were not nearly as orthodox as the history books would lead us to believe. It may be objected that there is nothing particularly profound or sinister in including such a stone – after all, during the war, this church was a meeting point for the Free French forces and a piece of Chartres was, surely, a poignant symbol of all the home country ever stood for. However, our research was to show that there was indeed more to it than that.

Day in and day out many people – Londoners and visitors alike – stop by Notre-Dame de France to pray and take part in religious services. The church seems to be one of the busiest in London, and it also acts as a convenient shelter for the dispossessed of the streets, who are treated with great kindness. But it is Cocteau's mural that acts as a magnet for most of those who go there as part of their trip to London, although they may well stay to take advantage of an oasis of calm in the midst of the capital's hustle and bustle.

Initially the fresco may disappoint, for – like much of Cocteau's work – it seems at first glance to be little more than a painted sketch, a scene simply outlined in a few colours on the plain plaster. It depicts the Crucifixion: the victim being surrounded by awestruck Roman soldiers, grieving women and disciples. It certainly has, one might think, all the ingredients of a traditional Crucifixion scene, but, like Leonardo's *Last Supper*, it repays closer, more critical – and even more commonsensical – scrutiny.

The central figure, the victim of this most horrible of deaths by torture, may well be Jesus. But equally it is true that we do not know his identity for certain simply because we see him only from the knees down. The top of the body is not shown. And at the foot of the cross is an enormous, blue-red rose.

In the foreground there is one figure who is neither Roman nor disciple, one who is turned away from the cross and who appears to be severely disturbed by the scene that is taking place behind him. True, it is a profoundly disturbing event – to witness the death of any man in such circumstances is surely harrowing enough, but to be present when God incarnate is shedding his blood would be indescribably traumatic. Yet this character's expression is not that of the appalled humanitarian, nor that of the bereft worshipper. If one is honest, the wrinkled brow and sideways glance are those of a disenchanted, even a disgusted, witness. This is not the reaction of someone who is remotely inclined to bend his knee in worship, but of someone who is expressing his opinion as equal to equal.

So who is this disapproving presence at Christianity's most sacred event? It is none other than Cocteau himself. And if one remembers that Leonardo painted himself looking away from the Holy Family in the *Adoration of the Magi*, and from Jesus in the *Last Supper*, there is at least, one might say, a family resemblance between the two paintings. And when one considers that it is claimed that both artists were high-ranking members of the same, heretical, secret society, further research becomes irresistible.

Glowering over the scene is a black sun, shedding its dark rays into the surrounding sky. Immediately before it stands a person – presumably a man – whose upraised, bulging eyes, silhouetted against the horizon, are remarkably like pert breasts. Four Roman soldiers strike epic poses around the cross, holding spears at odd, and apparently significant, angles – and one of them clutches a shield which bears the design of a stylized hawk. And by the feet of two of them lies a piece of cloth upon which are scattered dice. The sum total of the numbers shown on them is fifty-eight.

An insipid young man clasps his hands at the foot of the cross, his somewhat blank gaze vaguely centred on one of the two women at the scene. They in turn appear to be joined by a large 'M' shape just below the man with breast-like eyes. The older of the women looks down in her grief and appears to be weeping blood; the younger is literally more distant, and while she is standing close to the cross, her whole body is turned away from it. The spreadeagled 'M' shape is repeated on the front of the altar immediately before the mural.

The last figure in the scene, on the extreme right of the picture, is a man of indeterminate age, whose only visible eye is drawn in the distinct shape of a fish.

Some commentators[1] have pointed out that the angles of the soldiers' spears form the shape of a pentagram – in itself hardly an orthodox feature of such a traditional Christian scene. That, however intriguing, is not part of our present investigation. As we have seen, there do appear to be superficial links between the subliminal messages in Leonardo's and Cocteau's religious works and it is this shared use of certain symbols which drew our attention.

The names of Leonardo da Vinci and Jean Cocteau appear on the list of the Grand Masters of what claims to be one of Europe's oldest and most influential secret societies – the Prieuré de Sion, the Priory of Sion. Hugely controversial, its very existence has been called into question and therefore any of its alleged activities are frequently the subject of ridicule and their implications ignored. At first we sympathized with this kind of reaction, but our further investigations certainly revealed that the matter was not as simple as that.

The Priory of Sion first came to the attention of the English-speaking world as late as 1982, through the best-selling *The Holy Blood and the Holy Grail* by Michael Baigent, Richard Leigh and Henry Lincoln, although in its homeland of France reports of its existence gradually became public from the early 1960s. It is a quasi-Masonic or chivalric order with certain political ambitions and, it seems, considerable behind-the-scenes power. Having said that, it is notoriously difficult to categorize the Priory, perhaps because there is something essentially chimerical about the whole operation. There was nothing, however, illusory about the information given to us by the representative of the Priory whom we met in early 1991

– the meeting being the result of a series of rather bizarre letters sent to us after a radio discussion about the Turin Shroud.

What led up to this slightly surreal rendezvous is detailed in our previous book[2], but for the moment it will suffice to say that one 'Giovanni' – whom we only ever knew under this pseudonym – an Italian who claimed to be a high-ranking member of the Priory of Sion, had watched us carefully in the very early stages of our research into Leonardo and the Shroud. For whatever reason, he had finally decided to tell us about certain of that organization's interests and perhaps even to involve us in its plans. Much of that information was to lead eventually – after we somewhat tortuously checked it out – to our book on the Turin Shroud, but at least the same amount again had no relevance to that work, and was therefore omitted from it.

Despite the often startling, or even shocking, implications of Giovanni's information, we were compelled to take at least the major part of it seriously, simply because our independent research confirmed it. For example, the image on the Turin Shroud behaves like a photograph because, as we have demonstrated, that is precisely what it is. And if, as he claimed, Giovanni's information really did come from Priory archives, then there is reason to approach the notion of their existence – perhaps with a little healthy scepticism, but by no means with the out and out denial of many of their detractors.

When we first became involved in the secret world of Leonardo, we soon realized that if this shadowy society had really been an integral part of his life, then it might go a long way towards explaining his driving force. If he had really been part of a powerful underground network of some kind, his influential patrons – such as Lorenzo de Medici and Francis I of France – may also have been implicated. There did appear to be some shadowy organization behind Leonardo's obsessions: but was it, as some claim, actually the Priory of Sion?

If the Priory's claims are true, then it was already a venerable organization when Leonardo was recruited into its ranks.

But whatever its age, it must have exerted a powerful, perhaps a unique, attraction for the young artist and for several of his equally incredulous Renaissance colleagues. Perhaps, like the modern Freemasons, it offered material and social advancement, easing the young man's path through the most influential European courts, but that would not explain the evident depth of Leonardo's own strange beliefs. Whatever he was part of, it appealed to his *spirit* as much as to his material interests.

The underlying power of the Priory of Sion is at least partly due to the suggestion that its members are, and always have been, guardians of a great secret – one that, if made public, would shake the very foundations of both Church and State. The Priory of Sion, sometimes known as the Order of Sion or the Order of Our Lady of Sion as well as by other subsidiary titles, claims to have been founded in 1099, during the First Crusade – and even then this was just a matter of formalizing a group whose guardianship of this explosive knowledge already went back much further[3]. They claimed to be behind the creation of the Knights Templar – that curious body of medieval soldier-monks of sinister reputation. The Priory and the Templars became, so it is claimed, virtually the same organization, presided over by the same Grand Master, until they suffered a schism and went their separate ways in 1188. The Priory continued under the custodianship of a series of Grand Masters, including some of the most illustrious names in history such as Sir Isaac Newton, Sandro Filipepi (known as Botticelli), Robert Fludd, the English occult philosopher – and, of course, Leonardo da Vinci, who, it is alleged, presided over the Priory for the last nine years of his life. Among its more recent leaders were Victor Hugo, Claude Debussy – and the artist, writer, playwright and film-maker Jean Cocteau[4]. And although they were not Grand Masters, the Priory has, it is claimed, attracted other luminaries over the centuries such as Joan of Arc, Nostradamus (Michel de Notre Dame) and even Pope John XXIII.

Apart from such celebrities, the history of the Priory of Sion allegedly involved some of the greatest royal and aristocratic families of Europe for generation after generation. These include the d'Anjous, the Habsburgs, the Sinclairs and the Montgomeries.

The reported aim of the Priory is to protect the descendants of the old Merovingian dynasty of kings in what is now France – who ruled from the fifth century until the assassination of Dagobert II in the late seventh century. But then, critics claim that the Priory of Sion has only existed since the 1950s and consists of a handful of mythomaniacs with no real power – royalists with unlimited delusions of grandeur[5].

So on the one hand we have the Priory's own claims for its pedigree and *raison d'être* and on the other the claims of its detractors. We were faced with this apparently unbridgeable gulf, and – to be honest – we had doubts about continuing with this particular line of research. However, we realized that although an evaluation of the Priory logically falls into two parts – the questions of its existence in recent times and of its historical claims – the issue is complex and nothing connected with that organization is quite so clear-cut. One dubious connection or apparent contradiction concerning the Priory's activities inevitably leads sceptics to denounce the entire thing as arrant nonsense from beginning to end. But it must be remembered that we are dealing with *mythmakers*, who are often more concerned with conveying powerful and even shocking ideas through the use of archetypal images than with communicating the literal truth.

Of the Priory's modern existence we are in no doubt. Our dealings with Giovanni persuaded us that he, at least, was no random confidence trickster and that his information was to be trusted. Not only did he give us invaluable facts about the Turin Shroud, but he also supplied details about various other individuals who are currently involved with the Priory and other, perhaps allied, esoteric organizations, both in the UK and on the Continent. For example, he named as a fellow member a publishing consultant whom one of us had worked with in the 1970s. At first glance, Giovanni's statement about this man seemed like mere mischievous fantasy on his part, but within a few months something very strange happened.

By what was surely a striking synchronicity, that very publisher attended a party given by one of our friends in November 1991 at a restaurant she particularly liked – which was nowhere near her Home Counties house, but just round the corner from one of us. So it was especially astounding to find someone who had actually been named by Giovanni among the party-goers, as it were on our doorstep. We kept in touch with him afterwards and were invited to his home in Surrey. Always good company, it was no hardship to spend time with him and his wife, but gradually one fact became evident. He was a member of the Priory of Sion.

Our contact with him during this period culminated in an invitation to a post-Christmas party at his country house. The event was glamorous but friendly, and our fellow guests were charming cosmopolitans, who were all remarkably – perhaps, with hindsight, excessively – interested in our work on Leonardo and the Shroud. It was very flattering, but somewhat disquieting, especially as they were all members of the international banking scene.

Our host was already well known to us as a member of some kind of masonic organization, but despite his ready and often uproarious wit, he was also a practising occultist. We know this to be true, partly because he told us himself in what was clearly a deliberate move. Obviously he wanted us to know something about the occult leanings of himself and his circle – but what exactly? Whatever the nature of his hidden agenda we had learned that the Priory exists among cultivated and influential English-speaking men and women.

Giovanni also named a certain director of a London publishing company, who was also known to us, as a fellow Priory member. While we were unable to confirm his membership of that organization, we did discover that his interest in the occult extended beyond the occasional articles and books he wrote on the subject under other names. He also played a significant role in publicizing *The Holy Blood and the*

Holy Grail on its publication in 1982. (And it is surely no coincidence that he has a second home very close to a certain French village that has, as we shall see, a major part to play in the drama surrounding the Priory of Sion.)

The important fact to emerge from our dealings with these men is that the modern Priory of Sion is not, as critics claim, merely the invention of a handful of Frenchmen with monarchist fantasies. Because of our recent experience and contacts, there is no doubt in our own minds that the Priory exists *now*.

Its claimed historical pedigree, however, is quite another matter. It must be admitted that the Priory's critics have a point in that the first documented reference to it dates from as recently as 25 June 1956[6]. Under French law all associations must register themselves, paradoxical though this may seem in the case of so-called 'secret' societies. The Priory's claim at the time of registration was that its aim was to provide 'studies and mutual aid to members' – a statement which, although positively Pickwickian in its bland altruism, is also a study in careful neutrality. It declared only one activity, which was to publish a journal called *Circuit*, which was, in the Priory's own words, 'for information and defence of the rights and liberties of low-rent housing' (*foyers HLM* – literally the equivalent of British council housing). The declaration listed four officers of the association, the most interesting – and best known – of whom was one Pierre Plantard, who was also the editor of *Circuit*.

Since that obscure declaration, however, the Priory of Sion has become known to a much wider audience. Not only have its statutes appeared in print[7], complete with the signature of its alleged one-time Grand Master, Jean Cocteau (although, of course, this could be a forgery), but also the Priory has appeared in several books. Its début was in 1962 in *Les Templiers sont parmis nous (The Templars Are Among Us)* by Gérard de Sède, which included an interview with Pierre Plantard. The Priory, however, had to wait for twenty years to make an impact on the English-speaking world. In 1982 the phenomenal best-seller *The Holy Blood and the Holy Grail* by

Michael Baigent, Richard Leigh and Henry Lincoln hit the bookshops, and the ensuing controversy certainly made the Priory a fashionable subject for debate among a much wider public. What that book claimed for the organization and extrapolated from its alleged aims, will, however, be dealt with later.

Pierre Plantard emerges from the material in the public domain as a colourful character who has perfected the politicians' art of looking straight at the questioner while expertly dealing with the actual question in quite another way. Born in 1920, he first came to public notice in the Occupied France of 1942 as the editor of a journal called *Vaincre pour une jeune chevalerie* (*Conquest for a Young Knighthood*) – which was markedly uncritical of the Nazi oppressors, and which was actually published with their approval. This was officially the organ of the Order Alpha-Galates, a quasi-Masonic and chivalric society, based in Paris, of which Plantard became Grand Master at the age of just twenty-two. His editorials appeared first under the name of 'Pierre de France', then 'Pierre de France-Plantard' and finally simply 'Pierre Plantard'[8]. His obsession with what he deemed to be the correct version of his name can be seen once again when he adopted the more grandiose title of 'Pierre Plantard de Saint-Clair', which was the name under which he appeared in *The Holy Blood and the Holy Grail* – and which he used when he was Grand Master of the Priory of Sion between 1981 and 1984. (*Vaincre* is now the title of the Priory's internal bulletin, which Pierre Plantard de Saint-Clair edits with his son Thomas[9].)

This one-time draughtsman for a stove-fitting firm, who allegedly had difficulty paying the rent from time to time[10], nevertheless has exerted considerable influence on European history. It was Pierre Plantard de Saint-Clair – under the alias 'Captain Way' – who was behind the organization of the Committees of Public Safety which brought about the return to power of General Charles de Gaulle in 1958[11].

Let us now consider the essentially paradoxical nature of the Priory of Sion. First, where does the public information about that organization actually come from, and just how reliable is it? As cited in *The Holy Blood and the Holy Grail*, the primary source is a collection of just seven enigmatic documents lodged in the Bibliothèque Nationale in Paris, which are known as the *Dossiers secrets* (secret dossiers)[12]. At first sight they are a hotch-potch of historical genealogies and texts and more modern allegorical works that are attributed to anonymous authors or to authors with blatant pseudonyms, or bear the names of people who had nothing to do with them. Most of these entries concern the supposed Merovingian obsession of the society, and centre on the famous mystery of Rennes-le-Château, the remote Languedocian village that was the starting point for Baigent, Leigh and Lincoln's own investigation (of which more later). However, certain other major themes emerge that, to us, are far more significant and which we will deal with shortly. The first of the items in the secret dossiers was deposited in 1964, although it is dated 1956. The last item was deposited in 1967.

One might only too reasonably dismiss much of the contents of the dossiers as being some kind of joke. However, we caution against such an immediate reaction, because our experience of the Priory of Sion and its *modus operandi* is that it glories in quite deliberate and detailed misinformation. Behind this smokescreen of full-scale nonsense, prevarication and obfuscation, there lies a very serious, very single-minded intent.

However, what would not in a million years have fascinated and motivated such great names as Leonardo and Isaac Newton for so long was this supposed obsession with restoring the long-gone Merovingian bloodline to a position of power in modern France. On the evidence given in the secret dossiers, the case for the survival of the dynasty beyond King Dagobert II, not to mention the continuation of a clear line of descent right through to the late twentieth century, is at best fragile and at worst demonstrably fictitious[13]. After all, anybody who has ever tried to trace his or her family tree back beyond two or three generations soon discovers how complex and problematic the whole process is. So again, one is left with the question of just how such a cause could have inspired highly intelligent men and women for generation after generation. One can hardly imagine the likes of Isaac Newton and Leonardo being over-impressed by, for example, a British society whose aims were to restore to power the descendants of King Harold II (killed by William the Conqueror's men in 1066).

For the modern Priory of Sion, there are great difficulties in achieving their aims of restoring the Merovingian bloodline. Not only is there the problem of turning republican France back to the monarchy it rejected over a century ago, but even then (assuming that their Merovingian succession could ever be proved) that particular dynasty has no claim to the throne, because the French nation did not exist during the Merovingian era. As the French writer Jean Robin succinctly puts it: 'Dagobert was ... a King *in* France, but at no point King *of* France[14].'

The *Dossiers secrets* may appear to be complete nonsense, but the sheer scale of the effort and resources put into them, and into maintaining their claims, gives one pause. Even French writer Gérard de Sède, who devotes many closely argued pages to demolishing the alleged evidence for the Merovingian case given in the dossiers, has admitted that the scholarly and academic resources and research that went into them were disproportionately impressive. Although being scathing about 'this delirious myth', he nevertheless concludes that there is a real mystery behind it all[15]. One curious feature of the dossiers is the constant and underlying implication that the authors had access to official government and police files.

To take just two examples of many: in 1967 a booklet was added to the dossiers called *Le serpent rouge* (*The Red Serpent*), which was attributed to three authors – Pierre Feugère, Louis Saint-Maxent and Gaston de Koker – and dated 17 January 1967[16], although its deposit slip for the Bibliothèque Nationale is dated 15 February. This extraordinary thirteen-page text, which is generally most appreciated as an example of poetic talent, also encompasses astrological, allegorical and alchemical symbolism. What is sinister about it, however, is that the three authors were all found hanged within twenty-four hours of each other, on 6/7 March of that year. The implication is that their deaths were a result of their collaboration in writing *Le serpent rouge*. However, subsequent research has shown that the work was deposited among the dossiers on 20 March – *after* they were all found dead – and the deposit slip was deliberately falsified to bear the February date. But by far the most amazing thing about this whole strange business is that these three alleged authors actually had no connection with this pamphlet at all, or with the Priory of Sion . . . Someone had presumably seized on the fact of these three bizarrely synchronistic deaths and used them for their own strange purposes. But why? And, as de Sède points out, there were only thirteen days between the three deaths and the deposit of the pamphlet in the Bibliothèque Nationale – which was such fast work as to suggest strongly that the real author(s) had inside knowledge of confidential police investigations[17]. And Franck Marie, a writer and private detective, has established conclusively that the same typewriter was used to concoct both *Le serpent rouge* and some of the later documents in the secret dossiers[18].

Then there was the case of the forged Lloyds Bank Documents. Alleged seventeenth-century parchments found by a French priest at the end of the last century, which supposedly proved the continuing Merovingian line of descent, were acquired by an English gentleman in 1955 and deposited in a strongbox in a branch of Lloyds Bank in London. Although no-one has actually seen these documents, letters were known to exist that confirmed the fact that they were deposited and which were signed by three prominent British businessmen, all of whom had previous connections with British intelligence services. However, during their research for *The Messianic Legacy* (the sequel to *The Holy Blood and the Holy Grail*), Baigent, Leigh and Lincoln were able to prove that the letters were forgeries – although they incorporated parts of genuine documents bearing the real signatures, and copies of the birth certificates, of the three businessmen. The most significant and far-reaching point, however, is that whoever forged them seems to have obtained the genuine parts from documents in the files of the French government, in a way that strongly implicates the French Intelligence Service.[19]

Once again, one is faced with a sense of high strangeness. An enormous amount of time, effort and perhaps even personal danger must have been involved in setting up such an elaborate ploy. But at the same time, in the final analysis, it appears to be completely and utterly pointless. In that respect, however, the whole business is merely following the old tradition of intelligence agencies, in which few things are as they appear to be and the most seemingly straightforward matters may well be exercises in disinformation.

There are, however, reasons to make use of paradoxes – even blatant absurdities. We tend to remember the absurd, and, furthermore, illogicalities that are deliberately presented as scrupulously argued facts have a curiously powerful effect on our unconscious minds. After all, it is this part of ourselves that creates our dreams, which operate with their own kind of paradox and non-logic. And it is the unconscious mind that is the motivator, the creator, which, once it has been 'hooked', will continue to work even on the most subliminal message for years, extracting every last bit of symbolic meaning from a tiny scrap of apparent gobbledygook.

Sceptics, who pride themselves in general on their worldly wisdom, are often, in fact, curiously naive – for they see everything as starkly black or white, true or false, which is just how certain groups wish them to see it. For example, what better way of attracting attention on the one hand, but filtering out unwanted interlopers or the casually curious on the other, than to present the public with apparently intriguing but also virtually nonsensical information? It is as if even getting close to what the Priory is really about actually constitutes an initiation: if you are not meant for it then the smokescreen will effectively put you off deeper investigation. But if it is in some way meant for you then you will soon be given that extra material, or will discover for yourself, in some suspiciously synchronistic fashion, that extra insight into the organization which suddenly makes everything about it fall into place.

It is, in our opinion, a great mistake to dismiss the *Dossiers secrets* simply because their overt message is demonstrably implausible. The sheer scale of the work behind them argues in favour of their having *something* to offer. Admittedly many an unbalanced obsessive has spent all his time on some vast and doomed work, and the man-hours involved in it do not in themselves make the results any more worthy of our attention and respect. But here we are dealing with a *group* who are clearly working to some intricate plan, and, taken together with all the other available hints and clues (which will become evident in due course), it is clear that something is going on. Either they are trying to tell us something, or they are trying to conceal something – while still dropping hints about its importance.

So what do we make of the Priory's historical claims? Does it really go back as far as the eleventh century, and did its ranks actually include all the illustrious names given in the secret dossiers? First, one might say that there is always a problem in proving the existence, current or historical, of a secret society. After all, the more successfully secret it has been then the harder it is to corroborate its existence. However, where there can be shown to have been repeated interests, themes and aims among those who are claimed to have belonged to this group over the years, it is safe and even sensible to assume that such a group may actually have existed.

Unlikely as the rollcall of the Priory's Grand Masters (as given in the secret dossiers) may seem, the research of Baigent, Leigh and Lincoln has established that this is no random list[20]. There are indeed persuasive connections between succeeding Grand Masters. Besides knowing each other – and in many cases actually being related – these luminaries shared certain interests and preoccupations. It is known that many of them were associated with esoteric movements and secret societies such as the Freemasons, Rosicrucians and the Compagnie du Saint-Sacrement[21], all of which share some common aims. For example, there is a distinctly hermetic theme that runs through all their known literature – a sense of real excitement at the prospect of Man's becoming almost godlike in ever extending the boundaries of his knowledge.

Besides, our own independent research, which was presented in our last book, has confirmed that those individuals and families who were allegedly implicated in Priory business over the centuries were also the same prime movers who maintained what might be termed the Great Holy Shroud Hoax[22].

As we have already seen, both Leonardo and Cocteau employed heterodox symbolism in their supposedly Christian paintings. Separated by 500 years, their imagery shows remarkable consistency – and indeed, other writers and artists who have been linked with the Priory also work such motifs into their output[23]. This in itself suggests strongly that they really were part of some kind of organized underground movement, which was already well-established even in Leonardo's day. As both he himself and Cocteau have been claimed as its Grand Masters, and if one takes into account their shared preoccupations, it seems reasonable to deduce that they were indeed high-ranking members of some group at least very like the Priory of Sion.

The mass of evidence assembled by Baigent, Leigh and Lincoln in *The Holy Blood and the Holy Grail* for the historical existence of the Priory is unassailable. And yet more evidence – which had been amassed by other researchers – was published in the 1996 revised and updated edition of their book. (This is essential reading for anyone interested in this mystery.)

All this evidence shows that there was a secret society operating from the twelfth century – but is the modern Priory of Sion its true descendant? Certainly, while the two groups may not necessarily be linked as claimed, the modern Priory does have inside knowledge about the historical society. After all, it was only through today's members that we first heard of the Priory in the past.

But even access to the old Priory's archives would not necessarily imply a genuine continuation. In a recent conversation with the French artist Alain Féral – who, as Cocteau's protégé, worked with, and knew him very well – he told us adamantly that his mentor had *not* been Grand Master of the Priory of Sion. At least, Féral assured us, Cocteau had not been involved with the same organization that has since claimed Pierre Plantard de Saint-Clair as Grand Master. However, Féral has carried out his own investigation into certain aspects of the Priory of Sion story, especially those concerning the Languedocian village of Rennes-le-Château, and his opinion is that those listed as Priory Grand Masters in the *Dossiers secrets*, up to and including Cocteau, *were* connected by a genuine underground tradition[24].

At this stage in our research we decided to ignore the putative political ambitions of the modern Priory and concentrate instead on its historical aspects, which might, of course, help shed some light on the former.

The secret dossiers – apart from their Merovingian mythomania – lay great emphasis on the Holy Grail, the tribe of Benjamin and the New Testament character Mary Magdalene. For example, in *Le serpent rouge* this declaration appears:

> From the one that I wish to liberate, rise towards me the aromas of the perfume that impregnates the sepulchre. Formerly some called her; ISIS, queen of the beneficent sources, COME TO ME ALL YOU WHO SUFFER AND WHO ARE OVERWHELMED AND I WILL COMFORT YOU, others: MAGDALENE, of the famous vase full of healing balm. The initiates know her true name: NOTRE DAME DES CROSS[25].

This short passage is puzzling, not least because the last phrase – *Notre Dame des Cross* – makes no sense whatsoever (unless 'Cross' is a family name, in which case it becomes only slightly more intelligible). '*Des*' is the plural version of 'of the', but *cross* does not exist in French at all, and, of course, is in the singular in English. Then there is the peculiar confusion of Isis with Mary Magdalene – after all, one was a goddess and the other a 'fallen woman', and they are figures from different cultures with no apparent connection whatsoever.

Of course there is an immediate problem, one might think, in linking such apparently diverse subjects as the Magdalene, the Holy Grail and the tribe of Benjamin – not to mention the Egyptian mother goddess Isis – with that of the Merovingian line. The *Dossiers secrets* explain that the Sicambrian Franks, the tribe from which the Merovingians descended, were of Jewish origin; they were the lost tribe of Benjamin, who migrated to Greece and then on to Germany, where they became the Sicambrians.

However, the authors of *The Holy Blood and the Holy Grail* complicated the scenario still further. According to them, the importance of the Merovingian line was not merely the pipedream of a handful of eccentric royalists. Their claim took the whole issue into quite another realm – one that certainly captured the imagination of the millions of the book's enthusiastic readers. They alleged that Jesus had been married to Mary Magdalene and that there were offspring from this union. Jesus survived the cross, but his wife went without him when she took the children to an established Jewish colony in what is now southern France. It was their descendants who became the ruling family of the Sicambrians, thus founding the Merovingian line of kings.

This hypothesis may appear to make sense of the main Priory themes, but it does raise major questions of its own. As we have seen, it is impossible for any bloodline to survive in the 'pure' form necessary to support such a campaign, no matter from whom it was descended.

It is undeniable that there is a very good case for Jesus having been married to Mary Magdalene – or at least in some kind of intimate relationship with her – which we will discuss in detail later, and even for him having survived the Crucifixion. In fact, despite popular belief to the contrary, neither of these assertions relies upon the work of Baigent, Leigh and Lincoln, having been closely argued by several academics many years before the publication of *The Holy Blood and the Holy Grail*[26].

There is, however, a major problem in the assumptions that lie behind their arguments – one that they are clearly aware of even though they avoid drawing attention to it. To them, the Merovingians are important because they are Jesus' descendants. But if he survived the cross he could not be said to have died for our sins, could not have been resurrected – and therefore was not divine, not the Son of God. So why, one might ask, were his alleged descendants considered so important?

One of that hallowed group of descendants is believed to be none other than Pierre Plantard de Saint-Clair himself. Despite the inflated language employed about this hypothesis by some commentators, it must be stated that he himself has never claimed to be a descendant of Jesus. It cannot be stressed enough that it is not the *Christian* idea that Jesus was God incarnate – and therefore that his offspring were themselves divine in some way – which gives the idea of the Merovingian succession its alleged significance. The basis of this whole belief is that, as Jesus was of the line of David and therefore the legitimate King of Jerusalem, this title automatically falls, if only theoretically, on his future family. So it is political, rather than divine, power that is claimed for the Merovingian connection.

Baigent, Leigh and Lincoln clearly built their theory on the claims made in the *Dossiers secrets*, but in our opinion they have been somewhat selective in choosing just which of those claims to cite as evidence. For example, the *Dossiers* state that the Merovingian kings, from their founder Merovée to Clovis (who converted to Christianity in 496) were 'pagan kings of the cult of Diana'[27]. It is, surely, hard to reconcile this with the idea that they were descended from Jesus or a Jewish tribe.

Another example of this curious selectivity on the part of

Baigent, Leigh and Lincoln is that of the 'Montgomery document'[28]. This is, according to those authors, a 'narrative which had surfaced' among the family archives of the Montgomery family, a member of whom shared it with them. The date of its origins is uncertain, but the version they were shown came from the nineteenth century. Its value to them lay in the fact that, in essence, it backed up the theories put forward in *The Holy Blood and the Holy Grail*, although of course it could not be deemed to be proof of them. It did at least establish that such an idea – that Jesus was married to Mary Magdalene – was known a century at least before they began their research.

The Montgomery document tells the story of Yeshua ben Joseph (Jesus, son of Joseph) who was married to Miriam (Mary) of Bethany (the biblical character whom many people take to be the same as Mary Magdalene). As a direct result of a revolt against the Romans, Miriam is arrested and only released because she is pregnant. She then flees from Palestine, ending up in Gaul (what is now France), where she gives birth to a daughter.

While it is easy to see why the Montgomery document was seized on by Baigent, Leigh and Lincoln as support for their hypothesis, it is strange that they do not make more of certain aspects of the story. In this narrative, Miriam of Bethany is described as 'a priestess of a female cult'; like the Merovingians' worship of the goddess Diana, this adds a distinctly pagan gloss to the story which is hard to reconcile with the notion that the Priory is primarily concerned with the continuation of the bloodline of the Jewish King David – which included Jesus.

Interestingly, the modern Priory has neither confirmed nor denied the *Holy Blood and the Holy Grail* hypothesis – and once again one's suspicions are roused. Can it be that the Priory of Sion is playing games with us?

One thing became very clear to us: the Priory's motivating ambition is not the purely *political power* that Baigent, Leigh and Lincoln claim for it. Time and time again the dossiers mention people – either among the actual Grand Masters or those associated with the Priory – who are primarily not politicians, but *occultists*. For example, Nicolas Flamel, Grand Master from 1398 to 1418, was a master alchemist, Robert Fludd (1595–1637) was a Rosicrucian, and, nearer our own time, Charles Nodier (Grand Master from 1801–44) was a major influence behind the modern occult revival. Even Sir Isaac Newton (Grand Master 1691–1727), who is best known today as a scientist and mathematician, was a devoted alchemist and hermeticist, and certainly owned heavily annotated copies of the Rosicrucian manifestos[29]. Then of course there is Leonardo da Vinci, another genius whom moderns misunderstand completely, seeing his keen intellect as the product of materialist thinking only. In fact, as we have seen, his obsessions were drawn from quite other sources, and make him another ideal candidate for the list of the Priory's Grand Masters.

Surprisingly, while acknowledging the occult interests of many of these people, Baigent, Leigh and Lincoln do not seem to appreciate the full significance of their obsessions. After all, in many of these cases, the occult was no mere occasional hobby, but actually the main focus of their lives. And our own experience has indicated that the individuals concerned with the modern Priory are also committed occultists.

So what possible secret could have focused so many of the world's most brilliant occult minds for so long, given that it is unlikely to have been the implausible Merovingian cover story? Persuasive and ground-breaking though *The Holy Blood and the Holy Grail* may have been, its explanation of the Priory's aims and motives is basically unsatisfactory. Clearly there is something going on which is hardly likely, given the huge amount of time and energy it appears to have attracted over the centuries, to be merely about the legitimacy of the French monarchy. And whatever it is be must be such a threat to the status quo that, even after the Age of Enlightenment, it had to be kept secret, to be a matter closely guarded by an underground network of initiates.

Early in our research into Leonardo and the Turin Shroud we found ourselves faced, time and again, with the unavoidable feeling that there is a real secret that has been jealously guarded by the select few. As our investigations proceeded we could not shake off the suspicion that the themes we had detected in Leonardo's life and work closely paralleled those we had discerned in the material disseminated by the Priory. And, surely, it was at least worth double-checking the intimations that these very subjects were also interwoven in the work of Jean Cocteau.

We have already described that artist's mural in the church of Notre-Dame de France in London. But just what relevance does its strikingly peculiar imagery have to the much earlier work of Leonardo, and to some putative esoteric – and even heretical – movement?

The most obvious connection with the da Vinci opus is the fact that the artist painted himself looking away from the cross. Leonardo, as we have already mentioned, depicted himself in this way at least twice – in the *Adoration of the Magi* and in the *Last Supper*. Considering the expression on Cocteau's face, which surely implies deep unease about the entire scene, it may not be stretching a point too far to find a similar hostility in the violence with which Leonardo has turned away from the Holy Family in the *Adoration*.

In Cocteau's mural we see the man on the cross only from the thighs down, which implies some suspicion about his true identity. As we have seen in Leonardo's *Last Supper*, the curious overall lack of wine seems to imply a serious question about the nature of Jesus' sacrifice: here the artist goes further by not showing Jesus at all. Very similar, too, is the use of the giant 'M' shape – in Cocteau's work it links the two grieving women, presumably Mary the Virgin and Mary Magdalene. And again one may assume that it is the latter whom we see turned away from the Jesus figure. While his mother looks down, weeping, it is the younger woman who has her back to him. In Leonardo's *Last Supper* the 'M' links Jesus to the suspiciously female 'Saint John' – and this 'Lady M' is also leaning as far away as possible from him, while at the same time appearing to stay close.

The Cocteau mural also contains symbolism that is, once one is aware of the preoccupations of the Priory of Sion, quite explicitly connected to it. For example, there are fifty-eight dots shown on the dice that are being cast by the soldiers – and this is the esoteric number of the Priory[30].

The startlingly large blue-red rose at the foot of the cross is clearly an allusion to the Rosicrucian movement, which, as we shall see, has close links with the Priory and certainly with Leonardo.

As we have already seen, the members of the Priory believe that Jesus did not die on the cross, and some of its factions maintain that a substitute victim suffered what was meant to be his fate. Judging by the imagery in this mural alone, one might be tempted to think that those were Cocteau's own views. For example, not only do we not see the victim's face, but there is the inclusion of a figure not usually associated with the Crucifixion scene. This is the man on the far right whose one visible eye is drawn in an unmistakable fish-shape – surely an allusion to the early Christian code for 'Christ'. So who is this fish-eyed man supposed to be? In the light of the Priory's notion that Christ himself was never nailed to the cross, *could it not be that this extra figure is Jesus himself?* Was the would-be Messiah actually a witness to the torture and death of a surrogate? If this were true, one might well imagine his emotions.

Then again, in both the Leonardo and Cocteau murals, we see the Lady M – surely in both cases Mary Magdalene. Now, what we know of the Priory belief that she was married to Jesus would explain just why she was at the Last Supper, on her husband's right hand, and why she – as his 'other half' – is wearing the mirror image of his clothes.

Although there was a little-known tradition in medieval and early Renaissance times of depicting the Magdalene at the Last Supper, Leonardo made it known that the character on Jesus' right hand in his version was St John. So why did he set out to deceive in this way? Was this perhaps a subtle way of giving his imagery added subliminal power? After all if the artist tells us this is a man and our brain tells us it is a woman the confusion is likely to make us continue to ponder on it at an unconscious level for a long time.

In both the Leonardo and Cocteau murals, the Magdalene appears to be quietly expressing her own doubts through her body language about Jesus' supposed role. Was she indeed so close to him as to know the real story? Was the Magdalene really the wife of Jesus, and therefore party to inside information about the true outcome of the Crucifixion? Is this why she is turning away?

The Magdalene's role is cunningly – if subliminally – emphasized in the *Last Supper*, but Leonardo's major obsession would certainly appear to have been with that tragic New Testament character, St John the Baptist. If he was really a member of the Priory of Sion – and given their purported emphasis on the bloodline of Jesus – this obsession with the Baptist seems somewhat puzzling. But does it actually conform with the interests of the Priory of Sion?

Our mysterious informant Giovanni had left us with the tantalizing question: 'Why are the Grand Masters always called John?' At the time we thought this was some kind of semi-veiled allusion to his own choice of alias, and we duly took the point that he himself held no minor rank. But in fact he was drawing attention to another, much more significant issue.

While the Priory's Grand Masters are known in the organization as 'Nautonnier' (helmsman), they also take the name 'Jean' (John) or if female, Jeanne (Jean or Joan). Leonardo, for example, appears on their lists as Jean IX. It is worth noting that, peculiar though it may seem for such an ancient chivalric order, the Priory has always claimed to be an equal opportunities secret society, and four of its Grand Masters have been women. (Today, one of the French sections of the Priory is under the control of a woman[31].) However, this policy is totally consistent with the true nature and aims of the Priory – as we came to understand them.

The Priory's preoccupations are indicated by the titles used in their organizational hierarchy. According to their statutes, below the Nautonnier is a grade consisting of three initiates, called 'Prince Noachite de Notre Dame', and below that is a nine-strong grade called 'Croisé de Saint Jean', or 'St John's Crusader'. (The latter appears simply as 'Constable' in later versions of the statutes.)

There are six further grades, but the top three, comprising the thirteen highest-ranking members, form the ruling body. Collectively this is known as the Arch Kyria – the latter being a respectful Greek word for woman, the equivalent of the English 'lady'. Specifically, in the Hellenistic world of the early centuries BCE, it was an epithet of the goddess Isis[32].

The society's first Grand Master was, it must be said, a true John – Jean de Gisors, a French nobleman of the twelfth century. But the real riddle lies in the curious fact that his Priory title was actually 'Jean II'. As the authors of *The Holy Blood and* the *Holy Grail* muse:

> One major question, of course, was which John. John the Baptist? John the Evangelist – the 'Beloved Disciple' in the Fourth Gospel? Or John the Divine, author of the Book of Revelation? It seemed it must be one of these three . . . Who, then, was Jean I?[33]

Another thought-provoking 'John' connection is mentioned in the 1982 book *Rennes-le-Château: capitale secrète de l'histoire de France* by Jean-Pierre Deloux and Jacques Brétigny. Both authors are known to be closely involved with Pierre Plantard de Saint-Clair – they were, for example, among his 'entourage' when Baigent, Leigh and Lincoln met him in the 1980s[34] – and he certainly contributed enormously to the book. Clearly Priory propaganda, it explains how the society was formed. (Deloux and Brétigny also wrote articles relating to the Priory of Sion in the magazine *L'Inexpliqué* – the French version of *The Unexplained* – which, according to some, was set up and financed by the Priory[35].)

The main idea was, it is claimed, to form a 'secret government', with Godefroi de Bouillon – one of the leaders of the First Crusade – as the prime mover. In the Holy Land, Godefroi encountered an organization called the Church of John and, as a result, 'formed a great design'. He 'gave his sword to the service of the Church of John, that esoteric and initiatory Church which represented the Tradition, that which based its primacy on the Spirit.'[36] It was from this grand design that both the Priory of Sion – the organization that always names its Grand Masters 'John' – and the Knights Templar were formed.

And as Pierre Plantard de Saint-Clair says through Deloux and Brétigny:

> Thus, at the start of the twelfth century, were brought together the means, spiritual and temporal, which came to permit the realisation of the sublime dream of Godefroi de Bouillon; the Order of the Temple would be the sword-bearers of the Church of John and the standard-bearers of the premier dynasty, the arms that obeyed the spirit of Sion.[37]

The outcome of this fervent 'Johnism' was to be a 'spiritual renaissance' that would 'turn Christianity upside down'. Despite its obvious importance to the Priory, the emphasis on 'John' remained extremely obscure – at the beginning of this investigation we did not even know which John was so revered, let alone why. But what is the reason for this obscurity? Why don't they just tell us which John they are referring to? And why would reverence (however extreme) for any of the saints John even begin to threaten the very roots of Christianity?

It is at least possible to make a guess as to which John the Priory had in mind, if Leonardo's obsession with the Baptist is anything to go by. Yet, as we have seen, the Priory's idea of Jesus' role was hardly orthodox, and it seems illogical to find it according such reverence to the man who was allegedly only important as Jesus' forerunner. Could it be that the Priory, like Leonardo, secretly reveres John the Baptist over Jesus himself?

It is a very big thought. If there is any *reason* for believing the Baptist to have been superior to Jesus then the repercussions would be unimaginably traumatic for the Church. Even if the 'Johannite' view were based on a misunderstanding, there is no doubting the effects this belief would have if it were more widely known. It would be almost the ultimate heresy – and the *Dossiers secrets* emphasize repeatedly the anticlerical character of the Merovingian descendants and their positive encouragement of heresy. The Priory is keen to convey the idea that heresy is a good thing for some specific reason of its own.

We realized that the putative Baptist heresy had astounding implications, and that if we were to delve further into the Priory we would need to confront the John the Baptist issue head-on, although at the start we were not convinced that we would find any evidence to support the heresy.

At this point all we had as evidence for the Priory's beliefs about the Baptist was Leonardo's own manifest obsession with him, and the fact that it called its Grand Masters 'John'. Frankly, we had no serious hope then of finding anything more concrete than that, but as time went by, we were to uncover much more solid evidence that the Priory was indeed part of such a Johannite tradition.

With or without evidence to back it up, this heresy could still have been *believed* by generations of Priory members. But was it at least a part of the great secret they are supposed to possess and guard so tenaciously?

The other New Testament figure who is of immense significance to the Priory is, as we have seen repeatedly, Mary Magdalene. The authors of *The Holy Blood and the Holy Grail* have explained that her particular importance lies solely in the (alleged) fact that she was married to Jesus and was the mother of his children. But considering the Priory's less than total admiration for Jesus, this explanation seems weak. For that organization the Magdalene seems to have some importance in her own right, and Jesus himself is almost irrelevant – in the story of the 'Montgomery document', for example, his role is confined simply to being the father of her child and he plays no part whatsoever in the rest of the narrative. One might go so far as to say that even without Jesus there was something about this woman that makes her of supreme significance.

Later in our researches we managed to contact Pierre Plantard de Saint-Clair with some questions about the Priory's interest in Mary Magdalene. We received a reply from Plantard's secretary, Gino Sandri – an Italian who lives in Paris – which, although short and concise, was still redolent of the Priory's famed sense of mischief. In it Sandri said that it might be possible to help, but 'perhaps you yourselves already have information on this subject?'[38] Clearly this was a sly 'dig' at something he knew about us, but we took heart from the backhanded compliment. He seemed to be implying that we already had all the information we needed to know – but it was up to us to make sense of it. But Sandri's letter hid another piece of mischief: although postmarked 28 July, the letter itself bore the date 24 June – John the Baptist's Day.

To an outsider any particularly esoteric connection between Mary Magdalene and John the Baptist is a matter for fantasy, for the known Gospel texts do not even record that they ever met. Yet here we have an apparently ancient secret that involves – and honours – both of them in no uncertain fashion. What was it about these first-century characters that ensured this lasting, if 'heretical', tradition? What could they possibly even *represent* that would be so disturbing to the Church?

It was, as can be imagined, rather hard to know where to start. But wherever we delved into the story of the Magdalene one area that was considerably closer to home than Israel kept emerging as significant. The Priory particularly stressed the legend that took her to southern France, so that was where we had to go, if only to discover for ourselves if this story was merely a medieval fabrication that, like the Turin Shroud, was designed to attract a lucrative pilgrimage trade. But there was, from the beginning, something especially compelling about the connection of this enigmatic New Testament character with that particular area, something that went beyond such mercenary considerations. We set out to investigate the Magdalene's secret on her home ground.

CHAPTER THREE

In the Footsteps of the Magdalene

She is handsome – in the same way that the statues of Greek goddesses are handsome – rather than pretty in the modern fashion. Strong-featured, with hair falling from a centre parting, the impression she gives is one of almost school-marmish sternness and integrity. There is little here to suggest the voluptuous wanton of the legends. For this, we are told, is the head of Mary Magdalene.

The skull, normally on show in all its disturbingly grisly glory in the basilica, is now encased decently in its golden mask and paraded before the crowds in the town of St Maximin in Provence. This annual event takes place on the nearest Sunday to the Magdalene's feast day, 22 July. In 1995, the year of our visit, the parade took place on 23 July, in stifling heat and brilliant sunlight.

At nearly four in the afternoon, having just finished their lengthy French lunches, the townspeople finally brought out the relic on a suspiciously wobbly litter. Hundreds of people converged on the procession, perhaps just because it was there – everyone loves a parade – but there did seem to be many genuinely fervent pilgrims among the throng, eyes fixed joyously on the curious head that was being moved among them. We had to remind ourselves, however, that there are always pilgrims, always fervent believers, in any, or in every, thing, and that belief is in itself not a measure of historical authenticity. Nevertheless, coming as we do from a relatively Magdalene-free culture, the sheer power of this festival gave us pause. This is indeed serious Mary Magdalene country.

There was also a certain irony in our presence at St Maximin. The carbon dating of the Shroud of Turin in 1988, which had established that it was a fake – and which in turn led to our interest in it – had used, as a control sample, material from a thirteenth-century cope belonging to 'Saint' Louis IX that is kept in St Maximin's basilica.

For the purposes of this investigation, however, all thoughts of the Turin Shroud were put aside. We were there, in the South of France, to find the truth about Mary Magdalene, the woman believed to be at the heart of many ancient mysteries, and whose power extends to today's culture in a way we have not yet fully grasped. Standing there in the extreme, almost stupefying heat, we witnessed the annual procession of the alleged head of Mary Magdalene with mixed feelings. To those brought up in Protestant England, Catholic festivities and the whole ritual surrounding relics come as something of a culture shock. These things can appear tasteless, garish, even gruesome.

Yet here what hit one forcibly was not a ridiculous display of superstition, but the devotion and pride of the local people, whose enthusiasm for this particular saint cannot be said to be entirely solemn. Maybe the operative word here is 'local', for it is the Provençal, not the French, flag that flies overhead, and this is taken to be very much a local saint, even if she came to these shores somewhat late in life. Mary Magdalene, it is believed, came from Palestine by sea and settled in Provence, where she died. Such is her continuing power that she is not only revered, but *loved* with a curious passion, in the area to this day.

Certainly there is extraordinary, even fanatical, devotion accorded to her in Provence, and the legend of her dying in that area persists: many believe it as a matter of fact. Yet this is not merely another example of the pious continuation of a Catholic tradition. We were struck by the pervasive feeling here that something much more significant lay just under the surface. And it was precisely that submerged, *subterranean* vein of meaning that we were determined to uncover.

First, how could it be that the body of a first-century Jewess from Palestine came to be laid to rest in the South of France?

Just what is there about this woman, this particular saint, which evokes such passion and devotion so long after her death? And why – if indeed it is true – do the Priory of Sion accord her such unusual veneration?

Even before we made our first trip to France specifically to research the sites traditionally associated with her cult, we spent much time reflecting on her background. We needed to know how she was perceived historically in our culture – and how strong her continuing impact might be. For in contrast with the relative coolness with which she is received in modern Protestant England, to a great many hot-blooded European Catholics she is the object of fervent, even passionate, devotion. To them, she is the most important woman after the Virgin Mary.

Ask most educated people today who Mary Magdalene was and what she represented and the answers are very interesting. Almost everyone will reply that she was a prostitute, but after that – depending on the viewpoint of the person involved – there will usually be some comment about her ill-defined, but implicitly close, relationship with Jesus. This cultural assumption, confused though it may be, found expression in the Tim Rice/Andrew Lloyd Webber song 'I Don't Know How to Love Him' from the musical *Jesus Christ Superstar* (1970), in which she was portrayed as 'the tart with the heart' so beloved of British theatre, and in the role of Jesus' comforter, who was also given back her self-esteem by him. When the musical was first performed – and later made into a film – it caused something of a sensation among mainstream Christians, even among the characteristically unemotional British. This was, perhaps, mostly due to a sense of outrage that a story involving Jesus had been exploited for 'showbiz' and turned into a rock opera of all things!

A version of the Magdalene appeared in *Monty Python's Life of Brian* (1979), although that was not the reason for the howls of outrage that rose from the ranks of Christians around the world. Taking the character of Brian to be a thinly veiled allusion to Jesus himself, this clever and strangely disturbing comedy was widely deemed to be blatantly blasphemous. But all flippancy aside, the film never set out to portray Jesus, being a satirical comment on the Messiah cults of his day, which nonetheless, in our opinion, either by accident or design, incorporated some profound insights and some curiously well-researched detail. In it Brian's girlfriend Judith – surreally represented as being Welsh – was the real power behind him and his movement: indeed, her fiery rhetoric made a man of him, although it also ended by making him a martyr.

Christians picketed cinemas in several countries when they showed Martin Scorsese's *The Last Temptation of Christ* (1988). Although Jesus himself was portrayed as something of a simpleton, this does not seem to have been the reason for the widespread horrified reaction. This was rather more due to the explicit depiction of sex between Mary Magdalene and Jesus – even though it was merely a fantasy sequence. For reasons that we will analyze later, this whole concept is curiously repugnant to most Christians, probably because they take it to imply certain fundamental questions about Jesus' divinity. To them the notion of a sexually active Jesus, even within the context of a marriage, is automatically blasphemous: suggestions to that effect must imply that he could not also be the Son of God. But what was most significant to us about the making of *The Last Temptation* was Scorsese's obvious and persistent fascination with the Magdalene, and with the concept of her intimate relationship with Jesus. (And interestingly, the director is himself a Christian.)

It is not, however, merely modern permissiveness that has made the Magdalene something of an icon. Throughout history she has always somehow embodied the contemporary attitude to women – in ways not open to the only other significant female figure of the Gospels, the non-sexual and remote Virgin Mary. In Victorian times, for example, the Magdalene was a good excuse for depicting penitent prostitutes half-naked and ecstatic; at the same time somehow saint and sinner, knowing and unknown. It was a fashion in brothels at the time for some of the inmates to enact her penitence, although the precise details of those particular 'Mystery Plays' owed little to her story as told in the Gospels. In today's post-feminist times the emphasis is on her relationship with Jesus.

The Magdalene may have maintained her role as the litmus test of contemporary secular sexual mores, but her image throughout history has also reflected the Church's attitude to women and their sexuality. It is only as a *repentant* whore that she is admitted to the congregation of saints and the dissemination of her legend depends upon her penitence and uncomfortable, solitary lifestyle. Her sainthood rests on her self-abnegation.

In the last two decades, this Mary has become a focus for the way the Christian Church has dealt with its female followers, particularly when the ordination of women priests in the Anglican Church first became a controversial issue. It was no accident that when the first women were ordained as vicars in 1994 the lesson that was read was the New Testament story of how the resurrected Jesus met the Magdalene in the garden. Not unnaturally, being the only significant woman in the Jesus story apart from his mother, she is seized upon by many women activists within the modern Church as a potent symbol of their rights. For Mary Magdalene's continuing power is not imaginary: it has always existed and exerted a profound attraction throughout the centuries, as Susan Haskins makes clear in her recent study *Mary Magdalen* (1993)[1].

At first the Magdalene's sheer pulling power appears puzzling, especially as she is hardly mentioned in the New Testament. We were tempted to think that, as in the case of Robin Hood, the very paucity of information provided a temptation to invent mythical material to fill in the gaps. *Yet if anyone created a fantasy Mary Magdalene it was the Church.* The image of her as a repentant whore has nothing to do with her story in Matthew, Mark, Luke and John: the character described in the New Testament is quite different from the one conjured up by the Church.

The Gospels are the only texts relating to Mary Magdalene with which most people are familiar, so we turn to them now.

Until recently, her character has been regarded by most Christians as being marginal to the wider story of Jesus and his followers. But within the last twenty years there has been a distinct shift in scholars' perception of her. These days her role is seen as considerably more important, and it is in the light of these findings that we base our own hypothesis.

Apart from the Virgin Mary, Mary Magdalene is the only woman mentioned by name in all four Gospels. She first appears during Jesus' ministry in Galilee as one of a group of women who followed him – and 'ministered unto him of their substance'[2]. She it was who had 'seven devils' cast out of her. Tradition has also identified her with two other women of the New Testament: Mary of Bethany, sister of Martha and Lazarus, and an unnamed woman who anoints Jesus with spikenard from an alabaster jar. This connection will be explored later, but for the moment we will confine ourselves to the figure unequivocally identified as Mary Magdalene.

Her role takes on a totally new, profound and lasting significance when she is recorded as being present at the Crucifixion, and more especially when she becomes the first witness to the Resurrection. Although the four Gospel accounts of the discovery of the empty tomb are notoriously different, they nevertheless all agree on the identity of the first witness to the risen Jesus. This was undoubtedly Mary Magdalene. She was not merely the first *female* witness, but the first *person* to see him after he emerged from the tomb, a fact that has largely been obscured by the many who prefer to count only the men who followed Jesus as being his true Apostles.

The Church, in fact, has based its authority entirely on the concept of apostleship – Peter being the 'First Apostle' and therefore the conduit through which Jesus' own power was transmitted to posterity. His authority, although many believe it to come from the punning statement 'upon this Rock I will build my Church'[3], is officially believed to stem from him being the first of Jesus' disciples to see him in the resurrected state. But the New Testament account flatly contradicts the Church's teaching on this.

Clearly, on this one account alone, the Magdalene has suffered an enormous injustice, one with exceptionally far-reaching implications. But there is more. She was also the first disciple to receive a direct apostolic commission from Jesus by being instructed to take the news of his resurrection to the other disciples. Curiously perhaps, the very early Church recognized her true place in the hierarchy and gave her the title *Apostola Apostolorum* (Apostle of the Apostles), or even more explicitly 'The First Apostle'[4].

The reason why Jesus should have chosen to appear first in his resurrected form to a woman has always been a thorn in the side of theologians. Perhaps the most quaint explanation surfaced in the Middle Ages, when it was seriously suggested that the quickest way to spread the news was to tell it to a woman![5]

It is now generally understood by scholars that women played a much larger and more active role in Jesus' movement both in his lifetime and also later, when it spread among the Gentiles, than has generally been admitted by the Church[6]. Ironically, perhaps, the true picture of women's place then might not even be known now were it not for the controversy stirred up by the campaign for the ordination of women. It was only when the Church became a formalized institution – under the influence of St Paul – that the role of women was minimalized. And the process was also *retrospective*. In other words, although women had not been minor characters in the primary Christian drama, Paul and his henchmen made sure that they would be pushed to the margin throughout history.

It is true that the impression given by the Gospels alone is that Jesus' disciples were indeed all men. Only a single reference in Luke's gospel mentions women travelling with Jesus. This can be confusing when it later seems that women suddenly appear from nowhere to take the central place around the cross. Judging by the cavalier marginalization of women in the accounts in general, it is puzzling why they are so abruptly the centre of attention. Could this be because all his male followers had actually deserted him? Were the women left in the story at this crucial point *just because they were his only remaining faithful friends*?[7] The Gospel writers may have had to recount the role of the women at the Crucifixion simply because they were its only witnesses, and it was on their testimony alone that the story relies[8]. Significantly, women's testimony was not allowed in Jewish courts of law at that time, so their word about anything was not considered important. Among the many implications of this point is that the story of Mary Magdalene being the first to encounter the risen Jesus must have had some basis in fact. A story that was based primarily on the word of a woman is highly unlikely to have been fabricated.

Shining examples of loyalty, and of courage in standing by a convicted criminal, the women are all to be applauded. But one in particular towers above the others: Mary Magdalene. Her importance is suggested by the fact that almost without exception[9] her name comes first whenever a list is given of Jesus' female followers. Even some Catholics nowadays suggest that this was because she was the leader of the women disciples. In such a rigidly formalized and hierarchical society, this honour was neither minor nor accidental: the Magdalene comes first, even when listed by those with no regard for the place of *any* woman in the Jesus movement, and especially with no love for that woman in particular.

She it was, as we have seen, who 'ministered unto' Jesus and the male disciples. This has always been explained by the idea that she was a kind of devoted servant, constantly prostrating herself before the much more important men in the party. But the facts are very much otherwise: there is no doubt that the original words used actually mean 'supported' the others, and 'of their substance' means 'with their possessions'. In the opinion of many scholars, Mary Magdalene – perhaps like the other women of the Jesus movement – was no penniless hanger-on, but a woman of independent means who *kept Jesus and the other men*[10]. Although the biblical account also uses these words about other supportive women, it is, as we have seen, she who comes first.

Mary Magdalene is definitely and deliberately set apart from the other women by her very name. Every other woman who is mentioned by name in the canonical Gospels is defined by her relationship with a man, as 'wife of . . .' or 'mother of . . .' Only this Mary has what might be deemed a full name, although exactly what it means will be discussed later.

Yet this powerful and important character remains curiously enigmatic. After the somewhat backhanded compliment accorded to her in the Gospels when she appears to be singled out, she is never mentioned again – neither in the Acts of the Apostles nor in the writings of Paul (even in his description of the discovery of the empty tomb) nor in the letters of Peter. This might seem to be yet another mystery destined to be much discussed but never solved – until one turns to the writings known as the Gnostic Gospels, where the picture is suddenly clarified to a startling degree. These documents – of which there are over fifty – were discovered in 1945 at Nag Hammadi in Egypt and are a collection of early Gnostic Christian texts, the originals of some of which are acknowledged to date from roughly the same time as the canonical Gospels[11]. They are writings that were condemned as 'heretical' by the early Church and were therefore systematically sought out and destroyed, as if they contained some great secret that was potentially dangerous to the emerging Establishment.

What many of these forbidden texts proclaim was the pre-eminence of Mary Magdalene: one of them is even called *The Gospel of Mary*. The Mary of this gospel is not the Virgin, but Mary Magdalene.

Perhaps it is no coincidence that the four Gospels of the New Testament effectively marginalize her, while the 'heretical' writings emphasize her importance. Could it be that the New Testament is actually a form of propaganda on behalf of the anti-Magdalene party?

While we will be discussing the Gnostic Gospels in much greater detail in a later chapter, the following points are of immediate importance. The New Testament story, as we have seen, grudgingly implies that she had a major role in the Jesus movement, but the Gnostic Gospels openly proclaim and confirm her pre-eminence. Moreover, this superior status is not merely confined to her place among the womenfolk – she is *literally Apostle of the Apostles* and therefore acknowledged to be second only to Jesus, ranked above both male and female followers. She, it appears, was the one person who was effectively the bridge between Jesus and all his other disciples, and it was she who interpreted his words for their benefit. In these texts *it was not Peter who was Jesus' chosen second-in-command, but Mary Magdalene*.

She it was, according to the Gnostic *Gospel of Mary*, who rallied the despondent disciples after the Crucifixion and put some backbone into them when they were quite prepared to give up and go home after the apparent loss of their charismatic leader[12]. She countered all doubts, not only passionately but also with intelligence, and managed to inspire them to become true and devoted Apostles. This could not have been easy, for not only did she – presumably – have to counter the prevalent sexism of her day and culture, but she also had to contend with a powerful personal antagonist. This was Peter, the Big Fisherman of legend, the martyr and founder of the Roman Catholic Church. He, the Gnostic Gospels repeatedly claim, hated and feared her, although when his Master was alive he could only protest ineffectually at the extent of her influence[13]. Several of the texts recount heated exchanges between Peter and Mary, with the former demanding to know of Jesus why he apparently prefers the company of that woman. As Mary Magdalene says in another Gnostic Gospel, the *Pistis Sophia*: 'Peter makes me hesitate: I am afraid of him, because he hates the female race.'[14] And in the Gnostic *Gospel of Thomas* we find Peter saying: 'Let Mary leave us, for women are not worthy of life.'[15]

There is something else about the Gnostic accounts that makes them explosive where the Church is concerned. The picture they paint of Mary and Jesus' relationship was not merely that of teacher and pupil, or even guru and favourite student. They are depicted – often quite graphically – as being on more intimate terms. Take, for example, the Gnostic *Gospel of Philip*:

> But Christ loved her more than all the disciples and used to kiss her often on the mouth. The rest of the disciples were offended by it and expressed disapproval. They said to him, 'Why do you love her more than all of us?' The Saviour answered and said to them, 'Why do I not love you as I love her?'[16]

In the same Gnostic Gospel we read the apparently innocuous phrase: 'There were three who always walked with the Lord: Mary his mother, his sister and Magdalene, who is called his companion. His sister, his mother and his companion were all called Mary. *And the companion of the Saviour is Mary Magdalene.*'[17]

Whereas today the word 'companion' implies comrade, colleague and friend in a purely platonic sense, the original Greek word actually meant 'consort' or *sexual partner*[18] . . . Either the canonical Gospels were included in the New Testament because they and only they are the true word of God – and there are plenty of fundamentalists who believe this to be so – or the Gnostic Gospels contain at least as much valid information as Matthew, Mark, Luke and John. The balance of probability rests in favour of the Gnostic Gospels having just as much a claim on our respect as those in the New Testament.

If the Magdalene were really Jesus' lover or wife, then her enigmatic position in the New Testament is explained. She appears to be important, but the reason for her status is never clarified; perhaps the writers expected their audience to have prior knowledge of her relationship with Jesus. After all, it has been pointed out, rabbis were usually married as a matter of course: a bachelor preacher would have caused much more comment and a statement to that effect would almost certainly have been included in the Gospels. If Jesus had been celibate and childless in such a dynastic culture, not only would this have caused a stir, but it would have formed a much more obvious part of his reported teachings. In fact, celibacy was – and is – deemed so horrifying in the Judaic tradition as to be considered actually sinful. Jesus would have been notorious for preaching celibacy: this was never a charge levelled against him, even by his most implacable enemies. The monastic life was a much later accretion of Christianity – even the apparently misogynist Paul admitted that 'it is better to marry than to burn.'[19]

The very idea of Jesus as a sexual being is so antipathetic to most modern Christians that, as we have seen, Martin Scorsese's fantasy sequence of Jesus and Mary in bed provoked a mass howl of horror. Christians everywhere denounced it as sensationalism, sacrilege and blasphemy. But the real reason for this outrage was nothing less than the underlying atavistic fear and hatred of women. Traditionally they are seen as basically unclean and their physical proximity as polluting to the body, mind and spirit of naturally good pure men; surely the Son of God could never have put himself in such mortal danger. The horror felt at the idea of Jesus, of all men, being the sexual partner of any woman is multiplied a thousandfold when his lover is named as Mary Magdalene – *a known prostitute*.

Although we will be discussing this matter thoroughly later, suffice it to say here that the question of her being, or having been, a woman of the streets must remain open. There is evidence both for and against her one-time profession, but the most significant aspect of this matter is that the Church *chose to portray her as a prostitute*, if a repentant one. This at best highly selective interpretation of her character also served to convey two major messages: that the Magdalene in particular and all women in general were unclean and spiritually inferior to men, and that redemption is found only in the Church.

If it is unthinkable that Jesus and this (presumed) ex-whore were lovers, then to most Christians it is almost equally outrageous to suggest that they were man and wife. As we have seen, the authors of *The Holy Blood and the Holy Grail* argue that if the Magdalene were Jesus' wife then this would explain why she was so important to the Priory of Sion and its idea of a sacred bloodline. Yet that was by no means the first time that the idea had found its way into print.

It was in 1931 that D.H. Lawrence published his last novella, *The Man who Died*, in which Jesus survives the cross and finds true redemption through the sex act with Mary Magdalene, who is clearly identified as a priestess of Isis. Lawrence also associates Jesus with the dying-and-rising god Osiris, consort of that goddess. The story was originally entitled *The Escaped Cock*, and, as Susan Haskins writes:

> The cock is ... associated with the idea of the 'risen' body (the Christ-figure punningly exclaims 'I am risen!' on finally achieving an erection ...)[20]

(It seems strange that so much attention has been focused on *Lady Chatterley's Lover* when this other, potentially much more controversial, work has escaped censure.)

Although it is possible to make a good case for Jesus and the Magdalene being married – and, by implication, even having children – that in itself seems a weak reason for the Priory to invest so much passion in their devotion to her, because, as we saw in the last chapter, there are major reasons for discounting the idea that the Merovingian dynasty was descended from those two. Clearly her spell rests on something else, something elusive but not impossible to experience. Hints of it can be glimpsed in the power of her image in our culture, but it was in France that the real woman was supposed to have ended her days.

The most famous account of the Magdalene in France is Jacobus de Voragine's *Golden Legend* (1250)[21]. In it, de Voragine, the Dominican Archbishop of Genoa, refers to her as both *Illuminata* and *Illuminatrix* – the Illuminated and Illuminator – which is particularly interesting because these are the roles claimed for her throughout the 'forbidden' Gnostic texts. She is portrayed as being both enlightened and the bestower of enlightenment, initiate and initiatrix: there is no suggestion that she was spiritually inferior because she was a woman – quite the reverse.

As is the case with all legends, there are several variations on a central theme, which nevertheless remain remarkably constant. The main story is as follows: shortly after the Crucifixion, Mary Magdalene, together with her siblings Martha and Lazarus, plus several others – their identity varies depending on the version of the story – travelled by sea to the coast of what is now Provence. Among this moveable cast of extras is St Maximin, said to have been one of the seventy-two disciples of Jesus and the legendary first bishop of Provence; Mary Jacobi and Mary Salome, allegedly Jesus' aunts; a black servant girl called Sarah; and Joseph of Arimathea, a rich friend of Jesus who is more often linked to the Glastonbury story. The motive for what was supposedly a hazardous and uncomfortably long journey also depends on which version of the story you read. One is that this group had escaped from the persecution of the early Church by the Jews, and the other main motive given is that they had been deliberately set adrift by their enemies in a rudderless and oarless vessel. It was, of course, literally a miracle that they reached dry land.

The picture painted by the medieval story of the South of France in the days of the Magdalene was of a remote wilderness inhabited only by pagan savages. In fact Provence was a major part of the Roman Empire – a highly civilized area with flourishing Roman, Greek, and even Jewish communities; the Herod family owned estates in the South of France. And far from such a journey's being outlandishly arduous and off the map, it was a normal route for trading ships and no more difficult than the journey from say, Tyre or Sidon to Rome. If this particular party had come to Provence, they may well have done so voluntarily, without having been forced to flee.

The legends agree that they disembarked at what is now the town of Saintes-Maries-de-la-Mer, in the Camargue. Once there, the group split up and went their various ways to spread the Gospel. The story goes that the Magdalene preached throughout the region, converting the heathen before becoming a hermit in a cave at Sainte-Baume. Some stories have her living there for the implausible but biblically time-honoured period of forty years, spending what must have been very long days repenting of her sins and meditating on Jesus. To add a bit of spice to the story, she is believed to have spent all this time naked except for curiously abundant hair, which clothed her effectively in a way reminiscent of John the Baptist's animal skins. At the end of her life, we are told, she was carried by angels to St Maximin (by then the first bishop of Provence) who gave her the last rites just before she died. Her body was buried at the town named after him.

A pretty tale, but is there any truth in it? For a start, it is extremely unlikely that the Magdalene was a hermit, for however long, in a cave at Sainte-Baume. Even today's official guardian of the Catholic shrine admits that she was never there[22]. The site is not without significance, however. In Roman times it was far from the back of beyond hermitage of legend, being a well populated area, and that very cave was a centre for the worship of the goddess Diana Lucifera (the 'light bringer' or *Illuminatrix*). Although a naked – but unshorn – Magdalene would certainly have been the centre of attention, she would hardly have been alone in that place of worship, for many other priestesses and worshippers would have flocked to the cave. But while the Christianization of pagan sites, if only retrospectively, is a well-known historical practice, something else appears to be hinted at here.

(Interestingly, Arles – the nearest populous town to the place where the Magdalene is believed to have disembarked – was a major centre of the Isis cult[23]. This unwelcoming and marshy area appears to have been home to several goddess-worshipping groups, and no doubt continued to provide a refuge for cult members well into Christian times.)

In fact, the metamorphosis of the once splendidly voluptuous Magdalene into the gaunt, tearful hermit was the deliberate Christianization of a much more ambivalent story: all the key elements were taken from the legend of the fifth-century St

Mary the Egyptian, who was also a prostitute turned hermit and whose penitence in the wilderness of Palestine lasted forty-seven years. (Obviously, however, old habits died hard, because she financed her boat trip there by providing her usual personal services for the sailors – and even more remarkably, she was actually considered extra holy for doing so . . .)

Clearly – and in the light of other evidence given later – the 'penitent' part of the Magdalene story is a deliberate invention on the part of the medieval Church to make her more acceptable. But discovering what she was *not* did not in itself clarify either her story or her personality. Yet time and time again we were faced with the curious attraction of this woman, that goes beyond mere contemporary charisma, and whose appeal not only survived the centuries but actually appears to be on the increase in our own time.

There are thousands of saintly legends, some more believable than others, but sadly, most of them are mere fable. Why should the case of Mary Magdalene be any different? Why should there be any substance to this legend? Many commentators have claimed that the legend of the Magdalene in France was simply the invention of canny French publicists, eager to create a spurious biblical legacy for themselves (rather like the stories of the boy Jesus visiting England's West Country).

Undeniably, many of the details of the story of the French Magdalene are later accretions, but there are reasons to suspect that on the whole it is based on fact. For although it may be going too far to claim that Jesus visited the West Country – then a very remote area outside the Roman Empire – it is hardly the same thing to suggest that a woman of independent means would sail to a thriving culture on the shores of the romanized Mediterranean. But far more telling was the nature of her role in these tales: she is explicitly depicted as a preacher. As we have seen, the very early Church referred to her as 'the Apostle of the Apostles', but by the Middle Ages it would have been unthinkable to ascribe such a role to a woman. If, as critics maintain, the French Magdalene legend had been invented by medieval monks then they would hardly have granted her the by then emphatically male role of *Apostle*. This suggests that the story was based on a real memory, however embellished over the centuries, of the woman herself. And significantly, historians agree that Christianity was established in Provence in the first century[24].

Taking the city of Marseilles as our base, we set out to visit the main sites associated with the Magdalene legend.

The trail, like the story itself, began at Saintes-Maries-de-la-Mer, which lies some two hours' drive from Marseilles into the Camargue, the marshy area dotted with pools – *étangs* – where the mouth of the Rhône meets the Mediterranean. Saintes-Maries is the only town in an area otherwise effectively given over to the breeding of horses, for which the Camargue is famous, and which also provides sanctuary for many species of water bird, including flocks of flamingo which visit this coastline from Africa. It is a wild place, buzzing with clouds of mosquitoes at dusk, and after a long drive across the marshes from Arles it comes as something of a shock to arrive at Saintes-Maries and discover it to be a bustling tourist town, complete with funfair, bars and restaurants. Like the rest of the Camargue, it has a distinctly Spanish feel, even down to the bullring – which, here, is beside the beach.

The galleon-like church of Notre-Dame de la Mer rises abruptly above the low buildings of the town and it is no surprise to learn that this twelfth-century church was built complete with fortifications: being in a remote coastal town, it was under constant threat from pirates and other enemies[25].

Three Marys are venerated here: Mary Magdalene, Mary Jacobi and Mary Salome. The church was of particular interest to René d'Anjou (1408–1480), King of Naples and Sicily and, according to the Priory of Sion, its one-time Grand Master. 'Good King René' as he is known to history, was a passionate devotee of the Magdalene, and secured permission from the Pope to excavate the crypt. He found two skeletons, which were declared to be those of Marys Jacobi and Salome, but of the Magdalene he found no trace.

In the bowels of the church there is a curious altar dedicated to Sarah the Egyptian, supposedly the servant of the Marys. Traditionally believed to be black, she is the patron saint of the gypsies, who converge on the town in their thousands every 25 May for a festival in her honour. They elect that year's Gypsy Queen in front of Sarah's statue, which is then taken in procession and ceremoniously dipped in the sea. Naturally this event has become a major tourist feature of the area, and has attracted many famous names over the years – including Bob Dylan, who was inspired to write a song about his visit[26].

Among other illustrious visits is one commemorated by a plaque in the square outside the church: that of Cardinal Angelo Roncalli (1881–1963), then the Vatican's ambassador to France and later Pope John XXIII. It has been claimed that he was a member of the Priory of Sion, at the time when Jean Cocteau held the title of John XXIII as Grand Master[27].

Following what is claimed to have been the Magdalene's own itinerary, we went back to the heat and bustle of Marseilles, where she preached. Of the two cathedrals, which stand side by side, one is merely 150 years old and is still in use today. Although its decoration celebrates the Magdalene theme, this is presumably the result of local traditions and expectations. It is the older building, the Vieille Major, which is by far the more interesting of the two and contains apparently authentic depictions of the saint's life and work in the area. And, just like the dome of Notre-Dame de France in London, the ceiling has been decorated to look like a giant spider's web. By now deemed unsafe, however, this cathedral is no longer open to the public.

Built in the twelfth century on the site of a fifth-century baptistery, it is redolent of ancient Magdalenism. Not only is there a chapel dedicated to her specifically, but also St Serenus' chapel has a series of bas-reliefs depicting scenes from her life – which were commissioned by René d'Anjou. One of them actually shows her *preaching*, thus reinforcing the Gnostic

Gospels' image of her as Apostle. And, as she was presumably successful in converting the 'heathen', someone must have been on hand to baptize them into the Christian faith – but who was it? Could it possibly be that she, Apostle of the Apostles, took on that role herself?

Local tradition has her preaching on the steps of an old temple of Diana. This building did not, in fact, provide the actual foundations for either of the cathedrals of Marseilles, but is said to have been located at what is now the Place de Lenche – in a tangle of streets roughly 200 metres away. There is nothing there to commemorate its claim to historical fame, but there is something compelling in the locals' insistence that this unremarkable triangular spot is the place where the Magdalene once preached.

Past the fort of St John the Baptist and the picturesque old port with the world-famous, if malodorous, fish-market, is the abbey of St Victor. This is another important religious site – there has been a monastery there since the early fifth century, and that, in turn, was built on a pagan cemetery. The present building dates from the thirteenth century, but its crypt is much older and contains many ornate sarcophagi from the Roman period. The crypt also contains a cave-like chapel to the Magdalene. But to us, by far the most fascinating feature of this place was the thirteenth-century statue of Notre-Dame de Confession. Holding a child in her arms, she is shown as being black-skinned. She is one of the legendary – and controversial – 'Black Madonnas'.

To the east of Marseilles is Sainte-Baume – the large cavern where Mary Magdalene is supposed to have seen out her days as a hermit. A steep and winding road climbs sharply to nearly 1,000 metres, before levelling out onto a plateau and eventually conducting the visitor to a small cluster of buildings that constitute the village of Sainte Baume. From there it is a long, hot walk through woods to the grotto itself, now a Catholic sanctuary. However, there are no revelations to be had here, for, as we have seen, the Church grafted Sainte-Baume onto the Magdalene story to make it parallel the life of another prostitute-saint, Mary the Egyptian, and at the time of the Magdalene's supposed time there the grotto was a centre of pagan goddess worship. The myth had the double value of making the maverick Magdalene into someone easier for the Church to patronize, and of turning a former pagan site into a focus for Christian pilgrims.

From Sainte Baume the road continues on to the supposed site of the Magdalene's death and burial, Saint-Maximin-la-Sainte-Baume, where her annual festival was in full swing.

The glorious procession of the Magdalene's head begins with a service in the basilica Sainte-Marie-Madeleine, then the relics, which are normally locked in the sacristy, are mounted on litters and carried on a prescribed route through the winding, narrow streets of the town of St Maximin. A pipe and drum band, dressed in traditional Provençal costume, leads the parade, ushering in bishops, priests, Dominican monks and local worthies. As something of a 'warm-up' perhaps, there follow two litters bearing small statues of minor saints. Then, after a long wait, comes the head itself. Adorned with little gold medals around the edge of the canopy, the precious relic is clearly of enormous importance. Townsfolk bearing spears maintain a symbolic guard around it, and such is its drawing power that we spotted one young woman who completely forgot all ideas of modesty and leant out of her window to watch – without a stitch on. (There are those who might say this was only too appropriate where this particular saint is concerned.)

Everywhere the relic is taken the same haunting refrain wells up from the officiating clergy and the crowd, a special hymn to Mary Magdalene, which culminates in a soaring rendition within the basilica itself, led by its world-famous grand organ. But is all this flamboyance and ceremonial merely window dressing? Does it tell us anything at all about the real Mary Magdalene, the enigmatic woman from the New Testament who may actually have been the wife of Jesus?

Her relics were found, it is said, buried in the crypt of the church at St Maximin on 9 December 1279 by Charles II d'Anjou, Count of Provence. What was believed to be her skeleton was discovered in a costly alabaster sarcophagus dating from the fifth century. The explanation for this late entombment was found in documents discovered within it – saying that in 710 CE the Magdalene's body had been hidden in another sarcophagus to protect it from Saracen invaders and it was only at this later date that the record was set straight. The skeleton is still in its stone coffin in the crypt of the basilica, although the skull is in the ornate golden reliquary inside the sacristy. Charles d'Anjou sponsored the building of the basilica and he also – with papal approval – put it under the protection of the Dominican Order. The building, begun in 1295, was apparently completed after 250 years, but – as is the tendency with cathedrals – it has never actually been finished. Charles' original intention had been to make this a centre for Magdalene pilgrims, although it was not to achieve the same fame as, say, St James of Compostela.[28]

The medieval relic trade was, even at the time, infamous among the educated as being a blatant money-spinning exercise at the expense of simple piety. Thousands of pilgrims and believers poured money into the coffers of those Church authorities who claimed to have genuine holy relics on their premises. Of course by far the most lucrative sort of relic was the actual body of a saint, or at least a part of one. Wherever you went in Christendom, you were sure to find the toenail of some holy person and the earlobe of another. The irony was that even the most cynical and outrageous of exhibitors found it hard to convince the hordes of eager pilgrims that they had anything connected with Jesus himself, for had he not ascended bodily into heaven? The nearest they could manage were thorns from the 'crown' of thorns, or splinters from the True Cross – of which there were so many that it is estimated they would, if put together, make a veritable forest.

These days very few commentators, especially from outside the Catholic Church, have any qualms about denouncing almost all so-called relics as fakes, even admitting that they are such pathetic hoaxes that they add insult to injury. Sadly, the 'bones of Mary Magdalene' at St Maximin are definitely fakes, and it can be proved beyond doubt that the documents that apparently authenticated them are blatant forgeries – they used the dating system current in the thirteenth century, which was different from that of the eighth, and there was no Saracen threat in France at the time indicated[29].

There are, however, elements to this story that suggest that something more than simple venality was behind the hoax. It is true that the possession of relics was a lucrative business, but where the alleged bodies of great historical figures are concerned there is often another motive involved. For example, the alleged remains of King Arthur and his queen were found at Glastonbury in the eleventh century. Most people think this was merely the abbot's ruse to put his abbey on the map, but it had another dimension to it. At the time the English were involved in the conquest of Wales, and to the Welsh King Arthur was a legendary hero, a symbol of their defiance, who, it was popularly believed, had not died but would, at some point in the future, return to take their side against their enemies. By producing his corpse, the English delivered a psychological blow to the Welsh.

Mary Magdalene's bones were thought to be at Vézelay in Burgundy, where they had been taken from Provence and were kept under the altar of the abbey of Sainte-Marie-Madeleine and never seen. Then, in 1265, Saint Louis – a great collector and venerator of relics – ordered that they be exhumed and, two years later, that they be exhibited at a great ceremony, which he attended. Unfortunately all the monks of Vézelay could manage were a few bones in a metal coffer, not the complete skeleton that they were supposed to have had[30]. (This story is remarkable for the complete lack of resourcefulness shown by the monks in this situation.) As Louis' nephew, Charles II d'Anjou, then nineteen years old, would have been present at this ceremony.

After this event, Charles became convinced – for reasons that remain a mystery – that the real body of the Magdalene was still somewhere in Provence, and became obsessed with finding it. His passion for her has always puzzled scholars and has prompted one French historian to write: 'One would like to know from where the prince had drawn this devotion.'[31] Charles ordered the excavations beneath the church of St Maximin, digging with his own hands. Although the relics that were eventually unearthed, and which are revered today, are fakes, from Charles' actions it would seem that if there was any deception involved, it was played on, not by, him. However, there is another possibility: the 'discovery' of the relics at St Maximin was, in fact, a deliberate ploy to stop any further search for them. Meanwhile, Charles and his family would continue to look secretly . . .

When the bones were found, Charles lobbied the Pope to give official recognition to those relics over those at Vézelay – which he did in 1295 – and to approve the building of the basilica. However, it seems that something more was going on, as it is known that Charles made his plans in secret meetings with local archbishops. He was also keen to have the Dominican Order replace the Benedictines who were already installed at St Maximin, even though the former were reluctant to take over and eventually had to be ordered to do so by the Pope. The basilica was placed under the Pope's direct control, not the local archbishop's, but the change of auspices met with such fierce local resistance that Charles had to send troops in to help the new Dominican master and the representatives of the Pope and the king when they officially took charge.[32] One curious result of this was that the Dominicans adopted the Magdalene as their patron saint in 1297, with the epithet 'daughter, sister and mother' to the order[33].

As we have seen, a later descendant of Charles, René d'Anjou (an alleged Grand Master of the Priory of Sion), held the Magdalene in equally high esteem. He is said to have owned a Grail-style cup bearing the enigmatic inscription:

He who drinks deeply will see God. He who drinks it all in a single gulp will see God and the Magdalene.[34]

95

Mary Magdalene was clearly of great and abiding significance to the d'Anjou family: yet there is a mystery hidden in their fervour for her. The fact that René d'Anjou excavated at Saintes-Maries-de-la-Mer – apparently to search for the Magdalene's remains – was particularly odd because 200 years before Charles d'Anjou claimed to have found them at St Maximin. It seems that, despite the rival claims to have her remains, no-one had actually found them.

In Marseilles we had discovered one of the strange 'Black Madonnas' that we knew to be intimately connected with the Magdalene tradition, although quite why or how we were unsure.

These religious statues are precisely like the usual depictions of the Madonna and child, but for some reason the Madonna is shown as being *black-skinned*. They are not, it must be said, greatly beloved of the Church, which regards them with suspicion to say the least, and there are many theories to account for their blackness. What possible connection could they have to the Magdalene, a woman who is presumed to have been of Middle Eastern race – and who is traditionally thought to have been childless? We delved further into the cult of the Black Madonna in the hope of finding some clues.[35]

Known also as Black Virgins, each one of these statues has become the centre of a cult wherever it is located. Although Black Madonnas are found over a wide area in Europe, including sites in Poland and even in the UK, the highest proportion of them – around 65 per cent according to Ean Begg's 1985 survey – is found in France, and of those most are located in the south.[36]

Although these statues clearly still evoke huge, passionate followings, these are on a local scale and are *never* officially recognized or supported by the Catholic Church. There is, as we can vouch for in our own experience, something deemed 'not quite nice' about Black Madonnas. Ean Begg, in his book *The Cult of the Black Virgin* (1985), writes:

> ... there was no mistaking the hostility, when, on 28 December 1952, as [papers were presented] on Black Virgins to the American Association for the Advancement of Science, every priest and nun in the audience walked out.[37]

He goes on to mention that, active hostility apart, most modern priests profess either lack of interest or ignorance on the subject, and have no wish to investigate it.

During the research for his book, Begg frequently visited known Black Madonna sites only to discover that the local priest declared he had no knowledge of such a statue, or claimed that it had disappeared somehow or other. Yet wherever the Black Madonnas have existed or continue to be found, there is enormous local love and devotion showered upon them. So what is there about such cults that is so antipathetic to mainstream Catholicism?

There are many theories put forward to account for their blackness, ranging from the ridiculous to the sublime, although heavily weighted towards the former. Ean Begg cites a typical exchange between a colleague and a priest on the subject: to the question, 'Father, why is the Madonna black?' the priest's answer was, 'My son, she is black because she is black.'[38] Other explanations include the patronizing suggestion that such statues have only become black over the centuries because they have been subject to atmospheres that are thick with candle smoke. Of course the fact that every other statue of the same age and in the same place has remained at least *washable* poses fairly obvious questions. People are not so naive that they have mistakenly venerated dirty-faced Madonnas for centuries with such a rare and special passion. Besides, most of these statues were in fact deliberately painted black or made of black material such as ebony; therefore, one may reasonably suppose, they were intended to be black.

Perhaps more plausible, is the idea that these statues are dark because they were brought back by Crusaders from

97

places where people were dark-skinned. The fact is, however, that most of the Black Virgins were actually made in the places where they were to be worshipped, and that they were not copied from a design brought back from exotic foreign countries by the Crusaders.

Then there is another, considerably more persuasive, theory. Black Madonnas are almost always associated with much more ancient *pagan* sites[39]. And whereas the Christianization of such places has been a common enough phenomenon in Europe, the very blackness of these images suggests that they represent the continuation of pagan goddess worship that is dressed up as Christianity. This is, presumably, why the Church treats them with disdain, although the fervour accorded to them makes such worship nigh on impossible to ban. Besides, in order for a ban to take effect – certainly these days – reasons would have to be given which would merely draw attention to what has been going on for nearly 2000 years.

Pagan connections in themselves do not, of course, explain why the Madonnas are black – despite Christian apologists who claim that any such link must, at least symbolically, be 'dark'. Yet many of these sites have been associated with pre-Christian goddesses such as Diana and Cybele, who have been shown as black during the long period that they have been worshipped.

Another goddess who was sometimes represented as being black was Isis, whose cult lasted well into the Christian era around the Mediterranean. Sister of Nepythys, she was a multifaceted deity whose special gifts included magic and healing, and who was closely associated with the sea and the moon. Her consort, Osiris, who as god of the underworld and death was also represented as black, was foully betrayed and done to death by the evil god Set, but magically restored to life by Isis, in order to beget the child Horus.

It is acknowledged that the early Christians appropriated much of Isis' iconography for the Virgin Mary. For example, she was given several of Isis' titles – such as 'Star of the Sea'

(*Stella maris*) and 'Queen of Heaven'. And, traditionally, Isis was shown standing on a crescent moon, or with stars in her hair or around her head: so is Mary the Virgin. But the most strikingly similar image is that of the mother and child. Christians may believe that statues of Mary and the baby Jesus represent an exclusively Christian iconography, but in fact the whole concept of the Madonna and child was already firmly present in the cult of Isis.[40]

Isis, too, was worshipped as a holy virgin. But although she was also mother of Horus, this presented no problem to the minds of her millions of followers. For whereas modern Christians are expected to accept the Virgin birth as an article of faith *and* an actual historical event, the followers of Isis (Isians) and other pagans faced no such intellectual dilemma. To them, Zeus, Venus or Ma'at may or may not have once walked the earth: what mattered was what they *embodied*. Each of the pantheon ruled over his or her own area of human life; for example, the Egyptian goddess Ma'at dealt with the concept of justice, both in the material world and when the souls of the dead were weighed in the balance. The gods were understood to be living *archetypes*, not historical characters. Isians did not waste their time searching for cloths that may have wrapped the body of Osiris, nor did they consider it important to find splinters of the box in which he was confined. Far from being an unsophisticated and ignorant religion, theirs appears to have had a profound grasp of the human psyche.

Isis was worshipped as both Virgin and Mother – but not as a *Virgin* Mother. Isians would have considered the notion of the Virgin birth frankly ridiculous: the gods may be capable of wonders, but they do not demand that their worshippers suspend their disbelief quite so much. The worship of most major goddesses emphasized their essential femininity by dividing it up into three main aspects, each representing the lifecycle of real women. First, there is the Virgin, then the Mother, then the Crone; all three are also linked to the new moon, the full moon and the dark of the moon. Each goddess, including Isis, was understood to stand for the whole of female experience, including sexual love, and therefore could be invoked to help a woman with any kind of problem – unlike the Virgin Mary whose own presumed purity is an impenetrable barrier for those who would like to share their sexual problems with her.

Isis, a full-blooded woman who represents a complete female lifecycle, was sometimes represented as being black. And her cult was considerably more widespread than might be supposed. For example, a temple dedicated to her has been found as far north as Paris, and there is evidence to suppose that this was not an isolated establishment. Isis, the beautiful girl-goddess to whom women could pray – with a clear conscience – about absolutely anything, appealed to women from all cultures. When the patriarchal Church came along its first instinct was to eradicate pagan goddess worship. But the yearning for a goddess remained firm and posed a threat to the Church Fathers. So the Virgin Mary was permitted to exist as a kind of bowdlerized version of Isis, resolutely unacquainted with the biological, emotional and spiritual imperatives of real women, a makeshift goddess created by misogynists for misogynists. But it was unlikely that the sexless Virgin Mary would have taken over from Isis without some kind of backlash from her followers. How could the good, but essentially colourless, mother of Jesus fully take the place of the well-rounded Isis – not only Virgin, Mother and Crone, but also sexual initiatrix and controller of men's destinies? Could it be that the cult of Mary Magdalene, like that of the Black Madonna that is so despised by the Church, actually hides a much older and more complete idea of womanhood?

It has been well established that Black Madonna sites are associated with old pagan locations – but there is another link that is not so widely recognized. Time and time again these enigmatic statues and their age-old cults seem to flourish alongside that of Mary Magdalene. For example, the famous black statue of St Sarah the Egyptian is found at Saintes-Maries-de-la-Mer – the very place where the Magdalene is said to have disembarked after her journey from Palestine. And in Marseilles there are no fewer than three Black Madonnas, one in the crypt of the basilica of St Victor, immediately outside the underground chapel that is dedicated to Mary Magdalene. There is another in 'her' church in Aix-en-Provence (close to the place where she is believed to have been buried) and yet another in that town's main church of St Saveur.

The link between the cult of Mary Magdalene and that of the Black Madonna is undeniable. Ean Begg notes that no fewer than fifty centres of the former also contain shrines to the Black Virgin[41]. A study of the map of Black Madonna sites in France shows that the greatest concentration is in the Lyons/Vichy/Clermont-Ferrand area, centred on a range of hills called the Monts de la Madeleine. High concentrations of Black Madonna sites are also found in Provence and the eastern Pyrenees, both areas intimately connected with the Magdalene legend – so the association between the two cults is clear, although the reason for it is less so.

Here again we encounter the Priory of Sion, for – although this is not widely known – it is particularly interested in the Black Madonna cult. (It is curious that this is not mentioned in *The Holy Blood and the Holy Grail* because two of its authors, Michael Baigent and Richard Leigh, wrote articles on the subject for the weekly publication *The Unexplained* at the same time as their book came out[42].) Several of the places associated with the Priory have their own Black Madonnas, such as Sion-Vaudémont and the place where its members traditionally meet to elect Grand Masters, Blois in the Loire Valley[43].

The Black Madonna cult is central to the Priory. Its members single out the one at Goult, near Avignon, for special veneration; she is known as 'Notre-Dame de Lumières' (Our Lady of the Lights)[44]. To them, at least, there is no doubt about the real significance of the Black Madonna. Pierre Plantard de Saint-Clair writes explicitly, '*The Black Virgin is Isis* and her name is Notre-Dame de Lumière.'[45]

There appears to be a discrepancy here, for what possible link could there be between Isis/Black Madonnas and the

Priory's obsession with the Merovingian bloodline? Plantard de Saint-Clair explains the connection between the Priory and the Black Madonnas by claiming that their worship was promoted by the Merovingians. Even suspending disbelief about the reality of the bloodline, this fits awkwardly with the claims that it was descended from the Jews of the line of David. Begg notes another discrepancy: while the modern Priory's veneration of Isis may be seen as an attempt to provide themselves with a pedigree that goes back to Roman times and beyond, the female deities worshipped in Gaul were very largely Cybele and Diana, not Isis. Plantard de Saint-Clair insists that the Priory's involvement is specifically with Isis – but why? Begg suggests that it could be a device for hinting at some important ancient Egyptian connection[46].

If there is one legendary figure who can provide an answer to this riddle, or who represents the bridge between the pagan and Christian traditions that come together in the Black Madonna cult, it is surely Mary Magdalene. We have seen how important she is to the Priory, who see Isis in the Black Madonnas. But just why should this famous Christian penitent have come to be associated with ancient pagan sites?

One clue may lie in the Song of Songs, the collection of erotic poetry that is bizarrely included in the Old Testament and which is traditionally ascribed to King Solomon, writing to praise the Queen of Sheba's lavish charms. And, oddly, one of these passages is read out on the Magdalene's feast day in Catholic churches. It reads (Song of Songs 3:1–4):

> By night on my bed I sought him whom my soul loveth: I sought him, but I found him not.
>
> I will arise now, and go about the city in the streets, and in the broad ways I will seek him whom my soul loveth: I sought him, but I found him not.
>
> The watchmen that go about the city found me: to whom I said, Saw ye him whom my soul loveth?
>
> It was but a little that I passed from them, but I found him whom my soul loveth: I held him, and would not let him go,

until I had brought him into my mother's house, and into the chamber of her that conceived me.

The Song of Songs has been associated, from the early years of the Christian era, with the Magdalene[47]. In that case, perhaps there is some other connection hidden in the verses, for they also have the female lover saying 'I am black, but comely', which is yet another link with the Black Madonna cult[48], and, if the Priory is to be believed on this point, with the Egyptian goddess Isis.

This was bewildering, for if there appear to be few obvious connections between the Magdalene and the Black Madonnas, there are also few between the saint and the Song of Songs. Although, like the female lover who laments in those verses, Isis went out to search for her husband Osiris, what possible parallel is there in the story of Mary Magdalene? At first there appear to be no direct answers. It seems as if no one set of permutations fits all the known facts.

There is another, even more confusing element to take into account. Provence, home of Magdalenism and of several Black Madonnas, is also pervaded with a strong sense of another significant New Testament figure – John the Baptist. We were struck by the number of churches dedicated to, and places named after, him in the same area. In Marseilles, apart from a church dedicated to the Baptist, there is the old Knights Hospitaller fort of St John, which still guards the harbour entrance. In Aix-en-Provence we find the large church of St John of Malta; there is a bas-relief of John's beheading on the wall of a house in the street leading up to it. Elsewhere in our travels we were to come across the same inexplicable phenomenon; the highest concentration of Magdalene sites also contained more than the average number of churches dedicated to John the Baptist. Perhaps this apparently strange connection is what prompted Ean Begg to muse:

. . . the story of the Black Virgin may also include a heretical secret with the power to shock and astonish even current post-Christian attitudes, a secret, moreover, involving political forces still influential in modern Europe.[49]

Of course the prevalence of buildings dedicated to John the Baptist may easily be explained by the fact that the Knights Hospitaller (who were later known as the Knights of Malta) have always particularly venerated him and they have had a strong presence in the area. But another major chivalric Order who were a force to be reckoned with in the south of France were the more famous Knights Templar – and they, too, gave special homage to the Baptist.

While we were in Provence we could hardly miss the opportunity to visit the area of St-Jean-Cap-Ferrat, which Jean Cocteau made his home. The drive from Marseilles to Nice seemed to take forever, even though it is only a little further up the coastline towards the ritzier city-state of Monaco. St-Jean-Cap-Ferrat lies at the end of a peninsula and its history of providing a haven for film luminaries such as David Niven inevitably invokes cinematic imagery. Certainly it boasts some of the richest residences one could possibly imagine outside of a Bond movie[50] – and a certain Château St Jean that broods almost menacingly behind its sinister shades is like something out of a Hitchcock film. Yet even in this playground of the rich and famous all is not quite as materialistic as it seems: and the local emphasis on 'St Jean' is no accident.

The village itself has a church dedicated to John the Baptist, who is the saint after whom the area is named. Once again, this is thanks to the presence of the Knights of Malta, whose chapel of St Hospice still stands on the site of their original fort at the extreme tip of the peninsula, St John's Point – clearly an excellent place to keep lookout. The chapel walls are decorated with several plaques commemorating the visits of various Grand Masters of their Order over the years, and the area outside bears the name 'Place des Chevaliers de Malte' (Knights of Malta Square). This is dominated by the huge bronze statue of a Madonna and child which, although it has accrued a distinct dark-green patina, is known locally as *La Vierge*

Noire – The Black Virgin. Over five metres tall, she has over-looked the sea for nearly a century. Here is that strange phenomenon of the apparently symbiotic relationship of Black Madonna sites and those dedicated to the Baptist.

It is on the nearby mainland, however, that one finds an unexpected connection with the Priory of Sion. In the small town of Villefranche-sur-Mer there is a tiny harbourside chapel used by the fishing community. Because of that association it is dedicated to St Peter (the 'Big Fisherman'), but to us its main interest lay in the identity of the creator of its remarkable decor – it was designed and executed by Jean Cocteau, who completed it in 1958, although it had been a dream of his for many years. In the end he was personally responsible for every aspect of the chapel's decoration, down to the replastering of the walls and the design of the candle-sticks. And the end result is, not to put too fine a point on it, *weird*. There is a vague similarity to the decor of a Masonic temple, although the imagery is considerably more surreal. Staring eyes are painted everywhere: there are giant ones on either side of the altar, but a host of small ones are liberally dotted throughout, and peculiar figures – such as a woman raising three fingers very deliberately at the observer – grace the walls.

Of all the bizarre clusters of figures and symbols in the chapel, however, one in particular leapt out at us: it shows figures of gypsies dancing in the company of a goddess-like girl – clearly an allusion to the annual ceremony at Saintes-Maries-de-la-Mer. This is an odd reference to find at the other end of Provence, and in a chapel dedicated to St Peter – who, according to the Gnostic Gospels, was the enemy of the Priory's beloved Mary Magdalene.

Cocteau decorated this chapel immediately before working on the London mural, and in both cases the visitor goes away with an uneasy feeling, as if subliminal images are communi-cating something at an unconscious level that is quite different from the message supposedly contained within Christian buildings.

About thirty-five kilometres north of the luxury of Nice lies a cluster of villages that form part of the emerging pattern of coexisting Magdalene and John the Baptist sites. Along the valley of the River Vésubie runs the at one time important route from the Alps to the coast, and it is close to this area that we find evocative place names with the same associations as we found near St Jean-Cap-Ferrat. For example, the village of Sainte-Madaleine (sic) is found near to the places of *Marie* and *St Jean*.

That is not all. In the very same area there is the old Templar town of Utelle, whose medieval houses still bear the esoteric sigils of the alchemists, and further up the valley there is Roquebillière, another settlement of the chivalric brotherhood. The largest town is St-Martin-de-Vésubie, site of a legendary massacre of Templars in 1308.[51]

This is the homeland of a famous Black Madonna: la Madone des Fenestres (the Madonna of the Windows, although the actual derivation is contested), who was introduced to the area by the Templars. But the statue was, according to local tradition, brought to France by Mary Magdalene[52]. And while legends do not necessarily have any basis in fact, it is still interesting that the people here apparently found it natural to make associations between the Magdalene, the Black Virgin cult – and the Templars.

Just across the valley from St-Martin-de-Vésubie is the village of Venanson, where the chapel of Saint Sébastien is perched on a rock high above the one and only road. Inside, it boasts a picture of St Grat, a one-time local bishop, holding the head of John the Baptist. A mere five kilometres from this chapel there is, in the village of Saint-Dalmas, the Templar church of Sainte-Croix, one of the most ancient religious buildings of France. Its walls carry paintings of Salome presenting the head of John the Baptist to her mother Herodias and stepfather Herod.

Of course many churches, both Catholic and Protestant, carry some kind of representation of the Baptist, but they usually show John baptizing Jesus. Very few depict scenes of

John being beheaded, or feature his severed head, for it is only in those places where he is particularly venerated that such imagery is deemed appropriate. In this area of France, however, there are a number of such depictions – and this is by no means an accident for, as we have seen, it is a land where one once found a large concentration of Templars and associated Orders. John the Baptist has always been known to be the Templars' patron saint and is therefore especially revered by them. But just why was John the Baptist so important to the Templars and Knights of Malta? That was a question which was to assume a greater importance as our investigation proceeded.

Our trip to Provence had revealed that there was something substantial behind the Magdalene legends of the area, but it had also permitted tantalizing glimpses of something older, bigger, more organized – perhaps even darker. As we followed in her footsteps we began to find layer upon layer of esoteric associations that often went back centuries. Wherever the Magdalene was, there was usually a Black Madonna, and where that cult had operated there was once a thriving shrine to a pagan goddess. The other threads in the web connected this feminine triumvirate to the Priory of Sion, and – inexplicably – with the Templar's veneration of John the Baptist.

In those early stages of our investigation we recognized that such connections existed, but could make little sense of them. Sometimes, indeed, we feared we never would. But as we persisted in our research, apparently irreconcilable facts, legends and characters began to fall into place in the overall picture – and it was one of which Leonardo himself might have been proud.

With no idea just how disturbing our ultimate findings would be, we left Provence behind and headed deeper into the heartland of European heresy.

CHAPTER FOUR

Heartland of Heresy

The Magdalene legends stretch beyond Provence, although the sites associated with her earthly life in France are to be found only there. Stories of her abound right across the south, and are particularly concentrated close to the Pyrenees in the south-west, and in the Ariège. And it is to these lands that she is said to have carried the Holy Grail. Predictably, they are also home to a great many Black Madonnas, particularly in the eastern Pyrenees.

Heading west with Marseilles behind us, we approached the region of Languedoc-Roussillon, once the richest area of France, and now among its poorest. In this depopulated country, the land seems to echo with one's thoughts and little else for mile after mile, despite the increasing number of tourists who come to lap up its blood-soaked history – not to mention the local wine. And while we, as good Europeans, made our own contribution to the local economy, we were there first and foremost to examine the past.

Evidence of the region's turbulent history is everywhere. Ruined châteaux and ancient citadels, torn apart on the orders of kings and popes, litter the landscape and tell of brutalities that surpass even the usual medieval penchant for ruling by atrocity. For if anywhere in Europe could be said to have been a home for heresy, it is Languedoc-Roussillon. And it is this single fact of history that has been responsible for the systematic impoverishment of the area. Outside of regions such as Bosnia and Northern Ireland, rarely has religion made its mark on the fortunes of a country in quite such an obvious way.

Formerly just the Languedoc – from *Langue d'Oc*, the local language – it stretched from Provence to the area between

Toulouse and the eastern Pyrenees. Until the thirteenth century it was not properly part of France, but was ruled by the counts of Toulouse who, although nominally owing allegiance to the kings of France, were in practice even more wealthy and powerful.

In the eleventh and twelfth centuries this area was the envy of Europe for its civilization and culture. Its art, literature and science were by far the most advanced of the day – but in the thirteenth century this brilliant and glittering culture was ripped apart by an invasion from the barbaric north, causing a simmering resentment that persists to this day. Many of the inhabitants still prefer to regard the land as Occitania, its former name. It is, as we were to find, a region with a particularly long memory.

The old Languedoc has always been a heartland for heretical and unorthodox ideas, probably because a culture that encourages the pursuit of knowledge tends to tolerate radical new thought.

A central part of this milieu were the troubadours – those travelling minstrels whose songs of love were essentially hymns to the Feminine Principle. This whole tradition of courtly love centred on idealized womanhood, and on *the* ideal woman, the Goddess. Romantic they may have been, but the songs of the troubadours also conveyed real eroticism. The influence of the movement, however, extended beyond the Languedoc, and was particularly successful in Germany and the Low Countries where the troubadours were known as *minnesingers* – literally, 'lady-singers', although here the word carries the meaning of an idealized or archetypal woman.

The Languedoc saw the first act of European genocide, when over 100,000 members of the Cathar heresy were massacred on the orders of the Pope during the Albigensian Crusade (named after the town of Albi, a Cathar stronghold). It was specifically for the interrogation and extermination of the Cathars that the Inquisition was first created. Perhaps it is simply because the Albigensian Crusade took place way back in the thirteenth century that its impact has never been close to that of more modern holocausts. Many of the locals, however, still burn with the old passions, and some even suggest that there has been an official cover-up over the centuries, a conspiracy to prevent the Cathar story from being more widely known.

Besides the Cathars, the region was, and always has been, a centre of alchemy, and several villages attest to the alchemical preoccupations of its former residents, notably Alet-les-Bains near Limoux, where the houses are still decorated with esoteric symbolism. It was also in Toulouse and Carcassonne that the earliest known accusations of attending the so-called Witches' Sabbath appear, in the 1330s and 1340s. In 1335 sixty-three people were charged with witchcraft in Toulouse and confessions extracted from them by the usual guaranteed methods. The chief among them was a young woman named Anne-Marie de Georgel, who is thought to have spoken for the others when she described their beliefs. She said that they saw the world as a battleground between two gods, the Lord of Heaven and the Lord of this World. She and the others supported the latter because they thought he would win. This may have been 'witchcraft' to the ecclesiastical judges, but it was Gnosticism, pure and simple. Another woman, similarly arraigned, testified that she had attended the 'Sabbath' in order to 'serve the Cathari at supper'.[1]

Many pagan elements survive in this area, and are to be found in the most surprising places. For although carvings of the 'Green Man' – the vegetation god who has been venerated in most rural regions of Europe – can be seen in many otherwise Christian churches, such as Norwich Cathedral, he is not usually depicted as being the offspring of an Old Testament goddess. As A.T. Mann and Jane Lyle write:

> In the Pyrenean cathedral of St-Bertrand-de-Comminges, Lilith has found her way into a church: a carving there depicts a winged, bird-footed woman giving birth to a Dionysian figure, a Green Man.[2]

The same small town claims to have been the site of the tomb of no less a personage than Herod Antipas, the Palestinian ruler who had John the Baptist executed. According to the first-century Jewish chronicler Josephus, the wicked triumvirate of Herod, his wife, the scheming Herodias, and his stepdaughter Salome – she of the so-called 'Dance of the Seven Veils' – were all exiled to the Roman city of Lugdunum Convenarum in Gaul, which is now St-Bertrand-de-Comminges. Herod disappears without trace, but Salome died in a mountain stream, and Herodias lived on in local legend, becoming the leader of covens of 'night-hags'.[3]

Another colourful Languedocian legend concerns the 'Queen of the South' (*Reine du Midi*), a title of the countesses of Toulouse. In folklore, the protectrix of Toulouse is *La Reine Pedauque* (the Goose-foot Queen). This may be a reference in the punning, esoteric 'language of the birds' to the Pays d'Oc, but French researchers have identified this figure with the Syrian goddess Anath, who is in turn closely linked with Isis.[4] And there is also the obvious association with the bird-footed Lilith.

Yet another legendary character of the area is Meridiana. Her name appears to link her with both noon and the south (both *midi* in French). Her most famous appearance took place when Gerbert d'Aurillac (*c.*940–1003), who later became Pope Sylvester II, travelled to Spain to learn the secrets of alchemy. Sylvester, who owned an oracular talking head, received his wisdom from this Meridiana, who offered him 'her body, riches and her magical wisdom'[5] – clearly some form of alchemical and esoteric knowledge that was communicated through sexual initiation. The American writer-researcher Barbara G. Walker[6] derives the name Meridiana from 'Mary-Diana', thereby linking this composite pagan goddess with the legends of the Magdalene in the South of France.

It was also the Languedoc that was home to by far the highest concentration of Knights Templar in Europe until their suppression in the early fourteenth century, and the area is still studded with the evocative ruins of their castles and commanderies.

If, as we suspected, there existed many more 'heretical' branches of the Magdalene cult than those we found in Provence, then surely this would be where we would find them. Certainly one of the first major towns we were to pass on the autoroute from Marseilles had seen incredible passions roused in her name – and thousands of people had been horribly put to death because of what she meant to them.

Béziers today lies in the department of Hérault in Languedoc-Roussillon, a populous town roughly ten kilometres from the Gulf of Lions in the Mediterranean. But in 1209 every last inhabitant of the town was mercilessly hunted down and slain by the Albigensian crusaders. Even for the blood-soaked – and often frankly bizarre – annals of this lengthy campaign, this is a particularly odd story.

The tale was told by several contemporary commentators, but here we will confine ourselves to that of Pierre des Vaux-de-Cernat, a Cistercian monk writing in 1213[7]. He was not personally present at the events, but based his account on those of the crusaders who were.

Béziers had become something of a centre for heretics, which was why when the crusaders attacked it there was an enclave of 222 Cathars living there unmolested by the population in general[8]. Although it is not known whether or not the Count of Béziers was himself a Cathar or merely a sympathizer, what is certain is that he did nothing to persecute or suppress them, and it was this that particularly angered the crusaders.

They demanded that the townspeople – ordinary Catholics – either hand over the Cathars or leave the city so that the remaining Cathars could be more easily dealt with. Although this demand was made on pain of excommunication – no light matter in those days when hell was very much a reality – and the alternative option seemed generous enough in that it meant that the Catholics were given a chance to escape the coming massacre, an astonishing thing happened. *The townspeople refused to comply with either demand.* As des Vaux-de-Cernat wrote, they preferred 'to die as heretics rather than to live as Christians'. And according to the report sent to the Pope by his representatives, the townspeople took an oath to defend the heretics.

Accordingly, in July 1209 the crusaders marched into Béziers, and with no difficulty, took the city and killed everyone in it – men, women, children and priests – and the place was put to the torch. Between 15,000 and 20,000 people were slaughtered: of these just over 200 were heretics. 'Nothing could save them, not cross, nor altar, nor crucifix'. It was here that the Pope's legates were asked by the crusaders how they would know the heretics from the rest of the townsfolk and received the now notorious reply: 'Kill them all. God will know his own.'

While it is easy to understand that the townsfolk might have wanted to defend their city against the characteristic depredations of an army, it must be remembered that they had been given the opportunity to leave, and if the safety of their property was uppermost in their minds then they could have simply handed over the heretics and gone back to their daily lives without a backward glance. However, they stayed, and effectively signed their death warrants twice over by actively taking an oath of support for the Cathars. Just what was really going on in Béziers?

First, the precise date of the massacre must be taken into account. It was 22 July – the feast day of Mary Magdalene, which is pointed out as being of singular significance by all the contemporary writers. And it had been in the church of Mary Magdalene in Béziers forty years previously that the local lord, Raymond Trencavel I, had been slain – although the reason for this remains unclear. Yet in Béziers at least, the link between the Magdalene and heresy was no accident, and it provides an insight into the background to the Albigensian Crusade as a whole.

As Pierre des Vaux-de-Cernat wrote:

Béziers was taken on St Mary Magdalene's Day. Oh, supreme justice of Providence! . . . The heretics claimed that St Mary

113

> Magdalene was the concubine of Jesus Christ ... it was there-
> fore with just cause that these disgusting dogs were taken and
> massacred during the feast of the one that they had insulted ...

Shocking though this idea may have been to the good monk
and the crusaders, obviously it was no such thing to the vast
majority of the townsfolk, who had actively sided with the
heretics *unto death*. Clearly this belief was a local tradition of
almost unique power over the hearts and minds of the people.
As we have seen, the Gnostic Gospels and other early texts
have no hesitation in describing the relationship between
Mary Magdalene and Jesus as being overtly sexual. But how
on earth did those medieval French townsfolk get to hear of
this? The Gnostic Gospels had not been discovered (and even
if they had it is unlikely they would have been disseminated
to them). So where did this tradition come from?

This episode acted as a curtain-raiser for the whole
Albigensian Crusade, which was to ravage the Languedoc for
over forty years, causing scars so deep in the collective psyche
of the people that it is by no means whimsical to detect them
still. So just who were these Cathars – whose beliefs were to
cause a whole crusade to be mounted against them? What held
such terror for the Establishment that it created the Inquisition
specifically as a weapon against them?

No-one can, with any accuracy, pinpoint the genesis of the
Cathar faith, but it rapidly became a power to be reckoned
with in the Languedoc in the eleventh century. To the
Languedocians the Cathars were not treated with the disdain
or ridicule with which our own culture tends to consider
minority religious cults; they were the dominant religion of the
region and treated with the utmost respect locally. All the
noble families of the area were either known Cathars themselves, or Cathar sympathizers who gave them active support.
Catharism was virtually the state religion of the Languedoc[9].

Known as *Les Bonhommes* or *Les Bons Chrétiens* – good
men or good Christians – the Cathars would seem to have
offended no-one. Modern commentators, especially those with

a New Age perspective, claim that they represented a faultless move to return to the fundamentals of Christianity. Although, as we shall see, they did absorb many other ideas and had their own somewhat confused ideology, it is true that their way of life was an attempt to obey the teachings of Jesus. They accused the Catholic Church of having diverged much too far from the original concept of the Jesus movement. They regarded as anathema the wealth and pomp of the Church, which they saw as being the opposite of what Jesus had intended for his followers. Superficially, then, they may seem to have been the precursors of the Protestant movement, but despite certain similarities, this was not the case.

Cathars led very simple lives. They preferred to meet in the open air or in ordinary houses rather than in churches, and although they had an administrative hierarchy that included bishops, all baptized members were spiritually equal and regarded as priests. Perhaps more surprising for those days was their emphasis on equality of the sexes, although the cultured Languedoc did already have a more enlightened attitude to women than was usual. They were fish-eating vegetarians (for slightly ill-advised reasons, as we will discuss later) and pacifists, and they believed in a form of reincarnation. They were also itinerant preachers, travelling in pairs, living in the utmost poverty and simplicity, stopping to help and to heal wherever they could. In many ways the Good Men would have appeared to pose no threat to anyone – except the Church.

That organization found plenty of reasons to persecute the Cathars. They were vociferously antagonistic towards the symbol of the cross, seeing it as a gruesome and sick reminder of the instrument that tortured Jesus to death. They were also haters of the whole cult of the dead and its associated relic trade – a major means of lining the coffers of Rome in their day. But the overriding reason why the Cathars fell foul of the Church was that they refused to acknowledge the Pope's authority.

Throughout the twelfth century various Church councils

had condemned the Cathars, but finally in 1179 they and their protectors were pronounced 'anathema'. Until this point the Church had dispatched specific missionaries – talented orators of the day – to try to win back the Languedocians to the 'true faith', but such missions were greeted with apathy. Even the great St Bernard of Clairvaux (1090–1153) was sent to that area only to return exasperated at its intransigence. Significantly, however, his report to the Pope took care to explain that while the Cathars were doctrinally in error, if you were to 'examine their mode of life, you will find nothing more irreproachable.'[10] It was to be a common feature of the whole crusade that even the Cathars' enemies had to admit that their lifestyle was exemplary.

The Church's next tactic was to attempt to play the heretics at their own game by sending in its version of itinerant preachers. Among the first of these, in 1205, was the famous Dominic Guzman, a Spanish monk who went on to found the Order of Preaching Friars (later to become the Order of St Dominic, whose members still later manned the Holy Inquisition).

Then the two sides met in a series of open disputations, a sort of deadly earnest public debate, which resolved nothing. Finally, in 1207, Pope Innocent III lost patience and excommunicated the Count of Toulouse, Raymond VI, for failing to take action against the heretics. This was obviously an unpopular move, for the papal legate who delivered this news was killed by one of Raymond's knights. This was the last straw: the Pope declared an all-out crusade against the Cathars and those who supported and sympathized with them. The crusade was called on 24 June 1209 – the feast day of St John the Baptist.

Up until this point all the crusades had been called against the Muslims – against foreign 'savages' who lived in lands so distant as to be literally unimaginable. But this crusade was to be fought by *Christians against Christians*, almost on the Pope's own doorstep. There was every chance that some crusaders might know personally the heretics they were sworn to exterminate.

The Albigensian Crusade, which began in Béziers in 1209, proceeded with the utmost brutality, as city after city fell to the soldiers, under the command of Simon de Montfort. The campaign lasted until 1244 – a not inconsiderable period for the crusaders to do their very worst. There are places in the Languedoc where, even to this day, the name of Simon de Montfort evokes a response of mingled fear and loathing.

At the time overtly religious reasons for the campaign soon blended with more cynical political motives[11]. The majority of the crusaders came from the north of France and the wealth and power of the Languedoc was too attractive to be ignored. At the beginning of the crusade this area might have enjoyed considerable independence; by the end it was definitely part of France.

This episode in European history was, by anyone's standards, massively significant. Not only was it the first European genocide, but it was also a crucial move in the unification of France – and it provided the direct impetus behind the creation of the Inquisition. But in our opinion, there is much more to the Albigensian Crusade than a curiously forgotten campaign of atrocity.

The Cathars were pacifists, who so despised 'the filthy envelope of the flesh' that they were eager to shed it, even if the means of doing so meant martyrdom by being burnt alive. During the campaign countless thousands of Cathars ended their days at the stake, and of those many evinced not the slightest horror or fear when faced with it. Some apparently went further and showed *no pain*. This was particularly remarkable at the finale of the siege of their last refuge, Montségur.

An essential stop for the modern tourist, Montségur has become something of a mythical place, rather akin to Glastonbury Tor. But although those who are out of training may find the latter a stiff climb, it is as nothing compared with the road to the top of the 'château' of Montségur. A stone citadel, it is perched almost impossibly on the dizzying heights of a craggy mountain, roughly the shape of an old-fashioned sugar-loaf, which overlooks the village and a valley made dangerous by regular falls of rocks from the cliffs. Signs in several languages warn against rash attempts to climb to the 'château' by those whose stamina is in any doubt: even bronzed backpackers find the going remarkably tough. It is difficult to imagine how the Cathars and their supplies made it to the top. Once there, however, it was relatively easy to sit it out because the crusaders – with all their armour and horses – could not even attempt the climb.

By the early 1240s when the crusaders had forced the remaining Cathars further and further into the foothills of the Pyrenees, Montségur had become their headquarters. As home to about 300 Cathars, but more particularly their leaders, it was the glittering prize for the Pope's men. The Queen of France, Blanche of Castile, reinforced the importance of Montségur when she wrote of its capture, '[we must] cut off the head of the dragon'.

During the ten months of the siege of Montségur, a curious phenomenon took place. Several of the besieging soldiers *defected to the Cathars* despite the certain knowledge of how it would end for them. What could possibly have prompted this bizarre defection? Some have suggested that they were so impressed by the exemplary behaviour of the Cathars that they underwent a profound inner conversion.

As we have seen, the Cathars approached their certain death by torture not only with stoicism, but with total calm – even, it is said, when the flames actually began to lap around them. For those who can remember the 1970s this immediately calls to mind the haunting image of that lone Buddhist monk immolating himself as a protest against the Vietnam war. He sat perfectly still, in a trance born of long training and unimaginable discipline, as the fire killed him. And the Cathars consciously prepared for death, even taking an oath that specifically promised their allegiance to their faith in the face of all kinds of torture. Did they also practise a similar trance technique to enable them to overcome the most extreme of agonies? Surely this secret was something that soldiers since time immemorial have wanted to know.

Be that as it may, the fall of Montségur has created many more enduring mysteries that have exerted a fascination for generations, including Nazi treasure hunters and those searching for the Holy Grail. The most persistent mystery of all concerns the so-called Treasure of the Cathars, which four of them managed to carry off the night before the rest were massacred. These intrepid heretics somehow managed to get away by being lowered down on ropes over the particularly precipitous side of the mountain in the middle of the night.

Although they had formally surrendered on 2 March 1244, for reasons that have never been explained they were given permission to remain in the citadel for another fifteen days – after which time they gave themselves up to be burnt. Some accounts go further and describe them as having actually run down the mountainside and jumped into the waiting bonfires in the field below. It has been speculated that they asked for this extra time in order to perform some ritual, but no-one will ever know the truth of the matter.

The exact nature of the Cathar treasure is a matter of energetic speculation. Judging by the hazardous route taken by those four escapees, it can hardly have been bags of heavy gold bars. Some have speculated that it was the Holy Grail itself – or some other ritual object of great significance – while others claim that it took the form of writings, or knowledge, or even that the four Cathars were in themselves important in some way. They could have represented a line of authority, perhaps even literally embodying the legendary bloodline of Jesus.

But if the Cathar treasure were really *secret knowledge*, what form could it have taken? What did the Cathars actually believe? It is difficult to assess their beliefs with any accuracy, for they left few written records and much of what they were said to believe came from the writings of their enemies – the Inquisition. And as Walter Birks and R.A. Gilbert sagely point out in their *The Treasure of Montségur* (1987), too much emphasis has been placed on their putative theology when in all probability it was their *lifestyle* that was the attraction[12]. Yet the religion grew out of a specific world-view, and its precise origins remain debatable.

The Cathars were an offshoot of the Bogomils, an heretical movement that first flowered in the Balkans in the mid-tenth century, but which remained influential in the area until after the Cathars met their doom. Bogomilism spread widely – at least as far as Constantinople – and was regarded as a serious threat to religious orthodoxy.

The Bogomils of Bulgaria were themselves heirs to a long line of 'heresy', and had acquired a colourful reputation among their opponents. For example, our word 'bugger' is derived from the name Bulgar, and is meant both literally – all heretics are accused of sexual deviance, whether or not the accusation is justified – and in the general pejorative sense.

The Bogomils and their offshoots such as the Cathars were Dualists and Gnostics: to them, the world is inherently evil, the spirit being trapped in a body of filth, and the only way to become free is through *Gnosis*, the personal revelation that leads the soul to perfection and a knowledge of God. There are many possible roots of Gnosticism – ancient Greek philosophy, mystery cults such as Dionysianism, and dualist religions such as Zoroastrianism are likely candidates. (Further details can be found in Yuri Stoyanov's masterly study *The Hidden Tradition in Europe* (1994)[13].)

Faced with the kind of literature on the subject of Catharism that is found in many Languedocian tourist shops, one might be forgiven for thinking that it was a sort of dewy-eyed New Age religion with a clear-cut, simplistic theology. There are literally dozens of books and pamphlets that celebrate the Cathars' humanitarianism and beliefs in such 'modern' principles as reincarnation and vegetarianism. By and large, however, this is sentimental nonsense. The Cathars practised vegetarianism not because of their love for animals, but because of their hatred of procreation, and only ate fish under the mistaken belief that fish reproduced asexually. Again, their idea of reincarnation was based on the concept of 'the good end' (death), which usually meant being martyred for their faith. If they met with such an end there was no question of their being incarnated again in this despicable vale of tears; if they did not, then they would come back until they got it right.

Some have tried to argue that Catharism was entirely a local Languedocian product[14]: this is manifestly untrue, but it did incorporate home-grown material into its theology. Significantly, one thing that was unique to the Cathars was the belief that Mary Magdalene was Jesus' wife, or perhaps his concubine. This, however, was not deemed appropriate knowledge for all Cathars, but was reserved for high initiates – the inner circle – only. The Cathars were virulently anti-sex and even anti-marriage, so they were unlikely to have made this up; perhaps they were so horrified by it that they reserved it for those who had already proved themselves faithful.

The Cathars often found themselves in an awkward position theologically; for on the one hand they actively encouraged their followers to read the Bible for themselves (in contrast with orthodox Catholicism, which strenuously opposed popular access to the Scriptures), but on the other they had to radically reinterpret biblical events to make them fit their beliefs. The major example of their reinvention of the New Testament is that of their view of the Crucifixion, in which they posited a Jesus made of pure spirit being nailed to the cross. Although there is no biblical evidence for this whatsoever, they had to invent this 'other' Jesus because of their loathing for the physical body – to have a corporeal Christ was to them unthinkable.

So their idea of Jesus and Mary Magdalene being sexual partners can hardly have been the result of wishful thinking on their part. In fact they struggled with several different theological justifications to explain the marriage, something that would not have exercised them so greatly if they felt they could dismiss the story as complete nonsense.[15] What this would seem to point to is the prevalence of the idea of Jesus and the Magdalene's relationship in the Languedoc of the time – it was not only part and parcel of what ordinary people believed without question, but also so central to the whole Christian world in that place that it had to be dealt with rather than ignored. And as Yuri Stoyanov writes:

> The teaching of Mary Magdalene as the 'wife' or 'concubine' of Christ appears, moreover, an original Cathar tradition which does not have any counterpart in the Bogomil doctrines.[16]

Although the Magdalene was, and is still, a curiously popular saint in Provence where she is supposed to have lived, it is in the Languedoc that she has become the focus for overtly heretical beliefs, and – as we were to discover – it is also in this region that these beliefs have given rise to astonishing passions, wild rumours, and dark secrets.

As we have seen, the idea of Jesus and Mary Magdalene being lovers was also found in the Nag Hammadi Gospels, which were hidden in Egypt in the fourth century CE. Could it be that the similar Languedocian beliefs actually came from them or from a common source? Some scholars, notably Marjorie Malvern, have speculated that the Magdalene cult of the South of France did preserve those early Gnostic ideas[17]. And there is some evidence that this was indeed the case.

In the 1330s a remarkable tract called *Schwester Katrei* (*Sister Catherine*) was published in Strasbourg, allegedly written by the German mystic Meister Eckhart – but scholars agree that its real author was one of his female followers. It presents a series of dialogues between 'Sister Catherine' and her confessor about a woman's religious experience, and although it incorporates many orthodox ideas, it also features many that are decidedly less so. For example, it actually makes the statement: 'God is the Universal Mother . . .' and clearly reveals a strong Cathar inspiration, besides that of the troubadour/*minnesinger* tradition[18].

This unusual and outspoken tract links the Magdalene with *Minne* – the Lady-love of the *minnesingers*, but even more excitingly, it has given scholars pause for thought because it contains ideas about Mary Magdalene that are *only otherwise found in the Nag Hammadi Gospels*: she is portrayed as being superior to Peter because of her greater understanding of Jesus, and there is the same tension between Mary and Peter. Moreover, actual incidents that are described in the Nag Hammadi texts are mentioned in Sister Catherine's tract[19].

Professor Barbara Newman of Pennsylvania University highlights the academic quandary in the words: '"Sister Catherine"'s use of these motifs poses a thorny problem of historical transmission' and confesses that it is 'a real, if baffling, phenomenon.'[20] How on earth did the author of *Sister Catherine* in the fourteenth century get hold of texts that were not discovered until the twentieth? It cannot be coincidence that the tract shows the influence of the Cathars and troubadours of the Languedoc, and the obvious conclusion is that it was through them that knowledge of the Gnostic Gospels relating to Mary Magdalene was transmitted; their secrets may lie not only in what we know as the Nag Hammadi texts, but also in similar documents of equal value that have not yet been rediscovered.

It is interesting that there is an enduring belief in the sexual nature of the relationship between the Magdalene and Jesus in the South of France. John Saul's unpublished research has unearthed many references to such a union in the literature of southern France up until the seventeenth century – specifically in works by men associated with the Priory of Sion, such as César, the son of Nostradamus (which was published in Toulouse)[21].

We had seen in Provence that wherever there are Magdalene centres there are usually sites associated with John the Baptist. As the Cathars appeared to regard her highly, then perhaps they also showed the same veneration towards the Baptist. On the contrary, however, it seemed that the Cathars actively disliked the Baptist to the point of describing him as 'a demon'. This comes directly from the Bogomils, some of whom referred to him (somewhat confusingly) as 'forerunner of the AntiChrist'[22].

One of the few remaining holy texts of the Cathars is the *Book of John* (also known as the *Liber Secretum*), which is a Gnostic version of the Gospel of quite another John: much of it is exactly the same as the canonical Gospel but it contains some extra 'revelations' purportedly given privately to John the 'Beloved Disciple'. These are dualist-Gnostic ideas that accorded with the Cathar's general theology.[23]

In this book, Jesus tells his disciples that John the Baptist was, in fact, an emissary of Satan (the lord of the material world), sent to try to pre-empt his mission of salvation. This was originally a Bogomil text and was not completely accepted by either all Bogomils or all Cathars. Many Cathar sects entertained rather more orthodox ideas about John, and there are even signs that the Bogomils in the Balkans held rites on his feast day, 24 June.[24]

What is certain is that the Cathars did have a special regard for John's Gospel, which is generally accepted by scholars as being the most Gnostic of the New Testament. (In occult circles there is a long-standing rumour that the Cathars had another, now lost, version of John's Gospel, and many occultists have searched the area around Montségur hoping to find it – without success.[25])

Clearly the Cathars had unorthodox, if perhaps confused, ideas about John the Baptist. But was there anything at all in their concept of an evil John and a good Jesus? Perhaps not as such, but – as several modern commentators have suggested – the relationship between those two men may not have been quite as clear-cut as most Christians are led to believe[26]. The Cathar idea may have represented their dualist philosophy at its most simplistic: one of the pair is bad and the other good. But if so, then a logical conclusion is that they regarded them as opposite *but equal*. This implies that the Cathars thought of them as *rivals*, which is hardly the traditional Christian view – and it reveals that disconcerting doubts about John's alleged support of Jesus' mission had been recognized in that area a long time ago. Like the relationship of the Magdalene and Jesus, that of John and Jesus appears to have been perceived as radically different from the version taught by the Church.

Superficially it is disappointing to look to the Cathars for confirmation of John's importance to heretical movements. But there is one significant historical organization which does more than redress that balance. It is, of course, the Knights Templar, to whom John the Baptist has always been – inexplicably – an object of great devotion. And just as the Cathar crusade has left a visible legacy of its trauma on the landscape of the Languedoc, so the castles of those enigmatic knights still rise out of the mists in the more remote parts of that countryside.

The Templars are by now a sort of esoteric cliché, as anyone who is familiar with the fiction of Umberto Eco will know, and most historians feel no compunction in dismissing anything that claims to draw on their 'secrets' with utter disdain. However, any mystery connected with the Priory of Sion also involves those warrior-monks, and so they are an intrinsic part of this investigation.

A third of all the Templars' European property was once found in the Languedoc, and its ruins only add to the savage beauty of the region. One of the more picturesque local legends has it that whenever 13 October falls on a Friday (the day and date of the Order's sudden and brutal suppression) strange lights appear in the ruins and dark figures can be seen moving among them. Unfortunately on the Fridays when we were in that area, we saw and heard nothing except the alarming snufflings of wild boars; but the story shows how much the Templars have become part of local legend.

The Templars have lived on in the memories of the local people, and those memories are by no means negative. Even in this century, the famous opera singer Emma Calvé, who came from Aveyron in the north of the Languedoc, recorded in her memoirs that the locals would say of an especially good-looking or intelligent boy, 'He is a true son of the Templars'[27].

The main facts concerning the Knights Templar are simple[28]. Officially known as The Order of the Poor Knights of the Temple of Solomon, they were formed in 1118 by the French nobleman Hugues de Payens as knightly escorts for pilgrims to the Holy Land. Initially there were just nine of them, for the first nine years, then the Order opened up and soon it had established itself as a force to be reckoned with, not only in the Middle East, but also throughout Europe.

After the recognition of the Order, Hugues de Payens himself set out on a European trip, soliciting land and money from royalty and nobility. He visited England in 1129, when he founded the first Templar site in that country, on the site of what is now London's Holborn Underground Station.

Like all other monks, the knights were sworn to poverty, chastity and obedience, but they were in the world and of it and pledged to use the sword if necessary against the enemies of Christ – and the image of the Templars became inseparably linked with the crusades that were mounted in order to drive the infidel out of Jerusalem, and to keep it Christian.

It was in 1128 that the Council of Troyes officially recognized the Templars as a religious and military order. The main protagonist behind this move was Bernard of Clairvaux, the head of the Cistercian Order, who was later canonized. But as Bamber Gascoigne writes:

He was aggressive, he was abusive . . . and he was a devious politician who was quite unscrupulous in the methods he used to bring down his enemies.[29]

Bernard actually wrote the Templars' Rule – which was based on that of the Cistercians – and it was one of his protégés who, as Pope Innocent II, declared in 1139 that the Knights would be answerable only to the papacy from that time onwards. As both the Templars and the Cistercian Orders developed in parallel, one can discern a certain amount of deliberate co-ordination between them – for example, Hugues de Payens' lord, the Count of Champagne, donated to St Bernard the land in Clairvaux on which he built his monastic 'empire'. And significantly, André de Montbard, one of the nine founding

126

knights, was Bernard's uncle. It has been suggested that the Templars and Cistercians were acting together according to a pre-arranged plan to take over Christendom, but this scheme never succeeded[30].

It is hard to exaggerate the prestige and financial power of the Templars when they were at the height of their influence in Europe. There was hardly a major centre of civilization where they did not have a preceptory – as, for example, the wide scatter of such place names as Temple Fortune and Temple Bar (London) and Temple Meads (Bristol) in England still shows. But as their empire spread, so their arrogance grew and began to poison their relations with both temporal and secular heads of state.

The Templars' wealth was partly a result of their Rule: all new members had to hand over their property to the Order, and they also gained a considerable fortune through massive donations of land and money from many kings and nobles. Their coffers were soon overflowing, not least because they had also amassed impressive financial astuteness, which had resulted in them becoming the first international bankers, upon whose judgement the credit ratings of others depended. It was a sure way of establishing themselves as a major power. In a short space of time their title of 'Poor Knights' became a hollow sham, even though the rank and file might well have remained impecunious.

Besides their staggering wealth, the Templars were renowned for their skill and courage in battle – sometimes to the point of foolhardiness. They had specific rules to govern their conduct as fighters: for example, they were forbidden to surrender unless the odds against them were greater than three to one, and even then had to have their commander's approval. They were the Special Services of their day, an élite force with God – and money – on their side.

Despite their finest efforts, the Holy Land fell to the Saracens bit by bit until in 1291 the last Christian territory, the city of Acre, was in enemy hands. There was nothing for the Templars to do but to return to Europe and plot their eventual reconquest, but unfortunately by then the motivation for such a campaign had disappeared among the various kings who might have financed it. Their main reason for existing dwindled to nothing. Lacking employment, but still rich and arrogant, they were widely resented because they were exempt from taxation and their allegiance was to the Pope and to him alone.

So in 1307 came their inevitable fall from grace. The supremely powerful French king, Philip the Fair, began to orchestrate the downfall of the Templars with the connivance of the Pope, who was in his pocket anyway. Secret orders were issued to the king's aristocratic representatives and the Templars were rounded up on Friday 13 October 1307, arrested, tortured and burnt.

That, at least, is the story as told in most standard works on the subject. One is left with the idea that the entire Order met its horrible doom on that day long ago, and that the Templars were effectively wiped off the face of the earth for ever. Yet that is nowhere near the truth.

For a start, relatively few Templars were actually executed, although most who were captured were 'put to the question' – a well-worn euphemism for suffering excruciating torture. Relatively few faced the stake, although notably their Grand Master Jacques de Molay was slowly roasted to death on the Ile de la Cité, in the shadow of Notre-Dame Cathedral, in Paris. Of the thousands of others, only those who refused to confess, or recanted their confession, were killed. But how valid were the confessions wrung from them by the red-hot poker and the thumbscrews? And to what exactly were they expected to confess?

The accounts of Templar confessions are colourful, to say the least. We read of their having worshipped a cat, or indulging in homosexual orgies as part of their knightly duties, or venerating a demon known as Baphomet and/or a severed head. They were also said to have trampled and spat upon the cross in an initiatory rite. All of this, of course, would seem to make nonsense of the idea that they were devoted knights of Christ and upholders of the Christian ideal, and the more they were tortured the more this divergence became apparent.

This is hardly surprising: not many victims of torture manage to grit their teeth and refuse to agree with the words put in their mouths by their tormenters. But in this case there is more to the story than meets the eye. On the one hand, there have been suggestions that all the charges levelled against the Templars were trumped up by those envious of their wealth and exasperated by their power, and that they provided a good excuse for the French king to extricate himself from his current economic difficulty by seizing their wealth. On the other hand, although the charges may not have been strictly true, there is evidence that the Templars were up to something mysterious and perhaps 'dark' in the occult sense. Of course, these two alternative views are not mutually exclusive.

Much ink has been spilt on the debate over the charges made against the Templars, and their confessions. Had they actually committed the deeds to which they confessed, or did the Inquisitors invent the charges in advance and simply torture the knights until they agreed with them? (Some knights had testified that they had been told that Jesus was a 'false prophet', for example.) It is impossible to say one way or the other conclusively.

There is, however, at least one particular confession that must give pause for thought. This is that of one Fulk de Troyes, who said that he was shown a crucifix and told 'Set not much faith in this, for it is too young.'[31] Given the un-educated concept of history at the time, this enigmatic statement seems an unlikely thing for an Inquisitor to have made up.

Certainly the Priory of Sion claims to have been the power behind the creation of the Knights Templar: if so, then this is one of the best-kept secrets of history. Yet it is said that the two Orders were virtually indistinguishable until their schism in 1188 – after which they went their separate ways[32]. If nothing else there does seem to have been some kind of conspiracy about the conception of the Templars. Common sense suggests that it would have taken more than just the original nine knights to protect and provide refuge for all the pilgrims who visited the Holy Land, especially for *nine years;* moreover, there is little evidence that they ever made much of a serious attempt to do so. The Templars soon found themselves the pampered darlings of Europe, being given privileges and honours quite disproportionate to any actually earned. For example, they were granted an entire wing of the royal palace in Jerusalem itself – the place that was previously a mosque. This in turn was said, erroneously, to have been built on the foundations of the Temple of Solomon, from which the Templars took their full name.

Another mystery connected with their beginnings centres on the fact that there is evidence that the Order actually existed well before 1118, although why the date was falsified remains unclear. Many commentators have suggested that the first account of their creation – by William of Tyre and written a full fifty years after the event – was simply a cover story[33]. (Although William was deeply hostile to the Templars[34], he was, presumably, recounting the story as he understood it.) But once again, just what it was covering up is a matter for speculation.

Hugues de Payens and his nine companions all came from either Champagne or the Languedoc, and included the Count of Provence[35], and it is quite apparent that they went to the Holy Land with a specific mission in mind. Perhaps, as has been suggested, they were searching for the Ark of the Covenant[36], or for other ancient treasure or documents that might lead them to it, or for some kind of secret knowledge which would give them mastery of people and their wealth. And recently, Christopher Knight and Robert Lomas in their *The Hiram Key* have argued that the Templars sought and found a cache of documents from the same source as the Dead Sea Scrolls. However, intriguing though such a suggestion may be, they provide no convincing evidence for it – and, as we shall see, the whole subject of the provenance of the Scrolls is fraught with misconception and myth. But, there is indeed evidence that the Templars had sought out new knowledge from the Arabs and others on their travels.

To us one of the most fascinating things about the Templars was their unusually strong veneration of John the Baptist, who seems to be considerably more important to them than the average patron saint. The Priory of Sion – once, it is claimed, inseparable from them – calls its Grand Masters 'John', perhaps out of reverence for him. Yet it is virtually impossible to discover the reason for the Templars' allegiance in any of the standard histories; the usual explanation is that John was special to them because he was Jesus' teacher. Some have suggested that the severed head they were rumoured to have worshipped was that of the Baptist himself[37] – but the *worship* of such a totem implies, in any case, that the Templars were something quite other than uncomplicated Christian knights.

Even much of their apparently orthodox symbolism hides specifically 'John' allusions. For example, the Lamb of God was one of their most important images. Most Christians take this to mean Jesus – the Baptist having apparently said of him 'Behold the Lamb of God' – but in many places, such as the West Country of England, this symbol is taken to refer to *John* himself, and the Templars appear to have given it the same significance. The Lamb of God symbol was adopted as one of the Templars' official seals; this seal was specific to the Order in the South of France.

A clue that the Templars' veneration of John the Baptist was not a simple matter of paying homage to their chosen patron saint, but hid something rather more radical, is found in the work of a scholarly priest named Lambert de St Omer. Lambert was an associate of one of the original nine founding knights and Hugues de Payens' second in command, Godefroi de St Omer. In *The Hiram Key*, Christopher Knight and Robert

131

Lomas reproduce an illustration of Lambert's depicting the 'heavenly Jerusalem', and note that it:

> ... apparently shows the founder [of the heavenly Jerusalem] to be John the Baptist. There is no mention of Jesus at all in this so-called Christian document.[38]

As in the symbolism of Leonardo's paintings, the implication is that John the Baptist is important in his own right, and not merely for his role as Jesus' forerunner.

Two years after the mass arrests, while the knights were still on trial, the Catalan visionary and occultist Ramon Lull (1232–c.1316), previously a staunch supporter of the Order, wrote that the trials reveal 'dangers to the boat of St Peter', adding that:

> There are perchance among Christians many secrets, from which a [particular] secret may cause an incredible revelation, just as that [which is] emerging from the Templars ... such public and manifest infamy can of itself endanger the boat of St Peter.[39]

Lull seems to be referring not only to the dangers to the Church caused by the revelations about the Templars but also to other secrets, of equal magnitude. He also appears to accept the charges levelled against the Order – although, at that stage, it may have been unwise to question them.

Could the Languedoc, once home to the highest concentration of Templars in Europe, yield any clues as to the truth about the Order? Even after all this time, this was an area with very long memories and a healthy disregard for convention.

As we have seen, the Cathars and Templars flourished here at the same time, but, given what is generally understood of their relative values, it would seem that these two highly influential groups should be on opposite sides. Indeed, the Templar symbol of red cross on white background is often taken as that of a typical crusader. However, there are many indications that the Templars were, if not actively supportive, then certainly sympathetic to the 'heretics' in the mountains – and it is indisputable that the Templars were conspicuous by their absence in the Albigensian Crusade. Admittedly, the knights' primary interest at the time lay far away in the Holy Land, and many of them were drawn from the same families as the Cathars, but perhaps neither of these reasons totally explains their lack of interest in catching Cathars.

But what were the Templars' real interests and motives? Were they simply the warrior-monks they claimed to be, or was there a secret, occult dimension to their plans?

CHAPTER FIVE

Guardians of the Grail

The standard academic line is that 'occult' ideas about the Templars are nonsense: most historians state that they were merely the warrior-monks they claimed to be, and any suggestion that they were involved in anything remotely esoteric is the result of over-active imagination or sloppy research. Because this is the consensus, historians who have an interest in this side of the Order dare not show it openly for fear of losing their reputations (and academic funding). So such research is either avoided or, if it is done, it is never published. (There are several respected historians who privately acknowledge that the esoteric side of the Templars is important, but will never do so publicly.)

This attitude has led to a neglect of the study of certain important Templar sites. And we found that one region that suffered more than most from this phenomenon – to a mystifying degree – is the area of our particular interest: the Languedoc-Roussillon. Outside the Holy Land, this was the homeland of the Order – over 30 per cent of all Templar fortresses and commanderies in the whole of Europe were in this one small area. Yet only a negligible amount of archaeological work has been done there, and there are some key sites that have never been investigated.

Fortunately the official neglect is balanced by many private researchers with a passionate interest in these mysterious knights, and many locals see it as their duty to preserve and protect the old Templar sites. There are also several 'amateur' (in the sense that they are unfunded, but by no means in respect of the quality of their scholarship) research organizations, such as the Centre for Templar Studies and Research, run by Georges Kiess in Espéraza (Aude), which have put the academics to shame. The discoveries made by these enthusiasts, from a study both of the sites and of the many Templar documents stored untouched in local archives, are impressive – especially given the lack of funding and the sheer frustration of dealing with apathetic archivists and professional historians.

One such research group is Abraxas, run by British expatriate Nicole Dawe and Texan Charles Bywaters from the spa town of Rennes-les-Bains, Aude. Their researches, together with those of the network of similar groups, have made solid, documented discoveries that literally rewrite Templar studies. Struggling against the tide of official apathy on the one hand, and the over-enthusiasm of local treasure hunters – who pose a very real threat to the fabric of the sites – on the other, Nicole and Charles have discovered key Templar sites that have never yet been touched by archaeologists' spades. Much of their work has yet to be published, although they plan publication in the near future.

Therefore to find out more about the Templars in this heretical heartland of the Languedoc-Roussillon, it was not to academe that we went, but to Charles and Nicole.

Sitting in Charles' apartment on Rennes-les-Bains' main (and indeed almost only) street, we started by asking him and Nicole about the possible connection between the Templars and the Cathars. They replied that there were clear links between the two groups that went well beyond mere family ties and which are usually overlooked by historians – for example, even at the height of the Albigensian Crusade the Templars sheltered fugitive Cathars, and there are documented examples of them also giving succour to knights who actively fought for the Cathars against the crusaders.

As Nicole said:

You only have to scan the Cathar family names from the Inquisition documents and the names of Templars at the same period to find that they are the same. But, more particularly, it

135

is undeniable that certain Templar sites housed, gave shelter to, and even buried on sacred ground, Cathars.

Some have been cynical and suggested that this was because these people, in order to become lay members of the Temple, gave them their possessions and goods. In fact, we have proof of Cathars who came to the Templars after having been completely dispossessed, and were not only taken in and given shelter, but died and were buried there. Later, the Templars sometimes did what they could to make sure that Cathar families, or their descendants, got their land back.[1]

Charles went on:

In one area in particular the Templars very clearly allowed hostile activity from their location. Cathar knights continued to take part in the fight, then retired back to Templar property. It's very easily documented.

It seemed hugely significant to us that, given that some of the charges levelled at the Templars were definitely trumped up, the one thing that was not used in evidence against them was their close relationship with such outcasts as the Cathars. That the Inquisition was fully aware of this is revealed by their digging up Cathar bodies buried on Templar land in order to burn them as deterrents to other would-be heretics, even more than thirty years after the end of the crusade. (And it was the Inquisition which had tortured the Templars, so if anyone knew the connection with the Cathars, they did.) Clearly there was something else going on, perhaps even something known to the French Crown, but which was deemed so dangerous to make public that not a word about it has ever got out. In all our research into the Templars, in fact, we had the uneasy – but growing – feeling that there was some monumental secret lurking under the surface of the official story. Could it be that the Templars and the Cathars shared some potentially explosive knowledge? And could this secret have been Philip the Fair's real motive for mounting such a well-planned campaign against the Templars?

Not all Templars were destroyed on that fateful Friday the thirteenth. Many were allowed to live and re-form under a different name, and two countries in particular provided safe houses for the fleeing knights – Scotland and Portugal. (In the latter the Templars became known as the Knights of Christ.) The area around the Languedoc, we learned from Charles and Nicole, saw a curious exception to the overall pattern of the persecution. Roussillon, to the east of the area, actually came under the auspices of the Spanish kingdom of Aragon, although the northern parts, which included Carcassonne, were part of France. The Roussillon Templars were arrested and tried – but found innocent – and when the Pope officially disbanded the Order they either joined other similar brotherhoods or lived out the remainder of their lives with a pension on their lands.

As several commentators have suggested[2], the Templars survived the attempt to exterminate them totally and continue to exist to this day, although the evidence suggests that they have suffered many schisms and operate as different organizations, all claiming to be direct descendants of the original Order.

If the Templars were hiding something – which was deemed so dangerous by the French king that he took such drastic action against them – what could it be? Just who was using whom – the Pope or Philip? From whatever angle the story is viewed, there appears to be a crucial missing link.

Supposing that this elusive component concerned the Priory of Sion. As we have already seen, there are indications of a shadowy presence behind the very inception of the Templars, and this same puppet-master-group (whoever they were) appeared to direct the ensuing scenes. Certainly Charles and Nicole are in no doubt of the existence of an 'inner circle' that existed within the leadership of the Templars and which actually predated their official beginnings. They go so far as to argue that the whole Templar movement was created in order to give this inner circle a public face, just at the time when the Holy Land had been opened up to European travellers.

Other researchers have also come to the same conclusion. As French writer Jean Robin (drawing on the researches of Georges Cagger) says:

> The Order of the Temple was indeed constituted of seven 'exterior' circles dedicated to the minor mysteries, and of three 'interior' circles corresponding to the initiation into the great mysteries. And the 'nucleus' was composed of those seventy Templars 'interrogated' by Clement V [after the arrests of 1307].[3]

Similarly, in his *The Sign and the Seal*, British author Graham Hancock writes:

> ... the research that I had conducted into the beliefs and behaviour of this strange group of warrior monks had convinced me that they had tapped into some exceedingly ancient wisdom tradition ...[4]

It was possible to maintain a secret inner group because the Templars were essentially a mystery school – that is, they operated as a hierarchy that was based on initiation and secrecy. It is therefore likely not only that a Templar of the rank and file knew considerably less than his superiors, but that his actual beliefs were different. It is likely that the majority of the Knights Templar were no more than the simple Christian soldiers they appeared to be, but the inner circle was different.

The inner circle of the Templars appears to have existed in order to further active research into esoteric and religious matters. Perhaps one of the reasons for their secrecy was the fact that they dealt with the arcane aspects of the Jewish and Islamic worlds. They sought, literally, the secrets of the universe wherever they suspected they might be found, and in the course of their geographical and intellectual wanderings came to tolerate – perhaps even to embrace – some very unorthodox beliefs.

In those days there had to be a particularly strong driving force to pursue knowledge against all the odds, and the Templars were not concerned with the intricacies of research for its own sake – they were nothing if not intensely practical people. When they pursued a particular line of enquiry it was for a very good reason, and because of this they left certain clues as to what was particularly important to them.

One such clue lies in the obsessions of Bernard of Clairvaux, their early *éminence grise*. This intellectual but fiery monk was apparently utterly devoted to the Virgin Mary, as his many sermons show. However, it appears that the Virgin was not the true object of Bernard's spiritual love. It was another Mary altogether, one whose real identity is suggested by the fact that he was particularly fond of Black Madonnas[5]. He was also to write nearly ninety sermons on the subject of the Song of Songs, and preach many more explicitly linking the 'Bride' with Mary of Bethany[6], who in those days was unquestioningly assumed to be one and the same as Mary Magdalene.

'I am black, but comely' says the female lover, a phrase that also links the Song of Songs with the Black Madonna cult – to which Bernard (who was born at the Black Madonna centre of Fontaines near Dijon) was exceptionally devoted. He claimed to have received his inspiration as a child from having received three drops of miraculous milk from the breast of the Black Madonna of Châtillon. It has been speculated that this was a coded reference to his initiation into her cult[7]. And when Bernard preached the Second Crusade he chose to do so from the Mary Magdalene centre at Vézelay[8].

It is probable, therefore, that Bernard's apparent devotion to the Virgin was simply a smokescreen for his undoubted passion for the Magdalene, although of course the two are not mutually exclusive. However, in creating the Templar rule, Bernard commended the knights to 'the obedience of Bethany, the castle of Mary and Martha'[9] and he is known to have passed on this particular devotion to the Order. Even when faced with total extinction, the knights imprisoned with Grand Master Jacques de Molay in the dungeons of the fortress of Chinon composed a prayer dedicated to 'Notre Dame' (Our Lady) in which they remembered St Bernard as having founded the religion of the Blessed Virgin Mary[10]. But given all the other evidence, this could well have been another coded reference to the cult of the Magdalene.

It is significant that the Templar oath was sworn to 'God and Our Lady' – or often to 'God and the Blessed Mary'[11]. There is a suggestion that the 'Our Lady' spoken of in the oath is not the Virgin, which is also reinforced by the words of the Templar Absolution: 'I pray God that he will pardon you your sins as he pardoned them to St Mary Magdalene and the thief who was put on the cross'[12]. At the very least this shows the importance of the Magdalene to the Templars. (It is noteworthy that in the case of the Roussillon Templars during their captivity, the conditions in which they were chained up were deliberately worsened specifically – on the Pope's orders – *on the feast day of St Mary Magdalene*[13]. Remember that the massacre of Béziers took place on that feast day to make the point about the nature of the 'heresy'.)

In fact the Templars were preoccupied with the whole idea of the Feminine – a concept that may appear to be seriously at odds with their image as warriors. Yet, as Charles and Nicole have discovered, *the Order of the Temple included women*. Within the first years of its existence many women took the Order's oath, although they remained members of the lay persons' Temple. While there is no suggestion that there was a secret enclave of warrior queens within the Templar Order, as Michael Baigent and Richard Leigh write in *The Temple and the Lodge* (1989):

. . . a late twelfth-century account in England speaks of a woman being received into the Temple as a Sister, and seems quite clearly to imply some sort of feminine wing or adjunct to the Order. But no elaboration or clarification of the matter has ever been found. Even such information as might have been contained in official Inquisition records has long since disappeared or been suppressed.[14]

Nicole and Charles, from their close study of Templar documents, are more emphatic:

> If you go back to the twelfth-century documents, there are numerous instances of women having joined the Order, certainly in its first century. Anybody that joined had to take an oath to give 'my house, my lands and my body and soul to the Order of the Temple'. You have women's names at the end of these documents as well as men's, and you often have couples joining – so the women must have taken the oath too. These documents are mainly in this area [the Languedoc], and there are enough instances to show that there must have been quite a large number of women involved at one time.

They also point out that there was a later change to the rules, in which the Templars were specifically forbidden from accepting women – with the implication that up until that time they had been doing so.

When we expressed some surprise that this was not more widely known, and certainly, apart from some vague hints, the women's involvement does not feature in the standard works on the Templars, Charles explained:

> At times it appears as though a lot of this information has been intentionally overlooked. What you get in the books is a lot of redundant information, the same thing hashed over and over again. There are only two things it could be: either these people are blind, or for some very specific reason they are not focusing on that information. If you are a researcher, which supposedly these people are, it should leap off the page at you. But it's dismissed.

It *is* remarkable that the round-up of 13 October 1307 was so astonishingly bloodless. All across France, the king's seneschals opened their sealed orders, which commanded them to organize sufficient troops to arrest the best-trained warriors in Christendom – rather like the average neighbourhood police station in the UK being told to muster forces to arrest members of the SAS who were stationed in their area. And most of the Templars in France seem to have gone like lambs to the slaughter. It is strange that the knights did not call for reinforcements from outside France.

Significantly, some of the knights, including the Order's treasurer, managed to slip away in a manner that suggested they had been tipped off[15]. Besides, the famous Templar fleet, which had been based in France, simply disappeared at this time. In all the records of the French king's Templar depredations there is not a single ship listed. Where did the fleet go? It can hardly have disappeared into thin air.

The inner circle of the Templars, however, seemed to go to great lengths to preserve their secret knowledge. As the respected New Testament scholar Hugh Schonfield[16] has demonstrated, the Templars used the code known as the Atbash Cipher. This is truly remarkable because it had been used by the authors of some of the Dead Sea Scrolls at least *one thousand years* before the foundation of the Templar Order. Whatever else it may mean, this in itself reveals that the Templars were adept at keeping their secrets in the most ingenious ways – and also that their knowledge came from far-flung and esoteric sources. Schonfield reveals that when the code is applied to the name of the mysterious severed-head idol allegedly worshipped by the Templars – Baphomet – then it transforms into the Greek word *sophia*. Graham Hancock writes in *The Sign and the Seal* that *sophia* 'means nothing more nor less than "wisdom"'[17]. But in fact it means considerably more than that, and its full meaning adds a different gloss to the whole *raison d'être* of the Templars.

Simply alluded to as 'Wisdom', in Hebrew *Chokmah* – a feminine figure who appears in the Old Testament, specifically in the Book of Proverbs – Sophia has caused much embarrassment among both Jewish and Christian commentators because she is presented as being the partner of God. She it is who has influence over him and actually gives him advice.[18]

Sophia was also central to Gnostic cosmology – indeed, in the Nag Hammadi text called *Pistis Sophia* she was intimately associated with Mary Magdalene. And as *Chokmah* she is the key to the Gnostic understanding of the Cabala (the important and very influential occult system that formed the basis of medieval and Renaissance magic). To the Gnostics she was the Greek goddess Athena and the Egyptian goddess Isis – who was sometimes actually called Sophia[19].

Taken alone, of course, the Templars' use of the word Sophia – as encoded in 'Baphomet' – does not prove any special veneration on their part for the feminine. They may simply have admired the search for wisdom. However, there are many other indications that this was part of a profound obsession with the female principle, which extended well beyond mere semantics – as far as the Templars, and indeed other esoteric groups, were concerned.

As the Scottish researcher Niven Sinclair, whose knowledge of the Templars is particularly extensive, told us: 'The Templars were strong believers in the feminine side.'[20] To him there is no doubt about it, and there is nothing odd in it.

The Templars routinely made their churches *round*, because they believed that was the shape of Solomon's Temple. In turn, this may have symbolized the idea of a round universe, but it is more likely to have represented the *Feminine*. Circles and cycles have always been associated with goddesses and all things female, both esoteric and biological. It is an archetypal symbol that recurs throughout civilization: prehistoric grave mounds were round because they represented the womb of the earth, which would take the deceased back to be reborn as spirits. And everyone was familiar with the roundness of a pregnant belly, and the symbol of the 'Mother' phase of the goddess, the full moon.

Whatever the precise significance of roundness to the Templars, there is no question of its ever being *male*. And after the time of the Templars, the building of round churches was

143

officially deemed heretical by the Church[21]. However, as we have noted, the French Church in London is round, a feature that is repeated and reinforced by other decorative motifs both outside and in its interior.

The Templars, it seems, had acquired exotic and heretical knowledge, but was it by accident or design? The evidence points to the latter: they went looking for certain secrets that, once theirs, they were in a position to bestow or withhold. While many of their secrets remain in their keeping, they left clues to some of them in the form of codes – even carved in stone.

The Knights Templar were the prime movers behind the building of the great Gothic cathedrals, especially that of Chartres. As the predominant – often the only – 'developers' in large European centres of culture, they were behind the formation of builders' guilds, including that of the stonemasons – who became lay members of the Templar Order and who had all their advantages, such as exemption from paying tax.[22]

Throughout the long history of the great cathedrals, the strange symbolism of their decoration and design has been puzzled over by experts from many disciplines. It is only recently that it has been seen for what it undoubtedly was: the Templars' encoding of esoteric knowledge. Graham Hancock, when discussing the sacred architecture of the ancient Egyptians, notes that 'it has been equalled in Europe only in the great Gothic cathedrals of the Middle Ages such as Chartres' and poses the question: 'Was this an accident?' Hancock continues:

> I had long suspected that there had indeed been a connection and that the Knights Templar, through their discoveries during the Crusades, might have formed the missing link in the chain of transmission of secret architectural knowledge ... St Bernard, the Templars' patron, had defined God – astonishingly for a Christian – as 'length, width, height and depth'. Nor could I forget that the Templars themselves had been great

builders and great architects, or that the Cistercian monastic order to which Saint Bernard had belonged had also excelled in this particular field of human endeavour.[23]

The layout of the cathedrals was designed specifically to take into account – to *exemplify* – the principles of sacred geometry[24]. This is the idea that geometrical proportion has in itself a resonance with divine harmony, and that some particular proportions are more divine than others. This underlined Pythagoras' blunt statement that 'number is all', and reinforced the hermetic concept that mathematics are the code wherein the gods speak to Man. Particular adepts of this esoteric architecture were the Renaissance artists and designers, to whom the 'Golden Mean' – to them, the perfect proportion – was little short of a universal panacea. However, this was by no means the sum total of their thinking, and the whole concept of sacred geometry permeated all of their intellectual lives. Leonardo's drawings, be they of men or machines, the interior of flowers or the shape of a wave, communicate the artist's belief that there was meaning in pattern and harmony in proportion, and one of his most famous drawings, *Vitruvian Man*, literally embodies the Golden Mean[25].

The legendary Temple of Solomon was, to the Templars as to the later Freemasons, the finest flower and exemplar of all sacred geometry. It was not only a supreme delight to the eye of all who viewed or worshipped in it, but it went far beyond the mere five senses. It was deemed to resonate in a unique and transcendental manner with heaven's own celestial harmony; its length and breadth, height and depth being utterly in keeping with the proportions best loved by the universe. Solomon's Temple was, if you like, the very soul of God written in stone.

Many modern visitors have been perplexed by stone decorations of the old cathedrals that are clearly astrological in nature. Surely, one might think today, the unmistakable sign of Aries carved into the main doorway of such a venerable building must be an aberration, a personal foible on the part of an individual mason? Yet time and time again, in many different cathedrals, these signs appear – and they are never random.

All the lofty symbolism that can be found in the cathedrals was understood by the initiates at the time to reflect the age-old hermetic adage: *As above, so below.* The phrase was believed to have come from the *Emerald Tablet* of Hermes Trismegistus, the legendary Egyptian magician, or magus, although the words themselves may be much older. They mean that everything on earth has a counterpart in heaven and vice versa, something that Plato made popular with his notion of the *Ideal.* According to this, everything that exists, from a spoon to a man, was merely a version of its ideal, which existed in a sort of alternative dimension full of perfect templates. The magicians – or magi – went further, believing that every thought or act was mirrored on another plane, and that both dimensions somehow affected each other irresistibly. There are resonances of this concept in the modern scientific idea of parallel universes. Thus the stories of the ancient gods, with their petty jealousies and often sordid obsessions, were seen as being archetypal representatives of the human race. To the ancients, there was no discrepancy between abasing oneself before the great Olympian god Zeus and believing that he occasionally took the form of an animal in order to seduce earthly maidens. It was expected of a god that he behaved like a man – but the obverse of this concept was the idea, 'heretical' to Jews and Christians, that a man could become a god.

None of this was news to the Templars. The design of the cathedrals reveals an understanding of hermetic principles on the part of the stonemasons, and the knights who sponsored the building work[26]. They, of all medieval people, especially cherished the *practical application*, wherever possible, of any esoteric knowledge. To them, the encoding of secret messages in the very stone of the cathedrals went beyond mere fancy. As Baigent and Leigh say in their *The Temple and the Lodge*: '... God, had actually *taught* the practical application of sacred geometry through architecture.'[27] And once again, we find ourselves pointed in the direction of Solomon's Temple.

Son of the legendary Jewish hero, King David, Solomon built a Temple of surpassing beauty, using the finest and most costly materials[28]. Marble and precious stones, aromatic woods and the rarest fabrics were used to create a place that would make the worshippers' senses swim with delight, but also where God himself would feel at home. At its heart was the holy of holies, where the high priest could actually receive the Almighty through that most mysterious instrument, the Ark of the Covenant. This notoriously temperamental device was known on the one hand to bestow great blessings upon the 'righteous' and, on the other, to destroy either the evil-doer or those who had not been told how to combat the effects of its baleful presence. Perhaps to the Templars it sounded like the ultimate weapon, and so they went to find it, as some have suggested.

There are, perhaps, clues to what the Templars really believed to be the meaning of the 'Ark' in the decoration of the cathedrals. For example, Chartres Cathedral, the brainchild of their *éminence grise*, Bernard of Clairvaux contains a stone carving of what appears to be the Virgin Mary, with the carved 'label': *arcis foederis* – Ark of the Covenant. In itself this is not very significant, for it was a standard Christian symbol in medieval times. But as Chartres was a centre of the Black Madonna cult, is the Ark being equated with that other Mary, the Magdalene, or even with a much older, pagan goddess? Perhaps it is the Feminine principle itself that is being evoked, using the 'cover' of the Marian symbol. It cannot be a reference to the Virgin herself, for the architects of the Gothic cathedral had a special reason for evoking the archetype of a *sexually active woman*. (It is also significant that the first depictions of the legend of Mary Magdalene's life in France were in the stained-glass windows of Chartres Cathedral.)

It is in fact, the much-maligned and misunderstood discipline of alchemy that lay behind the often apparently bizarre decorations of the Gothic buildings (as, indeed, it was alchemy that seemed to be the common denominator of the majority of the Grand Masters of the Priory of Sion[29]).

Alchemy is believed to have come from the ancient Egyptians via the Arabs (the word itself derives from the Arabic). It was more than science: the practice embraced a fine web of interlinking activities and modes of thinking, from magic to chemistry, from philosophy and hermeticism to sacred geometry and cosmology. It also concerned itself with what people today call genetic engineering and methods of delaying the aging process, and of trying to attain physical immortality. Alchemists were hungry for knowledge and had no time for the Church's antagonism towards experimentation, so they went underground and continued their researches covertly. To the alchemist there was no such thing as heresy – while to the Church there was no such thing as an unheretical alchemist; hence the whole practice became known as 'the Black Art'.

There were many levels to alchemy: the outward, or exoteric, was concerned with working and experimenting with metals, but there were other, ever more secret levels that included the achievement of the mysterious 'Great Work'. This has been understood to be the crowning moment of an alchemist's life, when he finally turns base metal into gold. However, in esoteric circles it is also seen as the point when he becomes spiritually enlightened and physically revitalized – through a magical 'working' that revolves around *sexuality*. (This will be discussed in detail later.) It seems that the Great Work represented an act of supreme initiation.

Perhaps this rite was believed to bestow longevity: Nicolas Flamel, allegedly a Grand Master of the Priory of Sion, who achieved the Great Work in the company of his wife Perenelle on 17 January 1382, was rumoured to have lived for an exceptionally long time afterwards[30].

In alchemy, the symbol for the perfected Great Work is the hermaphrodite – literally the god Hermes and the goddess Aphrodite blended in one person. Leonardo was fascinated with hermaphrodites, even going so far as to cover sheet after sheet of his sketchpad with drawings of them – some pornographic. And recent work on the world's most famous portrait – the enigmatically smirking *Mona Lisa* – has shown persuasively that 'she' was none other than Leonardo himself. Researchers Dr Digby Quested of the Maudsley Hospital in London and Lillian Schwartz of Bell Laboratories in the USA used the most sophisticated computer techniques, independently of each other, to match the face of the portrait with the face of the artist and the result was a perfect fit[31]. Perhaps it was merely one of his exceptionally clever jokes on posterity, but there is also the possibility that Leonardo, as an alchemist, was also encapsulating his idea of having achieved the Great Work.

Some believe that this could bring about such a profound physical transformation that the successful alchemist might even change sex – perhaps this was the concept behind the *Mona Lisa*. But the symbol of the hermaphrodite also represents the moment of orgasm, when both male and female participants in the rite experience the sensation of blending into one another, of melting through their own boundaries into a mystical awareness of themselves and the universe.

The Gothic cathedrals boast many curious figures, from demons to Green Men. But some are passing strange: a carving in Nantes Cathedral shows a woman looking into a mirror, although the back of her head is in fact that of an old man[32]. And at Chartres the so-called 'Queen of Sheba' carving actually sports a beard![33] Alchemical symbols are found in many of the cathedrals that are associated with the Knights Templar.

Those are implicit links, but Charles Bywaters and Nicole Dawe have discovered Templar sites in the Languedoc-Roussillon with explicit alchemical symbolism:

> Our research has shown, among other things, that they were somehow very familiar with the properties of the soil. In one area in particular they created a hospital for Templars returning from the Holy Land, because the soil had healing

properties. There are alchemical signs at this site . . .

It's very clear that they were familiar with alchemy. It is significant when you find a location that was specifically chosen because of the nature of the soil, where there are clearly alchemical signs in the structure, and where there are tie-ins to both Cathars and Moslems. And this is hard, documented evidence; it's easy enough to prove.

During our travels in France, we repeatedly found that towns that had formerly been Templar property – such as Utelle in Provence and Alet-les-Bains in the Languedoc – subsequently became centres of alchemy. It is also significant that the alchemists, like the Templars, had a special veneration for John the Baptist[34].

As we have seen, the great cathedrals and many famous churches were built on sites known to have been sacred to ancient goddesses. For example, Notre-Dame in Paris rose up from the foundations of a temple of Diana, and St Sulpice in Paris was built on the ruins of a temple of Isis. In itself this is not unusual, for all over Europe Christian churches were built on old pagan sites, as a deliberate move on the part of the Church to show that it had triumphed over the heathen. But often what really happened was that the locals merely adapted their form of paganism to include Christianity, and saw the site of the new church as complementary to the Old Religion rather than the opposite. However, given the evidence for the deeper interests of the Templars, could it not be in the case of the cathedrals that they were intended to continue the worship of the feminine rather than to suppress it? Perhaps the cathedrals were goddess hymns carved in stone, and the 'Notre Dame' to whom so many of them were dedicated was really the feminine principle itself – *Sophia* . . .

Most people today think of Gothic architecture as being rather 'male' with its soaring spires and cross-shaped naves, but most of the decoration within is pervasively feminine, especially the splendid rose windows. Barbara G. Walker points out the significance of:

... the Rose, which ancient Rome knew as the Flower of Venus, [was] the badge of her sacred prostitutes. Things spoken 'under the rose' (*sub rosa*) were part of Venus' sexual mysteries, not to be revealed to the uninitiated ...

In the great age of cathedral building, when Mary was worshipped as a Goddess in her 'Palaces of the Queen of Heaven', or *Notre-Dames*, she was often addressed as the Rose, Rose-bush, Rose-garland . . . Mystic Rose . . . Like a pagan temple, the Gothic cathedral represented the body of the Goddess who was also the universe, containing the essence of male godhood within herself . . .[35]

The rose, as we will see, was also a symbol adopted by the troubadours, those singers of love songs from the South of France who are intimately connected with the erotic mysteries.

Other symbols found in the Gothic cathedrals convey strong subliminal messages about the power of the Feminine. Carved spiders' webs – an image repeated in the domed skylight of the church of Notre-Dame de France in London – represent Arachne, the spider goddess who rules Man's fate, or Isis, in her role as weaver of destiny. Similarly, the great maze or labyrinth drawn on the floor of Chartres Cathedral refers to the female mysteries, through which the initiate can find his way only by following the thread spun for him by the goddess. Clearly this place is not intended for the praise of the Virgin Mary, particularly because it is also home to a Black Madonna – Notre Dame de Souterrain (Our Lady of the Underworld). Also in Chartres is a stained-glass window depicting Mary Magdalene arriving in France by boat, thus combining a reference to the legend with that of Isis, for whom that was also a favoured means of transport. (Perhaps the Priory Grand Master's title of *Nautonnier*, 'helmsman' refers to its assumed role in the Ship of Isis.) This window is the oldest representation of the Magdalene legend in France, and, in a cathedral so many miles from Provence, was clearly deemed to be of great significance by the architects.

*   *   *

At the same time that the cathedrals were being built, heresy found another outlet, thus ensuring that its message would go down through history – although, like Leonardo's *Last Supper*, the codes through which it found expression are often misunderstood. This other heretical tradition was that of the Grail legends.

Today the term 'Holy Grail' is often used to signify an elusive goal, the glittering prize that will crown the work of a lifetime. Most people realize that it refers to something older, and religious in nature – usually the cup that Jesus drank from at the Last Supper. One legend has it that Joseph of Arimathea, Jesus' rich friend, collected in it the blood shed at the Crucifixion, which was then found to have healing properties. The search for the Holy Grail is understood to be a quest fraught with both physical and spiritual dangers, as the seeker fights with all sorts of foe, including those of the supernatural realm. In all versions of the story the cup is both a literal object and a symbol of perfection. It is seen to represent something that belongs to two dimensions at once – the actual and the mythical – and as such has a hold on the imagination that is second to none.

The Grail may be seen as a mysterious object, an actual treasure that exists in some cave somewhere, but it always carries the implicit idea that it symbolizes something ineffable, beyond the everyday world. This aura of spiritual questing arose, not only from the original Grail legends, but also from the culture in which they once flourished.

Of the millions of words that have been devoted to this subject over the course of centuries, in our opinion some of the wisest are to be found in *The Holy Grail* by Malcolm Godwin, published in 1994. It is a remarkable summary of all the disparate legends and interpretations, and perceptively sees right through the verbiage to the heart of the matter. Apart from the usual Christian and Celtic strands of the Grail romances of the late twelfth/early thirteenth centuries, Godwin also identifies a third, equally important strand – the alchemical. He reveals that the earliest versions of the Grail story undoubtedly drew on Celtic myths that involved the tales of that great hero King Arthur and his court, and many of the elements of these tales were focused on notions of Celtic goddess worship. The Grail stories redefined the old Celtic legends and extended them to encompass heretical ideas that were current in the thirteenth century.

The first of the Grail romances was Chrétien de Troyes' unfinished *Le Conte del Graal* (*c*.1190). It is significant that the town of Troyes, from which Chrétien took his surname, was a cabalistic centre and the site of the original Templar preceptory – and it was where the Count of Champagne held his court. (In fact, most of the original nine Templar knights were his vassals.) And the most famous church at Troyes is dedicated to Mary Magdalene[36].

In Chrétien's version of the story there is no mention of the Grail being a cup nor is any connection with the Last Supper or with Jesus ever explicitly described. In fact, there is no obvious religious connotation at all, and it has been said that its overall ambience is, if anything, distinctly pagan[37]. Here, however, the Grail object was a platter or dish – which, as we shall see, is highly significant. In fact, Chrétien had drawn on a much older Celtic tale that had as its hero Peredur[38], whose quest involved encountering a gruesome and apparently highly ritualistic procession in a remote castle. Carried in this were, among other things, a spear that dripped blood *and a severed head on a platter*. A common feature of the Grail stories is the critical moment when the hero fails to ask an important question, and it is this sin of omission that leads him into grave danger. As Malcolm Godwin says: 'Here the question which is not asked concerns the nature of the head. If Peredur had asked *whose* head, and how it concerned him, he would have known how to lift the enchantments of the Wasteland.'[39] (The land had been cursed and made infertile.)

Even without an ending, Chrétien's story was a runaway success and it gave rise to a huge number of copycat tales

– most of which were explicitly Christian. But, as Malcolm Godwin says, speaking of the monks who wrote them:

> They managed to cloud a work of the deepest heresy in such pious mystery that both legend and authors survived the fiery zeal of the Church Fathers. The orthodox minds of papal Rome, while never actually acknowledging the existence of the Grail, were surprisingly fainthearted about denouncing it either . . . Even more curiously the legend remained untainted by the fall of the heretical Cathars . . . and even the Knights Templar who feature implicitly within the various texts.[40]

One of these Christianized versions was *Perlesvaus*, which was, some say, written by a monk at Glastonbury Abbey in *c*.1205, while others believe it was the work of an anonymous Templar[41]. This tale is really about two quests that are interwoven. The Knight Gawain searches for the sword that beheaded John the Baptist, and which magically bleeds every day at noon. In one episode the hero encounters a cart containing 150 severed heads of knights: some were sealed in gold, some in silver and some in lead. Then there is a bizarre damsel who carries in one hand the head of a king, sealed in silver, and in the other that of a queen, sealed in lead.

In *Perlesvaus* the élite attendants of the Grail wear white garments emblazoned with a red cross – just like the Templars. There is also a red cross that stands in a forest, and which falls prey to a priest who beats it 'in every part' with a rod, an episode which has a clear connection with the charge that the Templars spat at and trampled on the cross. Once again, there is a curious scene involving severed heads. One of the Grail guardians tells the hero, Perceval, 'There are the heads sealed in silver, and the heads sealed in lead, and the bodies whereunto these heads belong: I tell you that you must make come thither the head both of the King and Queen.'

The alchemical symbolism is lavish: base and precious metals, kings and queens. Such imagery is also found in plenty in another major reworking of the Grail legend, as we shall see.

Despite the Church's tacit distaste for the Grail, the most Christianized version was actually written by a team of Cistercian monks. Called the *Queste del San Graal*, it is most remarkable for the fact that it draws on the Song of Songs for its powerful mystical symbolism[42].

Of all the frankly bizarre Grail stories the weirdest – and most provocative – was the Bavarian poet Wolfram von Eschenbach's *Parzival* (*c*.1220)[43]. In it the author states that he is deliberately correcting Chrétien de Troyes' version, which did not contain all the available information. He claims that his is the more accurate because he had obtained the real story from one Kyot de Provence – who has been identified as Guiot de Provins, a monk who was both a voice for the Templar Order and a troubadour[44]. As Wolfram writes in *Parzival*: 'The authentic tale with the conclusion to the romance has been sent to the German lands from Provence.'[45]

But what was this significant conclusion? In *Parzival* the Grail Castle is a secret place, guarded by the Templars (who, significantly, Wolfram calls 'baptised men') who are sent out to spread their faith in secret. *Secrecy* and the aversion of the Grail Company to being questioned are stressed.

At the end of the story Repanse de Schoye (the Grail bearer) and Parzival's half-brother Fierefiz go off to India and have a son called John – the famous Prester John – who is the first of a lineage *who always take the name John* . . . Could this be a coded reference to the Priory of Sion, whose Grand Masters always supposedly take this name?

It is the concept of lineage that is central to the theories of Baigent, Leigh and Lincoln concerning the Grail. As the title of their first book makes clear, to them the 'Holy Grail' was actually the 'Holy Blood'. This is based on the idea that the original French *sangraal*, which is usually taken as *san graal* (Holy Grail), should properly be rendered as *sang real* – the royal blood, which they took to mean a bloodline. Baigent, Leigh and Lincoln connected the Grail legends' emphasis on lineage with what they believe to be the great secret about Jesus and the Magdalene having been man and wife, and came up with their own theory: the Grail of the legends was a symbolic reference to the descendants of Jesus and Mary Magdalene. According to this theory, the Grail keepers were those who knew of this secret, sacred lineage – such as the Templars and the Priory of Sion.[46]

There is a problem with this idea, however: in the Grail stories the emphasis is on the lineage of the *Grail keepers* or *Grail finders*: the Grail itself is separate from them. While it could well be that the legends refer to a secret kept by certain families, and passed on from generation to generation, it seems unlikely that they really allude to a bloodline. After all, the idea just comes from playing around with a single French word *sangraal*, and we have already seen the difficulties that arise from any hypothesis that rests on the idea of the maintenance of a 'pure' bloodline through the ages.

The link between the Grail stories and the Templar legacy seems real enough. Wolfram von Eschenbach is believed to have travelled widely and to be no stranger to Templar centres in the Middle East, and his tale is by far the most explicitly Templar of all the Grail romances. As Malcolm Godwin says: 'Throughout *Parzival* Wolfram intersperses the account with allusions to astrology, alchemy, the Cabala and the new spiritual ideas of the East.'[47] He also includes obvious symbolism taken straight from the Tarot.

It is in this version that the Guardians of the Grail at the Castle Montsalvasch are explicitly called Templars[48]. The original castle has been identified with Montségur, the last major Cathar stronghold[49] – and, tellingly, in another of his poems Wolfram calls the Lord of the Grail Castle Perilla. The real Lord of Montségur in the poet's day was Ramon de Perella. Once again we find Templars and Cathars linked, both with each other and with some ill-defined but highly prized treasure.

There is no cup endowed with supernatural powers in Wolfram's version; here the Grail is a stone – *lapsit exillis* – which possibly means the Stone of Death, although this is mere speculation. No-one really knows. Other explanations have the stone as the jewel that fell from Lucifer's crown as he plummeted to earth from heaven, and the famed Philosopher's Stone (*lapis elixir*) of the alchemists. In the context, the last interpretation is the most likely: the text as a whole abounds with alchemical symbols.

Some writers have seen the character Cundrie, the 'messenger of the Grail' in *Parzival*, as representing Mary Magdalene[50]. (Certainly Wagner did – in his opera *Parsifal* (1882), his Kundry bears a flask of 'balsam' and washes the hero's feet which she then, Magdalene-like, dries with her hair.) Perhaps there is some resonance of the Grail cup in the alabaster jar that the Magdalene carries in traditional Christian iconography.

In all the stories, however, the quest for the Grail is an allegory of the hero's spiritual journey towards – and beyond – personal transformation. And as we have seen, one of the major motives of all serious alchemy was precisely that. But was it merely their alchemical subtext that made all the Grail legends 'heretical'?

The Church was no doubt mortally offended by the way in which the Grail stories ignored or abnegated its authority and that of the apostolic succession. The hero operates by himself – although occasionally with helpers – in the quest for spiritual enlightenment and transformation. So in essence the Grail legends are Gnostic texts, emphasizing the responsibility of the individual for the state of his own soul.

There is, however, much more to offend the sensibilities of the Church that is implicit in *every* Grail story. For the experience of the Grail is inevitably presented as being reserved for the highest initiate only, the cream of the élite – something that goes far beyond even the transcendence of the Mass. Moreover, in every Grail story the object itself – whatever it is deemed to be – is *kept by women*. Even in the Celtic story of Peredur the youths may bear the spear, but it is the maidens who carry what may be termed the *prototype Grail* – the platter with the head on it. But what were women doing taking such an authoritative role in something that was effectively a higher form of the Mass? (Remember that the Cathars, whose citadel of Montségur was almost certainly the original for Wolfram's Grail Castle, operated a system of sexual equality so that both men and women could be called 'priests'.)

Yet it is the connection with the Templars that is most pervasive in the Grail stories. As several commentators have pointed out[51], the charge that the knights worshipped a severed head – which was believed to be called Baphomet – has resonances with the Grail romances, in which, as we have seen, severed heads figure largely. The Templars were charged with ascribing Grail-like powers to this Baphomet: it could make the trees flower and the land fertile[52]. In fact, not only were the Templars accused of revering this idol head, but they also owned a silver reliquary in the form of a female skull which was labelled simply *caput (head) 58*[53].

Hugh Schonfield, when considering the implications of this female head, together with his 'decoding' of Baphomet as *Sophia*, writes:

> There would seem to be little doubt that the beautiful woman's head of the Templars represented Sophia in her female and Isis aspect, and she was linked with Mary Magdalene in the Christian interpretation.[54]

Templar relics are also reputed to have included the (alleged) right forefinger of John the Baptist. This may well be more significant than it seems. As we saw in Chapter One, Leonardo frequently depicted characters in religious scenes deliberately – and ritualistically pointing upwards with their right forefinger and this gesture appears to have been connected with John the Baptist. For example, we saw how an individual who appeared to be revering the carob tree in *The Adoration of the Magi* was making this gesture: both tree and gesture are linked with John. The relic said to have been owned by the Templars may have been the material reason for Leonardo's having espoused this imagery.

(Jacobus de Voragine in his *Golden Legend* chronicles a

tradition that John the Baptist's finger – the only part of the headless corpse to escape destruction by the Emperor Julian – was brought to France by St Thecla, so perhaps there may be some reason for believing that the Templar relic and that of the legend were one and the same. And de Voragine also records the legend that tells of the Baptist's head being buried under Herod's Temple in Jerusalem, where the Templars excavated.)[55]

The Templars are repeatedly linked with the Grail. British travel writer Nina Epton in her *The Valley of Pyrene* (1955) describes how she climbed up to the ruins of the Templar castle of Montréal-de-Sos in the Ariège to see murals that depicted a lance with three drops of blood and a chalice – an image clearly taken straight from the Grail legends.[56]

Other bizarre graffiti have been found in the château at Domme where many Templars were imprisoned. Ean and Deike Begg describe a strange Crucifixion scene in which Joseph of Arimathea (holding a cross of Lorraine) is shown, on the right, catching drops of Jesus' blood. On the left is a naked, pregnant woman holding a rod or wand.[57]

There are other, more curious, links. At St-Martin-du-Vésubie in Provence, which, as we have seen, is both a renowned Black Madonna and a Templar site, there is a legend that incorporates interesting elements of the Grail stories[58]. It is said that the Templars there were all beheaded during the suppression – something that, given the complete lack of official verification, seems highly unlikely – and that they cursed the land with blight. Men became impotent or sterile and the land infertile. Whatever the truth of the matter, it is an historical fact that in 1560 Duke Emmanuel Filibert of Savoy had the land exorcized, for it was in a pitiable state. In fact, one of its neighbouring peaks is still known as Maledia (roughly translated as 'sickness'). But the most significant part of this sorry tale is that it links Templars being beheaded with a blight upon the land – two major elements of the Grail canon. To the writers of the Grail stories there was something about severed heads, or perhaps a severed head, that brought doom upon the land, yet it could also provide largesse to those it favoured.

The different Grail stories and the various strands within them may appear confusing, but in his monumental study of the Holy Grail legends, *The Hidden Church of the Holy Graal* (1902), the great occult scholar A.E. Waite discerned the presence of a secret tradition within Christianity that was behind the whole concept of the legends. Waite was one of the first to recognize the alchemical, hermetic and Gnostic elements in the stories. Although he was certain that there are strong hints about the existence of such a 'hidden church' in the Grail legends, he does not come to any firm conclusion about its nature, but he does give a prominent place to what he called the 'Johannine [or Johannite] Tradition'[59]. He refers to a long-held idea in esoteric circles of a mystical school of Christianity that was founded by John the Evangelist, based on the secret teachings he had been given by Jesus. This arcane knowledge did not appear in the outward or exoteric Christianity that came down through the teachings of Peter. Significantly, Waite sees this tradition as having reached Europe via southern Gaul – the South of France – before filtering through to the early Celtic Church of Britain[60].

Despite the Celtic elements in the Grail stories, Waite sees their Johannite influence as originating from the Middle East, via the Templars. Cannily, he does not claim it as the only possible connection, because there is no conclusive evidence for it, but he admits that it is the most plausible. However, he is certain that the Grail romances were based on some kind of 'hidden Church' that was connected with the Templars.

Waite's emphasis on a 'Johannite' tradition was somewhat tantalizing – he did not elaborate on it and his source remains shrouded in mystery. But clearly it appeared to provide a potentially exciting link between the Grail stories and *a* Saint John – one which, as we shall see in the next chapter, was to make sense of much of the apparent confusion that surrounds this matter.

The Grail stories are yet another manifestation of the underground ideas that were circulating in medieval France under the auspices of the Templars, such as the Black Madonna cult. The connection between the two is striking. Both are based on earlier, pagan themes: the Grail stories on Celtic myths and the Black Madonna cult on pagan goddess shrines. Yet both flowered in the twelfth and thirteenth centuries because of contact – via the Templars – with the Holy Land.

The Templars were a repository of knowledge gleaned from many esoteric sources, including those of alchemy and sacred sexuality. (The connection between Black Madonnas, Templars and alchemy is the subject of a study by French historian Jacques Huynen in his *L'énigme des Vierges Noires (The Enigma of the Black Virgins)* (1972).) And the 'bridge' between their exotic and esoteric ideas and the Christian world of their day was embodied in the image of one woman: Mary Magdalene.

All this happened a long time ago. The Cathars have long been gone, and the Templar Order went not long afterwards. But is this secret knowledge, this mystical and alchemical awareness of the Feminine, also buried under the dust of centuries?

Perhaps not. Perhaps it has become the most exciting, and the most dangerous, secret kept alive in Europe's underground today.

CHAPTER SIX

The Templar Legacy

Most historians see the violent events of the early fourteenth century as the final curtain for the Templars – and therefore they do not look for any signs of their continuing existence. But the occult tradition has always spoken of spiritual descendants of those Templar knights who continue to live in our midst today, and there are modern societies that claim to be those descendants. Moreover, a welter of recent research has shown very persuasively that the Order did survive and exert an enormous influence on Western culture.

The implications of this are profound and far-reaching. For if they were, as we and other researchers believe, collectors of esoteric and alchemical knowledge, then any Templar survival points to some kind of continuation of great secrets through an occult tradition that may still exist to this day. These secrets – perhaps including scientific knowledge from the old alchemists and magical practices from Eastern esoteric traditions – may still live on, even in our own society. If this is so, then, as prime examples of an ancient heretical system of belief and practice, today's Templars could well have some light to shed on our own investigation. But first we had to convince ourselves that the Templars did not, in fact, die out.

Common sense dictates that the idea of the highly organized Templars just lying down and dying meekly is unlikely. For a start, not every single knight in Europe was rounded up simultaneously on that momentous Friday the thirteenth. That kind of cataclysm for the Order only happened in France – but even there some knights escaped. In other countries there was, as it were, a sliding scale of persecution and suppression. In England, for example, Edward II refused to believe that the

Templars were guilty as accused and even engaged in heated debate with the Pope about it. He flatly refused to use torture on the knights.

In Germany there was a wonderfully hilarious scene. Hugo of Gumbach, Templar Master of Germany, made a dramatic entrance into the council convened by the Archbishop of Metz. Arrayed in full armour and accompanied by twenty hand-picked and battle-hardened knights, he proclaimed that the Pope was evil and should be deposed, that the Order was innocent – and, by the way, his men were willing to undergo trial by combat against the assembled company . . . After a stunned silence the whole business was abruptly dropped and the knights lived to assert their innocence another day.

In Aragon and Castille the bishops conducted trials of the Templars – only to find them innocent. However, no matter how lenient or liberal the judges wished to be towards the knights, none of them could afford to ignore the Pope's command to dissolve the Order in 1312. But even in France only a relative few were executed – many being released after their recantation – and in other countries they simply reformed under another name, or they joined other existing orders such as the Teutonic Knights.

So historically there is slender evidence that the Knights Templar were ever effectively killed off. Of course they would have gone underground to regroup and re-form. In fact, the manner of their dissolution virtually guaranteed it.

Remember that the rank and file were very different from the inner circle, the élite knights who not only ran the organization but were also a repository for secret knowledge. It is very likely that knights from both these levels went off and founded their own underground movements, effectively starting two separate organizations, each claiming to have the true Templar pedigree.

After the disbanding of the Templars, most of their lands were given to their rivals, the Knights Hospitaller. In Scotland and England, however, much of this hand-over of property did not take place, and there is evidence that former Templar estates in London were still owned by families of Templar descent as late as 1650[1]. However, it was not continuity of ownership of land and buildings that we were interested in, but the perpetuation of the Templars' esoteric knowledge.

Although there is no conclusive evidence that the Templars were the masterminds behind the underground alchemical network, we do know that the 'inner circle' were interested in alchemy – as we have seen in the proximity of alchemical centres such as Alet-les-Bains to Templar commanderies. And, as we have seen, the alchemists – like the Templars – especially venerated John the Baptist.

Recently several commentators have presented persuasive evidence that Freemasonry had its origins in Templarism: both *The Temple and the Lodge* by Michael Baigent and Richard Leigh and *Born in Blood* by the American historical writer-researcher John J. Robinson have come to that conclusion even though approaching the subject from entirely different viewpoints.

The former traces the Templar continuity through Scotland, while the latter depends more on working back from modern Freemasonic ritual to its origins – and once again, ends up with the Templars. So these major books effectively complement each other, providing a more or less complete picture of the link between the two great occult organizations.

The only major point of disagreement between Baigent/Leigh and Robinson is that the former see Free-masonry as developing from isolated Templars in Scotland, then going to England in 1603 with the accession of the Scottish king, James VI, to the English throne and the ensuing influx of Scots aristocracy. Robinson, on the other hand, believes that the Templars developed into Freemasons in England. He argues persuasively that the Templars were behind the Peasants' Revolt of 1381, which specifically attacked the property of the Church and of the Knights Hospitallers – the two main enemies of the Templars – although it went to great lengths to avoid damaging former Templar buildings.

To many outsiders Freemasonry is simply a quaint old boys' club, an insiders' network that provides lucrative business contacts and influence for its members. Its ritual side is perceived as being ludicrous – with brothers rolling up one trouser leg and uttering archaic and meaningless oaths. Things may have changed, but in its earliest days Freemasonry was a mystery school with solemn initiations that drew on ancient occult traditions, and which were specifically designed to bring transcendental enlightenment, besides binding the initiate more closely to his brothers.

Originally it was an occult organization, explicitly concerned with the transmission of *sacred knowledge*. Much of what we would now call science actually came out of that brotherhood – as one can see from the formation of the Royal Society in England in 1662, which was and is concerned with the gathering and promulgating of scientific knowledge. It was the official establishment of the original 'Invisible College' of the Freemasons that had been formed in 1645[2]. (And just as in Leonardo's day, occult and scientific knowledge – far from being antithetical – were seen as one and the same.)

Although no doubt many modern Freemasons do undertake their initiations solemnly and with a sense of spirituality, the overall picture is one of an organization that has forgotten its original meaning. In fact, today's mainstream Freemasonry is that of Grand Lodge, which was only formed relatively recently, on John the Baptist's Day (24 June) in 1717. Before that time Freemasonry had been a *true* secret society, but the emergence of Grand Lodge marked an era when it had already become a glorified dining club, and which had gone semi-public because it no longer had any secrets to keep to itself.

So just how old is Freemasonry? The earliest acknowledged reference is in 1641[3], but if there is a link with the Templars it obviously does go back much further. John J. Robinson cites evidence of Masonic lodges existing in the 1380s[4] and an alchemical treatise dating from the 1450s explicitly uses the term 'Freemason'[5].

The Masons themselves claim that they emerged from the

English medieval stonemasons' guilds – which had developed secret gestures and codes of recognition because they possessed the potentially dangerous knowledge of sacred geometry. But, as John J. Robinson's extensive and meticulous research has shown, against all expectations, these guilds were conspicuous by their absence in medieval Britain[6]. Another Freemasonic myth is their claim that the stonemasons inherited their secret knowledge from the builders of the fabulous Temple of Solomon. If so, however, why did they ignore another group with more obvious links with that temple? They appear to be avoiding the most obvious link of all: the group whose full name was the Order of Poor Knights of Christ and the *Temple of Solomon* – in other words, the Templars.

Yet before the formation of Grand Lodge, the Freemasons actually promulgated the same kind of information about sacred geometry, alchemy and hermeticism as did the Templars. For example, the early Masons were very concerned with alchemy: a mid-fifteenth-century alchemical treatise alludes to Freemasons as 'workers in alchemy'[7] and one of the first Masonic initiates was recorded as being Elias Ashmole (inducted in 1646), founder of the Ashmolean Museum in Oxford, who was an alchemist, hermeticist and Rosicrucian[8]. (Ashmole was also the first person to write approvingly of the Templars since their suppression.[9])

A jewel in the crown of Masonry is the curious and compelling building called Rosslyn Chapel, a few miles out of Edinburgh. From the outside it looks so dilapidated as to be almost in danger of collapsing completely, but the interior is eye-openingly robust – as, indeed, it would have to be, for Rosslyn Chapel is the acknowledged focus for today's Freemasons and many Templar organizations.[10]

Built between 1450 and 1480 by Sir William St Clair, Laird of Rosslyn, it was originally intended to be simply the lady chapel of a much larger building that was supposed to be based on the design of the Temple of Solomon, but in the event it was to stand alone throughout the centuries. The St Clairs (later their name became Sinclair) were to be the hereditary protectors of Freemasonry in Scotland from the fifteenth century onwards[11]: surely it is no coincidence that before that time they served the same function for the Templars.

From its very beginnings the Templar Order was connected with the Sinclairs and Rosslyn: founding Grand Master Hugues de Payens was married to Catherine St Clair. Originally of Viking descent, the St Clairs/Sinclairs are one of the most intriguing and remarkable families in history, and were prominent in Scotland and France from the eleventh century. (Interestingly, their family name came from the Scottish martyr Saint Clair, who was beheaded.) Hugues and Catherine visited the St Clair estates close to Rosslyn and established there the first Templar commandery in Scotland, which became their headquarters.

(As we have seen, Pierre Plantard adopted the name 'de St Clair', thereby deliberately linking himself with the French branch of this ancient family. Several commentators have wondered whether he is entitled to use this designation, but there is at least a good reason for him to do so.[12])

The knights certainly made Scotland one of their major havens after their official suppression – perhaps because it was very much the land of Robert the Bruce, who had himself been excommunicated, so that the Pope for the moment held no sway in Scotland. And Baigent and Leigh argue persuasively that the missing Templar fleet turned up on Scottish shores.

One of the critical historic events of the British Isles was undoubtedly the Battle of Bannockburn, which took place on 24 June (John the Baptist's Day) in 1314, when Robert the Bruce's forces decisively overcame the English. However, the evidence suggests that they had formidable help – in the form of a contingent of Knights Templar who saved the day at the eleventh hour. Certainly, that is what today's Scottish Knights Templar (who claim descent from the fugitive knights) believe, as they commemorate the Battle of Bannockburn in Rosslyn Chapel on its anniversary as being the occasion when 'the Veil was lifted from the Knights Templar'. One of the knights who had fought alongside Robert the Bruce at Bannockburn was (another) Sir William St Clair, who died in 1330 and was buried at Rosslyn – in a characteristic Templar tomb[13].

Rosslyn Chapel itself contains some apparent anomalies in its decoration. Every square inch of the chapel's interior is covered in carved symbols and the building as a whole is designed to accord with the high ideals of sacred geometry. Much of this is undeniably Masonic. It boasts the 'Apprentice Pillar', an explicit parallel with the Masonic myth of Hiram Abiff[14], and the apprentice depicted on it is known as 'the Son of the Widow', a highly significant Masonic term (which is also important in this investigation). The lintel next to this pillar bears the inscription:

> Wine is strong, the King is stronger, women are strongest, but TRUTH conquers all.[15]

But while much of Rosslyn's symbolism is clearly Masonic, at least as much is definitely Templar: the floor plan of the chapel is based on the Templar cross, and there are carvings that include the famous two-men-on-a-horse image from their seal. And an ancient nearby wood was planted in the shape of the Templar cross.

All this is most curious, for according to standard history texts, Freemasonry dates from no earlier than the late 1500s, and the Templars were no longer a force to be reckoned with after 1312. Thus the imagery in the chapel, which dates from around the 1460s, should be too early for the former and too late for the latter.

There is, however, a great deal of symbolism found in Rosslyn Chapel that is not classically either Masonic or Templar. There is a plethora of pagan – and even some Islamic – imagery. And on the outside of the chapel is a carved representation of Hermes – a clear allusion to hermeticism – while the interior is adorned with over a hundred depictions of the Green Man, the pagan Celtic vegetation god. Tim Wallace-

Murphy, in his official history of Rosslyn Chapel, associates the Green Man with the Babylonian dying-and-rising god Tammuz. All such gods had similar attributes and were often depicted as having green faces – although the god who was most often depicted in this way was Osiris, consort of Isis.

When we visited Niven Sinclair, a member of that illustrious family, we found ourselves virtually bombarded with evidence that the Sinclairs had been not only Templar, but also *pagan*. Niven, who is a passionate researcher into the history of Rosslyn and the Sinclairs, offered some very revealing insights into what had happened to the lost Templar knowledge. He said that it was encoded in the fabric of Rosslyn Chapel in order to pass it on to future generations. As he said, 'Earl William St Clair built the chapel at a time when books could be burnt or banned. He wanted to leave a message for posterity.'[16]

As Niven warmed to his theme he impressed on us the sheer ingenuity of his ancestor Sir William in creating this book in stone. As he said, 'If you go to St Paul's Cathedral you can take it in in a single visit. If you go to Rosslyn Chapel you can't. I must count the number of times I've been there in hundreds, and every time I go I find something new. This is the beauty of the place.'

Rosslyn is far from being a typical Christian chapel. In fact, Niven went so far as to say, 'It was said that Earl William built Rosslyn Chapel to the "greater glory of God". If that is so, it is very remarkable how few Christian symbols you find within it.'

In the Middle Ages the Sinclairs actively promoted pagan celebrations and provided a haven for gypsies (of whom it has been said that they are 'among the last active preservers of Goddess-worship in Europe'[17]). And, tellingly, many authorities believe that there used to be a Black Madonna in the crypt of Rosslyn Chapel[18].

We had come to realize, with something of a shock, that the Templars were by no means the devoted Christian knights of popular imagination. The image they had created for themselves as cover had been extremely successful, but they had obviously intended to leave clues to their real preoccupations 'for those with eyes to see'. The decoration of Rosslyn Chapel was just one example of this cryptic but revelatory message.

The Templar love and preservation of knowledge meant that at Rosslyn we also find the 'Rosslyn-Hay Manuscript', which is the earliest known work in Scottish prose. It is a translation of René d'Anjou's writings on chivalry and government, and on its binding are found the words inscribed: 'JHESUS [sic] – MARIA – JOHANNES' (Jesus, Mary, John). As Andrew Sinclair says in his *The Sword and the Grail* (1992):

> The addition of the name of St John to that of Jesus and Mary is unusual, but he was venerated by the gnostics and the Templars . . . Another remarkable feature of the binding is the use of the Agnus Dei, the Lamb of God . . . In Rosslyn Chapel, the Templar Seal of the Lamb of God is also carved.[19]

Earl William and René d'Anjou were close, both being members of the Order of the Golden Fleece, a group whose avowed intent was to restore the old Templar ideals of chivalry and brotherhood.

It is clear that the Templars survived in Scotland and continued to operate openly, not just at Rosslyn but in several other locations[20]. However, in 1329 their charmed life was once again under threat when Robert the Bruce's excommunication was lifted and the shadow of the Pope's authority returned to haunt them. At one point there was even the distinct possibility that a crusade would be launched against Scotland, and although this did not materialize, the Scottish Templars thought it prudent to go underground like many of their European brothers; and it was this, it is claimed, that gave rise to the beginnings of Freemasonry.

Significantly, certain branches of Freemasonry have always claimed to be descended from the Templars and to have their origins in Scotland, but few historians – even within Masonry itself – have ever taken them seriously. These 'Templarist' Masons may well have inherited genuine Templar secrets, at least in part. Their knowledge, which includes hermetic and alchemical wisdom, besides that of sacred geometry, is still deemed valuable – perhaps more so because it addresses very different issues from those of the modern world at large.

It was a Scotsman, Andrew Michael Ramsay, who delivered what has become known as 'Ramsay's Oration' in 1737 to Freemasons in Paris[21]. A Knight of the Order of St Lazarus – and tutor to Bonnie Prince Charlie – 'Chevalier' Ramsay made a point of stressing to the brotherhood that they were descended from the *Crusader knights*, which was a thinly veiled reference to the Templars. It was in his interest to use this oblique terminology, for the Templars were still anathema in French society. The Oration also claimed, controversially, that the Masons originated in the mystery schools of the goddesses Diana, Minerva and Isis.

The Oration has attracted great scorn over the years, not only for the last statement about origins in Goddess worship, but because Chevalier Ramsay claimed that the Order was not descended from medieval stonemasons. Authorities on the subject homed in on this statement, saying that, as this was obviously untrue, it threw the whole of the Oration into question. But, as we have seen, recent research has shown that there were no medieval stonemasons' guilds in Britain, so perhaps the good Chevalier should be given at the very least the benefit of the doubt on that – and on his other statements.

The Oration of 1737 was the first public hint that Freemasonry was descended from the Templars – could there be any connection with the fact that just a year later the Pope denounced the whole brotherhood of Freemasons? Amazingly, even at this late date, the Inquisition arrested and tortured Freemasons as a direct result of this papal bull.

After Ramsay's heavy hints about the Templar connection, there came a more explicit and authoritative statement. In one of the most controversial episodes in the Freemasons' history,

Karl Gotthelf, the Baron von Hund und Alten-Grotkau, claimed that he had been initiated into a Masonic Order of the Temple in Paris in 1743, and that he was given the 'true' history of Freemasonry and authorized to set up lodges based upon this line of authority, which he called the 'Strict Templar Observance' – although, significantly, it was known in Germany as The Brethren of John the Baptist[22]. The true history that he had been given included the information that when the Templars had been suppressed, some of the knights had fled to Scotland and established themselves there. Baron von Hund possessed a list of what he claimed were the names of the Grand Masters who succeeded Jacques de Molay in the underground Templar movement after the suppression.

Von Hund's lodges were staggeringly successful almost immediately, but unfortunately he has won no friends among historians, who have denounced him as an out-and-out charlatan and dismissed his version of the 'true history' as complete nonsense[23]. They are equally scornful of his list of alleged Grand Masters. The main reason for this blanket dismissal was that his claims were based on the words of anonymous contacts – what he called 'Unknown Superiors' – and therefore it seemed as if he had simply made it all up. In fact, anonymous tip-offs are frequent occurrences within occult groups, as we can personally testify, and recently some very credible names have been ascribed to the Unknown Superiors, so it does look as if he might have been telling the truth about his contacts after all[24].

Significantly, historians have never been able to produce a definitive list of the Grand Masters of the historical Templars – due to the incomplete nature of the available archives. However, von Hund's list is identical to the one that appears in the *Dossiers secrets* of the Priory of Sion[25]. Baigent, Leigh and Lincoln's research[26] convinced them that the Priory's list is the most accurate available; although, due to the paucity of the records, we can never be sure, it certainly stands up to academic scrutiny and may well be correct. But while the Priory's list could – to be cynical – have been fabricated in the

1950s, it is unlikely that von Hund's could have been similarly invented back in 1750, when there were no available records and no historical research into the Templars. At the least, the link reveals a dovetailing tradition between the Strict Templar Observance and the Priory.

While many words have been written about von Hund's claims and his organization, there is a curious lack of speculation about what may have been his underlying motivation. In fact, his Strict Observance was basically an *alchemical network*, and he himself was first and foremost an alchemist[27]. Was von Hund carrying on the Templar tradition?

Whatever the truth behind von Hund's organization and preoccupations, Templarist Freemasonry was soon well established and was to become a major form of Masonry on both sides of the Atlantic. (The idea has been proposed that the Templars effectively 'hid' themselves within the high grades of Freemasonry.) Templarist Freemasonry also influenced another development that was to become important in our own line of research – Scottish Rite Freemasonry, especially the form known as the Rectified Scottish Rite, which is particularly strong in France.

French Freemasons have a curious legend about 'Maître Jacques', a mythical figure who was patron of the French medieval stonemasons' guilds. He was, according to the story, one of the master masons who worked on Solomon's Temple. After the death of Hiram Abiff he left Palestine and, together with thirteen journeymen, sailed to Marseilles. The followers of his great enemy, the master mason Father Soubise, determined to kill him, so he hid in the cave at Sainte-Baume – the same one that was later occupied by Mary Magdalene. All to no avail: he was betrayed and killed. The Masons still observe a pilgrimage to the site every 22 July.[28]

Another strong candidate for the role of heirs to the Templars' esoteric knowledge is the movement known as Rosicrucianism. Once much derided by historians as an invention of the early seventeenth century, the recognition is gaining ground that it has real roots in the traditions of the Renaissance. 'Rosicrucianism' as an ideal, or attitude – if not in name – is recognized as a driving force behind the Renaissance, an ideal typified by Leonardo. As Dame Frances Yates wrote:

> Might it not have been within the outlook of a Magus that a personality like Leonardo was able to co-ordinate his mathematical and mechanical studies with his work as an artist?[29]

Certainly Leonardo lived at a time when great intellectual and mystical movements acted like a magnet for those hungry after both knowledge and power. Because of the hostility of the Church, these movements had to remain underground, but the three main branches that flourished in secret were alchemy, hermeticism and Gnosticism. The hermeticism that provided such an important impetus for the Renaissance/Rosicrucian enlightenment, and the Gnosticism that gave rise to the Cathars, are two developments of the same cosmological ideas. The world of matter is the lowest in a hierarchy of 'worlds' – in their terms 'spheres', in today's terminology 'planes' or 'dimensions' – the highest of which is God. Man is a once-divine being who has become 'trapped' in his material body, but still retains a divine spark. (A much-quoted hermetic line was 'Know ye not that ye are gods?') It is possible – indeed, it is Man's duty – to try to reunite with the Divine. Gnostics expressed this in religious terms (seeing the reunion with the Divine as salvation), whereas the hermeticists thought of it in magical terms, but the basic idea is the same. It is impossible to draw a definite line between Gnosticism and hermeticism, just as it is impossible to draw a line between religion and magic.

Moreover, both Gnosticism and hermeticism can be traced back to the same time and place – the ferment of ideas that took place in Egypt, most especially in Alexandria, in the first and second centuries BCE. This huge melting pot of religious and philosophical ideas drew on the beliefs of many cultures –

Greek, Persian, Jewish, ancient Egyptian, even the religions of the Far East – to create ideas that underpin our whole culture. (The close relationship between Gnosticism and hermeticism is illustrated by the fact that the 'Gnostic Gospels' found at Nag Hammadi included treatises containing dialogues of Hermes Trismegistus.)

The cosmology of the *Pistis Sophia* – the Gnostic Gospel in which Mary Magdalene has such a key role – does not differ in any essential from that of the Renaissance magi such as Marsilio Ficino, Cornelius Agrippa or Robert Fludd. The same ideas, and the same culture, time and place gave rise to alchemy. Although it also drew on much earlier concepts, alchemy was – in the sense that it is understood today – a product of Egypt in the early centuries of the Christian era. The roots of alchemy, and its parallels with hermeticism and Gnosticism are explored in Jack Lindsay's *The Origins of Alchemy in Graeco-Roman Egypt* (1970).

It is not difficult to understand the appeal of Gnosticism, although it was no easy option – the emphasis being on personal responsibility for one's own actions – but at the same time the threat to the Church of Rome is obvious. As Hermes Trismegistus supposedly wrote: 'Oh! What a miracle is Man!', an exclamation that encapsulates the idea that mankind contains the divine spark. Neither Gnostics nor hermeticists grovelled before their God. Unlike Catholics, they did not think of themselves as lowly and evil creatures who were destined for purgatory, if not hell itself. Recognizing their divine spark automatically bestowed what we today would call 'self-esteem' or *confidence* – the magic ingredient in the process of fulfilling one's potential. This was the key to the Renaissance as a whole, and the fearlessness it induced can be seen in the sudden opening up of the world through circumnavigation and exploration. Worse still, as far as the Church was concerned, this notion of individual potential for godhood implied that *women* were as good as men, at least spiritually. Gnostic women had always had a voice, and even officiated at religious ceremonies: this was one of the major threats that

Gnosticism posed to the Catholic Church. Moreover, the idea of mankind's essentially divine status did not accord with the Christian idea of 'original sin' – the idea that all men and women are born sinful because of the Fall of Adam and Eve (especially the latter). Because all children are the result of the 'shameful' sex act, that idea inextricably linked women and children in a kind of everlasting conspiracy against pure men and a vengeful God. Gnostics and hermeticists, on the whole, had no truck with 'original sin'.

Each individual was encouraged to explore both outer and inner worlds for him/herself – experiencing *gnosis*, knowledge of the Divine. This emphasis on individual salvation was totally antithetical to the Church's insistence that only *priests* were the conduits through which God might communicate with mankind. The Gnostic idea of a direct line to God, as it were, threatened the Church's very existence. With no priestly hold over its flock, what chance did the Church have to maintain its control? As with alchemy, it was prudent to keep Gnosticism and hermeticism hidden from the eyes of the Church.

The combination of forbidden science and anathematized philosophy meant that the practitioners of these beliefs were beyond the pale, and clubbing together as an underground network was inevitable. Many such people (and Renaissance alchemists included women) also held unusual beliefs about such matters as architecture and mathematics, besides cherishing exceptionally unorthodox theological ideas. These people were dangerous, and made doubly so by the power of secrecy that has the habit of concentrating heterodoxy. One major manifestation of this heresy was the Rosicrucian movement.

The term 'Rosicrucian' dates only from the early seventeenth century, but it was certainly coined to describe a movement that was by then already well established. Its first major flowering, like those of so many other significant movements, was during the Renaissance – in fact it is scarcely an exaggeration to say that Rosicrucianism *was* the Renaissance.

The second half of the fifteenth century saw an explosion of interest in hermeticism and the occult sciences. Very little of the actual information involved was new, although of course there were many contemporary influences and personalities, and this era saw an unprecedented hunger to explore the wider implications of hermeticism. It was suddenly seen as something for intellectual debate beyond the secret enclaves that had, until then, been its guardians. If it had been left to its Renaissance enthusiasts, hermeticism would have been 'occult' no longer.

This upsurge of fascination with all things hermetic at this time was centred on the de Medici court at Florence (where it was a potent influence on Leonardo da Vinci among many other great thinkers)[30]. Under the patronage of the de Medicis – notably Cosimo the Elder (1389–1464) and his grandson Lorenzo the Magnificent (1449–1492) – the first great synthesis of many disparate occult ideas was undertaken. Not only did Cosimo send emissaries to look for legendary tomes such as the *Corpus Hermeticum*, allegedly written by Hermes Trismegistus himself, but he also sponsored their translation. The Medici court was a salon for famous – and perhaps notorious – occult thinkers such as Marsilio Ficino (1433–1499), translator of the *Corpus Hermeticum*, and Pico della Mirandola (1463–1494). The latter's greatest contribution was to introduce cabalistic theory and practice into this melting pot of daring ideas.

Mirandola, perhaps given a somewhat false sense of security by his aristocratic patron, was too outspoken in his occult ideas and soon found his books placed on the Papal Index, while he himself was under threat from Pope Innocent VIII. For a time it looked as if Mirandola would go the way of all who opposed the Vatican, but something strange happened. The new pope, Alexander VI – a member of the Borgia family – mysteriously dropped all the charges and threats against him, actually writing him a personal letter of support – but why? Perhaps a clue lay in the fact that this Pope decorated his private apartment in the Vatican with murals depicting ancient Egyptian themes, including the goddess Isis[31].

Modern historians tend to dismiss the power and influence of the occult. If they discuss it at all it is to underline, by comparison, the triumph of the Age of Enlightenment when all such 'superstitious nonsense' was rejected by anyone with a sense of reason. But occultism lived on, and in fact became the major influence on the Renaissance. A fascination with occultism was not merely a symptom of the new openness to ideas, it was actually the cause.

Dame Frances Yates charted the story of the occult's true role in the rise of the Renaissance in a series of books[32]. As she points out, the new occult philosophy spread from Italy throughout Europe, culminating in the European campaign of the great hermetic preacher, Giordano Bruno (1548–1600). Travelling widely throughout countries such as Germany and England, he preached a return to what was essentially the ancient Egyptian religion, and was characteristically outspoken about what he regarded as the evil of mainstream Christianity[33].

Hermeticism, as we have seen, was believed to have been founded by 'Thrice-great Hermes' himself via the fragment of the *Emerald Tablet* on which were inscribed many profound secrets. Although few hermeticists actually believed that myth, they did believe in the continuing significance of the Egyptian pantheon. But while most Renaissance hermeticists believed that their secrets came from the Pharaonic Egypt of the time of Moses, they came rather from a time closer to the era of Jesus. The roots of their ideas can be traced back to Egypt of the first–third centuries: beyond that we have to acknowledge the influence of many cultures. However, recent scholarship has recognized that, whereas previous generations tended to stress the influence of Greek philosophy, ideas ultimately dating back to the religion of the *ancient* Egyptians did have more influence on the development of hermetic ideas than previously thought[34].

Hermeticists recognized that, although ancient Greece had much to offer the thinking man, it was Egypt, above all, which held the keys to the knowledge they sought. They also realized that this knowledge was not simply there for the taking: the Egyptian system had been encoded in a *mystery school*, and the secrets required the dedicated student to earn them through the arduous stages of progressive initiation.

Giordano Bruno arrived in England in 1583 and rapidly made the acquaintance of such luminaries as Sir Philip Sydney, author of – among other works – *Arcadia*. Sydney, who was a student of the great English occultist Dr John Dee (1527–1606), was clearly a major figure in this shadowy world because Bruno dedicated two of his works to him while in England. It is also possible that another figure from the interlocking circles of Elizabethan society and the occult was present when Bruno and Sydney met – one William Shakespeare. (It is significant that the original Globe Theatre of London was built on the hermetic principles of sacred geometry[35], and perhaps also that Shakespeare's last play *The Tempest* is said to have been about Dr Dee, and to embody a great many Rosicrucian concepts[36].)

In Bruno we have a figure of similar stature as Luther or Calvin, but his name is rarely mentioned in the history that is taught in schools. Like them – and indeed like the great names of the Counter-Reformation – he was uncompromising and unforgiving in the manner of the time. But unlike them, Bruno was not preaching any version of accepted Christianity, and for that reason alone his days were numbered. Add to this his own bombastic nature and it is only too easy to predict his fate. Bruno was burnt at the stake in 1600 in Rome, after being betrayed and denounced to the Inquisition by a disenchanted follower.

Bruno established his own secret society, the Giordanisti, in Germany. Little is known about it but it became one of the major influences on the development of Rosicrucianism in Europe[37]. But equal credit should be given to the above mentioned Dr John Dee, a true Welsh wizard. A man of many parts, not only was he Elizabeth I's astrologer and counsellor, but he was also a spymaster – and an alchemist and necromancer[38].

(And something that is not generally known is that Dr Dee's codename as spy was '007'!)

From these roots grew Rosicrucianism, one of the most mysterious movements in history. Its existence first became known when two anonymous tracts, the *Fama Fraternitatis*, or *A Discovery of the Fraternity of the Most Noble Order of the Rosy Cross* and the *Confessio Fraternitatis*, or *The Confession of the Laudable Fraternity of the Most Honourable Order of the Rosy Cross* circulated throughout Germany in 1614 and 1615[39]. These publications announced the existence of a secret brotherhood of magical adepts – the Rosicrucians, who were named after their mythical founder, Christian Rosenkreutz (Christian RosyCross).

This hero had supposedly travelled throughout Egypt and the Holy Land collecting secret, or occult, knowledge that he passed on to a new generation of adepts. But if his life was unusual, his death and burial were even more bizarre. Rosenkreutz was said to have been 106 years old when he died in 1484, and was buried in a secret location that was kept lit by 'an inner Sun'. His body was also said to have been 'incorruptible' – it remained lifelike and did not decompose (a phenomenon that appears to attend the postmortem states of a surprising number of people, but mostly of Catholic saints).

These Rosicrucian Manifestoes, as the publications soon became known, did not themselves pass on any of the secrets, but in announcing the existence of the brotherhood they also suggested that anyone who wanted to know more got in touch with them. Presumably this was some kind of initiative test because no address for correspondence was given. This approach was enough to earn the Manifestoes the scorn of all mainstream historians, who dismissed them as some kind of weird hoax. But, as Frances Yates has shown[40], the writers of the Manifestoes revealed a profound and genuine knowledge of hermetic wisdom and alchemy. Significantly they regarded alchemy as *a spiritual* discipline and not at all concerned with the creation of gold, which they termed 'ungodly and accursed'[41].

Whatever the truth about the origins of the Rosicrucians, they did influence a great many world-renowned thinkers, such as Robert Fludd (1574–1637) and Sir Isaac Newton. Even, unexpectedly, the famed rationalist Francis Bacon was essentially a Rosicrucian[42]. Yet this makes sense, for the Rosicrucian movement was a synthesis of all hermetic and occult concepts: the only truly new thing about it was that it now had a name. And Frances Yates had no compunction in describing Leonardo – of all people – as 'an early Rosicrucian'[43].

As we have seen, Leonardo's name appears on the list of Grand Masters of the Priory of Sion, but he would not have called himself a Rosicrucian because the term had not been coined in his day. However, others on that list had no such problem – such as Johann Valentin Andraea (1586–1654), the German playwright and poet who had also been a Lutheran pastor. The *Dossiers secrets* claim that he was at the helm of the Priory from 1637 to 1654, but it is much more widely accepted that he himself wrote the Rosicrucian Manifestoes, or at least that he was behind them.

Andrea definitely wrote what was essentially the third Manifesto, *The Chemical Wedding of Christian Rosenkreutz*[44], in 1616, many years before he is said to have become head of the Priory. Perhaps it was his role as leading Rosicrucian that may have secured him the post. It certainly seems that the theme of Rosicrucianism was the common thread which bound together all four alleged Grand Masters whose periods of office spanned the seventeenth century. In a sense, therefore, this adds to the credibility of the list, for it was not until the 1970s that Frances Yates had established the existence and influence of the Rosicrucian legacy.

The Rosicrucian succession among Grand Masters of the Priory began, at least, with Robert Fludd, the English alchemist whose period of office was 1595–1637. Fludd claimed he had tried to find the Rosicrucians after reading their Manifestoes, with an eye to joining them, but he had failed. Nevertheless he wrote extensively on the subject and incorporated ideas from the Manifestoes in his own extremely influential works such as *Utriusque cosmi historia (History of the Two Worlds)* (1617)[45]. (Interestingly the occult commentator Lewis Spence noted that Robert Fludd, writing in the 1630s, uses 'language which smacks strongly of Freemasonry' and that he organized 'his society' in degrees.[46]) After Fludd came Andraea himself, who was Grand Master until his death in 1654, and he in turn was succeeded by Robert Boyle, the Oxford chemist.

As far as can be ascertained, Boyle never mentioned the word 'Rosicrucian' in his writings, but they show more than a passing familiarity with the contents of the Manifestoes[47]. And when he founded what was to become the Royal Society under the name The Invisible College, this was in itself an ironic reference to the common Rosicrucian description of themselves as an 'Invisible' society[48].

Then came Isaac Newton, said to be Grand Master of the Priory from 1691 to 1727. Long known to have practised alchemy, he also possessed a copy of the English translation of the Manifestoes, although there is evidence that he recognized the Rosenkreutz story as the myth it was meant to be. (Esoteric commentators, at least, have always realized that it was never intended to be taken as the literal truth.) It is only recently that the full extent of Newton's involvement with the occult has been recognized: over 10 per cent of his books were alchemical treatises. More tellingly perhaps, he also drew a reconstructed floorplan of the Temple of Solomon[49].

Rosicrucianism also had a strong connection with the blossoming of Freemasonry. The two earliest known English Freemasons – Elias Ashmole and the alchemist Sir Robert Moray – were linked with the Rosicrucian movement. Ashmole in particular was a known Rosicrucian, while Moray, according to Frances Yates, 'did more, probably, than any other individual to foster the foundation of the Royal Society.'[50] There were also several references in early Masonic literature that explicitly linked 'the Brothers of the Rosy Cross' with the Freemasons, although they seemed to indicate that they remained related – but distinct – societies[51].

The interconnection between Rosicrucianism, Free-masonry, hermeticism and alchemy – previously painstakingly pieced together by historians such as Frances Yates – has been dramatically confirmed in recent years by the discovery of a collection of documents that illustrate the extent to which such movements and subjects were integrated. In 1984 Joy Hancox, a music teacher from Manchester, as a result of researching the history of the house in which she lived, came across a collection of papers, mainly diagrams and geometrical designs, that had been amassed by John Byrom (1691–1763) and had been kept by his descendants, who were unaware of their significance. These papers, of which there are over 500, are chiefly concerned with sacred geometry and architecture, and cabalistic, Masonic, hermetic and alchemical symbols.[52]

The importance of the 'Byrom Collection' is the light that it sheds on the relationship between these subjects, and on the individuals – the cream of the intellectual and scientific establishment of the day – who were preoccupied with them. Byrom, a leading figure in the Jacobite movement that aimed to restore the Stuarts to the English throne, was a fellow of the Royal Society and a Freemason. He was part of the 'Cabala Club', otherwise known as the Sun Club, which met at a building in St Paul's Churchyard that was also the home of one of the four founding lodges of the Grand Lodge of English Freemasonry. His journal reveals him to have been in contact with the leading intellectuals of his time.

The work embodied in his collection is drawn from all the societies and individuals that we have discussed above, including the Rosicrucians, John Dee (to whom Byrom was related by marriage), Robert Fludd, Robert Boyle – even the Knights Templar.

It includes diagrams detailing the sacred geometry of numerous buildings from many periods, and therefore shows the continuity of knowledge of the principles underlying these buildings. For example, one diagram shows that the design of the mid-fifteenth-century chapel of Kings College, Cambridge – 'one of the last great Gothic structures built in this country'[53]

– was based upon the cabalistic Tree of Life (a conclusion that had already been arrived at by Nigel Pennick, an authority on esoteric symbolism). The design of the chapel was apparently derived from the fourteenth-century cathedral at Albi, in the Languedoc, previously one of the Cathar centres. The collection also includes a diagram of the Temple Church in London, as well as other Templar buildings, again demonstrating that all these buildings were part of a continuous tradition and that the members of the Rosicrucian/Masonic fraternities of the eighteenth century were aware of it. The Byrom collection also contains material relating to the Temple of Solomon and the Ark of the Covenant.

If, as appears to be the case, the Masons were descendants of the Templars, could it be that the Rosicrucians were also from the same lineage? The very name 'Rosy Cross' carries a potent suggestion of those knights with their emblem of a red, or *roseate*, cross. In Andraea's *Chemical Wedding* the red cross on a white background is a recurring theme, and his work in general carries strong connotations of the Grail stories – and therefore of the Templars. And the presence of Templar material in the predominantly Rosicrucian Byrom papers suggests that this fraternity and the Masons share a common origin.

However, while the Masons were, and are, a definite organization with known members and places where they met, the Rosicrucians have usually been seen as considerably more elusive, to the point where the word 'Rosicrucian' is taken to refer to an ideal rather than a description of membership – indeed, the Manifestoes themselves refer to the Rosicrucians as an 'invisible society'. But the 'first concrete and visible' Rosicrucian society was the Order of the Gold and Rosy Cross, founded in Germany in 1710 by Sigmund Richter, the primary purpose of which was alchemical research.[54] However, sixty years later this Order was transformed into a Strict Templar Observance Masonic Lodge, although it still maintained its alchemical nature. In this form it had many influential members, including Franz Anton Mesmer

(1734–1815), the discoverer of 'animal magnetism' (although not, as is frequently stated, the pioneer of hypnotism). The very fact that a Rosicrucian society could turn so readily into a Strict Templar Observance Lodge reveals their common heritage.

After 1750 the story becomes hopelessly muddled. Where once there were clear distinctions between Masons, Rosicrucians and organizations that claimed Templar origins, suddenly all such groups become so intimately entwined as to seem virtually one and the same. For example, in some forms of Freemasonry, initiates took the titles of 'Knight Templar' and 'Rose Cross', and it is impossible to work out whether this is so because there was a genuine line of descent or simply because these titles had a grandiose ring to them. It has been estimated that over 800 degrees and rituals were added to Freemasonry between 1700 and 1800.

Attempts to trace a direct line of Templar succession in Freemasonry and Rosicrucianism soon come to grief because of this enormous proliferation of Masonic rites and systems. This is particularly confusing because it is in many cases impossible to establish which systems were eighteenth-century innovations and which were genuinely older.

However, it is possible to find a common thread among certain Masonic systems that have been disowned or rejected by mainstream Freemasonry. These are the variations of 'occult' Freemasonry, all of which can be traced back to Baron von Hund's Strict Templar Observance, and whose development took place chiefly in France. The key to this is a Masonic system known as the Rectified Scottish Rite, which is specifically dedicated to occult studies and places most stress on its Templar origins. It is also this form of Freemasonry that had the closest links with the Rosicrucian societies.

Use of the word 'Templar' had become a problem for this school of Masonry. There was friction between its members and mainstream Freemasons, who officially rejected the suggestion of Templar origins – being especially irritated by von Hund's declaration that 'Every Mason is a Templar.' More worrying was the suspicion that they attracted from the authorities, as there were numerous rumours that the Templars had a secret plan to take revenge on the French monarchy and the papacy for the suppression of their Order and the execution of Jacques de Molay. Because of this, a Convent of 'Templarist' Masons was held in Lyons in 1778, at which the Rectified Scottish Rite was created, with an interior Order called the Chevalier Bienfaisant de la Cité Sainte. This was, however, simply another name for 'Templar'[55].

An important influence on the Convent of Lyons – and subsequent French esotericism – was the occult philosopher Louis Claude de Saint-Martin (1743–1804). Although he seems to have dedicated himself to celibacy, his philosophy centres on a veneration of the Feminine in the form of Sophia, whom he regarded as 'the feminine form of the Great Architect'[56]. 'Martinism' was the most influential occult philosophy, not only on these forms of occult Masonry, but also on the Rosicrucian societies of nineteenth-century France, which will be discussed fully in the next chapter.

A few years after the Lyons gathering, in 1782, another great Masonic conference – this time with representatives of all Masonic groups throughout Europe – was held at Wilhelmsbad in Hessen under the chairmanship of the Duke of Brunswick. Its purpose was to heal the deep divisions within Masonry by settling once and for all the question of the relationship between Freemasonry and the Knights Templar. The outcome was a humiliation for Baron von Hund, who came to argue the Templar case, and it was effectively the end of the Strict Templar Observance. However, the Templarists won one battle: the convent agreed to accept the Rectified Scottish Rite – which was just the Strict Templar Observance under another name.

Also important in occult Freemasonry are the systems known as 'Egyptian Rites', which were to assume importance in our investigation later. However, all of them derived from von Hund's beloved Strict Templar Observance, and are therefore *very* closely related to the Rectified Scottish Rite. Contrary to the usual image of Freemasonry they lay a special emphasis on the Feminine (some forms include active female lodges). All Freemasons revere the mysterious 'son of the widow'. In the Egyptian Rites, the 'widow' is *Isis*[57].

The Priory of Sion, with its own acknowledged emphasis on Isis, claims it began as the inner circle of the Templar Order, and naturally developed over the years and acquired other esoteric associations, some of which are telling in themselves. A major influence appears to have been Jacques-Étienne Marconis de Nègre (1795–1865), who founded one of the Egyptian Rites of occult Freemasonry in 1838, known as the 'Rite of Memphis'. This, too, claimed descent from von Hund's 'Templarist' tradition.

Marconis de Nègre outlined an elaborate 'foundation myth' for his organization, making the usual grandiose claim that the rite went back to antiquity, to a group called the Society of the Rosicrucian Brothers of the East. That in turn had been founded by a priest of the ancient Egyptian religion called Ormus, who was converted to Christianity by St Mark, and whose disciples included members of the Essenes[58].

The Ormus myth suggests four influences: Rosicrucian, Egyptian, Jewish esotericism such as the cabala (the Essenes were believed, rightly or wrongly, to have been cabalists), and Christian, perhaps of an heretical sort.

What really interested us about this myth was that – as readers of *The Holy Blood and the Holy Grail* will know – the Priory of Sion took the name 'Ormus' as its 'sub-title'. And we were later to learn that the Ormus story first appeared in connection with the Order of the Gold and Rosy, when it became a Strict Templar Observance Lodge in 1770.[59] But, as we shall see, the story behind this has very far-reaching implications where this investigation is concerned.

Not surprisingly, perhaps, there are societies that claim to be the Templars' official successors. Most of them can be easily dismissed, although the Ancient and Military Order of the

Temple of Jerusalem makes a persuasive case to be taken seriously. Today it is based in Portugal, where it claims to concentrate on charity work and historical research, although there is a splinter group that operates from the evocatively named Sion in Switzerland[60]. But its origins – in its resurrected form – were in France.

The Ancient and Military Order of the Temple of Jerusalem was founded in 1804 by a doctor with the sonorous name of Bernard Raymond Fabré-Palaprat, who alleged that he got his authority from *The Charter of Transmission of Larmenius*, usually known simply as the Larmenius Charter. If true, this would go a long way towards establishing that Fabré-Palaprat was indeed of the true Templar line, for this Charter claimed to have been written in 1324 by Johannes Marcus Larmenius, who had been appointed Grand Master by Jacques de Molay himself. The scroll allegedly bears the signatures of all the subsequent Grand Masters of the Order, which is significant because, after the execution of de Molay, there were not supposed to be any.

Predictably, historians have dismissed the Charter as a forgery[61]. Even more open-minded writers like Baigent and Leigh agree that it was a hoax[62]. But usually the critics have never actually seen it, basing their objections on a nineteenth-century translation of the original Latin[63]. (The document is written in Latin that has been transcribed into a code based on the geometry of the Templar cross.) One of the reasons it has been dismissed as a forgery is that the Latin is too good for the time – medieval Latin being notoriously haphazard – but in fact the translator had *corrected the grammar*. The critics have also dismissed the list of the declarations of Grand Masters because the form of words for each one is exactly the same, something that is unlikely over the timespan of 1324–1804. But again this is simply because the transcriber standardized them: in the original they were all different. So the two main reasons for rejecting the Larmenius Charter do not, in fact, hold water.[64]

Another reason why the Charter has been criticized is that

it carries a fulmination against 'the Scot-Templars deserters', who, Larmenius asserts, should be 'blasted by an anathema' (together with the Knights Hospitaller). Assuming that these schismatics were Baron von Hund's Strict Observance Masons, historians take this to be proof that the Charter was a fake – because they believe the baron invented the 'Scottish transmission' around 1750. But if he was telling the truth about the real origins of the Freemasons, a radically different picture emerges.

In fact, the Ancient and Military Order of the Temple claim that the Charter had been in existence at least a hundred years before Fabré-Palaprat made it public, when Philippe, Duke of Orléans – later Regent of France – used it as his authority to convene an assembly at Versailles of members of the Temple. If true, then this one event was in itself evidence for a continuing Templar presence in Europe. (It was the same Duke of Orleans who inducted Chevalier Ramsay into the Order of St Lazarus.)

Besides the Larmenius Charter, Fabré-Palaprat possessed another important document – which has also been dismissed out of hand by most commentators. This was the *Levitikon* – a version of John's Gospel with blatantly Gnostic implications – which he claimed to have found on a second-hand bookstall. Once again, this seems just a little too neat, but if the document is authentic, it throws some light on the real reasons for keeping much of the Gnostic knowledge secret. For the *Levitikon*, a version of St John's Gospel that some date as far back as the eleventh century[65], tells a very different story from that found in the more familiar New Testament book of the same name.

Fabré-Palaprat used the *Levitikon* as the basis for founding his Neo-Templar Johannite Church in Paris in 1828, into which his own followers were initiated in due course, and after his death ten years later Sir William Sydney Smith, the high-ranking Freemason and hero of the Napoleonic Wars, took over from him.

The *Levitikon*, which had been translated from Latin into

Greek, consists of two parts[66]. The first contains the religious doctrines that are to be given to the initiate, including rituals concerning the nine grades of the Templar Order. It describes the Templars' 'Church of John' and explains the fact that they called themselves 'Johannites' or 'original Christians'.

The second part is like the standard John's Gospel except for some significant omissions. Chapters 20 and 21 are missing, the last two of the Gospel. It also eliminates all hint of the miraculous from the stories of the turning of the water into wine, the loaves and fishes, and the raising of Lazarus. And certain references to St Peter are edited out, including the story of Jesus saying 'Upon this rock I will build my church'.

But if this is puzzling, the *Levitikon* also contains surprising, even shocking, material: *Jesus is presented as having been an initiate of the mysteries of Osiris*, the major Egyptian god of his day.

Osiris was the consort of his sister, the beautiful goddess Isis who governed love, healing and magic – among many other attributes. (Distasteful though such an incestuous relationship may seem to us today, it was part of the Pharaonic tradition, and would have seemed perfectly normal to any worshipper in ancient Egypt.) Their brother Set wanted Isis for himself, and plotted to kill Osiris. The latter was surprised by Set's henchmen, who dismembered his body and scattered the remains. Grieving terribly, Isis wandered the world looking for them, being assisted in her search by the goddess Nepthys, Set's wife, who disapproved of his crime. The two goddesses found all of the bodily parts of Osiris except his phallus. Reassembling them, Isis used an artificial phallus with which she magically conceived the child Horus. In some versions of the story she then had an affair with Set, although her motives seem unclear – there appears to be an element of revenge involved in this relationship. Horus, now a young man, was infuriated by this union, which he perceived as betraying his father Osiris' memory, so he had a duel with Set which resulted in the latter's death and left him with only one eye. He was healed, and the Eye of

Horus became Egypt's favourite magical talisman.

The *Levitikon*, besides making the extraordinary claim that Jesus was an Osiran initiate, also stated that he had passed this esoteric knowledge on to his disciple, John 'the Beloved'. It also claims that Paul and the other Apostles may have founded the Christian Church, but they did so without any knowledge of Jesus' true teaching. They were not part of his inner circle. According to Fabré-Palaprat, it was the *secret* teachings, as given to John the Beloved, which had been preserved and eventually influenced the Knights Templar.

The *Levitikon* records a tradition that was allegedly handed down through the generations of a sect, or Church, of Johannite Christians in the Middle East. They claimed to have been heirs to the 'secret teaching' and true story of Jesus, whom they refer to as 'Yeshu the Anointed'. In fact, if such a sect existed, their version of the Jesus story is so unorthodox that one wonders why they called themselves 'Christians' at all. For them, not only was Jesus an initiate of Osiris, but he was merely a man, not the Son of God. Moreover, he was the illegitimate son of Mary – and there was no question of the miraculous Virgin birth. They attributed all such claims to an ingenious – if outrageous – cover story that the Gospel writers had invented to obscure Jesus' illegitimacy, and the fact that his mother had no idea of the identity of his father!

The Johannite sect recognized that the title 'Christ' was not unique to Jesus: the original Greek *Christos* merely meant 'Anointed' – a term that could have been applied to many, including kings and Roman officials. Consequently, the Johannite leaders always took the title of 'Christ' themselves. (Significantly, the Nag Hammadi *Gospel of Philip* applies the term 'Christ' to all Gnostic initiates[67].)

The group was said to be a Gnostic sect that preserved various esoteric secrets, including those of the cabala. And they also conceived a plan to make themselves into an under-cover organization that would (in the words of the nineteenth-century writer Éliphas Lévi) 'be the sole repository of the great religious and social secrets, should make Kings and Pontiffs, without exposing it to the corruption of power'[68] – i.e. a mystery organization that would not be subject to the vagaries and uncertainties of political and social changes over the years. Their instrument was to be the Knights Templar, and Hugues de Payens and the other founding knights were, in fact, Johannite initiates. However, the Templars themselves became corrupt through their love of wealth and power, and were eventually suppressed. The French king and the Pope could not let the real nature of the Templar threat be known, so they concocted the charges of idolatry, heresy and immorality. But before his execution, Jacques de Molay, again in Lévi's words, 'organized and instituted Occult Masonry'.[69]

If true, this assertion alone changes the accepted version of history dramatically. It provides the direct and authoritative link between one type of Freemasonry and the old Templars – and therefore it might well follow that those particular Masons could have something to teach us about the Templar knowledge.

As we have seen, Éliphas Lévi devotes a section of his *History of Magic* to the Johannite tradition as described in the *Levitikon*. We first read this in A.E. Waite's English translation, but then we came across another translation of that particular section in a work by Albert Pike, the erudite Masonic scholar and Grand Master of the Ancient and Accepted Scottish Rite in America, *Morals and Dogma of the Ancient and Accepted Scottish Rite of Freemasonry* (1871). This version has several differences – but which of them was authentic?

We checked with the original French edition of Lévi's work[70] and found that Pike had made certain additions or corrections of his own, presumably based on his own understanding of this tradition. For example, he renders the last part of that historic sentence quoted above as 'Occult, Hermetic or Scottish Masonry'[71]. He also amends Lévi's words concerning a link between the Johannite Templars and the Rosicrucians. Lévi writes (in A.E. Waite's faithful translation):

The *School of Athens* by Raphael (above) *(Mansell Collection)*, depicting Leonardo da Vinci as Plato, to the left, pointing. In Leonardo's works the raised forefinger was always associated with John the Baptist, as for example in his last painting *St John the Baptist* (below, right) *(Réunion des Musées Nationaux)*. Another reference to the Baptist is in Leonardo's great hoax, the Shroud of Turin, where the head of 'Christ' is separate from the body, suggesting a beheading (below, left) *(Holy Shroud Guild)*.

In Leonardo's *Last Supper* (above) *(Mansell Collection)* 'St John' on Jesus' right is clearly a woman. Is this Mary Magdalene, believed to be the wife or lover of Jesus? Leonardo also painted himself as the second disciple on the right, looking away from Jesus. His denial of Jesus is also found in *The Adoration of the Magi* (below) *(Mansell Collection)*: he is in the bottom right corner. Note the 'John gesture' by the tree. One version of *The Virgin of the Rocks* (left) *(Réunion des Musées Nationaux)* appears to show Jesus blessing John – but as the child being blessed is with Mary, it may be that this is Jesus, and it is John who is blessing him.

A nineteenth-century Rosicrucian poster (above) *(Michael Holford)* depicts Leonardo, on the right, as 'The Keeper of the Grail'. Many believe that he was Grand Master of the Priory of Sion, as was the twentieth-century French artist Jean Cocteau, whose mural in the church of Notre-Dame de France, London (below) *(Clive Prince)*, also reveals heretical symbolism.

In the south of France – where Mary Magdalene is believed to have died – huge crowds attend the annual procession of her alleged skull (above) *(Clive Prince)*, behind a golden mask (below) *(Clive Prince)* in St Maximin, Provence.

In Marseilles a fifteenth-century bas-relief (centre) depicts her as 'Apostle of the Apostles'. Wherever her cult is found, there is also one of the mysterious Black Madonnas: both are linked to pagan goddess worship. The Priory of Sion particularly venerates Notre Dame de Lumières, near Avignon (right) *(Clive Prince)*. Mary Magdalene has always been regarded with unease by the Church, to whom she is an eternal penitent (bottom) *(Richard L. Feigen & Co.)*.

The Languedoc has always been the heartland of European heresy. The thirteenth-century Cathars, whose last stand against the papal crusade was at Montségur (above) *(Comstock)*, kept alive secret knowledge concerning Jesus and Mary Magdalene. The area was also a centre of the Knights Templar (left, their seal) *(British Library)*. Other clues about the Templars' beliefs can be found in the decoration of Rosslyn Chapel near Edinburgh (right) *(Derek Braid and Doug Corrance/Still Moving Picture Company)*, which is predominantly pagan, occult and Masonic.

ROSARIVM

CONIVNCTIO SIVE
Coitus.

A key element of Europe's underground tradition was sacred sexuality. This celebration of feminine wisdom or *Sophia* was depicted, for example, as Venus being adored by Grail Knights and heroes (right). Sexual secrets were fundamental to alchemy (top) *(Wellcome Institute Library, London)*. The power of female sexuality also lies at the heart of movements such as Rosicrucianism, Hermeticism and even certain forms of Freemasonry.

The successors of the old Rosicrucians, modifying little by little the austere and hierarchic methods of their precursors in initiation, had become a mystic sect and *had embraced zealously the Templar magical doctrines*, as a result of which they regarded themselves as the sole depositaries [sic] of the secrets intimated by the Gospel according to St John.[72]

Pike, tellingly, amends the italicized part of this to read:

... and had united with many of the Templars, the dogma of the two intermingling ...[73]

Pike's changes are significant because, whereas Lévi was an observer and commentator on the occult and Masonic world, and so to some extent an outsider, Pike was very much on the inside. He saw fit to correct Lévi's version, so that instead of talking of the Rosicrucians adopting 'Templar doctrines', Pike has them actually merging with surviving Templar groups.

But Pike's most significant amendment is something new entirely. After the sentence on Jacques de Molay's instigation of 'Occult, Hermetic or Scottish Masonry', Pike adds that this Order:

adopted Saint John the Evangelist as one of its patrons, associating with him, in order not to arouse the suspicions of Rome. Saint John the Baptist ...[74]

This is curious, to say the least. Seeing that both John the Evangelist and John the Baptist are recognized Catholic saints, why should the veneration of one be necessary as 'cover' for the reverence accorded to the other? Yet Pike, that most erudite of Masonic scholars, is not likely to have inserted this information for no good reason into the reproduction of passages from someone else's book. Clearly, we needed to delve further into this Johannite theme within the Masonic tradition.

As we saw in the last chapter, A.E. Waite had referred to a

'Johannite tradition' which had influenced the Grail legends, which at first seemed completely mystifying. Now, however, it was beginning to make sense: clearly the 'Johannite tradition' is somehow connected with either John the Evangelist or John the Baptist.

This underlying thread is, of course, not new to this investigation. The 'Johannite tradition' with its clear link with a Saint John is also central to the Priory of Sion – and to them, as we have discerned, it is John the Baptist who is pre-eminent.

As we saw in Chapter Two, the Priory claim that Godefroi de Bouillon met representatives of a mysterious 'Church of John' – in other words, the Brothers of Ormus – and as a result of that encounter decided to form a 'secret government'. The Knights Templar and the Priory of Sion were duly created as part of this master plan. It cannot be overemphasized that, at least according to this story, both the Priory and the Templars were created to conform to the ideals of this mysterious Church of John. Apart from some minor details, this story is identical to that of the *Levitikon*, and if nothing else, this at least establishes that the modern Priory and Templars are part of the same tradition.

The concept of the Templars as a secret organization with the authority to make and depose kings parallels that of the Templar Grail Knights of Wolfram von Eschenbach's *Parzival* – certainly there is evidence that the Templars did claim this right[75]. The problem is that most of these exotic claims for a long historical pedigree only date back to the Neo-Templar organizations of the nineteenth century. But they might hold water if they can be corroborated by independent evidence linking their movements with organizations that were definitely around centuries before, such as the Rosicrucian–Masonic link.

Another difficulty is that two different claims are being made: one is that certain forms of Freemasonry are directly descended from the Templars. The other is that the Templars themselves were a continuation of an older, heretical tradition that dated back to the time of Jesus. Unfortunately, proving the first does not automatically mean the second is true.

But the emphasis on an idiosyncratic version of John's Gospel is provocative, although there does seem to be some confusion between John the Evangelist and John the Baptist. Albert Pike's statement that the Masons adopted the Baptist as a cover for their secret veneration of John the Evangelist is, as we have seen, nonsensical. Why should they want to hide their reverence for either saint, when both of them were perfectly acceptable to the Church? All Pike has succeeded in doing is drawing attention to the two Saints John and shrouding both of them in an aura of mystery and intrigue. Perhaps that was his intention. Elsewhere A.E. Waite quotes Masonic writings about Johannite Masonry, which claims a connection with a Johannite Christianity centred on the *Baptist* and which regards him as 'the only true prophet'[76].

As we have seen, John the Baptist was patron saint of both Knights Templar and Freemasons. Indeed, the Grand Lodge of England was founded on 24 June – John the Baptist's Day. And the floor of every Masonic Temple bears two parallel lines: one represents the staff of John 'the Evangelist' (another name for John the Beloved), while the other line stands for the staff of the Baptist. Clearly both Johns are of special importance to the brotherhood, although it is the elder who takes precedence. Moreover, the Masonic oath is to 'the holy *Saints* John'[77]. But Masons today, by their own admission, have no idea why the two Johns are so venerated.[78] It may be that both these biblical characters have become confused over the years, and that the term 'Johannite', while taken to mean followers of the Beloved, may actually refer to those of the Baptist. But whether it is the younger or elder John – or both of them – who is revered by the Masons there is one name that is conspicuous by its virtual absence in lodges: Jesus himself does not figure largely. Allegedly this is because the Masons are not primarily a Christian organization; it is enough to be a theist to join their ranks. But in that case, why do they owe so much allegiance to the Christian Saints John?

The idea that John's Gospel conceals arcane secrets, or that there is another version of it, recurs throughout this investigation. The Cathars are said to have had a heretical alternative, and Sir Isaac Newton was obsessed with it. (As Graham Hancock writes: '. . . despite his own devoutly held religious convictions, he seemed at times to have seen Christ as an especially gifted man . . . rather than the Son of God.'[79])

So both the Scottish Rite Freemasons and the 'Larmenius Transmission' Templars may well have preserved the original Templar secrets, and both of them trace the Templars back to the 'Johannite sect'. Although there is nothing overtly Johannite in the Egyptian Rites of Freemasonry, these systems all derive from Baron von Hund's Strict Templar Observance. And the Priory of Sion links itself with all three of these systems.

As we have seen, Pierre Plantard de Saint-Clair has described the purpose of the Order of the Temple as being 'the sword-bearers of the Church of John and the standard-bearers of the premier dynasty, the arms that obeyed the spirit of Sion.' The outcome of this great plan was to be a 'spiritual renaissance' that would 'turn Christianity upside down'. Clearly this has not happened – yet, although our investigations show that the revelation that could lead to such an upheaval is already waiting in the wings to make a dramatic appearance on the world stage, perhaps in the form of the Priory or of allied mystery schools such as the Iohnists[80].

But in any case, we had come upon a most remarkable thing: we had begun with Leonardo's apparent obsession with John the Baptist and then followed up the slight hint that the Priory of Sion were somehow equally involved with that saint. At that stage it did not amount to much, but as we followed the clues from Templars to Masons and then to the occult groups, a much more persuasive connection took shape before our eyes. The Johannite heresy is there under all the various trappings of the occult underground – and it is to this tradition that the Priory, by its own admission, belongs.

Although many major questions still remained to be answered, a coherent picture was beginning to emerge, one that somehow linked John the Baptist with an intricately maintained occult tradition. Yet this was only part of what was emerging as a two-strand heresy, the other being the secret veneration of a goddess, of the Feminine principle.

Of course the latter strand is difficult to reconcile with the outward forms of organizations such as the Masons, which appear to be exceptionally male oriented. But clearly the secrets behind these two strands – the Feminine and the Johannite themes – are worth having, for they have been defended, guarded and protected against all the odds, and appear to have provoked particular hostility from the Church of Rome. This is not surprising, for the second strand of ancient esoteric secrets – the veneration of the Feminine principle – has taken the form of transcendental sex magic, with all its implications of the inherent power of the female.

CHAPTER SEVEN

Sex: The Ultimate Sacrament

Old alchemical texts are full of confusing and elaborate imagery – deliberately so, because they were meant to discourage the uninitiated from discovering their secrets. As we have seen, however, alchemy was concerned at its deepest level with personal, spiritual and sexual transformation, and its secrets concerned the techniques for achieving this 'Great Work'. Indeed, recognizing the profound non-material and sexual concerns of alchemy, the psychologist C.G. Jung saw it as the forerunner of psychoanalysis[1].

As we have seen, the 'Great Work' of the alchemists was a rare, life-changing experience and no-one knows for certain just what form it took. However, Nicholas Flamel (alleged Grand Master of the Priory of Sion), who achieved this glittering prize on 17 January 1382 in Paris, stressed that he did so in the company of his wife, Perenelle[2]. It seems that they were a particularly devoted couple: she appears to have been an alchemist too – many women were, in secret. But did Flamel emphasize her presence on that fateful day as a hint about the true nature of the Great Work? Is there a suggestion that it took the form of a sexual rite of some kind?

There is no doubt about the existence of at least a sexual component in the practice of alchemy, as the classic alchemical text *The Crowne of Nature*, quoted in Johannes Fabricius' *Alchemy*, reveals:

> White-skinned lady, lovingly joined to her ruddy-limbed husband, wrapped in each other's arms in the bliss of connubial union. Merge and dissolve as they come to the goal of

perfection: They that were two are made one, as though of
one body.[3]

Significantly, there are two Eastern disciplines that emphasize
the religious and spiritual transcendence of sexuality: the
Indian Tantra and the Chinese Taoism. Both of these are
ancient – and greatly respected in their cultures – and stress
the potential of certain sexual practices for achieving mystical
awareness, physical regeneration and longevity, and oneness
with God. Much of this is widely known today, but what is not
recognized beyond the groups of initiates themselves is that
there is, surprisingly, an alchemical branch of both Tantra and
Taoism. As we shall see, this dovetails with the true nature of
Western alchemy.

For example, in Tantrism, 'chemical' terminology is understood to represent sexual practices. As occult writer Benjamin
Walker says in *Man, Myth & Magic*:

> Though ostensibly concerned with the transmutation of baser
> metals into gold, and with the vessels, implements and appar-
> atus of commerce and the ritual movements of the alchemist in
> his workroom, this alchemy actually takes place within the
> body itself.[4]

The irony is that the sexual elements of Western alchemy have
usually been taken as a metaphor for chemical processes! As
Brian Innes observes in his article in *The Unexplained* on the
Tantric and Taoist sexual alchemy:

> The close similarity of the imagery – and the substances used
> – in alchemy in all these cultures is striking. A major differ-
> ence is equally striking: that medieval European alchemy does
> not seem to have had any explicit sexual basis.[5]

There was, however, a vast difference between the public
images and levels of acceptability of alchemy in the East and

West. In China and India it was not a forbidden science, and attitudes to sex were not as neurotic and repressed as they were in Europe; therefore it could be more open and honest about its work.

Recently, 'sacred sexuality' has been 'discovered' by the West. This is essentially the idea that sexuality is the highest sacrament, bestowing not only joy but also a oneness with the Divine and the universe. Sex is seen as the bridge between heaven and earth, bringing a release of enormous creative energy, besides revitalizing the lovers in a unique way – even down to their cellular level. Knowing about sacred sexuality means that the old alchemical texts can, at last, be fully understood in the West, although (as usual) it is the French researchers who are most willing to explore this aspect of them. Of the few Anglo-Saxon writers who have not fought shy of the subject, A.T. Mann and Jane Lyle say in their 1995 book *Sacred Sexuality:*

> It is hard to doubt that alchemical teachings concealed magical sexual secrets that were closely allied to tantric knowledge. Because of its complexity and diversity, alchemy certainly cloaked other mysteries in poetic allegory which only the mind of the initiate would be able to penetrate.[6]

One of the many French writers on the subject, André Nataf, says: '. . . the secret most alchemists pursued was an erotic one . . . alchemy is simply the conquest of love, an "alloy" of the erotic and spiritual.'[7]

Tantrism and Taoism have, of course, long been acknowledged as the conduits for the Eastern tradition of sacred sexuality, but there has been no such clear-cut and easily traceable tradition in the West – *unless it was simply known as alchemy.*

The sexual imagery of alchemical texts seems only too blatant to this post-Freudian age: the Moon says to her spouse, the Sun: 'O Sun, thou dost nothing alone if I am not present with my strength, as a cock is helpless without a hen.'[8] Chemical experiments take the form of 'marriages' or 'copulations', just as Johann Valentin Andraea's tract was called *The Chemical Wedding*.

Of course it might simply be that such imagery meant what it said: a 'copulation' being just that, and that there was no secret at all hidden in the alchemical symbolism. However, the words were carefully chosen to convey complex instructions, covering both a sexual and a chemical meaning. Essentially the alchemical texts contained lessons in sex magic and chemistry at the same time.

Perhaps curiously, given the obvious sexual tone of much of the work, the standard historical idea of alchemy was that it was merely chemical, and that all the symbolism was merely fanciful. The reason for this was that until the mysteries of the East were more widely known, there was no framework in which to set the whole idea of sexual alchemy. Now, however, we have no such problem, and this concept is rapidly gaining recognition.

Barbara G. Walker seizes on the underlying significance of alchemy:

> Some of the secret is given away by the preponderance of sexual symbolism in alchemical literature. 'Copulation of Athene and Hermes' might mean mixing sulfur [sic] and mercury in a retort; or it might mean sexual 'working' of the alchemist and his lady-love. Illustrations in alchemical books suggested sexual mysticism more often than not.
>
> Mercurius or Hermes was the alchemical hero who fertilized the Holy Vase, a womb-like sphere or egg from which the *filius philosophorum* was to be born. This vessel may have been real, a laboratory flask or retort; more often, it seemed to be a mystical symbol. The Royal Diadem of its offspring was said to appear *in menstro meretricis*, 'in the menstrual blood of a whore', who may have been the Great Whore, an ancient epithet of the Goddess . . .[9]

(Walker, however, misses the point when she goes on to suggest that in seeking the *vas hermeticum* – the Vessel of

Hermes – they identified it with the *vas spirituale*, the spiritual vessel or womb, of the Virgin Mary. For which other Mary is routinely depicted as carrying a vase or jar? Who is tradition-ally shown as wearing a blood-red dress or as covered in her long red hair? Which other Mary is associated with the idea of whoredom and sexuality? Once again we find the Virgin Mary as a cover for the secret cult of the Magdalene.)

Today we often talk of 'sexual chemistry', but to the alchemist this had a more profound meaning than the idea of immediate attraction. In the French esoteric magazine *L'Originel*, Denis Labouré, the occult authority, discusses the notion of 'internal' as opposed to 'metallic' alchemy and its parallel with Tantrism, but insists that it is a part of a 'tra-ditional *Western* heritage' (our italics). He says:

> If internal alchemy is well-known in Taoism or Hinduism, historical constraints [i.e. the Church] have obliged Western authors to make use of the greatest prudence. Nevertheless, certain texts make a clear allusion to this alchemy.[10]

He then goes on to cite a treatise of Cesare della Riviera, dated 1605, and adds:

> In Europe, the tracks of these ancient [sexual] rituals pass through the Gnostic schools, the alchemical and cabalistic currents of the Middle Ages and Renaissance – where numerous alchemical texts can be read on two levels – until we find them again in occult organisations formed and organised, principally in Germany, in the seventeenth century.

In fact, the use of 'metallurgical' symbolism dates back to the very inception of alchemy in first–third-century Alexandria. Metallurgical metaphors for sex are found in Egyptian magic spells: alchemists simply adopted the imagery. This is an example of an Egyptian love spell attributed to Hermes Trismegistus, dating from at least the first century BCE, which centres on the symbolic forging of a sword:

Bring it [the sword] to me, tempered with the blood of Osiris, and put it in the hand of Isis . . . all that forge in this stove of fire, breathe it also into the heart and liver, into the loins and belly of [woman's name]. Lead her into the house of [man's name] and let her give in to his hand what is in her hand, to his mouth what is in her mouth, to his body what is in her body, to his wand what is in her womb.[11]

The alchemy as practised by the medieval underground network originally took shape in the Egypt of the early centuries of the Christian era. Isis played an important role in the alchemy of that time. In one treatise entitled *Isis the Prophetess to her son Horus*, Isis tells how she obtained the secrets of alchemy from an 'angel and prophet' through her feminine wiles. She encouraged him to build up his lust for her until it could not be contained any longer, but refused to give herself to him until he gave her his secrets – a clear reference to the sexual nature of alchemical initiation[12]. (This recalls the story of Pope Sylvester II and Meridiana discussed in Chapter Four, where he received his alchemical knowledge through having sex with this archetypal female figure.)

Another early treatise, attributed to a woman alchemist called Cleopatra – an initiate of the school founded by the legendary Maria the Jewess[13] – contains explicit sexual imagery: 'See the fulfilment of the art in the joining together of the bride and bridegroom and in their becoming one.' This is strikingly similar to a contemporary Gnostic text that reads:

When the male attains to the supreme moment and the seed springs forth, at that moment the woman receives the strength of the male and the male receives the strength of the woman . . . It is because of this that the mystery of bodily union is practised in secret so that the conjunction of nature should not be degraded through being seen by the multitude who would despise the work[14].

Early alchemical texts are saturated with symbolism that hint at the secret techniques of sacred sexuality, which were probably derived from an Egyptian equivalent of Tantrism and Taoism. The existence of such a tradition is revealed in the text known as the 'Erotic Papyrus of Turin' (where it is now kept), which has long been regarded as an example of Egyptian pornography. However, once again this reaction is a prime example of Western academic misunderstanding: what is deemed pornographic was in fact a religious ritual. Some of the most sacred ancient Egyptian rites were sexual – for example, a daily religious observance on the part of the Pharoah and his consort that probably involved him being masturbated by her. This was a symbolic re-enactment of the god Ptah's creation of the universe, which he effected by similar means. Religious imagery in palaces and temples unequivocally depicted this act, yet it was deemed so outrageous by archaeologists and historians that it is only recently that its significance has been acknowledged – and even so, the subject is still discussed in hesitant and apologetic tones. Clearly, the West has a long way to go before it catches up with the Egyptians' total acceptance of sex as a sacrament.

This reluctance to accept the significance of sex to the ancients is not a new phenomenon. To scholars of the first and second centuries the subject was not a problem, but as Jack Lindsay notes, by the seventh century, sexual symbolism in alchemical works is being treated in a 'hidden allusive way'[15].

So from its very beginnings, Western alchemy had a strong sexual side. Are we really to believe that by the Middle Ages this profound and influential tradition had totally died out?

Some of the early Gnostic sects – such as the Carpocratians of Alexandria – practised sexual rites. Not surprisingly they were condemned as debased and disgusting by the Church Fathers, and in the absence of less hostile records we have no way of knowing exactly what form they took.

Throughout the history of Christianity, 'heretical' sects incorporating a more libertarian attitude to sex sprang up but were invariably condemned and suppressed – for example, the Brothers and Sisters of the Free Spirit, also known as the Adamites, were said to practise a 'sexual secret' as far back as the thirteenth and fourteenth centuries.[16] The philosophy of the Adamites was a marked influence on the tract *Schwester Katrei* – which, as we have seen, includes evidence of familiarity with the Gnostic Gospels' portrayal of Mary Magdalene – and the female author appears to have been a member of this sect.[17]

Another group involved with erotic mysticism – although not known as a religious sect – were the troubadours, those famed singers of the love-cult in the south-west of France, whose German equivalents were the *minnesingers* – Minne being an idealized woman or goddess[18]. The love of the knight for his lady reflects a devotion to, and reverence for, the Feminine Principle. And the content of the poems – a mixture of 'spirituality and carnality'[19] – can be seen as a series of thinly veiled allusions to sacred sexuality. Even the academic Barbara Newman, in summing up this tradition, could not escape from using language redolent of sacred sexuality when she described it as:

> . . . an erotic game with a bewildering variety of moves: one could become the bride of a God or the lover of a Goddess, or merge utterly with the Beloved and become oneself divine . . .[20]

Much of the courtly love tradition involves the understanding of specific techniques, for example, that of *maithuna*, the deliberate withholding of orgasm to induce sensations of bliss and mystical awareness.

As the British author and poet Peter Redgrove says:

> It is possible to trace a whole tradition of *maithuna* (Tantric visionary sexuality) in the literature of Romance.[21]

The troubadours took the rose as their symbol, perhaps because its name (in French as in English) is an anagram of

Eros, the god of erotic love. There is also the possibility that their ubiquitous 'lady' – she who must be obeyed, if only from a chaste distance, was meant to be understood at an esoteric level as something else, as their German name of *minnesinger* suggests.

This archetypal lady could not have been the Virgin Mary, for although the rose was widely thought of as her symbol in the Middle Ages, her cult did not need to hide itself in codes. Besides, the flower most descriptive of her qualities was not the erotic rose, but the more evocative Easter Lily: beautiful but austere, with no hint of carnality. So who else could the troubadours' songs celebrate? Who else was a 'goddess' much beloved of heretical groups at the time? Who else but Mary Magdalene?

The great rose windows of the Gothic cathedrals always face west – traditionally the direction sacred to female deities[22] – and are never far from a shrine to the Black *Madonna* ('My Lady'). And, as we have seen, these enigmatic statues are pagan goddesses in another dress, an embodiment of the old celebration of female sexuality.

Apart from the sacred rose, the Gothic cathedrals also contained other pagan imagery – for example, the spider's web/maze symbolism of Chartres and other cathedrals is a direct reference to the Great Goddess in her manifestation as spinner and mistress of Man's fate, but many other churches also contain a host of feminine images. Some of them are so graphic that, once they are understood, Christians may not feel quite the same about their churches again. For example, the great Gothic doorways, through which generations of Christians have passed so innocently, are actually representations of the most intimate part of the goddess. Drawing the worshipper into the dark and womb-like interior of Mother Church, they are carved with funnelling ridges, and more often than not even carry a clitoris-like rosebud at the top of the arch. Once inside, the Catholic churchgoer pauses at the stoup of Holy Water, which is often represented as a giant shell, symbol of the goddess' nativity – as Botticelli, alleged Grand Master of the Priory of Sion immediately before Leonardo, so stunningly depicted it in his *The Birth of Venus*. (And the cowrie shell, once the emblem of Christian pilgrims, is acknowledged as being a classic symbol for the vulva[23].) All these symbols were employed deliberately by the adherents of the Feminine Principle, and even though they communicate at a subliminal level, they still have an unsettling effect on the unconscious. Taken together with soaring music, candlelight and the scent of incense, no wonder churchgoing once inspired such peculiar fervour!

To initiates into the mysteries, the Feminine was a concept that was carnal, mystical and religious at the same time. Its energy and power came from its sexuality, and its wisdom – sometimes known as the 'whore wisdom' – came from a knowledge of the 'rose', *eros*.

As the saying goes, 'Knowledge is power', and secrets of this nature wield a power unlike any other, so they posed a unique threat to the Church of Rome, and indeed to all shades of Christian opinion. Sex was – and in many cases still is – deemed only acceptable between those whose unions are likely to result in procreation. For this reason, there is no Christian concept of sex for joy only, let alone the idea – as in Tantrism or alchemy – that it can bring spiritual enlightenment. (And while the Catholic Church notoriously forbids contraception, other Christian groups go even further: for example, the Mormons frown on post-menopausal sex.)

What all these inhibitory rules are really about, however, is *control over women*. They must learn to view sex with apprehension – either because it is joyless, their marital duty and nothing else, or because it leads inevitably to the pain of childbirth. This was central to the way women were viewed by the Church, and by men in general throughout the centuries: if women were to have the fear of childbirth removed from them, chaos would undoubtedly ensue.

One of the major motives behind the atrocities of the witch-hunts was the hatred and fear of midwives, whose knowledge of alleviating the pain of birthing was deemed a threat to decent civilization: Kramer and Sprenger, authors of the infamous *Malleus Maleficarum* – the handbook of European witchfinders – particularly singled out midwives as deserving of the worst possible treatment at their hands. The terror of women's sexuality ended with hundreds of thousands dead, most of them women, over the course of three centuries of witch trials.

Since the misogynist days of the early Church Fathers, when it was even doubted that women had souls, everything was done to make them feel profoundly inferior on every level. Not only were they told they were naturally sinful in themselves, but they were also the greatest – sometimes the *only* – cause of men's sinning, too. In feeling honest-to-goodness lust, men were taught that they were only reacting to the devilish wiles of the woman, who bewitched them into acts that they would not otherwise have considered. An extreme expression of this attitude can be found in the medieval Church's idea that a woman who was raped was responsible not only for provoking the act against herself, but also for the loss of the rapist's soul – for which she would have to make reparation on Judgement Day[24].

As R.E.L. Masters writes:

> Almost the entire blame for the hideous nightmare that was the witch mania, and the greatest part of the blame for poisoning the sexual life of the West, rests squarely on the Roman Catholic Church.[25]

The Inquisition – which had been created specifically to deal with the Cathars – swung easily into its new role as witch-finder, torturer and murderer, although the Protestants were also to join in with gusto. Significantly, the first witch trials took place at Toulouse, headquarters of the anti-Cathar Inquisition. Was it merely spite at some kind of residual Catharism that led to this crucial trial, or was it a symptom of the fear that Languedocian women instilled in the sex-obsessed Inquisitors?

Underlying the hatred and fear of women was the knowledge that they have a unique capacity to *enjoy* sex. Medieval men might not have had the benefit of today's anatomical education, but personal investigation could not have failed to reveal the existence of that curiously threatening organ, the clitoris. That tiny protuberance, so cleverly – if subliminally – celebrated as the rosebud atop the Gothic arch, is the only human organ whose function is *solely to give pleasure*. The implications of this are, and always have been, enormous, and are at the heart of all patriarchal suppression on the one hand, and all Tantric and mystical sex rites on the other. The clitoris, which even now is deemed hardly a fit subject for discussion, reveals that *women were meant to be sexually ecstatic*, perhaps unlike men, whose own sexual equipment doubles up for the purposes of urination and procreation.

Yet the misogynistic tradition of the Judaeo-Christian patriarchy has been so successful that it was not until the twentieth century that the notion that women enjoy their sexuality has become acceptable in the West, and even now this is not the case where the Church is concerned. While it is true that sexual inequality and prudery are not an exclusive development of the three great patriarchal religions of Christianity, Judaism and Islam – one has only to look at the wife-burning customs of India – nevertheless the idea that sex is inherently dirty and shameful is a Western tradition. And wherever such an attitude prevails there will always be the sort of repressed desire and guilt that will inevitably give rise to crimes against women, perhaps even witch manias. The West's puritanical background and its hatred and fear of sex have brought a terrible legacy to the end of the millennium in the form of wife battering, paedophilia and rape. For wherever sex is distrusted, childbirth and children will also be seen as intrinsically dirty, and youngsters will fall prey to violence just like their mothers.

The somewhat contradictory and irascible Yahweh of the Old Testament created Eve – and clearly lived to regret it. Almost as soon as she was 'born' she revealed a capacity to think for herself that was well beyond Adam. Eve and the 'serpent' made a powerful team: this is hardly surprising because snakes were ancient symbols of *Sophia*, representing wisdom, not wickedness. But was God pleased that the woman he had created showed initiative and autonomy in eating of the Tree of Knowledge – *wanting to learn?* After revealing a curious lack of foresight about Eve's capabilities, especially for an omnipotent and omniscient maker of universes, God condemns her to a life of suffering, beginning, one must note, with the curse of *sewing*... (For she and the hapless Adam had to make loincloths of figleaves in order to cover their nakedness.) Adam and Eve were thus introduced to the idea of *shame* about their bodies, and of course about their sexuality. Bizarrely, one is given to understand that it was God himself who was horrified by the sight of the naked flesh he had himself created.

This simple-minded myth has provided a retrospective justification for the degradation of women, and discouraged the alleviation of gynaecological and birthing agonies. It has denied women a voice for thousands of years – and it has demeaned, degraded and even demonized the sex act, which should be joyful and *magical*. It has substituted shame and guilt for love and ecstasy, and it has inculcated a neurotic fear of a male God who was apparently so full of self-hate that he loathed even his best creation – humanity.

From this one poisonous tale has come the concept of original sin, which condemns even innocent newborns to purgatory; it has, until recently, shrouded the awesome miracle of birth in a pall of embarrassment and superstition, and it has removed the unique power of the female – which is, of course, why it was concocted in the first place.

Although there is still a staggering amount of fear and ignorance about sex in our culture, matters are a lot better now than they were even ten years ago. Several major books have broken new ground – or perhaps old ground anew. Among them are *The Art of Sexual Ecstasy* by Margo Anand (1990) and *Sacred Sexuality* by A.T. Mann and Jane Lyle (1995), both of which celebrate sex as a means to spiritual enlightenment and transformation.

As we have seen, other cultures do not suffer from the same problem (unless contaminated by Western thinking). And in certain cultures sex was elevated even beyond an art: it was deemed to be a sacrament – something that enables the participants to become one with the Divine. This is the *raison d'être* of Tantrism, that mystical system of union with the gods through sexual techniques such as *karezza* or achieving bliss without orgasm. Tantrism is the 'martial art' of sexual practice, involving astonishingly disciplined and lengthy training for both men and women – both of whom are deemed *equal*.

The art of Tantrism, however, is not exclusive to the exotic world of the East. Today one can find schools of Tantra springing up in London, Paris and New York, although the extreme rigorousness of the art is offputting to many; it can, for example, take months just to learn to breathe in the right way. Yet the use of sex as a sacrament is *not new to the West*.

We have seen how sexual the roots of alchemy were, and how the troubadours' cult of the rose can be understood as the worship of *eros*. We have noted how the builders of the great cathedrals, such as Chartres, invested so heavily in the symbol of the red rose, and set up shrines to the Black Madonnas with their potent pagan associations.

We can also see that the Grail as cup is a female symbol, and – in an exceptionally blatant move – in the story of *Tristan and Isolde*, the great Grail hero, Tristan, changes his name to *Tantris*[26] . . . In fact, the novelist Lindsay Clarke describes the troubadours' love poetry as 'Tantric scripts of the West'[27].

In the Grail legends the blight on the land is due to the loss of the king's sexual potency, often symbolized by him being 'wounded in the thigh'. In Wolfram's *Parzival* it is more explicit; the wound is in the genitals. This has been taken as a response to the Church's repression of natural sexuality[28]. The resulting spiritual stagnation can only be lifted through a quest for the Grail, which, as we have seen, is always specifically linked to women. In one fifteenth-century Italian painting of the Grail knights adoring Venus (see first illustration section) there is no room for doubt as to the nature of the quest.

What is stressed in both the Grail legends and the courtly love tradition of the troubadours is the spiritual elevation of, and respect for, women. It is, we suggest, significant that both strands of this tradition had at least some of their roots in the south-west of France.

Most modern researchers believe that Tantrism came to Europe via contact with the mystical Islamic sect of the Sufis, who incorporated ideas of sacred sexuality into their beliefs and practices. It is, indeed, undeniable that there are close parallels between the forms of language used to express these ideas by the troubadours and the Sufis. But did the Sufic Tantrism take root in Provence and the Languedoc because there was *already* a similar tradition in that area? We have already seen how the Languedoc had a tradition of upholding the equality of women. And when the witchcraft mania first cast its black shadow in Toulouse, what did it really hope to eradicate? Once again, we find ourselves facing the embodiment of that cult of love – Mary Magdalene.

Another woman who had an appreciation of the mystical potential of sex was the, until recently, relatively little-known St Hildegard of Bingen (1098–1179). As Mann and Lyle write:

A great visionary, Hildegard wrote of a feminine figure, an unmistakable image of the goddess, who came to her during deep contemplation: 'Then I seemed to see a girl of surpassing radiant beauty, with such dazzling brightness streaming from her face that I could not behold her fully. She wore a cloak whiter than snow, brighter than stars, her shoes were of pure gold. In her right hand she held sun and moon, and caressed them lovingly. One her breast she had an ivory tablet, on which appeared in shades of sapphire the image of a man. And all creation called this girl sovereign lady. The girl began to speak to the image on her breast: "I was with you in the beginning,

212

in the dawn of all that is holy, I bore you from the womb before the start of day." And I heard a voice saying to me "The girl whom you behold is Love: she has her dwelling in eternity."'

Hildegard, like all medieval courtly lovers, believed men and women could attain divinity through loving each other, so that 'the whole earth should become like a single garden of love'. And this love was to be whole, a complete expression of union involving both body and soul for, as she wrote, 'It is the power of eternity itself that has created physical union and decreed that two human beings should become physically one.'[29]

Hildegard was a remarkable woman: immensely learned, especially in medical matters. Her degree of education cannot be explained – she herself ascribed it to her visions. Perhaps this was a veiled reference to some mystery school or similar repository of knowledge. Significantly, many of her writings show acquaintance with hermetic philosophy.[30]

This acclaimed abbess also wrote detailed – and accurate – descriptions of the female orgasm, uterine contractions and all. It seems that hers was more than a theoretical knowledge, which is, it is claimed, unusual for a saint. Whatever the secrets of her inside information, she was a great influence on St Bernard of Clairvaux, patron and inspiration of the Templars.[31]

Those warrior-monks might appear to be a major objection to the idea of the continuing underground tradition of an heretical love cult. Ostensibly celibate (although there were persistent rumours of widespread Templar homosexuality), it does seem unlikely that they were, at least, practical exponents of a philosophy that celebrated feminine sexuality. But there are clear hints of such a link in the works of one of their most devoted supporters – the great Florentine poet, Dante Alighieri (1265–1321).

His writings have long been recognized as containing Gnostic and hermetic themes – for example, a century ago Éliphas Lévi described Dante's *Inferno* as being 'Johannite and Gnostic'[32].

The poet was directly inspired by the troubadours of the

South of France, and was a member of a society of poets who called themselves the *fidele d'amore* – 'the faithful followers of love'. Long regarded as an aesthetic circle, recent scholars have begun to discover more secret and esoteric motivations behind them.

The respected academic William Anderson, in his study *Dante the Maker*, describes the *fidele d'amore* as 'a close brotherhood devoted to achieving a harmony between the sexual and emotional side of their nature and their intellectual and mystical aspirations.'[33] He draws on the research of French and Italian scholars, who have concluded that 'the ladies all these poets worshipped were not flesh-and-blood women but, instead, were all masks of the ideal Feminine, Sapientia or Holy Wisdom' and 'that the Lady of these poets was . . . an allegory of the Divine Wisdom also sought.'[34]

Anderson – along with fellow scholar Henry Corbin – sees Dante's spiritual path as seeking enlightenment through sexual mysticism, as did the troubadours. Henry Corbin says:

> The *fidele d'amore*, companions of Dante, profess a secret religion . . . the union that joins the possible intellect of the human soul with the Active Intelligence . . . Angel of Knowledge, or Wisdom-Sophia, is visualised and experienced as a love-union.[35]

More remarkable, however, is the link that Dante and his fellow mystics provide with the Knights Templar. He was one of their most enthusiastic supporters, even after their suppression, when it was inadvisable to be connected with them. In his *Divine Comedy* he brands Philip the Fair as 'the new Pilate' for his actions against the knights. Dante himself is thought to have been a member of a tertiary Templar Order called La Fede-Santa. The connections are too suggestive to be dismissed – perhaps Dante was not the exception, but the *rule*, of Templars who were involved in a love cult.

Anderson says:

On the face of it the Templars, as a celibate military order . . .
would appear to be a most unlikely channel for themes devoted
to the praise of beautiful ladies. On the other hand, many
Templars were soaked in the culture of the East and some may
well have come into contact with Sufi schools . . .[36]

He goes on to summarize the conclusions of Henry Corbin:

> The link between Sapientia [Wisdom] and the imagery of the
> Temple of Solomon together with its associations with the
> Great Circle pilgrimage lead to the supposition of a connection
> between the *fidele d'amore* and the Knights Templar, even to
> the extent of regarding them as a lay confraternity of the
> order.[37]

Together with the revolutionary evidence that has been uncovered by such researchers as Niven Sinclair, Charles
Bywaters and Nicole Dawe, this suggests strongly that at least
the inner order of the knights was indeed part of a secret tradition that venerated the Feminine Principle.

Similarly, that disputed branch of the Templars – the Priory
of Sion – has always had women members, and the list of its
Grand Masters includes four women, which is particularly
strange because their names appear in the medieval period,
when one would have expected sexism to be at its most prevalent. As Grand Masters these women would have wielded real
power – and this role no doubt demanded particularly high
standards of integrity and the ability to deal with many levels
of conflicting interests and egos. While it does seem strange
for women to have been at the helm of such an allegedly
powerful organization at a time when even female literacy was
by no means common, it seems less peculiar in the context of
a secret tradition of goddess worshippers.

Underpinning many of the later mystery schools were the
Rosicrucians, whose interest in sexual mysticism is present in

their very name: the phallic cross and the female rose conjoined. This symbol of sexual union is reminiscent of the ancient Egyptian looped cross (*ankh*): the upright being the phallus and the almond-shaped loop being the vulva. Rosicrucians, with their blend of alchemical and Gnostic wisdom, fully understood the underlying principles, as the seventeenth-century Rosicrucian alchemist Thomas Vaughan explained: '. . . life itself is nothing but a union of male and female principles, and he that perfectly knows this secret knows . . . how he ought to use a wife . . .'[38] (Remember the huge rose at the foot of the cross in Cocteau's London mural – clearly this is a Rosicrucian allusion. And significantly, the rose-cross image is found on the Templar tomb of Sir William St Clair[39] . . .)

Even if there is, as we have seen, evidence for the Templars, the alchemists and the Priory being devotees of a love cult, there seems little possibility that the resolutely male line of hermetic philosophers had any link with a feminine – or perhaps a feminist – organization. Yet here too their superficial image is misleading.

Leonardo himself is widely considered to have been a homosexual misogynist, and it is true that he evinced little outward love for women, as far as we know. His mother, the mysterious Caterina, appears to have abandoned him to his fate as an infant, although she may have gone to live out her days with him many years afterwards – certainly Leonardo had a housekeeper whom he referred to ironically as 'la Caterina', and whose funeral he paid for. He may have been a homosexual, but that has never stood in the way of men's adoration of the Feminine Principle – often quite the reverse. Gay icons are classically strong and colourful women who have had traumatic lives – just like Mary Magdalene and Isis herself. Besides, Leonardo is known to have been very close to Isabella d'Este, an educated and intelligent woman. Although it would be carrying speculation too far to suggest that she was a member of the Priory or some other 'feminist' underground school, this may imply at the very least that Leonardo approved of female literacy.

The Florentine hermeticist Pico della Mirandola devoted many words to the theme of female power. His book *La Strega* (*The Witch*) relates the story of an Italian cult based on sexual orgies and presided over by a goddess. More remarkably, he equated this goddess with the 'Mother of God'.[40]

Even the notably masculine Giordano Bruno was heavily involved with the feminine. During his stay in England in 1583–85 he published several major works that outlined the hermetic philosophy that can be found in any history textbook. However, what is routinely ignored is the fact that he had also published a volume of passionate love poetry called *De gli eroici furori* (*On the Heroic Frenzy*), which was dedicated to his friend and patron Sir Philip Sydney. This was no hymn to a passing infatuation, or even merely a glimpse into the hitherto unknown secret life of a philanderer. Although it is recognized that there was a deeper level to this poetry, most authorities believe it to be merely an allegorical expression of the hermetic experience. In fact, the love expressed in these works was not allegorical, but literal.

The *furori* of the title is, to quote Frances Yates: 'An experience which makes the soul "divine and heroic" and can be likened to the trance of the *furor* of passionate love.'[41] In other words, what we are looking at once again is a knowledge of the transmutational powers of sex.

In these poems Bruno was referring to an altered state of consciousness in which the hermeticist realizes his potential divinity. This is expressed as the ecstasy of complete union with one's *other half*. As Dame Frances says: '. . . I think that what the religious experience of the *Eroici furori* really aims at is the Hermetic gnosis; this is the mystical love poetry of the Magus man, who was created divine, with divine powers, and is in the process of again becoming divine, with divine powers.'[42]

Yet looking at the tradition that Bruno was following, it is clear that such sentiments were not merely metaphorical. This emphasis on enlightenment through sex was part and parcel of the hermetic philosophy and practice. The concept of sacred sexuality accords totally with the words of Hermes Trismegistus himself in the *Corpus Hermeticum*: 'If you hate your body, my child, you cannot love yourself.'[43]

Hermeticists such as Marsilio Ficino identified four types of altered state in which the soul becomes reunited with the Divine, each of which was associated with a mythological figure: poetic inspiration under the Muses, religious enthusiasm under Dionysus, prophetic trance under Apollo and all forms of intense love under Venus. The last is the climax in all senses, for this is when the soul actually achieves its reunion with the Divine.[44]

Significantly, historians have always taken the first three of these altered states literally, but have chosen to read the last, the rite of Venus, as a mere allegory or as some kind of impersonal or spiritual love. But if this were the case the hermeticists would hardly have categorized it under Venus! The historians' apparent coyness on this point is due to the widespread ignorance of the underground tradition. This is yet another example of concepts that were once thought to be obscure becoming crystal clear once the idea of sacred sexuality is taken into account.

The great hermetic magician Henry Cornelius Agrippa (1486–1535), makes the matter quite explicit. He wrote in his classic work *De occulta philosophia*: 'As for the fourth *furor*, coming from Venus, it turns and transmutes the spirit of man into a god by the ardour of love, and renders him entirely like God, as the true image of God.'[45] Note the use of the alchemical term *transmutes*, which is usually taken to refer to the foolish and futile preoccupation with trying to turn lead into gold. Here, however, quite another sort of precious commodity is sought. Agrippa also stressed that sexual union is 'full of magical endowment'.[46]

The place of Agrippa in this heretical tradition should not be underestimated. His treatise *De nobilitate et praecellentia foeminei sexus* (*On the Nobility and Superiority of the Female Sex*), which was published in 1529 but based on his disser-

218

tation of twenty years earlier, is much more even than a remarkably modern appeal for the rights of women. This astonishing work of Agrippa's has gone largely neglected until very recently for one, sadly predictable, reason. Because it advocated sexual equality – even arguing for the ordination of women – it has been taken as a *satire*! It is a grim reflection on our culture that such a passionate work in favour of women should be dismissed as a joke. But it seems clear that Agrippa was not joking.

He was not merely arguing the case for what we would call women's rights – for the political status of women to be re-defined – but was trying to convey the principle behind such a campaign. As Professor Barbara Newman of Northwest University, Pennsylvania, says in her study of this tract:

> ... even a sympathetic reader might be uncertain whether Agrippa was calling for a gender-blind, equal-opportunity Church or a form of woman-worship.[47]

Newman and other scholars have traced Agrippa's inspiration back to several roots including the cabala, alchemy, hermeti-cism, Neo-platonism and the troubadour tradition. And, once again, the quest for *Sophia* is cited as being a major influence.

It would be a mistake to think Agrippa was merely arguing for respect and equality for women. He went much further. His point was that women should literally be *worshipped*:

> No one who is not utterly blind can fail to see that God gath-ered all the beauty of which the whole world is capable together in woman, so that all creation might be dazzled by her, and love and venerate her under many names.[48]

(And it is significant that Agrippa, like the alchemists, believed that menstrual blood had a particular practical and mystical application[49]. They believed that it contained some unique elixir or chemical and that ingesting it in a certain manner, using ancient techniques, would guarantee physical

219

rejuvenation and bestow wisdom. Of course, nothing could be further from the attitude of the Church.)

Agrippa was no mere theorist, and also no coward. Not only was he married three times, but he also succeeded in what might have been the impossible: he defended a woman accused of witchcraft – and *won*.

Of course Vaughan, Bruno and Agrippa were all men, and it is tempting to suspect that they enjoyed this sexual bliss simply for their own benefit, even if that were profoundly spiritual. However, while it is true to say that any woman daring to write about such matters would have been arrested for witchcraft, it is also the case that the rite of Venus was only deemed to have 'worked' if both partners attained the same goals. The idea was one of opposites and equals working towards the same goal and receiving the same enlightenment as partners, just as in the Chinese idea of the whole being made up of Yin and Yang.

Giordano Bruno was not one to keep his beliefs to himself. In his later published works he employed yet more explicitly sexual imagery[50] – but even this has been sidelined by historians; if it is mentioned in standard works it is usually explained as being allegorical. Not only this but other explicit – and associated – references in his works are also routinely misunderstood. When Bruno wrote of a 'goddess' as the anonymous lady to whom his love poetry was written, this has been understood as being an affectionate epithet. And later, when he gave his farewell address to Germany, saying bluntly that the goddess Minerva was *Sophia* (wisdom), this was also taken to be another allegory. But his actual words were unmistakably those of a goddess worshipper:

> Her have I loved and sought from my youth, and desired for my spouse, and have become a lover of her form . . . and I prayed that . . . she might be sent to abide with me, and work with me, that I might know what I lacked . . .[51]

More compelling, however, is the fact that in his dedication of the *Eroici furori* he specifically likens it to the Song of Songs[52]. Once again, we find ourselves faced with the cult of the Black Madonna, and by association, that of the Magdalene. (Of course that other great hermetic/Rosicrucian writer of the day, who was known as William Shakespeare, dedicated his sonnets to a mysterious Dark Lady, the identity of whom has provided generations of critics with endless fuel for debate. While it may well have been the case that she was a real woman – or even a man – it is also likely that she represented *au fond* the Black Madonna, the dark goddess. Indeed, the hermetics symbolized a particular altered state – a kind of specialized trance – as a lady of dark complexion.[53])

Bruno's robust attacks on Christian belief and *mores* led him to a terrible death, and acted as a warning to other would-be brave souls. The atrocious holocaust of the witch trials, as we have seen, also reinforced the necessity for circumspection among 'heretics' (and it must be remembered that, although burnings had long since ceased, the last prosecution of a woman under the Witchcraft Act in the UK was as recent as 1944). But transcendental lovemaking, as a specific secret of the occult underground, was not confined to individuals, and it did not die out with them.

There is some difficulty in tracing a direct tradition of sacred sexuality in Europe because of the Church's antagonism to it and the consequent need for secrecy among the guardians of this knowledge. However, in the seventeenth and eighteenth centuries, Germany seems to have become home for this tradition, although little research was done into this until recently. According to modern French researchers – such as Denis Labouré – the practice of 'internal alchemy' became focused on Germany in various occult societies. Other recent research, including that of Dr Stephen E. Flowers, has confirmed that German occultism of this period was essentially sexual in nature.[54]

A problem for investigators into this area is that evidence for sex cults tends to come from the Church, or at least from those

221

who saw Satanism in anything connected with sex. When such movements find themselves persecuted their records are either destroyed or censored, and all that is left is the version of events as told by their enemies. This happened to the Cathars and the Templars, and of course reached its terrifying zenith in the witch trials. We see this process in effect whenever ideas about sacred sexuality are expressed – as happened once again in France in the nineteenth century.

At that time, several interconnected movements emerged that – although they blossomed within the Catholic Church and centred on people who considered themselves to be good Catholics – included concepts of sacred sexuality and of the elevation of the Feminine (usually in the outward form of the Virgin Mary) and were associated with a shadowy 'Johannite' society – this time specifically concerned with John the Baptist.

This is an enormously complex series of events to unravel, largely because, apart from the unorthodox religious ideas and concepts of sexuality that led the movement to be branded immoral, they were also bound up with political causes that attracted the hostility of the authorities. Therefore almost all the accounts we have of them come from their enemies.

The political motives of these groups are outside the scope of the present investigation, although it was very important to those involved at the time. Suffice it to say that they backed the claims of one Charles Guillaume Naündorff (1785–1845), who boasted that he was Louis XVII (who was thought to have been killed as an infant with his father, Louis XVI, during the French Revolution).

One of these groups was the Church of Carmel, also known as the Oeuvre de la Misericorde (Work of Mercy), which was established in the early 1840s by one Eugène Vintras (1807–1875). A charismatic and compelling preacher, Vintras attracted the cream of high society into his movement, which nevertheless soon became the focus for accusations of diabolism. Certainly his rituals had some kind of a sexual content, in which (in Ean Begg's words) 'the greatest sacrament was the sexual act'.[55]

To make matters worse as far as the authorities were concerned, Vintras and Naündorff endorsed each other. So, inevitably, Vintras found himself in what was clearly a show trial. Accused of fraud – although even the alleged victims denied that any crime had taken place – he was sentenced to five years in jail in 1842. On his release he went to London and it was at that time that one of the former members of his Church – a priest called Gozzoli – wrote a pamphlet accusing him of sexual orgies of all kinds. While this seems to have been mostly the product of an over-heated imagination, some of it may have been based on fact. Then in 1848 the sect was declared heretical by the Pope and all its members were excommunicated. As a result it became independent and boasted both male and female priests – like the Cathars, although whether Vintras' cult followed their high principles is unclear.

Behind Vintras and Naündorff was a shadowy sect known as 'the Saviours of Louis XVII', or as the *Johannites*. This group can be traced back to the 1770s, and appears to have had some part in the civil unrest that preceded the Revolution. Unlike the 'Masonic' Johannites discussed earlier, it had no doubt which Saint John it venerated – it was the Baptist.[56]

After the Revolution the Johannites became concerned with the restoration of the monarchy. They were largely responsible for the promotion of Naündorff as pretender to the throne, and also behind 'prophetic' movements such as that of Vintras. Another self-styled 'guru' of the day – Thomas Martin, who had risen meteorically from peasant to king's adviser[57] – was supported by the Johannites, and they appear furthermore to have somehow 'stage managed' certain visions of the Virgin – such as that of La Salette in the foothills of the western Alps in 1846[58]. Just what was going on is hard to say precisely, but it is possible to identify the main threads running through certain apparently associated events.

First, there was an attempt to regenerate Catholicism from within. This involved replacing mainstream dogma – based on the authority of Peter – with a mystical and esoteric

Christianity in the belief that an age was dawning in which the Holy Spirit would be in the ascendant. A feature of this was the elevation of the Feminine, in the outward form of the Virgin Mary, but this soon took on a more overtly sexual character and began to seem actively hostile to the Church. The vision of La Salette – which was condemned by the Church – was central to this plan. And somehow John the Baptist's role in these developments was crucial.

The movement was also allied with the attempt to have Naündorff recognized as the legitimate king of France, probably because, if it had succeeded, he would have been favourable to this new form of religion (having already endorsed Vintras). Significantly Melanie Calvet, the girl who had the vision at La Salette, had herself come out in favour of Naündorff. And it is interesting that the Church reacted by shipping her off to a convent in Darlington, in the north-east of England, where she could do no more harm.[59]

The combined forces of Church and State prevented the movement's grand plan from being fulfilled, and whatever really happened is now buried under an avalanche of scandal and innuendo. But no doubt it is significant that the Church's reaction to this threat was to make the Immaculate Conception of Mary an article of faith in 1854. (This doctrine was to be conveniently endorsed by the Virgin Mary herself when she appeared to the peasant girl Bernadette Soubirous at Lourdes some four years later, although the latter at first simply described her vision as 'that thing'.)

Prophets such as Martin and Vintras appear to have been 'managed' by the Johannites, rather than actually being part of the sect themselves. Vintras' link with them was his mentor, a certain Madame Bouche, who lived in the Place St Sulpice in Paris, and went under the splendidly evocative name of 'Sister Salome'. (Vintras' Church of Carmel was still operating in Paris in the 1940s, and there was rumoured to be a group in London in the 1960s.[60])

Another movement merged with the Church of Carmel but had actually been founded earlier, in 1838. This was the

Brothers of Christian Doctrine which had been established by the three brothers Baillard, all priests. They set up two religious houses – again, regarding themselves as Catholics – on mountains: St Odile in Alsace and Sion-Vaudémont in Lorraine. Both were important sites in their regions, and it is a mystery how the Baillard brothers managed to acquire them.

Sion-Vaudémont was an important pagan site in antiquity, sacred to the goddess Rosamerta, and – as can be guessed from its name – has a long association with the Priory of Sion. In fact, a historically recognized Ordre de Notre-Dame de Sion was established there in the fourteenth century by Ferri de Vaudémont, whose charter linked it to the abbey of Mount Sion in Jerusalem – from which the Priory claims to have originally taken its name. Ferri's son married Iolande de Bar, the Grand Master of the Priory between 1480 and 1483, who was also the daughter of René d'Anjou, the previous Grand Master. Iolande promoted Sion-Vaudémont as an important centre for pilgrimage, focusing on its Black Madonna. The statue itself was destroyed during the Revolution, and replaced by a medieval – not black – Virgin, taken from the church of Vaudémont, which is dedicated to John the Baptist.[61]

So it appears to be significant that one of the Baillard brothers' new churches was based in that place. They had similar ideas to those of Vintras, including the emphasis on the coming age of the Holy Spirit and on sacred sexuality, so it is not surprising that they sprang from the same source. Their movement attracted great support, including that of the House of Habsburg. But it, too, was suppressed in 1852.

After Vintras' death in 1875 the movement was taken over by the Abbé Joseph Boullan (1824–1893) – an even more controversial figure. Previously he had seduced a young nun at the convent at La Salette, Adèle Chevalier, and the two of them set up the Society for the Reparation of Souls in 1859. This was definitely based on sexual rites, its overall philosophy being that humanity would find redemption through sex if used as a sacrament. While this may in itself seem pure and alchemical in nature, unfortunately Boullan extended the benefits of this rite to the animal kingdom.

Boullan and Adèle Chevalier are reported as having sacrificed their infant child during a Black Mass in 1860. However, although this is presented as fact in all the modern literature, it is impossible to trace it back to a reliable source. If Boullan was known to have committed such a crime he seems to have escaped prosecution. It is true that he was suspended from his offices as priest in that year, but this was reversed after a few months. In 1861 he and Adèle were jailed for fraud (perhaps the authorities' usual way of dealing with those they disliked but could pin nothing on). On his conviction Boullan was yet again suspended from his priestly duties, but once more the decision was reversed. After his release from prison he *voluntarily* presented himself to the Holy Office (then the official name of the Inquisition) in Rome, which found no fault in him and let him return to Paris.[62]

While in Rome Boullan wrote his doctrines down in a notebook (known as the *cahier rose*, overtly after the colour of the cover), which was found by the writer J.K. Huysmans among his papers after his death in 1893. The precise details of the contents are unknown – though it was described as a 'shocking document' – and it is now locked away in the Vatican Library. All applications to see it are refused.[63]

There is clearly more to the Boullan story than meets the eye. Superficially it seems to be yet another story of a perverts' club. However, it does seem that the Church actually protected Boullan to some extent. For example, it issued an instruction that he should not be harassed, and there are hints that he possessed some kind of secret that protected him.[64] Boullan's story fits the classic pattern of the *agent provocateur*, who infiltrates an organization with the deliberate aim – on behalf of a quite different group – of discrediting it. This would explain the glaring discrepancies in his life and in the official attitudes towards him.

After his return from Rome, Boullan joined Vintras' Church of Carmel and became its leader. This caused a schism: those cult members who did accept him accompanied him to Lyons, where they set up their headquarters. Wild scenes of sexual licence followed – which, once again, may seem remarkably at odds with Boullan's declaration that he was the reincarnation of John the Baptist.

That idea may well have been the inspiration behind at least the name chosen by J.K. Huysmans (a devotee of the Black Madonna cult), who used Boullan as the model for 'Dr Johannès' (one of Boullan's aliases) in his novel about Satanism in Paris, *Là-Bas* (*Down There*) (1891). However, it would be a mistake to jump to the obvious conclusion – Dr Johannès was portrayed as a priest who practised magic to *counter* Satanism and who was misunderstood by the Church, which, of course, denounced all magic as being of the Devil. Huysmans befriended Boullan and stayed with him in Lyons while researching his novel, but although he was certainly very knowledgeable about magic, theoretically at least, he always remained a true son of the Church.

Là-Bas is remembered these days mainly for its lurid description of a Black Mass, which appears to be an eyewitness account. However, the real villains of the piece are the Rosicrucians because of the notorious magical battle between Boullan and members of certain Rosicrucian Orders that flourished in France at that time. It might seem incongruous that the Rosicrucians of all people were so opposed to Boullan and all he appeared to stand for. Of course the conflict may have been merely one of those clashes of personality that characteristically afflict such movements – but perhaps certain Rosicrucians were alarmed at Boullan's openness with their secrets.

France had become home to a number of occult lodges. Several Rosicrucian Orders represented a development of the blend of Templarist–Masonic–Rosicrucian movements found in the south-west of France. Although these were not strictly Masonic Orders, they were certainly allied to the occult Masonic systems such as the Rectified Scottish Rite and the Egyptian Rites. Both the Masonic and Rosicrucian groups embraced the Martinist philosophy – the occult teachings of

Louis Claude de Saint-Martin. In fact, the significance of Martinism should not hardly be underestimated: the Rectified Scottish Rite Freemasons of today recruit exclusively from among the Martinists.[65]

The first of these Rosicrucian organizations appears to have been an offshoot of a somewhat irregular Masonic lodge known as La Sagesse (Wisdom or *Sophia*) in Toulouse. Around 1850 one of its members, the Vicomte de Lapasse (1792–1867), a well-respected doctor and alchemist, founded the Ordre de la Rose-Croix, du Temple et du Graal (Order of the Rose-Cross, the Temple and the Grail)[66]. A subsequent head of this order was Joséphin Péladan (1859–1918), who was also from Toulouse and became what might be termed godfather of the French Rosicrucian societies of that time.

Péladan was a great occult expert, having been inspired by the French writer Éliphas Lévi (real name Alphonse Louis Constant, 1810–75). Péladan developed a magical system that has been described as 'erotic Catholicism-cum-magic'[67] and organized the popular Salon de la Rose + Croix. (Interestingly, it was on a poster advertising one of these meetings that Dante is portrayed as Hugues de Payens, first Grand Master of the Templars, and Leonardo is depicted as the Keeper of the Grail. [see illustration] He believed that the Catholic Church was a repository of knowledge that it had itself forgotten, and he was particularly interested in John's Gospel[68]. He was also ahead of modern scholarship in that he perceived the *fidele d'amore* as an esoteric society, which he specifically linked to the seventeenth-century Rosicrucians.[69]

Péladan met another occultist, Stanislas de Guaïta (1861–1898), and in 1888 the two of them formed the Ordre Kabbalistique de la Rose-Croix (cabalistic Order of the Rose-Cross). It was Guaïta who infiltrated Boullan's Church of Carmel and together with Oswald Wirth, a disenchanted member of that cult, wrote the book *The Temple of Satan*, which exposed the movement as being diabolic. This led to the magical battle, in which Boullan and Guaïta accused each other of using magical means to murder the other.

Disappointingly, Boullan seems to have died of natural causes, but equally inevitably the feud led to two flesh-and-blood duels, one between Guaïta and one of Boullan's disciples, Jules Bois, and the other between the latter and one of the Rosicrucians, Gérard Encausse (better known as Papus). Both of these events ended in draws.

This episode is a favourite with writers on the occult, but it is never satisfactorily explained. Why should Guaïta and the Parisian Rosicrucians undertake a vendetta against Boullan? (Remember in this context that we only have the word of Guaïta and Wirth for the depravities allegedly committed by Boullan and his followers.) On the face of it, there is no real connection, or grounds for dispute, between the occult lodges and Boullan's essentially religious Order.

However, a little more digging reveals the reason: de Guaïta and a tribunal of Rosicrucians had initially condemned Boullan for 'profaning' and revealing 'cabalistic secrets' – that is, the teachings that were deemed to be the province of the Rosicrucians[70]. (And their condemnation was on 23 May 1887, *before* Guaïta infiltrated Boullan's group.) This was the real reason why they felt Boullan had to be stopped.

Other commentators seem not to have noticed the implications of this: if Boullan's rites were deemed to be something that belonged to the Rosicrucians *then they, too, must have practised sexual rites*. Boullan's error, in their eyes, lay in making them public.

The Paris of the late nineteenth century was home to much learned occultism and philosophy – reflecting, perhaps, the *fin de siècle* quest for a deeper meaning to life. It attracted all manner of thinkers and artists such as Oscar Wilde, Debussy and W.B. Yeats. (As ever, the true European Union was an occult brotherhood.) The salons were packed with famous faces who were as eager to pick up magical formulae as they were to pick up gossip, among them Marcel Proust, Maurice Maeterlinck and the opera singer, Emma Calvé (1858–1942). A famed beauty, she eventually held her own soirées for anyone who had anything interesting to share – preferably some great

229

occult secret. These circles also included the likes of Joséphin Péladan, Papus and Jules Bois (who was one of Emma Calvé's many lovers).

Many of the prime movers in this circle were from the Languedoc, including Emma Calvé herself. (She was no stranger to mysticism: it was a relative of hers, Melanie Calvet, who had had the famous vision at La Salette. And interestingly, Adèle Chevalier, the nun who had been seduced by Boullan and became his partner, was one of Melanie's friends.) It was Emma Calvé who was to play a significant role in the tangled tale of the Abbé Saunière, parish priest of the Languedocian village of Rennes-le-Château, which we will discuss later.

Suggestively, in 1894 she bought the château of Cabrières (Aveyron), near her birthplace of Millau, which was said in the seventeenth century to have been the hiding place of the long-sought-after Book of Abraham the Jew, which had been used by Flamel to achieve the Great Work[71]. In her autobiography, Calvé records that the château 'was the refuge of a certain group of Knights Templar'[72], but tantalizingly, does not elaborate further.

Certain other important occult groups had begun in the Languedoc and became connected with the Rosicrucian societies. These were influenced by the Strict Templar Observance Freemasonry of Baron von Hund, although the main influence came through that much maligned figure, Count Cagliostro (1743–1795)[73].

Widely denounced as a charlatan, this natural showman was a genuine seeker after occult knowledge. Born Giuseppe Balsamo, he took the title of Count Alessandro Cagliostro from his godmother. He was introduced to the occult when he was twenty-three during a visit to Malta, where he met the Grand Master of the Knights of Malta – an alchemist and Rosicrucian. Cagliostro himself caught the occult bug and became an alchemist and Freemason and was heavily influenced by von Hund's Strict Templar Observance. His introduction to Freemasonry came in Gerrard Street in London's Soho, where he was initiated into a Strict Templar Observance lodge in April 1777. He travelled widely through Europe, but spent most of his time in Germany, specifically searching out the lost knowledge of the Templars. He also gained a reputation as a healer.

After receiving the Pope's permission to visit Rome in 1789, on his arrival he was promptly handed over to the Inquisition on a charge of heresy and political conspiracy – on the orders of the Pope – and sentenced to life imprisonment. He died in the dungeons of the fortress of San Leo in 1795.

Cagliostro had established the system of 'Egyptian' Freemasonry (the mother lodge was set up in Lyons in 1782) which consisted of both male and female lodges, the latter being headed by his wife Serafina. Lévi described this as an attempt 'to resuscitate the mysterious worship of Isis.'[74]

The fruits of Cagliostro's researches into the occult societies of Europe were a body of knowledge known as the *Arcana Arcanorum* (Secret of Secrets), or A. A. He took this term from the original Rosicrucianism of the seventeenth century, but his corpus consisted of descriptions of magical practices that especially stressed 'internal alchemy'. As we have seen, these are essentially *sexual* techniques, akin to Tantrism – yet Cagliostro had learned them in *Germany* among the Rosicrucian groups.[75]

It was under Cagliostro's authority that the Rite of Misraïm (Hebrew for 'Egyptians') was created in Venice in 1788. Around 1810 the three Bédarride brothers brought the system to France, where it was incorporated into the Rectified Scottish Rite of Freemasonry[76].

The Rite of Misraïm was the direct antecedent of the Rite of Memphis – which had, as we have seen, been founded by Jacques-Étienne Marconis de Nègre and with which the Priory of Sion has associated itself. (The two systems unified as the Rite of Memphis-Misraïm in 1899 under the Grand Mastership of Papus, who remained at the helm until his death in 1918.) The Rite of Memphis was also closely associated with a secret society called the Philadelphians that had been founded by the

Marquis de Chefdebien in 1780 – another offshoot of von Hund's Strict Templar Observance, although it was specifically formed to acquire occult knowledge. Marconis de Nègre stressed the close ties with the Philadelphians and named one of the grades of his movement 'The Philadelphes'.[77]

Neither rite – of Memphis or Misraïm – was in itself particularly influential. But taken together, as Memphis-Misraïm, they were a power to be reckoned with, and their influence spread like tidal waves through the occult underground of Europe. Among their members were such dark stars as the British occultist Aleister Crowley and mystic luminaries like Rudolf Steiner. And there was also Karl Kellner, who was eventually, with Theodore Reuss, to found the Order of the Templars of the Orient, better known simply as the OTO.

This organization was – and is – explicitly about sex magic. And although it is widely thought to represent the Westernizing of Tantrism, it was also very much the logical development of secrets taught in Memphis-Misraïm – which themselves derived from the knowledge acquired by Cagliostro from the alchemical Rosicrucian groups of Germany and the Strict Templar Observance lodges.

Crowley left Memphis-Misraïm to join the OTO and then became its Grand Master, and another influential figure who crossed from the former to the OTO was Rudolf Steiner. He is most famous for his 'pure' brand of mysticism – Anthroposophy – and deliberately played down his association with the OTO, so successfully that many of his most ardent modern followers have no knowledge of it. When he died, however, he was buried in his OTO regalia[78].

Significantly, Theodore Reuss wrote that the sex magic of the OTO was: 'the KEY which opens up all Masonic and hermetic secrets . . .'[79] He also said bluntly that sex magic was the secret of the Knights Templar.[80]

Another offspring of the Memphis/Misraïm movement took shape in England in the late nineteenth century. This was the hermetic Order of the Golden Dawn, whose members included Bram Stoker the theatre manager most famous for being the author of *Dracula*; Aleister Crowley the Irish poet, patriot and mystic, W. B. Yeats, and sociable Constance Wilde, wife of the doomed Oscar. Founded in 1888 by Macgregor Mathers and W. Wynn Westcott, its direct line of descent went back to the Gold and Rosy Cross, the Strict Templar Observance order from Germany discussed in the last chapter, as did many of its actual grade names and rituals[81]. The Golden Dawn also used rites taken from Memphis/Misraïm. In the end, however, the order owed its birthright to Baron von Hund – both German and French influences ultimately go back to him and his Templarist rites[82].

The Golden Dawn is much more well known in the English-speaking world than those other, more exotic European groups. It has a reputation for great integrity and appears at first glance to be a society of esotericists who liked robing up and uttering incantations, but who were basically little more than after-dinner occultists with high ideals. However, among French occult scholars the Golden Dawn has a much more sinister reputation; when it opened its Paris branch in 1891 it accepted many of the more dubious characters discussed above, including the seemingly ubiquitous Jules Bois.

In fact, even the English Golden Dawn had a little-known, more profound aspect. It was effectively two separate Orders: on the one hand it had a well-known, respectable public face, and on the other there was an inner order called the Rose of Ruby and the Cross of Gold, into which initiation was by invitation only. The outer Order seems to have acted as a recruiting ground for the inner, secret circle whose practices included sex rites.

Certainly the Golden Dawn guarded its inner secrets well. For years even those writers, such as Katan Shu'al[83], who are themselves part of the occult world could only speculate about sex rites in that Order. However, it seems that they did exist, although the evidence is piecemeal. In fact, it seems that sexual elements were present from the very foundation of the Order. The Golden Dawn grew out of another society, the Societas Rosicruciana in Anglia, which had among its founders one

Hargrave Jennings (1817–1890), whose writings were as explicit as a Victorian gentleman's could be on the subject of sex magic. In his massive work *The Rosicrucians: Their Rites and Mysteries* (1870), Jennings, in the words of author Peter Tompkins, 'hinted as strongly as he could that these rites and mysteries were of a fundamentally sexual nature'.[84] For example, in discussing the sexual symbolism of the interlinked triangles that make up the Seal of Solomon (or the Star of David), Jennings adds explicitly:

> . . . the pyramid indicates the female corresponding tumefactive or rising power – not submissive, but answeringly suggestive, synchronized in the anatomical clitoris . . . that eccentric minute object, meaning everything in the Rosicrucian anatomy.[85]

On 18 July 1921 Moina Mathers – one of the founders of the Golden Dawn (and sister of the philosopher Henri Bergson) – wrote to Paul Foster Case, who was tutor to the New York branch of the Order, on hearing that he was teaching sex rituals:

> I regret that anything on the Sex Question should be entered into the Temple at this stage for we only begin to touch on sex matters directly, in quite the higher grades . . .[86]

Then when the occult writer and Golden Dawn member Dion Fortune (real name Violet Firth) wrote articles about sex, Moina wanted to expel her for betraying the Order's secrets. But eventually she had to acknowledge that Dion Fortune could not have known them because she had not reached the necessary grades[87].

Commentators such as Mary K. Greer[88] now accept that there is evidence to support the idea that the Golden Dawn did indeed practise sex magic, which it clearly regarded as being too potent and precious to be squandered on its newest recruits and lowest grades.

Hints about the inner secrets of the Golden Dawn are also to be found in the words describing a joint vision that Florence Farr and Elaine Simpson, two adepts of that system, had in the 1890s. The former, a famous actress of the London stage, was also renowned for her affairs with a number of men, including George Bernard Shaw and brother occultist W.B. Yeats. Florence and her magical colleague Elaine undertook an astral journey together – a sort of twin adventure on the Inner Planes or a shared hallucination. This phenomenon is a common enough part of magical training, and is usually part of caba-listic 'pathworking', a sort of mental projection or association of images that is set in the classic framework of the 'Tree of Life'.

Florence and Elaine set out to visit the 'sphere of Venus' in their joint minds' eye. The culmination of their astral journey took the form of an encounter with a striking female archetype, who smilingly said:

> I am the mighty Mother Isis; most powerful of all the world, I am she who fights not, but is always victorious. I am that Sleeping Beauty whom men have sought for all time. The paths which lead to my castle are beset with danger and il-lusions. Such as fail to find me, sleep; or may ever rush after the *Fata Morgana* leading astray all who feel that illusory influence. I am lifted up on high and draw men unto me. I am the world's desire, but few there be who find me. When my secret is told, it is the secret of the Holy Grail . . .

> I have given my heart to the world, that is my strength. Love is the Mother of the Man-God, giving the quintessence of her life to save mankind from destruction, and to show forth the path to eternal life. Love is the Mother of the Christ-Spirit, and this Christ is the highest love. Christ is the heart of love, the heart of the Great Mother Isis, the Isis of Nature. He is the expression of her power. She is the Holy Grail, and He is the life blood of Spirit that is found in the cup.[89]

Accompanying these words were vivid images of a cup holding ruby-coloured fluid and a three-barred cross.

At first glance this may seem a rather 'New Age' sort of mish-mash, with Jesus and the Egyptian goddess Isis being mixed up with the notion of the Holy Grail simply because it sounds arcane and mystical. But, as the late occult expert Francis X. King wrote, there are two significant points in this: 'The first is the identification of the Blessed Virgin, "Mother of the Man-God", with Venus, goddess of love – that is, *sexual* love, *eros* not *agapé*. The second is the identification of the Grail . . . with Venus, the archetypal *yoni* or female organ of generation.'[90]

Modern readers might cynically interpret those ladies' vision as a sort of wish fulfilment, a joint sexual fantasy – especially when considering Florence Farr's colourful reputation as the British counterpart of Emma Calvé. Yet the vision was supposed to have revealed a secret that was in keeping with the magical philosophy of the Golden Dawn, and certainly Francis X. King expressed puzzlement as to where the women could have got the imagery from, considering that the society was not, supposedly, connected with any kind of sexual rite. This vision, however, indicates strongly that it *was*, although, again, the rites concerned seemed to be only for initiates into the highest grades, the inner circle.

It is significant that the vision links Isis with the Grail and with sex, which would not have been strange to alchemists, Gnostics or troubadours. That the Grail – seen here as the traditional cup – is a feminine symbol is easily understood by our post-Freudian world, but it was still revelatory to those who came before. But here the red fluid, the blood it contains, is carried by *Isis* . . .

Interestingly, the theme of the Sleeping Beauty, which is mentioned in the account of the women's vision, also figures largely in *Le serpent rouge*, that key text of the Priory of Sion. The search for the Sleeping Beauty is a repeated motif and is entwined with that of the quest for the queen of a lost kingdom. As we have seen, that document also reveals a preoccupation with Mary Magdalene and Isis, characteristically combining them into the same figure.

The quest for a queen is alchemical imagery, so we should not be surprised to find those embodiments of sexuality – the Magdalene and Isis – as its object. Curiously, although even today the role of sexuality in heretical and occult movements is barely recognized or acknowledged, its importance can hardly be overestimated. Sex has never been a side issue or merely a matter of personal foible, but it has been at the heart of *most* powerful underground organizations.

The tradition that most interests us and which lies behind this investigation is actually dependent on the notion of sacred sexuality. As we have seen, this tradition appears to be made up of two main strands – that of reverence for the Magdalene and that of reverence for John the Baptist. At this stage in our research we faced the possibility that the Magdalene was simply a symbolic figure that represented the idea of sacred sex, and that the image of her did not relate to any actual historical character. In any case, the connection between Mary Magdalene and sex is not hard to understand and seems perfectly natural.

This is not so, of course, when considering the John the Baptist strand and the idea of sacred sexuality. The biblical account, and Christian tradition, have created a compelling and enduring image of a man who was ascetic in the extreme – a sort of John Knox figure – of uncompromising morals and unflinching celibacy. How on earth could he, of all people, have been important to any cult based on sexual practices? Superficially it seemed as if there was not, and never could be, any such connection – and yet time and time again our investigation revealed that generation after generation of occultists at least believed that it existed. And, as we have seen in the case of the Golden Dawn, first impressions of even occult groups can be very misleading. Their true *raison d'être* may have surprising implications.

Florence Farr and her colleagues in the Golden Dawn belonged to a wide circle of international occultists, which included Péladan and Emma Calvé. The societies with which they were associated were extremely influential, and it was that network of societies which provided the framework for one of France's most famous mysteries; one that intimately concerns the Priory of Sion.

The focus for all the *Dossiers secrets* and allied material emanating from the Priory of Sion is unequivocally the mystery of Rennes-le-Château. For example, *Le serpent rouge* repeatedly alludes to places in and around that village. We could hardly avoid turning our attention to Rennes-le-Château, and once again we found ourselves in the Languedoc – the heartland of heresy.

CHAPTER EIGHT

'This is a Terrible Place'

Rennes-le-Château is an occult cliché, almost – by now – in the same league as the Grail itself, and just as elusive. Yet it is a real location, and it is here that we, too, found ourselves as our own quest unfolded. This place could be compared with Britain's Glastonbury, for both places appear to hold close to their hearts profound mysteries, while to both have accrued the most ludicrous, yet widespread, myths and suppositions.

Rennes-le-Château is in the department of the Languedoc known as the Aude, close to the town of Limoux, which gives its name to the famed *blanquette*, or sparkling wine, in the area known in the eighth and ninth centuries as the Razès. From the small town of Couiza, large signs point to a minor road, advertising the '*Domaine de Abbé Saunière*'. Following these signs, drivers find themselves on the curious corkscrewing road up to the hilltop village of Rennes-le-Château.

To us, as to many these days, it is an exciting journey. Thanks mainly to *The Holy Blood and the Holy Grail*, but also to word-of-mouth legend, this simple drive up a French hill rapidly takes on the feeling of an initiation in itself. Yet the place where visitors usually stop is very prosaic. The approach road leads inevitably up to the lone car-park, through a narrow '*grand rue*' that offers no post office or even a general store – but which does boast an esoteric bookshop, a bar/restaurant, the ruined château that gives the village its name, and alleys leading to the notorious little church and the presbytery.

This place has a sinister history and an even murkier, if somewhat vague, reputation. In brief, the story is that François Bérenger Saunière (1852–1917), an ordinary priest, born and raised in the village of Montazels, just three kilometres from Rennes-le-Château, made a discovery of some kind during renovations to his dilapidated tenth-century parish church[1] just over a hundred years ago. As a result of this discovery – either because of its intrinsic value or because it led him to something that could be turned to financial advantage – he became immensely wealthy.

Speculation has varied over the years as to the true nature of Saunière's discovery: most prosaically it has been suggested that he found a horde of treasure, while others believe it was something considerably more stupendous, such as the Ark of the Covenant, the treasure of the Jerusalem Temple, the Holy Grail – or even the tomb of Christ, an idea that found most recent expression in *The Tomb of God* by Richard Andrews and Paul Schellenberger (1996). (For our discussion of their theory see Appendix II.)

We had to go to Rennes-le-Château because, according to the *Dossiers secrets* and to *The Holy Blood and the Holy Grail*, it was of particular significance to the Priory of Sion – although the precise reasons for this remained obscure. The Priory claim that what Saunière had discovered were parchments containing genealogical information that prove the survival of the Merovingian dynasty, and establish that certain individuals have a right to claim the throne of France – such as Pierre Plantard de Saint-Clair. However, as no-one outside of the Priory has actually set eyes on these parchments, and the whole idea of the continued Merovingian line is dubious to say the least, there is little reason to set much store by this claim.

There is yet another major flaw, a glaring inconsistency, in the Priory's story. If they had really existed for many centuries solely to protect the Merovingian descendants, it is curious that they welcomed information telling them who those descendants were. Surely they knew whom they were sworn to uphold – otherwise they would hardly have had the kind of fanatical zeal that over the centuries had maintained their own organization for so long! To rely – apparently – on what is essentially a retrospective *raison d'être* is suspicious, to say the least.

Nevertheless, we were intrigued by the importance invested in the village by the Priory. There are two possible reasons for this: one is that the village is indeed significant, but not for the reasons stated in the *Dossiers* – while the other is that the Saunière story has no real connection with the Priory and that it hijacked the mystery for its own ends. We had to find out which of those alternatives was nearer to the truth.

Arriving in the village's car-park, one is faced with a stunning view over the Aude Valley to the snow-capped peaks of the Pyrenees. It is easy to see why, in the past, this apparently inconsequential hamlet was deemed of such strategic importance, for surely the view of any enemy approaches would have been hard to equal. This was why Rennes-le-Château was once a major Visigothic stronghold: some go so far as to identify it as the lost city of Rhedae, which was the equal of Carcassonne and Narbonne – although it is hard to see such a bustling metropolis in this peculiarly deserted cluster of houses today. Yet the place still exerts a magnetic influence: although only under a hundred people actually live in Rennes-le-Château, it has over 25,000 visitors a year.

The water tower, which rises out of the car-park itself, bears the signs of the zodiac – a motif that is also repeated above the doors of some of the cottages – but, disappointingly, this turns out to be a common custom of the area. But all eyes are drawn to the quaint folly-like building that seems to grow out of the very cliff-edge of the village, hanging over the sheer drop. This was Saunière's private library and study, known as the Tour Magdala (the Magdala Tower). It is part of his *domaine*, recently opened to the public. Like a small medieval turret, the tower on one side gives on to lengthy ramparts, leading to a now derelict glasshouse. In the rooms underneath the ramparts there is a museum now, which is dedicated to Saunière's life and the mystery that surrounds him. A garden separates the tower from the rather grand house that he had built with his unexplained wealth, the Villa Bethania, some

241

rooms of which are open to the public. Just beyond, round a gravel path, lies a small grotto made by the priest himself from stones carried up specially, and presumably with great effort, from a nearby valley. Then one comes to the village graveyard and the dilapidated church. This is dedicated to St Mary Magdalene.

Given the fame of the church it is astonishing to find that it is so small, but any disappointment is more than made up for by the justly famed bizarre character of the decorations made by the Abbé Saunière. In this, at least, the Abbé still manages to amaze.

Over the porch, with its almost comical second-rate white plaster birds and broken yellow tiles, are carved the words: *Terribilis est locus iste* ('This is a terrible place'), a quotation from the Book of Genesis (28:17) that is completed, in Latin, on the arch of the porch: 'It is the house of God and the Gate of Heaven'. A statue of Mary Magdalene presides over the door, while the tympanum is decorated with an equilateral triangle, and carved roses with a cross. But much more startling is the sight of a plaster demon, hideously contorted, apparently guarding the doorway immediately inside the porch. Horned and grimacing, he crouches in a clearly meaningful manner, while bearing the stoup of holy water on his shoulders. This is surmounted by four angels, each making one of the gestures involved in the sign of the cross, while the words *Par ce signe tu le vaincras* ('By this sign shall you conquer him/it') are inscribed under them. Against the far wall is a tableau showing the baptism of Jesus – who is depicted in a position that is precisely the mirror image of the demon. Both the demon and Jesus are gazing at a specific part of the floor, which is laid out like a chessboard. In the tableau, John the Baptist towers over Jesus, pouring water onto him from a shell, thus repeating the motif of the shell-shaped water stoup that is bearing down upon the demon. Clearly some parallel is being drawn between the two sets of images, between the demon and the baptism of Jesus. (In April 1996, in one of the many acts of vandalism to which the church is prone, the demon had his head lopped off – and stolen – by an unknown attacker.)

Standing on the black-and-white chequered floor and looking around at this tiny parish church of St Mary Magdalene, it seems at first glance to be fairly typical of a Catholic church of its time and place. Over-decorated with garish plaster saints – such as St Anthony the Hermit and St Roche – it contains the usual quota of church furnishings. Yet they repay more careful scrutiny, for most of them bear at least one idiosyncratic touch. For example, the Stations of the Cross, which unusually run anti-clockwise, here include a boy in a kilt and a small black child. And the awning over the pulpit takes the form of Solomon's Temple.

The bas-relief on the front of the altar was, so it is said, Saunière's pride and joy: he put the finishing touches to it himself. It shows a golden-garbed Magdalene kneeling in prayer, an open book before her and a skull by her knees. Her fingers are curiously intertwined in the manner usually described as *latté*. A cross apparently made out of a spindly live tree – with a leafy shoot halfway up – rises in front of her, and beyond the rocky grotto where she kneels one can see the distinct shape of buildings silhouetted against the sky-line. Curiously, although the skull and open book are both accepted parts of the Magdalene's iconography, the usual jar of spikenard is missing here.

She also appears in the stained-glass window above the altar, where she is apparently emerging from under a table to anoint Jesus' feet with the precious ointment. In all there are four images of the Magdalene in the church, which, even given her status as its patron saint, might seem excessive for such a tiny building. Saunière's commitment to her is reinforced by the naming of his library – the *Magdala Tower* – and of his house, the *Bethany, Villa*. Bethany being the biblical home of the family which included Lazarus, Martha and Mary.

There is a secret room hidden behind a cupboard in the sacristy, but even the latter is rarely seen by the public. Its one window, which cannot be seen clearly from the outside, appears to depict in stained glass the usual Crucifixion scene.

But, like virtually everything else in this 'terrible place', it is not quite what it seems. The eye is drawn to the distant land- scape, which can be seen under the arms of the man on the cross; clearly this is the real focus of the picture. There, once again, is the Temple of Solomon.

Even the entrance to the graveyard is unusual: the archway is decorated with a metal skull and crossbones, an emblem of the Knights Templar – although an unusual touch is the grin which shows off twenty-two teeth. The graves, floridly topped with elaborate floral tributes and photographs of the departed as in many other French churchyards, include those of the Bonhommes family. Anywhere else, perhaps, this would hardly cause comment, but here this linguistic reminder of the Cathars – *les Bonhommes* – seems particularly poignant. Saunière's grave, with its bas-relief of his profile – slightly damaged by vandalism in recent times – lies up against the wall separating the cemetery from his former *domaine*. Marie Dénarnaud, his faithful housekeeper (if not considerably more), is buried at his side.

It is not our purpose to go over in detail what is by now a thoroughly hackneyed story. But in suspecting that the Rennes mystery would yield some clues about the continu- ation of the underground tradition, we were neither mistaken nor disappointed. As we have seen, we had found evidence for a complex series of connections that led back to a *Gnostic* tradi- tion in the area, a place that has always been notorious for its 'heretics', be they Cathars, Templars or so-called 'witches'. Since the trauma of the Albigensian Crusade the local people have never totally trusted the Vatican, so it has provided the perfect home for unorthodox ideas, besides those with minority political interests. In the Languedoc, with its long and bitter memories, heresy and politics have always gone hand- in-hand, as perhaps they still do.

In Saunière we find an extravert rebel priest. He was hardly a typical village clergyman, being familiar with Greek as well as Latin and a regular subscriber to a contemporary German newspaper. Whether or not he discovered some treasure or secret, it is unlikely that the whole 'Rennes business' is a complete fabrication. There are, however, several reasons for thinking that the story as it is generally told is largely misunderstood.[2]

The exact sequence of events is notoriously difficult to reconstruct, as it relies largely on the memories of the villagers rather than on documentary evidence. Saunière took up his post as parish priest in early June 1885. Within a few months he was in trouble for preaching a fiercely anti-Republican sermon from his pulpit (during the elections of that year) and was temporarily deprived of his position. Reinstated in the summer of 1886, he received a gift of 3000 francs from the Countess de Chambord, widow of a pretender to the French throne – Henri de Bourbon, who claimed the title Henri V – in recognition of his services to the monarchist cause. Apparently he used the money to renovate the ancient church, and in most accounts this was when the Visigothic pillar that supported the altar was removed – in which, it is said, he found certain coded parchments. But this seems unlikely, because his eccentric behaviour and ambitious projects did not begin until 1891. It was around that time that the bell-ringer, Antoine Captier, found something of importance. Some say it was a wooden cylinder, while others claim it was a glass phial: whatever it was, it is believed to have contained rolled-up parchments or documents that he gave to Saunière. And it appears to be *this* discovery that prompted the priest's peculiar actions.

The usual version is that Saunière presented the parchments to his bishop at Carcassonne, Félix-Arsène Billard, and that this precipitated a trip to Paris. It is usually said that Saunière had been advised to take the documents to be decoded by an expert, one Émile Hoffet, who was then a young man studying for the priesthood, but who already had a deep knowledge of occultism and the world of secret societies. (He later taught at the church of Notre-Dame de Lumières in Goult, a Black Madonna site that is especially important to the Priory of Sion[3].) Hoffet's uncle was the director of the Seminary of Saint Sulpice in Paris.

The church of St Sulpice is distinguished by the fact that the Paris meridian – which passes close to Rennes-le-Château – is marked by a copper line across its floor. Built on the foundations of a temple of Isis in 1645, it was founded by Jean-Jacques Olier, who had it designed according to the Golden Mean of sacred geometry. It was named after a bishop of Bourges at the time of the Merovingian king, Dagobert II, and his feast day is 17 January – a date that recurs in the Rennes-le-Château and Priory of Sion mysteries. Much of J.K. Huysmans' satanic novel *Là-Bas* is set in Saint Sulpice, and the seminary attached to it was notorious for unorthodoxy (to say the least) in the late nineteenth century. It also served as the headquarters for the mysterious seventeenth-century secret society called the Compagnie du Saint-Sacrement, which, it has been proposed, was a front for the Priory of Sion.

During Saunière's stay in Paris – which was either in the summer of 1891 or the spring of 1892 – Hoffet introduced him into the flourishing occult society that was centred on Emma Calvé, and which included such characters as Joséphin Péladan, Stanislas de Guaïta, Jules Bois and Papus (Gérard Encausse). There is a persistent rumour that Saunière and Emma became lovers.

Saunière is said to have visited the church of Saint Sulpice and studied certain paintings there, and – according to the usual story – bought reproductions of specific paintings in the Louvre (which will be discussed later). On his return to Rennes-le-Château, he began the decoration of his church and the building of his *domaine*.

The visit to Paris is a crucial part of the Saunière mystery, and has been the subject of intense scrutiny by researchers ever since. There is no direct evidence that it ever actually happened. A portrait photograph of Saunière bearing the name of a Paris studio, long taken as proof of the trip, was recently shown to be of his younger brother Alfred (also a priest)[4]. It has also been claimed that Saunière's signature appears in the Mass book at Saint Sulpice, but this has never been confirmed. The writer Gérard de Sède[5], who owns some of Émile Hoffet's papers, claims that they contain a note of a meeting with Saunière in Paris (undated, unfortunately), but as far as we know there is no independent corroboration of this. As with much of this story, it rests on the memories and testimony of the villagers and others. For example, Claire Captier, née Corbu, daughter of the man who bought Saunière's *domaine* from Marie Dénarnaud in 1946 – the latter lived with the Corbus until her death in 1953 – is emphatic that the Paris trip *did* happen[6].

Whatever Saunière had found, it appeared to have made him extremely wealthy very quickly. When he had first taken up his post his stipend was 75 francs a month. Yet between 1896 and his death in 1917 he spent a vast sum – perhaps not the 23 million francs that some claim, but certainly as much as 160,000 francs a month. He had bank accounts in Paris, Perpignan, Toulouse and Budapest and invested heavily in stocks and shares and securities – not the customary financial standing of a country priest. It has been said that he made his money from trafficking in Masses (charging to say Masses that were believed to let the payee off a number of years in purgatory), but although he certainly did so, as French historian René Descadeillas – usually regarded as the leading debunker of the Saunière affair – says, this could not have 'produced sufficient sums to enable him to erect such constructions and at the same time live so grandly. Therefore there was something else.'[7] In any case, one might ask why so many people should have wanted to have Masses said by Saunière – an insignificant rural priest from a remote parish.

He and Marie attracted criticism because of their lavish lifestyle: she always dressed in the latest Paris fashions (it is said that this was the reason for her nickname of 'la Madonne', the Madonna) and they entertained on a scale that was completely disproportionate to their supposed income or social status. Moreover, the rich and famous made the incredibly difficult journey to Rennes-le-Château to stay with them. (For some strange reason, however, Saunière only entertained in the Villa Bethania, preferring to live in the run-down presbytery

247

attached to the church.) Their visitors included a Habsburg prince – who rejoiced in the curiously evocative name of *Johann Salvator* von Habsburg – a government minister and Emma Calvé.

But it was not just the lavish scale of their hospitality that invited hostility: Saunière and Marie took to digging at night in the graveyard. Although on the whole what they were up to is a matter for speculation, it is certain that they erased the inscriptions on the headstone and the slab that covered the grave of the evocatively named Marie de Nègre d'Ables, a noblewoman of the area who died on 17 January 1781, presumably in order to destroy the information it contained. Little did they realize that all this effort was for nothing – a copy of the inscription already existed thanks to visiting members of a local antiquarian society. As we will see, however, Saunière's eagerness to destroy the inscription is of great significance to our investigation.

At around the time of the alleged Paris trip, Saunière also found the 'Knight's Stone' face down near the altar, a carved slab dating from Visigothic times, which depicted a knight on a horse with a child. He seemed to have found something of great importance under it – perhaps another cache of documents or artefacts, or the entrance to a crypt. No-one knows for sure as Saunière had the floor replaced, but his diary records the enigmatic entry for 21 September 1891: 'Letter from Granès. Discovery of a tomb. It rained.'

Saunière's nocturnal excavations caused a local scandal, but it was his trafficking in Masses that eventually provoked the wrath of the Church authorities to the extent that he was stripped of his priestly office. He was even assigned to another parish, but refused point-blank to comply, and stoutly lived on in Rennes-le-Château with Marie. When the Church sent another priest to the village, Saunière celebrated Mass in the Villa Bethania unofficially for the villagers, who remained loyal to him.

Of all the mysteries surrounding Saunière, perhaps one of the most enduring is that which followed his death. He fell ill on 17 January 1917: he died five days later and his body was sat upright in a chair in the open air, on the ramparts of the terrace of his *domaine*, while the villagers – and others who had already made much lengthier journeys – filed past, plucking red pom-poms from his cloak. His last confession was heard by the priest from nearby Espéraza, and whatever was said had such a profound effect on him that, as René Descadeillas says '. . . from that day, the old priest was no longer the same man; he had manifestly received a shock.'[8]

After his death, the faithful Marie Dénarnaud lived on in the Villa Bethania. Saunière who, as a priest, could not own anything, had bought all the land in her name. She became increasingly reclusive and gained a reputation for irascibility, resisting the many attempts to buy the increasingly derelict *domaine* from her. But finally, in 1946, on the feast day of Mary Magdalene[9], she sold it to Noël Corbu, a businessman, on the understanding that she could live out the remainder of her life there.

Corbu's daughter Claire Captier recalled living there as a child. According to her, Marie visited Saunière's grave every day – and in the middle of every night. Marie told the young Claire of an extraordinary phenomenon that attended some of those visits. She would say, 'Tonight I was followed by the will-o'-the-wisps of the cemetery.' Asked if she was afraid, she replied, 'I am used to it . . . I walk slowly, they follow me . . . when I stop, they stop as well, and when I close the cemetery gate, they always disappear.'[10]

Claire Captier[11] also recalls that Marie said, 'With what Monsieur the Curé has left, one could feed all of Rennes for a hundred years and it would still remain.' And when asked why, if so much money had been left to her, she still lived like a pauper, she replied, 'I cannot touch it.' And in 1949, when she knew that Corbu's business was in difficulties, she said, 'Do not worry so much, my good Noël . . . one day I will tell you a secret that will make you a rich man . . . very rich!' Unfortunately, in the months leading up to her death from a stroke in January 1953, she became senile, and the secret died with her.

What was the Saunière story all about? Certainly it seems as if he was being paid by some outside agency to stay in the village (even when rich and no longer the parish priest he chose to remain), although the payments may have been erratic. His wealth did not consist of one large lump sum, as some have suggested, because his cash flow was variable. He often went through lean patches, only to recover his lavish lifestyle once again in a matter of months. At the time of his death he was committed to ambitious new projects that would have cost at least eight million francs[12] – to build a decent road up to the village for a motor car he intended to buy, lay water to all the houses and create an outside baptismal pool, and erect a seventy-metre tower from which he planned to call his parishioners to prayer.

Strong candidates for the role of paymaster are the monarchists, in which case there is a different mystery. What possible service could Saunière have provided for them that resulted in payments on such a grand scale? Could his obsession with the Magdalene somehow suggest the underlying reason for their lavish rewards? Certainly there was more to this wealth than an involvement with a political plot. And his few surviving memoirs, in the words of Gérard de Sède, reveal:

a curious devotion to the *Bona Dea*, to the eternal feminine principle which, in the mouth of Bérenger [Saunière], seems to transcend belief and faiths.[13]

Once again we find secrets surrounding the Feminine Principle as embodied in Mary Magdalene . . . and a distinct connection with the Priory of Sion, who claim to venerate Black Madonnas and Isis. And, as we shall see, the area around Rennes-le-Château contains many more clues to the continuation of this form of goddess worship.

* * *

What of the famous parchments allegedly found by Saunière (according to Priory of Sion sources)? They are said to have consisted of two genealogies concerning the survival of the Merovingian dynasty and two consisting of extracts from the Gospels in which certain letters, which are marked out, yielded coded messages. The parchments themselves have never seen the light of day, but alleged copies of the coded texts have been widely published, their first appearance being in 1967 in *L'Or de Rennes* by Gérard de Sède and his wife Sophie. (In fact, although he is not credited as such, Pierre Plantard de Saint-Clair has stated that he was the co-author of this book[14].)

These texts have been the subject of thousands of words and much ongoing speculation. From the New Testament account of Jesus and the disciples in the cornfield on the Sabbath, the marked letters, when simply read in order, spell out:

A DAGOBERT II ROI ET A SION EST CE TRESOR ET IL EST LA MORT
(TO/FOR DAGOBERT II KING AND TO/FOR SION IS THIS TREASURE
AND IT IS DEATH/HE IS THERE DEAD)

The other text overtly describes Jesus' anointing by Mary of Bethany, and the decoded version is usually given as:

BERGERE PAS DE TENTATION QUE POUSSIN TENIERS GARDENT LA
CLEF PAX 681 PAR LA CROIX ET CE CHEVAL DE DIEU J'ACHEVE CE
DAEMON DE GARDIEN A MIDI POMMES BLEUE
(SHEPHERDESS NO TEMPTATION THAT POUSSIN TENIERS HOLD
THE KEY PEACE 681 BY THE CROSS AND THIS HORSE OF GOD I
COMPLETE [or KILL] THIS GUARDIAN DEMON AT MIDDAY [or IN
THE SOUTH] BLUE APPLES)

The deciphering of this code was far more complex than the first. By reading the marked letters in this case you get 'REX MUNDI' (Latin for 'King of the World' – a Gnostic term for the god of this earth, which was used by the Cathars), but 140 extraneous letters have been added as well, making the

251

decoding an immensely tortuous process to get the 'Shepherdess no temptation' message[15]. (Interestingly, the system used had been devised by the French alchemist Blaise de Vignère, who was secretary to Lorenzo de Medici.) The final message is a perfect anagram of the inscription on Marie de Nègre's tombstone (which is discussed in the next chapter).

Although there is little doubt that the decoding of the message is accurate, there have been many ingenious – and often highly imaginative – attempts to *explain* or make sense of it. None of these has been completely satisfactory. (The most recent, by Andrews and Schellenberger, is discussed in Appendix II.)

The problem with these parchments is that Philippe de Chérisey, an associate of Pierre Plantard de Saint-Clair (and probably his successor as Grand Master of the Priory of Sion in 1984), later admitted that he had fabricated them in 1956[16]. (When confronted with this by the authors of *The Holy Blood and the Holy Grail* in 1979, Plantard de Saint-Clair claimed that de Chérisey had simply copied them, but this is not entirely convincing[17].) Whichever way one looks at the parchments, it has to be admitted that they are hugely successful as classic time-wasting devices, and are far too unreliable to provide major guidelines for an investigation into the Saunière story.

But if the priest had not found parchments, perhaps he did find treasure of some sort – as many people firmly believe. Certainly he found a small cache of old coins and jewellery in the church, but as the area as a whole is rich in archaeological finds, such a discovery would hardly have excited the interest that has surrounded the Saunière story. Many people believe that he found a veritable Aladdin's cave of sumptuous treasure, so much that even he and his glamorous friends failed to squander it, and that some of it is still there for the enterprising seeker to find. It has been suggested that the elaborate symbolism in the church, together with the various coded messages such as the 'Blue Apples' parchment, are intended to provide the enterprising seeker with clues as to where the rest of the treasure might be found.

Romantic though this notion may be, it is nonsense. First, this scenario is unlikely to explain his recurring cash flow problems; secondly, he created the so-called treasure maps – the church symbolism – which is not a very intelligent thing to do if he was intent on keeping the money for himself. Lastly, if the church is essentially one large treasure map then the symbolism used is bizarre and esoteric in the extreme. If he wanted to keep the money for himself he would hardly have designed a treasure map for public consumption (no matter how arcane), and if he wanted only certain people to find it then why didn't he just tell them? And his finding of treasure would hardly explain why rich and influential people wanted to visit him in his remote hilltop parish.

Given all the evidence, it seems that Saunière was being paid by someone for something – some service that involved his staying in Rennes-le-Château, where he insisted on living even when ordered to move away. His activities reveal that he was definitely looking for something: his nocturnal excavations in the churchyard, his lengthy tours of the immediate neighbourhood, and even lengthier trips to places further afield, which lasted several days at a time. But it was so important that he was thought to be still at Rennes-le-Château that during his absences Marie Dénarnaud regularly sent out prepared letters in reply to correspondence received, implying that he was simply too busy to respond personally at that time. (Some of these stock replies were found in his papers after his death.)

A new addition to the Saunière story emerged in 1995, when esotericist André Douzet produced a *maquette*, or plaster model, representing a landscape in relief, which Saunière had allegedly commissioned just before his death[18]. It shows hills and valleys and what appear to be roads or rivers running through them. There is a single, square building on one of the hillsides. Ostensibly, it depicts the area around Jerusalem, as biblical sites such as the Garden of Gethsemane and Golgotha are indicated. However, the landscape of the *maquette* does not in any way match that of Jerusalem: perhaps it really shows the area around Rennes-le-Château. Could Saunière have envisaged turning his homeland into the New Jerusalem?[19]

It is possible to spend an entire lifetime studying the possibilities of the Rennes-le-Château mystery: indeed, perhaps that is its function – to be a glorified red herring. For while it is undoubtedly of significance, it draws attention away from the equally suggestive involvement of others in the surrounding area.

Other priests in the neighbouring parishes were implicated in the affair, including Saunière's superior, Félix-Arsène Billard, the Bishop of Carcassonne. He allegedly sent Saunière to Paris and turned a blind eye to his eccentric and scandalous behaviour. (It was on Billard's death in 1902 and the appointment of his successor that Saunière was prosecuted.) And Billard himself was involved in some dubious financial dealings[20].

The best known of this coterie of priests around Saunière is the Abbé Henri Boudet (1837–1915), who had been priest of Rennes-les-Bains since 1872. A wise, scholarly and reserved man – temperamentally the very opposite of Saunière – he was also engaged in strange activities. In 1886 he published a bizarre book, *Le vraie langue celtique et le cromleck de Rennes-les-Bains* (*The True Celtic Language and the Cromlech of Rennes-les-Bains*), which has perplexed researchers ever since. Ostensibly the book deals with two subjects: a perverse theory that many ancient languages – Celtic, Hebrew and so on – were derived from Anglo-Saxon, including often hilarious examples of how place-names in the vicinity of Rennes-les-Bains came from English roots; and a description of various megalithic monuments in the area. Boudet was a respected local historian and antiquarian, and the theories he propounded are so unlikely that many have concluded that they must conceal a deeper, secret message – a literary counterpart of the decor of Saunière's church. Some have even suggested that the two complement each other, and that when put together they encode directions to the 'treasure'. If so, no-one has come up with a satisfactory deciphering, and Boudet's book is as puzzling today as it was when it was first published. His other activities, however, also run parallel to Saunière's, as he is known to have altered inscriptions on gravestones in his churchyard and moved landmarks in the area.

Some have seen Boudet as the real mastermind behind Saunière's building work, and there have been suggestions, such as that of Pierre Plantard de Saint-Clair – so far unsubstantiated – that Boudet was Saunière's 'paymaster'[21]. But Boudet is also significant to another major player in this complex mystery: Plantard de Saint-Clair himself wrote the preface to a 1978 facsimile edition of *Le vrai langue celtique . . .* and owns land close to Rennes-les-Bains. One can also see in the graveyard of Boudet's old church a marker indicating the plot that Plantard de Saint-Clair has reserved for himself.

Another clerical contemporary of Saunière's was the Abbé Antoine Gélis, who was parish priest of the village of Coustassa, which lies across the valley of the River Sals from Rennes-le-Château. On 1 November 1897 the elderly Gélis (then aged seventy) was found savagely murdered, having died from repeated and vicious blows to the head, apparently delivered by an assailant whom he had let into his presbytery and with whom he was chatting. Gélis was a friend of Saunière's – the latter records a meeting with him and several others in his diary of 29 September 1891, just eight days after the entry concerning the 'discovery of a tomb'. In the period before his murder, Gélis was apparently living in fear, keeping his door locked and seeing only his niece, who brought him his meals. And he had recently come into a great deal of money – some 14,000 francs – that nobody could account for. He had hidden it in his house and church, and papers were found that revealed the hiding places. Yet virtually all the money was still there after his murder. The murderer – who was never caught – had searched the house, but had left nearly 800 francs lying about. Stranger still, he had ritualistically laid out the body, crossing the arms across the chest, and leaving a piece of paper with the words *'viva Angelina'* written on it.

255

No motive was ever discerned behind this crime.

There are a couple of particularly strange elements interwoven in the Gélis murder. His gravestone, in the churchyard at Coustassa, has been positioned – alone of all the graves – so that it faces Rennes-le-Château, which is clearly visible on the hillside opposite. The grave also bears a rose-cross insignia. And, although this brutal murder of an elderly and fragile priest shocked the local populace, the diocese seemed to have wanted the matter forgotten as swiftly as possible. When Gérard de Sède tried to investigate it in the early 1960s, he found no record of the murder in the diocesan archives at Carcassonne. It was not until 1975 that two lawyers reconstructed the story from local police and court records.[22]

It has even been suggested that Saunière was responsible for the Gélis murder, but this is pure speculation. It does seem, however, that something sinister was going on that involved local priests beyond the confines of Rennes-le-Château.

Undoubtedly the village of Rennes-le-Château is important in itself, but perhaps too much emphasis has been placed on it, for the whole region around it is also steeped in mystery. Most researchers recognize the fact that there are other, equally compelling and strange sites nearby, but tend to see them merely as a backdrop for the Saunière story. However, if he made a discovery, there are many places where he could have made it. Apart from his several lengthy absences from the village, sometimes for days or even weeks, he was also known to take long walks in the immediate vicinity. (And his enthusiastic hunting and fishing excursions may well have been a cover for some other activity.)

The *Dossiers secrets* baldly state that Saunière had been working for the Priory of Sion, but is there any evidence for its influence in the surrounding area? We have seen that Pierre Plantard de Saint-Clair owns land close to Rennes-les-Bains and has bought a plot in the graveyard there, but are the organization's apparent preoccupations actually reflected in the area?

Given the extraordinary cross-culture of secret societies in the Languedoc it would be surprising if they were not. In fact, a study of the area close to Rennes-le-Château yields many clues not only about the Priory, but also about a broader underground tradition – one that we had suspected might exist. We were to find that what might be called the Great European Heresy – the extreme veneration, even the covert worship, of Mary Magdalene and of John the Baptist – is well represented here.

There is a remarkable proliferation of churches dedicated to the Baptist in this region. They are often found in clusters – for example, there are three 'John' churches in the small area of Belvèze-du-Razès. (Interestingly, a large part of this area is called *La Magdalene*.)

It is also interesting that the current 'Magdalene' church in Rennes-le-Château was once merely the chapel of the château, while another church graced the village – which was dedicated to John the Baptist[23]. This was destroyed in the fourteenth century when Rennes-le-Château was captured by the troops of a Spanish nobleman, apparently being demolished stone by stone in the belief that some kind of treasure was hidden inside[24].

An unexplained volte-face took place in nearby Arques, when the original St John the Baptist Church was rededicated to St Anne. This is particularly odd because it still houses a relic of the Baptist.

Arques and Couiza – where there is another 'John' church – was owned by the de Joyeuse family until 1646, when Henriette-Catherine de Joyeuse sold all her land in the Languedoc to the French monarchy. Interestingly, she was the widow of Charles, Duke of Guise, who had been tutored by Robert Fludd – who had been specially brought from England to do the job[25].

Either in Couiza or in Arques there was once a Black Madonna, known as Notre-Dame de la Paix, which was taken to Paris in 1576 by the de Joyeuse family, where it can still be seen in the church of the Sisters of the Sacred Heart (in the

Twelfth arrondisement)[26]. Strangely, Saunière corresponded with the superior of this order, to whom he was clearly someone special. A letter to him from Sister Augustine Marie, Secretary of the Order, dated 5 February 1903[27], asks him to say Masses specifically in honour of their Black Madonna, offers to sell him a statue of the Petit Jésus de Prague (which can still be seen in the Villa Bethania) – and, somewhat mysteriously, thanks him 'for the devotion that you show to our kind King'. This could refer to some pretender to the French throne or to Jesus, although, as we shall see, there was another 'King' who was honoured by heterodox groups. Yet there is a suggestion of a different, perhaps coded, meaning in Sister Augustine Marie's words and the curious implication that there is something special about the parish (and parishioners) of Rennes-le-Château.

The de Joyeuse family also built the John the Baptist Church in Arques, which was constructed from the ruins of the ancient château that had been destroyed by Simon de Montfort's men. Indeed, the present bell tower and main wall were actually part of the original château. As we have seen, the church was once dedicated to John the Baptist but is now dedicated to St Anne – although even the mayor of Arques could not tell us why the change had been made.

His predecessor in the 1930s and 40s was Déodat Roché, a great student of the esoteric history of the area who was behind one of the more earnest attempts to re-establish a Cathar Church in the area[28]. One of Roché's uncles was Saunière's doctor, and another was his notary.

Midway between Rennes-le-Château and Limoux is the thermal spa town of Alet-les-Bains. Formerly the site of the local bishopric (before it moved to Carcassonne), Alet was, in the Middle Ages, a renowned alchemical centre. Nostradamus' family came from this town, and it is possible that the famous seer himself lived there for a while. The town has Templar connections, going back to the very earliest years of the Order – several important acts granting them land were signed there in the 1130s – and Templar symbols can be seen carved on the timbers of some of the picturesque medieval houses to this day; indeed, the town's coat of arms features a Templar cross. The imposing church, St Andrew's, has a curious connection with that Order. Writer and researcher Franck Marie[29] has demonstrated that (like Rosslyn Chapel) its design is based on the geometry of the Templar cross – yet the church was built in the late fourteenth century, *after the suppression of the Order*. The building is also notable for windows that bear the sign of the six-pointed star, the Star of David. Apart from its obvious Jewish associations (which are, to say the least, extremely unusual in a medieval Christian church), the symbol also has traditional magical connotations – symbolizing the union of male and female principles.

The main street of Alet-les-Bains is the Avenue Nicolas Pavillon, named after its most famous bishop (whose incumbency lasted from 1637 to 1677). He is a significant figure who was involved in events connected to the Priory of Sion. Pavillon, together with two other clerics, the famous St Vincent de Paul and Jean-Jacques Olier (the builder of St Sulpice), were the driving force behind the Compagnie du Saint-Sacrement, which was also known among its members as 'the Cabal of the Devout'. Ostensibly a charitable organization, it is now recognized by historians as having been a politico-religious secret society that manipulated prominent leaders of the time and even had influence over the monarch. So well did the Compagnie hide its true motives that historians still cannot agree on exactly what they were – at times it appears to be fiercely mainstream Catholic, but at others thoroughly heretical. It has been argued that it was, in fact, a front for the Priory of Sion[30]. As we have seen, its headquarters were at the seminary of St Sulpice in Paris.

One of these conspirators, the mysterious St Vincent de Paul (*c.*1580–1660) – who claimed, bizarrely, to have been schooled in alchemy – is honoured at another site that ranks as one of the most enigmatic in the Languedoc. This is the basilica of Notre-Dame de Marceille, which lies to the north of Limoux, just outside the town. A statue of St Vincent stands in its grounds, to mark the fact that he founded the Order of the Lazarist Fathers, who, since 1876, have been in charge of the basilica. (Significantly, the Lazarist Father from Notre-Dame de Marceille was prominent among those invited to Saunière's ceremonies to open various parts of his *domaine*.)

This site has many provocative links with the 'heresies' we were investigating[31]. For a start, despite the difference in spelling, this 'Marceille' (the derivation of which is unknown) evokes the Magdalene through the connection with 'Marseilles'. The basilica was built on the site of an ancient pagan sanctuary, centred on a spring that is reputed to have healing properties, particularly for the eyes. The church takes its name from an eleventh-century Black Madonna that is still on display inside, and with which many miracles have been associated. Perhaps, with that background, it should be no surprise to discover that the site formerly belonged to the Templars. For centuries it was a centre for pilgrims.

Over the years, for some reason, there have always been struggles between various religious bodies for the control of this site. It originally belonged to the nearby Benedictine abbey of St Hilaire, which during the Albigensian Crusade attracted hostile comment because of its policy of neutrality towards the Cathars. (The entire population of Limoux was excommunicated at one point for sheltering them.) In the thirteenth century the struggle was among the Archbishop of Narbonne, the Benedictine Order and the Dominicans. Later the king had to intervene in a dispute over ownership of the site among the Archbishop, the Lord of Limoux and Guillaume de Voisins, Lord of Rennes-le-Château. On 14 March 1344 (the hundredth anniversary of the mysterious Cathar ceremony on Montségur the night before they gave themselves up to the flames) Pope Clement VI gave the church to the College of Narbonne in Paris, in whose possession it stayed until the mid-seventeenth century, when it passed to the Bishop of Alet-les-Bains. (Interestingly, the main source of income for the College of Narbonne was revenue from the church of Mary Magdalene in Azille, in the Aude.[32]) During the

Revolution the church and lands were sold, but the Black Madonna was hidden by a Priory of the Order of the Blue Penitents, a curious group who have links with the Free-masons of the Rectified Scottish Rite and the Chefdebien family – who, as we shall see, are significant players in this drama[33]. The church was restored as a place of worship in 1795.

Yet another dispute took place during Saunière's time, and involved his superior, Monseigneur Billard, Bishop of Carcassonne. The site was then owned by several proprietors, but through a series of shrewd – and not always ethical – moves, he employed the services of a banker as 'front man' to buy up all the shares. Interestingly, the sale took place on 17 January 1893 (although Billard somehow got hold of the Black Madonna, which was kept in Limoux for a while). Within four months, however, the new owner had sold the land back to the bishopric and Billard had the sole control that he wanted.

In 1912 Pope Pius X decreed that the church should be elevated to the status of a basilica, a rare honour and one that is completely inexplicable for such a relatively humble site. The status of basilica is usually only granted to churches of special significance – as in the case of St Maximin's in Provence, which houses the (alleged) relics of Mary Magdalene.

The area around Notre-Dame de Marceille is also notable for having been, until very recently, a place of particular interest to gypsies, who used to have a camp in the field between the church and the River Aude, which runs a few hundred metres to the west.

Notre-Dame de Marceille is specially mentioned in Abbé Boudet's enigmatic book, *Le vraie langue celtique* ... and it was this that brought the late Belgian researcher Jos Bertaulet, to the site[34]. He made an interesting discovery: on the former church lands, now in private hands, on the banks of the Aude there is an underground vault. This consists of two large chambers that date from either the late Roman or early

Visigoth period (third–fourth century). Around six metres in height, the first of these chambers has a shaft in the vaulted roof, but the only entrance is a narrow, one-metre-high tunnel, apparently of later construction and which was hidden inside a small, now ruined house (which seems to have been built expressly for this purpose). The function of the vault is unknown. There are speculations that it acted as a Visigoth burial chamber – although it is now empty – or as a place of initiation into some mystery school. Whatever its function, there is some evidence that it was in use until the early part of the twentieth century, although its existence was so secret that – as we were to discover in traumatic circumstances – even the priests of the basilica itself do not know of it. Perhaps it was this curious underground chamber that Billard was so keen to get his hands on.

During a research trip to France in the summer of 1995, Clive Prince visited the area with his brother Keith. We had been given information about the vault, including directions on how to find it – which proved invaluable as the entrance was overgrown with a formidable tangle of weeds – by Belgian researcher Filip Coppens. Jos Bertaulet had partially covered the skylight shaft of the first chamber with stone slabs to prevent accidents. There was, as we were to find out the hard way, a sheer drop of six metres beneath.

Keith, having descended into the first chamber using a climbing rope (any wooden stairs having long since rotted away), stumbled on the rubble littering the floor and fell heavily. Lying in the dark among the debris of the ages, at first it seemed as if Keith had broken his leg, and although it was later discovered that he had merely torn a ligament, he was unable to stand, let alone climb out of the vault. Clive had no option but to call the emergency services (who arrived in such numbers that it seemed Keith's predicament was the most exciting thing to happen for a long time in Limoux). After four hours a cave rescue team finally winched him out through the top shaft, and off to Carcassonne hospital. (One thing that did emerge from this episode was that when Clive went for help to the basilica, the officials there did not know that the vault existed.)

Sadly, because of this incident further investigation of the underground chambers was impossible. Perhaps a more serious consequence was the threat by the authorities to seal them up to prevent further accidents. It came as a relief to discover that this had not, in fact, happened, although the entrances had been covered over by the time we returned with Charles Bywaters in the spring of 1996. On this occasion, although we made no attempt to explore the main chambers, we did investigate the tunnel that led into them – and made a very significant discovery.

The tunnel appears to lead off from a blank wall, but, following a suggestion made by Filip Coppens, we examined this wall and found that it had once been a doorway. It had been deliberately sealed up – apparently relatively recently – and iron bars that were set into the stone may have served as handles. Judging by the local authorities' manifest ignorance of the existence of the vault, it could not have been they who sealed up this doorway. So who did so – and in any case, why seal up just one of the chambers in this way?

From the condition of the iron bars we estimated that the doorway had been sealed up roughly a hundred years ago, when Billard had sole control of the property. Did he hide something behind that bricked-up doorway? Perhaps he did, but his actions revealed a virtual desperation to own that particular place, which suggests he was not hiding, but *looking for* something. And whatever it was, there must still be at least some clues as to its nature in that damp and secret place, because he took pains to seal it up.

Shortly before his death from cancer in 1995, Jos Bertaulet claimed to have decoded Boudet's strange work *La vraie langue celtique* . . . and concluded that it told that a reliquary containing the head of 'a sacred King' was hidden in that underground vault. He further stated that Boudet linked this chamber with the Holy Grail legends. As we have seen, the theme of decapitated sacred kings runs through these stories (and Saunière was thanked for the devotion that he had shown to 'our kind King' by the Sisters of the Sacred Heart in Paris). And, significantly, Notre-Dame de Marceille was once owned by the Templars.

Further research depends on getting through the sealed doorway, and it seems unlikely – at the time of writing – that permission for that will be granted. But so many themes that are central to this investigation appear to come together in this place: the Black Madonnas, Templars, the Magdalene and the Grail legends. And the story of a severed head, in an area so replete with churches dedicated to him, surely evokes the figure of John the Baptist. Clearly, the region in general, and the site of Notre-Dame de Marceille in particular, still holds some profound secret.

It is difficult to see just how Saunière fits into this picture, but equally it appears that he had to be part of it. It is very likely that he found something of great significance, but it is impossible to say what it was with any certainty. However, our investigation has yielded several very telling clues from the kind of company he kept and the contacts he deliberately sought. In fact, the evidence we painstakingly pieced together concerning Saunière's true affiliations changes radically and for ever the standard image of a humble country priest who stumbled upon a treasure trove. Whatever he was really up to, its significance extends well beyond the confines of the curious village of Rennes-le-Château.

CHAPTER NINE

A Curious Treasure

Sceptics allege that there is no Rennes-le-Château mystery. To them, Saunière made his money simply by trafficking in Masses – or perhaps through some other shady deals – and the treasure story was cynically fabricated as a tourist attraction. As for the emphasis on the village and its myth in the *Dossiers secrets*, this, they say, was simply the Priory creating an air of mystery for itself. Besides, the story as we know it can be traced back only to 1956, when Noël Corbu taped an account with which to entertain guests at the Villa Bethania, which he had turned into a hotel-restaurant.

However, investigation shows that there *is* a mystery: indeed, the village was clearly a focus for esoteric researchers before that time. For example, in 1950 someone went there specifically to search for the fabled Cathar treasure, which he believed had been carried there from Montségur[1]. Perhaps this also explains the otherwise curious presence of German officers in the Villa Bethania, where they were billeted, during the Second World War. As many people are now aware, the Nazis had an obsession with occult and religious artefacts and spent many wartime months actually excavating at Montségur. It is rumoured that they were looking for the Holy Grail: certainly Otto Rahn, the Nazi archaeologist, had concentrated his efforts to find it in that area in the 1930s.

Noël Corbu is a major player in the Rennes-le-Château story. His role goes well beyond that of local hotelier and teller of tall tales – as can be seen from his part in the publication of the notorious coded parchments. As we have seen, these first appeared in a book by Gérard de Sède published in 1967, but later a colleague of Pierre Plantard de Saint-Clair and fellow member of the Priory of Sion, Philippe de Chérisey, confessed to having made them up.

In his most recent book on the Rennes-le-Château affair in 1988, Gérard de Sède states that he published the texts in good faith, having been given them by someone connected with Rennes-le-Château who claimed that they were copies that Saunière had given to the village's mayor before taking the originals to Paris. But de Sède is careful to avoid naming this 'someone'.[2]

However, his identity *is* given in the work of Jean Robin: he was Noël Corbu[3]. This is significant because if de Chérisey *did* forge the parchments, then Corbu could only have got them through contact with the Priory of Sion.

The more the circumstances in which Corbu came to own Saunière's *domaine* are investigated, the more intriguing they become. The usual story is that he happened on the village by chance during the Second World War, befriended the elderly Marie Dénarnaud, and decided that the villa would make a good home. But the real story appears to be that he had been interested in the Saunière story for some time, and in the early 1940s had gone out of his way to make friends with Marie to find out more.[4]

The plot thickens: the Church had, for some reason, always been keen to get its hands on Saunière's former property, but was equally eager not to be seen to do so. In fact, it made several attempts to persuade Marie to sell, but she refused. It appears that, through the mediation of a priest named Abbé Gau, it had persuaded Corbu to act on its behalf, presumably with the agreement that when Marie had sold the property to him, he would pass it over. Something seems to have gone wrong: perhaps Corbu reneged on the deal with the Church[5].

Later he applied directly to the Vatican for a grant, which was obviously deemed to be of unusual importance because the Vatican despatched the papal ambassador in person to Carcassonne to make enquiries of the diocese. And this ambassador was none other than Cardinal Roncalli – later to be Pope John XXIII (who, according to *The Holy Blood and the*

Holy Grail may have been a Priory man himself). The diocese apparently gave a negative report, and recommended that the grant be refused. But oddly, the Vatican gave it to him anyway.

Clearly, the Corbu connection makes a difference to an understanding of the Rennes-le-Château story: the mystery did not end with the death of Saunière. And as Corbu lived with Marie Dénarnaud for roughly seven years, it seems that he was in a good position to discover the secret. Whatever it was, he did not invent it. (Interestingly, it has been stated that Corbu, with Pierre Plantard de Saint-Clair, was a prime mover in the Priory's emergence into the public eye in the 1950s, but these rumours have never been substantiated.[6])

In the last chapter we saw that Saunière was just one individual involved in a wider mystery of the area – in events that involved large sums of money and that led some to resort to murder.

Undoubtedly the mystery also involved the groups in Paris with which Saunière was in contact. But it is interesting that many of the leading figures in the circles surrounding Emma Calvé were – like Emma herself – of Languedocian origin. It has been remarked that it was not, in fact, necessary for Saunière to have gone to Paris to meet most of these figures, as they often visited Toulouse, the 'cradle of their circle'[7]. Once again the trail leads back to people and groups whose names and affiliations are already familiar to this investigation.

These connections are exceptionally significant: not only do they shed some much-needed light on Saunière himself, they also show that the Rennes-le-Château story really does belong in this investigation. Tracing the priest back to the elaborate 'family tree' of occult groups we discussed earlier was to provide us with completely unexpected insights and revelations about the true nature of the wider Languedocian mystery, which to our knowledge has never been published in English before.

Strangely, given all the time and trouble that has been invested in trying to unravel the mystery, some of the answers are literally staring the investigator in the face. Clues to

Saunière's own particular affiliation can be found within the Rennes church itself. For while sceptics have suggested that the whole of the garish and peculiar decor could be put down either to Saunière's bad taste or to mental aberration, other research has indicated that there is more, rather than less, mystery to the 'terrible' place.

We suspected that the church and its immediate environs had been designed and laid out according to a very specific, arcane plan. Its major themes appear to have been inversion, mirror imaging and the balance of opposites: for example, the counterpart of the Tour Magdala is the glasshouse at the other end of the ramparts. Whereas the former is built of solid stone and has twenty-two steps going up to the top of the turret, the latter is of insubstantial material and its twenty-two steps descend into a room underneath. And the layout of Saunière's garden and the Calvary outside the church clearly conform to a preconceived – and presumably meaningful – geometrical pattern.

These observations of ours were confirmed by Alain Féral[8], a well-known artist who lives in the village – and who is the protégé of none other than Jean Cocteau. Féral, who has lived in Rennes since the early 1980s, has made the most detailed measurements of the plans for the church and surrounding buildings and has concluded that they reveal recurring themes. (It may not, of course, have been Saunière himself who was responsible for this – it may have been Henri Boudet, or the architect he brought in to do the work, or even the superiors of whatever group Saunière may have been involved with.)

Reinforcing our idea of the theme of mirror imaging, Féral points out that the Visigoth pillar (which formerly supported the altar), bears a carved cross, which Saunière placed upside down outside the church. He also cites the significance of the number twenty-two: apart from the steps of the tower and glasshouse, the number appears elsewhere in the *domaine*. Two flights of steps lead from the garden to the terrace, each of eleven steps. The two inscriptions in the church that have attracted the most attention – *Terribilis est locus iste* over the porch and *Par ce signe tu le vaincras* above the Holy Water stoup – are both made up of twenty-two letters. (The Latin phrase, which is more usually rendered as *Terribilis est hic locus*, and the extraneous *le* in the French phrase, seem to have been contrived to give each of them twenty-two letters.) There is a good reason for the emphasis on eleven and twenty-twos: these numbers are both 'Master numbers' in the occult. They are particularly significant in cabalistic studies.

Then there is the curiously heterodox pattern created by four objects, two inside and two outside the church: the confessional, which is directly facing the altar; the alter itself; the statue of Notre-Dame de Lourdes (with its inscription of 'Penitence! Penitence!') which is outside the church on the inverted Visigoth pillar and the 'Calvary' in the little garden Saunière painstakingly constructed himself. These four objects not only form a perfect square, but also carry a symbolic message. The confession box and the 'penitence' inscription both refer to *repentance* and they face, respectively, the altar and the Calvary, both symbolic of *salvation*. So each pairing appears to symbolize a spiritual journey, path or initiation – from repentance to forgiveness and then to salvation[9]. This is so carefully contrived that it *must* have had some message. Is Saunière trying to say that forgiveness and salvation can also be found outside the Church? And is there something else being hinted at here, something connected with figures who represent *repentance and penitence* – John the Baptist and Mary Magdalene?

The phrase 'Penitence! Penitence!' was that allegedly spoken by the Virgin Mary during the apparitions at La Salette. Of the two young visionaries, one was a shepherdess called Melanie Calvet, who was related to Emma Calvé. (Emma changed the spelling of her name when she became an opera singer.) For a time the La Salette vision threatened to rival that of Lourdes, but the Catholic Church decided it was just a hoax. The La Salette vision, however, was championed by the Johannite/Naündorff/Vintras movement (see Chapter Seven). Saunière also wrote approvingly of the La Salette visions[10].

As we have seen, the celebrated decorations in the church itself seem unlikely signposts to the location of some great treasure. If Saunière had found something that had made him rich, he was hardly likely to decorate his church with coded directions to the place where it used to be. It is more likely that the decorations are trying to *conceal* something, or at least make a statement that would only be obvious to another initiate. The best analogy – and in the circumstances probably a particularly apt one – is with a Masonic lodge room. To a non-initiate the various symbols employed in such a temple – the compasses, set-squares and other regalia – simply cannot be 'decoded' to give any coherent picture of what Masons are really about. One has to know the underlying philosophy, history and secrets that they symbolize to understand what they are doing there.

Many have discerned the symbols of various occult and secret societies – the Rosicrucians, the Knights Templar and the Freemasons – in the church's decor. The roses and cross on the tympanum clearly refer to the Rosicrucians. One of the most frequently cited anomalies in the Stations of the Cross is that of the Eighth Station, in which Jesus (effortlessly carrying his cross) meets a woman who is wearing what appears to be a widow's veil, and who has her arm around a little boy who is swathed in what seems to be some tartan material. This is taken to be a reference to the Freemasons, who call themselves 'Sons of the Widow'. (And perhaps there is significance in the fact that the Eighth House of astrology rules the mysteries of sex, death and rebirth – and the occult.) The black-and-white chessboard floor of the church and the blue ceiling with its gold stars above the altar recall the standard decorations of a Masonic lodge.

In our opinion, one of the most important elements of the whole church is the first the visitor sees on entering it. The recently vandalized demon in the doorway has always been called 'Asmodeus', he who traditionally guards buried treasure – although there is nothing to link this statue explicitly with the devil of that name. But we discussed this with

270

Robert Howells, who, as manager of one of London's most famous occult bookshops, has an extraordinarily extensive knowledge of esoteric symbolism, and whose own researches into the Rennes-le-Château mystery are scholarly, sane and far-reaching. He pointed out that there is an ancient Jewish legend about the building of the Temple of Solomon in which the king prevented various demons from interfering in the work in a number of different ways – one of them, Asmodeus, was 'bound' by making him carry water, the one element that could be used to control him[11]. Significantly, such legends have been incorporated into Masonic lore, and it is surely no coincidence to find this tableau in Saunière's church where Asmodeus is being controlled by carrying water – under the words 'By this sign you will conquer him'. And the decorations of the water stoup – angels, salamanders, water stoup and demon – represent the classic four elements of air, fire, water and earth that are essential to any occult work.

If the Asmodeus link is correct then it is very curious, for the tableau of the demon and that of Jesus' baptism are, as we have seen, clearly intended to be taken together. As the demon is being tamed by water, is the same thing happening when John pours water over Jesus? Then there is the peculiar reversal of the usual order of the two Greek letters *alpha* and *omega*, the first and the last, which are associated with Jesus. One would expect that alpha would be shown under John – the alleged forerunner – and omega under Jesus, the culmination. But here the reverse is true.

The prevalence of images suggesting the Temple of Solomon both inside and outside the church could refer either to the Masons or to the Knights Templar. The fact that the anomalous letters in the misquoted phrase *Par ce signe tu le vaincras*, which is found between the four angels and the demon are the thirteenth and fourteenth letters (the '*le*' is entirely superfluous and changes the meaning of the sentence) is thought by some to invoke the year 1314, when Jacques de Molay, head of the Templars, was burnt at the stake.

All of this symbolism has been painstakingly researched by

271

dozens of competent investigators over the years and the results have been almost as many diverse interpretations. Yet the answers may be very simple and perhaps disappointingly obvious. In fact, the symbolism of the Rennes-le-Château church has never been a mystery to those versed in Masonic lore. It is simply the indication of Saunière's particular affiliation, which was *Masonic*. This is confirmed by his choice of the sculptor for the Stations of the Cross and the other statues – one Giscard, who lived in Toulouse and whose bizarrely decorated house and studio can still be seen in the Avenue de la Colonne in that city. Giscard was a known Freemason, although admittedly he specialized in church decorations and other examples of his work can be found throughout the Languedoc. Interestingly, in the church of John the Baptist at Couiza, which lies at the foot of the hill below Rennes, one can find identical Stations of the Cross that had been supplied by Giscard – but these are monochrome versions and the anomalies so noticeable in Saunière's church are absent. It is almost as if the two churches, which are only a couple of kilometres apart, are intended to be compared in order to highlight the oddities in Saunière's version.

Jean Robin, in his book on Rennes-le-Château, states that Saunière's Masonic affiliations are confirmed by records in the archives of the diocese[12]. As we have seen, however, Freemasonry consists of a number of separate traditions. To which did Saunière belong? Here again, knowledgeable French researchers are in agreement: his affiliation was to the Rectified Scottish Rite, the branch of 'occult' Freemasonry that specifically claims descent from the Knights Templar.

Antoine Captier, the grandson of Saunière's bell-ringer, who acts as a focus for research into Rennes-le-Château and the Saunière affair, said to us: 'We know that he belonged to a Masonic lodge. He was sent to a place where there was something [significant]. He found certain things. But once again he wasn't alone. He didn't work alone.'[13] Later in our conversation he was more precise: Saunière's links were with the Rectified Scottish Rite; he added, however, 'It's not a secret.' This was also the conclusion reached by Gérard de Sède, who has researched the affair for thirty years. In fact, de Sède believes that some of the symbolism in the Ninth Station of the Cross directly evokes the grade of Chevalier Bienfaisant de la Cité Sainte – the euphemism for 'Templar'[14].

There is another indication of Saunière's possible affiliation. His choice of saintly statues in the church, Magdalenes apart, has been keenly debated by researchers: they are St Germaine, St Roch, two Antonys – of Padua and the Hermit – and, above the pulpit, St Luke. Alain Féral has pointed out that, if these are joined up with an 'M' shape on the floorplan of the church, their initials spell *graal*.[15]

With the rose-cross symbols on the tympanum and the prevalence of images of the Temple of Solomon, this points in the direction of the Ordre de la Rose-Croix, du Temple et du Graal – an Order founded in Toulouse around 1850 and later headed by none other than Joséphin Péladan, the godfather of the erotic occult groups of the day.

At the start of our investigation we had thought that the tendency for many other researchers to believe that all roads lead to Rennes-le-Château was mistaken. But in a sense they are right, although mostly for the wrong reasons. Certainly, it was astounding to uncover the intricate network of occult and Masonic groups that we discussed previously and trace them back to Saunière and his village. This is no coincidence: it was part of an elaborate and meticulous plan that was well established before he was born and which continues to this day.

We have seen that Saunière showed great interest in the tomb of Marie de Nègre d'Ables, Dame d'Hautpoul de Blanchefort, which had been erected by Antoine Bigou, parish priest of Rennes-le-Château, in 1791. She was the last of the direct line that had held the title to Rennes-le-Château, although other branches of the family continued. Marie de Nègre d'Ables had married the last Marquis de Blanchefort in 1732, the name coming from the nearby 'château' (although it appears to have been merely a tower of some kind) of Blanchefort, whose ruins can still be seen. Marie's own family, however, had some very interesting connections. We have already discussed the influential Rite of Memphis, which later merged with that of Misraïm. This was founded in 1838 by Jacques-Étienne Marconis *de Nègre*, who was indeed of the same family as the Marie of the Rennes-le-Château story[16]. And it was one of the Hautpouls – Jean-Marie-Alexandré – who was instrumental in the creation of the Rectified Scottish Rite grade of the Chevalier Bienfaisant de la Cité Sainte, the euphemism for *Templar*, in 1778[17]. Members of the same family were prominent in the La Sagesse Masonic lodge out of which grew the Ordre de la Rose-Croix, du Temple et du Graal[18]. Marie de Nègre's nephew and heir, Armand d'Hautpoul, was certainly connected with individuals linked to the Priory, including Charles Nodier, who was Grand Master from 1801 to 1844[19]. Armand d'Hautpoul was also tutor to the Count de Chambord, whose widow was so generous to Saunière.[20]

Marconis de Nègre's Rite of Memphis was closely connected with the society known as the Philadelphians, which was created by the Marquis de Chefdebien – a Rectified Scottish Rite Mason – in Narbonne in 1780[21]. This is another of the Templarist Masonic societies influenced by the ideas of the Baron von Hund: Chefdebien had been present at the famous Convent of Wilhelmsbad of 1782, which tried to settle once and for all the question of the Masons' Templar origins, and had spoken out on von Hund's side. The Philadelphians, like the Rite of Memphis, were primarily concerned with the acquisition of occult knowledge – both had grades solely dedicated to this task. The Philadelphians, moreover, aimed to try to untangle the complicated history of Freemasonry, with its proliferation of competing hierarchies, grades and rituals, in an attempt to discover its original purpose and secrets. They became a repository for information about Masonry and similar societies, which was either given to them in good faith or came to them as a result of infiltration. So it is significant that Saunière's brother Alfred (also a priest) was tutor to the

Chefdebien family – and that he was dismissed for stealing part of their archives.[22]

Alfred Saunière is undoubtedly a key figure in the strange events in which his elder – and more famous – brother was involved, and would repay further research. However, it is difficult to find out much about him, although it is known that he was the lover of the occultist, the Marquise du Bourg de Bozas, one of the visitors who had been entertained at the Villa Bethania. Alfred died an alcoholic in 1905, after being excommunicated.

After Alfred's death Saunière, in a letter to his bishop, referred to a local feeling that he 'should be expected to atone for the errors of my brother, the Abbé, who died too soon.'[23]

Once we had learned of Saunière's connections with Scottish Rite Freemasonry, much of the wider picture began to become clearer. And, far from being a personal obsession, Saunière's special reverence for the Magdalene truly emerged as being part of the Great European Heresy. The key to his affiliations lay in the people he knew.

In fact, it is possible to go further and connect Saunière with Pierre Plantard de Saint-Clair through just one man: Georges Monti[24]. Also known under the aliases Count Israël Monti and Marcus Vella, he is one of the most ruthless and powerful figures in twentieth-century secret societies – although by no means the best known. In the time-honoured way of such *magi*, he preferred to exercise his influence from the shadows rather than seek publicity in the manner of his associate Aleister Crowley. Throughout his life he rose through the ranks of many occult, magical and Masonic societies, often in order to infiltrate them on behalf of others. He was also a double agent for both French and German intelligence agencies; as in the case of John Dee and possibly also of Leonardo, the two worlds of espionage and the occult frequently go hand in hand. He led such a complex life that it is impossible to gauge where his true allegiance lay. In all probability it lay with himself and his love of intrigue and personal power.

Whatever Monti's true motives, he was amazingly

successful in his secret life, often holding high ranks in societies that were mutually hostile, either without one knowing about the others, or with each believing that he was infiltrating the other groups on its own behalf. For example, although some of the groups were, like Monti himself, markedly anti-Semitic, he also succeeded in holding high rank in B'nai B'rith, a Jewish quasi-Masonic society founded in the USA – even converting to Judaism to do so.

Monti was born in Toulouse in 1880, abandoned by his Italian parents and brought up by the Jesuits. From an early age he was interested in the shadowy world of occult secret societies. He travelled throughout much of Europe, spending time in Egypt and Algeria. Among the many societies he joined was the Holy Vehm, a German organization that specialized in political assassinations. He was also said to 'hold the keys' of Italian Freemasonry. Among his many acquaintances was Aleister Crowley – in fact, he has been described as Crowley's 'representative in France'[25], and was a member of the OTO when that flamboyant Englishman was Grand Master. Not surprisingly, Monti's dubious life eventually caught up with him and he was poisoned in Paris in October 1936.

He enters this investigation because his earliest role in the Parisian occult world was as secretary to Joséphin Péladan, and therefore an intimate of Emma Calvé's circle. As we have seen, Saunière was known to have connections with Péladan and his group, and to have known Emma Calvé, so he must have met Monti. Besides, the latter was a Languedocian, and often lived in Toulouse or elsewhere in the Midi.

In 1934 Monti founded the Ordre Alpha-Galates, of which Pierre Plantard de Saint-Clair became Grand Master in 1942, at the tender – but perhaps significant – age of twenty-two. And even though Plantard was only sixteen when Monti died, he knew him: Plantard de Saint-Clair's ex-wife, Anne Léa Hisler, in a 1960 article wrote unequivocally that he 'knew Count Georges Monti well'[26]. Monti may even have been his occult teacher and mentor.

So it seems that there was a clear link between Saunière and Plantard de Saint-Clair in the form of Georges Monti, perhaps representing a continuation of a certain underground tradition.

So what can one make of the Saunière story? To cut through all the obfuscations, myths and layers of guesswork is no small task, but it did seem that the priest had been *looking for something*, and that he was not working alone. The evidence points to the existence of a secret paymaster, very possibly linked to the influential occult societies of Paris and the Languedoc. Not only is this the most logical explanation, it is also the one that Saunière himself gave. When Billard's successor as the Bishop of Carcassonne demanded that Saunière account for his extravagant lifestyle, the priest spiritedly answered:

> I am not obliged ... to divulge the names of my donors ... To bring them into the open without permission would run the risk of bringing discord to certain families or households ... the members of whom gave without their husbands', childrens' or heirs' knowledge.[27]

Later, however, he said he would give the bishop the names of his donors – but only in the secrecy of the confessional. The wording of a supportive letter written to Saunière by a close friend in 1910 employs more suggestive language:

> You have had the money. It is not for anybody to penetrate the secret that you keep ... If someone has given you the money under natural secrecy, you are obliged to keep it, and nothing can release you from this secrecy ...[28]

Saunière's brother Alfred had also, it appears, been in on the secret. In reply to the authorities' questions about his extravagance, Saunière replied:

My brother being a preacher had numerous contacts. He served as intermediary for these generous souls.[29]

But although Rennes-le-Château may have been the start of Saunière's mysterious quest – which, it seems, was undertaken on behalf of these elusive others – it appears that the object of the search may have lain elsewhere.

Recently many researchers have found intriguing clues about Saunière's real interests and motivations scattered about his *domaine*. During one of our trips to the area in 1995 we took with us Lucien Morgan, a television presenter and Tantric authority, who was amazed to discover that the Tour Magdala and ramparts were built according to the ancient principles of a certain kind of sex rite. He believes that Saunière and his secret circle practised occult sexual rituals that were designed to facilitate clairvoyance, put them in contact with the gods – achieving in effect the old alchemists' Great Work – and secure material power and influence. Others have recognized indications of sex magic: British authors Lionel and Patricia Fanthorpe quote occult expert Bremna Agostini, who says that Saunière was carrying out a sex magic ritual known as the 'Convocation of Venus' in which Marie Dénarnaud and Emma Calvé participated.[30]

As far as this investigation is concerned, the really significant point in all of Saunière's building in Rennes-le-Château was his emphasis on Mary Magdalene. True, the village church was dedicated to her long before he was born, but even this was no mere coincidence, for it had been the chapel of the local ruling family – that of Marie de Nègre. And given their close association with the Rectified Scottish Rite, the dedication would seem to be significant. Saunière also named his library tower after her, and called his house after the one in which, according to one interpretation of New Testament events, she had lived with her brother Lazarus and her sister Martha. And out of all the decorations in the church it was the bas-relief in front of the altar, depicting the Magdalene, which he chose to paint himself.

278

We discovered that he had also had made a small bronze statue of the Magdalene, which he placed outside the grotto by the church. It was just under a metre high and weighed around eighty-five kilos, and was the mirror image of, but otherwise identical to, the bas-relief. This statue has long since disappeared, but André Galaup, a retired journalist from Limoux, has photographs of it.[31]

The legend '*Terribilis est locus iste*' is prominent above the church door. As Keith Prince pointed out to us, the phrase comes from Genesis 29:17 and tells how Jacob dreams of a ladder on which angels ascend and descend. On waking, he utters these words. He goes on to name the place Bethel, meaning House of God. But in the Old Testament Bethel becomes a rival power-centre to Jerusalem – giving the concept of Bethel the connotation of alternative or rival to the 'official' religious centre. In France, however, the implication is more obvious: one French dictionary actually defines 'Bethel' as a '*temple of a dissident sect*'[32]. Could this be what Saunière was trying to communicate? Interestingly, the *Dossiers secrets* claim that Saunière, in his latter years, planned to set up 'a new religion' and mount a crusade throughout the area. The final building work planned for his *domaine* – the tall tower and the outside baptismal pool – was part of this ambition.[33]

We decided to concentrate on what Saunière had found on his arrival at Rennes-le-Château, and what may have inspired him in his search. Leaving aside the red herring of the parchments, we were struck by the apparent contradiction in Saunière's behaviour. Many people think he was trying to leave clues in the decoration of his church, yet he is also known to have carefully *destroyed* certain things he found there – specifically the inscriptions on two stones that had marked the grave of Marie de Nègre. He also moved them from the grave, which suggests that he wanted to obscure its exact location.

As we have seen, these stones – a headstone and a horizontal slab – were placed on Marie de Nègre's grave by the Abbé Antoine Bigou about a hundred years before Saunière arrived. But there was already an oddity involved: Bigou erected the stones in 1791 – ten years after the death of the woman supposedly in the grave – at the same time as he had the 'Knight's Stone' placed face down in the church. (The raising of this stone appears to have been an important step in Saunière's search.) There is yet another indicator that Saunière was in some way following in Bigou's footsteps: before becoming parish priest of Rennes, Bigou had served at the small mountain village of Le Clat, about twenty kilometres away. Saunière, too, had been priest at Le Clat immediately before coming to Rennes-le-Château. Could Saunière have been looking for something connected with Bigou and, therefore, with the d'Hautpoul or de Nègre families?

Bigou's work on the grave may have been prompted by events in France that took place between Marie's death and 1791 – the beginning of the terror of the French Revolution. The revolutionaries were hostile to the Catholic Church, and many relics, icons and decorations were destroyed or looted in this period. Interestingly, shortly after his work in Rennes-le-Château, Bigou, who was opposed to the Republic, fled across the border to Spain, where he died in 1793.

There was another oddity about Marie de Nègre's interment. The lords of Rennes, the d'Hautpoul family, were customarily placed in the family vault, which is said to be beneath the church. So why should Marie's burial have departed from this custom? We know that the crypt existed, as it is referred to in a parish register that covers the years 1694 to 1726 and which is on display in the museum. According to this the entrance to the crypt is within the church. However, the entrance is now lost, although it seems certain that Saunière discovered it; perhaps the documents he discovered told him where to look.

The account of the Saunière story recorded by the brothers Antoine and Marcel Captier and based on their family's memories[34] was that the priest had discovered the entrance to the crypt beneath the Knight's Stone, and that he had actually gone down into it. But he then hid the entrance again under the new floor of the church, presumably not wanting its whereabouts to be known. Antoine Bigou must have had the same preoccupation, because it was he who had placed the Knight's Stone face downwards in 1791, covering the entrance. Why should both priests, a century apart, have been so concerned that nobody else should enter the crypt of the lords of Rennes-le-Château?

There is a simple answer. If Saunière had gone into the vault and found the tomb of Marie de Nègre where it ought to have been in the first place, he would have realized immediately that something very odd was going on: *the woman had two graves*. But the second, the one in the graveyard, was put there by Bigou ten years after her death. Obviously, Marie was not buried in the graveyard – in which case, who or what was?

A reasonable hypothesis is that Bigou, presumably due to the upheavals of the Revolution of 1789 that threatened him personally, had hidden something in the Rennes-le-Château graveyard before fleeing to Spain. But what could it have been – another body, an object or documents of some kind? Perhaps it was something too difficult for Bigou to take with him to Spain, or perhaps it was something that really *belonged* in Rennes-le-Château. We may never know, but it seems that Saunière did, because he opened the grave up to look for it. And he had been keen that the message of the two gravestones should be lost – at least that of the horizontal slab, on which he obliterated the inscription. Could the message yield some clue as to what the grave had really contained?

The inscription that was on the headstone of Marie de Nègre's grave contains a great many mistakes, which cannot be merely the result of sloppy workmanship[35]. Words are misspelled, letters missed out, spaces either omitted or added where they are not needed. Out of the twenty-five words on the inscription, no fewer than eleven contain mistakes. Some seem fairly innocuous, but one in particular was so bad that it should have caused grave offence to the family. The final words should have read as the conventional REQUIESCAT IN PACE – 'rest in peace' – but they appear as REQUIES CATIN PACE. The French word *catin* is slang for 'whore'. This is reinforced by an error in her husband's family name: d'Hautpoul appears as DHAUPOUL. This may not change the meaning significantly, but it does successfully draw attention to the word. And *poule* (hen) is another slang term for a prostitute; in fact, *hautpoul* could mean 'high prostitute' . . .[36]

In the same way the name on the tombstone resonates with important themes in this research. It is even tempting to think that Marie de Nègre existed only as a name, the code for something quite astonishing. For Blanchefort, although certainly the name of a local landmark, means either 'white tower' or '*strong white*' – an alchemical term. And 'Marie de Nègre' evokes the Black Madonnas and their association with Mary Magdalene, which is reinforced by the *hautpoul* reference to 'high prostitution', whore wisdom. Once again, we find apparent connections that are evocative of sacred sexuality, and perhaps – in the context of rumours of 'treasure' – of the sexual aspects of the alchemical Great Work. And yet more significantly perhaps, there is another misspelling on the tombstone: D'ABLES is rendered as D'ARLES. If this is, as we suspect, a reference to the town of Arles in Provence, it may evoke the fact that it was an old centre for the cult of Isis. In any case, Arles is very close to Saintes-Maries-de-la-Mer.

The design of the second stone on Marie de Nègre's grave, the horizontal slab, is more contentious, as there are some discrepancies in the various published accounts of it[37]. In most versions this bears two main inscriptions: the phrase – in Latin but, curiously, inscribed in Greek characters – *Et in Arcadia ego*, and the four Latin words *Reddis Regis Cellis Arcis* across the stone. The meaning of the latter is not clear, and has been the subject of many different interpretations, but it seems to refer to a royal vault or tomb, perhaps connected with Rhedae and/or the village of Arques. (The word *Arcis* has many possible meanings, from words connected with the English 'arc', or words meaning 'enclosed' or 'within', or it could simply be an allusion to Arques, either its ancient name of Archis or a phonetic rendering of the modern name).

The *Et in Arcadia ego* motto is also found on the tomb in the painting *The Shepherds of Arcadia* by Nicolas Poussin (1593–1665), which so remarkably resembled one which seems always to have stood – in one form or another – by the road from Rennes-le-Château and Couiza to Arques. (The most recent version was dynamited in 1988 because the farmer on whose land it stood was no longer willing to tolerate hundreds of tourists trespassing. Unfortunately, this drastic measure was in vain: now the tourists arrive to take photographs of where the tomb *used* to be.)

Saunière is said to have brought back from his trip to Paris copies of certain paintings, one of which was Poussin's *The Shepherds of Arcadia*.[38] This painting, dating from around 1640, shows a group of three shepherds examining a tomb, watched by a woman who is usually taken to be a shepherdess. The tomb bears the Latin inscription *Et in Arcadia ego*, an oddly ungrammatical phrase that has been interpreted in several ways but is generally taken to represent a *memento mori*, a meditation on mortality: even in the paradisiacal land of Arcadia death is present. The motto has a close connection with the Priory of Sion story, and features on Pierre Plantard de Saint-Clair's coat of arms. It is also, as we have seen, said to have been incorporated into the decoration on the horizontal stone on the grave of Marie de Nègre. The theme of the painting was not invented by Poussin, the earliest known example of it being one by Giovanni Francesco Guercino, about twenty years before. However, the man who commissioned the Poussin version, Cardinal Rospigliosi, is also thought to have suggested the theme to Guercino. And the earliest known appearance of the phrase *Et in Arcadia ego* in art is in a sixteenth-century German engraving, entitled *The King of the New Sion dethroned after having inaugurated the Golden Age* ...[39]

While discussing Poussin it is interesting to note a letter that Abbé Louis Fouquet wrote from Rome to his brother Nicolas, Louis XIV's Superintendent of Finances, in April 1656:

[Poussin] and I have planned certain things that I will speak to you in detail about soon, [and] which will give you, through M. Poussin, advantages that kings would have great trouble in drawing from him, and that, after him, perhaps nobody in the centuries to come will ever recover; and what is more, this would be without great expense yet would turn a profit, and these things are so difficult to find that nothing on this earth now could have a better, nor perhaps equal, fortune.[40]

Significantly, it was Charles Fouquet, brother of Louis and Nicolas, who, as Bishop of Narbonne, later took sole control of Notre-Dame de Marceille for a period of fourteen years.[41]

The reason why the Poussin painting is of interest to Rennes researchers is that the landscape as seen in the painting appears to be very similar to that of the area around the site of the Arques tomb, and Rennes-le-Château itself can be seen in the distance. However, the landscape, if similar, is not identical, and this has been taken by some as proof that the resemblance is coincidental. But in our opinion Poussin's depiction of the countryside is close enough to the original to allow the possibility that he was trying to convey the area around Rennes.

The plot thickens, however: the Arques tomb is known to date only from the early years of the twentieth century. It was built in 1903 by a local factory owner, Jean Galibert, and subsequently sold to an American named Lawrence. There are, though, rumours that this tomb merely replaced an earlier version that had stood on the same spot, which in turn had replaced the one before. Our friend John Stephenson, who has lived in this area for many years, confirmed that the locals say there has 'always been a tomb on that spot'. So it is possible that Poussin really had simply painted what he had seen there. John Stephenson also told us that the connection with Poussin's painting had been known in the area for a long time, which certainly argues against the sceptics' idea that it was an invention of the 1950s or 60s. The place has always been regarded as significant.

It has also been claimed the *Arcadia* motto was only adopted by Plantard de Saint-Clair and the Priory of Sion in the twentieth century, as was its alleged link with the Poussin painting and the tomb of Marie de Nègre. But the phrase had been connected with the area well before Saunière's time. In 1832 one Auguste de Labouïse-Rochefort wrote a book entitled *Voyage à Rennes-les-Bains* which included references to a hidden treasure linked with Rennes-le-Château and Blanchefort. Labouïse-Rochefort wrote another book, *Les Amants, à Éléonore* (*The Lovers, to Eleonore*) which included the phrase on its title page.

The tomb is known locally as the 'Arques tomb', which, although more accurate than the phrase the 'Poussin tomb', is still not precisely true, for the village of Arques is three kilometres further east along the main road. Although the tomb is much nearer to the village of Serres, the word *Arques* is too close to that of *Arcadia* not to be exploited.

According to Deloux and Brétigny, in their *Rennes-le-Château: capitale secrète de l'histoire de France*, the slab on Marie de Nègre's tombstone was actually brought to her grave by the Abbé Bigou from an earlier version of the Arques tomb[42]. If true, this raises an intriguing possibility. Could Poussin simply have painted something he had actually seen – a tomb with the words *Et in Arcadia ego* on it?

John Stephenson told us an astounding local legend relating to the Arques tomb: that it was either the resting place of Mary Magdalene or acted as a marker or pointer in some way to it – the inscription on the Marie de Nègre slab actually had an arrow running down the centre. But, tantalizingly, the stone slab has been moved, so we no longer know in which direction the arrow originally pointed.

The evidence suggests that Saunière believed that Mary Magdalene's body was somewhere to be found; either it was in the actual vicinity of Rennes-le-Château, or the village provided some kind of clue to its whereabouts. What was concealed in Marie de Nègre's second tomb? Did the coded inscription that apparently referred to a 'high prostitute' really signify the Magdalene? (Perhaps the term could be read as 'High Priestess', thus linking the concept of sacred sexuality with ancient, rather than modern, occult practices.)

Saunière certainly seemed to be looking for something special and potent, something precious that was connected with his beloved Mary Magdalene – and what could be more precious than her actual bones? Of course this might simply have been a personal obsession on his part and he may have imagined that the relics were there to be found. On the other hand, as we have seen, Saunière was working for, and probably financed by, a larger, shadowy organization. Were they similarly deluded? Perhaps not. The evidence suggests that the priest was acting on inside information about a real object.

As our investigation proceeded, we became increasingly convinced of this Magdalene hypothesis, but soon discovered that – at least among British researchers into the subject – we were alone. So it was encouraging to find that French researchers were working along the same lines. To them as to us it was not inconceivable that Saunière and his mysterious backers were searching for *Mary Magdalene herself*.

During one of our trips to the area in spring 1995, Nicole Dawe kindly arranged a dinner party for us to meet Antoine and Claire Captier, together with Charles Bywaters. Antoine, grandson of the bell-ringer who found the wooden cylinder containing the documents that he gave to Saunière, has lived with the mystery all his life, as has Claire, who is the daughter of Noël Corbu.

Antoine was frank: he had no interest in stirring up yet more mystery. 'I won't tell you what I don't know,' being his way of opening the discussion[43]. He said he thought it unlikely that we would ask anything new, but was surprised when we asked him about Saunière's possible connection with the Magdalene cult – because it had been an angle that had been ignored until recently, but our interest in it strangely paralleled that of certain French researchers.

Antoine told us that Saunière *had* researched the Magdalene legend, having, for example, visited Aix-en-Provence and the surrounding area. This was emerging in a journal called *Cep d'Or de Pyla*, which is produced by André Douzet – the man who found the *maquette* discussed in the last chapter – who lives in Narbonne. Douzet and his circle are enthusiastic and knowledgeable researchers into the esoteric history of France. Antoine said that the next issue of the journal 'will be interesting to you . . . because you will find something deeper, concerning the Magdalene.'

Again thanks to Nicole, we later met André Douzet, who told us that he and some others, notably Antoine Bruzeau, had undertaken research specifically into Saunière's interest in the Magdalene – but it seemed as if the key to the mystery lay some distance away from Rennes-le-Château. André had not, initially, been drawn to the Saunière mystery, but arrived at it by a circuitous route: certain sites of interest to him in his home city of Lyons directed him there.

The connection goes back to Gérard de Roussillon – who, in the ninth century, had founded the abbey in Vézelay in Burgundy where, it was later claimed, he had taken Mary Magdalene's body. We recall (see Chapter Three) that this claim was later outdone by St Maximin in Provence, when the monks at Vézelay could not produce the relics. We also recall that this event prompted Charles II d'Anjou to undertake a feverish search for them, convinced that they were still somewhere in Provence.

Gérard de Roussillon was Count of Barcelona, Narbonne and Provence – a vast area. His family also owned estates in the Le Pilat region – now the Le Pilat National Park – to the south of Lyons. They were passionate devotees of the Magdalene, and the area was a centre for her cult. (A Sainte-Madeleine Chapel in the Le Pilat region held what were said to be the relics of Lazarus.)

In the thirteenth century the reigning count, Guillaume de Roussillon, died in the Crusades and his mourning widow Béatrix retreated to the hills of Le Pilat, where she founded a Carthusian monastery, Sainte-Croix-en-Jarez, in which she lived out the rest of her life. But thereafter the monastery seemed to have a strange association with Mary Magdalene.

Antoine Bruzeau argues that the family had possessed the true relics of Mary Magdalene, and that Béatrix had taken them to Sainte-Croix. (Or perhaps she had simply entrusted the abbey with the secret of their location.) He also suggests that the real site for the Magdalene's landing in France was not the Camargue, but the coast of Roussillon, at a place still called the *Mas de la Madeleine*. According to his theory, she had lived out her life not in Provence but in the Languedoc – around the area of Rennes-le-Château.[44]

For some reason the Roussillon family felt it was their duty not only to keep the relics but also to keep them secret. This is extremely odd at a time when relics were so lucrative, and suggests that they had motives other than the simple veneration of a New Testament saint. Perhaps it was something connected with the Magdalene's true role.

In the fourteenth century a curious mural was added to the abbey at Sainte-Croix, showing Jesus being crucified on *living wood*. This was later plastered over, but rediscovered in 1896 – shortly before Saunière personally painted the bas-relief on his altar, showing the Magdalene contemplating a cross made of still-growing wood.

Later, in the seventeenth century, one of the friars at Sainte-Croix, Dom Polycarpe de la Rivière, a renowned scholar, undertook renovations in the monastery and may have unearthed something. He was particularly interested in the Magdalene – he wrote a book about her that is, unfortunately, now lost, besides one on the area around Aix-en-Provence, St Maximin and Sainte Baume, *which the Vatican suppressed*. De la Rivière was also connected with Nicolas Poussin, and Bruzeau's research suggests that they were both part of a secret society known as the Société Angélique.[45]

In the hills of Le Pilat an ancient road climbs Mont Pilat to a chapel dedicated to Mary Magdalene. The road begins at the village of Malleval, whose church contains statues of St Anthony of Padua and Sainte Germaine that are identical to those at Rennes-le-Château. The trail passes a chapel dedi-

cated to Saint Antony the Hermit – another saint venerated in
Saunière's church (and whose feast day is 17 January). And in
the Magdalene Chapel is a tableau of the saint in her grotto that
is strikingly similar to the one at Rennes-le-Château. Bruzeau
points out that in the background of Saunière's altar piece
there is an arch and column: in Celtic the first is *pyla*, in Latin
the second is *pila* – phonetically pointing to the area of Le Pilat.
And the peaks shown on the horizon seem to be those of the
area around Mont Pilat.

It had always struck us as odd that, in his bas-relief,
Saunière should have left out Mary Magdalene's most characteristic piece of iconography – her jar of holy balm, or *sainte
baume* . . . Could this be his way of saying that her true relics
were not at St-Maximin-la-*Sainte-Baume* in Provence after all?

Certainly, judging by invoices for the hire of coach and
horses in the Lyons area in 1898 and 1899[46], it appears that
Saunière scoured the region of Le Pilat, looking for what was
left of his beloved Mary Magdalene.

The overriding question is why anyone should go to so
much trouble to find what would be, essentially, just a box of
bones. For although Catholics have always had a fondness for
saintly corpses, it must be remembered that many of those
who apparently sought the Magdalene's remains were either
occultists or *rebel* Catholics. Either way, they do not appear to
have been sentimental people and the age of relics as big business is long over – so why did they devote so much time and
trouble to this search?

Perhaps it was not simply a skeleton they were looking for:
the coffin or tomb may have been believed to hold some secret,
either something having to do with the body itself or something that was with it. Henry Lincoln, presumably with tongue
in cheek, suggested to the French press that this 'something'
might be the marriage certificate of Jesus and the Magdalene[47].
More seriously, the secret has to be something similar to this
– something evidential and unequivocal that, once made
public, would cause an enormous furore.

Given the interests of the specific groups we have been

investigating, it must be something *heretical*, the nature of which would prove profoundly unsettling to the established Church. But what could possibly pose such a threat? Why should something that – presumably – is roughly 2000 years old have any significant bearing on modern society?

CHAPTER TEN

Divining the Underground Stream

At this point in our investigations we again found ourselves confronting the apparent significance of Mary Magdalene to an underground, heretical network. This is where we had begun, with Leonardo's cunning and subliminal symbolism of the 'Lady M' in his *Last Supper*. Yet in the years that had elapsed since we first found ourselves drawn to the shadowy world of European heresy, we had covered a huge amount of ground, in all senses of the word. It was time to take stock: what had we discovered?

The 'Lady M', whom we took to be Mary Magdalene, was clearly of enormous importance to Leonardo, who, it is claimed, was Grand Master of the Priory of Sion. Certainly, our own encounters with members of today's Priory had reinforced our suspicion that she was highly significant to them. And the same applies to John the Baptist – a figure who dominated Leonardo's work and whom the Priory appears to venerate with special devotion.

Our many trips to the South of France revealed that there was some basis for taking the legends of Mary Magdalene living there seriously, but her links with the Black Madonna cult point to a *pagan* connection. Everything about the veneration of the Magdalene is highly charged sexually – something that is particularly evident in the association of her with the Old Testament erotic love poem, the Song of Songs.

But there is an apparent paradox. For on the one hand there is evidence that the Magdalene was Jesus' wife – or at least, his lover – but on the other she is persistently associated with pagan goddesses. This seems totally irrational – why on earth should the wife of the Son of God be linked in this way with such figures as Diana the Huntress and the Egyptian goddess of love and magic, Isis? This was a question that haunted our researches.

Throughout our investigation, individuals and groups, such as the Templars, St Bernard of Clairvaux and the Abbé Saunière, have persistently been found to revolve intimately around the central theme of the Feminine. Although to some of them this may have been merely a philosophical ideal, the very fact that it was given a recognizable female face points to a more specific devotion. She was, if not the Magdalene, then Isis, ancient Queen of Heaven and consort to the dying-and-rising god Osiris. Certainly, this chain of associations – Magdalene/Black Madonna/Isis – has always been what the Priory are about. To them a Black Madonna represented both the Magdalene and Isis simultaneously. Yet this is very odd, for the first is a Christian saint and the latter a pagan goddess: surely there is no feasible connection?

As we have seen, the Cathars appeared to hold unacceptable and heterodox views about the Magdalene: indeed, the entire town of Béziers was put to the sword because of this heresy. To them, she had been Jesus' concubine – an idea curiously echoing that of the Gnostic Gospels, which describe her as the woman whom Jesus frequently kissed on the mouth, and whom he loved above everyone else. The Cathars believed this to be true, albeit with the greatest reluctance, for their own version of Gnosticism regarded all sex and procreation as, at best, a necessary evil. This idea of the Magdalene's relationship with Jesus did not come from their Bogomil forerunners, but was actually current in the South of France – in a culture that sought to elevate the Feminine in all ways, as the blossoming of the troubadour tradition reveals. And, as we have seen, the 'Sister Catherine' tract reveals that the ideas about Mary Magdalene found in the Gnostic Gospels had somehow been transmitted to the fourteenth century.

Curiously, we discovered that those most apparently masculine of men, the Knights Templar – or at least their inner order – were also heavily committed to the elevation of the

Feminine. The intensity of their veneration for Black Madonnas was second to none, and their knightly quest for transcendental love was behind the great Holy Grail legends.

The Templars were hungry for knowledge, and their search for it was their main driving force. They seized knowledge wherever they found it: from the Arabs they took the principles of sacred geometry, and their apparent close contacts with the Cathars added an extra Gnostic gloss to their already heterodox religious ideas. From their very beginnings the interests of this order of knights were essentially occult: the unconvincing story of their origins as protectors of Christian pilgrims to the Holy Land if anything draws attention to the anomalies surrounding the Order.

The largest concentration of Templar properties in Europe was to be found in the Languedoc, that strange region in the south-west of France that appears to have acted like a magnet for many heretical groups. Catharism, at its height, became virtually the state religion of that area, and it was there that the troubadour movement was born and flourished. And recent research has shown that the Templars practised alchemy. The buildings of several towns in the Languedoc, such as Alet-les-Bains, still bear complex alchemical symbols and also have strong Templar connections.

After the sinister events surrounding the official suppression of the Templars, the Order went underground and continued to exert its influence on many other organizations. How the Templars did this, and who inherited their knowledge, has never been known for certain, until the last ten years. Gradually it has emerged that the Templars have continued to exist as Rosicrucianism and Freemasonry, and the knowledge they had acquired passed into these societies.

We discovered that careful examination of these groups revealed their underlying and consistent preoccupations. One of these is a great, perhaps even an excessive, veneration for one or both of the Saints John – John the Evangelist (or the 'Beloved') and John the Baptist. This is puzzling, for the very groups that appear to hold them so sacred are hardly orthodox

Christians, and even seem to regard Jesus with some coolness. One of these groups is the Priory of Sion, but most bewildering in this context is the fact that although the Priory calls its successive Grand Masters 'John', Pierre Plantard de Saint-Clair claims that the title of the first of this line – 'John I' – is 'symbolically reserved for Christ'[1]. One wonders why Christ should be honoured by being called John.

Perhaps the answer lies in the idea, shared by these societies, that Jesus passed on his *secret* teachings to the young Saint John, and it is this tradition that is guarded so jealously by the Templars, Rosicrucians and Freemasons. And it seems that John the Evangelist has become confused, apparently deliberately, with the Baptist.

The very concept of there having been a secret Gospel of John was common among the 'heretics', from the Cathars of the twelfth century to the *Levitikon*. It is curious that this Johannite thread runs so pervasively and consistently through all these groups, because it is also one of the least known. Perhaps this is simply because the shroud of secrecy has been particularly successful in concealing it from the eyes of the world for so long.

The other major theme that is carried through the various tributaries of the 'underground stream' of heresy is that of the elevation of the Feminine Principle, and specifically the acknowledgement of sex as a sacrament. The alchemists' Great Work, for example, has clear parallels with Tantric sex rites – although it is only recently that these connotations have been understood. Ironically it was only when our culture became aware of Tantrism that the practices of many old Western traditions finally made sense.

Female wisdom has long been sought after, both in the philosophical sense and as that which was believed to be bestowed magically, through the sex act. This search for female wisdom – *Sophia* – is the thread that draws together all of the groups we have investigated: for example, early Gnostics, hermetic groups, the Templars and their successors in Rectified Scottish Rite Freemasonry. The Gnostic text, the

Pistis Sophia, links Sophia to Mary Magdalene and Sophia was also closely associated with Isis – perhaps this helps to explain the Priory of Sion's apparent blend of the saint with the goddess. However, this is only a clue; it is not the answer.

The Magdalene's continuing significance is not in doubt. Yet her remains have been sought – and possibly are still being sought – with an unaccountable fervour. In the thirteenth century Charles II d'Anjou undertook the quest with fanatical zeal, although he was clearly disappointed, for about two centuries later his descendant, the more famous René d'Anjou, was still looking for them. Even at the end of the nineteenth century the same burning desire – to find the physical remains of his beloved Magdalene – seems to have consumed the Abbé Saunière of Rennes-le-Château.

One way or another, the Magdalene holds the key to a great mystery, one that has been jealously and ruthlessly guarded for centuries. And part of this secret intimately involves John the Baptist (and/or perhaps John the Evangelist). Once we realized that there was such a secret, we were keen to dust off the cobwebs of history as quickly as possible and throw some light on it. But this was no easy task: the groups and organizations who have guarded this knowledge over the years have developed ways of keeping outsiders well away from the truth. Although a few have given us hints and clues, no-one was going to hand the central secret over to us. All we knew was that all the evidence points to the mystery being constructed over a foundation that essentially comprised *Sophia* and John. Those themes were central – but we had no idea why, although one clue lay in the fact that whatever the secret is, it is certainly not one that would reinforce the Church's authority. Indeed, this great unknown heresy would seem to pose the greatest threat, not just to Catholicism, but to Christianity as we know it. The groups who kept the secret clearly believed themselves to have been in possession of some knowledge about the real origins of Christianity, and even about Jesus himself.

Whatever the nature of this secret, clearly it is something that was relevant – and significant – to the nineteenth and twentieth centuries. In Rennes-le-Château, Saunière entertained not just representatives of Parisian high society such as Emma Calvé, but politicians and members of imperial families. In our day, Pierre Plantard de Saint-Clair and the Priory of Sion have been associated with figures such as Charles de Gaulle and Alain Poher, a prominent French statesman who was twice Provisional President[2]. Recent rumours have even linked the late President François Mitterand with Pierre Plantard de Saint-Clair[3]. Certainly, Mitterand paid a visit to Rennes-le-Château in 1981, when he was photographed on the Tour Magdala and next to the statue of Asmodeus in the church[4]. It may be significant that he was born in Jarnac, where he was laid to rest in a private ceremony while world leaders attended a service at Notre-Dame in Paris. According to the Priory of Sion's statutes of the 1950s, Jarnac has long been one of their centres.[5]

The Priory of Sion is widely believed to have real influence in European, indeed world, politics. But why should the matters that we had been investigating, no matter how interesting from an historical and philosophical perspective, matter to it? Is this linked to the 'turning upside down of Christianity' promised by the union of the Priory of Sion and the 'Church of John' that we discussed earlier?

The one thing that Mary Magdalene and John the Baptist had in common was that they were saints, and were apparently historical characters who could be found in the New Testament. The only logical avenue for further research was to look at their lives and roles, in the hope that this might reveal the reason for their enduring appeal to the heretical underground traditions. If we had any hope of ever understanding their supreme importance to the initiates of the most solemn and knowledgeable esoteric groups, then we had to begin reading the Bible in earnest.

PART TWO

The Web of Truth

CHAPTER ELEVEN

Gospel Untruths

At Easter 1996 the British media[1] devoted much attention to what seemed like an amazing discovery – that of ossuaries, found in Jerusalem, that contained the bones of a small group of people among whom was 'Jesus the son of Joseph'. The others were two Marys (one whose inscription was in Greek) – in this context possibly the Virgin and the Magdalene – one Joseph, a Matthew and a 'Jude, son of Jesus'. Obviously these names, all found together in this way, held some excitement for Christians, although the implications of this discovery were not necessarily to their liking – after all, Christianity itself was founded on the idea that Jesus rose from the dead and ascended bodily into heaven. To find his bones would be devastating. But were they really his – and those of his family?

It has to be admitted that in all probability they were not. It may well have been mere coincidence that the names have a particular resonance for Christians, for they were all common names in the Palestine of the first century. But the reason why this discovery was significant was the sheer scale and intensity of the debate that it caused. Television programmes and the quality broadsheets seized on the question: if these could have been proved to have been those particular bones, what would it have meant to Christianity? And to us, one of the most revealing aspects of the matter was how astonished and affronted many Christians are when confronted with the idea that Jesus may have been a normal man. It even came as a surprise to many that his was a common name.

While it is understandable that committed Christians would wish to maintain their view of Jesus as Son of God and perhaps decide as a matter of policy to ignore what outsiders might say about him, it is still odd that so many Christians actually do not know just how much of the Gospel account has been shown to be inaccurate. Never has there been so much information available: books have been written over the last fifty or so years that have taken a huge range of positions about Jesus and his movement, and have presented many diverse (and sometimes entertaining) theories. Among them have been ideas such as that Jesus was a divorced father of three, a Freemason, a Buddhist, a conjuror, a hypnotist, the progenitor of a line of French kings, a Cynic philosopher, an hallucinogenic mushroom – and even a woman! This explosion of weird and wonderful ideas may be partly a result of the modern willingness to question, but the reason that such ideas have been able to arise is that recent scholarship has revealed that the traditional story of Jesus is radically flawed and therefore very weak. However, although such ideas can flourish because this vacuum exists, they do depend on the Gospels having to be, not only reinterpreted, but virtually rewritten.

This vacuum could only be discerned once the background research provided a context for the story. Archaeological discoveries such as the Nag Hammadi texts and the Dead Sea Scrolls have revealed much more about the time and culture in which Jesus lived – and suddenly it seems that many of the aspects of Christianity that used to be considered unique were no such thing. Even the most well-worn and familiar Christian concepts can now be seen as having had a completely different meaning in the context of first-century Palestine.

For example, a slogan that evangelical Christians are particularly fond of exhibiting outside their churches is 'Jesus Christ is Lord'. To them this phrase encapsulates the idea that Jesus was literally divine – *the* Lord, God incarnate. It was taken from the Gospels in the belief that it was a title given to Jesus by his followers in recognition of his unique status. But as the highly respected biblical scholar Geza Vermes has shown, it was merely a common term of respect such as children used to their father or a wife to her husband – the equivalent of 'sir'[2]. It implies nothing beyond mere custom, and certainly nothing spiritual or divine. But over the centuries this phrase has taken on a life of its own and is taken almost as proof that Jesus is Lord of All.

Another example of the way Christian tradition has become historical fact is that of the main festivals such as Easter and Christmas. Every year millions of Christians the world over celebrate the birth of the baby Jesus on 25 December. The story of the Nativity is one of the most familiar in the world: Mary was a Virgin who conceived through the intervention of the Holy Spirit; there was no room at the inn for her and her husband Joseph so the child was born in a stable (or in some versions, a cave), and the magi and the shepherds came to worship the newborn Saviour. This story may not be favoured by the more sophisticated Christians and by theologians, but it is one of the first tales children are told, and it becomes 'Gospel' at an early age.

When the Pope deemed it prudent to explain that Jesus had not actually been born on 25 December, but that the date was chosen because it was already a mid-winter festival for the old pagans, the announcement caused something of a stir. To most ordinary Christians even this came as a great revelation. That this announcement should have come as late as 1994 is barely credible. Yet it is only the tip of the iceberg, for theologians have known for a very long time that the whole Christmas story is a myth.

The extent to which most Christians are deliberately kept in ignorance by those who know better goes much, much further: the Christmas date of 25 December is not only the alleged birthday of Jesus: it was also that of many pagan gods such as Osiris, Attis, Tammuz, Adonis, Dionysus and many others.

They, too, were born in humble dwellings such as caves, and shepherds attended their births, which had been heralded by signs and wonders, including the sighting of a new star. And among their many titles were those of 'Good Shepherd' and 'Saviour of Mankind'. If confronted with the evidence for Jesus having been just one in a long line of 'dying-and-rising-god' traditions, the clergy tend to take refuge in the unsatisfactory

301

concept that the pagans of old somehow dimly perceived that one day there *would* be a real saviour god, but had to make do with a grotesque parody of the Christianity that was to come.

Although we will be dealing in detail with the real origins of Christianity later, suffice it to say that the shared birthdate of 25 December is not the only similarity between the Jesus story and that of the pagan gods. Osiris, for example – consort of Isis – died at the hands of the wicked *on a Friday* and was magically 'resurrected' after being in the Underworld *for three days*. And Dionysus' mysteries were celebrated by ingesting the god through a magical meal of bread and wine, symbolizing his body and blood. These 'dying-and-rising gods' have been recognized as such for many years by theologians, historians and biblical scholars, yet it seems there has been a tacit conspiracy to keep such knowledge from the Church's 'flock'.

With all the welter of new material emerging about the origins of Christianity, it is only too easy to get carried away with enthusiasm and embrace one particular idea without the necessary caution and discernment. If the source material is misinterpreted then the conclusions reached can be very wide of the mark. For example, a vast number of words have been devoted to the Dead Sea Scrolls, which were discovered in 1947: some of them appear to throw new light on early Christianity. Certain passages of the Scrolls have convinced many people that Jesus and John the Baptist were members of the Essenes, a sect based at Qumran by the Dead Sea. It is no exaggeration to say that this is now believed by many people to be unassailably proven.

In fact, there is no proof that the Scrolls themselves were of Essene origin – this was simply the immediate assumption when they were found. There is another assumption: that the documents were the writings of just one sect, either the Essenes or one of the many others that are known to have retreated to that area. However, the foremost professor of Jewish history, Norman Golb, who has closely observed the discovery of the Dead Sea Scrolls and the development of their study, has recently challenged this assumption. He has demonstrated that the case for them having come from one community – or even that a religious community ever existed at Qumran – is not supported either by archaeological evidence or by the evidence in the Scrolls themselves. Golb believes that the Scrolls are in fact part of the Temple library, which had been hidden there during the Jewish Revolt in 70 CE[3].

If Golb is right, and there is every indication that he is, then virtually every book written on the Dead Sea Scrolls is redundant. Essentially what most writers have done is try to reconstruct the beliefs of one putative sect from a collection of documents that actually have their origins among a variety of different groups. This is like deducing someone's *beliefs* from looking at what is on their bookshelves: our own personal library, for example, easily reveals our interest in religious and esoteric subjects, but as our books cover a variety of viewpoints – sceptical, rational, credulous – they clearly cannot represent what we actually believe. (By comparison, the Nag Hammadi texts have never been regarded as the product of a single sect.)

Although the 'Essene' connection of the Dead Sea Scolls is fallacious, despite its status as a modern myth, they remain of profound historical significance for the understanding of Judaism at that time. But as they are unlikely to be of great use to any study of the origins of Christianity, the Scrolls will not figure largely in this investigation.

The dangers of basing far-reaching conclusions on faulty premises are exemplified by *The Hiram Key* by Knight and Lomas. Their argument is that as some of the Dead Sea Scrolls contain ideas that are similar to those of Freemasonry, and as they claim 'that the authors of the Dead Sea Scrolls . . . were Essenes is now beyond doubt'[4] then it would follow that the Essenes were the forerunners of Freemasonry. Add to that their certainty that Jesus was an Essene and the conclusion is clear: Jesus was a Freemason.

However, as we have seen, the Scrolls were not written by the Essenes and Jesus has not been proved to be one of that sect, so the whole argument collapses. If nothing else, this provides the over-enthusiastic researcher with a cautionary tale.

We had reached the point where we realized that a radical re-evaluation of the status of both John the Baptist and Mary Magdalene was long overdue. After all, it did seem that both these historical figures had some persuasive claim to be taken very seriously – at least by a tenacious underground movement in Europe which had included some of the finest minds of all time.

The main theme of what we term the Great European Heresy was the inexplicable veneration – amounting in many cases to actual worship – of Mary Magdalene and John the Baptist. But did this represent anything more than some kind of wilful unorthodoxy, a persistent rebelliousness against the Church merely for the sake of it? Was there anything of substance behind these heresies? To find out if there was any factual basis for these beliefs, we turned to the New Testament, and in particular to the four canonical Gospels of Matthew, Mark, Luke and John.

We confess to an initial bewilderment at this 'heretical' connection between the Baptist and the Magdalene. Not only was there nothing in the received version of Christianity to link them – apart from their apparent devotion to Jesus – but a superficial investigation of the heresies themselves also failed to provide any plausible common ground. Their images were poles apart. John the Baptist comes over as an ascetic who died because of his uncompromising moral standards, although, perhaps tellingly, he did not die as a *Christian* martyr. (In fact there is no suggestion that he invoked the teachings or morals of Jesus when he took his fatal stand against Herod Antipas.) And on the other hand, the Magdalene is believed to have been a prostitute, although, according to the traditional story, she reformed and spent the rest of her long life as a penitent. Somehow John and Mary do not seem to be natural allies: according to the Gospels, certainly, there is no suggestion that they even met.

However, there are indications that they probably did at least know of each other. The Baptist is acknowledged by scholars to have had a widespread fame in his time and place as a righteous preacher who came out of the wilderness to call men to repentance, while Mary was one of Jesus' female followers or disciples, holding an important role in his entourage. And, it is believed, John and Jesus were cousins, or at least in some way blood relatives. From reading between the lines one can imagine that perhaps John knew of Mary Magdalene as someone who washed the men's feet and brought them clean towels and cooked their meals. Perhaps he vaguely knew of her past reputation and frowned upon her presence as 'unclean' – unless, of course, he had baptized her himself. There are no records of this, but then there are no records even of Apostles such as *St Peter* having been baptized.[5]

However, deeper investigation into the background of the Bible story does yield some clues about the connection between the Magdalene and the Baptist. The first major link is that of their complementary roles in Jesus' career as a preacher. It is John who represents its beginning and Mary who symbolizes its end.[6]

It is John who initiates Jesus' ministry through the rite of baptism. It is Mary who is central to the events surrounding his death and resurrection. The major connection is that they both officiate at a species of *anointing*. John's baptism with water is clearly analagous to the anointing with spikenard by Mary of Bethany, who is generally assumed to be the same as Mary Magdalene, and it is the latter who anointed Jesus' dead body with myrrh and aloes for burial.

The one major similarity between these two curiously compelling characters, however, is that although they both obviously fulfilled a major ritual function in Jesus' life, they have only been included in the Gospel story on sufferance. They come and go from the pages of the Bible with such abruptness as to create a peculiarly jarring effect. On the one hand one reads of John's execution at the hands of Herod's men, but on the other there is no word of how Jesus grieved at this, or how he exhorted his followers to show reverence for John's memory. The Magdalene suddenly appears in the story at the time of the Crucifixion in what is clearly a role of some intimacy with Jesus and is the first person to witness the Resurrection – yet why is she not specifically mentioned previously? Perhaps this is because the Gospel writers were obliged to admit that both John and Mary Magdalene fulfilled roles so central to the Jesus story that they could not be totally written out, but otherwise would never have mentioned them. So what was there about both John the Baptist and Mary Magdalene that was so offensive to the Gospel writers and the early Church Fathers?

It is easy to see this deliberate marginalization in the case of the Magdalene. On the one hand she is clearly important in the Jesus story, but on the other there is virtually no information about her in the Gospels. Apart from one mention of her in Luke, for example, she makes her first real entrance as a witness to the Crucifixion. We are not told how she came to be a follower, except for the implication in the 'casting out of seven devils' story that she had been healed by Jesus at some point. Nor are we told what her exact role was, especially at Jesus' burial.

At first we assumed naively that any female follower of Jesus would have received this slighting treatment simply because she was a woman and therefore a second-class citizen as far as first-century Jews were concerned. Yet if so, things must have changed since the days of Ruth and Naomi, whose Old Testament lives were so well chronicled. Then there is the curious emphasis on this Mary's surname or title, *Magdalene*. For, although we will discuss its derivation later, it is still possible to see in the very fact that it was used by the Gospel writers an indication that she was a woman of independent means. Every other woman in the Gospels is defined by her status as a wife, mother or sister of some important man. But here we have simply *Mary Magdalene*. It is as if the Gospel writers expected their readers to know who she was.

The Gospels say of Jesus' women followers that they 'ministered unto him of their substance' – indicating that they had some substance to minister unto him with. Was she one of a group of independent women of some means who essentially *kept* Jesus' group? Certainly many scholars believe this to be the case[7]. But whatever her financial status, Mary Magdalene, when mentioned at all by name, is always at the top of the list of women disciples, even before Mary the Mother – except where there is a specific reason for placing the Virgin first.

The Priory of Sion believe that Mary Magdalene is one and the same as Mary of Bethany, the sister of Lazarus, and the one who anoints Jesus' feet. If this is the case, then her brusque treatment at the hands of the Gospel writers becomes yet more apparent. They appear to have deliberately made her identity and role even more difficult to determine. The Synoptic Gospels go so far as to make the woman who anoints Jesus anonymous, although it is highly likely that the writers knew who she was and why she was important.

This process of marginalization appears also to have been applied to John the Baptist. Modern New Testament scholars acknowledge that the precise relationship between John and Jesus is hard to define. Many of them point to John's apparent over-emphasis on his role as mere forerunner, suggesting that he 'protests too much'. Significantly, Mark's Gospel – which was probably the earliest, and the one on which Matthew and Luke were based – is less insistent on John's subordinate role than the later texts. This has led many scholars to conclude that John's subservience to Jesus, which is repeated ad nauseam, was actually a cover-up for a rivalry between the two men, and their respective groups of disciples.

Close scrutiny of the Gospels themselves reveals hints of such a rivalry. For a start, an unbiased reading reveals that many of Jesus' first – and most famous – disciples actually came from the ranks of John's followers. For example, young John 'the Beloved' (who, as we have seen, was central to many 'heretical' beliefs), is widely acknowledged to have been one of the Baptist's acolytes and could even have taken his name as a mark of respect for him. John's disciples continued after their leader's beheading as a separate group: we are told that some of them went to take away his body, and there are New Testament passages in which Jesus' followers dispute with John's over their respective lifestyles[8].

More tellingly, however, John is recorded as having had his doubts about Jesus as Messiah – in a passage that, not surprisingly, is given few airings by the Church. When John is incarcerated in Herod's prison he sends two of his disciples to ask Jesus: 'Art thou he that should come, or do we look for another?'[9] This is a particularly embarrassing episode for theologians. On the one hand they see John the Baptist as having been appointed by God to pave the way for the Messiah, and to point him out as such to the people, thereby recognizing in him too some measure of divine guidance – yet the 'forerunner' then questions whether or not he has made the right choice!

There are some less obvious, but equally telling, signs of the rivalry that existed between the two men even in the recorded words of Jesus. The first is in the well-known passage in which Jesus appears to praise John to the crowds, telling them that 'Among them that are born of women there hath not risen a greater than John the Baptist'[10]. However, he then adds the puzzling qualification that 'he that is least in the kingdom of heaven is greater than he'. The exact meaning of this has been the subject of much debate. The eminent New Testament scholar Geza Vermes compared this use of the phrase 'least in the kingdom of heaven' with other examples and concluded that it was a circumlocution – a formal and impersonal phrase – which stood for the speaker himself[11]. In other words, Jesus was telling the crowd 'John may have been a great man but *I am greater.*'

However, there is another, much more obvious interpretation, which we have never seen discussed by any biblical scholars. It is acknowledged that the phrase 'born of women' could be taken as an insult because it implied weakness[12] – in which case, the whole passage takes on an entirely different hue. Perhaps Jesus' statement 'Among them that are born of women there hath not risen a greater than John the Baptist' maybe taken as a *direct insult*. This slur seems to have been reinforced by the next comment – 'he that is least in the kingdom of heaven is greater than he.' If Geza Vermes is right, and Jesus was saying that he was greater, then it was hardly a compliment to John. But it may have been a stronger insult, meaning 'even the least of my followers is greater than him.'

It has been suggested[13] that there is also another thinly veiled slight on John – which would have been obvious to first-century Jews – in Jesus' comments during a discussion between his disciples and those of John: 'no man putteth new wine into old skins'[14]. In that time and place wine was often carried in 'bottles' made of animal skins – and John wore animal skins . . . In the context of that particular discussion, it is very likely that this comment referred to John.

It is clear that this rivalry was well known to the Gospel writers at least fifty years after the Crucifixion (which is roughly when the books were written). Perhaps the four Gospels were actually written with the hidden agenda of mini-mizing this infamous rivalry and ensuring that Jesus came out in the superior position. In fact, no doubt the Gospel writers would have been a lot happier if they could have left John out altogether.

So it is clear that the Baptist and the Magdalene – the one who baptized Jesus and the other who was the first witness to the whole point of Christianity, the Resurrection – are united by the fact that the Gospel writers were, to say the least, uncomfortable about them. But is it possible to discover why, and to reconstruct their true roles and re-establish their original significance?

The main problem is that the books of the New Testament are a very unreliable source of information. Like all ancient texts they have, of course, been subject to a relentless process of editing, selection, translation and interpretation. Over the centuries parts have been added to the original works that are sometimes unimportant, but on occasion highly significant. For example, in the First Epistle of John, the sentence 'For there are three that bear record in heaven, the Father, the Word and the Holy Ghost and these three are one' is known to have been added later[15]. Then again, the story of 'the woman taken in adultery' appears only in John's Gospel – and its earliest known versions do not contain this episode[16]. It is a matter of great debate whether or not it is authentic.

A major example of the confusion that is due to the vagaries of translation is that of the common misconception that Jesus was a humble carpenter. The word used in the original Aramaic was *naggar*, which can mean either a worker in wood *or* a scholar or learned man[17]. In the context, the latter makes the most sense, for there is no other hint anywhere else that Jesus was any kind of a craftsman – and his learning caused special comment from those who heard him: the word *naggar* is only used when the people are specifically discussing his erudition[18]. Yet the idea that Jesus was a carpenter is now just as indelibly written into the Christian story as the 'fact' that he was born on 25 December.

The dates at which the canonical Gospels were written have been the subject of great debate and controversy. As A.N. Wilson writes:

> One of the most curious features of New Testament scholar-ship is the fact that, though learned men have pored over documents for centuries, they have never managed to establish beyond doubt such simple questions as where the Gospels were written, or when they were written, still less, by whom they were written.[19]

The earliest surviving complete manuscripts are from the fourth century, but they are clearly copies of older texts. So scholars have had to try to establish their provenance by analysing the language of the surviving Gospel fragments. Although the question has not been conclusively resolved, the current consensus is that Mark's Gospel is the earliest, having been written perhaps as early as 70 CE. It is also agreed that Matthew and Luke were based largely on Mark and therefore must have been composed later, although they do incorporate material from other sources. John's Gospel is thought to be the last to have been written – somewhere between 90 and 120 CE.[20]

The fourth Gospel – John's – has always been something of an enigma. Matthew, Mark and Luke, known collectively as the Synoptic Gospels, tell more or less the same story, putting the events in much the same sequence and depicting Jesus in a similar way – although there are still many discrepancies and inconsistencies in individual episodes. A good example of this is the different number and names of the women who attended Jesus' tomb according to the three authors. John's Gospel, however, tells Jesus' story in a very different order and also includes events that the others do not mention.

Two examples are the wedding at Cana, in which Jesus performs his first miracle – turning the water into wine – and the raising of Lazarus that becomes, in John, one of the pivotal events. That the other chroniclers should have been unaware of such important episodes has always puzzled biblical historians.

However, John's Gospel also differs in the image that it presents of Jesus. While the Synoptic Gospels tell the story of a religious teacher and miracle-worker that largely fits within a Jewish framework, John's Gospel is much more mystical and more Gnostic in attitude, placing far more emphasis on Jesus' divinity. It also seeks to explain the meaning behind the story as it unfolds.[21]

The standard view today is that Jesus was a Jewish religious leader who was mostly rejected by his own people. Many modern commentators do not even think that he intended to found a new religion, and that Christianity almost happened by accident, because Jesus' teachings took hold in the rest of the Roman Empire. This explains, they say, ideas such as Jesus' deification: he had to become known as the Son of God – literally God incarnate – to appeal to the romanized world, which was used to the idea that its rulers and heroes became

311

gods. Because John's Gospel dwells on such themes, it has been assumed that it was written at a later stage in the development of Christianity, when the fledgling religion was finding its feet within the wider context of the Roman Empire.

The problem is that John's is the only Gospel that actually claims to be based on the eyewitness testimony of someone who had been present at the major events of Jesus' life: 'the beloved disciple', who is traditionally taken to be the young John, hence the attribution of the Gospel.

John's Gospel certainly contains the most circumstantial detail, such as the naming of individuals who appear anonymously in other versions. So some scholars[22] have argued that John is the earliest Gospel, although there are other interpretations, ranging from the idea that John simply had the best imagination to his having used first-hand testimony but added his own interpretation to it later.

John's Gospel is, by any standards, very strange. It has long bewildered even the most erudite of scholars because of its confusing messages: in fact, its tone – which is unmistakable – is flatly contradicted by the facts it is careful to set before the reader. Because of the detailed information it gives, John's Gospel is recognized as the most valuable historically, and yet it is also regarded as the most distant in time from Jesus' life. It shows more precise knowledge about Jewish religious practices, yet it is the least Jewish, and most Hellenistic, in outlook. It is by far the most hostile to the Jews – its diatribes against them reveal real hatred – yet makes it clearer than the other Gospels that it was the Romans, not the Jews, who were responsible for the execution of Jesus. And it is also the most strident in its marginalization of John the Baptist, devoting many words to his apparent inferiority and completely ignoring the Baptist's subsequent fate – yet, unlike the Synoptic Gospels, it tells us that Jesus recruited his first disciples from John's group and that the followers of both leaders continued to be rivals, thereby revealing that John was important in his own right.

This evident confusion, however, is easily explained by the

many sources that were used in order to compile John's Gospel – including its eye-witness account of Jesus' mission. And as we will see, some of these sources are particularly revealing.

Many modern Christians believe that the New Testament was somehow divinely inspired. However, the facts argue against this: it was only in 325 CE that the Council of Nicaea met to debate which out of many books would be included in what was to become the New Testament. There is no doubt that the men present at the Council brought to the task their own prejudices and agendas, of which we are still reaping the sorry harvest. Eventually the Council established that only four Gospels would be included in the New Testament and rejected forever over fifty other books with more or less equal claim to be considered authentic[23].

At a stroke the views expressed, either implicitly or explicitly, in the rejected material became synonymous with heresy. (In fact, the word *heresy* originally just meant *choice*.) In a sense the same kind of selection process as that which was employed by the Council of Nicaea in the fourth century continues to this day. The public at large is not, on the whole, allowed to make up its own mind about the surviving texts. For example, the *Gospel of Thomas*, the existence of which had been known about for a long time, was only discovered in full when the Nag Hammadi texts were uncovered in 1945. But any rejoicing at its discovery must surely be tempered by recognition of the reason for its acceptance by theologians: it agreed with the existing four Gospels, and that was why it was allowed to pass into the unofficial canon (although the Catholic Church itself pronounced it heretical). Other texts, dating from roughly the same time, were discarded because the religious views in them do not accord with those of the New Testament. These are generally the texts that come from a Gnostic background.

Christians are brought up with the notion of the 'Gospel truth' meaning the literal, unequivocal, unambiguous and divinely inspired *facts*. Very few modern scholars, however, accept that the New Testament is God's word, as they know that the words of the New Testament are no more or less valid than any other account given by people fifty or more years after the events they describe.

Is it any coincidence that the Gospels were written only after the first missionary, Paul, had evangelized many of the countries of the eastern Mediterranean? Certainly in his letters Paul gives no clue at all that he knew anything of the life and deeds of Jesus other than that he was killed and rose from the dead. So were the Gospels created to reinforce his version of Christianity or to counter it? The authors could hardly have been unaware of Paul's ministry.

The Gospel accounts were, as we have seen, written at least four decades after the Crucifixion, and things had moved on since then – not least because the 'coming of the kingdom of God', as promised by Jesus, had not actually materialized. This very time lapse, of course, presents enormous problems in assessing the authenticity of the Gospels because there is no way of knowing which passages were based on real historical events, on rumour and extrapolation from rumour – or on complete fabrication. Many of the words we now think of as having come from the very lips of Jesus himself may not have been recorded verbatim, or may not have been said by anyone, ever.[24] Some of them may have been misremembered even by his followers (although it is possible that people with an oral tradition, like the Jews, kept it considerably 'purer' for longer than we would today), and someone else's words altogether may have been ascribed to Jesus. Ironically, however, one of the few ways of testing that a saying is genuine is the 'principle of dissimilarity': that is, seeing if it *contradicts* the overall message of the Gospels. After all, if it goes against the spirit of most of the text the author is unlikely to have made it up[25].

For most of the last two thousand years, the Gospels were assumed to have been divinely inspired and to contain the unadulterated truth about Jesus, his teachings and message for mankind. He was, it was understood, the Son of God, sent to save Man from his sins by a supreme act of sacrifice and to establish a new Church to supersede the religion of the Old Testament – and, by implication, that of all the pagans of the Greek and Roman world. It has only been in the last two hundred years that the Bible has been subjected to the same critical scrutiny as other historical documents, and that an attempt has been made to fit the life and teachings of Jesus into the context of his time.

It might be expected that such a process would have clarified much about Jesus' character and motivation. In fact, the opposite has been the case. Although this approach has revealed that many assumptions are wrong – for example, Jesus was *not* executed on the initiative of the Jewish religious leaders but because of accusations of political intrigue by the Romans[26] – it has totally failed to answer some of the most fundamental questions about him. We can say what Jesus *was not*, but it is still difficult to say what he *was*.[27]

The result of this is that, today, New Testament scholarship is in crisis. It is unable to agree on such fundamental questions as: did Jesus himself claim to be the Messiah? Did he claim to be the Son of God? Did he claim to be the King of the Jews? And it is completely unable to explain the significance of many of the things he did. It cannot even provide a convincing explanation for his Crucifixion, because there is nothing that Jesus said or did – as reported in the Gospels – that would have offended either the Jewish religious leaders or the Roman overlords to the point that they would have wanted his blood[28]. Many of his symbolic actions, such as the overturning of the moneylenders' tables in the Temple, or even the crucial event of the inauguration of the eucharist at the Last Supper, cannot be related to anything in Judaism.

Most amazing of all, however, is the fact that New Testament scholarship has great difficulty in explaining why a religion should have been founded in Jesus' name in the first place. If Jesus really was the long-expected Jewish Messiah, then he failed in that role because he was humiliated, tortured and killed. And yet his followers not only continued to venerate him but were also led by their devotion to him to set themselves up as being different from other Jews.

A good example of this academic confusion can be seen in the works of two of the most prominent New Testament scholars of recent times, Hugh Schonfield and Geza Vermes. The parallels between the two professors are striking. Both were Jewish scholars who, at an early age, developed an interest in the origins of Christianity, and devoted the majority of their distinguished working lives to the subject. Both of them realized that most Christian scholars had failed to put the search for the historical Jesus into the wider context of the Jewish culture of his own time and place. Both hoped to find the answer through a careful comparison of the Gospel accounts and the Judaism of Jesus' time, and both, besides their many academic works, published enormously successful popular books which presented the result of their life's work – Schonfield with his *The Passover Plot* (1965) and Vermes with his *Jesus the Jew* (1973). The conclusions they came to, however, could hardly have been more different.

Vermes presents Jesus as a Hasid – one of the rather shaman-like heirs to the Old Testament prophets who were noted for their independence from institutional Judaism and for their miracles. He argues that there is nothing in the New Testament to suggest that Jesus ever claimed to be the Messiah, still less the Son of God – those titles were retrospectively applied to him by his followers. Schonfield, on the other hand, has Jesus as primarily a political figure working for Palestine's independence from Rome, who *consciously* shaped his own career to fit that of the expected Messiah, even to the point of voluntarily engineering his own death by crucifixion.

It was Schonfield's *The Passover Plot* that revealed yet more reasons to be cautious about accepting the 'Gospel truth'. His work demonstrated that there existed behind Jesus and his known followers another, shadowy group with their own agenda and interest in manipulating his story. Although his argument is familiar, it is worth briefly summarizing here.

Throughout the Gospel stories Jesus repeatedly encounters

316

certain people who are neither his closest disciples nor part of the mass of his followers, and who are usually well off – such as Joseph of Arimathea, who emerges abruptly from nowhere to monopolize Jesus' burial arrangements. The central characters in this organization were the group at Bethany, which Schonfield calls Jesus' 'base of operations'[29].

This group appear to have ensured that Jesus fulfilled the role of the expected Messiah, especially the entry into Jerusalem. The ass on which he sat, thus fulfilling the prophecy of Zechariah (9:9), had clearly been prearranged, complete with a password in order for it to be handed over – although Jesus' disciples knew nothing about it[30]. Then the room for the Last Supper is ready and waiting, although it is the busiest time of the year and Jerusalem is packed to overflowing. Jesus tells his disciples to go into the city and look for a *man* carrying a pitcher of water (who would have stood out like a sore thumb because only women did such menial tasks); again, passwords were to be exchanged, and he would then take them to the upper room.[31]

This indicates that the disciples were unaware of much of what was really going on, and that Jesus was working to some kind of preplanned programme, in which the Bethany family were main players. This is another example of how the Gospels do not give a complete picture of Jesus' story.

Most people today are aware that political motives have been ascribed to Jesus. It is now understood that his disciples included members of different factions – some of them so extreme that we would call them terrorists today. Judas' second name, which is usually given as 'Iscariot' is now believed by the majority of scholars to derive from *sicarii*, the name of one such group. Simon the Zealot is another example of how close the men of violence were to Jesus.[32]

The works of Schonfield and Vermes are relatively well known and easily available. The work of another biblical researcher, however, while deserving of a much wider audience, has in fact received a considerably smaller one.

A highly significant discovery was made in 1958 by Dr

Morton Smith (subsequently Professor of Ancient History at Columbia University, New York) in the library of Mar Saba, an isolated and closed community of the Eastern Orthodox Church about a dozen miles from Jerusalem. Smith had first gone to the monastery during the Second World War when, as a student, he was stranded in Palestine. Realizing the potential importance of the documents that had been accrued in that library over the centuries, he went back there in 1958.

His most significant discovery at Mar Saba was of some fragments of a 'Secret Gospel' said to have been written by Mark[33]. What he actually found was a copy of a letter from the second-century Church Father, Clement of Alexandria. The copy dated from, at the earliest, the second half of the seventeenth century, and had been written on the end-papers of a book dating from 1646 (a common practice when very old documents began to deteriorate). However, from analysis of the style – which contains many of Clement's known idiosyncrasies – paleographers have established that the original had indeed been written by him. There are also peculiarities in the extracts from this 'Secret Gospel' quoted in the letter that makes it probable that they are genuine. (For example, it describes Jesus as becoming angry. Of the canonical Gospels only Mark attributes normal human emotions to Jesus – the others excised such elements from their accounts, and it is hardly something that the Church Fathers such as Clement would have invented.)

Clement's letter is a reply to someone called Theodore, who had apparently written to him for advice on how to deal with a heretical sect known as the Carpocratians (after their founder, Carpocrates). This was a Gnostic cult whose practices included sexual rites, which were, predictably, condemned by Clement and the other Church Fathers. The sect's doctrines were apparently based on an alternative Gospel of Mark. In his letter Clement admitted that this Gospel existed and was authentic – although he accused the Carpocratians of misinterpreting and falsifying some of it – and that it represented a Gospel written by Mark that contained the esoteric teachings

318

of Jesus that were not intended to have been revealed to the average Christian. This 'Secret Gospel of Mark' was very similar to the better-known, canonical version, except that it contained at least two passages that had been deliberately excised from it to keep them from the eyes of the 'uninitiated'.

The discovery is significant for three reasons. First, for the insight it gives into the formative years of the Christian Church, and the methods used by the Church Fathers to establish the canon of Christian dogma. It shows that texts *were* being edited and censored, and that even works recognized as being of equal value to the canonical Gospels were being withheld from the ordinary worshippers. Moreover, it reveals that even such an august figure as Clement was prepared to lie to prevent such material from becoming more widely known: although he admits to Theodore that Mark's Secret Gospel does exist, he advises him to deny it to everyone else.

The second significant aspect is that it confirms that the canonical Gospels, and the other books of the New Testament do not give a complete picture of the teachings and motivation of Jesus, and that (as suggested by some reports of his words in the canonical Gospels) there were at least two levels of teaching. One was the exoteric for the ordinary followers, and the other was the esoteric, for the special disciples – or the true inner circle of *initiates*.

The third significant point about the discovery of Mark's Secret Gospel – and one of particular relevance to our own enquiry – is the nature of the two passages that Clement quotes in his letter.

The first is an account of the raising of Lazarus, although in this version he is not named, simply being described as a 'youth' of Bethany. The account is very similar to that in John's Gospel, except that in this version there is a follow-up to the actual miracle – it says that six days afterwards the youth came to Jesus 'wearing a linen cloth over his naked body' and remained with him for a night, during which he was 'taught . . . the mystery of the kingdom of God'[34]. Rather than a miraculous resurrection, therefore, the raising of Lazarus seems to have been part of some kind of initiatory rite in which the initiate undergoes a symbolic death and rebirth before being given the secret teachings. Such a rite is a common part of many of the mystery religions that were widely practised in the Greek and Roman worlds – but did it, as some readers may deduce, also include a homosexual initiation?

Morton Smith certainly speculated that this might have been so, judging by the specific allusion to a single cloth covering the youth's nakedness and the fact that he spent a night alone with his teacher, Jesus. In our opinion, however, this is too modern – and too glib – an interpretation, for the mystery schools routinely involved both nudity and long hours' seclusion with one's initiator without any sexual activity necessarily having been involved.

The fact that this account is of the raising of Lazarus is also important. As we have seen, this is one of the episodes in John's Gospel that does not appear in any of the others, and is cited by critics as proving that the Gospel is not authentic. The very fact that it once appeared in at least one of the other Gospels, but was then deliberately removed, supports John's authenticity, and explains why such significant events were censored from them, as they gave clues to a secret teaching that had been reserved for Jesus' inner circle.

The other, shorter, passage quoted by Clement is also interesting, because it fills a notorious gap in the story that was already recognized by scholars. In the canonical Mark (11:46) there is the curious statement: 'And they [Jesus and his disciples] came to Jericho: and as he went out of Jericho with his disciples and a great number of people, blind Bartimeus, the son of Timaeus, sat by the highway side begging.' As there was no point in telling us that Jesus went to Jericho then immediately left it, it is obvious that something is missing from the account. Clement's letter confirms that this was the case by giving the censored passage, which is:

And the sister of the youth whom Jesus loved and his mother and Salome were there, and Jesus did not receive them.

This omitted verse seems innocuous enough, and it has not attracted the interest of the 'Lazarus' passage – but it is, in fact, considerably more significant than it first seems. The 'youth whom Jesus loved' is Lazarus, as he is referred to by this phrase in John's Gospel. (And, as the phrase is also used of the disciple on whose testimony the Gospel is based – 'John' – there is at least a good case for supposing that the 'Beloved Disciple' and Lazarus are one and the same.) Lazarus' sisters are Mary and Martha of Bethany, and if it is accepted that this Mary is the same as Mary Magdalene, then she would be one of the three women whom Jesus avoided at Jericho.

Because of its brevity, this passage does not contain the theological implications of the longer account about Lazarus quoted above. What is significant, however, is that, for some reason, such an apparently harmless sentence should have been suppressed so early. What possible reason could the Church Fathers have had to deny their followers the knowledge that there had been some kind of situation involving Jesus and Lazarus' sister – possibly Mary Magdalene – his mother and a woman named Salome?

Scholars have reacted to Smith's discovery of this material by ignoring the implications and declaring it too insubstantial to be analysed properly. But, in our opinion, it does raise some interesting questions.

Clement believed that Mark had written this 'Secret Gospel' when living in the Egyptian city of Alexandria. Bearing it in mind that the 'foundation myth' of both the Priory of Sion and the Rite of Memphis links the Egyptian priest Ormus with St Mark – could it be a veiled reference to this secret tradition?

The finding of the Secret Gospel of Mark confirms that the books of the New Testament as we know them today are *not* dispassionate, true records of Jesus and his ministry. To an extent, they are works of propaganda. It might seem impossible even to hope to reconstruct an accurate picture of the early days of Christianity from their pages. But the situation is not completely hopeless. Propaganda *can* be used to draw reasonable conclusions provided it is recognized for what it is.

321

It can be made to reveal what it sets out to conceal if it is analysed carefully – for example, suspicious passages are those where obfuscations are obvious or where names are omitted for no apparent reason.

It is, however, heartening to know that much of the 'forbidden' material that had been edited out of the original New Testament texts or that appeared in the entire Gospels that had been voted out of the New Testament by the Council of Nicaea has been kept secretly by the so-called 'heretics', whose heresy in many cases was due simply to the fact of their knowing the truth about these censored passages. What could this edited material possibly contain that was so potentially damaging to the Church that those who knew it were ruthlessly hunted down and burnt to death?

Taking the clues from our investigation of European underground movements we set out to reassess the story of Jesus and his teachings. For years we had struggled with the mass of diverse information we had assembled from many sources – everything from standard theological texts to interviews with the 'heretics' themselves, from the pages of the New Testament and from Apocryphal and Gnostic texts to the works of the alchemists and hermeticists. A pattern eventually began to emerge – and it was so startling, so different from the version of events taught in the churches, that at first we doubted our own conclusions.

What if many of those so-called 'heretics', with their secret knowledge of the original Jesus story, were actually *the real Christians?* What can a truly dispassionate analysis of the story tell us about those momentous events in first-century Palestine? It was time to cast off the blinkers of prejudice and see beyond the myth.

CHAPTER TWELVE

The Woman Whom Jesus Kissed

The woman known as Mary Magdalene is clearly of enormous, if initially puzzling, significance to the ancient 'heretical' underground movements of Europe. Her links with the Black Madonna cult, with the medieval troubadours and the Gothic cathedrals, with the mystery surrounding the Abbé Saunière of Rennes-le-Château – and with the Priory of Sion – imply that there was something about her that has always been deemed *dangerous* by the Church.

As we have seen, many legends have grown up around this enigmatic and powerful woman. But who was she, and what is her secret?

There are, as we have seen, few explicit references to 'Mary Magdalene' in the New Testament Gospels. Yet it is clear from the way she is mentioned that she was the most important of Jesus' female disciples – all of whom are even now almost totally ignored by the Church. If it does draw attention to them it is usually with the tacit understanding that somehow the word 'disciple' carries more weight when applied to men. In fact the role of the female disciples has been minimized to the most culpable extent by commentators who came well after the Gospel writers. For while the first-century Jews may have had sociological and religious problems with the concept of *important* women simply because of their culture, more recent critics have no such excuse. Yet the debate about women priests in the Anglican ministry – to cite just one example – shows that little has changed in 2000 years. To churchgoers everywhere 'the disciples' are automatically and exclusively the prominent male characters Peter, James, Luke and so on, and *not* 'Mary Magdalene, Joanna, Salome . . .' despite the fact that these women are listed even by the Gospel writers.

During the neverending arguments about women priests (even the women concerned were mostly scrupulous about not using the 'pagan' term *priestess*), extraordinary misrepresentations of Jesus' followers were cited as 'proof' that women were not meant to be members of the clergy. For example, Jesus was said to have chosen his disciples from men only, despite the fact that, as we have seen, women are listed *by name* as being part of his entourage, and despite the fact that the Jewish tradition of the day meant that if it had been possible for the Gospel writers to ignore them entirely they would have done so. The fact that they were named indicates that they had an unavoidably significant part in the ministry – something that was certainly the case in the following generations of Christians. For as Giorgio Otranto, an Italian professor of Church history, and others have shown conclusively, for several hundred years women were not only members of the congregation, they were actually *priests* and even *bishops*.

As the authority on women in early Christianity, Karen Jo Torjesen, writes in her book *When Women Were Priests* (1993):

> Under a high arch in a Roman basilica dedicated to two women saints, Prudentiana and Praxedis, is a mosaic portraying four female figures: the two saints, Mary, and a fourth woman whose hair is veiled and whose head is surrounded by a square halo – an artistic technique indicating that the person was still living at the time the mosaic was made. The four faces gaze out serenely from a glistening gold background. The faces of Mary and the two saints are easily recognizable. But the identity of the fourth is less apparent. A carefully lettered inscription identifies the face on the left as Theodora Episcopa, which means Bishop Theodora. The masculine form for bishop in Latin is *episcopus*; the feminine form is *episcopa*. The mosaic's visual evidence and the inscription's grammatical evidence point out unmistakably that Bishop Theodora was a

woman. But the *a* on Theodora has been partially effaced by scratches across the glass tiles of the mosaic, leading to the disturbing conclusion that attempts were made to deface the feminine ending, perhaps even in antiquity.[1]

Male priests may tie themselves in logical knots trying to explain away such graphic depictions of women priests – some even tried to write Theodora off as the *mother* of the male bishop – but the facts speak for themselves. Women were not merely useful in doing the first-century equivalent of making the coffee and sandwiches; they officiated at the eucharist, and led the congregations in worship. There was no suggestion, in those early days, that a menstruating female priest would somehow taint the symbolic wine and bread, as in recent times[2].

It was only in November, 1992 that the Church of England finally voted on the thorny question of women priests and, by a mere two-vote margin, decided to allow them to be ordained. Although it is not our intention to dwell on the controversy over women priests, we do express our sympathy with the many women who have tried against all the odds to explain to their male 'superiors' that all they are asking for is a *return* to the way it was at the beginning, not some radical twentieth-century reinterpretation. In demanding to be allowed to be ordained, these women were asking for no more than the rights they would have had centuries ago. (Amazingly, the real status of women in the early Church seems to have been known in the sixteenth century: Agrippa's treatise on the superiority of women, discussed in Chapter Seven, includes the words '[we are not] ignorant of so many holy abbesses and nuns among us, whom antiquity did not scorn to call priests.[3])

There were, however, very good reasons for women being so prominent in the Jesus cult – which, unfortunately, made it inevitable that certain types of men would seek to demote and denigrate them. Although we will deal with that issue later, suffice it to say now that there is no doubt that women played a priestly role in the earliest Christian Church, one that was at least equal to that of the men.

One of the more patronizing assumptions of male priests is that the women named in the Epistles and Acts were merely the providers of hospitality for the male Apostles as they went about preaching and baptizing. Women with names such as Luculla and Phillippa are thanked for their patronage, and it is clear that many such women were rich and perhaps surprisingly independent for their time and culture. Although we challenge the view that this was their only function, it is clear from the way Mary Magdalene is described that she was one of the earliest female patrons.

She and other women 'ministered unto them [Jesus and his male disciples] of their substance', indicating that they supported them financially. Elsewhere the women are described as 'following him', and the original words actually implied full participation in the activities and practices of the group.

As we have seen, Mary Magdalene is the only woman in the Gospels not identified by her relationship with a man – as sister, mother, daughter or wife. She is simply named. While this may reflect ignorance on the part of the chroniclers about her identity, it is more likely that she was so well known in her day that it was inconceivable that any early Christian would not know immediately who she was.

But while her relationships with others are open to debate, one thing emerges clearly from the Gospel accounts: Mary Magdalene was an independent woman. And, as Susan Haskins points out, this carries a clear implication that she was 'of some means'[4].

Significantly, very few other Gospel characters are named like Mary (the) Magdalene, and of that handful the two that leap from the page are Jesus the Nazorean and John the Baptist (or, as is becoming the preferred description, the Baptizer).

What does her name signify? 'Magdalene' seems to mean 'of Magdala', and it is always said that this refers to the fishing town of el Mejdel in Galilee. But there is *no evidence* that this is so, or that it was known as Magdala in Jesus' time. (In fact, el Mejdel was called Tarichea by Josephus.) There was, however, a town of Magdolum in the north-east of Egypt, near the border with Judaea – probably the Migdol mentioned in Ezekiel[5].

The meaning of Magdala itself has been open to several possible interpretations, such as 'place of the dove', 'place of the tower' and 'temple-tower'[6].

It may even be that Mary's name was both a reference to a place and a *title*, for in the Old Testament there is a telling prophecy (Micah 4:8):

> And thou, O tower of the flock, the strong hold of the daughter of Zion, unto thee shall it come, even the first dominion; the kingdom shall come to the daughter of Jerusalem.

For, as Margaret Starbird notes in her 1993 study of the Magdalene cult, *The Woman with the Alabaster Jar*, the words translated as 'tower of the flock' are *Magdal-eder*, adding:

> In Hebrew, the epithet *Magdala* literally means 'tower' or 'elevated, great, magnificent'.[7]

Was the Magdalene's connection with towers and, more significantly, with the restoration of Sion, known in her own lifetime? It is also very telling that *Magdal-eder* meant 'tower of the flock', with its implication of watch-tower or guardian of lesser beings – even perhaps of being a 'Good Shepherd'.

Mary Magdalene has already caused a commotion in our own time, when it was claimed in *The Holy Blood and the Holy Grail* that she had been Jesus' wife. Although this suggestion was, in fact, not new, it was the first most people had heard of it, and predictably it caused a stir. The guilt associated with sex is so deeply ingrained in our culture that any suggestion that Jesus had had a sexual partner – even in the context of a monogamous and loving marriage – is seen by many as somehow sacrilegious and disgusting. The concept of a married Jesus continues to be regarded on the whole as unlikely at best and the work of the Devil at worst. Yet there are many reasons for believing that Jesus was indeed in a close relationship – and very probably with Mary Magdalene.

Many commentators have pointed out that the complete silence on the part of the New Testament about Jesus' marital status is very odd. Chroniclers of his time and place routinely described people in terms of what made them *different* from others – and for a man of over thirty not to have been married would have been virtually unique. It must be remembered that we rely on the picture of Jesus that was painted by the Gospel writers and their sources: their perspective was essentially Jewish. The Jews regarded celibacy as *improper*, for it suggested an unwillingness to father the next generation of the Lord's chosen people, and was a matter for rebuke from the elders of the synagogue. Some second-century rabbis, according to Geza Vermes, 'compare deliberate abstention from procreation to murder'[8]. The often gratuitous genealogies in the Bible prove that the Jews were a proudly dynastic race and, indeed, they still greatly value close family ties. Marriage has always been central to the Jewish way of life – never more so than when the nation was under threat, as it was under Roman rule. For a charismatic and famous preacher *not* to have been a husband and father would have been nothing short of a scandal, and it would have been a miracle for his group to have lasted very long, certainly beyond the death of its founder.

According to the New Testament, Jesus and his followers had many enemies. Yet there are no surviving accusations of them being a homosexual enclave – as doubtless there would have been if they had been a group of celibate men: had there ever been such a scandal it would surely have reached Rome and we would have known about it today. Slurs of this sort are not reserved for modern tabloid newspapers – Pilate and his cohorts were sophisticated and worldly Romans – and the Jews acknowledged the existence of homosexuality, if only to condemn it. If Jesus and his male disciples were celibate and preached celibacy, this alone would have caused a stir among the authorities.

Scholars usually avoid the celibacy question, taking on trust the Church's tradition that Jesus was unmarried. But when the subject *is* discussed, the difficulties in proving his marital status emerge very clearly. For example – as we have seen – Geza Vermes, in his attempt to define the historical Jesus, came to the conclusion that he best fitted the mould of the Hasidim, the heirs to the Old Testament prophets. In doing so he tries – sometimes successfully, sometimes less so – to account for Jesus' actions and teachings in terms of such a role, by comparing them with those of other known Hasidim of that time and place. However, when he comes to the question of Jesus' celibacy (which he accepts) he runs into difficulty. He has to admit that most of the individual Hasidim he is using as comparisons were married and had fathered children. In fact, he is only able to come up with one other holy person of that culture who extols celibacy – Pinhas ben Yair – who lived a full century after Jesus, and was not even a Hasid![9] Astoundingly, this was enough for Vermes to conclude that Jesus had a similar lifestyle, but others may not be so easily persuaded. In fact, Pinhas' celibacy was so unusual that it won him notoriety *on those grounds alone*. There is no suggestion that Jesus' lifestyle or message emphasized or promoted celibacy: if it had, we would certainly have known about it.

It is true that there were some Jewish sects such as the Essenes, who were celibate – although, once again, we know this only because it was so unusual as to attract specific comment. Some have used this in favour of the argument that Jesus himself was an Essene. However, the sect is not mentioned once in the entire New Testament, which would hardly have been the case if Jesus had been its most famous member.

The case for Jesus being married has been cited by several modern commentators, but the Gospels' silence on the subject does have another possible interpretation. He could have had a sexual partner who was not his wife, or had been through a form of marriage that was not recognized by the Jews.

(It must be remembered that the heretical tradition stressed that Jesus and the Magdalene were sexual partners, not that they were husband and wife; as we have seen, the Gnostic Gospels, the Cathars and others of the underground network either specifically referred to her as Jesus' 'concubine' or 'consort', or were careful to use such ambiguous words as their 'union'.)

As for positive evidence of Jesus' marital status, it has been argued that the wedding at Cana, at which Jesus turned the water into wine, was in fact his own[10]. In the account, his status appears to be that of the bridegroom. He is expected, for otherwise inexplicable reasons, to supply the wine for the wedding feast. Again, it is interesting that this key event, in which Jesus performs his first public miracle, appears only in John's Gospel and is not mentioned in the other three. There may, however, be another interpretation of this event, which we will discuss later.

Balancing these arguments are the questions: if Jesus were married, then why is there no specific mention of his wife or family in the Gospels? If he was married, who was his wife? Why on earth should his followers have wanted to delete any mention of her? Perhaps they avoided her because her relationship with Jesus offended them and would prove embarrassing to their mission. If they were not married, but had an intimate sexual and spiritual relationship, then the male disciples would have preferred to forget it.

This is precisely the situation that is described so vividly in the Gnostic Gospels, in which the identity of Jesus' partner is clarified. Mary Magdalene was the *sexual partner* of Jesus, and the male disciples resented her influence on their leader.

As for the reason why Jesus' relationship with the Magdalene was covered up, what may seem obvious today will not do in the context of the first century. We might think that the cover-up was because the Christian Church has always, apparently, made women subordinate and looked upon procreation as a necessary evil. However, the evidence is that this anti-marriage attitude is the *result* of this cover-up, not its cause. In fact, the very early Church, before it became an institution and established a hierarchy, did not have any prejudices against women, as we have already seen.

That there was a deliberate cover-up about the Magdalene and her relationship with Jesus is evident, but straightforward misogyny does not explain it. There must have been some other factor that inspired this anti-Magdalene campaign. Presumably this was connected with her character or identity in some way, and/or the nature of her relationship with Jesus. In other words, it was not the fact that Jesus was married, it was whom he was married to that was the problem.

Time and time again during the course of this investigation we had come across these hints that the Magdalene was somehow deemed to be unsavoury. Now we had to find out what there was about her that created this aura of danger, what factors other than mere misogyny lay behind the curious age-old fear of this powerful female friend of Jesus.

The identification of Mary Magdalene, Mary of Bethany (Lazarus' sister) and the 'unnamed sinner' who anoints Jesus in Luke's Gospel has always been hotly debated. The Catholic Church decided at an early date that these three characters were one and the same, although it reversed this position as recently as 1969. The Eastern Orthodox Church has always treated Mary Magdalene and Mary of Bethany as separate characters.

Certainly, discrepancies and contradictions obscure the matter – but such confusion is significant in itself because the Gospels, like a guilty person, tend to become obviously evasive when trying to hide something. The fact that such evasiveness surrounds every description of Bethany, the family that lived there – Lazarus, Mary and Martha – and the events that took place there makes the whole subject more, rather than less, suggestive.

As we have seen, Morton Smith's discovery proves that the removal of the story of the raising of Lazarus from Mark's

Gospel was a deliberate act of censorship. Yet in its only surviving canonical version – in the Gospel of John – it is one of the most pivotal events of the whole story. So why were the early Christians, who took pains to remove it from at least one of the other Gospels, made so uncomfortable by it? Was it, yet again, because the story included *Mary*? Or was the place, Bethany, also somehow tainted?

Luke's Gospel (10:38) describes an episode in which Jesus visits the house of two sisters named Mary and Martha, but there is no mention of a brother, nor – significantly – is the place actually named. It is just called 'a certain village' so offhandedly as to rouse immediate suspicions. After all, it is not as if the name of the place were totally unknown to the other chroniclers. Lazarus, too, is deliberately omitted from Luke. What was there about that place and the family who lived there? (Perhaps there is a clue in the fact that John the Baptist began his ministry in a place called *Bethany*.)

It is also Luke's Gospel (7:36–50) that gives the most obscure account of the anointing of Jesus' feet. Alone of all the Gospel writers he places the event in Capernaum, at the beginning of Jesus' ministry, and he does not name the woman who apparently intruded on his meal by anointing his head and feet with the precious ointment spikenard, and dried him with her hair.

John's Gospel (12:1–8), however, is explicit on the matter. The anointing takes place at the Bethany home of Lazarus, Mary and Martha, and it is Mary who performs the anointing. John's account (11:2) of the raising of Lazarus also stresses that the latter's sister Mary was the woman who later anointed Jesus.

Neither Mark (14:3–9) nor Matthew (26:6–13) name the woman concerned, but they agree that it happened at *Bethany* two (as opposed to John's six) days before the Last Supper. Even so, according to them the anointing took place at the house of one Simon the Leper. It seems that everything about Bethany and that family caused great disquiet among the Synoptic chroniclers to the extent that they 'fudged' the issue, although they had to include the event. They were disturbed by the Bethany story – perhaps for the same reasons as those that made it so important to the heretical underground.

Bethany is also significant because Jesus set out from there on his fatal journey to Jerusalem – to the Last Supper, and on to his arrest and Crucifixion. And although the disciples appear to have known nothing about the coming tragedy, there are suggestions that the family at Bethany were not so unprepared, and, as we have seen, may have made some of the arrangements, such as supplying the donkey on which Jesus rode into the capital.

Mary of Bethany and the unnamed woman who anoints Jesus were clearly one and the same – but was she also Mary Magdalene? Most modern scholars believe that Mary of Bethany and Mary Magdalene were two separate women. But the question remains, why should the Gospel writers have wanted to 'fudge' this issue?

Some scholars, certainly, take the view that the Magdalene and Mary of Bethany were the same. William E. Phipps, for example, believes it is strange that Mary of Bethany – who was clearly a very close friend of Jesus – was not specifically named as being present at the Crucifixion, and that Mary Magdalene suddenly appears at the cross without any major mention beforehand[11]. Phipps also points out that it is possible for two separate epithets – 'of Bethany' or 'of Magdala' – to be applied to the same person, depending on the context. This becomes even more likely if the writers are deliberately trying to obscure the issue.

However, scholars do not, on the whole, even consider the possibility of the Gospel writers' censorship, of deliberately misrepresenting certain aspects of the story they have chosen to tell. (Some, notably Hugh Schonfield, do admit that there is something the Gospel writers are either wilfully withholding from us about the Bethany group, or that there is something about it that the writers simply did not know or understand.) Once such 'fudging' is recognized, then it becomes possible that Mary of Bethany and Mary Magdalene *were* the same person.

This investigation began with an examination of the underground tradition, as exemplified by Leonardo da Vinci and his alleged brotherhood, the Priory of Sion. As we have seen, the first time most English-speaking readers heard of the Priory was in *The Holy Blood and the Holy Grail* – and that book unequivocally argues that Mary Magdalene and Mary of Bethany were the same. Significantly, the 1996 revised version presents new material, including the 'Montgomery document' which, as we have seen, appears to reinforce the whole basis of *The Holy Blood and the Holy Grail*. Specifically, in this context, the document states that Jesus was married to 'Miriam of Bethany' and that she went to France and bore a daughter. Clearly this is supposed to be Mary Magdalene – although the important point here is that Priory apologists *believe* that to be the case. And it must be remembered that in all the traditional accounts of Mary Magdalene going to France – such as *The Golden Legend* – it is assumed that she is the same as Mary of Bethany. But is there any evidence to back this up?

There is a clue in Luke, who, after describing the anointing of Jesus by the 'unnamed sinner', immediately introduces the Magdalene for the first time (8:1–3). It seems that, unconsciously at least, for Luke the association was too strong to be ignored.

Significantly, Jesus himself links not only the *act* of the anointing but also the *person* of the anointer with his forthcoming burial, as, for example, in Mark (14:8): 'She hath done what she could: she is come aforehand to anoint my body to the burying.' This is an implicit connection between this woman of Bethany and Mary Magdalene, for the latter it is who goes to the tomb to anoint Jesus' body for burial just days afterwards. Both the anointing of the live Jesus and the intended anointing of his corpse are ritual acts of great significance, and if nothing else they connect the two women. In any case, it is of supreme importance that the person who anoints Jesus – marking him out for his true destiny – *is a woman*.

While it is not impossible that they were one and the same, it is best to keep an open mind on the issue, as we delve further into the biblical account of the characters and roles of the Magdalene and Mary of Bethany.

Significantly, the persistent idea that Mary Magdalene was a prostitute comes from the traditional association of (or confusion with) her character with Mary of Bethany, who is described as 'a sinner'. Of course, if Mary of Bethany was a prostitute and was also the same person as Mary Magdalene then this would go a long way towards explaining the Gospel writers' extreme caution – and deliberate obfuscation – about the latter. We need to examine the character of Mary of Bethany to see what light it can shed on this matter.

In the Synoptic Gospels the woman who anoints Jesus is not named, although they make the point that she is a sinner, but in John's Gospel she is explicitly identified as Mary of Bethany and her moral status is not mentioned. This in itself might seem somewhat suspicious.

In Luke, the anointing woman is described as 'a woman in the city, which was a sinner'. Although the original Greek for 'sinner' in this context – *harmartolos*, meaning one who has transgressed and placed him or herself outside the law – does not necessarily imply prostitution, the other associated emphasis on her wearing her hair loose – something not done by respectable women – does imply some kind of sexual sin, at least in the eyes of the Gospel writers[12].

In the context of the Jewish culture of those days, there was something unsavoury about Mary of Bethany, but it would not necessarily suggest she was a common whore plying her trade in the street. (Spikenard, which came from a very rare and prized Indian plant, was so prohibitively expensive as to have been outside the resources of a common streetwalker. According to William E. Phipps the spikenard cost her the equivalent of a year's wages for an agricultural labourer[13].) It also seems unlikely that even if Mary were a wealthy 'madam' of a brothel she would openly live with her brother Lazarus and her sister Martha, neither of whom appears to have had any kind of bad reputation, and who are clearly great friends of Jesus, who stayed with them. So just what was the real nature of her 'sin'?

Harmartolos was a term taken from archery, meaning to miss the target: in this context it simply means someone who does not adhere to the Jewish law or ritual observances – either because he or she has failed to keep the prescribed practices, or because he or she is not Jewish at all[14]. If the woman was not, in fact, Jewish then at the very least this may explain the attitude of the Gospel writers towards her. However, it is the detail of her having unbound hair – and the attitude of the disciples towards her – that has given rise to the implication of her transgression being somehow sexual.

It is this air of distastefulness that, intentionally or otherwise, has effectively detracted from the true significance of the anointing of Jesus. There is one major point about this act that has attracted very little attention, but upon which much of Christianity actually depends. It is well known that the term 'Christ' comes from the Greek *Christos*, which in turn is a translation of the Hebrew 'Messiah'. But, despite the widespread belief to the contrary, it carries no implications of divinity: *Christos* simply means 'Anointed One'. (Using this interpretation any anointed functionary is a 'Christ' – from Pontius Pilate to the British Queen.) The idea of a *divine* Christ was a later interpretation of the Christians: the *Jewish* Messiah was expected to be merely a great political and military leader, albeit chosen of God. In his own time, the term 'Messiah' or 'Christ', when applied to Jesus, would simply have meant 'anointed'.

There is, of course, only one anointing of Jesus mentioned in the Gospels. While some have argued that his 'anointing' was in fact the baptism by John, on that reasoning all the multitude who flocked to the Jordan would also have been 'Christs'. The awkward fact remains that the one person who 'Christ-ened' Jesus *was a woman*.

Ironically, Jesus is reported as having remarked at his anointing (Mark 14: 9):

Verily I say unto you, Wheresoever this gospel shall be preached throughout the whole world, this also that she hath done shall be spoken of for a memorial of her.

It is curious that the Church, which has traditionally believed that the anointing woman was *Saint* Mary Magdalene, has ignored this injunction. Considering how the Magdalene is patronized in general from pulpits the world over, it seems that the words of Jesus themselves, are, like everything else in the New Testament, subject to a relentless process of selectivity. In this case Jesus' words are mostly totally ignored. But even on the rare occasions when she is given her due for this episode, there is silence on its implications.

Only two people are named in the New Testament as having officiated at major rites in Jesus' life: John, who baptized him at the beginning of his ministry and Mary of Bethany, who anointed him at the end. Yet, as we have seen, both these people have been marginalized by the Gospel writers – it is as if they have only been included because what they did was too important to have been left out. And there is one major reason for this: the baptism and the anointing *imply authority on the part of those who officiated*. For though a baptizer and an anointer *bestow* authority – in much the same way as the Archbishop of Canterbury conferred the regal status on Queen Elizabeth II in 1953 – *they themselves must have had authority to do so.*

We will be dealing with the issue of John's authority later, but consider the curious fact that the anointing story is even included. If the anointing of Jesus had been a frivolous or meaningless gesture it would never have been recorded at all. Yet here we are told that the disciples, especially Judas, condemned Mary for using the rare and expensive unguent of spikenard to anoint Jesus on the grounds that it could have been sold to raise money for the poor. Jesus responds that there will always be poor people, but he will not always be there (to be so honoured). This rebuke – apart from arguing against any

337

notion that Jesus was some kind of proto-Marxist – not only justifies Mary's action, but also implies strongly that only he and she actually understood it. The male disciples – as usual – seem at a loss to comprehend the finer points of this highly significant ritual, and were actively hostile to Mary's actions, although Jesus himself took care to uphold her authority. This event had another importance: it marked the moment when Judas became the betrayer – immediately afterwards he sells Jesus to the priests.

Mary of Bethany 'Christ-ened' Jesus with the spikenard, an unguent that had, very likely, been kept for that specific occasion, and was an ointment associated with burial rites. Jesus himself remarked of the anointing (Mark 14:8): '. . . she has come aforehand to anoint my body to the burying'. In his mind, at least, it was intended to be a *ritual*.

Clearly, the anointing carried a profound significance – but what was its precise purpose? And why, in that society at that time, was it done by a woman? Given the gender and reputation (however ill-deserved) of the anointer, the ceremony is hardly typical of Judaic practice. Perhaps there is a clue to the real nature of the anointing in the 'Montgomery document'.

As we have seen, this account tells of the marriage of Jesus to Miriam of Bethany, who is described as a 'priestess of a female cult' – a goddess-worshipping tradition. If true, this may explain why the anointing seemed so foreign to the other disciples, although there is still the apparent problem as to why Jesus should be so tolerant of it. And if she really were a pagan priestess this would explain why the male disciples thought of her as being of dubious morals and character.

If Mary of Bethany were really a pagan priestess, why was she anointing Jesus? More to the point, why did he allow her to do so? And are there any parallels between this ritual and those commonly associated with the paganism of that day? In fact, there is one ancient rite that is strikingly relevant: the anointing of the *sacred king*. The idea behind this was that a true king or priest could only receive his full divine power through the authority of the high priestess. This traditionally took the form of the *hieros gamos*, or sacred marriage: the king-priest uniting with the queen-priestess. It was through sexual union with her that he actually became the acknowledged king. Without her he was nothing.

There is nothing in the modern life of the West that echoes this concept or practice, and it is difficult for people today to begin to understand the whole notion of the *hieros gamos*. Outside the intimate world of individual couples, we have no concept of sacred sexuality. Yet this is not merely about sex or eroticism, no matter how elevated it is believed to be: in the sacred marriage the man and woman *actually become the gods*. It is the high priestess who becomes the goddess herself, who then bestows the ultimate blessing of regeneration – as in alchemy – on the man, who embodies the god. Their union was believed to infuse both themselves and the world around them with a regenerative balm, and actually echo the creative impulse of the birth of the planet.[15]

The *hieros gamos* was the ultimate expression of what is termed 'temple prostitution', where a man visited a priestess in order to receive gnosis – to experience the divine for himself through the act of lovemaking. Significantly, the original word for such a priestess is *hierodule*, which means 'sacred servant'[16]; the word 'prostitute', with all its implied moral judgement, was a Victorian rendering. Moreover, this temple servant is, unlike the secular prostitute, acknowledged to be in control of both the situation and the man who visits her, and both of them receive benefits in terms of physical, spiritual and magical empowerment. The body of the priestess had become, in a way almost unimaginable to today's Western lovers, literally and metaphorically a gateway to the gods.

Of course nothing could be further from the attitude of even the modern Church both to the sex act and to women. For not only did the so-called temple prostitution bestow spiritual enlightenment – a process known as *horasis* – but without car-nal 'knowledge' of the hierodule a man would remain spiritually unfulfilled. Of himself he had little hope of ecstatic contact with God or the gods, but women had need of no such ceremony: to these pagans women are naturally in touch with the Divine.

It is possible that the 'anointing' performed on Jesus was symbolic of the sexual act of penetration. Yet although it is not necessary to think in those terms to comprehend the solemnity of the ritual, there are unavoidable associations with the ancient rites in which the priestess, who represented the goddess, was physically prepared to 'receive' the man who had been chosen to symbolize the sacred king, or saviour god. All the mystery schools of Osiris, Tammuz, Dionysus, Attis and so on included a rite – enacted by their human stand-ins – in which the god was anointed by the goddess prior to his actual or symbolic death, which would make the land fertile once more. Traditionally it was *three days afterwards* that, thanks to the magical intervention of the priestess/goddess, he rose again and the nation could heave a sigh of relief until the next year. (The mystery plays have the goddess saying, 'They have removed my Lord and I do not know where to find him' – virtually the same words as those ascribed to Mary Magdalene in the garden. We will be discussing this in detail later.)

Clues to the real significance of the anointing of Jesus can be found in the Old Testament book of the Song of Songs (1:12), where the 'Beloved' says: 'While the *King* sitteth at his table, *my spikenard* sendeth forth the smell thereof.' It must be remembered that Jesus himself associated his anointing with his burial, so the very next verse assumes another significance: 'A bundle of myrrh is my well-beloved unto me: he shall lie all night betwixt my breasts.'

This is a clear link between the anointing of Jesus and the Song of Songs. Many authorities believe the Song of Songs actually to have been the liturgy from a sacred marriage rite, pointing to its many similarities to such liturgies from Egypt and other Middle Eastern countries.[17]

There is one particularly striking resonance: as Margaret Starbird says:

Lines that are identical and parallel to those in the Song of Songs are found in the liturgical poem from the cult of the

Egyptian goddess Isis, the Sister-Bride of the mutilated . . . Osiris.[18]

The goddess/priestess unites with the god/priest in the sacred marriage for complex reasons. Superficially it is a fertility rite, to ensure personal and national fecundity, to secure the future of the people and their land. But it is also through the ecstasy and intimacy of the sex rite that the goddess/priestess bestows wisdom on her partner. The Jungian analyst Nancy Qualls-Corbett in her *The Sacred Prostitute* (1988) lays great emphasis on the link between the sacred whore and the Feminine Principle as symbolized by Sophia (Wisdom)[19]. As we have seen, Sophia repeatedly occurred in our investigations – she was particularly venerated by the Templars – and is strongly associated with both the Magdalene and Isis.

The anointing of Jesus was a pagan ritual: the woman who performed it – Mary of Bethany – was a priestess. Given this new scenario it is more than likely that her role in Jesus' inner circle was as sexual initiatrix. But let us remember that both the heretics and the Catholic Church have long believed that Mary of Bethany and Mary Magdalene were the same person: in this figure of sexual initiatrix we finally have the missing reason for the confusion about the Magdalene's true role and significance in Jesus' life. If she really were a hierodule operating in the patriarchal world of Judaism she would inevitably be thought of as a moral outcast. But as long as she was with Jesus she was protected, if only just, from the effects of that righteous outrage, as her various interchanges with Simon Peter (as given in the Gnostic Gospels) clearly show.

The Priory of Sion, as we have already noted, are devotees of the goddess – in the form of the Black Madonna, as Mary Magdalene or as Isis herself. They clearly associate Mary Magdalene with Isis: this is central to their very *raison d'être*, although at first this seems distinctly puzzling. However, it is clear that they see the Magdalene as a pagan priestess – at the very least, this is another parallel between her and Mary of Bethany.

Mary Magdalene's role as pagan priestess is recognized by Baigent, Leigh and Lincoln but, while raising the subject, they appear to deem its implications unworthy of further attention. For example, while they argue that the Magdalene was connected with a goddess cult, they conclude that 'prior to her affiliation with Jesus, the Magdalene may well have been associated with such a cult.'[20] And then they drop the matter. However, the crucial phrase here is *prior to* her affiliation with Jesus', assuming that he converted her, and echoing the traditional view that she was a reformed character through her relationship with him. This view, however, may be somewhat naive – although to challenge it is to evoke a profoundly disquieting alternative scenario.

Qualls-Corbett also cites the connection between the Sacred Whore, Sophia and the Black Madonna, thus underlining the links we described in Part One[21]. This multifaceted personification of the Female Principle sheds light on the great, and jealously guarded, erotic secret of the Western occult tradition. For Sophia *is* the Whore, who is also the 'Dearly Beloved' of the sacred marriage, and who is Mary Magdalene, the Black Madonna and Isis. The sacred sexuality implicit in the alchemists' Great Work is a direct continuation of this ancient tradition, in which the sex rite bestows spiritual enlightenment and even physical transformation. It is after this supreme experience with the goddess/priestess that the god/priest is so changed that he may no longer be recognizable and is 'resurrected' unto a new life.

Significantly, as Nancy Qualls-Corbett and other recent commentators have pointed out, the portrayal of Mary Magdalene in the Gnostic Gospels is that of illuminatrix and illuminator – Mary Lucifer, the light-bringer – the bestower of enlightenment through sacred sexuality. And taken with our conclusions about Mary of Bethany, it seems that she and Mary Magdalene are indeed the same woman.

This scenario also reinforces the idea that Mary was Jesus' wife, although it essentially redefines that word. She was his partner in a *sacred* marriage, which was not necessarily a love match. Interestingly, as we have seen, the Song of Songs is a sacred marriage liturgy – and this has always been linked with Mary Magdalene.

Sacred sexuality – anathema to the Church of Rome – finds expression in the concept of the sacred marriage and 'sacred prostitution', in the ancient Oriental systems of Taoism and Tantrism, and in alchemy.

As Marvin H. Pope says in his exhaustive work on the Song of Songs (1977):

> The Tantric hymns to the Goddess offer some of the most provocative parallels to the Song of Songs.[22]

And as Peter Redgrove explains in his *The Black Goddess* (1989), while discussing the sexual arts of Taoism:

> It is interesting to compare this with Middle-Eastern sexual religious practices, and the image of them which we have inherited. Mari-Ishtar, the Great Whore, anointed her consort Tammuz (with whom Jesus was identified) and thereby made him a Christ. This was in preparation for his descent into the underworld, from which he would return at her bidding. She, or her priestess, was called the Great Whore because this was a sexual rite of *horasis*, of whole-body orgasm that would take the consort into the visionary knowledgeable continuum. It was a rite of crossing, from which he would return transformed. In the same way Jesus said that Mary Magdalene anointed him for his burial. Only women could perform these rites in the goddess' name, and this is why no men attended his tomb, only Mary Magdalene and her women. A chief symbol of the Magdalene in Christian art was the cruse of holy oil – the external sign of the inner baptism experienced by the Taoist . . .[23]

There is something else that is of great importance about that cruse of oil with which the Magdalene anointed Jesus. As we have seen, the Gospels tell us that it was spikenard – an

343

unguent that was exceptionally costly. The reason for its high price was that it had to come all the way from India, home of the ancient sexual art of Tantrism. And in the Tantric tradition different perfumes and oils are assigned to specific areas of the body: *spikenard was for the hair and feet* . . .

In the Epic of Gilgamesh, the sacrificial kings are told: 'The harlot who anointed you with fragrant oil weeps for you now', while a similar phrase was used in the mysteries of the dying god Tammuz, whose cult was prevalent in Jerusalem in Jesus' time[24]. And significantly the 'seven devils' that Jesus allegedly cast out of the Magdalene may be seen as the seven Maskim, Sumero-Akkadian spirits who ruled the sacred seven spheres and who had been *born of the goddess Mari.*[25]

In the tradition of the sacred marriage, it was the bride of the sacrificial king – the High Priestess – who chose the moment of his death, who attended his burial and whose magic brought him out of the underworld to new life. In most cases, of course, this 'resurrection' was purely symbolic, being seen in the new life of springtime – or, in the case of Osiris, in the annual flooding of the Nile valley that would renew the fertility of the land.

So we may see Mary Magdalene's anointing for what it was – both as an announcement that the moment for Jesus' sacrifice had arrived, and as a ritual setting-apart of the sacred king, by virtue of her own authority as priestess. That this role is diametrically opposed to the one that the Church has traditionally assigned to her should, by now, come as no surprise.

In our opinion, the Catholic Church never wanted its members to know about the true relationship between Jesus and Mary, which is why the Gnostic Gospels were not included in the New Testament and why most Christians do not even know they exist. The Council of Nicaea, when it rejected the many Gnostic Gospels and voted to include only Matthew, Mark, Luke and John in the New Testament, had no divine mandate for this major act of censorship. They acted out of self-preservation, for by that time – the fourth century – the power of the Magdalene and her followers was already too widespread for the patriarchy to cope with.

According to that censored material, which was deliberately rejected to prevent the true picture being known, Jesus gave the Magdalene the title of 'Apostle of the Apostles' and 'the Woman Who Knew All'. He said that she would be raised above all the other disciples and rule the forthcoming Kingdom of Light. As we have seen, he also called her *'Mary Lucifer'* – 'Mary the Light-bringer' – and it was claimed that he brought Lazarus back from the dead simply out of love for her, there being nothing he would not have done for her, nothing he could refuse her. The Gnostic *Gospel of Philip* describes how the other disciples disliked her, and how Peter in particular sought to argue about her status with Jesus – even, rather ingenuously, on one occasion asking him why he preferred her to the other disciples and why was he always *kissing her on the mouth*! In the Gnostic *Gospel of Mary*, the Magdalene says that Peter hated her and 'all the race of women' and in the *Gospel of Thomas*, Peter says 'Let Mary leave us, for women are not worthy of life' – a foretaste of the grim battle between the Church of Rome, which was founded by Peter, and the heretical underground that belonged to Mary. (It is instructive to remember that this began as the personal clash of two individuals – and one of them was Jesus' *consort*.)

Significantly, the Gnostic *Gospel of Philip* (which specifically describes the Magdalene as Jesus' sexual partner), is replete with allusions to unions between men and women, between bride and bridegroom. Ultimate enlightenment is symbolized by fruits of the union of the bride and bridegroom: here Jesus is the bridegroom, his bride is Sophia – and Jesus making her pregnant is the coming of gnosis[26]. (And interestingly, even in the canonical Gospels Jesus frequently speaks of himself as 'the Bridegroom'.) The Gospel of Philip also clearly associates Mary Magdalene with Sophia[27].

That Gnostic Gospel lists five initiatory rites or sacraments: baptism, *chrism* (anointing), eucharist, redemption – and the highest of all, 'the bridal chamber':

> The chrism is superior to baptism ... and Christ is (so) called
> because of the chrism ... He who is anointed possesses the All.
> He possesses the resurrection, the light, the Cross, the Holy
> Spirit. The Father gave him this in the bridal chamber.[28]

If the rite of sacrament of *chrism* was superior to that of baptism, then this implies that Mary's authority was actually greater than John the Baptist's. Even more significantly, however, the *Gospel of Philip* makes it clear that *all* the Gnostics who followed that system, not just Jesus, became 'Christs' upon their anointing. And the highest sacrament was that of the 'bridal chamber' – which is never explained and remains a mystery to historians. However, in the light of this investigation, one can make a shrewd guess: certainly the words of the passage contain a clue to the true nature of the relationship between Jesus and Mary. As we have seen, the latter was also known in the Gnostic Gospels as 'the woman who knows the All', and here we are told that 'he who is anointed *possesses the All*'. And the *Gospel of Philip* states bluntly: 'Understand what great power undefiled intercourse possesses'.[29]

The third-century Gnostic scripture known as the *Pistis Sophia* sets forth what claimed to be the teachings of Jesus twelve years after his resurrection. In this the Magdalene is portrayed in the archetypal role of catechist, questioning him to elicit his wisdom – just like the Oriental Shakti or goddess ritually questioning her divine consort. It is remarkable that in the *Pistis Sophia* Jesus uses the same term for Mary as the one used of those goddesses – 'Dearly Beloved'. These are also the words used of one partner for the other in a sacred marriage.

The intimacy of Jesus and Mary carries another profound implication. A comparison of their relationship and that of Jesus and his disciples leaves little doubt as to who was really privy to his ideas, thoughts and secrets. The male disciples are frequently portrayed as being rather *dim*. Time and time again they 'knew not what he meant' – hardly an inspiring quality in the men who would one day, apparently, found their leader's

Church. True, the Acts of the Apostles tell of the heavenly fire of Pentecost that bestowed some wisdom and power on the disciples, but the Gnostic Gospels tell of the one disciple who was in no need of such heavenly intervention. According to that censored material it was the Magdalene who rallied the stricken disciples after the Crucifixion and, by dint of her stirring words only, inspired them to take up the cause when they seemed more than ready to give up. Admittedly she had seen the risen Jesus with her own eyes, but once again one is left with the curious sense of their lack of motivation, faith and courage compared with hers.

Could it be that the Twelve were not, in fact, the inner circle of Jesus' followers at all but were at best simply the most loyal of his *uninitiated* devotees? In retrospect their ignorance was astonishing. For example, although Jesus' death and resurrection were quintessentially what his mission was all about, the men did not expect it to take place: 'They knew not the scripture, that he must rise again from the dead.'[30]

It was Mary Magdalene and her women followers who went to the tomb. Perhaps her words to the 'gardener' – in reality the risen Jesus – about her 'Lord' having been taken away and that she 'knew not where they have laid him' could mean that she was just as unaware of what was going on as the men. But there are compelling reasons for seeing her words in the context of her being privy to, perhaps a priestess of, the inner mysteries. Mary Magdalene was in all probability Jesus' consort and the first Apostle, and it seems likely that her role comprised another, older and more pagan ritual significance.

It is assumed that no men attended Jesus' tomb because that was not the kind of thing that men did in those days. But, judging from the Gnostic accounts of the stunned apathy of the male disciples after the Crucifixion, mere custom was not the explanation for their absence. In the tradition of the mysteries, only priestesses proclaimed the climax of the king's sacrifice – his miraculous resurrection.

Even if the apparent similarities between Jesus' anointing, death and resurrection and the pagan traditions prevalent in

347

his day are accepted, the question remains as to why a Jewish preacher could possibly have become involved in such a scenario. For although Mary Magdalene does appear to have been part of some cult involving sacred harlots, and her influence over her consort was undoubtedly great, what possible reason could Jesus have had to turn his back on centuries of ingrained Jewish tradition? How could he, of all people, have participated in a *pagan* rite?

This very question confronts us with a hitherto unimaginable possibility. As we have seen, the reality concerning Jesus and his mission may be very different from the one taught by the Church. Even to suspend disbelief and consider *what if* the hypothesis offered above is true is to create a completely new scenario. *What if* Jesus was a partner in a sacred marriage and therefore a willing participant in pagan sexual rites; *what if* Mary Magdalene was really a high priestess of a goddess cult and *at least Jesus' spiritual equal*, and *what if* Peter and the other male disciples were not, in fact, part of the inner circle of the movement? There is another question to be asked: with such a radical new framework in place – however hypothetically – what kind of man was really at its centre? Who was the real Jesus?

CHAPTER THIRTEEN

Son of the Goddess

As we have seen, modern historical scholarship has presented a mass of thought-provoking new discoveries about the origins of Christianity, and yet the gulf between what biblical scholars know about the religion and what Christians themselves know, is, if anything, widening. Burton L. Mack, Professor of New Testament Studies at Claremont School of Theology, California, recently lamented 'the frightful lack of basic knowledge about the formation of the New Testament among average Christians.'[1]

That New Testament analysis as we know it only began in the nineteenth century reflects the almost superstitious reluctance to examine the original texts that came of the Church's age-long prohibition on Bible reading for the masses. For centuries only priests read the Scriptures – in fact, in most cases they had the monopoly of literacy. The rise of Protestantism partly overcame this exclusivity, and gave many more people access to the texts that they deemed sacred. However, all extreme forms of the Protestant movement – from Puritanism to what is now known as Fundamentalism – have stressed the divine inspiration behind the words of the New Testament, and on those grounds alone forbade any suggestion that they might *not* be the literal truth. To this day, millions of Christians ignore the evidence for the New Testament being a mixture of myth, fabrication, garbled versions of eyewitness accounts and material taken from other traditions. But in avoiding this evidence they are not only missing the point but also maintaining a belief system that is increasingly vulnerable to criticism.

When nineteenth-century scholars did begin to employ the

same criteria that are routinely used to analyse other historical texts, the results were extremely telling. One of the first developments to emerge was the assertion that Jesus never actually existed, and that the Gospels were simply composed of mythological and metaphorical material. Nowadays few New Testament scholars agree with this view – although, as we shall see, it still has its advocates. The case for an historical Jesus is sound enough, but it is still instructive to look into the reasoning of those who believed it was not, and that Jesus was a complete invention of the early Christians.

Advocates of this view say that, outside the Gospels themselves, there is no independent evidence that Jesus ever actually existed. (This in itself comes as a shock to many Christians who assume that, because he is central to their world, he must have been very famous in his day: in fact he is not mentioned in *any* contemporary text.) The other books of the New Testament – for example, Paul's Epistles – take Jesus' existence for granted but offer no solid evidence for it. Paul, whose letters are the oldest known Christian writings, gives no biographical details about Jesus at all apart from those surrounding his Crucifixion – nothing about his parents, his birth or the background of his life. But then Paul, like the other New Testament authors, is concerned more with theology, with maintaining the Jesus movement and explaining its teachings, than with the biography of its founder.

Many nineteenth-century historians were worried about the lack of any contemporary record of Jesus. As we have seen, no first-century chronicler mentions him at all. And, as Bamber Gascoigne has written: 'For the first fifty years of what we now call the Christian era, not a word survives about Christ or his followers.'[2]

The Roman writer Tacitus (in his *Annals*, c115 CE) records the growth of Christianity – which he calls a 'dangerous superstition' – in both Jerusalem and Rome, and refers in passing to the execution of its founder, but gives no details and refers to him simply by the title 'Christ'[3].

Suetonius, in his *Lives of the Caesars* (c.120), refers to unrest among Jews in Rome in 49 CE at the instigation of 'Chrestus'. This is often quoted as evidence for an early Roman branch of Christianity, but it is not necessarily so. There were many self-proclaimed Messiahs among the Jews at that time, all of whom could be termed, in Greek, 'Christs', and Suetonius writes as if this particular one was actively, and in person, inciting Jewish rebellion in Rome at the time.[4]

Another notable Roman who had dealings with the Christians in the early years of the first century was Pliny the Younger, but beyond saying that their movement was founded by 'Christ' he gives no other information about them. What is particularly interesting about his account, however, is the fact that it shows that this Christ was already regarded as a god.[5]

These were Roman writers, and, as Palestine was something of a backwater of their empire, it is not surprising that they should neglect Jesus and the early days of the Christian Church. (Besides, rebels and criminals were not so readily given the limelight as they are in our own celebrity-minded age. Even the rebellion of the ex-slave Spartacus was given relatively little chronicle space.) However, one would have imagined that the life and ministry of Jesus might have been quoted in the works of Flavius Josephus (38–c100), a Jew who switched sides in the Jewish Revolt and wrote two books chronicling the history of the period. His *Antiquities of the Jews* (written around 93 CE) does, in fact, mention other characters from the Gospel story, most significantly John the Baptist and Pontius Pilate. There is one reference to Jesus, but unfortunately it has long been recognized to have been added to Josephus' work by a much later Christian writer, probably in the early fourth century – precisely in order to overcome the otherwise embarrassing silence on the subject[6]. In fact that reference to Jesus is far too reverential, to the extent that commentators have wondered why, if Josephus really thought of him in such glowing terms, he himself was never converted to Christianity! The real question, however, was whether or not this insertion merely provided a reference where none existed, or was a substitute for one that was less than flattering about Jesus and his movement. We cannot be sure either way, although the weight of evidence is in favour of its being a complete invention; the passage is not even in Josephus' style and it fits awkwardly into the flow of the story. Moreover, the Christian writer Origen, in the late third century, does not seem to have been aware of any reference to Jesus in Josephus' work[7]. (Although Eusebius does quote the reference when writing in the following century.) However, Josephus' reference to the preaching of John the Baptist and his execution by Herod Antipas is not disputed.[8]

Of course the lack of contemporary references to Jesus outside the Gospels does not mean that he never existed. It could simply mean that his impact on his time and place was not great enough. After all, there were many other would-be Messiahs around at the time who have escaped our attention.

There is also the problem why, if no such person existed, anyone should have invented him, and why so many people should have believed the story to the extent that a religion in his name flourished so quickly. As Geoffrey Ashe points out, the concept of fictional characters, which is so much a part of our own culture, was not familiar at all to ancient authors[9]. Even if they were writing what was essentially fiction, it was always based on a real character, such as Alexander the Great. For this reason alone it seems highly unlikely that Jesus was a complete invention – and if there had simply been any great cultural or spiritual demand for a 'Dying God', there were already enough to choose from, as we shall see. There was no necessity to invent another one.

It is significant, too, that the Gospel writers set Jesus against a background of known historical characters, such as John the Baptist and Pilate. This also argues in favour of his actuality, and besides, not one of the early critics of Christianity challenged the existence of its founder, which they certainly would have done if there had been any doubt on the matter.

And the very way in which Jesus is portrayed indicates that he was a real man. No writer would have gone to the trouble of creating a fictitious Messiah and yet depict him as being so ambiguous, even elusive, about his role, nor would he leave quite so many impenetrable sayings and allusions among his alleged teachings. The ambiguity, the apparent contradictions and the sometimes downright unintelligible turns of phrase mark the Gospels out as the – somewhat muddled – accounts of the words and deeds of a genuine historical character.

Paul's lack of any mention of Jesus' biographical details has been taken by the sceptics as evidence that Christ did not exist. But no-one argues that Paul was himself a fabrication – and he definitely knew people who had met Jesus. For example, Paul not only met Peter but fell out with him (and this less than seemly behaviour is evidence that *they* were real – no writer in those days would have made his heroes so flawed). So it seems likely that Jesus did exist – but of course that does not in itself mean that everything in the Gospels is true.

But there was another reason for many nineteenth-century scholars to doubt the existence of Jesus. As historical knowledge grew and the New Testament was increasingly subjected to critical analysis, it became obvious that the Jesus story had uncannily close parallels with those of famous mythological figures; specifically with the dying-and-rising gods of the ancient Middle East, who were worshipped in the mystery cults that flourished at the same time as Christianity, and which long predated it.

One of the most erudite and persuasive expositions of this argument is J.M. Robertson's *Pagan Christs*, published in 1903. In his introduction to a recent abridgement, Hector Hawton summarized the position in the form of the question:

> . . . no one seriously claims that Adonis, Attis and Osiris were historical characters . . . why, then, is an exception made of the alleged founder of Christianity?[10]

These parallels relate to Christianity in two ways. First, in the accounts of the events of Jesus' life, such as his death and Resurrection and his inauguration of the eucharist at the Last Supper, and secondly in the meaning invested in those events by the early Christians. A brief résumé of the main relevant points made by Robertson and other leading commentators underlines the fact that many of the most sacred parts of the Jesus story are identical to those from other ancient religions.

Robertson says:

> Like Christ, and like Adonis and Attis, Osiris and Dionysus also suffer and rise again. To become one with them is the mystical passion of their worshippers. They are all alike in that their mysteries give immortality. From Mithraism Christ takes the symbolic keys of heaven and assumes the function of the virgin-born Saoshayant, the destroyer of the Evil One . . .[11]
>
> In fundamentals, therefore, Christism is but paganism reshaped.[12]
>
> The Christian myth grew by absorbing details from pagan cults . . . Like the image of the child-god in the cult of Dionysus, he was pictured in swaddling clothes in a basket manger. He was born in a stable like Horus – the stable-temple of the Virgin goddess Isis, queen of heaven. Again like Dionysus, he turned water into wine; like Aesculapius, he raised men from the dead and gave sight to the blind; and like Attis and Adonis, he is mourned and rejoiced over by women. His resurrection took place, like that of Mithra, from a rock-tomb . . .[13]
>
> [our italics] *There is not a conception associated with Christ that is not common to some or all of the Saviour cults of antiquity.*[14]

If it is astonishing that the points raised by Robertson and others made such little impact at the time, it is even more astounding that they are still largely unknown today. A more recent voice on the subject is that of Burton L. Mack, writing in 1994:

> Study after study has shown that early Christianity was not a unique religion but had been 'influenced' by the religions of late antiquity . . . unsettling was the discovery that early Christianity bore a distinct resemblance to the hellenistic

354

mystery cults, particularly where it mattered most, namely their myths of dying and rising gods and in their rituals of baptism and sacred meals.[15]

Hugh Schonfield says in his *The Passover Plot*:

> Christians continue to be troubled today by the Church's contradictory doctrines, which arose from the unhappy endeavour to blend incompatible Pagan and Jewish ideals.[16]

Scholars such as Robertson found it inconceivable that it was a coincidence that so many elements from dying god cults could be found in the Jesus story. They concluded that the Gospels had taken the key events from the stories of Osiris, Attis and the like and grafted them onto a 'home-grown' hero – Jesus – who never existed.

A recent advocate of this idea is Ahmed Osman, who, in his *House of the Messiah*, advances the theory that the Gospel stories actually recorded a mystery play dating back many centuries to the time of Ancient Egypt. Like his predecessors, Osman builds his case on the striking parallels between Jesus' myth and the stories of the ancient Egyptian religion, and on the doubts about Jesus' historical existence.[17]

But why would anyone hijack a mystery play from another tradition and introduce real people into it such as John the Baptist? Osman thinks that the Gospel story was *an invention of the followers of John the Baptist*. According to his thesis, they invented Jesus in order to fulfil their masters' prophecy about one who was to come after him, and whose predicted advent was, presumably, conspicuous by its absence. However, this is implausible for several reasons: the followers of John would hardly have fabricated a story in which their own beloved master was so marginalized – only being included at all in order to set the scene for the glorification of somebody else. And, as we shall see, it is by no means even certain that John ever made his famous prophecy about a greater one who was to come after him.

According to Osman, no-one would have known about Jesus' mission as Redeemer until after he had actually died, so he would have had no large following in his lifetime. Osman clearly thinks that the Jews were expecting a Messiah who would die for them. This is simply not the case – the Jews never expected their hero-king to be sacrificed or shamed in this way. The whole idea of the redemptive death as we know it is a later Christian interpretation.

Few other scholars today doubt that Jesus existed, although the majority of them still have problems with the clear examples of mystery school references in the Gospels. Finding it impossible to reconcile them with the more obvious Jewish material, they tend to reject the pagan allusions. They claim that these were added as the early Christians came into contact with the wider Roman Empire, particularly as a result of Paul's travels. The accepted view is that the Jerusalem Church, led by Jesus' brother James the Just, represented the 'pure', original form of Christianity. Unfortunately, due to an accident of history, James' Church was wiped out during the Jewish Revolt, so the nature of its beliefs must remain a matter for speculation. We do know, however, that its followers worshipped in the Jerusalem Temple, so it is reasonable to assume that their beliefs were based on Judaic practices. After the collapse of the Jerusalem Church, the stage was clear for Paul's to take over. On the face of it, this seems to provide an elegant solution to the problem of why so much mystery school material can be found in the Gospels as we know them.

There might be another explanation – if the argument is turned on its head. What if *Paul's* version of Christianity were the nearer to Jesus' own teaching and it was the Jerusalem Church that had got it wrong? Brothers do not inevitably understand each other, and certainly there was a marked coolness between Jesus and his family, so there is no reason to assume that James' Christianity was any closer than Paul's to Jesus' original teachings.

The accepted view of the development of early Christianity

fails to explain why Paul, who was a Jew himself, should have felt the need to preach a paganized form of the fledgling religion. His famous conversion on the road to Damascus probably happened within, at the most, five years of the Crucifixion – and, as his previous role had been that of persecutor of the Christians presumably he had a sound idea of what he was persecuting them for.

Our discoveries about the Magdalene being an initiatrix of a mystery school carry the implication that Jesus himself was also an initiate – perhaps because she initiated him. But how could he be so deeply involved with a pagan cult when everyone knows that he was Jewish?

We have discovered that nothing at all should be taken for granted in this story. We thought it worth challenging the usual preconceptions about Jesus' own religious background head on. As Morton Smith says ironically in his *Jesus the Magician* (which we will be discussing in detail shortly)

> Of course Jesus was a Jew, and so were all of his disciples –
> presumably. The presumption is not certain.[18]

To start with, it is worth asking *how* we 'know' these things about Jesus.

The accepted academic view of Jesus discussed above is based on two assumptions that try to make sense of the evident contradiction between Jewish and pagan elements in his story.

The first assumption is that Jesus was Jewish – although exactly which sect he belonged to is a matter of dispute. As we have seen, the second assumption is that the overtly pagan, mystery-cult aspects of the Gospel stories are the result of later inventions. The argument is that, as Christianity began to spread in non-Jewish communities within the Roman world, affinities with the mysteries were perceived and elaborated upon, especially as they could help to explain away Jesus' conspicuous failure to fulfil the role of Jewish Messiah.

It came as a shock to us to realize that these really were just assumptions, and not solid proven fact. Neither of them is based on the quality of evidence normally demanded by historians. There is no solid evidence that the pagan elements came from Paul. They may, of course, have come from one of his fellow missionaries – the spread of Christianity was, despite the success of Paul's own publicity, not entirely due to him. When he arrived in Rome, for example, he discovered that there were already Christians there.

It seems that even in the sceptical twentieth century there is such widespread tacit acceptance of the Christian story that even normally critical academics fail to see their own preconceptions for what they are. For example, A.N. Wilson, usually a shrewd and analytical commentator, wrote the following two sentences one after the other without apparently noticing the contradiction between them:

> ... it is necessary, before one starts [to try to answer the questions about the historical Jesus], to empty the mind and take nothing for granted. The centre of Jesus' teaching was his belief in God, and his belief in Judaism.[19]

We decided to see just what would happen if we *did* question these assumptions.

The standard version of the early development of Christianity always relies on the basic premise that Jesus was of the Jewish religion, which meant that many otherwise intriguing aspects of the Gospel story have automatically been rejected. We looked more closely at the assumption of Jesus' Jewishness – which of course implies both an ethnic and a religious background – and soon found ourselves challenging it. (He may have been ethnically a Jew, but not of the Judaic religion: for the purposes of this argument we will use the term 'Jewish' when referring to Jesus in the latter sense only, unless otherwise stated.)

Of course our challenging this assumption was not without trepidation: we were, after all, taking on the full weight of over a century of New Testament scholarship. So we were more than a little relieved to discover that the latest trend in New Testament studies was based on exactly the same question: was Jesus really a Jew?

The first such work to reach a popular audience was Burton L. Mack's *The Lost Gospel* in 1994, although several other scholars had been publishing the results of their research along similar lines in learned journals since the late 1980s.

Mack approached the problem from the viewpoint of Jesus' teachings rather than his life story. He bases his argument on the lost source for the Synoptic Gospels, known as Q (from the German *Quelle*, meaning 'source'), or as much of it as can be reconstructed from a comparison of those Gospels. He concludes that Jesus' teachings did not come from Judaism, but were more closely related to the concepts, and even the style, of certain Greek philosophical schools, especially that of the Cynics.

Q is reliably believed to have been a collection of the sayings and teachings of Jesus, fitting neatly into the specific genre of contemporary writings known as 'wisdom literature' that was known to exist in ancient Hebrew, but which was by no means unique to the Jewish religion or culture. It was also popular throughout the Hellenistic world, the Near East and Ancient Egypt. One authority, Kloppenborg, has argued that Q most closely follows the model of Hellenistic 'handbooks of instruction'. Q does differ from those handbooks in its inclusion of prophetic and apocalyptic material, but Mack believes that the 'wisdom teaching' alone formed the original Q, and that the other material was added later.

Mack and the other scholars working along the same lines base their conclusions on the teachings and sayings of Jesus. They still reject the *events* as reported in the Gospels because they do not fit the traditions of either Jews or Cynics, and suggest that the dying-and-rising god and mystery school themes are later inventions of the early Christians.[20]

We asked ourselves the following questions: is there any evidence to show that Jesus was *not* Jewish? On the other hand, was there any evidence to show conclusively that he *was*? Do the mystery school elements make things easier to explain, or harder?

Admittedly, Jesus' ministry took place in a Jewish context – first-century Judaea – and most of those who followed him were also Jewish. His immediate disciples and those who wrote the Gospels seem to have believed him to have been a Jew. However, his followers seem to have considered him something of an enigma – for example, they were uncertain about him being the Messiah – and the Gospel writers clearly had an enormous struggle to reconcile the contradictory elements of his life and teaching. It seems that they were unsure just how to deal with him.

At first glance it would seem that there is a very good case for believing that Jesus *was* Jewish. He often spoke of Old Testament religious figures such as Abraham and Moses, and frequently engaged in debate with Pharisees about points of Jewish law – if he was not a Jew surely there would have been no reason for him to have done this so obsessively.

But most scholars agree that these passages are the least likely to be genuine words of Jesus. They were added later because the *Apostles* found themselves arguing points of Jewish law and felt the need to create a retrospective justification for their case by using Jesus himself. The proof of this is that the antagonists in the New Testament stories are usually Pharisees, who actually had no special function or authority – especially in Galilee – in Jesus' time, whereas by the time the Gospels were being compiled they were in the ascendant[21]. As Morton Smith says:

> Almost all Gospel references to the Pharisees can be shown to derive from the 70s, 80s and 90s, the last years in which the Gospels were being edited.[22]

The only way to understand Jesus' true origins is to set him in the context of his time and place. Although there is continuing debate about where he was born and raised, as we shall see, the Gospels agree that he launched his mission from Galilee. It is unlikely, though, that he was a local, because while the Gospels refer to the disciples' distinctive Galilean accent – which was considered humorously rustic by the Judaeans – significantly this was not said of Jesus himself[23].

So what do we know of Galilee in Jesus' day? Mack neatly summarizes the current academic view of that place and time:

> In the world of the Christian imagination Galilee belonged to Palestine, the religion of Palestine was Judaism, so everyone in Galilee must have been Jewish. Since this picture is wrong . . . the reader needs to have a truer picture in mind.[24]

What we think of as Judaism at the time of Jesus – from the picture presented by the Gospels – was really only the Temple Judaism of Judaea, whose worship centred on the Jerusalem Temple. It was first established by the Jews after their traumatic Captivity in Babylon, and was in a constant state of flux. But not all Jews had been exiled, and their version of Judaism developed separately and was very different from that of the ex-captives who returned. The religion of the non-exiles was particularly practised in Samaria and Galilee to the north, and in Idumaea to the south of Judaea.

Galilee, however, was hardly a hotbed of fervent Judaism – of any sort. It had, in fact, only briefly been part of the kingdom of Israel many centuries before Jesus, since when it had come under the influence of several different cultures. Not for nothing was Galilee known as 'the land of the Gentiles'[25]. It was even more cosmopolitan than Samaria, which lay between Judaea and Galilee. As Mack says: 'It would be wrong to picture Galilee as suddenly converted to a Jewish loyalty and culture.'[26]

Galilee, with its good climate for agriculture and lucrative fishing in Lake Galilee, was a rich and fertile area. It had extensive trade links with the other cultures of the Hellenistic world, and stood at the heart of a network of trade routes leading to the rest of Syria, Babylonia and Egypt. It was home to peoples of many lands and cultures, and even Bedouin tribesmen were familiar visitors. As Morton Smith points out, the main influences on Galilean religion at that time were 'native, Palestinian, Semitic paganism, Greek, Persian, Phoenician and Egyptian'.[27]

Galileans were known for their fierce independence. But, in Mack's words, the area had 'no capital city, no temple and no hierarchy of priests'[28]. Significantly, the oldest-known synagogue in Galilee dates only from the third century of the Christian era.[29]

The region had been annexed to Israel in 100 BCE, and soon afterwards, in 63 BCE, the Romans conquered all of Palestine and made it into a province of their empire. At the time of Jesus' birth the whole of Israel was ruled by the Romans' puppet-king, Herod the Great – who was actually a polytheistic Idumidaean – but by the time of his ministry the land had been divided among Herod's three sons. Herod Antipas ruled Galilee, and (after his brother Archelaus had been forcibly retired to the Herod family estates in the South of France) Judaea was ruled directly by Rome, through its governor, Pontius Pilate.

In Jesus' day Galilee was a cosmopolitan and wealthy region – hardly the rustic backwater of popular imagination – which was not even predominantly Jewish and to which the authorities in Jerusalem would have been no more popular than their Roman masters.

Once Galilee is understood to have been very different from the traditional image of the place in which Jesus began his ministry, questions immediately arise about his real aims and motives. If Galilee were really a sophisticated culture without any fanatically anti-Roman and pro-Jewish bias, then was Jesus really trying to rouse its population to rebellion against the Romans, as some modern commentators suggest? And was Galilee the wisest place to begin some kind of campaign to reform Judaism, as others believe?

Although there were Jews in Galilee, there were also many other religions co-existing in an enviable atmosphere of tolerance. There were even 'heretical' forms of Judaism that flourished there, which makes it still more implausible that it was promising soil in which to plant any kind of Judaic reform. In an area where, it seems, virtually anything went where religion was concerned, an attempt to redefine mainstream Judaism would have fallen on stony ground indeed. And it would have made even less sense of the culmination of Jesus' mission in Jerusalem.

As Schonfield says in his *The Passover Plot:*

> ... the Jews regarded northern Palestine as the natural home of heresy ... We do not know so much about the old Israelite religion, but it would appear to have absorbed a good deal from the worship of the Syrians and Phoenicians, and this was not to nearly the same extent eradicated, as it was in the south, by the reforming zeal of Ezra and his successors.[30]

Another northern territory that was to be important to Jesus was Samaria, made famous in the story of the Good Samaritan. Because of innumerable sermons on the subject, churchgoers understand that Samaritans were reviled by the other Jews, and that the story of the Samaritan who crossed the road to help the victim of a mugging is a perfect example of the need to recognize the potential for good in everyone.

However, there is another reason to take Samaria seriously in the context of this investigation. The Samaritans had their own expectations of an imminent Messiah, whom they called the Ta'eb, and who was considerably different from the Judaic version. In John's Gospel (4:6–10) we read how Jesus met a Samaritan woman at a well, who recognized him as the Messiah – presumably as the Ta'eb – which hints that his Judaism was, at the very least, unorthodox. Perhaps Jesus invented the parable of the Good Samaritan as a 'thank you' to the Samaritans for their support.

Yet another misconception about Jesus' background is the idea that he was 'Jesus of Nazareth' – i.e. that he came from the town of that name, which exists in modern Israel. But in fact there are no records of any such place until the third century.

The word should be *Nazorean*, which identifies Jesus as a *member* of one of several sects that collectively used that name – but not, significantly, as its founder. The Nazoreans were a group of related sects about whom little is known. However, the word itself is telling, as it derives from the Hebrew *Notsrim* signifying 'Keepers or Preservers ... those who maintained the true teaching and tradition, or who cherished certain secrets which they did not divulge to others ...'[31]

This in itself runs counter to one of the major tenets of Christianity, which is that the religion is for everyone, and has no secrets – the polar opposite of the mystery schools, which offered different grades of knowledge or enlightenment to those who climbed the ever-steeper rungs of initiation. To those cults, wisdom is offered only if it is *earned*, and a pupil receives insight only when he is deemed ready for it by his spiritual masters. This was a common enough notion in Jesus' day: the mystery schools of Greece, Rome, Babylon and Egypt routinely employed this structured teaching, and guarded their secrets jealously. To this day the mystery school approach is employed by many Eastern religions and philosophical schools (including Zen Buddhism) – and also by groups like the Freemasons and Templars. The whole notion of initiation is also what gave the *occult* its name, for, as we have seen, the word itself simply means 'hidden' – the mysteries remain secret until the moment is right, and the student ready. If Jesus' teaching was not *meant* to be for the masses then by its very nature it was élitist and hierarchical – and *occult*. And, as we have seen when re-evaluating the true status of Mary Magdalene, there are just too many similarities between the mystery schools and the Jesus movement to be ignored.

There are many other misconceptions about Jesus. For example, the Christmas story is mostly a fairy tale – belonging with the nativity myths of the other dying gods – but there is even doubt about Jesus being born in Bethlehem. In fact, John's Gospel (7:42) explicitly states that he was *not* born there.

While most of the elements of the Nativity have clearly been derived from the birth myths of other dying-and-rising gods, the visit of the Wise Men from the East was based on a contemporary account from the life of the Emperor Nero[32]. Sometimes these figures are known as the magi, which is a specific title given to a tradition of Persian magicians – or sorcerers. It seems very odd to have the equivalent of three Aleister Crowleys visiting the baby Jesus to give him gifts, without any word of criticism or censure from the Gospel writers. And judging by the fact that they claimed to have followed a star to Bethlehem, they were also astrologers (astronomy as a separate discipline was unknown in those days). We are definitely expected to be *impressed* by the story of sorcerers giving Jesus gold, frankincense and myrrh. (But as we have seen, Leonardo in his *Adoration of the Magi* omitted the gold, symbol of kingship and of perfection.)

As we have seen, Jesus is referred to as a *naggar*, which means both a carpenter and a scholar or learned man – in his case, probably the latter. Neither were Jesus' most famous disciples likely to be the humble fishermen of legend: A.N. Wilson points out that they actually owned a fishing business on Lake Galilee[33]. (Besides, as Morton Smith remarks, some of the disciples were clearly non-Jewish: Philip is a Greek name, for example[34].)

Many commentators have used the parables as evidence that Jesus came from a humble background: he routinely used analogies that revolved around everyday rural and domestic situations, and this is taken as proof that he had personal experience of such things[35]. However, others[36] have pointed out that his imagery actually reveals only a superficial acquaintance with the mundane realities of life – it is as if he were really a much grander person who was deliberately trying to speak down to the masses, like an aristocratic Conservative candidate addressing working-class voters in terms he hopes they will find familiar.

Even if the wedding at Cana was not, as some believe, the occasion of his own marriage to the Magdalene, it still shows that he moved in 'society' circles, judging by the scale of the celebrations. And the incident of the Roman soldiers playing dice at the foot of the cross for Jesus' clothes implies that they were worth winning. Nobody gambles for inferior rags.

So a picture is emerging of Jesus' background that is significantly different from the one with which most of us have grown up. The next question is whether there is any assumption about Jesus that we *are* justified in making? For example, is there any positive evidence in the Gospels for the idea that Jesus was a non-Jew?

After his baptism, Jesus retired into the desert where he was tested by the Devil, who tried to seduce him into revealing his divinity. Once again, however, this is by no means straightforward. Some have even suggested that the temptation reveals nothing less than Jesus' implicit rejection of Yahweh himself[37]. That may be arguable, but one episode definitely reflects his attitude to the Jewish God.

One of the most famous events of the New Testament is when Jesus, full of righteous rage at the sight of the money-changers in the Temple, overturns their tables. While this appears to be a straightforward enough episode, it does in fact pose a major problem, one that has long been recognized by theologians and New Testament scholars alike.

Although Jesus' actions are usually explained by his horror at seeing such a holy place contaminated by financial transactions, this is a very Western attitude, and a recent one at that. For the changing of money in order to buy animals to sacrifice in the Temple at Jerusalem was neither a corruption nor an abuse. It was a fundamental part of the worship there. As the Professor of Biblical Studies at Chicago University, John Dominic Crossan stresses, 'There is not a single hint that anyone was doing anything financially or sacrificially inappropriate.' As he goes on to say, it was 'an attack on the Temple's very existence . . . a symbolic negation of all that . . . the Temple stood for.'[38]

Some have attempted to explain the action – which was pivotal to Jesus' ministry – by arguing that it expressed his dissatisfaction with the contemporary regime at the Temple. But in the context of that time and place it would have been such an overreaction as to suggest mental imbalance. To take a modern analogy: it would be like an Anglican who is opposed to the ordination of women expressing his protest by going into Westminster Abbey and trampling the cross on the altar. It would not happen, simply because worshippers know where to draw the line between action that is appropriate – however symbolic it may be – and protest that is actually sacrilegious. What Jesus did was the latter.

So Jesus' Judaism was, at the very least, unorthodox. This clears the ground for new suggestions as to what he actually *was*. And there are clear indications that he was part of a mystery school. But are there any episodes in the Gospels themselves that hint that this might have been the case?

Early in our investigation it came as something of a shock to discover that very few other researchers appear to have asked one of the questions that was, to us, utterly basic: namely, 'Where did John the Baptist get the ritual of baptism from?' Further delving revealed that it had absolutely no precedent in Judaism, although references to ritual washing – repeated immersions symbolizing purification – are found in the Dead Sea Scrolls. However, it is inaccurate to describe these rites as 'baptisms': what John advocated was a single, life-changing act of initiation that was preceded by confession and repentance of sins. The fact that this ritual was without Jewish precedent is indicated by his title or nickname – John *the* Baptist – the only one, not one of many. Indeed, it has often been taken as an innovation of his, although there are, in fact, many precedents and exact parallels *outside* the Jewish world.

Baptism as the outward and visible symbol of an inward spiritual renewal was a feature of many of the mystery cults that existed throughout the Hellenistic world at the time. It had a particularly long tradition in the ancient Egyptian mystery cult of Isis and, significantly, baptism in her temples on the banks of the Nile was preceded by public repentance and confession of sins to the priest. (This is discussed more fully in the next chapter.)

Moreover, that was the only period in the lengthy history of the Isis religion during which it sent missionaries into countries beyond Egypt, so it seems likely that John had been particularly influenced by their ritual of baptism. He may, as we shall see, have had personal experience of the Egyptians' religion on their home ground, for there are old Christian traditions that *John's* family fled into Egypt to escape Herod's wrath – traditions which found expression in Leonardo's *Virgin of the Rocks*.

Jesus' baptism presents several problems. First and by no means least is the idea of a sinless Son of God actually *needing* to have his sins washed away. It simply will not do to explain it away, as many have tried to do, by saying that Jesus was giving a good example to his followers, for nowhere in the Gospel accounts is that point made. There are also, however, significant anomalies in the very imagery that the Gospel accounts employ when describing Jesus' baptism by John. While Morton Smith[39] points out that the image of the descending dove has no parallel or precedent in Jewish tradition, Desmond Stewart goes further, finding definite links with the symbolism and practices of Egypt. He says:

> Although Yahweh supposedly sent ravens to feed one prophet, he did not customarily manifest himself in descending birds. Doves, in any case, were sacred to the pagan goddess of love, whether known as Aphrodite or Astarte . . .
>
> For what Jesus thought he saw, Egypt provides better guidance . . . When Re [or Ra, the Egyptian sun god] held his beloved, the pharaoh, to his bosom, he did so in the guise of Horus, whose commonest symbol was the hawk . . . The adoption, in a baptismal rite, of a mortal by a deity posed no major problem to Egyptians.[40]

The one major Egyptian deity who is usually associated with the symbol of a dove is, however, once again Isis, who was known as 'Queen of Heaven', 'Star of the Sea' (*Stella Maris*) and 'Mother of God' long before the 'Virgin' Mary was born. Isis was frequently portrayed as suckling Horus, the magical offspring of herself and the dead Osiris. It was in the annual festival that marked his death, and, three days later, his resurrection, that the sun was described as turning black when he died and entered the Underworld. (And it is a black sun that glowers over the Crucifixion scene in Jean Cocteau's mural in London.)

Given the unusual missionary zeal of some groups of Isians at the time, and the geographical proximity of Egypt – not to mention the cosmopolitan nature of Galilee – it is not surprising that John, Jesus and those who followed them would have been influenced by the Isis cult.

What is remarkable is that most Christians are still encouraged to think of their belief as being totally and in every respect unique, untainted by any other philosophy or religion, when clearly this is not the case. Take, for example, the Last Supper, at which Jesus is believed to have inaugurated the sacred meal of wine and bread, which was to represent his sacrificial blood and body.

A.N. Wilson writes, 'This smacks strongly of the mystery cults of the Mediterranean, and has little in common with Judaism.'[41] He then uses this as evidence for his idea that the Last Supper was an invention of the Gospel writers – but what if it really happened *as a pagan rite?*

Desmond Stewart strengthens the parallel, saying:

[Jesus] took bread and wine, elements of everyday sociability which yet mark the heights of Osiran symbolism and transformed them, not into a sacrifice, but a bond between two states of being.[42]

Christians see the sacred meal of wine and bread – the climax of the Protestant communion and the Catholic Mass – as being unique to Jesus. In fact it was already a *common practice* of all the major Dying God mystery schools, including those of

Dionysus, Tammuz and Osiris. In every case it was understood to be a way of becoming one with the god concerned and of achieving spiritual elevation (although the Romans expressed horror at the implicit cannibalism involved). All of the other cults were well represented in Palestine at the time of the Last Supper, so their influence is understandable.

Of all the four Gospels, it is perhaps significant that it is John's that tells of the Supper but omits any mention of the ceremony of the bread and wine – perhaps because that was not the occasion when it was actually inaugurated. Elsewhere in John's Gospel (6:54) it is implied that the sacred meal of bread and wine was promoted from the earliest days of Jesus' career in Galilee.

The very concept of eating and drinking the god – the ritual of the Mass – is abhorrent to Jews. As Desmond Stewart says:

> The notion that the corn *was* Osiris was common to Egyptians while a similar notion attached itself to [the goddesses] Demeter and Persephone in Hellas [Greece] itself.[43]

Another parallel with the mystery schools – and one which has no parallel with Judaic belief or practice – is the story of the raising of Lazarus. This is clearly an initiatory act: Lazarus is 'raised' in the *symbolic* death and rebirth that was a common feature of the mystery schools of the time, and which has echoes in certain rituals of modern Freemasonry. The only canonical Gospel to record this event – John's – makes it miraculous, a literal raising from the dead. But the Secret Gospel of Mark makes it clear that it is a symbolic act only, marking the 'death' of Lazarus' old self and his rebirth as a more spiritual being. Presumably this episode was edited out of the other Gospels because it was such an obvious allusion to mystery school activities. But as far as this investigation is concerned, the most significant point about this ritual is that its most direct parallel was with the 'rebirth' ceremonies of the Isis cult of Egypt. As Desmond Stewart says (referring to the first-century Isian mystic):

> . . . the evidence of Bethany indicates that Jesus practised a
> species of mystery akin to what Lucius Apuleius experienced
> in the cult of Isis.[44]

Even the Crucifixion reinforces the Jewish denial that Jesus
was the expected Messiah, for dying in such shameful circumstances was the last thing that an all-conquering Messiah was
expected to do. That in itself does not concern Christians
unduly, for they maintain that his Messiahship went far
beyond, in spiritual terms, what the Jews expected of it.
However, there are other problems with the New Testament
account of Jesus' death. It appears that the Christian interpretation of it as being the supreme mystical sacrifice was
actually invented later *in order* to account for the discrepancy
between what Jewish expectations were of their Messiah and
what actually happened to Jesus.

It has been suggested that Jesus, and those of his circle,
developed their own concept of the Messiah, by incorporating
into it the ideal of the Suffering Just One, as derived from the
figure of Joseph in apocryphal Jewish writings. But significantly, in the heretical north of Palestine – Galilee – the
'suffering' Joseph had absorbed some of the characteristics of
the Syrian cult of Adonis-Tammuz[45]. Scholars have also noted
the influence of the *shepherd* god Tammuz on the Song of
Songs[46], which is, as we have seen, so important to the Black
Madonna cult. It is likely that Jesus called himself the Good
Shepherd after Tammuz, and that his followers at the time
would have been familiar with the term – Bethlehem was
a major cult centre of Adonis-Tammuz. (Interestingly,
Christians such as St Jerome were incensed by the existence of
a Temple to Tammuz on the alleged site of Jesus' birth in
Bethlehem.)

It is remarkable, however, that although many modern
commentators acknowledge the presence of strong pagan
influences in Jesus' life and teachings, they fail to explore
them beyond a superficial mention. For example, as Hugh
Schonfield says:

It took a Nazorean of Galilee to apprehend that death and resurrection was the bridge between the two phases [of Suffering Just One and Messianic King]. The very tradition of the land where Adonis yearly died and rose again seemed to call for it.[47]

While Geoffrey Ashe admits: 'Christ became a Saviour with a perceptible likeness to the dying-and-rising gods of the Mysteries, Osiris, Adonis and the rest.'[48]

However, the archetype that fits most closely with Jesus' life and story as it has come down to us is that of the Egyptian god Osiris, consort of Isis. Traditionally he was killed on a Friday, and rose again after three days[49]. And there are hints that in the early days of Christianity the title *Christos* became confused with another Greek word, *Chrestos*, which means gentle or kind. Some early Greek manuscripts of the Gospels used this word in place of *Christos*. But *Chrestos* was one of the epithets traditionally ascribed to Osiris – and, significantly, there is also an inscription in Delos to *Chreste Isis*.[50]

Jesus' cry from the cross is also open to a pagan interpretation. Both the version of Mark '*eloi eloi!*' and that of Matthew, '*eli eli!*', are translated as 'My God! My God! [why hast thou forsaken me?]', although some of the bystanders are reported to have misunderstood the word and thought that he was calling upon the prophet Elias, whom Jesus himself had specifically linked with John the Baptist[51]. But in Aramaic 'My God' should have been *ilahi*. Desmond Stewart[52] suggests that the word was, in fact, *Helios* – the name of the sun god, which is particularly interesting because the cry was linked to the anomalous period of darkness at noon. In fact, one of the earliest-known New Testament manuscripts has bystanders thinking he is calling on Helios, whose cult – which was widespread in Syria until the fourth century – was Christianized by substituting the name Elias. And obviously a *sun* god is quintessentially about cyclical dying and rising again.

So we can see that Jesus fits easily into the tradition of the dying god, but this archetype does not constitute the whole picture of the ancient mysteries. The god – Osiris, Tammuz,

Attis, Dionysus or any of the others – was inevitably associated with his consort, the goddess, who usually fulfilled the principal role in the drama of his resurrection. As Geoffrey Ashe puts it:

> Always the companion-god was the Goddess' doomed and tragic lover, who died annually with the green life of nature and was reborn in the spring . . .[53]

Clearly, if Jesus were really fulfilling a 'Dying God' tradition there was, apparently, something missing. As she goes on to say:

> In his role as dying-and-rising Saviour he could not readily be perceived as standing alone. Such gods had never normally done so . . . You could not have Osiris without Isis, or Attis without Cybele.[54]

Critics may say that because Jesus had no companion-goddess figure, he could not have been enacting a dying-god role. He was, they say, unique in his true divinity and needed no woman to share it with him. But what if he *did* have such a partner? And of course he did, and this knowledge is what has been cherished in secret by generations of 'heretics'. *Jesus' 'Isis' was Mary Magdalene*.

Egyptians addressed their Queen Isis as 'Mistress of the gods . . . thou lady of red apparel . . . mistress and lady of the tomb . . .'[55] Traditionally the Magdalene has been depicted as wearing a red dress, which has been taken to refer to her having been a 'scarlet woman'. And it was the Magdalene who presided over the ceremonies in Jesus' tomb.

Understand this, and much of what has been lost, deliberately obscured and distorted finally falls into place, including the very nature of what may be termed true Christianity.

Despite first impressions, the Feminine Principle is not absent from the Gospels – at least in their original form. The famous opening words of the Fourth Gospel are 'In the beginning was the Word, and the Word was with God, and the Word was God.' While the concept of the Word (*Logos*) is derived from the ideas of the Neo-Platonic Jewish philosopher Philo of Alexandria, a contemporary of Jesus, in this – John's version – it appears to be explicitly *Feminine*. *Logos* is a masculine noun but paradoxically the concept it is describing appears to be feminine. Clearly some confusion has taken place when the Gospel was taken from its source material – and later we came to realize the significance of the real origins of this passage.

The phrase 'and the Word was with God' is a radical mistranslation, which changes the true meaning completely, but in doing so conveniently removes some very awkward implications. For the original Greek words are *pros ton theon*, which literally means 'going towards God', and carries the meaning of a man seeking unity with a woman. As George Witterschein puts it:

> . . . we can even use the word *erotic* to describe a yearning for unity to overcome separation.
>
> The key to it all . . . was the attraction between man and woman, which parallels . . . the attraction between the Word and God.[56]

In other words, the Word is female. And significantly, the accurate translation of the opening lines of the Gospel of John is:

> In the beginning was the Word, and the Word was toward God, and God was what the Word was. It was with God in the beginning.[57]

Therefore the Word was a force that is distinctly separate from God. Significantly, it is generally understood that the Word and the Holy Spirit were one and the same, although the original term for the latter was unambiguously feminine. It was *Sophia*.[58]

The concepts evoked in these lines are clearly non-Jewish. But neither are they original to the early years of the emerging 'new' religion of Christianity. The American anthropologist and Professor of Religious History, Karl Luckert, who has made a major study of the Egyptian religion and its influence on later theological and philosophical concepts, is in no doubt about their true origin, when he writes:

> . . . in all the religious literature from the so-called Hellenistic Period, there is no better summary of ancient orthodox Egyptian theology than the prologue to the Gospel of John.[59]

Desmond Stewart, in *The Foreigner*, argues that Jesus was brought up, if not actually born, in Egypt. However, he could still have been Jewish, for there were large and flourishing Jewish communities in Egypt at that time. Stewart points out that many things about Jesus, from the lack of a Galilean accent to the emphasis and implicit background of his parables, suggest an Egyptian upbringing. And of course, the New Testament tells us that Mary, Joseph and the infant Jesus fled into Egypt to escape Herod's wrath. Apart from the incident of Jesus arguing with the elders in the Temple at Jerusalem at the age of twelve, there is no mention of his young life at all. However, even this episode is clearly an invention, for it has Mary and Joseph expressing their ignorance of Jesus' divinity – immediately after the story of his miraculous birth, which surely they, if anyone, would have known about! So there is nothing authentic about Jesus in the canonical Gospels from his infancy until his mature manhood. Where had he been? Why is there this silence about his childhood and teenage years? If he was out of the country and involved in another culture altogether, however, the writers may have felt it was not their place – or, more likely, beyond their talents – to fabricate a whole series of incidents to fill the gap.

Other sources confirm this view. The Jewish holy book, the *Talmud*, does not refer to Jesus as either a native Galilean or as coming from Nazareth, but it does state dogmatically that he came *from Egypt*[60]. Moreover, and perhaps most tellingly, the *Talmud* states unequivocally that the reason for Jesus' arrest was a charge of *sorcery*, and that he was an initiate of Egyptian magic. This concept was also the main thrust of Morton Smith's 1978 book *Jesus the Magician*, in which he suggests that such miracles as turning water into wine and walking on water were just as much a part of the usual repertoire of Egyptian conjurors as the Indian rope trick is of Eastern fakirs.

Smith gives many examples of the similarity between Jesus' miracles and the magic spells and incantations found in contemporary papyrus texts, as well as parallels with the life and works of the famous magician Apollonius of Tyana (a younger contemporary of Jesus) and Simon Magus. Both of these men were credited with abilities almost identical to those of Jesus.

Christians might say that it was only a misunderstanding on the part of the credulous masses that gave rise to the image of Jesus as an occultist: his miracles were really the gift of the Holy Spirit. However, that is as much a subjective interpretation as the other and actually has fewer arguments in its favour. And Morton Smith draws our attention to a major paradox of Christianity:

> ... we have to reckon not only with a tradition that tried to clear Jesus of the charge of magic, but also that revered him as a great magician.[61]

There were many itinerant magicians – sorcerers – of greater or lesser celebrity, in the Graeco-Roman world at the time of Jesus, and a commonplace part of their repertoire was healing and exorcism, as it is today with Indian holy men and voodoo priests, among others. (That the alleged cures are genuine is a matter for debate, but the amazement of the crowds is mostly real enough, and word-of-mouth does much to build up the reputation of the wonder-worker.)

Smith suggests that the term 'Son of God' – which has

always puzzled theologians and New Testament scholars, because it has no Jewish precedent and was not a concept associated with the Messiah – is itself derived from the Graeco-Roman-Egyptian tradition. The successful magician gained his abilities through allowing himself to become the conduit for a god, as with tribal shamans. So, Smith suggests, Jesus became the Son of God as the result of *a magical possession* by the deity.

The 'water into wine' miracle of the wedding at Cana has been shown to be suspiciously similar to an account of a Dionysiac ceremony held at Sidon, even down to the words used[62]. And, in the Hellenistic world, Dionysus was explicitly associated with Osiris[63]. Smith also quotes from two Egyptian magical texts that parallel the eucharist, the ritual taking of bread and wine that is held so sacred by Christians as having been uniquely instigated by Jesus. Smith says – and the italics are his:

> *These are the closest known parallels to the text of the eucharist.* In them as in it a magician-god gives his own body and blood to the recipient who, by eating it, will be united with him in love.[64]

Even the words spoken by Jesus are similar to those of the magical texts.

There are other hints – actually in the Gospels themselves – that Jesus was widely thought of as a magician at the time. In John's Gospel, the words addressed to Pilate when Jesus is handed over to him is that he is 'a doer of evil'. In Roman law this was the term for a *sorcerer*[65].

The most significant aspect of Morton Smith's research in this context is that, although based entirely on a comparison between the Gospels and the magical papyri, his conclusions match *exactly* the way Jesus is portrayed in the Jewish *Talmud* and early rabbinical writings. These never depicted Jesus as a Jew who invented a heretical form of Judaism, as many modern Christians believe him to be. Instead, those Jewish texts regard him either as a Jew who converted to another religion entirely, or as someone who was never a Jew at all. In fact, they specifically denounce him as a practitioner of Egyptian magic. The *Talmud* itself states unequivocally that Jesus spent his early manhood in Egypt and that he learned magic there.

In one tale from the rabbinical literature, Jesus is likened to an earlier figure named Ben Stada. He was a Jew who had tried to introduce the worship of other, pagan, deities alongside that of Yahweh, and who had specifically brought magical practices from Egypt. The tale emphazises that, in a similar way, Jesus brought Egyptian magical practices from Egypt to the Jews. Other rabbinical texts are equally explicit on this point: Jesus 'practised magic and deceived and led astray Israel.'

Clearly the view of Jesus held by contemporary Jews was that he was an Egyptian magical adept. His crime, in their eyes, was that he tried to introduce *pagan ideas and pagan gods* into the Jewish lands.

The *Talmud* and other collections of rabbinical texts can be traced back only to the third century CE, giving rise to accusations of deliberate defamation on the part of Jesus' enemies, the Jews. However, these accusations of what is essentially *witchcraft* might not have arisen out of pure malice as might at first appear. The accusation of sorcery is a curious one to have trumped up – and there is evidence that such ideas about Jesus were current earlier.

Justin Martyr, writing *c.*160 CE, reports a discussion with a Jew, Trypho, who calls Jesus a 'Galilean magician'. The Platonic philosopher Celsus, writing around 175 CE, states that, although Jesus grew up in Galilee, he worked for a time as a hired labourer in Egypt, where he learned the techniques of magic.

As we have seen, the Gospel writers saw nothing shameful or shocking in recording that the *magi* paid homage to Jesus with their gold, frankincense and myrrh. These were emphatically not merely Wise Men or kings, but members of a specific occult fraternity that originated in Persia. And while some commentators may try to explain this as the sorcerers' symbolic acknowledgement of the superiority of the infant Son of God, there is no hint at such an interpretation in the Gospels themselves, where the visit of the magi is clearly intended to provoke awe and admiration.

Morton Smith points out that – although history has tended to play this down – the earliest Christians, especially those in Egypt, practised magic. Some of the first-known Christian artefacts are magical amulets, bearing images of Jesus with written spells. The implication is clear: Jesus' first generation of followers recognized him as a magician, either because they knew him to be one, or simply because he fitted the role to perfection.[66]

There is, however, a much darker rumour that was current in Jesus' own day about his involvement with sorcery, one that not only reinforces that of the rabbinical writings but which, if true, would also solve an enduring biblical problem. This bizarre and shocking accusation, which will be discussed later, may well prove to hold the key to much of the mystery surrounding the relationship of Jesus and the Baptist, and the possible reason for John's importance to occult groups over the centuries.

As we have seen, there are remarkably clear parallels between the life of Jesus and the story of Osiris. But perhaps even more tellingly, many of his actual words appear to have come unchanged from the tradition of the Egyptian religion. For example, Jesus said (John 12:24): 'Except a corn of wheat fall into the ground and die, it abideth alone: but if it die, it bringeth forth much fruit.' This imagery and concept comes undeniably from the Osiran cult[67]. And Jesus' words 'In my Father's house are many mansions' (John 14:2), which have puzzled generations of Christians, is explicitly Osiran and come *directly* from the Egyptian *Book of the Dead*[68].

More properly called *Coming Forth By Day*, this work was made up of a series of spells with which the soul could overcome the terrors of the afterlife, and was read to the dying by a priest or priestess. Jesus' knowledge of *Coming Forth By Day* suggests a familiarity not only with the religious writing of the Isis/Osiris cult, but also with their magic – as we have seen, religion and magic were the same to the Egyptians.

Osiris was killed on a Friday and his dismembered body was scattered. After three days, he rose again – thanks to the magical intervention of Isis, who had mourned him throughout the land. In the annual Osiran mystery plays of Egypt, the high priestess who played Isis lamented 'Evil men have killed my beloved, and where his body is I know not': when she finally reassembles his body, she says 'Behold I found thee lying there . . . O Osiris, live, stand up the unfortunate one that liest there! I am Isis.' The priest playing Osiris then stood up and showed himself to his followers, who expressed their doubt and awe at the miraculous resurrection.[69]

Compare the first sentence with the words of Mary Magdalene to the 'Gardener' (who turns out to be Jesus): 'They have taken my Lord and I know not where they have lain him'. ('My Lord' was a common form of words used by a wife of her husband in that culture.[70]) Perhaps there was also a ritual in Jesus' tomb in which the Magdalene uttered the words of the Egyptian goddess, before proceeding to heal him of his wounds. In the Dying God mysteries it is the goddess who, with her female attendants, goes into the Underworld to bring out the resurrected god, and that dark Hades was usually represented as a *tomb*.

As, in our opinion, Jesus and the Magdalene were living out the story of Osiris' death and resurrection, the choice of crucifixion made perfect sense – *for the cross was already an ancient Osiran symbol*.

It was Mary Magdalene and her women who attended the burial of Jesus, not simply because, as has been suggested, it was women's work in those days, but because they were consciously enacting their own part in the story of Osiris. Jesus was playing the role of a Dying God who was resurrected thanks to the intervention – magical or otherwise – of his 'goddess', his sexual and spiritual partner, Mary Magdalene. She it was who bestowed his Messiahship by ritually anointing him with spikenard, and if the idea that she was wealthy is correct, then perhaps her influence made the initiatory and magical rite of the Crucifixion possible.

With his heavy reliance on Osiran imagery and putative Egyptian background, Jesus may well have undergone the horrors of crucifixion willingly, but for reasons that are somewhat ironic considering how he is perceived by Christians. To them, Jesus is God incarnate, but perhaps he believed that, through a symbolic death and rebirth, he could *become* a god. The Crucifixion may well have been deliberately set up and organized – with the help of a certain amount of bribery – so that Jesus, like Lazarus, could be reborn in the manner of the Osiran mystery school, resurrecting into the form of Osiris himself. This is all the more likely if Jesus really did consider himself to be royal – of the line of David – for a dead Pharaoh automatically became 'an Osiris' and became ruler of the heavens and harrower of the Underworld, through the magical intervention of Isis. Did Jesus expect to emerge from the tomb imbued with divine power? Perhaps this idea explains one of the most enduring mysteries of Christianity – whether or not Jesus died on the cross.

Many people believe that Jesus did not. Certain Gnostic Gospels, the *Koran* and some early Christian heretics – and perhaps the Priory of Sion – have taken the view that a substitute (possibly Simon of Cyrene) took his place, while others think he suffered crucifixion but was taken down alive and that his 'resurrection' simply referred to him being healed of his wounds. Certainly Leonardo believed he had been taken down from the cross and lived: the blood is still running on the image of the man on his faked 'Holy' Shroud of Turin, and blood does not continue to run on a corpse. (Even if our thesis is wrong, and Leonardo did not fake the Shroud, whoever did do so must also have believed that Jesus did not die on the cross – and if, against all the evidence, it really is the Shroud of Jesus then it *clearly proves that he was alive in the tomb*.)

Of course it could have been an accident that Jesus was taken down alive, and that the standard version of his arrest and Crucifixion are the nearest to the truth that we have. But there are too many logical objections. The Roman occupying forces were a practical people, and their functionaries were experienced torturers and executioners. Yet we are told that they hastily concluded the executions on that Friday – breaking the legs of the crucified thieves, for example, so that they would be buried before the Sabbath began. Are we seriously to believe that the Romans of all people would care about Jewish custom to that extent, or if they did, that they would somehow forget that Friday night dusk signalled the end of the torture of crucifixion, even if it had begun just hours before?

Crucifixion was the worst death imaginable because it routinely took days for the victims to die. That was the whole point. So in that case, why was anyone, ever, crucified on a Friday in Palestine when they would have to have been taken down, alive or dead, at sunset of that same day?

Certainly there was a trial and there was a crucifixion. But it appears that Jesus and his inner circle – which included the 'Bethany Family' – deliberately engineered the events to fulfil some plan of their own. Hugh Schonfield's *The Passover Plot* elegantly and persuasively explains how this happened, but fails to explain why, if Jesus were setting himself up to be the Messiah, he should choose to be crucified, because such a shameful death would never have been the fate of that longed-for Jewish hero.

Yet the stage-management goes beyond having Jesus arrested and crucified. There are anomalies in the Gospel account that arouse grave suspicions. The length of time allotted to Jesus' Crucifixion was, as we have seen, noticeably short, and we are also told that, whereas the thieves had to be given the *coup de grâce* by the Roman soldiers to finish them off before the Sabbath, Jesus simply obliged them by dying before sunset. Many people have suggested that some drug – a powerful narcotic – may have been given to Jesus on the sponge as he hung on the cross, which gave him the appearance of death. In this case, it must be presumed that the plotters had bribed the guards to look the other way. These clues suggest that the plot was essentially about mounting a very cynical performance: crucifixion was the most public way to announce a death, and having done that, any apparent return to life would be deemed miraculous.

The very nature of this arrangement reveals why it had to be the Romans, not the Jews, who had arrested and sentenced Jesus. If the Jews had found him guilty he would have been stoned, and it would have been impossible to fake a death by stoning.

But what were the conspirators hoping to achieve by this elaborate – and risky – subterfuge? After all, as we have seen, a crucified criminal could never be accepted as the Messiah: the Jews did not expect the Messiah to be crucified, nor did they look to him to return from the dead. This interpretation of their expectations simply did not exist.

The plan was not, therefore, one that fitted into the mould of Jewish tradition. Yet it *did* conform to a non-Jewish concept – that of the dying-and-rising god, which was at the heart of the great mystery school cults. Jews would have none of this: to them there was only one God and it was inconceivable that he would ever be part of a bloodshedding cult, for they regarded anything connected with blood and the grave as unclean and abhorrent. Yet the Middle Eastern and Mediterranean countries of the day abounded with the worship of such deities.

It cannot be stressed too much that there is no question of the story of Jesus' death and resurrection being unique. In the context of the proliferation of dying god cults at that time, he was obviously intending to be associated with one of them. But which one? And what did he hope to gain by this painful and dangerous plan?

As we have already seen, Jesus' cry from the cross can be interpreted as being '*Helios! Helios!*' ('O Sun! O Sun!') The death of Osiris is traditionally represented as a *black sun* – in other words, the forsaking of the light, which has at least equal claim on Jesus' cry of '*O Sun! O Sun! Why has thou forsaken me?*'

Certainly it seems that Jesus was in some way living out the story of Osiris on that Friday long ago.

There are many unanswerable questions surrounding the Resurrection, assuming that the Christian idea of Jesus' actual death and literal resurrection is wrong. For example, what state was he in when taken down from the cross – was he in a coma in the tomb, or simply injured but conscious? What happened to him then? Did he, as some have suggested, leave Palestine and travel to far-flung places, such as India? And what happened to his relationship with the Magdalene, for she appears to have sailed to Gaul without him? Whatever the truth of the matter, the Jesus of the Gospels disappears from history after his alleged resurrection.

Essentially, the Gospels fall apart after the discovery of the empty tomb. The New Testament accounts of the risen Jesus' appearances to his disciples and alleged ascension into heaven are a hopeless muddle – inconsistent even as myths. Of course non-Christians seize on this tangle of stories as proof of their fabrication, and certainly we would agree with that. Yet despite this mess, as Hugh Schonfield points out, one source *can* be clearly discerned: the risen Jesus' meeting two disciples on the road to Emmaus was taken from Lucius Apuleius' Isian work. *The Golden Ass*[71].

Although the concept of a future bodily resurrection is part of Judaic belief, what happened when Jesus was allegedly resurrected certainly does not conform with Jewish thinking. The traditional view is that all the righteous will be resurrected together at the end of time: Jesus apparently defied this plan, being restored to life while his fellows still lay mouldering in their tombs. Then he ascended into heaven, leaving no bodily remains behind, although he promised that his spiritual self was readily available to his followers – indeed, this continuing spiritual presence was one of the main reasons why the fledgling Christian religion proved so attractive to the Roman world, and very largely why it still has such a hold over millions of hearts and minds.

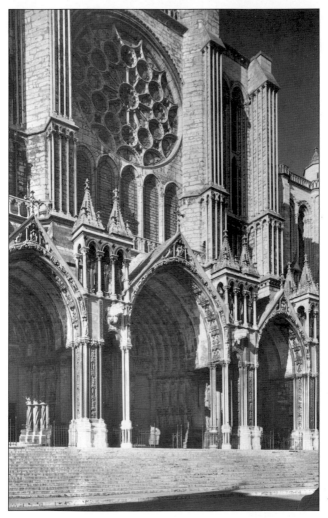

Sexual symbolism is even found in the great Gothic cathedrals, which were masterminded by the Knights Templar. Common features include rose windows and Gothic arches (as seen here at Chartres) *(A.F. Kersting)*, both of which represent intimate female anatomy: the arch, which draws the worshipper into the body of Mother Church, evokes the vulva. The rose was also used by the troubadours and alchemists as an anagram for *eros*, or sexual love.

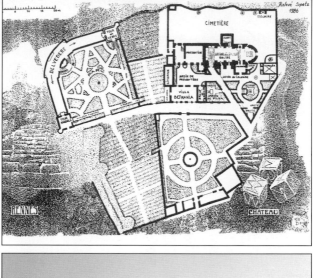

The inexplicable wealth of Abbé Saunière of Rennes-le-Château allowed him to build an elaborate domain (top: seen here in the ground plan drawn by French artist *Alain Féral*), laid out according to occult and Masonic principles. For example, his Magdala Tower contrasts with an insubstantial glass tower, symbolizing the Gnostic concept of the balancing of opposites (bottom) *(Clive Prince)*. In his church the demon bearing the holy water stoup (opposite, bottom left) *(Mary Evans Picture Library)* embodies occult and Masonic concepts. Saunière was obsessed with Mary Magdalene: he himself put the finishing touches to this bas-relief in the church (opposite, top) *(Clive Prince)*. The mystery attracted even François Mitterand, weeks before his election as President in 1981 (opposite right, bottom) *(André Galaup/Midi Libre)*.

Underlying European 'heresy' is a secret devotion to the ancient Egyptian goddess Isis (above left) *(British Museum)*, often concealed behind the cult of Mary Magdalene or the Black Madonnas (above right). Research reveals that Jesus was an initiate of the Egyptian religion of Isis and Osiris (below) *(British Museum)*. Archaeological discoveries have shown that Judaism itself had its roots in the religion of Egypt. For example, the 'cherubim' found in a ninth-century BC Jewish palace (opposite, below) are strikingly similar to winged Egyptian goddesses (opposite, above) *(British Museum)*. Was Jesus attempting to take Judaism back to its true roots?

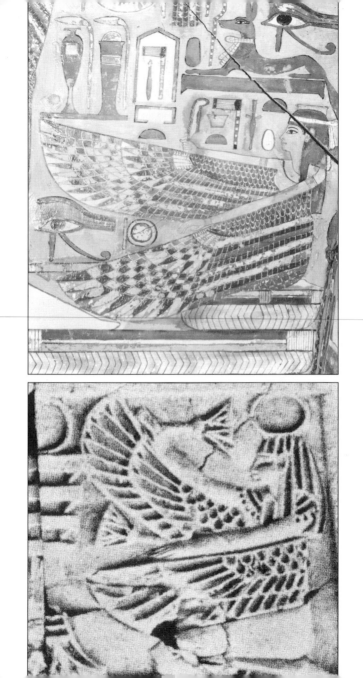

John the Baptist has always been central to heretical groups including the Knights Templar and the Priory of Sion – as, for example, in Leonardo's sculpture outside the Baptistery in Florence (opposite, below) *(Bridgeman Art Library)* and in the church at Rennes-le-Château, where the Baptist towers over Jesus (opposite, above) *(Clive Prince)*. The Lamb of God on the Languedocian Templar Seal (right) *(British Library)* reveals their devotion to John. The idea of his superiority is not confined to Europe: the Mandaeans of Iraq and Iran also regard Jesus as John's usurper. Their rites centre on baptism (above left) and ritual handshakes (above right). Are the Mandaeans the remnants of the 'Church of John' which influenced the Knights Templar?

John the Baptist's beheading has always exerted a powerful influence on artists, writers and musicians, as exemplified in Gustave Moreau's *L'Apparition (Réunion des Musées Nationaux)*, although the biblical accounts contain deliberate obfuscation. Many modern commentators believe there was something suspicious about John's death: could the jealously guarded secrets of the heretics hold the truth about his beheading? And is this secret the revelation that the Church has always feared?

As Karl Luckert points out, modern commentators, while acknowledging that this concept of Jesus' continued spiritual presence is not Jewish, do not provide any ideas as to its true context and background. So where did this idea come from?

Luckert's erudite analysis[72] shows conclusively that the twin concepts of Jesus' unique Resurrection and his continued spiritual presence can be traced without a shadow of doubt to Egyptian theology. As he explains, ancient Egyptian theology:

> ... made it possible to believe that the Son of God rose from death ... and thus returned to the Father. It explained also why for a while, before he completely ascended into heaven, some of the Christ apparitions have been seen ... Also in tune with Egyptian logic was the notion that, even though Christ Jesus had now returned to the Father he nevertheless eternally remains present among his followers.

Once again, we see that concepts that are central to the Christian religion – which have long been cherished as evidence of Jesus' uniqueness and divinity – did not leap fully formed from his life and teachings. Neither were they born of the sort of heretical Judaism that is so frequently evoked to explain their genesis.

The concept of individual resurrection and of the eternal life of the spirit in the afterworld came from Egypt: there it was accepted as a given fact. And the notion of the continuing, comforting presence of the spirit after death was directly taken from beliefs surrounding the death of the Pharoahs, who were thought to guide the people from the invisible world.

We have seen how the crucial events of Jesus' life appear to fit the story of Osiris, and how the role of his partner, Mary Magdalene, dovetailed with that of Isis. But there is one other major point to be made in this context.

While the Osiris archetype clearly matches Jesus' conscious fulfilment of his role – by 'dying' on a Friday, being mourned by 'Isis' and coming back to life three days later – it was the goddess whose magic made the resurrection possible. That hers was no subordinate role cannot be over-emphasized.

Isis was seen as the *Creator*: as the Egyptian scriptures said: 'In the beginning there was Isis, Oldest of the Old.' She was the goddess 'from whom all becoming arose', and a traditional invocation says: '. . . thou are creator of all good things.' But more than that, Isis – not Osiris – was the original *Saviour*, being described by Aristides, an initiate of her mysteries, as 'a Light and other unutterable things conducing to salvation', while Lucius Apuleius addressed her thus: 'O Thou Holy and eternal Saviour of the human race . . . thou givest light to the Sun . . . Thou treadest death underfoot.'[73]

Scholars accept that the early Christians absorbed certain aspects of the Isis cult into their own movement, such as the concept that a belief in the goddess bestowed eternal life. They also took over many of her temples. One such shrine was at Sais, an old capital of Egypt, which became a church of the Virgin Mary in the third century. A thousand years previously, as a temple to the great goddess Isis, it had carried the inscription 'I am all that was, that is, and that is yet to come' – which much later found its way into the Book of Revelation (1:8) as the words of Yahweh.

The influence of the Isis cult can be found openly even in the canonical Gospels. For example, one of the most famous sayings of Jesus is 'Come to me all you who are heavy laden, and I will refresh you'. Because of its offer of comfort and love in the midst of life's struggle, it is often found on posters outside churches, and prefixed by the phrase 'Jesus said'. In fact, that very phrase – word for word – was lifted entirely from the sayings of Isis. It can still be seen inscribed over the door to a temple dedicated to her at Dendera. In any case, the succour offered in the sentence is surely that of a *mother*.

If, as we believe, Jesus and Mary Magdalene were initiates of the Isis and Osiris mysteries then 'Christianity' must have been very different from the patriarchal, God-*fearing* religion it soon became. And their essentially pagan background finally sheds some light on some of the New Testament's most enduring enigmas.

The basic dilemma has always been to try to reconcile the existence of an historical Jesus with the obvious Egyptian mystery school elements of the stories about him. As a direct result of this problem commentators have gone in one of two ways: either, as with Ahmed Osman, they have concluded that Jesus did not exist, or, like A.N. Wilson, they maintain that the mystery school references were never part of the original story, but were added later.

However, these two apparently irreconcilable elements can, as we have demonstrated, make sense when taken together. The assumption that Jesus was of the Jewish religion is what has prevented a clear and simple solution from being recognized. If, on the other hand, his religion came from outside the Jewish tradition, then it all falls into place.

This is not to claim that Jesus' disciples were not Jewish, or that he was not deliberately targeting the Jews with his campaign. Yet, as we have seen, it is evident that there was a 'puppet-master-group' behind the movement, part of which was almost certainly the 'Bethany Family'.

The Jesus movement comprised an inner and an outer circle, the esoteric and exoteric versions of the cult. Ironically, most of the disciples and the sources from which the Gospels were drawn were part of the latter, the group that Jesus deliberately kept in the dark about his true message and agenda. Radical and bizarre though that may at first appear, this is precisely the situation that is portrayed repeatedly in the Gospels – in which disciples such as Peter often confess themselves totally perplexed about Jesus' teachings and his intentions. More crucially, the outer circle disciples were uncertain about Jesus' ambitions and even his true role.

Scholars have confessed themselves puzzled over the basic question as to why Christianity – out of all the Messiah cults of that time and place – should have been the one to survive and flourish. As we have seen, the reason why the Jesus movement was almost the only such group to have gained lasting ground outside Judaea was that it was already recognizable as a mystery cult. The secret of its appeal was that it was essentially a *hybrid*, a blend of certain aspects of Judaism and of pagan, mystery school elements. Christianity was unique because it was reassuringly familiar to many Jews and also to Gentiles, while at the same time being excitingly different.

Christianity as a new religion was created out of the dynamic that arose as the various ethnic and religious converts struggled to make their own kind of sense out of the individual – and often contradictory – elements of the hybrid. The followers constantly faced the struggle to force the archetypal dying-and-rising god into the classic mould of the Messiah and vice versa, and it is this impossible blend that has become the Church's Christ.

Of course many might dispute the Egyptian background of Christianity, citing the generally Jewish tone of the Gospels. This, they might reasonably point out, is all the evidence we have for the nature of the early religion, and that certainly implies it had Judaic roots. However, the New Testament Gospels do *not* comprise the only available evidence, although they are all the Church would prefer us to have. As we have seen, the large body of work known collectively as the Gnostic Gospels has been deliberately withheld from Christians for many centuries – and the picture they summon up of very early Christianity is certainly not that of a Jewish schismatic sect. What the Gnostic Gospels describe is an Egyptian mystery school.

Scholars such as Jean Doresse – in his study of the Nag Hammadi documents – acknowledge the pervasive influence of Egyptian theology on the Gnostic writings. Time and time again in these long-ignored Gospels we find obvious Egyptian concepts. This is most notable in the *Pistis Sophia*, the cosmology of which matches that of the Egyptian *Book of the Dead*. The Gnostic Gospels even employ the same terminology: for example, they use the Egyptian word for 'hell', *Amente*.[74]

For centuries Christians have understood that the Gospels

of the New Testament are 'right' – historically and spiritually – while the Gnostic books are 'wrong'. Matthew, Mark, Luke and John have been believed to be divinely inspired, whereas the others (if known about at all) are widely regarded as nonsense. Yet, as we have hoped to show, there are compelling reasons to consider the Gnostic works as at least equally worthy of our attention.

The Gnostic Gospels were rejected by the Church Fathers for reasons of self-preservation, for these writings presented a very different image of Christianity, one that it would not be in their interests to support. Not only do those suppressed books tend to stress the importance of Mary Magdalene (and the other women disciples), they also present a religion that had its roots – unlike that of the New Testament books – in Egyptian theology. Christianity was intended to be neither a patriarchy nor a development, however heretical, of Judaism. There is no denying that the Gospels of the New Testament were written by Jesus' Jewish followers, but, ironically, they seem to be the ones with the least grasp on what he stood for, the ones who tried to explain him in their own cultural and religious context. On the other hand, it appears that the Gnostic Gospels present a more authentic picture of the origins of their religion – and even of Jesus' own background and beliefs.

But the question remains: what did Jesus and his inner circle hope to gain by disseminating what was essentially a pagan message in the heartland of Judaism?

The original religion of the Hebrews was, like that of all other ancient cultures, polytheistic – venerating *both gods and goddesses*. Only later did Yahweh emerge as the pre-eminent deity, and the priests effectively rewrote their history to erase – not very comprehensively – the earlier worship of goddesses. (And as a result, the status of women declined sharply as it did in early Christianity for the same reason.)

The Hungarian-born anthropologist and biblical scholar Raphael Patai, in his major work *The Hebrew Goddess*, has conclusively demonstrated that Jews once worshipped a female deity. Among the many examples he cites of Hebrew goddess worship is that concerning Solomon's Temple: despite the tradition, it was *not* built to honour Yahweh alone, but also to celebrate the goddess Asherah. Patai says:

> . . . the worship of Asherah as the consort of Yahweh . . . was an integral element of religious life in ancient Israel prior to the reforms introduced by King Josiah in 621 BCE.[75]

Solomon's Temple was built on the model of the Phoenician temples, which in turn were themselves modelled on those of ancient Egypt.[76] And several scholars believe that the images carved on the Ark of the Covenant actually depicted Yahweh and a female deity. The cherubim featured on the Ark were also images of the goddess – carvings of two 'cherubim' found in King Ahab's palace in Samaria are identical with classic representations of Isis.

Heretical, goddess-worshipping Jews continued to thrive in several areas, notably Egypt.[77] Even in mainstream Judaism the goddess survived 'under cover' in two main forms. One is the personification of Israel as a woman; the other, the figure of Wisdom – in Hebrew *Chokmah*, or in Greek *Sophia*. Although usually explained as an allegory for God's divine wisdom it is clear that *Chokmah* has another meaning: wisdom is portrayed as female, and as having co-existed with Yahweh from the beginning.[78]

This figure is now widely acknowledged to have her origins in the goddesses of the surrounding cultures. In particular, Burton L. Mack has uncovered the influence of the Egyptian goddesses Ma'at and Isis.[79]

By Jesus' time Judaism had not completely lost its pagan origins: in any case, Jews converted to foreign religions during the periods of Greek and Roman domination – for example, the Maccabean Revolt of mid-second century BCE was largely about the rift caused by apostate Jews who worshipped, among other gods, Dionysus.

The pagan, goddess-worshipping element of heretical

Judaism could explain much about Jesus, his true motives and his mission. Without this consideration there is an apparent contradiction: while, if taken in isolation, virtually everything that Jesus said or did can be traced back to a mystery school – most likely that of Isis and/or Osiris – yet there is also evidence that he consciously played the role of Jewish Messiah and that the majority of people who followed him believed him to be their king. Even very respected scholars have rejected all the Messianic material when it failed to fit their hypotheses: if they are correct in doing so then Jesus was certainly an initiate of a mystery school. But to us, rejecting this material is unsatisfactory, because it would mean that several Gospel episodes – such as Jesus' entry into Jerusalem on an ass – are complete fabrications. Although there are some demonstrably fictitious tales in the Gospels (mainly concerning Jesus' infancy) there is persuasive evidence that these particular parts are authentic. As we saw in Chapter Eleven, the events leading up to Jesus' triumphal entry in Jerusalem appear to have been pre-arranged, for example in the provision of the ass on which Jesus was to ride in fulfilment of the Messianic prophecies. The evidence of this pre-arrangement lies within the Gospel accounts themselves, yet the writers clearly do not understand its significance. If the Gospel writers had made this episode up, they would certainly not have invented such evidence.

So what were Jesus' real aims and motives? It could be that he was using the Messianic mania current at the time in order to reintroduce goddess-worship – after all, even if he were really, as was claimed on his behalf, of the royal line of David, this was hardly an obstacle, for King David himself had been a goddess-worshipper, as had King Solomon. Perhaps Jesus was an Isian priest who was trying to present an acceptable version of the Isis/Osiris religion to the Jews, or to use the craving for a Messiah to further more secret long-term plans that involved esoteric initiations, perhaps culminating in the Crucifixion. And, as 'Jesus the Nasorean', he was part of a primitive 'family' of Jewish heretical sects who are believed to have passed on the original form of the religion. We can only speculate about the nature of the Nasorean beliefs, but where Jesus was concerned, they clearly dovetailed with his mystery school convictions. Whatever the truth of the matter, Jesus was not so much the Son of God as a devoted Son of the Goddess.

The idea that Jesus was trying to reintroduce goddess worship to the people of Israel fits the case remarkably well. It is also precisely the idea ascribed to Jesus in the *Levitikon*, that key text of the Johannite movement. In it Jesus is an Osiran initiate who realizes that the original religion of Moses and the Tribes of Israel was that of Egypt and that the Jews had forgotten that there was also a goddess. Of course none of this adds up to definite proof, but there is – as we shall see in the next chapter – strong support for this hypothesis from some very surprising quarters.

Astounding though it may seem now, the similarities between early Christianity and Isis and Osiris worship were actually recognized by the early Church. In fact, the two religions were open competitors for the hearts and minds of the same people; apart from the Christians' insistence that their founder had been a real man, their doctrines were virtually identical.

The Isis cult that existed at the time of Jesus was not precisely the same as that which flourished in Egypt before the rise of the Hellenistic empire – her attributes had changed as she absorbed those of other goddesses. In the fourth century BCE, during the Greek rule of Egypt, a new cult of Isis and Serapis (the Greek form of Osiris) emerged, which was essentially a blend of the separate mystery schools. This cult reached Rome before the year 200 BCE, having already cut a swathe throughout the empire. The major cult centre, however, remained in Egypt, at the Serapeum in Alexandria, while there was another centre at Delos.[80]

The lower classes of Rome loved the Isis cult and embraced it wholeheartedly. Such mass movements were always treated with suspicion by the authorities, who saw in them the potential for large-scale subversion, so the Isians of Rome suffered frequent persecutions. Finally, the Senate ordered the destruction of the temples of Isis and Serapis in Rome – but, despite full knowledge of the consequences, no workman could be found to do the job. The cult was officially abolished by Julius Caesar.

However, in 43 BCE the triumvirate unexpectedly ordered the construction of a new Isis-Serapis temple. This may have been the direct result of the notorious liaison between Mark Antony and Cleopatra – she often had herself depicted as Isis and her lover as Osiris or Dionysus. Mark Antony himself preferred to be known as the New Dionysus. During her reign, Cleopatra made sure that the worship of Isis was the national religion of Egypt.

The most severe persecution of the Isians in Rome came under the Emperor Tiberius in 19 CE, when their priests were crucified and 4000 of them were exiled. This persecution coincided with that of the Jews in Rome. The reason for this double overreaction is, however, unclear. Josephus records the story and attributes it to a scandal in which one of the Isian priests helped a Roman noble seduce another man's wife in their temple, but given the usual standard of morals in Roman high society this would normally have hardly caused a raised eyebrow. It seems that Josephus was trying to make a distinction between the persecution of the Isians and that of the Jews, but the real reason appears to be that the former had been involved in a civil disturbance[81].

Something unusual was happening to the Isian religion at the time. As R. Merkelbach, writing in *Man, Myth & Magic*, says:

It is clear that the 'church' of Isis had a 'mission' during the imperial period . . . There is therefore no doubt that propaganda was being spread.[82]

In the first century CE fortune smiled on the cult, and it gained some support among the upper classes and even among emperors. Caligula – hardly, however, a good example –

promoted the building of temples and established Isian festivals. Claudius and Nero were both attracted to the mystery cults in general, and expressed interest in that of Isis. Several of the later Roman Emperors were devotees.

Isis worship continued openly until the end of the fourth century, but its greatest rival was Christianity. In 391 CE the Christians destroyed the Serapeum in Alexandria and took measures to suppress the cult wherever it was found. The last official Isian festival of the old days was celebrated in Rome in 394.

Why was the Isis cult so popular – what did it have to offer its followers?

As we have seen, it was concerned with personal salvation and redemption, and bestowed on its devotees the blessings of an eternal afterlife. As Sharon Kelly Heyob says in *The Cult of Isis among Women in the Graeco-Roman World* (1975):

> Isis eventually became a saviour goddess in the essential meaning of the word. Individual redemption could be attained through participation in her mysteries. The belief that immortality could be obtained was the most persistent of its doctrines.[83]

While Merkelbach says of the Isis cult:

> It was popular because it appealed to the desire for personal salvation (like Christianity), and Platonic philosophical ideas became associated with it [as they did with Christianity].[84]
>
> Sins were confessed and forgiven through immersion in water . . .[85]

S.G.F. Brandon stresses that the two concepts – immersion to symbolize spiritual purification and consequent regeneration – were put together in Egypt in the rituals of the Osiris mystery school, and that:

> This two-fold process for the achievement of a blessed immortality is not found again until the emergence of Christianity.[86]

394

Indeed, there are close parallels between the description of baptism as given by Paul and that of the Osiran mystery schools.[87]

As in Christianity, the personal salvation of the worshipper was linked to his or her *repentance*. In fact, in the later Roman world, only these two religions shared such an emphasis on repentance.[88]

There is another striking – and unique – similarity between the practices of the Isis cult and later Catholic Christianity. This was the concept of *confession*: the devotee would admit to a wrong-doing to the priest, who would then make a plea to Isis on his or her behalf for her forgiveness.[89]

Another custom that the early Church shared with the Isians – despite the modern misconception – is the active role played by women, although some estimates suggest that in both cases priests outnumbered priestesses. Even so, in terms of participation and spiritual status the sexes were deemed to be equal.

The Isis cult generally emphasized the goddess's maternal aspect, celebrating her attributes as wife and mother, although it did not neglect the other sides of the female nature. Consequently, as we have seen, the family trinity of Isis, Osiris and Horus exerted a potent influence over the worshippers' family life: men, women and children alike felt they were understood by their gods. The laity in general played a very active part in the religion – unlike the total control exercised by the male priests of Rome – and there were many 'lay' associations connected to the temples.

Sexually, the Isians were encouraged to be monogamous and to uphold the sanctity of the family. And although several Roman authors condemned them for immoral behaviour, the same writers complained about the regular periods of sexual abstention required of their Isis-worshipping mistresses.

In the Egyptian heyday of the religion, the greatest Isian celebration came on 25 December, when the birth of Isis' son Horus was commemorated – and then, twelve days later, on 6 January, that of her other son, Aion. Both these dates have

395

been taken over by Christians – the Orthodox Church celebrates Christmas on 6 January. In Egypt, Christians in the fourth century celebrated the epiphany of Jesus on that day, also adopting elements from the Aion festival, including baptismal rites using water from the Nile. In *Man, Myth & Magic*, S.G.F. Brandon notes the 'evident influence of the festival of Isis on popular Christian customs associated with the Epiphany'[90].

However, many of the mystery cults of Jesus' time involved similar practices. For example, they commonly declared that their initiates had been 'born again', and, as Marvin W. Meyer says in his *The Ancient Mysteries:*

> Ordinarily, the *mystai* [initiates] partook of food and drink in the ritual celebrations, and sometimes they may have become one with the divine by participating in a sacramental meal analagous to the Christian Eucharist. The wild maenads of Dionysus, for example, were said to have devoured the raw flesh of an animal in their *omophagia*, or feast of flesh . . . the descriptions of the raw feast suggest that participants believed they were consuming the god himself . . . In the mysteries of Mithra, the initiates partook of a ceremony that was so reminiscent of the Christian 'Lord's Supper' that it proved an embarrassment to the Christian apologist Justin Martyr. According to Justin, the Mithraic *mystai* ate bread and drank water (perhaps a mixed cup of water and wine) at an initiatory meal – in diabolical imitation, he hastily adds, of the Christian Eucharist.[91]

Yet no matter how similar other mystery cults appear to be to early Christianity and the teachings of Jesus, it is that of Osiris which has, as we have seen, the greatest claim to be their most direct inspiration. S.G.F. Brandon describes Osiris as 'a prototype of Christ'.[92]

The history of the early Church in Egypt is very suggestive where the similarities between Christianity and the Isis/Osiris mystery school are concerned. Historians recognize that there is a great mystery about the origins and development of Christianity in Egypt: all they can be sure about is that it was a very early offshoot of the movement. Indeed, for such a large and influential metropolis, Alexandria is virtually ignored by the writers of the New Testament, being mentioned just once. (But that reference, as we shall see, is of particular significance to this investigation.) There is also a complete absence of written records about the Church until the third century CE: scholars ascribe this to some wholesale destruction of the archives by the dominant Christian faction[93]. Clearly there was something abhorrent about the Egyptian branch of the movement. Perhaps a clue about its nature is implicit in the fact that when the Serapeum was destroyed in 391 CE many of the worshippers went over to the Coptic (Egyptian) Christian Church[94].

The Coptic Church remained a distinct entity, independent of the Church of Rome or the Eastern Orthodox Church. Significantly, its doctrines are an obvious blend of traditional Egyptian and Christian beliefs – and the two were assimilated with extraordinary ease. After 391 the Coptic Church adopted the *ankh* – the Egyptian looped cross – as its symbol and still uses it today. And Mircea Eliade states bluntly: 'The Copts regard themselves as the true descendants of the ancient Egyptians'.[95]

It was at the same time and in the same place that so many essential pieces of our jigsaw were being created. The Alexandria of that time was a crucible for the synthesis of much knowledge and many ideas, out of which came hermeticism, the Gnosticism of the Nag Hammadi texts and alchemy in its 'modern' form. They were, in essence, all expressions of the same emphasis on the transcendental power of the Feminine, and the magic of blending the goddess with her god.

The sad fact is that, while all the connections between Christianity and the Isis/Osiris religion have been well known to scholars for at least sixty years, few Christians know of them. Of course they may not care that Jesus was one of a long line of saviours, of dying-and-rising gods, for to them *faith* is more important than historical fact. On the other hand, many modern Christians have felt distinctly cheated by the Church as they have made such discoveries for themselves.

Christianity was not the religion founded by the unique Son of God who died for all our sins: it was the worship of Isis and Osiris repackaged. However, it rapidly became a personality cult, centred on Jesus.

But if he was essentially an Egyptian missionary, was he simply a selfless worker on behalf of his gods? Was it enough for Jesus to reach the hearts and souls of the masses? There is something missing from the picture, something central to our understanding of both the man and his mission. Clearly Jesus also had his eyes set on a worldly goal: there *was* a political agenda that ran parallel with his ambitions as Isian/Osiran proselytizer. It was no accident that he was a prominent leader and that he took his message to many parts of Palestine, reaching as many people as possible. In that time and place politics and religion were inseparable. If you were a great religious leader then you were also a political power to be reckoned with.

However, every campaign with such high stakes inevitably faces challenges to its leadership; voices are raised in dissent. In this case the voice was one that had come before, one that could be heard crying in the wilderness. And it is to that voice, to John the Baptist – that we now turn.

In Part One we identified two main strands – centred upon Mary Magdalene and John the Baptist – that ran, like underground streams, through all the heresies we have investigated. And clearly both of these strands hid some powerful and dangerous knowledge, something that would threaten the very foundations of the Church if they were made public. Certainly in the case of Mary Magdalene our investigation has shown this to be true. She herself is now revealed as a major key to Jesus' own long-hidden secrets. Through her we finally see that he was a priest of the Egyptian religion, a magical adept whom she initiated through the rite of sacred sex. This is what the heretical cult of the Magdalene actually meant, and what it effectively encoded for generations of heretics. Not only did she represent the pagan tradition to which she and Jesus belonged; where most of the heretical underground were concerned, Mary Magdalene *was* the goddess Isis.

But the heretics also kept another strand of secrets close to their hearts, and this was embodied and encoded in the figure of John the Baptist. And just as in the case of the Magdalene, he was a real person who knew and interacted with Jesus. So what revelations does he have to offer?

CHAPTER FOURTEEN.

John Christ

When researching Leonardo da Vinci's role in faking the Shroud of Turin we were amazed at how often John the Baptist appears in his story. Not only was the artist himself a great admirer of the saint, but many of the places connected with the Maestro were, perhaps coincidentally, dedicated to him. Foremost among them is Leonardo's beloved city of Florence, which boasts the extraordinary Baptistery at its heart. In 1995, when making a television documentary about the Shroud, we visited it with a film crew, which – the magic acronym 'BBC' being virtually an 'open sesame' – ensured that we had the place to ourselves for some time before the doors were opened to the public. The Baptistery is a strange, octagonal building that dates from the period of the First Crusade and may well owe its unusual shape to the Templars, who (as well as their characteristic round churches) also promoted the octagonal form, based on what they believed was Solomon's Temple in Jerusalem. We had especially wanted to see it because Leonardo's only surviving sculpture (a joint work with Giovanni Francesco Rustici) decorated one outside wall of this strange, octagonal building. It was, of course, a statue of John the Baptist. And, as in all Leonardo's depictions of John, he is shown with his right forefinger raised.

As we have seen, the European Heresy is partly centred on the Baptist, although the real reasons for this are deliberately kept unclear: indeed, even when we began to research this matter some years ago it soon became apparent that this constituted an inner secret of such organizations as the Knights Templar and the Freemasons. But why is it still deemed prudent to keep this secret so zealously guarded?

*　　*　　*

The traditional Christian view of John the Baptist is straightforward enough. It is agreed that his baptism of Jesus marked
the start of the latter's ministry – in fact, two of the canonical
Gospels begin with John preaching by the River Jordan. The
image that the writers conjure up of John is that of a fiery,
ascetic evangelist who emerged from a hermit-like existence in
the desert to call the people of Israel to repent of their evil ways
and be baptized. From the very beginning, there is something
so uncompromising and cold about John that he makes the
modern reader uncomfortable; indeed, there is *nothing* in the
Gospels to justify the extreme veneration shown him by generations of heretics – certainly not that shown him by men of
such supreme intellect as Leonardo da Vinci.

The Gospel accounts, in fact, reveal little about the Baptist.
They tell us that the baptism he performed was an outward
sign of repentance, and that a great many answered his call
and were ritually immersed in the Jordan – including Jesus.
According to Matthew, Mark, Luke and John, the Baptist
proclaimed that he was only the forerunner of the prophesied
Messiah, and that he recognized Jesus to be this figure. Having
fulfilled his role, he fades almost entirely from the picture,
although there are implications that he continued to baptize for
a while.

Luke's Gospel makes Jesus and John cousins, and, interwoven
with the account of the former's conception and birth, gives a
description of those of John – which parallel Jesus', but are
markedly less miraculous. John's parents, the priest Zacharias
and Elisabeth, are childless and advanced in years, yet are
informed by the angel Gabriel that they have been chosen to bear
a son, and shortly afterwards the post-menopausal Elisabeth
conceives. It is to Elisabeth that Mary goes when she finds herself pregnant with Jesus. Elisabeth is six months pregnant at
the time, and at Mary's presence her unborn child 'leaped in
her womb'; thus she knows that the latter's child is to be the
Messiah. Elisabeth praises Mary, which inspires her to proclaim
the 'song' that is now known as the *Magnificat*[1].

We read in the Gospels how, shortly after he baptized Jesus, John was arrested on the orders of Herod Antipas and imprisoned. The reason given is that John had openly condemned Herod's recent marriage to Herodias, the former wife of his half-brother Philip – a marriage that, since she had divorced Philip first, was against Jewish law. After an unspecified period in prison, John was executed. In the familiar story, Herodias' daughter by her earlier marriage, Salome, dances for her stepfather at his birthday feast, and he is so delighted that he promises her whatever she desires, up to 'half his kingdom'. On Herodias' prompting, she asks for the head of John the Baptist on a platter. Unable to go back on his word, Herod reluctantly agrees – having come to admire the Baptist – and has John beheaded. His disciples are permitted to take the body away for burial, although whether this includes the head is unclear.[2]

The story has everything – a tyrannical king, a wicked stepmother, a nubile dancing girl and the horrific death of a famous holy man – and has therefore provided fertile material for generations of artists, poets, musicians and playwrights. It seems to have an eternal fascination, which is perhaps curious for an episode that consists of just a few verses in the Gospels. Two adaptations in particular scandalized audiences at the beginning of the twentieth century: Richard Strauss' opera *Salome* portrayed a promiscuous girl trying to seduce John in prison and, when spurned, demanding his head as revenge, then kissing its lifeless lips triumphantly afterwards. Oscar Wilde's play of the same name had only one performance due to the horror roused by its pre-publicity, which centred mostly on the fact that he himself played the title role. However, Aubrey Beardsley's famous poster for the play remains a graphic depiction of Wilde's interpretation of the biblical story, and once again, centres on Salome's supposed necrophiliac lust.

This heady cocktail of imagined eroticism has little connection with the bald account in the New Testament, whose sole purpose appears to be to establish in no uncertain terms that

John was Jesus' forerunner and spiritual inferior – and also to fulfil the prophesied role of the reincarnated Elias, who would precede the advent of the Messiah.

However, there is another easily accessible source of information about John: Josephus' *Antiquities of the Jews*. Unlike his alleged reference to Jesus, the authenticity of this is not disputed because it fits naturally into the narrative and is an impersonal account that does not eulogize John, and also differs from the Gospel accounts in significant ways.[3]

Josephus records John's preaching and baptizing, and the fact that his popularity and influence over the masses alarmed Herod Antipas, who had John arrested and executed in a 'pre-emptive strike'. Josephus gives no details of his imprisonment or the circumstances or manner of his execution, and makes no mention whatsoever of the alleged criticism of Herod's marriage. He highlights John's enormous popular support, and adds that, not long after his execution, Herod suffered a serious defeat in battle – which the people took as a sign of retribution for his crime against the Baptist.

What can we conclude about John from the Gospel accounts and Josephus? To begin with, the story of his baptism of Jesus must be authentic, for its inclusion argues that it was too well known to leave out altogether – we have noted earlier the tendency of the Gospel writers otherwise to marginalize John wherever possible.

John was active in Peraea, east of the Jordan, a territory under Herod Antipas' rule along with Galilee. Matthew's description is contradictory[4]; the Gospel of John is more specific and names two small towns where John baptized: 'Bethany across the Jordan' (1:28) – a village near the main trade route – and Aenon in the north of the Jordan Valley (3:23). The two places are a fair distance apart, so John appears to have travelled extensively during his mission.

The impression of hermit-like asceticism fostered by the English translations of the Gospels may, in fact, be a misconception. The original Greek *eremos*, given as either 'desert' or 'wilderness', can mean any place of solitude. The same word, significantly, is used of the place in which Jesus feeds the five thousand[5]. Carl Kraeling, in his study of John, which is considered the standard academic text, also argues that the diet of 'locusts and honey' that John is said to have favoured does not argue an especially ascetic lifestyle.[6]

It is also likely that John's mission was not confined solely to Jews. In Josephus' account, although he initially has him exhorting 'the Jews' to piety and a life of virtue, he adds that 'others gathered together [i.e. around him] (for they were also excited to the utmost by listening to his teachings)'[7]. Some scholars think that these 'others' can only be non-Jews, and according to the British biblical scholar Robert L. Webb:

> . . . there is nothing in the content to suggest that they could not have been Gentiles. The location of John's ministry suggests that he could have contact with Gentiles who travelled the trade routes coming from the East, as well as the Gentiles living in the region of the Trans-Jordan.[8]

Another misconception is that of John's age, which is usually taken to be roughly the same as Jesus'. However, the implication of all four Gospels is that John had been preaching for several years before he baptized Jesus and that he was, perhaps by a large margin, the elder of the two[9]. (The story of John's birth in Luke's Gospel is, as we shall see, highly contrived and unlikely to bear much resemblance to the facts.)

Like Jesus', John's message was an implicit attack on the Jerusalem Temple cult – not simply on the possible corruption of its officials, but on all it stood for. His call to baptism may have angered the Temple authorities, not merely because he claimed it was spiritually superior to their rites, but also because his was *free*.

Then there are the anomalies in the descriptions of his death, especially when compared with Josephus' account. The respective motives ascribed to Herod – fear of John's political influence (Josephus), and anger at his criticism of the ruler's marriage (the Gospels) – are not mutually exclusive. Herod

Antipas' marital arrangements did, in fact, have political implications, but not because of whom he had married. The problem lay with whom he had *divorced* in order to do so. His first wife was a princess of the Arabian kingdom of Nabataea, and the perceived insult to this royal family had precipitated a war between the two kingdoms. Nabataea actually bordered on Herod Antipas' territory of Peraea, where John was preaching. Therefore John's denunciation of the marriage effectively put him on the side of the enemy king, Aretas, with the implicit threat that, if the populace were to agree with him, they might end up supporting Aretas against Antipas.[10]

Perhaps this seems academic, but it is puzzling that the Gospels should 'soften' Herod's real motive for having John killed. If we recognize that they are essentially works of propaganda, and that when they obscure some event they do so deliberately, the alternative raises questions about why, in this instance, the Gospel writers should bother.

It is understandable that the Gospel writers would have wanted to censor any suggestion that John had a huge popular following – it fits their general policy towards him – but if they were going to fabricate anything, one might have expected them to concoct a story that supported Jesus in some way. For example, they might have had John arrested for proclaiming Jesus as the Messiah.

The Gospel accounts also make a mistake. They say that John criticized Herod Antipas on the grounds that the latter had married his half-brother Philip's ex-wife. But although the circumstances of the marriage are historically accurate, the half-brother in question was actually another Herod, not Philip. It was this Herod who was Salome's father.[11]

Despite the fact that John – like the Magdalene – has been deliberately marginalized by the Gospel writers, one can still find hints about his influence on contemporaries of Jesus. In one episode, the implication of which appears not to have impinged on most Christians, Jesus' disciples say to him: 'Lord, teach us to pray, the same as John taught his disciples.'[12] This request can actually be understood in two ways: as 'teach us prayers as John taught his disciples' or 'teach us the *same prayers* as John taught . . .' We then read that Jesus taught them what has become known as the Lord's Prayer ('Our Father, which art in Heaven, Hallowed be thy name . . .').

As long ago as the nineteenth century the great Egyptologist Sir E.A. Wallis Budge[13] noted the origins of the opening of the 'Lord's Prayer': an ancient Egyptian prayer to Osiris-Amon begins 'Amon, Amon who art in heaven . . .' Clearly this predated both John and Jesus by centuries, and the 'Lord' who is invoked in the prayer is neither Yahweh nor his alleged son, Jesus. So in any case, the 'Lord's Prayer' was not composed by Jesus.

John is most widely considered to have been overcome by awe at the very sight of Jesus before he baptized him. We are left with the impression that his whole mission, perhaps his entire life, was geared to that one event. In fact, however, there are clear indications that John and Jesus, although closely associated at the beginning of the latter's career, were *bitter rivals*. This has not escaped many of today's most respected biblical commentators. As Geza Vermes writes:

> The aim of the Gospel writers was, no doubt, to give an impression of friendship and mutual esteem, but their attempts smack of superficiality and close scrutiny of the admittedly fragmentary evidence suggests that, at least on the level of their respective disciples, sentiments of rivalry were not absent.[14]

Vermes also describes Matthew and Luke's insistence on Jesus' precedence over John as 'laboured'. Indeed, to objective readers, there is something deeply suspicious about John's repeated, and rather sickening, emphasis on the superiority of 'one that cometh after'. Here we have a John the Baptist who is actually *grovelling* before Jesus.

However, as Hugh Schonfield says:

> We are made aware from Christian sources that there was a considerable Jewish sect in rivalry with the followers of Jesus,

who held that John the Baptist was the true Messiah . . .[15]

Schonfield also notes the 'bitter rivalry' between their respective followers, but adds that, because the influence of John on Jesus was too well known: 'They could not therefore disparage the Baptist, and had to contrive instead to emphasize his secondary place.'[16]

(Without an understanding of this rivalry neither John's nor Jesus' true roles can be fully grasped. Apart from the far-reaching implications for Christian theology itself, the failure to recognize the Jesus/John hostility makes most radical new theories ultimately unsatisfactory. For example, as we have seen, Ahmed Osman actually argues that Jesus was invented by John the Baptist's followers in order to fulfil his prophecy about one who was to come. Similarly Knight and Lomas' *The Hiram Key*[17] goes so far as to maintain that Jesus and John were co-Messiahs working in partnership, a theory that demands that the two preachers were close colleagues; but nothing could be further from the truth.)

The most logical conclusion is that Jesus began as one of John's disciples, and broke away later to form his own group. (It is very likely that he *had* been baptized by John, but as an acolyte, not as the Son of God!) Certainly, the Gospels record that Jesus recruited his first disciples from among the hordes of John's disciples.

In fact, the great English biblical scholar C.H. Dodds translates the phrase from John's Gospel, 'He that cometh after me' (*ho opiso mou erchomenos*), as '*he that follows* me'. This could, for the ambiguity is the same as in English, mean 'disciple'. Indeed, Dodds himself thought that this was the case.[18]

The most recent Bible criticism points to the notion that John never made his famous proclamation about the superiority of Jesus, or even hinted that the latter was the Messiah. This is supported by several facts.

The Gospels (rather ingenuously) record that John, when in prison, questioned the authenticity of Jesus' Messiahship. The implication is that he doubted whether he had been right in his

407

original endorsement of Jesus, but this could equally be another example of the Gospel writers having had to adapt a real episode for their own purposes. Could it be that John had unequivocally *denied* Jesus' Messiahship – maybe even denouncing him?

From the point of view of the Christian message the implications of the whole episode are – or should be – deeply disturbing. For on the one hand Christians accept that John had been divinely inspired to recognize Jesus as the Messiah, but John's question from prison reveals, at the very least, that he had doubts. Clearly his incarceration had given him time to think, or perhaps divine inspiration had deserted him.

As we shall see, later followers of John, who were encountered by Paul during his missionary work at Ephesus and Corinth, knew nothing of John's alleged proclamation of a greater figure who was to come after him.

The single most compelling piece of evidence that the Baptist never proclaimed Jesus as the coming Messiah is that Jesus' *own disciples did not acknowledge him as such*, at least at the beginning of his ministry. He was their leader and their teacher, but there is never any suggestion that they originally followed him because they believed he was the long-awaited Jewish Messiah. Jesus' identity as the Messiah seems to have gradually dawned on the disciples as his ministry progressed. Yet Jesus began his mission after his baptism by John: so why, if John had really announced Jesus' Messiahship, did no-one else know of it at the time? (And the Gospels themselves make it clear that the people followed him not because he was the Messiah, but for some other reason.)

Then there is another, very thought-provoking, consideration. When Jesus' movement first began to make an impact, Herod Antipas became afraid and appeared to think that Jesus was John resurrected or reincarnated (Mark 6:14):

> And King Herod heard of him (for his name had spread abroad) and he said, That John the Baptist was risen from the dead, and therefore mighty works do shew themselves in him.

These words have always been a source of puzzlement. What did Herod mean by them – that Jesus was in some way John reincarnated? But this can hardly have been the case, for both John and Jesus had been alive at the same time. Before examining this story further, let us note some important implications of Herod's words.

The first is that clearly he does not know that John had foretold that 'one greater than he' was to follow him, otherwise he would have drawn the obvious conclusion that Jesus was this person. If the coming of the Messiah had been a conspicuous part of John's teaching – as the Gospels claim – then Herod would have known about it.

The second is that Herod says that 'John ... was risen ... and *therefore* mighty words do shew themselves in him [Jesus] ...' This implies that John had enjoyed a reputation on his own behalf for miracle-working. This, however, is flatly denied in the Gospels – in fact, in the Gospel of John (10:41) it is so emphatic as to suggest a cover-up. Had John the Baptist turned water into wine, fed thousands from a handful of food, healed the sick – even raised the dead? Perhaps he had. One thing is certain, however: the New Testament, being the propaganda of the Jesus movement, is not the place in which we may expect to read of it.

One possible explanation of Herod's otherwise puzzling words about John somehow being reborn through Jesus is, superficially at least, incredible – both literally and metaphorically. But remember that we are dealing with a culture and an era that was so different from ours as to be in many ways another world entirely. As Carl Kraeling, in 1940, pointed out, Herod's words only make sense if understood as reflecting *occult* ideas that were current in the Graeco-Roman world of Jesus' time[19]. This suggestion was taken up and expanded upon by Morton Smith in his *Jesus the Magician* in 1978[20]. As we have already seen, Smith has concluded that the answer to the enigma of Jesus' popularity lay in his displays of Egyptian magic.

At that period it was believed that, in order to work magic, a sorcerer needed to have power over a demon or spirit. In fact, this is alluded to in the Gospel passage in which Jesus refers to the accusation made against *John* that 'he had a demon'. This does not, as might appear, refer to possession by an evil spirit, but rather to the claim that John had *power* over one.

Kraeling's suggestion in this context was that the words of Herod Antipas could be understood as a reference to this concept, because it was not only demons who could be 'enslaved' in this way, but also the spirit of a human being, especially one who had been murdered. A spirit or soul thus enslaved would, it was believed, carry out its master's bidding. (Such a charge was later made against Simon Magus, who was said to have 'enslaved' the spirit of a murdered boy.)

Kraeling writes:

> John's detractors used the occasion of his death to develop the suggestion that his disembodied spirit was serving Jesus as the instrument for the performance of works of black magic, itself no small concession to John's power.[21]

With this explanation in mind, Morton Smith's rendering of Herod's words is:

> John the Baptist has been raised from the dead [by Jesus' necromancy; Jesus now has him]. And therefore [since Jesus-John can control them] the [inferior] powers work [their wonders] by him [i.e. his orders].[22]

In support of this idea, Smith cites a magical text on a papyrus now in Paris. The invocation is made – significantly perhaps – to the sun god Helios:

> Give me the authority over this spirit of a murdered man, a part of whose body I possess . . .[23]

Especially interesting in this context are the gifts that this magical operation is intended to confer on the magician: the ability to heal and to tell if a sick person will live or die, and the promise that 'you will be worshipped as a god . . .'[24]

Another episode serves to underline the fact that John's popularity was, if anything, greater than Jesus'. This takes place near the end of the latter's ministry, when he is preaching to the crowds in the Temple in Jerusalem[25]. The 'chief priests and elders' come to confront him publicly and pose trick questions in the hope of trapping him – questions that Jesus sidesteps with the alacrity of a seasoned politician. They demand that he identify the authority with which he speaks. Jesus responds with a counter-question: 'The baptism of John, whence was it? from heaven or of man?'

This gives his opponents pause for thought:

And they reasoned with themselves, saying, If we shall say, From heaven; he will say unto us, Why did ye not then believe him?
   But if we shall say, Of men; we fear the people; for all hold John as a prophet.

Faced with this quandary, they decline to answer.

What is significant in that exchange is that Jesus used the priests' fear of *John's* popularity with the crowds against them, not of his own. As we have seen, Josephus stressed the extent of John's influence and support among the people: clearly the Baptist was no common itinerant preacher, but a leader of great charisma and power who, for whatever reason, commanded a huge following. In fact, according to Josephus, both Jews and Gentiles 'were excited to the utmost by listening to his teachings'.

A curious episode in the apocryphal Gospel called the Book of James or the Protoevangelium indicates that John was important in his own right[26]. Admittedly, this Gospel was compiled fairly late and includes many accounts of Jesus' childhood that no-one now takes seriously – but it does incorporate material from several sources and could therefore include at least hints of well-known traditions. It is certainly difficult to see how someone familiar with the canonical Gospels could have made it up.

In this tale of the infancies of Jesus and John – after the familiar story of the birth of Jesus and the visit of the Wise Men – Herod orders the Massacre of the Innocents. So far, this sounds identical to the version found in the New Testament. However it soon takes a radically different line.

When Mary hears of the massacre her reaction is simply to wrap her baby in swaddling clothes and place him in an ox manger – presumably in order to hide him from the soldiers. But it seems that *John* is the object of their search. We read how Herod sends his men to question John's father Zacharias, and they report back that he does not know where his wife and child are:

> Herod was wroth and said: His son is to be king over Israel.

In this version, it is Elisabeth that flees with John into the hill country. There are clear hints here of a parallel, perhaps even a rival, 'Holy Family'.

As we have seen, John had a large popular following, which, like Jesus' movement, consisted of a circle of disciples who accompanied him everywhere and of members of the general public who came to listen to his words. Also as in the case of Jesus, after John's death his disciples began to write accounts of his life and teaching in what were effectively *scriptures* of John.

Scholars recognize that such a corpus of 'John literature' existed – once, but we do not have it today. Possibly it was destroyed, or kept secretly by 'heretics'. It does seem, however, that it must have contained some material that did not agree with the New Testament accounts of John and Jesus – otherwise it would have been preserved in the public domain in some form.

Luke's account of the 'joint' conceptions of Jesus and John is extremely interesting. From an analysis of the story, scholars have established beyond doubt that this is actually a combination of two separate stories, one telling of John's conception and the other of that of Jesus, which are (according to Kraeling) 'held together by materials basically unrelated to the thread of either series'[27]. In other words, Luke (or the source he used) took two distinct stories and tried to join them together using the literary device of the meeting of the two expectant mothers, Elisabeth and Mary. The logical conclusion is that the story of John's infancy was originally independent of the Gospel, and that it probably *predated* the story of Jesus' Nativity. This carries important implications. One is that stories concerning John were already in existence. The other is that Luke's version of the Nativity has been evoked specifically in order to 'trump' the one that was current about John. After all, the 'miracle' of John's birth is simply that he was born to such aged parents, whereas Luke has Jesus actually being born of a virgin. And the only motive that Luke could have had for telling the story in this way was that John's following still existed as a rival to that of Jesus.

This is supported by another fact that has been established by scholars – but which remains unknown to most Christians. The much-loved 'song' of Mary's, the *Magnificat*, was in fact *Elisabeth*'s, and referred to *her* child. The wording links the woman to the Old Testament character Hannah, who was childless until her latter years, so it is more appropriate for Elisabeth's situation. In fact, some early New Testament manuscripts actually state that it is Elisabeth's song, and the Church Father Irenaeus (writing *c.*170) also states that she, not Mary, spoke those words.[28]

Similarly, at the circumcision ceremony for John, his father Zacharias proclaims a 'prophecy', or hymn, which is known as the Benedictus, in praise of his new-born son[29]. Obviously this must once have been part of the original 'John the Baptist' nativity story. Both the Magnificat and the Benedictus appear to have been separate 'hymns' to John that have been incorporated into a 'John Gospel' which was then adulterated by Luke to make it more acceptable to the followers of Jesus. This indicates that people were not only writing accounts of John's life but also eulogizing him in song and verse. But did these traditions about John actually provide the later Gospel writers with the material on which to base their tale about Jesus? As Schonfield says in his *Essene Odyssey*:

> Contact with followers of John the Baptist . . . acquainted the Christians with the Nativity stories of John in which he figured as the infant Messiah of the priestly traditions, born at Bethlehem.[30]

Besides this, the early Church texts known as the Clementine Recognitions actually state that some of John's disciples believed *him* to be the Messiah.[31] And Geza Vermes believes that some episodes in the Gospels and Acts themselves hint that John's followers believed he was the Messiah.[32]

The knowledge that such a thing as 'John literature' ever existed supplies an answer to the many problems about the Fourth Gospel – which was attributed to the disciple John. As we have seen, there are several internal contradictions in this Gospel. Although it is the only one to be based on an eye-witness account – a claim supported by the circumstantial detail in the text itself – it contains conspicuously Gnostic elements that are at odds both with the other Gospels and with the matter-of-fact tone of the rest of the book itself. This is particularly noticeable in the 'prologue' concerning God and the Word. John's Gospel is the most vociferously anti-Baptist of all four, and yet is the only one that tells us explicitly that Jesus recruited his first disciples from John's followers – including the supposed author and eyewitness, the 'beloved disciple' himself.[33]

These contradictions, however, do not necessarily invalidate the Gospel. It is clear that the author compiled the text from several sources, which he wove together and interpreted according to his own beliefs about Jesus, rewriting material where he felt it to be necessary. Whoever the author was, the Gospel seems to contain the 'beloved disciple's' first-hand testimony. But many of the most influential New Testament scholars think that the author also used some of the texts written by followers of the Baptist, which, according to the authority on Middle Eastern studies, Edwin Yamauchi, 'The Fourth Evangelist . . . demythologized and Christianized.'[34]

The Baptist material is chiefly the prologue and some of what are called 'the revelation discourses' between Jesus and his disciples. The great German biblical scholar Rudolf Bultmann argued that these were:

> . . . believed to have been originally documents of the followers of John the Baptist who had exalted John and originally given John the role of a Redeemer sent from the world of Light. Therefore a considerable part of the Gospel of John was not originally Christian in origin but resulted from the transformation of a Baptist tradition.[35]

Note that these elements in John's Gospel are the most Gnostic, and have therefore caused the most problems, where that Gospel is concerned, for historians. It has often been assumed that, as these elements are so out of keeping with the theology of the other Gospels and the rest of the New Testament, this book must have been written considerably later than the others. However, recognizing that they came from a source other than Jesus' followers changes the picture, and several commentators have linked the Fourth Gospel to a 'pre-Christian Gnostic source' which was adapted by the writer. That source would seem to be John the Baptist and his followers, who would appear to have been Gnostic themselves.

(These discoveries may provide a solution to the controversy over the dating of John's Gospel. As we have seen, the standard view has long been that, because of the Gnostic and non-Jewish material in this Gospel, it was written after the Synoptic Gospels. However, if Jesus was not a Jew, and as much of the material derives from the followers of John the Baptist – who, as we shall see, were Gnostic – it is entirely possible that this Gospel is contemporary with, or even predates, the others.)

Not only did John have a large and devoted following during his lifetime, but it continued to grow after his death in a manner that is curiously parallel to the growth of Christianity. There is evidence that John's movement had become a Church in its own right and that it was not confined to Palestine. In his 1992 book *Jesus* A.N. Wilson writes:

> If the John the Baptist religion (and we know there was one) had become the dominant cult of the Mediterranean rather than the Jesus religion, we should probably feel that we knew more than we do about this arresting figure. His cult survived until at least the mid-50s, as the author of Acts is guileless enough to let on . . . In Ephesus, they thought 'The Way' (as the religion of these early believers was known) meant following 'the Baptism of John' . . . Had Paul been a weaker personality . . . or had he never written his epistles, it could easily have been the case that the 'Baptism of John' would have been the religion which captured the imagination of the ancient world, rather than the Baptism of Christ . . . The cult might even have developed to the point where present-day Johnites, or Baptists, would have believed that . . . John was Divine . . .
>
> This accident of history, however, was not to be.[36]

So even the New Testament describes the existence of the Church of John beyond the boundaries of Israel. Bamber Gascoigne writes:

> A group of people whom Paul met in Ephesus give an intriguing glimpse of one such potential religion developing – and one that Paul nipped quickly in the bud.[37]

That group of people was, of course, John's Church. Their very existence as a separate entity after the death of Jesus argues that John had never preached of 'one greater' coming after him, or that if he had, that person could not have been Jesus. It

416

seemed that when the Johannites met Paul they had no idea of any such prophecy. Theirs was no insignificant cult. It has been described as 'an international following'[38] and it stretched from Asia Minor to Alexandria. The Acts record that John's religion had been brought to Ephesus by an Alexandrian named Apollos – suspiciously the only reference to Alexandria in the whole of the New Testament.

So John the Baptist had a distinct and strong following of his own, which survived him as a veritable Church. However, it has been assumed – as in A.N. Wilson's comments above – that it was absorbed into the Christian Church early on. Certainly some of its communities were, like those encountered by Paul, superseded by his own version of the Jesus movement. But there is strong evidence that the Church of John actually *survived*.

This body of evidence, however, emphasizes the role of a character who, at first, might seem very out of place in this story, someone who has been reviled throughout Christian history as 'the father of all heresies', and a black magician of the worst kind. He has even given his name to a sin: that of trying to *buy* the Holy Spirit: simony. We are referring, of course, to Simon Magus.

Unlike the other two major figures we have been discussing – Mary Magdalene and John the Baptist – Simon Magus was not someone who has been marginalized by the first Christian chronicles, but was actually allowed to feature quite prominently in early Christian writings. However, he is still unequivocally denounced as evil, as the man who attempted to ape Jesus, and who at one point even infiltrated the embryonic Church in order to learn its secrets – until, of course, he was exposed by the Apostles.

Sometimes known as 'the First Heretic', Simon Magus is deemed to be almost beyond redemption. Yet a clue as to why this should be so lies in the fact that the early Church Fathers regarded the word Gnostic as being synonymous with 'heretic' – and Simon was a Gnostic (although, not, as they believed, the founder of Gnosticism).

Simon makes only a brief appearance in the New Testament, in the Acts of the Apostles (8:9–24). He was, significantly, a Samaritan, who, according to the Acts, had been using sorcery to 'bewitch' the people of Samaria. When the Apostle Philip preaches there, Simon is so impressed that he is baptized by him. But this turns out simply to be a cunning ruse so that he can learn how to secure the power of the Holy Spirit for himself. He offers money to buy it from Peter and John, and is soundly rebuked. So Simon, fearing for his soul, repents and asks them to pray for him.

However, the early Church Fathers knew rather more about this character, and their accounts contradict the simple morality tale of the book of Acts[39]. He was a native of the village of Gitta, who was renowned for his abilities as a magician (hence his title of *Magus*). During the reign of Claudius (41–54 CE, i.e. within ten years of the Crucifixion) he went to Rome, where he was honoured as a god, and a statue was even raised to him there. The Samaritans had already recognized him as a god.

Simon Magus travelled with a woman named Helen, a former prostitute from the Phoenician city of Tyre, whom he called the First Thought (*Ennoia*), the Mother of All. This arose out of his Gnostic beliefs: he taught that God's 'first thought' – just like the Jewish figure of Wisdom/Sophia discussed earlier – had been female, and that it was she who had created the angels and other demigods, who are the gods of this world. They created the Earth under her instructions, but rebelled and imprisoned her in matter, the material world. She was trapped in a series of female bodies (including that of Helen of Troy), each enduring increasingly unbearable humiliations, and eventually ended up as a whore in the seaport of Tyre. But all was not lost, because God was also incarnate, in the form of Simon. He had sought her out and rescued her.

The concept of a cosmological system that encompassed a series of higher and lower worlds and planes is one with which we are now familiar. Although the precise details vary, it is the common Gnostic belief that reached as far as the medieval Cathars, and which underlies the hermetic cosmology that is the basis of Western occultism, running through alchemy to the hermeticism of the Renaissance. There are also exact and striking parallels with other systems that we have discussed. The most significant is the similarity with the Coptic Gnostic *Pistis Sophia*, in which it is Jesus who comes in search of the trapped Sophia, a figure explicitly linked in that text with the Magdalene[40]. (Simon also called Helen his 'lost sheep'.)

The personification of Wisdom as a woman – and a whore at that – is by now something with which we are familiar in this investigation, and which runs like a thread through it. In Simon's case, this embodiment was literal, in the person of Helen.

As Hugh Schonfield writes:

> . . . the Simonians worshipped Helen as Athena (Goddess of Wisdom), who in turn was identified in Egypt with Isis.[41]

Schonfield also links Helen with Sophia herself and with Astarte.

Karl Luckert also traces Simon's concept of the *Ennoia*, as incarnated in Helen, to Isis[42]. Geoffrey Ashe agrees, adding: '[Helen] is set on a pathway back to glory as *Kyria* or heavenly Queen'[43].

Another apocryphal source, dating from around 185, describes Helen as being 'black as an Ethiopian' and has her dancing in chains, adding: 'The whole Power of Simon and of his God is this Woman who dances.'[44]

Irenaeus writes that Simon's initiated priests 'lived immorally'[45], although, disappointingly, he does not enlarge on this. But they obviously practised sexual rites, as Epiphanius reveals in his monumental work *Against Heresy*:

> And he enjoined mysteries of obscenity and . . . the shedding of bodies, *emissionum virorum, feminarum menstruorum*, and

that they should be gathered up for mysteries in the most filthy collection.[46]

(G.R.S. Mead, a good Victorian, left this rather coy translation with those Latin phrases, but it appears that Simon's sect used sex magic, involving semen and menstrual blood.)

The Church Fathers were obviously deeply afraid of Simon Magus and his influence. It appears to have been a serious threat to the early Church, which may seem odd – until one realizes just how much Simon actually had in common with Jesus.

The Fathers were at pains to point out that, although Simon and Jesus said and did much the same things, including miracles, the source of their power was very different. Simon did his through wicked sorcery, whereas Jesus did his through the power of the Holy Spirit. In effect, Simon was a Satanic parody of Jesus. So we find, for example, Hippolytus stating bluntly of Simon: 'He was not Christ'[47].

Epiphanius writes more revealingly:

From the time of Christ to our own day the first heresy was that of Simon the magician, and though it was not correctly and distinctly of the Christian name, yet it worked great havoc by the corruption it produced among Christians.[48]

Moreover, according to Hippolytus:

... by purchasing the freedom of Helen, he thus offered salvation to men by knowledge peculiar to himself.[49]

Another account credits Simon with the ability to work miracles, including turning stones into bread. (This may account for the Temptation of Jesus when he is offered the power to do the same, but turns it down. However, we are later told that he fed five thousand people from five loaves and two fishes, which is much the same thing.)

Hieronymus quotes from one of Simon's works:

I am the Word of God, I am the glorious one, I am the Paraclete, the Almighty. I am the whole of God.[50]

In other words Simon proclaimed himself as being divine, and promised salvation to his followers.

In the Apocryphal Acts of Peter and Paul, Simon Magus and Peter engage in a contest to raise a dead body to life. Simon, however, can only manage to reanimate the head whereas Peter does the trick perfectly.[51] There are many such Apocryphal tales of magical battles between Simon Magus and Simon Peter, all of them ending with the required Christian triumph. What they do show, however, is that the former was so influential that the stories *had* to be concocted in order to counter his power over the masses.

The Magus was no simple itinerant sorcerer, but a philosopher who wrote his ideas down. Needless to say, his original books have been lost, but there are some extensive quotations from them in the works of the Church Fathers, where they were included in order to be roundly condemned. These fragments, however, clearly reveal Simon's Gnosticism and emphasis on the existence of two opposite but complementary forces – one male and one female. For example, this is quoted from his *Great Revelation:*

> Of the universal Aeons there are two shoots . . . one is manifested from above, which is the Great Power, the Universal Mind ordering all things, male, and the other from below, the Great Thought, female, producing all things. Hence pairing with each other, they unite and manifest the Middle Distance . . . in this is the Father . . .
>
> This is He who has stood, stands and will stand, a male-female power in the pre-existing Boundless Power . . .[52]

Here we can see echoes of the alchemical hermaphrodite, of the symbolic androgyne that was to so fascinate Leonardo. But where did Simon Magus' ideas come from?

Karl Luckert[53] traces the 'ideological roots' of Simon's

teachings to the religions of ancient Egypt, and it does seem to be the case that they reflect, perhaps even continue in an adapted form, those cults. Although, as we have seen, the Isis/Osiris schools emphasized the opposite and equal nature of the female/male deities, this is sometimes understood to be blended in the one character and body of Isis. She is occasionally portrayed as being bearded, and is believed to have said: 'Though I am female, I became a male . . .'

Simon Magus and Jesus were, as far as the early Church was concerned, dangerously alike in their teaching, which is why Simon was accused of having tried to steal the Christians' knowledge. This is a tacit admission that his own teaching was, in fact, *compatible* with that of Jesus – even that he was part of the same movement. The implications of this are disturbing. Were the sexual rites of Simon and Helen for example, also practised by Jesus and Mary Magdalene? According to Epiphanius, the Gnostics had a book called the *Great Questions of Mary*, which purported to be the inner secrets of the Jesus movement and which took the form of 'obscene' ceremonies.[54]

It might be tempting to dismiss such rumours as merely scurrilous scandal-mongering – but, as we have seen, there is evidence that the Magdalene was a sexual initiatrix in the tradition of the *temple prostitute*, whose function was to bestow upon men the gift of *horasis*: spiritual enlightenment through sexual intercourse.

John Romer, in his book *Testament*, makes the parallel clear:

> Helen the Harlot, as the Christians called her, was Simon Magus' Mary Magdalene.[55]

Then again, there is another link: that of their probable Egyptian origins. Karl Luckert says of Simon:

> As the 'father of all heresy' he must now be studied not merely as an opponent, but also a conspicuous competitor of Christ in the early Christian church – possibly even as a potential ally . . .

422

From the fact of their common Egyptian heritage may be derived the very strength of Simon Magus' threat. The danger amounted to the possibility that he could be confused with the Christ figure himself . . .[56]

And Luckert sees a close parallel in what he perceives as being the real mission of the two men. He acknowledges the apparent dichotomy in Jesus' preaching an essentially Egyptian message to a Jewish audience, but perceives the close connection between the *original* Hebrew theology, and that of Egypt. He says of Simon Magus:

[he] . . . saw it as his mission to fix that which . . . must have gone wrong; namely, the estrangement of the entire female Tefnut-Mahet-Nut-Isis dimension from the masculine godhead.[57]

This, of course, is precisely the motive that we have hypothesized for Jesus' mission in Judaea, and that is ascribed to him in the *Levitikon*. Luckert concludes that Jesus won out over Simon Magus only by going to the extreme lengths of including his own death in the picture. The emphasis shifts radically, however, when one takes into consideration the idea that the Crucifixion may not have ended in Jesus' death.

Apart from the parallels with Jesus, there is another disquieting – and for us, revealing – fact about Simon Magus: *he was a disciple of John the Baptist*. Not only that, but he was actually named by John *as his own successor* (although, for the reasons given below, it was not to be a direct succession).

The implications of this are astounding. For Simon had been known as a sorcerer and sex magician all along, and not merely in the years after John died. This was hardly a case of a disciple kicking over the traces once the puritan guru is removed from the frame. John must have known and approved of Simon's teaching. And if Simon were a member of John's inner circle, he would have learned his magic from the Baptist – as would other disciples in a similar position. Such as Jesus . . .

The following is taken from the third-century *Clementine Recognitions*:

> It was at Alexandria that Simon perfected his studies in magic, being an adherent of John, a Hemerobaptist ['Day-baptist': little is known about this term], through whom he came to deal with religious doctrines. John was the forerunner of Jesus . . .
> . . . Of all John's disciples, Simon was the favourite, but on the death of his master, he was absent in Alexandria, and so Dositheus, a co-disciple, was chosen head of the school.[58]

This account also goes into extremely convoluted numerological reasons for why John had thirty disciples – presumably of the inner circle only – although it was really twenty-nine and a half because one was a woman who did not count as a full person. Her name was Helen . . . This is interesting because it implies, in the context, that this was Simon Magus' Helen, and that she, too, had been a disciple of John. All of which leaves the distinctly uneasy feeling that the Baptist, who has always been presented as an ascetic, monk-like puritan, was in fact something quite other.

When Simon returned from Alexandria, Dositheus yielded the leadership of John's Church to him, although not without a struggle. Once again, we find that the Egyptian city of Alexandria is important in this story, presumably because that is where the main protagonists learned their magic.

Dositheus also had a sect named after him, which succeeded in surviving until the sixth century. Origen records:

> . . . a certain Dositheus of the Samaritans came forward and said that he was the prophesied Christ: from that day until now there are Dositheans, who both produce writings of Dositheus and also relate some tales about him, as that he did not taste of death, but is still alive.[59]

Simon's own traceable following continued until the third century. His immediate successor was one Menander.

The Dositheans 'worshipped John the Baptist' as the 'righteous teacher . . . of the Last Days'[60]. Yet both Simon's and Dositheus' sects were eventually eradicated by the Church.

The clear implication is that John the Baptist was not the occasional preacher to a rabble: he was the head of an *organization* – and it was based in Alexandria. As we have seen, the first proselytizers of the Jesus movement were amazed to discover a 'John Church' at Ephesus, which had been taken there by Apollos of Alexandria. It was that metropolis that was also the base for Simon Magus – John's official successor and a known rival of Jesus – who was also a Samaritan. Interestingly, Christians venerated the Baptist's alleged tomb in Samaria until it was destroyed in the fourth century by the Emperor Julian, which at least suggests an early tradition linking John the Baptist with that land. (Perhaps the parable of the Good Samaritan was really a shrewd attempt to appease the disciples of John or Simon Magus.)

However, there is no suggestion that Simon Magus was a Jew, even one from Samaria. Even in their most virulent attacks on him, the Church Fathers never once attack him for being Jewish – and given the violence with which Jews have been accused of having murdered the Son of God over the centuries, this is particularly telling. As we have seen, John preached to non-Jews and he attacked the Jerusalem Temple cult – the very foundation of the Jewish religion. He had, in all probability, strong links with Alexandria – but more significantly, his successor was also a Gentile. All of this implies that John himself was not a Jew, and that he was familiar with the Egyptian culture.

It is particularly odd that the early Church Fathers, such as Irenaeus, should have traced the origins of 'heretical' sects back to John the Baptist, of all people. After all, the Gospels have him apparently inventing baptism and virtually living just to pave the way for Jesus. But did they know the truth about John? Did they realize that he was no forerunner but a bitter rival, who was worshipped in his own right as Messiah?

Did they recognize the astounding fact that John was *not, in fact, a Christian at all*?

The Gospel writers have, in effect, got their revenge on John. They have rewritten him and in the process 'tamed' and realigned him, so that the one-time rival – perhaps even enemy – of Jesus is seen as kneeling before him in awe at his divinity. They have removed John's real motives, words and actions and replaced them with those that fit the image they deliberately created of Jesus and his movement.

As a piece of propaganda it has been startlingly successful, although perhaps this has been partly due to the earlier Church's tendency to answer any 'heretical' questions with the thumbscrews and flaming pyre. The Christian story we receive on trust today is the result of the Church's previous reign of terror as much as of the propaganda of the Gospels.

But well away from the baleful influence of the established Church, some of John's followers faithfully kept his memory as 'true Messiah' alive. And they still exist today.

CHAPTER FIFTEEN

Followers of the King of Light

In the seventeenth century, Jesuit missionaries returning from the area around the southern reaches of the Euphrates and Tigris rivers, in what is now Iraq, brought back tales of a people whom they called 'St John's Christians'. Although this group lived in the Moslem world, and were surrounded by Arabs, they still adhered to a form of Christianity in which John the Baptist was pre-eminent. Their religious rites all centred on baptism, which was not a once-only ceremony initiating and welcoming a new member into the congregation, but played an important part in *all* their sacraments and rituals.[1]

Since those first contacts, however, it has become apparent that the term 'St John's Christians' is a great misnomer. The sect in question do especially venerate John the Baptist – but they cannot be called 'Christians' in the usual sense at all. For they regard Jesus as a false prophet, a liar who deliberately misled his own – and other – people. But having lived under the constant threat of persecution from Jews, Moslems and Christians for centuries, they have adopted the strategy of presenting themselves to visitors in the least offensive guise. It was for this reason that they took the name 'St John's Christians'. Their policy is encapsulated in these words from their sacred book, the *Ginza*:

> When Jesus oppresses you, then say: We belong to you. But do not confess him in your hearts, or deny the voice of your Master, the high King of Light, for to the lying Messiah the hidden is not revealed.[2]

Today, this sect – which still survives in the marshes of southern Iraq and, in smaller numbers, in south-west Iran – is known as the Mandaeans. They are a deeply religious and peaceable people, whose code forbids war and the shedding of blood. They mostly live in their own villages and communities, although some of them have moved to the cities, where they traditionally work as gold- and silversmiths, work in which they excel. They retain their own language and script, both of which were derived from Aramaic, the language spoken by Jesus and John. In 1978 their numbers were estimated at fewer than 15,000, but the persecution of the marsh Arabs by Saddam Hussein after the Gulf War may well have brought them close to extinction – political circumstances in Iraq make it impossible to be precise on the subject.[3]

The name Mandaean literally means *Gnostic* (from *manda*, gnosis) and properly refers to the laity only, although it is often applied to the community as a whole. Their priests are called *Nasoreans*. The Arabs refer to them as *Subbas*, and they appear in the Koran under the name of *Sabians*.

No serious scholarly work was done on the Mandaeans until the 1880s. Even so, the most extensive studies to date are still those of Ethel Stevens (later Lady Drower) in the years immediately before the Second World War. Academics still rely heavily on the material she collected, which includes many photographs of their rituals and copies of the Mandaean holy books. Although welcoming strangers, they are naturally – and with good reason – a closed and secretive people, and Lady Drower spent much time winning their confidence to the point that they revealed their beliefs, doctrines and history to her, and allowed her access to the secret scrolls containing their sacred texts. (In the nineteenth century, French and German scholars had tried unsuccessfully to breach this wall of secrecy.) But undoubtedly there remain inner mysteries that have not yet been shared with outsiders.

The Mandaeans have a number of sacred texts – all their literature is religious – the most important of which are the *Ginza* (*Treasure*), also known as the *Book of Adam*; the *Sidra d'Yahya*, or *Book of John* (also known as the *Book of Kings*), and the *Haran Gawaita*, which is a history of the sect. The *Ginza* certainly dates from the seventh century CE or earlier, while the *Book of John* is thought to have been compiled from that time onwards. The John of the title is the Baptist, who in the Mandaean text is referred to by two names, Yohanna (which is Mandaean), and Yahya, which is the Arabic name by which he appears in the Koran. The latter is used more often, indicating that the book was written after the Moslem conquest of the region in the middle of the seventh century, although the material in it is much earlier. The important question is just how much earlier.

It used to be thought that the Mandaeans had created the *Book of John* and elevated the Baptist to the status of their prophet as a cunning ploy to avoid persecution by the Moslems, who only tolerated those whom they called 'people of the Book' – that is, people with a religion that had a holy book and a prophet; otherwise they were regarded as heathens. However, the Mandaeans appear in the Koran itself, under the name of Sabians, as a 'people of the Book', proving that they were known as such long before they came under threat of Moslem rule. In any case, they *did* suffer persecution, particularly in the fourteenth century, when their Islamic rulers nearly wiped them out.

Constantly retreating from persecution, the Mandaeans finally arrived in their current homeland. Their own legends, and modern scholarship, show that they came originally from Palestine, out of which they were forced in the first century CE. Over the centuries they moved east and south, moving on as they met with persecution. What we have today is effectively the remnant of a much more widespread religion.

Today the Mandaean religion is, frankly, a hopelessly confused hotchpotch: various fragments of Old Testament Judaism, heretical Gnostic forms of Christianity and Iranian dualist beliefs are all mixed into their cosmology and theology. The problem lies in ascertaining which were their original beliefs, and which came later. It seems that the Mandaeans themselves have forgotten much of the initial meaning of their religion. But it is possible to make some generalizations about it, and painstaking analysis has enabled scholars to come to some conclusions about their beliefs in the distant past. It is this analysis that has provided us with some exciting clues about the importance of John the Baptist and his real relationship with Jesus.

The Mandaeans represent the world's only surviving Gnostic religion: their ideas concerning the universe, the act of creation and the gods are familiar Gnostic beliefs. They believe in a hierarchy of gods and demigods, both male and female, with a fundamental split between those of light and those of darkness.

Their supreme being, who created the universe and the lesser deities, appears under various names that translate as 'Life', 'Mind' or 'King of Light'. He created five 'beings of light', which automatically brought into being five equal but opposite beings of darkness. (This emphasis on light being equated with the highest good is characteristically Gnostic: virtually every page of the *Pistis Sophia*, for example, uses this metaphor. To the Gnostics being *enlightened* meant literally and figuratively entering a world of light.) As in other Gnostic systems, it is these demigods who created and rule the material universe and this earth. Mankind was also created by one such being called either (depending on the version of the myth) Hiwel Ziwa or Ptahil. The first humans are the physical Adam and Eve – Adam Paghia and Hawa Paghia – and their 'occult' counterparts, Adam Kasya and Hawa Kasya. The Mandaeans believe themselves to be descended from parents from both physical and spirit 'sets' – Adam Paghia and Hawa Kasya.

Their nearest equivalent to the Devil is the dark goddess Ruha, who rules over the realm of darkness, but she is also regarded as the Holy Spirit. This emphasis on equal and opposite forces of good and evil, male and female, is characteristically Gnostic and is exemplified in the words:

... the earth is like a woman and the sky like a man, for it makes the earth fecund.[4]

An important goddess, to whom many prayers can be found in Mandaean books, is Libat, who has been identified with Ishtar.

To the Mandaeans, celibacy is a sin; men who die unmarried are condemned to be reincarnated – but otherwise the Mandaeans do not believe in the cycle of rebirth. At death the soul returns to the world of light from which the Mandaeans once came, and it is helped on its way with many prayers and ceremonies, many of which clearly originate from ancient Egyptian funerary rites.

Religion permeates every aspect of the Mandaeans' daily lives, but their key sacrament is baptism, which features in marriage and even funeral services. The Mandaean baptisms are complete immersions in specially created pools that are connected to a river, which is known as a *Jordan*. Part of every ritual is a series of complex handshakes between the priests and those who are being baptized.

The Mandaeans' holy day is Sunday. Their communities are ruled by the priests, who also take the title 'king' (*malka*), although some religious duties may be carried out by the laity. The priesthood is hereditary and consists of three tiers: the ordinary priests, who are called 'disciples' (*tarmide*), bishops and an overall 'head of the people' – although no-one has been deemed worthy to fill this role for over a century.

The Mandaeans claim to have existed long before the time of the Baptist, whom they see as a great leader of their sect, but nothing more. They say they left Palestine in the first century CE, having originated in a mountain region that they call the Tura d'Madai, which has not as yet been identified by scholars.

When the Jesuits first came across them in the seventeenth century, it was assumed that they were the descendants of Jews whom John had baptized, but now their claims to have existed before that time and indeed, in another place, are taken seriously by scholars. But they do still retain traces of their time in first-century Palestine: their writing is similar to that of Nabataea, the Arabic kingdom that bordered Peraea, where John the Baptist first appeared.[5] Clues in the *Hawan Gawaita* suggest that they left Palestine in 37 CE – roughly the time of the Crucifixion, but whether this was merely a coincidence it is impossible to say[6]. Were they driven out by their rivals, the Jesus movement?

Until recently academics thought that the Mandaean's denial that they came from a breakaway Jewish sect was untrue, but now it is recognized that they have no Judaic roots. For although their writings do include the names of some Old Testament characters, they are genuinely ignorant of Jewish customs and ritual observances – for example, their males are not circumcised and their Sabbath is not on a Saturday. All of this indicates that they once lived close to the Jews, but were never actually part of them.[7]

One thing that has always puzzled scholars about the Mandaeans is their insistence that they originally came from *Egypt*. Indeed, in Lady Drower's words, they consider themselves to be, in some ways, 'co-religionists' with the ancient Egyptians, as one of their texts says that 'the people of Egypt were of our religion.'[8] The mysterious mountain region, the Tura d'Madai, which they cite as their original home, was where the religion emerged – among people, they say, who had come from Egypt. The name of their demigod who rules the world – Ptahil – bears a striking similarity to that of the Egyptian god Ptah and, as we have already seen, their funerary ceremonies appear to owe much to those of the ancient Egyptians.

After their flight from Palestine, the Mandaeans lived in the lands of the Parthians and in Persia under the Sassanid rulers, but they also settled in the city of Harran – which, as we shall see, has some significance to this investigation.

The Mandaeans have never claimed that John the Baptist was their founder or that he invented baptism. Neither do they regard him as anything more than a great – in fact, the greatest – leader of their sect, a Nasurai (adept). They claim that Jesus, too, was a Nasurai, but became 'a rebel, a heretic, who led men astray, [and] betrayed secret doctrines . . .'[9]

Their *Book of John*[10] tells the story of John and Jesus. John's birth is foretold in a dream and a star appears and hovers over Enishbai (Elisabeth). His father is Zakhria (Zachariah), and both parents, as in the Gospel story, are elderly and childless. After his birth, the Jews plot against the child, who is taken by Anosh (Enoch) for protection and hidden in a holy mountain, from which he returns at the age of twenty-two. He then becomes the leader of the Mandaeans – and, interestingly, is represented as a gifted healer.

John is called *The Fisher of Souls* and *The Good Shepherd*. The former term has been used of both Isis and Mary Magdalene[11], besides – as 'Fisher of Men' – Simon Peter, and the latter of many old Mediterranean gods, including Tammuz and Osiris – and, of course, Jesus. The *Book of John* includes the Baptist's lamentation for one lost sheep who becomes stuck in the mud, because he bows down to Jesus.

In the Mandaean legend, John takes a wife, Anhar, but she does not play a prominent role in the story. One strange element in the legend is that the Mandaeans appear to have no knowledge of John's death, which is, of course, very dramatic in the New Testament. There is a suggestion in the *Book of John* that John dies peacefully and that his soul is led away by the god Manda-t-Haiy in the form of a child, but this appears to be a poetic prefiguring of what they think *should* happen to the Baptist. Many of their writings about John were never intended to be taken as biographical fact, but it is still puzzling that they ignored what was essentially a martyr's death. On the other hand, it may be that the episode is central to their most secret, inner mysteries.

What of Jesus in the Mandaean *Book of John*? He appears under both the names Yeshu Messiah and Messiah Paulis (this is thought to derive from a Persian word meaning 'deceiver'), and sometimes as 'Christ the Roman'. He first appears in the story applying to become a disciple of John – the text is unclear, but the implication is that Jesus was not a member of the sect, but an outsider. When he first goes to the Jordan and requests baptism, John is sceptical about his motives and worthiness and refuses, but Jesus eventually persuades him. As Jesus is baptized, Ruha – the dark goddess – appears in the form of a dove and throws a cross of light over the Jordan.

After becoming John's disciple, however – in an astonishing parallel with the stories told by Christians about Simon Magus – Jesus (in the words of Kurt Rudolph) 'proceeds to pervert the word of John and change the baptism of the Jordan, and become wise through John's wisdom.'[12]

The *Hawan Gawaita* denounces Jesus in these words:

> He perverted the words of the light and changed them to darkness and converted those who were mine and perverted all the cults.[13]

The *Ginza* says: 'Do not believe him [Jesus] because he practises sorcery and treachery.'[14]

The Mandaeans, in their confused chronology, look forward to the coming of a figure called Anosh-Uthra (Enoch) who will 'accuse Christ the Roman, the liar, son of a woman, who is not from the light' and who will 'unmask Christ the Roman as a liar, he will be bound by the hands of the Jews, his devotees will bind him, and his body will be slain.'[15]

The sect has a legend about a woman called Miriai (Miriam, or Mary), who elopes with her lover and whose family desperately seek to get her back (but not before giving her a piece of their mind, expressed in colourful language, calling her 'a bitch in heat' and a 'debauched trough'). The daughter of 'the rulers of Jerusalem', she goes to live with her Mandaean husband at the mouth of the Euphrates, where she becomes a kind of prophetess, seated on a throne and reading from 'the Book of Truth'. If, as seems most likely, the story is an allegory of the sect's own travels and persecutions, it would indicate that a Jewish faction had once upon a time joined forces with a non-

Jewish group, the merging of the two resulting in the Mandaeans. However, the name Miriai and her depiction as a misunderstood and persecuted 'whore' are also suggestive of the Magdalene tradition, as are the details about her leaving her homeland and becoming a preacher or prophetess. In any case, it is interesting that the Mandaeans should want to symbolize themselves as a woman.[16]

The Mandaeans may appear to be simply an anthropological curiosity, a lost and confused people who are frozen in time and who have picked up some bizarre beliefs over the years. However, careful study of their sacred texts has revealed some exciting parallels with other ancient literature that have a bearing on our investigation.

Their sacred scrolls are illustrated with depictions of gods that bear a striking similarity to those in Greek and Egyptian magical papyri – of the kind used by Morton Smith in his research[17]. Comparisons have been made between the doctrines of the Mandaeans and those of the Manicheans, the followers of the Gnostic teacher Mani (c.216–76); indeed, the consensus is that the baptismal sect of the Mughtasilah to which Mani's father belonged and among whom Mani himself was brought up, were the Mandaeans (either during their long exodus towards southern Iraq or in a now-extinct community)[18]. Mani's doctrines were undoubtedly influenced by the Mandaeans – and it was his doctrines, in turn, that exerted a strong influence on European Gnostic sects down to, and including, the Cathars.

Scholars such as G.R.S. Mead have pointed out striking similarities between the sacred texts of the Mandaeans and the *Pistis Sophia*. In fact, a section of the *Book of John* called the *Treasury of Love* is regarded by him as 'the echoes of an earlier phase' of that work.[19] There are also strong parallels with several Nag Hammadi documents which have been linked to 'baptismal movements' that existed at the time. And close similarities have been noted between Mandaean theology and that of some of the Dead Sea Scrolls.[20]

Another thought-provoking connection is that the Mandaeans are known to have settled in Harran in Mesopotamia. Until the tenth century, this was the centre of a sect or school known as the Sabians, who are very important in the history of esotericism[21]. They were hermetic philosophers and heirs to Egyptian hermeticism, and were extremely influential on Moslem mystical sects such as the Sufis, whose influence in turn has been traced to the culture of southern France in the Middle Ages – for example, as exemplified in the Knights Templar. As Jack Lindsay says in his *The Origins of Alchemy in Graeco-Roman Egypt*:

> A strange pocket of Hermetic beliefs, including much connected with alchemy, persisted among the Sabians of Harran in Mesopotamia. They survived as a pagan sect inside Islam . . . for at least two centuries.[22]

The Mandaeans, as we have seen, are still termed 'Sabians' (or Subbas) by modern Moslems, so it is clearly *their* philosophy that was so influential at Harran. And besides their hermeticism, what other legacy did they bestow on the Templars? Did they pass on their reverence for, and perhaps even secret knowledge of, John the Baptist?

The most exciting links, however, are with the enigmatic fourth Gospel. Kurt Rudolph, who is probably the foremost expert on the Mandaeans today, writes:

> The oldest elements of Mandaic literature have preserved for us a witness from the Oriental milieu of early Christianity which can be utilized in the interpretation of certain New Testament texts (in particular the Johannine corpus).[23]

We have already seen that many of the most respected and influential twentieth-century New Testament scholars regard parts of John's Gospel – notably the 'In the beginning was the Word . . .' prologue and some of the theological discussions – as having been 'lifted' from texts written by followers of John the Baptist. Many of the same academics agree that these texts shared a common origin: the Mandaeans' sacred books. As early as 1926, H.H. Schaeder suggested that the prologue of John's Gospel – with its feminine Word – was 'a Mandaic hymn taken over from Baptist circles'.[24] Another scholar, E. Schweizer, pointed to the parallels between the discourse on the Good Shepherd in the New Testament Gospel of John and the Good Shepherd section in the Mandaean's *Book of John*, and concluded that they came from the same original source[25]. Of course this original source did not apply the Good Shepherd analogy to Jesus, but to John the Baptist: the New Testament Gospel of John effectively *stole* it from the Mandaeans/Johannites.

Commentators such as Rudolf Bultmann have concluded that the modern Mandaeans are truly the descendants of the followers of the Baptist – they are the elusive Church of John which was discussed earlier. Although there are compelling reasons for thinking that the modern Mandaeans are merely one branch of the surviving Johannite Church, it is still instructive to note W. Schmithals' summary of Bultmann's conclusions:

> On the one hand John [the Gospel] manifests close contacts with the Gnostic conception of the world. The source of the discourses, which John takes over or to which he adheres, is Gnostic in outlook. It has its closest parallels in the Mandaean writings, the oldest strata of whose traditions go back to the time of primitive Christianity.[26]

Even more comprehensively, it has also been argued that the apocalyptic material in the *Q*, the source document for the Gospels of Matthew, Mark and Luke, comes from the same source as the Mandaean *Ginza*[27] – and it has even been suggested that the Christian baptism developed from Mandaean rites.[28]

The implications of this scriptural plagiarism are striking. Could it really be that much of the material so cherished by

437

generations of Christians as concerning, or even representing, the actual words of Jesus was about another man entirely? And was that other his bitter rival, the prophet who did *not* foretell the coming of Jesus, but who was revered as the Messiah himself – John the Baptist?

Continued investigation reveals more and more evidence that the Mandaeans represent a direct line back to John's original followers. In fact, the earliest reference to the Mandaeans dates from 792 CE, when the Syrian theologian Theodore bar Konai, quoting from the *Ginza*, explicitly states that they are derived from the Dositheans[29]. And, as we have seen, the Dositheans were a heretical sect actually formed by one of John's first disciples, alongside Simon Magus' group.

There is more. We have already seen that Jesus was called 'the Nazorean' or 'Nazarean', which was also a name that was applied to the early Christians – although it was not coined to describe them. It was a term that already existed and was used of a group of related sects from the heretical regions of Samaria and Galilee who regarded themselves as preservers of the true religion of Israel. When used of Jesus, the term 'Nazorean' identifies him as an ordinary member of a cult that, from other evidence, seems to have been in existence for at least 200 years before he was born.

But remember that the Mandaeans also call their adepts 'Nasurai': this is no coincidence. Hugh Schonfield, in discussing the pre-Christian Nasoreans, states:

> There is good reason to believe that the heirs of these Nazareans . . . are the present Nazoreans (also known as Mandaeans) of the Lower Euphrates.[30]

The great British biblical scholar C.H. Dodds concluded that the Nazoreans were the sect to which John the Baptist belonged – or, more correctly, which he *led* – and that Jesus began his career as a disciple of John, but went on to start his own cult and took the name with him.[31]

It is possible that the Mandaeans are not confined exclusively to Iraq and Iran these days (if, indeed, they have managed to survive Saddam's depredations), but may also be represented by another highly secretive sect that still exists in modern Syria. They are the Nusairiyeh or Nosairi (sometimes also known as the Alawites after the mountain range in which they live). The name is obviously close to 'Nazorean'. Again outwardly Islamic, they are known to have adopted the trappings of that religion to protect themselves from persecution. Although it is known that they have a 'true' religion that they keep secret, its details – for obvious reasons – are hard to come by. It is believed, however, to be some form of Christianity.

One of the few Europeans who have ever managed to get close to the Nosairis' inner teachings is Walter Birks, who writes an account of them in *The Treasure of Montségur* (co-written with R.A. Gilbert)[32]. He spent some time in the area during the Second World War, and befriended some of the priests. His account is very circumspect, as he has always honoured the pledge of secrecy he gave them, but from what he does say it would seem very likely that they are a Gnostic sect that is very like that of the Mandaeans. What is particularly interesting is an interchange between Birks and one of the Nosairi priests after they had discussed the subject of the Cathars and the possible nature of the Holy Grail (he had noticed that some of their rituals centred on the use of a sacred chalice). The priest told him 'the greatest secret' of their religion, which was that: 'This grail that you speak of is a symbol and it stands for the doctrine that Christ taught to John the Beloved alone. We have it still.'[33]

We remember the 'Johannite' tradition of some forms of European occult Freemasonry, and of the Priory of Sion – that the Knights Templar had adopted the religion of the 'Johannites of the East', which was composed of the secret teachings of Jesus as given to John the Beloved disciple. Once it is clear that John's Gospel was originally *Baptist* material, then the apparent confusion we had noted earlier between John the Beloved and John the Baptist is clarified.

* * *

439

The Mandaeans' traditions about John the Baptist and Jesus fit astonishingly well with the conclusions we outlined in the last chapter: Jesus was originally a disciple of the Baptist but set up in his own right, in the process taking with him some of John's disciples. The two schools were rivals, as were their respective leaders.

Taken together, all this adds up to a remarkably consistent picture. We know that John the Baptist was a highly respected figure with a large following – a veritable Church, in fact – which however, disappears from the 'official' records after a brief mention in Acts. But this movement had a literature of its own, which was suppressed, although some elements of it were 'borrowed' by the Christian Gospels, specifically the 'John Nativity' in Luke (or his source) and Mary's 'song' of the *Magnificat*. More startling is the evidence, given above, that the myth of Herod's massacre of the innocents was, however fictitious, previously linked with the birth of *John*, who Herod feared was the true 'King of Israel'.

Two other movements that posed a great threat to the emerging Christian Church were founded by other disciples of John – Simon Magus and Dositheus; both of these were *Gnostic* sects that were influential in Alexandria. Significantly, the 'Baptist' material that was incorporated into the New Testament Gospel of John is also Gnostic, and the Mandaeans are Gnostics. The obvious conclusion is that John the Baptist himself was a Gnostic.

There are also telling parallels between the writings of the Mandaeans, Simon Magus, John's Gospel and the Coptic Gnostic texts, chiefly the *Pistis Sophia*, which plays an important part in our investigation of Mary Magdalene.[34]

None of the sects – Mandaeans, Simonians and Dositheans – which were associated with John the Baptist is part of the Jewish religion, although they all began in Palestine, two of them in the heretical northern land of Samaria. And if those groups were not of the Jewish religion, the clear inference is that John was not Jewish either. For although the development of Gnostic ideas can be traced to other places and cultures –

notably Iran – there is a clear line of influence from the religion of ancient Egypt. It is there that we have found the closest parallels with the ideas and actions of Jesus, and, significantly, the Mandaeans themselves trace their ancestry back to Egypt.

Despite the confused state of their texts, much of what the Mandaeans say about themselves is borne out by modern scholarship – which was, if anything, initially sceptical about their claims.

The Mandaeans claim that the precursors of their sect came from ancient Egypt, although the sect itself originated in Palestine. They were not Jews, but lived alongside Jews. Their sect, known then as the Nazoreans, was led by John the Baptist, but it had existed long before him. Interestingly, they honour him, but do not consider him to be anything greater than a leader and prophet. They suffered persecution, first from Jews, then from Christians, and were driven out of Palestine, further and further eastwards to their current, precarious homeland.

The Mandaean view of Jesus – that he was a liar, a deceiver and evil sorcerer – agrees with that of the Jewish *Talmud*, in which he is condemned for 'leading astray' the Jews, and in which his death sentence is ascribed to him having been condemned as an occultist.

All the sects connected with John the Baptist, while individually relatively small, if taken together were a huge movement. The Mandaeans, the Simonians, the Dositheans – and, arguably, even the Knights Templar – were ruthlessly persecuted and suppressed by the Catholic Church because of their knowledge about, and reverence for, the Baptist, leaving only the small group of Mandaeans in Iraq. Elsewhere, particularly in Europe, the Johannites may have gone underground, but they do continue to exist.

In European occult circles, the Knights Templar were said to have derived their knowledge from 'the Johannites of the East'. Other esoteric and secret movements, such as the Freemasons – specifically those orders that claim a direct descent from the

Templars, and also the Egyptian Rites – and the Priory of Sion, have always particularly venerated John the Baptist.

To summarize the main points of this Johannite tradition:

1. It lays a special emphasis on John's Gospel, because they claim it retains secret teachings given to John the Evangelist ('the Beloved disciple') by 'Christ'.
2. There is evident confusion between John the Evangelist (the presumed author of the Fourth Gospel) and John the Baptist. This confusion remains a feature of mainstream Freemasonry.
3. The 'secret traditions' referred to are specifically Gnostic.
4. Although claiming to represent an esoteric form of Christianity, one that guards the 'secret teachings' of Jesus, the tradition shows a marked lack of respect for Jesus himself. At best, it seems to regard him as merely mortal, illegitimate, and perhaps even as having suffered from delusions of grandeur. To Johannites, the term 'Christ' does not signify any divine status, but is taken simply as a term of respect – in fact, every one of their leaders is known as 'Christ'. For this reason when a member of such a group calls himself a 'Christian', this may not mean quite what it seems to.
5. The tradition also regards Jesus as an adept of the Egyptian mystery school of Osiris, and the secrets he passed on as being those of the Osiran inner circle.

In its original form, the New Testament Gospel of John was not a Jesus movement scripture, but a document originally belonging to the followers of John the Baptist. This explains not only the reason for the high regard that Johannites have shown for this Gospel, but also the confusion between John the Evangelist and John the Baptist. However, where the Johannite tradition is concerned, this confusion was *deliberate*.

There is no evidence for a movement of Eastern 'Johannites' who formed an esoteric Church founded by John the Evangelist. There is, however, considerable evidence for the existence of such a Church inspired by John *the Baptist*. This is still represented by the Mandaeans and perhaps by the Nosairi. Undoubtedly the Mandaeans were found elsewhere in the Middle East – the locations are not known – but today they are confined to small communities in Iraq and Iran. It is more than possible that they still existed at the time of the Crusades, and therefore could have come into contact with the Templars, and it is also likely that the Western Church of John went underground in the early centuries of the Christian era.

Even given the atrocious treatment they have received from Christians, it is hard to explain why the Mandaeans at least continue to express a burning hatred towards Jesus himself. True, they regard him as a false Messiah who stole their Master John's secrets and used them to lead astray some of their own number, but after all this time the sheer vehemence of their hostility seems inexplicable. Neither does their history of persecution quite explain why they still fulminate against Jesus *personally* with such heat. What could he possibly have done to deserve such continued vilification for century after century?

CHAPTER SIXTEEN

The Great Heresy

We are aware that much in the last few chapters may have come as a shock to many readers, particularly if they are not familiar with recent biblical scholarship. To claim that the New Testament misrepresented the Baptist as being subservient to Jesus, and that John's official successor was the Gnostic sex magician Simon Magus is so much at odds with the 'traditional' story as to suggest outright fabrication. But as we have seen, many highly regarded New Testament scholars made these discoveries quite independently: we have merely collated and commented on them.

The majority of modern biblical scholars agree that John the Baptist was a prominent political leader, whose religious message somehow threatened to destabilize the status quo of Palestine at that time – and it has long been recognized that Jesus was a similar figure. But how does this political dimension to his mission relate to what we have uncovered about his Egyptian mystery school background?

It must be remembered that religion and politics were one and the same thing in the ancient world, and any charismatic crowd-puller was automatically deemed a political threat by the powers that be. And those very crowds would have looked to the leader for guidance, which was likely, at the very least, to upset the authorities. The blending together of religion and politics was exemplified in the concept of the Divine King, or Caesar as god. In Egypt the Pharaohs were believed to be deities from the moment of their succession: they began as Horus incarnate – the magical offspring of Isis and Osiris – and after the sacred rites of death had been completed, they *became* Osiris. Even in the days of the Roman Empire, the ruling family of Egypt, the Greek Ptolemy dynasty – of which Cleopatra is the best-known member – were scrupulous in maintaining the Pharaoh-as-god tradition. The Queen of the Nile identified closely with Isis, and was often portrayed as the goddess.

One of the most enduring concepts connected with Jesus is that of his *kingship*. 'Christ the King' is frequently used by Christians interchangeably with the term 'Christ the Lord', and although both are used symbolically, there is still a pervasive sense that he was somehow royalty – and the Bible agrees.

The New Testament is unequivocal on this point: Jesus was a direct descendant of King David, although the accuracy of this statement cannot be verified. The crucial point is that Jesus himself either believed he was of the royal line, or wanted his followers to believe it. In any case, there is no doubt that Jesus was claiming to be the legitimate king of all Israel.

On the face of it, this would seem to be at odds with our idea that Jesus was of the Egyptian religion – for why would the Jews even listen to a non-Jewish preacher, let alone accept him as their rightful King? As we have seen in Chapter Thirteen, many of Jesus' followers seemed to think he was Jewish: presumably this was an essential part of his plan. However, the question remains – why would he want to be king of the Jews? If we are right and he wanted to restore what he believed to be the original religion of the people of Israel, to bring back to the fierce patriarchy the lost goddess of Solomon's Temple, what better way than to establish himself in the hearts and minds of the masses as their rightful ruler?

Jesus wanted political power; perhaps this explains what he hoped to achieve by undergoing the initiatory rite of the Crucifixion and the subsequent 'Resurrection' through the intervention of his priestess and partner in the sacred marriage, Mary Magdalene. He may have truly believed that by 'dying' and rising again, he would become – in the age-old manner of the Pharaohs – Osiris the god-king himself. As a deified immortal, Jesus would then have unlimited worldly power. But obviously something went badly wrong.

As a power-raising exercise the Crucifixion was something of a debacle, and presumably the expected rush of magical energy did not materialize. As we have seen, scholars such as Hugh Schonfield suggest that Jesus is very unlikely to have perished either on the cross or as a direct result of its torments. But he appears to have been laid low or in some way incapacitated, for not only does the great push for political power not materialize, but also the Magdalene left the country, eventually arriving in France. One may speculate that without Jesus – her protector – she suddenly found herself threatened by her old opponents, Simon Peter and his allies.

The idea that any Jews would have been receptive to a non-Jewish leader does seem unlikely at first glance. However, this scenario is not impossible – *because it actually happened*.

Josephus in *The Jewish War* records that, about twenty years after the Crucifixion, a figure known to history only as 'the Egyptian' entered Judaea and raised a sizeable army of Jews in order to overthrow the Romans. Referring to him as 'a false prophet', Josephus says:

> Arriving in the country this man, a fraud who posed as a seer, collected about 30,000 dupes, led them round by the wild country to the Mount of Olives, and from there was ready to force an entry into Jerusalem, overwhelm the Roman garrison, and seize supreme power with his fellow-raiders as body-guards.[1]

This army was routed by the Romans under Felix (Pilate's successor as governor) although the Egyptian himself escaped and fades completely from history.

Although there were Jewish colonies in Egypt and so this foreign upstart may therefore have been a Jew, this episode is still instructive because someone who was at least perceived to be an Egyptian was able to rally a substantial number of Jews in their own country. Other evidence, however, suggests that this leader was not a Jew: the same figure is mentioned in the Acts of the Apostles (21:38). Paul has just been rescued

from the mob at the Temple in Jerusalem and placed in 'protective custody' by the Romans, who are clearly unsure of his
identity. The captain of the guard asks him:

> Art not thou that Egyptian, which before these days madest
> an uproar, and leddest out into the wilderness four thousand
> men[2] that were murderers?

Paul replies that 'I am a man which am a *Jew* of Tarsus . . .'

This episode poses some interesting questions: why should
an Egyptian bother to lead a Palestinian revolt against the
Romans? And perhaps even more pertinently, why should the
Romans connect Paul – a Christian preacher – with this rabble-
rousing Egyptian? What on earth could they have in common?
Then there is another significant point: the word translated as
'murderers' in the King James version is actually *sicarii*[3],
which was the name of the most militant Jewish nationalists,
who were notorious for their terrorist tactics. The fact that
they were able to rally behind a foreigner on this occasion
demonstrates that it is possible that they would have done so
in Jesus' case.

Our investigation into Mary Magdalene and John the Baptist
has shed new light on Jesus. We now perceive him as radically
different from the Christ of tradition. There appear to be two
main strands to the mass of information about him that has
emerged: one that connects him to a non-Jewish, specifically
Egyptian, background – and the other in which he is seen as
John's rival. What picture emerges if we combine the two?

The Gospels are very careful to present a Jesus who was literally divine; therefore everyone – John included – was his
spiritual inferior. But once this is seen as mere propaganda, the
story finally falls into place. The first major difference from the
commonly accepted story of Jesus is that, preconceptions aside,
he was not marked out from the beginning as the Son of God,
nor was his birth attended by angelic hosts. In fact, the story of
his miraculous Nativity was in part complete myth, and in part

447

'lifted' from the (equally mythical) tale of John's birth.

The Gospels say that Jesus' career began when John baptized him, and his first disciples were recruited from among the Baptist's followers. And it is also as a disciple of John that Jesus figures in the Mandaean texts.

However, it is very likely that Jesus was a member of the Baptist's *inner* circle – and, while John's proclamation of Jesus as the awaited Messiah never happened, the story may echo some genuine commendation by him. There is even the possibility that he really was the Baptist's heir apparent for a while, but something very serious happened that caused John to have second thoughts and nominate Simon Magus instead.

There does appear to have been a breakaway movement from John's group: presumably it was Jesus himself who led the schism. The Gospels record antagonism between the two sets of disciples, and we know that John's movement continued after his death, independent of the Jesus cult. Certainly there was some kind of major dispute or power struggle between the two leaders and their followers: witness John's doubts, when in prison, about Jesus.

There are two possible scenarios. The schism could have happened before John's arrest, and been a clean break. This is hinted at in John's Gospel (3:22–36), but not in the others (they concentrate on Jesus alone after his baptism). Alternatively, after John was arrested Jesus could have tried to assume the leadership – either on his own initiative, or as John's legitimate second-in-command. But, for some reason, he was not accepted by all John's followers.

As we have seen, Jesus appeared to have complex motives, but it seems undeniable that he consciously enacted two main religio-political dramas, one esoteric and one exoteric – respectively the story of Osiris and the prophesied role of the Jewish Messiah. His ministry suggests a definite strategy, which was carried out in three main stages: first, attracting the masses by performing miracles and healings; then, once they started following him, making speeches promising them a Golden Age (the 'Kingdom of Heaven') and a better life; and finally getting them to recognize him as Messiah. Because of the authorities' hypersensitivity concerning potential subversives, no doubt he had to make his claim to Messiahship implicit rather than state it boldly.

Many people today accept that Jesus had a political agenda, but this is still regarded as secondary to his teaching. We realized that we needed to set our hypothesis about his character and ambitions against the context of what he preached. The belief that he advocated a coherent ethical system based on compassion and love is so widespread that it is taken as read. To virtually everybody, from most religions, Jesus is the epitome of gentleness and goodness. These days even if he is not thought of as the Son of God, he is still seen as a pacifist, a champion of outcasts and a lover of children. To Christians and very largely to non-Christians too, Jesus is perceived to be the one person who almost *invented* compassion, love and altruism. Clearly, however, this is not the case: obviously there have always been good people in every culture and religion, but specifically the Isian religion of that time placed great emphasis on personal responsibility and morality, on upholding family values and respect for all people.

An objective examination of the Gospel stories reveals something quite other than the consistent moral teacher Jesus is believed to have been. Even though the Gospels are effectively pro-Jesus propaganda, the picture that they paint of the man and his teachings is inconsistent and elusive.

Briefly, Jesus' teachings as presented in the New Testament are contradictory. For example, on the one hand he tells his followers to 'turn the other cheek' and forgive their enemies, and to hand over all their possessions to the thief who steals some of them[4] – but on the other, he declares 'I have come not to bring peace but a sword.'[5] He upholds the commandment to 'honour thy father and thy mother'[6] but then he also says:

> If any man come to me, and hate not his father, and mother, and wife, and children, and brethren, and sisters, and his own life also, he cannot be my disciple.[7]

449

His followers may have been urged to hate their own lives, but at the same time they are told to love their neighbours *as themselves*.

Theologians try to explain such discrepancies by claiming that some of the sayings are to be taken literally, but others metaphorically. The problem with this, however, is that theology was invented to cope with such contradictions. Christian theologians start from the assumption that Jesus was God. This is a prime example of circular reasoning: to them, everything that Jesus says must be right because he said it, and he said it because it was right. However, the theory falls to the ground if Jesus was not God incarnate, and the glaring contradictions in the words attributed to him can be seen in the harsh light of day.

Christians today tend to think that the image of Jesus has remained unchanged for 2000 years. In fact, the way he is thought of now is vastly different from the way he was perceived just two centuries ago, when the emphasis was on him as stern judge. It changes from era to era and place to place. Jesus as judge was the concept behind such atrocities as the Cathar Crusade and the Witch Trials, but since Victorian times he has been 'gentle Jesus, meek and mild'. Such contradictory images are possible because his teachings, as given in the Gospels, can be all things to all men.

Curiously, this very nebulous quality may actually hold the key to understanding Jesus' words. Theologians tend to forget that he was addressing real people and living in a real political environment. For example, his pacifist speeches may have been an attempt to dispel the authorities' suspicions about his subversive potential. Because of the turmoil of the time, his rallies would have included informers and he had to watch what he said.[8] (After all, John had been arrested because of suspicions that he might have led a rebellion.) Jesus had to be very careful: on the one hand he had to build up popular support, but on the other he had to come over as representing no threat to the *status quo* – until he was ready.

It is always important to understand the *context* of any point

Jesus makes. For example, the phrase 'Suffer the little children to come unto me'[9], is almost universally taken to be a fine example of his gentleness, approachability and love for the innocent. Leaving aside the fact that astute politicians have always kissed babies, it must be remembered that Jesus enjoyed flouting convention – he kept company with women of dubious morals and even tax collectors. When the disciples tried to keep back mothers and children, Jesus stepped in immediately and told them to come forward. This could have been another example of his delight in breaking conventions, or simply letting the disciples know who was boss.

Similarly, when Jesus says of the children:

> Whosoever shall offend one of these little ones that believe in me, it is better for him that a millstone were hanged around his neck, and he were cast into the sea.[10]

Most people read this as a statement of his/God's love for children. But few people notice the qualification – *'that believe in me'*. Not all children qualify for his love, only those who belong to *his followers*. In fact, he is playing on the insignificance of children, saying in effect 'even a child who follows me is important.' The emphasis is not on little ones – it is on his own importance.

As we have seen with the Lord's Prayer, the most familiar – and well-loved – words of Jesus are also, ironically, the most open to question. 'Our Father who art in Heaven' was not a form of words that was invented by Jesus: it seems that John the Baptist was also using them at the time and, in any case they originated in prayers to Osiris-Amon. So it is with the Sermon on the Mount – as Bamber Gascoigne says in his *The Christians*, 'Nothing in the Sermon on the Mount is exclusively original to Christ.'[11] Once again, we find that Jesus speaks words that are first attributed to John the Baptist. For example, in Matthew's Gospel (3:10) John says, '. . . every tree which bringeth not forth good fruit is hewn down, and cast into the fire.' Then, later in the same Gospel (8:19–20), in the Sermon

451

on the Mount, Jesus repeats this metaphor word for word, adding 'Wherefore by their fruits ye shall know them.'

Although it is unlikely that Jesus ever made one single speech that was what we know today as the Sermon on the Mount, it is probable that it did represent the key points of his teaching – as understood by the Gospel writers. Although at least one of those strands was already acknowledged to be part of John's message, the Sermon is undoubtedly complex: it includes ethical, spiritual – and even political – statements, and therefore repays closer scrutiny.

The evidence for Jesus having a political agenda is exceptionally strong. Once this is understood, many of his more elusive sayings fall into place. The Sermon on the Mount appears to consist of a series of one-line statements, which are particularly comforting because of the authority with which they were uttered, such as 'Blessed are the pure in heart for they shall see God'. However, cynics may see them merely as a string of platitudes, or rather absurd promises ('Blessed are the meek for they shall inherit the earth'). After all, every revolutionary in history has tried to make himself popular with the common people, especially by appealing to the dissatisfied and dispossessed, just as today a politician might make promises to the unemployed. This fits in with his agenda as a whole: his repeated attacks on the rich are an essential part of his appeal to popular support, since the rich are always the focus for discontent.

The fact remains that Jesus' words – 'love your enemies/ blessed are the peacemakers/blessed are the merciful' – do appear to be those of a genuinely compassionate, loving and caring man. Whether or not he was the Son of God, he does appear to have embodied a remarkable spirit. If we seem to express some cynicism about both the man and his motives, we do so only because we believe the evidence suggests that this is justified. For a start, as we have seen, Jesus' words – at least as reported in the Gospels – were often ambiguous and sometimes flatly contradictory, and occasionally they can be shown to have originated with John the Baptist.

Even so, it might be thought that our own suggestions are contradictory: on the one hand questioning Jesus' motives and even his integrity, while on the other aligning him firmly with the loving and compassionate cult of Isis. Yet there is no contradiction in this: throughout history men and women have been attracted to a host of different religions or political systems and have become fervent converts to them, only at a later date to use them in order to further their own causes, perhaps even persuading themselves that they had only the organization's best interests at heart. Just as history has shown that Christianity – which proclaims itself *the* religion of love and compassion – has produced sons and daughters who have led less than exemplary lives, so the Isian religion has fallen foul of the depredations of human nature over the years.

So, Jesus was a wonder-working magician who pulled in the crowds because he *entertained* them. Casting out demons must have been spectacular and ensured that the exorcist was talked about for months after he had left the village. Having got the attention of the crowds, Jesus began to teach them, in order to build himself up as the Messiah.

But, as we have seen, Jesus started as a disciple of John, which prompts the question – did the Baptist have the same ambitions? Unfortunately, given the scant information available, it is impossible to do more than speculate. And although the image we have of John is hardly that of a worldly political go-getter, our conception of that coldly righteous figure comes from the pages of the Jesus movement's propaganda – the New Testament Gospels. On the one hand, Herod Antipas had John arrested (according to the more reliable account of Josephus) because he thought him a potential subversive, but this may have been a pre-emptive move rather than a reaction to anything actually said or done. On the other hand, John's followers, including the Mandaeans, did not seem to recognize any political ambitions on their leader's part, but this may have been because he had been arrested before he could show his hand – or simply because they were unaware of his secret motives.

453

The event that marked the moment when Jesus went into action appears to have been the Feeding of the Five Thousand. The Gospels portray this as being just a sort of miraculous picnic, with their host amazing the people by multiplying a meagre supply of five barley loaves and two small fishes so that it fed them all, but at the time the story had a profound significance that has been lost: first, the miracle is totally unlike any other reported of Jesus – the others that were intended for the public at large all concerned healing in one form or another. Secondly, the Gospels themselves suggest that there is something significant about this event that even they do not grasp. Jesus himself reinforces this by saying mysteriously: 'Ye seek me, not because ye saw signs, but because ye ate of the loaves.'[12] In Mark's Gospel at least, nobody is amazed by the event. As A.N. Wilson says:

> The miracle or sign concentrates on the feeding, and not on the multiplication of bread. Indeed, it is noticeable that in Mark's account, no-one expresses the slightest astonishment at this incident. When Jesus cleanses a leper, or heals a blind man, the event is usually enough to 'astound' or 'amaze' everyone who hears about it. There is no amazement at all in Mark.[13]

The significance of the feeding of the crowd was not its paranormal nature. It is possible that the Gospel writers invented the miracle part of the story because they knew they had to make it stand out for some reason, but did not quite know why.

The key point is that there were, according to the Gospels, five thousand *men* – there may also have been an unspecified number of women and children, but they are irrelevant to this particular story.[14] The account may begin by telling of five thousand *people*, but later specifies that this was a crowd of *men*. There is a special significance in this: it is stressed that Jesus made them all sit down together. As A.N. Wilson says:

> Make the men sit down! Make the Essenes sit down! Make the Pharisees sit down! Make Iscariot sit down . . . and make Simon

the Zealot sit down, with his patriotic band of terrorist guerrillas! Sit down, O men of Israel![15]

In effect, Jesus was getting the hitherto warring factions to sit down peaceably and take a ritual meal together. As A.N. Wilson argues, it appears to have been literally a gathering of the clans – a massive rally of old enemies, at least temporarily united by Jesus, the former disciple of John the Baptist.

The very language that Mark (6:39–40) uses is highly suggestive of a military event:

> And he commanded [the disciples] to make all sit down by companies upon the green grass. And they sat down in ranks, by hundreds, and by fifties.

According to the Gospel of John (6:15) it was as a direct result of 'the loaves' that the people wanted Jesus to be king. It was clearly a great event, but it appears to have more than the obvious significance – because it follows *immediately* after John's beheading. As the story goes in Matthew (14:13):

> When Jesus heard of it [John's death], he departed thence by ship into a desert place apart: and when the people had heard thereof, they followed him on foot out of the cities.

Jesus may have been so overcome with grief at the news of John's death that he needed the peace of the wilderness, which was unfortunately shortly to be shattered by the arrival of a horde of people who wanted to hear him preach. Perhaps they needed to be reassured that John's ideals were not dead and that their continuity was ensured through Jesus.

In any case, John's death was very significant to Jesus. It paved the way for him to become leader of the group and possibly to stand at the helm of all the people. It is likely that he had already taken over John's movement after his arrest, and when the people heard of the Baptist's subsequent execution, they rushed to follow his second-in-command – Jesus.

There are many unanswered questions that arise concerning the whole episode of John's incarceration; once again, it seems as if the Gospels are hiding something from us. They say that the reason for John's arrest was that he had spoken out against Herod's illegal marriage to Herodias, whereas Josephus' account states that John was arrested because he was seen either as an actual or potential threat to Herod's rule. Josephus gives no details in his account of the circumstances of the Baptist's death or the way in which he was executed. Then there is John's apparently abrupt change of heart about Jesus' Messiahship: perhaps he had heard something about Jesus while in jail that cast doubt on it. And, as we have seen, there is something clearly unsatisfactory about the reasons given for John's death: according to the Gospels, Herod was *tricked* into having John killed by Herodias, with Salome as the intermediary.

There are several problems with the Gospels' story of John's death. We are told that Salome, acting on the instructions of her mother Herodias, asks Herod for John the Baptist's head – and he complies, albeit reluctantly. This is an extremely unlikely scenario: given what is now known about the extent of John's popularity, Herod would hardly be fool enough to have him killed for such a perverse whim. John the Baptist may have been a threat while alive, but, one might think, he should have become much more of a danger as a martyr. Herod may, of course, have deemed the risk worth taking and exerted his authority, no matter how great the Baptist's following was. If so, he would have had John executed unequivocally on his own orders: certainly he would not have acted on such a grave matter simply to keep his sadistic step-daughter happy. Given the circumstances, it seems strange that there was no large-scale civil unrest, or even an uprising. As we have seen, Josephus records that the people attributed the crushing defeat of Herod's army soon afterwards to divine retribution for John's death, which at the very least reveals that the tragedy had a powerful and lasting impact.

However, there was no uprising. Instead, any tension was

diffused by Jesus, who, as we have seen, immediately presided over the Feeding of the Five Thousand. Did he calm the people down? Did he manage to comfort them about the death of their beloved Baptist? He may well have done, but there is no mention of any such thing in the Gospels. Clearly, however, many of John's disciples perceived Jesus as having taken on their dead leader's mantle.

So the Gospel writers' version of John's death makes little sense. Why should they have felt it necessary to invent such a convoluted story? After all, if their intention was simply to play down the size of John's following, they could have made his death into the first Christian martyrdom. As it turned out, they describe it as the result of a sordid palace intrigue – Herod is content to have imprisoned John, so he has to be tricked into having him killed. But why should they go out of their way to insist that Herod comes out of it as a decent man trapped by scheming women into ordering a dreadful deed? It seems, therefore, that there *had* been a palace intrigue surrounding John's death, which was too well known for the Gospel writers to ignore. But in rewriting the story to suit their own ends, they unwittingly created a nonsense.

Herod Antipas did not benefit in any way from John's death – his speaking out against the marriage was presumably already widely known and the damage done. If anything, the reverse was true: John's death made the situation more difficult for him.

So who *did* benefit from John's death? According to Australian theologian Barbara Thiering, rumours had circulated at the time that Jesus' faction was to blame.[16] Shocking though this may appear at first, no other known group would have benefited more from the removal of John the Baptist. For this reason alone, the supporters of Jesus should not be overlooked, if – as we suspect – John's death was actually a cleverly contrived murder. After all, we do know the identity of the rival leader he chose to cast doubts on from prison, in what was possibly the last public utterance he ever made.

Yet harbouring suspicions is one thing, and finding

457

supporting evidence for them is quite another. After the passage of 2000 years it is, of course, impossible to find fresh and direct clues about the truth of this matter, but it is still possible to uncover a skeleton framework of circumstantial evidence that certainly gives one pause for thought. After all, as we have seen, there must have been specific reasons for the Johannite tradition, for the heretics' – at best – coolness towards Jesus, and, at the most extreme, the Mandaeans' active hostility towards him. The reasons must lie in the circumstances surrounding John's death.

Curiously, although this must be one of the most well-known of all New Testament episodes, we only know the name of Herodias's daughter – Salome – thanks to *Josephus*. The Gospel writers carefully avoid mentioning it at all, even though they record the names of all the other major players in the scene. Could it be that they were deliberately concealing her name?

Jesus had a disciple called Salome. However, although she is listed as one of the women who stood of the foot of the cross and went with the Magdalene to the tomb in *Mark's* Gospel, in Matthew and Luke – who used Mark as their source – she has mysteriously disappeared. Moreover, we saw earlier the curious omission of the apparently innocuous episode in Mark's Gospel, which is revealed in Morton Smith's *The Secret Gospel*:

> Then he came into Jericho. And the sister of the young man whom Jesus loved was there with his mother and Salome, but Jesus would not receive them.

Unlike the deletion of the raising of Lazarus, there is no obvious reason for the editing out of this incident. So it seems that the Gospel writers had their own motives for not letting us know about Salome. (She does, however, feature in the *Gospel of Thomas* – one of the Nag Hammadi texts – where she lies on a couch with Jesus[17], in the otherwise lost *Gospel of the Egyptians*[18], and in the *Pistis Sophia* where she is portrayed as a disciple and catechist of Jesus.) Admittedly, Salome was a common name, but the very fact that it was clearly important enough to be removed so carefully by the Gospel writers actually has the effect of drawing our attention to the Salome who followed Jesus.

Certainly John the Baptist had become something of an embarrassment for the breakaway Jesus movement. Even when incarcerated he still managed to voice his doubts about his former disciple's status – which were clearly so worrying that, as we have seen, his official successor was not Jesus, but Simon Magus. Then this charismatic prophet, with his considerable following is, we are told, killed on a whim by the Herod family who could not have been so naive as to underestimate the potential reaction of the people.

As we have seen, scholars such as Hugh Schonfield have argued convincingly that there was a shadowy group who appear to have facilitated Jesus' mission – and they could have deemed it prudent to remove the Baptist permanently. History is replete with instances of convenient deaths, such as those of Dagobert II and Thomas à Becket, which at a blow removed both dissent and the final obstacle to the ambition of the new regime. Perhaps John's execution falls into that category. Could this group have decided it was time to remove Jesus' great rival from the scene? Of course Jesus himself may have been in total ignorance of the crime committed to his advantage, just as Henry II had never intended his knights to kill Archbishop Thomas à Becket.

The group behind Jesus appear to have been wealthy and influential, so they may well have had contacts within Herod's palace. We know that this is not impossible because even Jesus' immediate following had at least one known contact inside the palace: the Gospels list his disciple Joanna as being the wife of Chuza, Herod's steward[19].

Whatever the truth of the matter, the fact is that there was *something* seriously amiss in the relationship between the Baptist and Jesus, something that heretics have believed for centuries, and that scholars are at last beginning to acknowledge, if only that they were rivals. At the very least, the heretics' antipathy to Jesus may be based on the idea that he had been nothing more than an unscrupulous opportunist, who exploited John's death to his own advantage by taking over the movement with indecent haste – especially if John's legitimate successor was really Simon Magus. Perhaps the mystery surrounding John's death provides the key to the otherwise inexplicable emphasis on venerating the Baptist over Jesus among the groups we have discussed throughout this investigation.

As we have seen, the Mandaeans uphold John as the 'King of Light', while vilifying Jesus as a false prophet who led the people astray – just as he is portrayed in the *Talmud*, where he is also described as a sorcerer. Other groups, such as the Templars, have taken an apparently less extreme view, but nevertheless have venerated John over Jesus. This found supreme expression in Leonardo's *Virgin of the Rocks*, and is reinforced by elements in the other works that we discussed in Chapter One.

When we first noticed Leonardo's obsession with the supremacy of John the Baptist we wondered if it was merely a whim on his part. But after sifting through the mass of evidence for the existence of a wider John cult, we had to conclude not only that there was such a thing, but also that it has always existed parallel to the Church, keeping its secret safe. The Church of John has had many faces over the centuries, such as that of the warrior-monks of old and their political arm, the Priory of Sion. Many secretly worshipped John when they bowed the knee to 'Christ' – as we have seen, the Priory, which gives its Grand Masters the title of 'John', began this tradition with 'Jean *II*'. Pierre Plantard de Saint-Clair explains this with what appears to be a *non sequitur*: 'John *I*' is reserved for *Christ*.

Of course presenting a sound case for the existence of groups who have *believed* Jesus to be a false prophet, or even to have had a hand in the murder of John the Baptist, is by no means the same thing as proving that these things were actually so. What is certain is that the two Churches have existed side by side for two thousand years; the Church of Peter that upholds Jesus as not only the perfect man but also as God incarnate – and the Church of John that sees Jesus as quite the reverse. It may be that neither has the monopoly of the truth, and that what we are seeing reflected in these opposing factions is merely the continuation of the old feud between the disciples of the two teachers.

Yet the very fact of the existence of such a tradition as the Church of John argues forcibly that the time is long overdue for a radical re-evaluation of the characters, roles and legacies of John the Baptist and Jesus 'Christ'. But there is much more than that at stake here.

If the Church of Jesus is built on the absolute truth, then the Church of John is built on a lie. But if the situation is reversed then what we are faced with is the *possibility* of one of history's most terrible injustices. We are not saying that our culture has been worshipping the wrong Christ, for there is no evidence that John sought that role, or that it even existed, in the terms that we understand it today, until Paul invented it for Jesus. But in any case, John was killed for his principles, and we believe that they arose directly out of the tradition from which he took the ritual of baptism. This was the ancient religion of personal *gnosis*, of *enlightenment*, the spiritual transformation of the individual – the mysteries of the worship of Isis and Osiris.

Jesus, John the Baptist and Mary Magdalene preached essentially the same message – but, ironically, it was not the one most people assume it to be. This first-century group took their form of intense Gnostic awareness of the Divine to Palestine, baptizing those who sought this mystical knowledge for themselves – initiating them in the ancient *occult* tradition. Also part of this movement were Simon Magus and his consort Helen, whose magic and miracles were, like those associated with Jesus, an intrinsic part of their religious practices. Ritual was central to this movement, from the first baptism to the enactment of the Egyptian mysteries. But the

461

supreme initiation came through sexual ecstasy.

However, no religion, no matter what it professes, guarantees moral or ethical superiority. Human nature always intrudes, creating its own hybrid system, or, in some cases, the religion becomes a personality cult. This movement may have been essentially Isian, with all the emphasis on love and tolerance that religion sought to instil, but even in its homeland of Egypt there were many recorded cases of corruption among the priests and priestesses. And in the turbulent days of first-century Palestine when men fervently sought a Messiah, the message became confused in a surge of personal ambition. As ever, the higher the stakes, the more likely it is that power is abused.

The conclusions and implications of this investigation will be new to most readers, and no doubt shocking to many. Yet, as we have hoped to show, these findings arose step by step as we looked at the evidence. In a great many cases, there was what will be to many people a surprising amount of support from modern scholarship. And in the end, at the very least, the picture that emerges is very different from the one with which we are familiar.

This new picture of the origins of Christianity and of the man in whose name the religion was founded carries the most astonishingly far-reaching implications. And although these implications may be new to most people, they have been recognized by a particularly tenacious stratum of Western society for centuries. It is strangely disturbing to consider, even for a moment, the possibility that the heretics were right.

CHAPTER SEVENTEEN

Out of Egypt

Two thousand years after Jesus, John and Mary lived out their strangely significant lives in a backwater of the Roman Empire, millions of people still believe in the story as told in the Gospels. To them, Jesus was the Son of God and of a virgin, who happened to be incarnated as a Jew, John the Baptist was his forerunner and spiritual inferior, and Mary Magdalene was some woman of dubious reputation whom Jesus healed and converted.

However, our investigation has revealed the picture to be very different. Jesus was not the Son of God, and neither was he of the Jewish religion – although he may have been ethnically a Jew. The evidence points to his preaching a foreign message to the land in which he mounted his campaign and began his mission. Certainly his contemporaries thought of him as being an adept of Egyptian magic, a view that is also expressed in the Jewish *Talmud*.

This may simply have been malicious rumour, but several scholars, notably Morton Smith, have agreed that Jesus' miracles were part and parcel of the typical Egyptian magician's repertoire. Besides, he was actually delivered to Pilate with the words that he was 'a doer of evil' – in Roman law that specifically meant a sorcerer.

John did not recognize Jesus as the Messiah. He may well have baptized him, because Jesus was one of *his* disciples, perhaps even rising through the ranks to become his second-in-command. Something went wrong, however: John changed his mind and nominated Simon Magus as his successor. Shortly afterwards John was killed.

Mary Magdalene was a priestess who was Jesus' partner in

a sacred marriage, just as Helen was Simon Magus's. The sexual nature of their relationship is attested in many of the Gnostic texts that the Church prevented from being included in the New Testament. She was also 'Apostle of the Apostles' and a renowned preacher – even rallying the despondent disciples after the Crucifixion. Simon Peter hated her, as he hated all women, and she may have fled to France after the Crucifixion because she feared what he might do to her. And although it is impossible to know exactly what her message was, it is certain that it would have borne little relationship to what is now known as Christianity. Whatever else she was, Mary Magdalene was not a *Christian* preacher.

The Egyptian influence in the Gospel story is undeniable: Jesus may well have been consciously fulfilling the prophesied role of Jewish Messiah to gain popular support, but he and Mary seem also to have been enacting the myth of Isis and Osiris, probably for initiatory purposes.

Egyptian magic and esoteric secrets were behind their mission, and their teacher was John the Baptist. Two of his disciples – his successor Simon Magus and the ex-prostitute Helen – were an exact parallel to Jesus and the Magdalene. Perhaps they were supposed to be. The underlying knowledge was sexual – that of *horasis*, enlightenment through transcendental sex with a priestess, which was a familiar concept in the East and also just across the border in Egypt.

Despite the Church's claims, it was not Peter who was Jesus' closest ally, nor – judging by his repeated failures to understand his master's words – was he even in the inner circle. If anyone was Jesus' successor it was the Magdalene. (It must be remembered that they were actively spreading the teachings and practices of the already very ancient Isis/Osiris cult, not some kind of Jewish heresy as is often thought.) Mary Magdalene and Simon Peter set out on different journeys, ending with one of them founding the Church of Rome, and the other entrusting her mysteries to generations of those who understood the value of the Feminine Principle: the 'heretics'.

John, Jesus and Mary were linked together inextricably by

their religion (that of ancient Egypt) which they adapted for the Jewish culture – as were Simon Magus and Helen, who targeted Samaria for their message. Definitely not part of this inner circle of Egyptian missionaries were Simon Peter and the rest of the Twelve.

Mary Magdalene was revered by the underground movement in Europe because she founded her own 'Church' – not a Christian cult in the generally accepted sense of the term, but based on the Isis/Osiris religion. Something very like it had been preached by both Jesus and John.

John was venerated by the same tradition of 'heretics' because they were the direct spiritual descendants of those to whom he was their 'sacrificial king', the martyr of their cause who had been cut down in his prime. The shock and atrocity of his death were underscored by the highly dubious circumstances that surrounded it, and by what was perceived to be the subsequent callous manipulation of John's followers by his old rival.

There is however, another side to this story. As we have seen, there was a rumour circulating during his lifetime that claimed Jesus had worked black magic on the dead Baptist. Certainly, the work of Carl Kraeling and Morton Smith has shown that Herod Antipas believed that Jesus had enslaved his soul (or consciousness) in order to gain magical powers, for it was understood among Greek and Egyptian magicians that the spirit of a murdered man was easy prey for sorcerers – especially if they owned a part of the victim's body. Whether or not Jesus went through any such magical ceremony, a rumour that John's soul lived on under the control of his erstwhile rival would have done the Jesus movement no harm. In that magically-minded era it would have virtually ensured that the majority of John's disciples would have gone over to Jesus, particularly as he seemed to have miraculous powers. And as Jesus had already told his followers that John had been the reincarnated prophet Elias, he would have seemed to be all the more authoritative to the masses.

Yet despite the peculiar notion of a Jesus who was believed to have had control of the souls of at least two other prophets, the secret of the underground tradition is not concerned with him. In fact, even though the heretics revere John and the Magdalene as real historical individuals, they have also always seen them as *representatives* of an ancient belief system. It is what they stood for that was most important to them – as High Priest and High Priestess of the Kingdom of the Light.

The two traditions – one centring on the Baptist and the other on the Magdalene – only really became discernible around the twelfth century, when, for example, the Cathars emerged in the Languedoc and the Templars rose to the pinnacle of their power. There is an apparent gap in the transmission of the traditions: it is as if they disappear into a black hole roughly between the fourth and twelfth centuries. It was around 400 CE that the Nag Hammadi texts – which emphasized the role of Mary Magdalene – were buried in Egypt: as we saw in Part One, strikingly similar ideas about her importance persisted in France, having some influence with the Cathars. And although the Church of John apparently disappeared after approximately 50 CE, its continued existence can be deduced from the Church Fathers' fulminations against John's successors – Simon Magus and Dositheus – for about another two hundred years. Then, again in the twelfth century, this tradition also surfaces once more in the Templars' mystical veneration of John.

It is impossible to say with any certainty just what happened to both traditions in those missing years, but at the end of our investigation we feel we can hazard an educated guess. The Magdalene 'line' continued in the South of France, although any records confirming this would have been destroyed during the systematic devastation of the Languedocian culture that accompanied the Cathar crusade. But echoes of the tradition have come down to us through the Cathar beliefs about the Magdalene's relationship with Jesus and the Cathar-influenced tract *Schwester Katrei*, some of whose ideas were clearly taken from the Nag Hammadi texts.

It is likely that the John tradition survived independently in the Middle East through the ancestors of the Mandaeans and the Nosairi, yet we know that it appears in Europe centuries later. But how did it come to Europe? Who saw its value and decided to uphold its beliefs in secret? Once again we find the answer in the warrior-monks, whose Middle Eastern military operations hid their driven quest for esoteric knowledge. The Knights Templar brought the John tradition to Europe to join that of the Magdalene, thus making sense of what might appear to have been separate male and female mysteries. And it must be remembered that the original nine Templar knights had emerged from Languedocian culture, the heart and soul of the Magdalene cult – and that occult tradition has it that they learned their secrets 'from the Johannites of the East'.

In our opinion it is highly unlikely that the Templars' uniting of these two traditions was merely coincidental. After all, their primary aim was to seek out and make use of the most arcane knowledge. Hugues de Payens and his eight brother knights went to the Holy Land with a purpose in mind: they sought the power of knowledge and may have also looked for some artefact of great value, which was unlikely to have been simply monetary. The Templars appeared to know of the existence of the Johannite tradition before they found it, but how they learned of it no-one can say.

Clearly what was at stake was much more than some vague religious ideals: the Templars were nothing if not practical men – primarily concerned with the acquisition of material power – and the penalty for upholding their secret beliefs was unimaginably horrific. It cannot be over-emphasized that these beliefs were not merely some spiritual notions they had decided to espouse for the good of their souls. These were *magical* and *alchemical* secrets that, at the very least, may well have given them the edge in what we would now call science. Certainly the superiority of their knowledge in such matters as sacred geometry and architecture found expression in the Gothic cathedrals that are still with us today, those secret books of stone that contain the fruits of their adventures into the esoteric. In their trawl of the world's knowledge the Templars sought to expand their understanding of astronomy, chemistry, cosmology, navigation, medicine and mathematics – the benefits of which are self-evident.

But the Templars were even more ambitious in their quest for hidden – *occult* – knowledge: they sought the answers to the great eternal questions. And in alchemy they may have found at least some of them. That mysterious science, which they espoused, has always been thought to yield the secrets of extending life itself, of longevity, if not actual physical immortality. Far from simply extending their philosophical or religious horizons, the Templars sought the ultimate power: the actual mastery over time itself, over the tyranny of life and death.

And after the Templars came generation after generation of 'heretics' who took up the gauntlet and carried on the tradition with equal fervour. Those fanatically sought-after secrets obviously had an appeal that inspired incalculable numbers of people to risk everything – but what was it? What was there about the Magdalene and Johannite traditions that provoked such zeal and devotion?

There is no one reply to these questions, but there are three possible answers.

The first is that the Magdalene and John the Baptist stories offer between them the secret of what 'Christianity' – their original mission – was supposed to have been, in stark contrast to what it actually had become.

While all around them women were demeaned and sex degraded, and priests held the keys to heaven and hell, the heretics looked to the secrets of the Baptist and the Magdalene for comfort and enlightenment. Through these two 'saints' they could covertly join the unbroken line of Gnostic and pagan worshippers that ran right back to ancient Egypt (and possibly beyond): as Giordano Bruno taught, the Egyptian religion was far superior to Christianity in every way; and, as we have seen, at least one Templar rejected the primary symbol of Christianity, the cross, as being 'too young'.

Instead of the stern patriarchy of Father, Son and (by now male) Holy Spirit, the adherents of this secret tradition found the natural balance of the old trinity of Father, Mother and Child. Instead of feeling guilt-stricken about sex, they knew by their own experience that it was actually a gateway to God. Instead of being told the state of their souls by priests, they found their own salvation by direct *gnosis* or knowledge of the divine. All this was punishable by death throughout much of the last 2000 years, and all this came from the secret traditions of the Baptist and the Magdalene. No wonder they had to be kept underground.

The second reason for the continued appeal of these traditions is that these heretics also kept *knowledge* alive. It is very easy for us today to underestimate the sheer power of learning throughout most of history: The invention of printing caused a furore, and even the ability to read and write – especially for women – was rare and frequently regarded with the gravest suspicion by the Church. Yet this underground tradition actively encouraged a hunger for knowledge even among its womenfolk: both male and female alchemists worked long hours behind closed doors to discover great secrets that crossed the boundaries between magic, sex and science – and frequently seemed to have found them.

The unbroken line of this underground tradition encompassed the builders of the pyramids, perhaps even those who raised up the Sphinx, those who built according to the principles of sacred geometry and whose secrets found expression in the soaring beauty of the great Gothic cathedrals. These were *the makers of civilization*, upholding it through the secret tradition. (Surely it is no coincidence that Osiris was believed to have given mankind the knowledge necessary for culture and civilization.) And, as the recent works of Robert Bauval and Graham Hancock[1] reveal, the ancient Egyptians possessed scientific knowledge that was even beyond that of our own age. An inextricable part of this line of heretical scientists were the Renaissance hermeticists, whose elevation of Sophia, quest for knowledge and belief in the divine nature of Man had originally developed from the same roots as Gnosticism.

Alchemy, hermeticism and Gnosticism all lead back inevitably to the Alexandria of Jesus' day, where an extraordinary mixture of ideas was fermenting. And so we find that the same ideas permeate the *Pistis Sophia*, the *Corpus Hermeticum* of Hermes Trismegistus, what survives of the works of Simon Magus and the Mandaean sacred texts.

As we have seen, Jesus has been explicitly linked with the magic of Egypt, and the Baptist and his successors, Simon Magus and Dositheus, have also been cited as 'graduates' of the occult schools of Alexandria. And all the Western esoteric traditions can be traced back to the same root.

It would be a mistake, however, to think that the knowledge sought by the Templars or the hermeticists was simply what we today would call philosophy – or even science. It is true that those disciplines were part of what they hungered for, but there is also another dimension to their secret tradition, one that it would be wrong to omit. Underlying all the heretics' architectural, scientific and artistic endeavours was a passionate search for *magical power*. Could the clue as to why this was so important to them lie in the rumour of Jesus' 'magical enslavement' of John? Perhaps it is significant that the Templars, whose reverence for the Baptist was known to be second to none, were accused of worshipping a severed head in their most secret rituals.

The question of the validity and effectiveness (or otherwise) of ceremonial magic is outside the scope of this book: what matters is what others have *believed* over the centuries, and what part it has played in their motives, their conspiracies and the plans that they put into action.

Occultism was the real driving force behind many apparently 'rationalist' thinkers – such as Leonardo da Vinci and Sir Isaac Newton – and behind the *inner circle* of organizations such as the Templars, some chapters of Freemasonry, and the Priory of Sion. And this long line of secret magicians – *magi* –

may well have included both the Baptist and Jesus.

One of the least known Grail stories has, as the object of the quest, the severed head of a bearded man on a platter. Was this a reference to John's head, to the strange enchanted power it was supposed to possess and bestow on whoever found it? Once again, it is too easy to indulge in late twentieth-century scepticism. What is important is that, in some way, John's head was *deemed* not only sacred, but also *magical*.

The Celts also had a tradition of bewitched heads, but more pertinently, there was a severed head kept at the Osiran temple of Abydos that was believed to prophesy.[2] In another associated myth, the head of that other dying-and-rising god, Orpheus, was washed upon Lesbos, where it began to predict the future[3]. (And is it merely a coincidence that one of Jean Cocteau's most enigmatic and surreal films was *Orphée*?)

Leonardo depicted 'Jesus' on his fake Shroud of Turin as beheaded. At first we thought that this was no more than a visual device to convey the idea that, in Leonardo's heretical Johannite opinion, one who was beheaded was (morally and spiritually) 'over' one who was crucified. Certainly the demarcation line between 'Shroudman's' head and body is deliberate, but Leonardo might be suggesting something else. Perhaps it was a reference to the idea that Jesus *owned* John's head, and that he had somehow absorbed him, becoming – in the words of Morton Smith – 'Jesus-John'. Remember that, in the nineteenth-century poster of the Salon de la Rose + Croix, Leonardo is depicted as the *Keeper of the Grail*.

We saw how, in Leonardo's work, the raised forefinger symbolizes the Baptist: John is making this gesture in the Maestro's last painting, and in his sculpture of John in Florence. That is not so unusual, for other artists have depicted him in this way, but in Leonardo's works characters other than John himself are shown as using it in what is clearly meant to be a *reminder* of the Baptist. The figure in the *Adoration of the Magi* standing next to the elevated roots of the carob tree (which traditionally symbolizes John) raises his forefinger in the direction of the Virgin and child; Elisabeth, John's mother, is doing this right into the face of the Virgin in the cartoon for *The Virgin and Child with St Anne*, and the disciple who so rudely thrusts his face into Jesus' in the *Last Supper* pierces the air in no uncertain terms with his forefinger. And while they may well be saying, in effect, 'John's followers do not forget', this repeated motif may also be a reference to an actual relic – to the finger of John that was believed to have once been among the Templars' most cherished relics.

(In Nicolas Poussin's painting *La Peste d'Azoth – The Plague of Azoth* – a giant statue of a man has lost a hand and his bearded head. But the forefinger of the severed hand is shown specifically making the 'John' gesture.)

During the course of this investigation we have heard an alleged Templar saying – 'he who owns the head of John the Baptist rules the world' – and at first dismissed it as fanciful or at best metaphorical in some way. But one must not forget that certain objects, at once mythical and real, have always exercised a tremendous hold over human hearts and minds – among them the 'True Cross', the Holy Shroud, the Grail and of course, the Ark of the Covenant. All of these legendary objects encompass a curiously compelling mystique, as if they themselves are gateways where the human and divine worlds meet, real solid objects that exist in two realities at once. But if artefacts such as the Grail are believed to possess magical power, how much more sought-after are the actual physical remains of people who are believed to have embodied supernatural energy and possessed hidden knowledge.

Certainly we have seen how the Magdalene's relics have been of supreme importance to those of the secret tradition, and it may be that they, too, are deemed to possess some actual magical power. In any case, Mary's bones would seem to be objects of great veneration and, like John's grisly relic, would no doubt act as a totem behind which the heretics would rally. With or without the concept of magical power, to stand before the head of John and the bones of the Magdalene would have an enormous impact on those of the secret tradition: it would be a highly charged emotional moment even to consider that here, together, were the remains of the two human beings who had been treated with such ruthless, and calculated, injustice over the centuries, and in whose names countless 'heretics' had suffered.

The third reason for the enduring appeal of the secret tradition is its own self-generating moral certainty: these 'heretics' believe they are right and the established Church wrong. But they were not merely keeping alive another religion in a 'foreign' culture. They were keeping alive what they believed to be the sacred flame of the true origins and purpose of 'Christianity'. However, this all-pervasive sense of righteousness when faced with what was to them the 'heresy' of the Christian Church explains only why it had such a hold in the past. In this day and age, with its much more tolerant approach to religion, why on earth should this tradition need to remain secret?

We began this investigation by examining the modern Priory of Sion and its continued activities. Whatever that organization is really about, Pierre Plantard de Saint-Clair has indicated that it has a definite programme, a schedule within which it intends to bring about certain concrete changes in the world at large, although their precise nature can only be a matter for speculation[4].

Whatever the Priory's master plan may be, it does appear to concern the heresy that we have uncovered. Indeed, hidden in the *Dossiers secrets* are certain quite unambiguous statements to the effect that the Priory has been responsible, throughout history, for masterminding the secret tradition. These statements, which allude directly or indirectly to the Priory, include: '[They are] the supporters of all heresies . . .'[5]; 'behind all heresies, passing through the Cathars and the Templars to Freemasonry . . .'[6]; 'secret agitators against the Church . . .'[7] And another Priory document, *Le cercle d'Ulysse* (*The Circle of Ulysses*), published in 1977 under the name of Jean Delaude, includes the ominous words:

What are the Priory of Sion planning? I do not know, but it represents a power capable of taking on the Vatican in the days to come.[8]

And, as we saw earlier, the Priory-inspired work *Rennes-le-Château: capitale secrète de l'histoire de France*, in discussing the Priory's connections with the 'Church of John', refers to events that will 'turn Christianity upside down'.

At the beginning of this investigation we considered the possibility that the Priory suffered from collective delusions of grandeur, and – like most people – found it hard to envisage what kind of secret it could have so jealously guarded that could possibly have the power to threaten such a vast and well established organization as the Church of Rome. Now, after all our researches and experiences, we have come round to the view that the Priory's agenda – whatever that might be – should at least be taken seriously.

In fact, the concept of an organized body that is sworn to topple the Church is not new. For example, in the eighteenth century, when secret societies claiming Templar ancestry began to emerge, paranoia swept through both the Church and several European states. France in particular sweated under the vengeful shadow of Jacques de Molay – were the Templars coming back, literally with a vengeance? There were even rumours that the knights were behind the French Revolution.

However, there are problems with the Templar revenge scenario. No intelligent organization would fuel the white heat of hatred against all the odds and over the centuries simply to kill off a future French monarch and an individual pope, neither of whom had anything to do with their suppression all those hundreds of years before. This idea relies on the Templar suppression being the *reason* for their hatred of the Church – but what if they had already hated it on principle? (And according to the *Levitikon* the Templars were against the Church of Rome from their very inception, not because of the way they were suppressed.)

Our research has shown not only that the Templars believed

474

themselves to possess secret knowledge about Christianity, but also that they are its real and proper guardians. And it must be remembered that the Templars and the Priory of Sion have always been inextricably entwined; any plan or programme of one is very likely also to belong to the other. And in the Priory of Sion we find an organization in which the two heretical strands – of the Magdalene and the Baptist – come together.

It may be that the Priory/Templars are planning to present to a startled Christendom some form of proof for their age-old beliefs, some tangible support for their goddess-worshipping, Johannite tradition. Even given their apparent obsession with searching for relics, it is difficult to imagine what this concrete evidence could possibly be, or – at first glance – how any object could pose a threat to the Church.

But, as we have seen in the case of the alleged Holy Shroud, religious relics do possess a unique and potent hold over hearts and minds. In fact, *anything* supposedly connected with the central characters of the Christian drama is invested with a singularly magical resonance – even the 'anti-relics' of those ossuaries found in Jerusalem recently immediately became the focus for an intense debate and widespread Christian soul-searching. It is instructive to imagine how public interest would have escalated if the ossuaries had been more persuasively linked to Jesus and his family. It would surely have fuelled mass hysteria among Christians, who would have felt betrayed, bereft and spiritually destabilized.

People love a quest – a search for something that is tantalizingly elusive, but perhaps still almost within reach. Seeking an ever-receding Holy Grail or Ark of the Covenant seems almost to be programmed into us, as the enthusiasm that greeted Graham Hancock's *The Sign and the Seal* reveals. Yet deep down there is also a recognition that these objects, although they may – excitingly – actually exist somewhere, are merely symbols, foci or embodiments of some arcane secrets. While the Priory of Sion and their allies may be about to reveal some concrete justification for their beliefs, history itself has, as we have hoped to show, yielded some clues as to the strength of that justification.

Of course such plans are of the utmost interest, but they are no longer necessary in order to understand the putative threat to the Church – and, by implication, to the roots of the whole of our Western culture. So much is based on assumptions about the Christian story, and so much intensely personal emotion is invested in such concepts as a Jesus Christ who was the Son of God and of the Virgin Mary, the humble carpenter who died for our sins and was resurrected. His life of humility, tolerance and suffering has become the image of human perfection and the spiritual model for millions. Jesus Christ, from his place at his Father's right hand in heaven, looks upon the poor and downtrodden and gives them comfort – for did he not say 'Come unto me all ye who are heavy laden and I shall refresh you'?

In fact, although it is very likely Jesus did utter those words, it is simply not true that they originated with him. For, as we have seen, they – and presumably many others like them – came from the words attributed to *Chreste Isis*: Gentle Isis, the supreme mother goddess of the Egyptians. To Jesus, as to any other Isian priest, those words would have been very familiar.

As we have seen, most modern Christians are surprisingly badly informed about developments in biblical scholarship. To many, notions such as Jesus as an Egyptian magician, or the rivalry between Jesus and John the Baptist, must appear as little short of blasphemous – yet these are not the inventions of fiction writers or of the enemies of their religion, but the conclusions of respected scholars, some of whom are Christians themselves. And it was well over a century ago that the pagan elements of Jesus' story were first recognized.

When we first began to study the subject, we were amazed at just how much scholars have *questioned* the standard Christian story, presenting detailed and meticulously argued cases for an almost unrecognizable version of Jesus and his movement. We were particularly astonished to discover that

476

there was already abundant scholastic evidence for Jesus' not being Jewish – and for him actually being of the Egyptian religion. Yet, because our cultural assumption that Jesus was a Jew is so strong, even those who have amassed this evidence fail to take the final logical step and conclude that the weight of this material actually reveals that Jesus was not of the Jewish religion, but of the Egyptian.

There are many who have made a major contribution towards the creation of a radically new picture of Jesus and his movement. Desmond Stewart argued superbly in his *The Foreigner* that Jesus had been influenced by the Egyptian mystery schools, but again, Stewart only sees the Egyptian connection as a modification to Jesus' essential Judaism. And Professor Burton L. Mack, although arguing that Jesus was not of the Jewish religion, also rejects the mystery school material in the Gospels on the grounds that it was a later addition – an assumption that is not reinforced by any evidence whatsoever.

Even Professor Karl W. Luckert writes:

> These birth pangs [of Christianity] . . . were nevertheless real labour pains on the part of Christendom's mother, the expiring religion of ancient Egypt. Our old Egyptian mother died in the centuries during which her vigorous offspring emerged and began prospering in the Mediterranean world. Her labour pains were her death pangs.
>
> Throughout her life of almost two millennia, this Christian daughter born of Mother Egypt has remained relatively well informed about her ancient Hebrew paternal tradition . . . [but] to this day has not been told about the identity of her deceased mother religion . . .[9]

Yet having magnificently argued the case for Christianity's Egyptian roots, Luckert still manages to miss the point. He sees the Egyptian influence as indirect, a distant echo of Judaism's own origins in Egypt. But if Jesus taught Egyptian mystery school material, surely it makes more sense that he learnt it first-hand, from just across the border, rather than piecing it together from fragmentary and uncertain Old Testament allusions.

Out of all these authorities, only one has actually taken that daring last logical step. Morton Smith, in his *Jesus the Magician*, states unequivocally that Jesus' own beliefs and practices were those of Egypt – and, significantly, he based this assertion on material from certain Egyptian magical texts.

Morton Smith's work, while ignored completely by many biblical commentators, has been greeted with cautious approval by some.[10] Yet the views of academics are, as we have seen throughout our investigation, by no means the entire picture. Over the centuries, many groups have shared a secret belief in the Egyptian background of Jesus and others in the first-century drama – and these 'heretics' have also provided us with many more insights into the origins of Christianity. It is interesting that these ideas are now being borne out by modern New Testament scholarship.

If Christianity were really an offshoot of the Egyptian religion, and not the unique mission of the Son of God – or even a radical development of a form of Judaism – then the implications for our whole culture are so basic and enormously far-reaching that they can only be touched on here.

For example, by turning its back on its Egyptian roots the Church lost the fundamental understanding of the archetypal equality of the sexes, for Isis was always balanced by her consort Osiris, and vice versa. In principle at least this concept encouraged due respect to be given equally to both men and women, for Osiris represented all men and Isis all womankind. Even in our secular age we are still suffering the consequences of this denial of the Egyptian ideal: for while sexism is not exclusively a Western phenomenon, its direct manifestations in the West owe much to the Church's teachings about the place of women.

Moreover, in denying its Egyptian background, the Church also rejected – frequently with a special virulence – the whole concept of sex as a sacrament. In setting up a celibate Son of

God at the head of a misogynist patriarchy, they perverted the original 'Christian' message. For the gods that Jesus himself venerated were a sexual partnership and this sexuality was a matter for celebration and emulation among their worshippers – yet significantly, the Egyptians were not known as a particularly licentious people, but were remarkable for their spirituality. The consequences of the Church's attitude to sex and sexual love for our culture have, as we have seen, been terrible: repression on such a scale has been responsible, not only for personal torment and unnecessary soul-searching, but also for countless crimes against women and children – many of which the authorities have chosen to ignore.

There have been other bitter harvests of this great mistake, of a Christian Church that has denied its true roots. For centuries the Church has routinely perpetrated atrocities against Jews, based on the belief that Christianity and Judaism were in competition. Traditionally the Church considered the Jews blasphemers for denying Jesus' Messiahship – but if Jesus had not been a Jew, then there was even less reason for the horrors committed against millions of innocent Jews. (The other major accusation used to justify attacks on Jews – that they had killed Jesus – has long been recognized as fallacious, simply because it was the Romans who executed him.)

Then there was another group that has attracted the Church's hostility over the years. In its fervour to establish itself as the one and only religion, Christianity has always waged war on pagans. Temples were destroyed and people tortured and killed, from Iceland to South America, from Ireland to Egypt in the name of Jesus Christ.[11] Yet if we are right, and *Jesus himself was a pagan* then this Christian fervour was not only once again a denial of common humanity, but also of their founder's own principles. This issue is still relevant, for modern pagans continue to be harassed by Christians in today's society.

Our whole culture is unquestioningly understood to be Judaeo-Christian, but what would it mean if we are right and it should be, in fact, *Egypto*-Christian instead? Of course this can only be a hypothetical question, but perhaps it is more appealing to base our dream of religion on the magic and mystery of the pyramids than on the wrathful Yahweh. Certainly, the religion that has as its trinity Father, Mother and Child must always exert a powerful attraction and a profound sense of comfort.

We have traced the continuing line of 'heretical' belief in Europe, the underground stream of goddess mystery, of sexual alchemy and of the secrets that surround John the Baptist. The heretics have, we believe, held the keys to the truth about the historical Church of Rome. We have presented their case in these pages, step by step as we ourselves made the discoveries and saw the overall picture emerging from the welter of information – and, indeed, of misinformation.

We believe that, on the whole, the heretics have a case worth making. Certainly, grave injustice has been done to the historical figures of John the Baptist and Mary Magdalene, and the time to set the record straight is long overdue. Respect for the Female Principle and the whole concept of sexual alchemy needs to be understood if Western mankind has a hope of entering the new millennium free from repression and guilt.

Yet if any one lesson can be gleaned from the journey we undertook in this investigation and the discoveries we made, it is not so much that the heretics have been right and the Church wrong. It is that there is a need, not for more jealously guarded secrets and holy wars, but for *tolerance* and an openness to new ideas, free from prejudice and preconception. With no limits on the imagination, the intellect, or the spirit, perhaps the torch once kept alight by such luminaries as Giordano Bruno, Henry Cornelius Agrippa – and Leonardo da Vinci – may be ours to carry forward. And we may even come to appreciate fully that old hermetic adage: *Know ye not that ye are gods?*

APPENDIX I

Continental Occult Freemasonry

Tracing the spread of Freemasonry from the British Isles to the Continent, and its development in Europe, is a complicated process, which is hampered as much by modern 'mainstream' Masonry's desire to disassociate itself from its esoteric origins as by the unwillingness of historians to take the subject seriously.

The first officially recognized Masonic lodges in France were established in the 1720s, under the control of Grand Lodge of England. However, at this time there were already lodges in France, which owed their origins to the (predominantly Scottish) supporters of Charles I who fled to France around 1650. The history of Freemasonry in France has therefore been one of two distinct streams, those descended from the English lodges (which formed their own Grand Lodge in Paris in 1735) and those descended from the Scottish Lodges, with periods of mutual hostility alternating with attempts at reconciliation. The foundation of the Grand Lodge of France in 1735 represented a break with the English Grand lodge, the source of friction being precisely London's objections to 'their' lodges entertaining good relations with the Scottish lodges.

Scottish Masonry would seem to have been closer to Freemasonry's original character as an occult secret society, whereas in England it had transformed itself into an association for mutual aid and advancement, or at best a philosophical society. Certainly, Scottish Masonry has always had a markedly occult character.

Baron von Hund's creation of the Strict Templar Observance in the late 1740s represented a new development within Scottish Freemasonry. Von Hund claimed his authority derived from members of the exiled Stuart supporters in Paris, a circle centred on Charles Edward Stuart (1720–1788), the 'Young Pretender'. If true – and recent research tends to support his claims – his system would derive from the same circles as the already existing Scottish system.

Although von Hund was initiated in Paris and first began promoting his new system in France, the Strict Templar Observance had its greatest initial success in his native Germany, where it was known at first as the Brethren of St John the Baptist. (The title 'Strict Templar Observance' was not actually adopted until 1764, the system prior to this being called simply 'Rectified Masonry') Von Hund created the first German lodge, the 'Lodge of the Three Pillars' in Kittlitz on 24 June (John the Baptist's Day) 1751. The German lodges had close links with the Rosicrucian societies, particularly the Order of the Gold and Rosy Cross (see Chapter Six).

In France, a rival authority to the Grand Lodge, the Grand Orient, was created in 1773. The principal point of disagreement between the two systems was the involvement of women in Freemasonry – the Grand Orient included all-female lodges. However, the Grand Orient was plunged into turmoil because of what was perceived as an attempt by the Strict Templar Observance to take it over. The resistance was, in part, due to nationalism, as it was regarded as a foreign, German system. In consequence, a new 'Scottish' system, the Ancient and Accepted Scottish Rite (which was subsequently to become very popular in the USA), was created in 1804. (To confuse matters further, there is today a French National Grand Lodge – as distinct from the Grand Lodge of France – which, although representing a minority of lodges, is allied to the English Grand lodge.)

Martinès de Pasqually (1727–1779) founded another form of occult Freemasonry, the Order of the Elect Cohens, in 1761. Very little is known of de Pasqually's background, although he was probably Spanish. Some researchers believe that de Pasqually was connected with the Dominican Order – the former Inquisition – and that he was able to draw upon heretical and magical material in their archives. He was also able to produce, for the Grand Lodge of France, a licence granted to his father by Charles Edward Stuart, which links him to the Scottish Masonry that was behind Baron von Hund.[1]

De Pasqually's secretary was Louis Claude de Saint-Martin, an important and influential occult philosopher, who was known as the 'Unknown Philosopher'. Saint-Martin formed a new system of Scottish Masonry, the Reformed Scottish Rite, and this was united to the French branch of the Strict Templar Observance at the 1778 Convent of Lyons, a gathering of Scottish Rite masons that also included representatives of Swiss Freemasonry. The main driving force behind the Lyons meeting was Jean-Baptiste Willermoz (1730–1824), who was also a member of the Elect Cohens. At the meeting, von Hund's Strict Templar Observance and Saint-Martin's Reformed Scottish Rite were united under the name of the Rectified Scottish Rite. (Saint-Martin's philosophy – Martinism – was a major influence on the French occult revival of the late nineteenth century, especially on the 'Rosicrucian' groups discussed in Chapter Seven, and the links between the Martinist Orders and the Rectified Scottish Rite remain close to this day.)

The Strict Templar Observance was abolished at the Convent of Wilhelmsbad in 1782, although the Rectified Scottish Rite system (which was essentially the Strict Observance under a new name, with the addition of certain Martinist beliefs) was recognized as legitimate.

The Strict Templar Observance also lived on through its influence on another form of 'occult' Freemasonry, the Egyptian Rites that were created by Count Cagliostro (see Chapter Seven.) After his induction into a Strict Observance lodge (Esperance 369) in London in 1777, Cagliostro developed his own system that incorporated alchemical and other ideas that he had learned from German occult groups. He created the 'mother lodge' of the Egyptian Rite in Lyons in 1782. The distinctive feature of this system – apart from its use of ancient

Egyptian symbolism – was the equal role of women.

The date of the founding of this system is also significant. Sceptics attribute the foundation of Egyptian Rite Freemasonry to the European vogue for all things Egyptian that followed Napoleon's campaign in Egypt (during which the famous Rosetta Stone was discovered). However, this took place in the years 1798–99, *after* the instigation of the Masonic system.

The Rite of Misraïm was created in Venice in 1788, under a licence granted by Cagliostro. This was brought to France in 1810 by three brothers from Provence – Michael, Joseph and Marcus Bedarride.

They established a Grand Chapter in Paris and negotiated to join the Grand Orient. It also established links with the Rectified Scottish Rite – an acknowledgement of the two systems' common origins in the Strict Templar Observance. The four highest grades of the Rite of Misraïm were called the Arcana Arcanorum.

Another important Egyptian Rite was that of Memphis, created in Montauban in 1838 by Jacques-Étienne Marconis de Nègre (1795–1865), a former member of the Rite of Misraïm. This system, too, had close ties with the Rectified Scottish Rite.

In 1899 the Rites of Memphis and Misraïm were united by Gérard Encausse (Papus), who had previously founded and led the Martinist Order (see Chapter Seven).

Thus the Rectified Scottish Rite, the Egyptian Rites and the Martinist Orders form an interconnected group of societies, all owing their origins to the Strict Templar Observance of Baron von Hund – which in turn derives from the Scottish Knights Templar – and the Rosicrucian lodges of Germany.

APPENDIX II

Rennes-Le-Château and the 'Tomb of God'

As we were preparing the final draft of this book, Rennes-le-Château returned to the headlines with the publication of *The Tomb of God* by Richard Andrews and Paul Schellenberger (1996). Its highly controversial thesis is that the secret found by the priest Bérenger Saunière was nothing less than the location of the tomb of Jesus, which they believe is to be found on Pech Cardou, a mountain just five kilometres to the east of Rennes-le-Château. But Christianity, of course, demands a belief in Jesus' *bodily* ascension into heaven, so there should have been nothing to bury. The very idea of Jesus' body existing *anywhere* is profoundly shocking – and threatening – to orthodox Christendom.

The idea that Jesus' tomb is in the Rennes-le-Château area is not new. If anything, it is something of a cliché in France, where there are already at least two books and half a dozen unpublished theories claiming the same thing, although each favours a different location. (One of them actually suggests that the Son of God's last resting place is under what is now the public toilet in Rennes-le-Château's car-park![1]) The idea derives from the sheer *significance* of the rumoured secret and the prevailing belief that it is connected with a tomb (as, for example, in Poussin's *Shepherds of Arcadia*, which has a tomb as its central feature). And what could be more significant than the discovery of the tomb of Jesus?

But how do Andrews and Schellenberger's theories work as a solution to the Rennes-le-Château mystery? Their conclusions are based on their discovery of complex geometric designs hidden within the two 'coded parchments' supposedly found by Saunière and in various paintings that have been connected with this story, such as Poussin's *Shepherds of Arcadia*. They interpret these as a set of 'instructions' that, when applied to the map of the Rennes-le-Château area, lead to the site on Pech Cardou where the 'secret' is to be found.

There are, to say the least, a host of problems with this. First, although the geometric 'code' does seem to exist in many (but not all) of the works, it is by no means obvious that these are intended as a map – there could well be some esoteric significance based on the principles of sacred geometry. Secondly, even if they are right, their reasons for applying these 'instructions' in the way that they do are obscure and often arbitrary. It is, in fact, only the parchments that make the connection between geometry and landscape and, as we have seen in Chapter Eight, these are of extremely dubious provenance.

Even if Andrews and Schellenberger have found the right spot, their final deduction – that the secret is that Jesus is buried there – is remarkably feeble. They interpret the famous 'Blue Apples' message as a set of instructions, the goal of which is to find these *pommes bleues*. They claim that this phrase, upon which much of their argument hangs, is the local argot for 'grapes'. Unfortunately this term is emphatically *not* local slang for grapes. And even if it were, it takes a quite amazing leap of logic to claim that *pommes bleues* actually refers to Jesus! In fact, the authors bewilder the reader with their certainty, writing of '. . . the symbolism of the body inherent in the message *pommes bleues* . . .'[2] and elsewhere making the bald statement, 'from the grapes that symbolise his [Jesus'] body, the *pommes bleues*'.[3]

The authors also claim confirmation of their reasoning in their own interpretation of the *Et in Arcadia ego* . . . motto. They assume it should be completed by the word *sum*, making the phrase into 'And *I* am in Arcadia' – which they turn into an anagram of 'I touch the tomb of God, Jesus' (*Arcam Dei tango, Iesu*). But this depends on the assumption that it is an anagram, and on the addition of a word that has to be guessed at.

Andrews and Schellenberger interpret the 'Blue Apples' message as references to various locations that, when joined up on the map, form a perfect square. However, their interpretations are very forced. For example, the Latin numerals for 681 are taken to be a reference to a specific spot height to the north-east of Rennes-le-Château. This only appears as such, however, on the current edition of the IGN map (the equivalent of the British Ordnance Survey map). All other editions and a sign at the spot itself give the correct height as *680* metres. This leads Andrews and Schellenberger to conclude that some 'initiate' at the Institut Géographique Nationale doctored the current edition to fit the message! (Wouldn't it have been considerably easier just to give the correct height in the first place?)

Then Andrews and Schellenberger ignore the fact that the coded message is a perfect anagram of the inscription on Marie de Nègre's headstone, which dates from 1791. This would be a truly amazing piece of work by the codemakers, to turn an eighteenth-century inscription into a message that indicates precisely those four sites – one of which is a modern spot height and another a railway bridge built in the 1870s!

Besides such tortuous reasoning, they also rely on many well-worn fallacies of the Saunière story. For example, they repeat the rumour that Marie Dénarnaud ordered Saunière's coffin several days before his death – while he was in perfect health. Apart from the fact that his excessive lifestyle had ruined his constitution, it is now well known among Rennes researchers that the story comes from a misreading of the date on the receipt for the payment for his coffin: *12 juin* (June) was taken as *12 jan* (January).

The authors claim to have become interested in this mystery in the first place because of the intrigue surrounding the suspicious deaths of three priests in the area – Saunière himself, and the Abbés Gélis and Boudet. Andrews and Schellenberger believe that the trio were all murdered because of their knowledge of the great secret. This would indeed be the stuff of a truly gripping murder mystery were it not for the fact that only one of those priests was murdered: the Abbé Gélis. As we have seen, Saunière's lifestyle virtually guaranteed him a relatively early grave, and Boudet died of natural causes at an advanced age (in a very unmysterious retirement home).

So, their solution to the enduring Rennes-le-Château mystery is ultimately unsatisfactory. But does the hypothesis about Jesus' body hold up?

Andrews and Schellenberger offer three alternative scenarios: Jesus survived the cross and fled to Gaul where he lived out the rest of his life; his family and/or disciples brought his remains to France; or the Templars discovered the remains in Jerusalem and took them to the Languedoc. While none of these is impossible, the authors offer no direct or compelling evidence for any of them.

The idea of Jesus being buried in the South of France is plausible, although it might be argued that it makes more sense in the context of our own conclusions. It is possible that the Magdalene took Jesus' body with her or was even accompanied by him. (Andrews and Schellenberger, in the mainstream Christian fashion, totally ignore her.) However, we find no evidence, even of a *tradition* to support their idea: what traditions there are place the emphasis firmly on Mary Magdalene. The heretical underground of the South of France was and is, first and foremost, a Magdalene, not a *Jesus*, cult.

But even if a body that could perhaps be that of Jesus is found there, how could it ever be positively identified as such? Andrews and Schellenberger, once again, apply their unique logic to the problem. Although they describe the first-century Jewish burial practice (for them, Jesus was a Jewish Essene) of gathering the bones of the decomposed corpse and placing them in a stone jar or ossuary, they suddenly switch to discussing Jesus' *embalmed* body. (Irrelevantly, they note that the Templars are known to have had knowledge of embalming; it would have been rather late for the laying out of Jesus' body.) They even suggest that the body might be identified by comparing it with the image on the Turin Shroud!

Of course, any amount of speculation about Jesus' tomb must remain in the realms of wishful thinking until, or unless, it is actually found and investigated. Andrews and Schellenberger do not claim to have found, but merely located, it. They plead for a full-scale archaeological dig which will, they are confident, confirm their hypothesis.

However, the local traditions are primarily concerned with two people: Mary Magdalene and John the Baptist, and *not* Jesus. In the light of our research, rumours of *Christ's* remains being in the area may actually refer to someone nearer to the hearts of the locals than Jesus.

Notes and References

CHAPTER ONE: THE SECRET CODE OF LEONARDO DA VINCI

1   See Augusto Marinoni, 'The Bicycle', in Reti (ed.), *The Unknown Leonardo*, 1974.

2   Picknett and Prince, *Turin Shroud: In Whose Image?*

3   Ibid., chapter 8.

4   For example, by Maria Corti, an Italian researcher who agrees that the Shroud image is a self-portrait of Leonardo, but prefers to ascribe his motives to his wish to identify with the sufferings of Jesus. Corti outlined her views in the BBC documentary 'Double Exposure', broadcast as part of the *Everyman* series, 15 October 1995 (directed by Nikki Stockley and produced by Trevor Poots).

5   See Picknett and Prince, p178.

6   Ibid., pp151–152.

7   Ibid., pp132–133.

8   Bramly, *Leonardo: The Artist and the Man*, p163.

9   Ibid., pp184–186.

10 Ibid., p190.

11 At the age of twenty-four, Leonardo was arrested on charges of sodomy, for which the penalty was death. The charge was dropped, as one of the young men arrested with him was related to the ruling family of Florence, but the experience seems to have had a profound effect on his later life, fostering his obsession with privacy and secrecy.

12 Yates, *Giordano Bruno and the Hermetic Tradition*, p435.

13 Picknett and Prince, chapter 5.

14 See chapter 6.

15 Picknett and Prince, pp153–155.

CHAPTER TWO: INTO THE UNDERWORLD

1 Lincoln, *The Holy Place*, pp158–160.

2 Picknett and Prince, chapter 4.

3 On the origins and history of the society – as claimed by the Priory of Sion itself – see Baigent, Leigh and Lincoln, *The Holy Blood and the Holy Grail*, chapters 4–7.

4 For a complete list of the alleged Grand Masters of the Priory of Sion, see the appendix to *The Holy Blood and the Holy Grail*.

5 See, for example, 'The Myth of the Priory of Sion' by British researcher Paul Smith, *The Rennes-le-Château Observer*, no. 1.7 (March 1995).

6 The Priory of Sion registered itself at the Sub-Prefecture of Saint-Julien-en-Genevoise (Haute Savoie) on that date. The announcement of its registration appeared in the *Journal officiel de la République Française* on 20 July, 1956.

7 The statutes bearing Cocteau's signature and dated 5 June, 1956, are reproduced in Baigent, Leigh and Lincoln, *The Holy Blood and the Holy Grail*, pp225–228. Confusingly – and typically – there are a second set of statutes, unsigned and deposited with the official registration, which differs in several respects from the 'Cocteau' statutes. These were printed in an article by Jean-Luc Chaumeil, 'Les archives du prieuré de Sion', in the journal *Le Charivari*, no. 18 (Winter 1973).

8 See de Sède, *Rennes-le-Château: le dossier, les impostures, les phantasmes, les hypothèses*, pp130–133.

9 Robin, *Le royaume du graal*, p37.

10 Brian Innes, 'Names to Conjure With', *The Unexplained*, no. 126, p2516, quoting French researcher Franck Marie.

11   Baigent, Leigh and Lincoln, *The Messianic Legacy*, chapter 23.

12   The 'secret dossiers' consist of: Henri Lobineau, *Généalogie des rois mérovingiens* . . . (dated 1956, deposited 1964); Madaleine Blancasall, *Les descendants mérovingiens ou l'énigme du Razès wisigoth* (1965); Antoine l'Ermite, *Un trésor mérovingien à Rennes-le-Château* (dated 1961, deposited 1966); Eugène Stublein, *Pierres gravées du Languedoc* (supposed re-edition of 1884 work, deposited 1966); S. Roux, *L'affaire de Rennes-le-Château: réponse à Lionel Burrus* (1966); Pierre Feugère, Louis Saint-Maxent and Gaston de Koker, *Le serpent rouge* (1967); Philippe Toscan du Plantier, *Les dossiers secrets d'Henri Lobineau* (1967).

   The full texts of the *dossiers*, as well as other similar documents relating to the Priory of Sion, are reprinted in Jarnac (ed.) *Les mystères de Rennes-le-Château: mélanges sulfureux*.

13   For detailed discussions of the historical errors in the claims of Merovingian descent in the *Dossiers secrets* and other Priory-inspired works, see de Sède, *Rennes-le-Château*, pp134–144 and Robin, *Le royaume du graal*, pp621–623.

14   Robin, *Le royaume du graal*, p621.

15   De Sède, *Rennes-le-Château*, p127.

16   Great significance is attached to the date 17 January by the Priory of Sion. As will be seen, it frequently recurs in this story.

17   De Sède, *Rennes-le-Château*, pp123–127.

18   Appendices to Franck Marie's re-edition of *Le serpent rouge* (S.R.E.S., Malakoff, 1979), cited in Jarnac, *Les archives du trésor de Rennes-le-Château*, volume 1, pp188–190.

19   Baigent, Leigh and Lincoln, *The Messianic Legacy*, chapter 18.

20   Baigent, Leigh and Lincoln, *The Holy Blood and the Holy Grail*, chapters 6 and 7.

21   A secret society of the seventeenth century, whose headquarters were at the Seminary of Saint Sulpice in Paris. (See chapter 8.)

22   Picknett and Prince, chapter 6.

23 See, for example, Baigent, Leigh and Lincoln, *The Holy Blood and the Holy Grail*, chapter 6.

24 Conversations between Alain Féral and Clive Prince at Rennes-le-Château, 2 June 1995 and 5 March 1996.

25 Entry for Leo in *Le serpent rouge*, (authors' translation.)

26 For example, Phipps, *Was Jesus Married?*

27 'Henry Lobineau', *Généalogie des rois mérovingiens . . .*, table 4.

28 Baigent, Leigh and Lincoln, *The Holy Blood and the Holy Grail*, pp487–488.

29 This side of Newton's life is explored in the recent biography, *The Last Sorcerer* by Michael White.

30 Wood, *Genisis*, p218.

31 Baigent, Leigh and Lincoln, *The Messianic Legacy*, p345.

32 Our thanks to Keith Prince for pointing this out to us.

33 Baigent, Leigh and Lincoln, *The Holy Blood and the Holy Grail*, p164.

34 Baigent, Leigh and Lincoln, *The Messianic Legacy*, p295.

35 The allegation was made in anonymous tracts circulated in Paris on 1983. (Ibid., p334.)

36 Deloux and Brétigny, *Rennes-le-Château: capitale secrète de l'histoire de France*, pp44–45.

37 Ibid., p45.

38 Letter from Gino Sandri to the authors, dated 24 June 1995.

CHAPTER THREE: IN THE FOOTSTEPS OF THE MAGDALENE

1 Haskins, *Mary Magdalen*.

2 Luke 8:3. (Except where noted, all quotations from the Bible are the King James' version.)

3   Matthew 16:18.

4   Haskins, chapter III.

5   Ibid., p155.

6   For a study of the importance of women in the early Church, see Torjeson, *When Women Were Priests*.

7   Even the Catholic Church has officially recognized this. In his 1987 encyclical *Mulieries dignitatem* which reiterated the traditional view of women as inherently subordinate to men, Pope John Paul II conceded that Jesus' female followers had shown more loyalty than the men – but then goes on to assert that Jesus called 'only men' as his apostles.

8   Ricci, *Mary Magdalene and Many Others*, p193.

9   The single exception is John 19:25, where Jesus' mother is placed at the head of the list. Even here, Mary the Mother is only listed first because there is a specific reason to do so. See Witherington, *Women and the Genesis of Christianity*, p115.

10 Haskins, p12.

11 On the Nag Hammadi texts, see: Pagels, *The Gnostic Gospels*; Schneemelcher (ed.), *New Testament Apocrypha* and Layton, *The Gnostic Scriptures*.

12 Schneemelcher, pp391–395.

13 For example, in the Gospel of Mary. (See Schneemelcher, p395).

14 Pagels, p85.

15 Haskins, p43.

16 Pagels, p84.

17 Gospel of Philip, vs 32. (See Schneemelcher, p192.)

18 R. McL. Wilson, *The Gospel of Philip*, pp96–98; see also Haskins, p40.

19 I Corinthians 7:9.

20 Haskins, p373.

21 De Voragine, *The Golden Legend*, vol. 1, pp374ff.

22 Father Philippe Devoucoux du Buysson, writing in *Dieu est amour*, no. 115 (May 1989).

23 Walker, *The Woman's Encyclopedia of Myths and Secrets*, p455.

24 Ricci, p151.

25 Buenner, *Notre-Dame de la Mer et les Saintes-Maries*.

26 Dylan's song, 'One More Cup of Coffee' (1975), is a haunting evocation of the dark power of female sexuality, personified by a gypsy princess.

27 Baigent, Leigh and Lincoln, *The Holy Blood and the Holy Grail*, pp164–167.

28 Moncault, *La basilique Sainte-Marie-Madeleine et le Couvent royal*.

29 Haskins, p131.

30 From *7eme Centenaire*, a commemorative history produced by the Association du 7e de Saint-Maximin et de la Sainte-Baume (1995), pp9–10.

31 Victor Saxer, quoted in Haskins, p131.

32 *7eme Centenaire*, pp14–16.

33 *La revue du rosaire* (journal of the Dominican Order at St Maximin), May 1995, p13.

34 Baigent, Leigh and Lincoln, *The Holy Blood and the Holy Grail*, p141. (Our translation.)

35 For a detailed study of the Black Madonna cult, including its links with Mary Magdalene and the Priory of Sion, see Begg, *The Cult of the Black Virgin*. This includes a detailed gazeteer of Black Madonna sites.

36 From analysis of the sites listed in the gazeteer section of Begg's book.

37 Ibid., pp8–9

38 Ibid., p8.

39 This is explored in the two main French studies of the Black Madonna cult, *Étude sur l'origine des Vierges Noires* by Marie

Durand-Lefèbvre (1937) and *Nos Vierges Noires, leurs origines* by Emile Saillens (1940). (Cited in Begg.)

40 See entry for 'Isis' in Walker, p453.

41 Begg, p99.

42 Richard Leigh and Michael Baigent, 'Virgins with a Pagan Past' (*The Unexplained*, no. 3, p61), 'The Goddess Behind the Mask' (no. 5, p114) and 'Guardians of the Living Earth' (no. 7, p154).

43 Deloux and Brétigny, pp42–44.

44 Ibid., p47.

45 Begg, p14.

46 Ibid., p15.

47 The earliest Christian commentary on the Song of Songs, dating from the late second century, associates the 'bride' of the Song with Mary Magdalene. (Haskins, p63.)

48 The Black Madonna in Tindari, Sicily, makes the connection explicit by bearing an inscription of this phrase.

49 Begg, p13.

50 St-Jean-Cap-Ferrat and Villefranche-sur-Mer did, in fact, feature as locations in the 1984 Bond film *Never Say Never Again*.

51 Tarade and Barani, *Les sites magiques de Provence*, pp134–135.

52 Ibid., p136.

CHAPTER FOUR: HEARTLAND OF HERESY

1 H.T.F. Rhodes, 'Black Mass', *Man, Myth and Magic*, no. 10 (1971), pp274–278.

2 Mann and Lyle, *Sacred Sexuality*, p137.

3 Begg, p39.

4 Robin, p266.

5 Begg, p113.

6 Walker, p650.

7   Reproduced on pp110–112 of Wolff (ed.) *Documents de l'histoire du Languedoc*, which includes three other contemporary accounts of the massacre. The following extracts are the authors' translation.

8   The Bishop of Béziers, Renaud de Montpeyroux, who sided with the Crusaders, drew up a list – still extant – of known Cathars that he demanded be handed over. (Ibid., p110.)

9   See bibliography for sources on the Cathars.

10 Quoted in Birks and Gilbert, *The Treasure of Montségur*, p59.

11 To illustrate this point, at one stage during the Crusade the Count of Toulouse made an alliance with the Catholic King of Spain against the Crusaders.

12 This often overlooked point is discussed in detail in Birks and Gilbert, chapter 8.

13 Stoyanov, *The Hidden Tradition in Europe*.

14 For example, Baigent, Leigh and Lincoln in *The Holy Blood and the Holy Grail*, p52.

15 See Stoyanov, pp222–223.

16 Ibid., p223.

17 Malvern, *Venus in Sackcloth*.

18 Newman, *From Virile Woman to WomanChrist*, pp172–181.

19 For example, *Sister Catherine* uses the phrase that women should 'become male' in order to enter the Kingdom of Heaven, which is identical to the Gospel of Thomas. Even more striking, the tract tells a strange, metaphorical anecdote in which Jesus tells his disciples to eat the corpse of a dead man; this very image is used in two of the Nag Hammadi texts, the Gospel of Philip and the Gospel of Thomas.

20 Newman, p178.

21 Cited in Baigent, Leigh and Lincoln, *The Holy Blood and the Holy Grail*, pp469–470.

22 Stoyanov, p129.

23 See Birks and Gilbert, pp80–81, and Stoyanov, pp214–219.

24 Stoyanov, p173.

25 Birks and Gilbert, p36.

26 The true nature of the relationship between Jesus and John the Baptist is explored in Part Two.

27 Calvé, *My Life*, p3.

28 See bibliography for works consulted on the history of the Templars.

29 Gascoigne, *The Christians*, pp78–79.

30 Baigent, Leigh and Lincoln, *The Holy Blood and the Holy Grail*, pp83–90.

31 Ibid., p83, citing M. Michelet, *Procès des Templiers* (Paris, 1851).

32 Philippe Toscan du Plantier, *Dossiers secrets d'Henri Lobineau*, plate 4. See also *The Holy Blood and the Holy Grail*, pp120–123.

33 The evidence for this is discussed in chapter 6 of our *Turin Shroud: In Whose Image?*

34 Barber, *The Trial of the Templars*, p12.

35 Sinclair, *The Sword and the Grail*, p9.

36 Hancock, *The Sign and the Seal*, chapter 5.

37 See Baigent, Leigh and Lincoln, *The Holy Blood and the Holy Grail*, p80.

38 Knight and Lomas, *The Hiram Key*, p269 and plate 21.

  Knight and Lomas surmise that Lambert's illustration was copied by him from one of the 'Essene Scrolls' that the Templars found beneath Herod's Temple in Jerusalem. However, this is unlikely: Lambert died in 1121, while the nine founding ˡⁿ ights were still excavating; the illustration is clearly of medieval European style; and none of the Dead Sea Scrolls contain illustrations of any kind. It is, in any case, very debatable whether the Dead Sea Scrolls, and hence the cache of documents hypothesized by Knight and Lomas, were Essene texts – see chapter 11.

39 From Lull's *Liber de acquisitione terrae sanctae* (March 1309), quoted in Hillgarth, *Lull and Lullism in Fourteenth Century France*, p104. The original Latin text is as follows:

Pars ista ostendit pericula navicule Sancti Petri et primo sic: Inter christianos sunt forte multa secreta de quibus secretis poterit orribilis revelatio sicut de Templariis evenire . . . hoc etiam dico de quibusdam palam turpissimus et sensibus manifestis, propter que periclitatur navicula Sancti Petri.

Our thanks to Keith Prince for the translation.

CHAPTER FIVE: GUARDIANS OF THE GRAIL

1 Quotes from Nicole Dawe and Charles Bywaters in this chapter are taken from an interview in Rennes-les-Bains, 4 August 1995.

2 See chapter 6.

3 Robin, *Le royaume du graal*, p229.

4 Hancock, p333.

5 Begg, p104.

6 For example, Sermon 57, reproduced in Matarasso, *The Cistercian World*. On St Bernard and the Song of Songs, see Pope, *Song of Songs*, pp122–124.

7 Norvill, *Hermes Unveiled*, pp125–126.

8 Haskins, p122.

9 Begg, p103.

10 Ibid., p24.

11 See, for example, the reception ceremony described in appendix B of Barber, *The Trial of the Templars*.

12 Ibid., pp167 and 213.

13 Information supplied by Nicole Dawe and Charles Bywaters.

14 Baigent and Leigh, *The Temple and the Lodge*, p95.

15 Ibid., p84.

16 Schonfield, *The Essene Odyssey*, pp162–164.

17 Hancock, p334.

18 See chapter 13.

19 See Lee Irwin, 'The Divine Sophia: Isis, Achamoth and Ialdabaoth', in Fideler (ed.), *Alexandria 3*.

20 Interview with Niven Sinclair, 4 May 1996.

21 Spelman Timmins, 'Celestial Harmonies', *The Unexplained*, no.153, p3041.

22 Andrew Sinclair, p110.

23 Hancock, p306.

24 For a discussion of sacred geometry, especially as applied to the architecture of Templar buildings, see Hancock, *The Byrom Collection*, chapter 5. In discussing the implications of the possession of this knowledge by the Templars, Hancock (p157) poses the question: 'did they constitute part of a wider philosophy which the Church could only brand as heresy?'

25 Nataf, *The Occult*, pp38–39.

26 Baigent and Leigh, p188.

27 Ibid., p189.

28 The building of Solomon's Temple is described in the First Book of Kings, chapters 5–7.

29 See chapter 6.

30 For details of Flamel's life and his achieving of the Great Work, see Holroyd and Powell, *Mysteries of Magic*, pp171–182. This book also includes an alleged nineteenth-century account of a meeting with the still-living Nicolas and Perenelle Flamel. We note, however, that the 'little-known work' cited is entitled *The Lying Raven* and is by one Ninian Bres, which happens to be an anagram of the real name of one of the authors of *Mysteries of Magic*!

31 See our *Turin Shroud: In Whose Image?*, p95.

32 See the illustration accompanying Kenneth Rayner Johnson's article 'The Image of Perfection', *The Unexplained*, no. 45, p828.

33 See plate 13 in Hancock's *The Sign and the Seal*.

34 St Victor, *Epiphany*, p90.

35 Walker, pp866–867.

36 Ean and Deike Begg, *In Search of the Holy Grail and the Precious Blood*, p79.

37 Godwin, *The Holy Grail*, p16.

38 The tale of Peredur is one of the collection of Welsh folk-tales known as the *Mabinogion*. See the translation by Gwyn Jones and Thomas Jones.

39 Godwin, p47.

40 Ibid., p80.

41 Baigent, Leigh and Lincoln, *The Holy Blood and the Holy Grail*, p302, citing R. Barber.

42 Godwin, p104.

43 Wolfram von Eschenbach, *Parzival*, translated by A.T. Hatto.

44 Baigent, Leigh and Lincoln, *The Holy Blood and the Holy Grail*, pp307–308.

45 Wolfram von Eschenbach, *Parzival*, p410.

46 Baigent, Leigh and Lincoln, *The Holy Blood and the Holy Grail*, chapter 11.

47 Godwin, p176.

48 For example, Wolfram von Eschenbach, *Parzival*, p405.

49 Godwin, p206.

50 C. de Hoghton, 'Parsifal', *Man, Myth and Magic*, no. 76, p2143.

51 For example, Ian Wilson, *The Turin Shroud*, pp205–206.

52 See the Articles of Accusation against the Templars, reproduced in Appendix A of Barber, *The Trial of the Templars*.

53 Ibid., p163.

54 Schonfield, *The Essene Odyssey*, p165.

55 De Voragine, vol.2, p132.

56 Upton, *The Valley of Pyrene*, pp135–138.

57 Ean and Deike Begg, p42.

58 Tarade and Barani, pp134–137.

· 59   Waite, *The Hidden Church of the Holy Graal*, p561.

60   Ibid., p448.

CHAPTER SIX: THE TEMPLAR LEGACY

1   Hancox, pp183–185.

2   Yates, *The Rosicrucian Enlightenment*, chapter XIII.

3   This was the induction of Sir Robert Moray into the Mary's
Chapel Lodge of Edinburgh. The lodge was obviously already
established prior to this date.

4   Robinson, *Born in Blood*, pp55–62.

5   Cited in Spence, *An Encyclopaedia of Occultism*, p174.

6   Robinson, p199.

7   Thomas Norton's *Ordinall of Alchemy* (see note 5).

8   Yates, *The Rosicrucian Enlightenment*, Chapter XIV.

9   In Ashmole's history of the Order the Garter (1640). Frances
Yates has found a strong connection between the seventeenth-
century Rosicrucians and the Order of the Garter. This in
itself is suggestive, since the Order of the Garter has been
seen as a continuation at least of the ceremonial of the Knights
Templar.

10   On Rosslyn Chapel and the St Clair family, see Sinclair, *The
Sword and the Grail* and Wallace-Murphy, *The Templar Legacy
and the Masonic Inheritance within Rosslyn Chapel.*

11   *Kenning's Masonic Cyclopaedia and Handbook of Masonic
Archaeology, History and Biography*, p558. The 'St Clair Charter',
which declares the St Clair/Sinclair family hereditary patrons of
Freemasonry, is alleged to date from 1441, although the earliest
known copy is from around 1600.

12   See Baigent, Leigh and Lincoln, *The Messianic Legacy*,
pp361–367. Niven Sinclair, who has researched his family's
genealogy extensively, told us that Plantard has 'a reasonably
good link' with the French branch of the St Clairs.

13 Sinclair, p3.

14 The legend of the murder of Hiram Abiff, chief architect of the Temple of Solomon, and the search for his body, forms the central theme of Masonic initiation rituals. See Robinson, pp217–223.

15 Sinclair, p171.

16 The following quotes are from an interview with Niven Sinclair at his home in Surrey, 4 May 1996.

17 Walker, p360.

18 For example, Sinclair, p86.

19 Ibid., p77.

20 See Baigent and Leigh, chapter 6.

21 Robinson, p182.

22 Pennick, *Hitler's Secret Sciences*, pp9–10

23 For example, Partner, *The Murdered Magicians*, p117.

24 Baigent and Leigh, pp267–269.

25 The Priory of Sion's list covers the first eight Templar Grand Masters, from 1118 to 1188, and appears in Philippe Toscan du Plantier, *Dossiers secrets d'Henri Lobineau*, plate 4 (See chapter 2, note 12). This claims to be based on the *Book of Constitutions* of the 'Commanderies of Geneva'. On the link with Baron von Hund's list, see Baigent and Leigh, p267.

26 Baigent, Leigh and Lincoln, *The Holy Blood and the Holy Grail*, pp129–132.

27 Partner, p118; J.M. Roberts, *The Mythology of the Secret Societies*, p98.

28 Nataf, p146.

29 Yates, *Giordano Bruno*, p449.

30 See Yates, *The Occult Philosophy in the Elizabethan Age*, chapter II.

31 Yates, *Giordano Bruno*, pp111–115.

32 See bibliography.

33 Yates, *Giordano Bruno*, p215.

34 For example, Luckert, *Egyptian Light and Hebrew Fire*.

35 This suggestion was put forward by Frances Yates in 1966 in *The Art of Memory*, but remained a speculation until receiving remarkable confirmation from the 'Byrom Papers' (discussed below), which contain a plan of the Globe and other Elizabethan theatres.

36 Yates, *The Occult Philosophy*, chapter XV.

37 Yates, *Giordano Bruno*, p312.

38 On Dee's part in the foundation of the Rosicrucians, see Yates, *The Rosicrucian Enlightenment*, chapter III, and *The Occult Philosophy*, chapters VIII and IX.

39 The texts of the two Rosicrucian manifestoes are reproduced in the appendices of Yates' *The Rosicrucian Enlightenment*.

40 Ibid., p38.

41 Quoted in ibid., p44.

42 Ibid., p118.

43 Quoted in Baigent, Leigh and Lincoln, *The Holy Blood and the Holy Grail*, p449.

44 *The Chemical Wedding* is summarized in Yates, *The Rosicrucian Enlightenment*, chapter 5.

45 Ibid., chapter VI.

46 Spence, p174.

47 Yates, *The Rosicrucian Enlightenment*, pp182–185.

48 Ibid., p183.

49 Hancock, p335.

50 Yates, *The Rosicrucian Enlightenment*, p210.

51 Ibid., p211.

52 Hancox, *The Byrom Collection*.

53 Ibid., p131.

54 See Ellic Howe, 'German Occult Groups', in Cavendish (ed.), *The Encyclopedia of the Unexplained*, p89; Ellic Howe, 'Rosicrucians', *Man, Myth and Magic*, no. 87, p2426; J.M. Roberts, *The Mythology of the Secret Societies*, p102.

55 See Findel, *The History of Freemasonry*, pp233–234 and Robert Amadou, 'Martinès de Pasqually et l'Ordre des élus Cohen', *L'Originel*, no. 2 (Autumn 1995).

56 Nataf, p177.

57 See the interview with Sebastiano Caraccioli (present head of the Ancient and Original Oriental Rite of Misraïm and Memphis), *L'Originel*, no. 2 (Autumn 1995), p38.

58 De Sède, *Rennes-le-Château*, pp205–206. The connection between Ormus and the Order of the Gold and Rosy Cross can be found in the researches of Jean-Pierre Bayard into the Rosicrucians.

59 Our thanks to Filip Coppens for bringing this to our attention.

60 Baigent, Leigh and Lincoln, *The Messianic Legacy*, pp426–428.

61 For example, Partner, p135.

62 Baigent and Leigh, p113.

63 For examples of the standard criticisms of the Larmenius Charter, see Findel, *A History of Freemasonry* and Grégoire, *Histoire de sectes religieuses*, vol. 2, pp401–402.

64 These points are argued in detail in F.J.W. Crowe, 'The "Charta Transmissionis" of Larmenius', *Transactions of the Quatour Coronati Lodge*. (Our copy omits publication details and date.) Our thanks to Guy Patton for supplying us with a copy of this immensely useful paper, which contains reproductions of the Larmenius Charter as well as the original Latin text.

65 The *Levitikon* is agreed to date from at least the fifteenth century. Some scholars have placed it in the thirteenth century, others the eleventh – see Grégoire, vol. 2, p407. (Grégoire, a bishop, is hostile to the content of the *Levitikon*, but accepts that it is of at least thirteenth-century origin.)

66   The following summary of the *Levitikon* is taken mainly from Grégoire, vol. 2, pp407–422.

67   R. McL. Wilson, p43.

68   Lévi, *The History of Magic*, translated by A.E. Waite, p264.

69   Ibid., p271.

70   Lévi, *Histoire de la magie*.

71   Pike, *Morals and Dogma of the Ancient and Accepted Scottish Rite of Freemasonry*, p821. (Our thanks to Filip Coppens for directing us to this work.)

72   Lévi (Waite translation), p405.

73   Pike, p821.

74   Ibid.

75   Arkon Daraul, in *Secret Societies*, records the words of the English Master of the Temple to Henry III in 1252: 'So long as thou dost exercise justice thou wilt reign; but if thou infringe it, thou will cease to be King!'

76   In Waite's notes to his translation of Lévi's *The History of Magic*, p174.

77   Robinson, p206.

78   Ernest Beha, in *A Dictionary of Freemasonry* states: 'The reason for adopting the two Saints John is obscure.' The question was the subject of a study by the Reverend George Oliver in 1848, entitled *A Mirror for the Johannite Masons*, which concluded that the Masons' reverence for John the Baptist is due to the fact that he was Grand Master of Freemasonry in his day!

79   Hancock, p335.

80   Iohnism is a mystery school with branches in several countries, mainly France and the UK. It claims to be an offshoot of the original Church of John, and also includes the worship of the goddess Isis. However, because it offers no proof of its claimed pedigree, or even a foundation myth, we considered it to be outside the scope of this investigation.

CHAPTER SEVEN: SEX: THE ULTIMATE SACRAMENT

1   Jung, *Psychology and Alchemy*.

2   Holroyd and Powell, pp175–176.

3   Mann and Lyle, p175.

4   Benjamin Walker, 'Tantrism', *Man, Myth and Magic*, no.109, p2780.

5   Brian Innes, 'Alchemy: Sex and Symbol', *The Unexplained*, no. 50, p988.

6   Mann and Lyle, p170.

7   Nataf, pp6–7.

8   Walker, p19.

9   Ibid., pp9–10.

10 Denis Labouré, 'De Cagliostro aux Arcana Arcanorum', *L'Originel*, no. 2 (Autumn 1995), p20.

11 Lindsay, *The Origins of Alchemy in Graeco-Roman Egypt*, p171. (Our thanks to Steve Moore for directing us to this work.)

12 Ibid., p195.

13 On Mary the Jewess, see ibid., chapter 11.

14 Ibid., p285.

15 Ibid., p372.

16 Redgrove, *The Black Goddess and the Sixth Sense*, p131.

17 Newman, p172.

18 For a discussion of the religious elements of the troubadour and *minnesinger* traditions, see ibid., chapter Five.

19 Walker, pp859–864.

20 Newman, p167.

21 Redgrove, p135.

22 Walker, p866.

23 Ibid., pp182–183.

24 Newman, p25.

25 Quoted in Walker, p910.

26 Significantly, Tristan reveals the secret of his alternative name by whispering it to his lover, to reassure her when she fears becoming pregnant. See Roger S. Loomis and Laura H. Loomis, *Medieval Romance*, and H.A. Guerber, *Legends of the Middle Ages*. Our thanks to Jane Lyle for this information.

27 Quoted in Mann and Lyle, p169.

28 Godwin, pp24–25.

29 Mann and Lyle, p162.

30 Riffard, *Dictionnaire de l'ésotérisme*, p154.

31 Ean Begg, p114.

32 Lévi (trans. Waite), p345.

33 Anderson, *Dante the Maker*, p85.

34 Ibid., p84.

35 Ibid., p111.

36 Ibid., p85.

37 Ibid., p412.

38 Quoted in King and Sutherland, *The Rebirth of Magic*.

39 Sinclair, p44.

40 Walker, p1085.

41 Yates, *Giordano Bruno and the Hermetic Tradition*, p280.

42 Ibid., p281.

43 Nataf, p70.

44 Yates, *Giordano Bruno*, p281.

45 Quoted in ibid., p281.

46 Quoted in King and Sutherland, p170.

47 Newman, p227.

48 Quoted in ibid., p230.

49 Ibid., p232.

50 Yates (*Giordano Bruno*, p332), discussing Bruno's last published work, refers to 'violent sexual' imagery, but does not elaborate.

51 Ibid., p311.

52 Ibid., p284.

53 See Yates, *The Occult Philosophy*, chapter VI.

54 Flowers, *Fire and Ice*.

55 Ean Begg, p12.

56 The Johannites were created in the early 1770s, and were ostensibly based on the visions of one Loiseaut, who claimed to have had visions of John the Baptist prophesying an imminent period of upheaval, chaos and the overthrow of the monarchy. This, of course, soon came to pass in the French Revolution. On the Johannites' links with Naündorff and Vintras, see Webb, *The Occult Underground*, pp298ff.

57 Ibid., p299.

58 Ibid., pp136–137.

59 Ibid., p301.

60 Griffiths, *The Reactionary Revolution*, p145.

61 Ean Begg, pp12–13.

62 Griffiths, pp129–135.

63 Ibid., p131.

64 Information supplied by researcher Jonothon Boulter.

65 Rémi Boyer, 'Le Monde secret: pour une compréhension du monde des sociétés secrètes', *L'Originel*, no. 2 (Augumn 1995), p12.

66 De Sède, *Rennes-le-Château*, pp207–208.

67 King and Sutherland, p63.

68 Nataf, p162.

69 De Sède, *Rennes-le-Château*, p211.

70 Griffiths, p134.

71 De Sède, *Rennes-le-Château*, p32.

72 Calvé, *My Life*, p155.

73 On Cagliostro's life and career, see: Colin Wilson, *The Occult*, part 2, chapter 5,; F. Ribadeau Dumas, 'Cagliostro', *Man, Myth and Magic*, no. 14, p388; and Tompkins, *The Magic of Obelisks*, pp108–151. On his connections with the Strict Templar Observance, see Tompkins, p109 and Findel, p231.

74 Lévi, p409.

75 Denis Labouré, 'De Cagliostro aux Arcana Arcanorum', *L'Originel*, no. 2 (Autumn 1995).

76 Marie-Jean Vinciguerra, 'Garibaldi héros du Risorgimento et la maçonnerie italienne', *L'Originel*, no. 2.

77 De Sède, *Rennes-le-Château*, pp204–206.

78 Frater U∴ D∴, *Secrets of the German Sex Magicians*, pp3–4.

79 Quoted in William Sargent, 'Sex', *Man, Myth and Magic*, no.91, p2541.

80 Quoted in Tompkins, p423.

81 De Sède, *Rennes-le-Château*, pp208–209; Daniel Wagner, 'La Golden Dawn et ses descendants', *L'Originel*, no. 2 (Autumn 1995).

82 Howe, 'German Occult Groups' in Cavendish (ed.), *Encyclopedia of the Unexplained*; Daniel Wagner, 'La Golden Dawn et ses descendants', *L'Originel*, no. 2 (Autumn 1995), p76.

83 Shu'al, *Sexual Magick*.

84 Tompkins, p413.

85 Quoted in ibid., p413.

86 Quoted in Greer, *Women of the Golden Dawn*, p352.

87 Ibid., p357.

88 Ibid., p451.

89 Quoted in King and Sutherland, pp26–29.

90 Ibid., p30.

CHAPTER EIGHT: 'THIS IS A TERRIBLE PLACE'

1   The church is generally dated to the tenth or eleventh century, although recent work indicates that some parts may be as early as the fifth century. See Sipra, *L'architecture insolité de l'église de Rennes-le-Château.*

2   Piecing together an accurate account of the Saunière affair is notoriously difficult, as the exact order of events is not easy to reconstruct and the story has acquired many spurious elements in the retelling. Space does not allow a detailed discussion of each and every point, and the following account is intended as a summary only. For works consulted, see the bibliography. We are also grateful for the many discussions we have had with researchers in France and Britain (see the acknowledgements) which have helped clarify many of the details.

    There is a vast literature on Rennes-le-Château in France, ranging from sceptical debunking to credulous fantasy. Among these works, those of Pierre Jarnac (see bibliography) are indispensable to the researcher. Jean Robin's *Rennes-le-Château: la colline envoûtée* is also recommended.

    Works in English tend (as here) to give summary accounts only. For a good introduction and overview see Gay Roberts, *The Mystery of Rennes-le-Château: A Concise Guide,* published by the British-based Rennes-le-Château Research Group.

3   Descadeillas, *Mythologie du trésor de Rennes-le-Château.* (See Chapter Three on the Priory and Notre-Dame de Lumière.)

4   Alain Féral, 'Deux abbés Saunières à Rennes-le-Château', *Association Terre de Rhedae Bulletin,* no. 8 (October 1994), p34. (The Association Terre de Rhedae, based in Rennes-le-Château, is dedicated to research into the village and the Saunière mystery.)

5   De Sède, *Rennes-le-Château,* pp27–28.

6   Interview with authors, 25 May 1995.

7 Descadeillas, *Notice sur Rennes-le-Château et l'abbé Saunière*, p11.

8 Ibid., p11.

9 The official date of the change of ownership was 26 July 1946, but Marie Dénarnaud's handwritten testament is clearly dated 22 July.

10 Corbu and Captier, *L'héritage de l'abbé Saunière*, p13.

11 Ibid., pp12 and 43.

12 Ibid., p59.

13 De Sède, *Rennes-le-Château*, p26.

14 In a letter to Pierre Jarnac dated 22 May 1985, reproduced in Jarnac, *Les archives du trésor de Rennes-le-Château*, vol. 2, p547.

15 See Lincoln, *The Holy Place*, Appendix 1.

16 Robin, *Le royaume du graal*, p36. De Chérisey's admission was in a pamphlet entitled *L'Enigme de Rennes* (1978).

17 Baigent, Leigh and Lincoln, *The Messianic Legacy*, p301.

18 Benoist Rivière, 'Où il est question d'une maquette', in Rivière (ed.) *Lumières nouvelles sur Rennes-le-Château*, p101. (See the translation by Clive Prince in *Le Reflet*, no. 5 (Autumn 1995).)

19 For more on this idea, see Keith Prince, 'Terribilis Est Locus Iste', *Le Reflet*, no. 5 (Autumn 1995).

20 Billard influenced several elderly churchgoers to amend their wills in his favour, the money being left to him as a private individual, not in his capacity as bishop. The Vatican also suspended him from performing the holy offices for three months for mismanagement of funds. Nothing actually illegal could be established, but his financial dealings were regarded as unethical by many; less than a month after his death one of his own priests wrote that 'the diocese could even view his death as a blessed release.' (See Jarnac, *Les archives du trésor de Rennes-le-Château*, vol 2., pp457–470.)

21 Deloux and Brétigny, p8.

22 Julien Coudy and Maurice Nogué, *Midi Libre*, 3–5 October 1975,

cited in Jarnac, *Les archives du trésor de Rennes-le-Château*, vol. 2, p443.

23 Sipra, p5.

24 De Sède, *Rennes-le-Château*, p173.

25 Robin, *Le royaume du graal*, p122.

26 Begg, p209.

27 The letter is reproduced in Corbu and Captier, p37.

28 Birks and Gilbert, pp.33–35.

29 Marie, *Alet-les-Bains*.

30 Baigent, Leigh and Lincoln, *The Holy Blood and the Holy Grail*, pp178–183.

31 Except where noted, details of the history of the site are taken from Migault, *Notre-Dame de Marceille, Limoux*.

32 Paul Smith, 'Verdict on Notre-Dame de Marceille', *The Rennes-le-Château Observer*, no. 11 (June 1996), p13. (*The Rennes-le-Château Observer* is the journal of the Rennes-le-Château Research Group.)

33 See Gay Roberts, 'The Brotherhood of the Blue Penitents of Narbonne', *The Rennes-le-Château Observer*, no. 1.8 (September 1995), p6.

34 See Jos Bertaulet, *De Verloren Konig en de bronnen van de graallegende*, and Filip Coppens, 'The Vault at Notre-Dame de Marceille'. *The Rennes-le-Château Observer*, no. 1.7 (March 1995), p27.

CHAPTER NINE: A CURIOUS TREASURE

1 Corbu and Captier, p278.

2 De Sède, *Rennes-le-Château*, p187.

3 Robin, *Le royaume du graal*, p36.

4 De Sède (*Rennes-le-Château*, pp79–80) tells the story of Corbu's previous interest in the Saunière affair, his deal with Abbé Gau, the investigation of Archbishop Roncalli, and the Vatican grant, but carefully avoids naming him. Jania Macgillivray (quoted in

Deloux and Brétigny, p33) names Corbu when describing his dealing with Gau and the Vatican grant.

5   De Sède states that the anonymous subject of his story had 'duped' the bishopric, but does not elaborate.

6   Paul Smith, in 'The Plantard Grail' (*Pendragon*, vol. XVII, no. 3), refers to this claim being made in the Belgian magazine *Bonne Soirée* (14 August 1980) Christopher Scargill, in an article in *Popular Archaeology* (April 1985) entitled 'The Abbé Saunière's "Treasure"' makes the same assertion, but on what grounds is not known.

7   De Sède, *Rennes-le-Château*, pp201–202.

8   Féral's work, under his pseudonym of Spatz, is published in Göte and Spatz, *Rennes-le-Château: clef du royaume des morts*. See especially volume 3.

9   Jonothon Boulter, 'Jansenism and Rennes', *The Rennes-le-Château Observer*, no. 1.7 (March 1995), p18.

10 De Sède, *Rennes-le-Château*, pp25–26, citing a collection of Saunière's writings published as *Mon enseignement à Antugnac* (Éditions Bélisane, Nice, 1984).

11 See Rappoport, *Ancient Israel*, vol. 1, p94.

12 Robin, *Rennes-le-Château: la colline envoûtée*, p142.

13 Interview in Rennes-les-Bains, 25 May 1995.

14 De Sède, *Rennes-le-Château*, pp189–194.

15 See Guy Patton, 'Mary Magdalene and Rennes-le-Château', The *Rennes-le-Château Observer*, no. 1.8 (September 1995), p15.

16 De Séde, *Rennes-le-Château*, pp218–219.

17 Ibid., p194.

18 Ibid., pp207–208.

19 Baigent, Leigh and Lincoln, *The Holy Blood and the Holy Grail*, pp477–479.

20 Ibid., p480. On the Count de Chambord's connection with the Rennes-le-Château affair, see Guy Patton, 'Saunière and the

Count de Chambord', *The Rennes-le-Château Observer*, no. 11 (June 1996), p20.

21 Robin, *Rennes-le-Château*, p60.

22 De Sède, *Rennes-le-Château*, p218, from information supplied by Aynard de Bissy, a descendant of the Chefdebiens.

23 Quoted in Robin, *Rennes-le-Château*, p62.

24 Because of the nature of Monti's life and activity, biographical information is hard to come by. The following account is drawn from Gérard de Sède (*Rennes-le-Château*, pp225–236), which is taken from a dossier compiled by Émile Hoffet and now in de Sède's possession.

25 Robin, *Rennes-le-Château*, p151.

26 From the journal *Circuit*, no. 8, quoted in de Sède, *Rennes-le-Château*, p236.

27 Descadeillas, *Notice sur Rennes-le-Château et l'abbé Saunière*, p12.

28 Corbu and Captier, p216.

29 Descadeillas, *Notice sur Rennes-le-Château et l'abbé Saunière*, p8.

30 Lionel and Patricia Fanthorpe, *Rennes-le-Château: Its Mysteries and Secrets*, pp3 and 180.

31 Interview with André Galaup, Rennes-les-Bains, 28 July 1995.

32 J.E. Mansion, *New Standard French and English Dictionary* (George G. Harrap & Co., London, 1939). Our thanks to Keith Prince for bringing this reference to our attention.

33 'Madeleine Blancasall', *Les descendants mérovingiens ou l'énigme du Razès wisigoth*. (See chapter 2, note 12.)

34 Antoine Captier, Marcel Captier and Michel Marrot, *Rennes-le-Château: le secret de l'abbé Saunière*. Although this tells the story of Saunière in comic book form, it represents the most accurate account of the events according to the memories of the villagers.

35 The inscription is as follows:

CE GIT NOBLE M/ ARIE DE NEGRE/ DARLES DAME/ DHAUPOUL/ DE/

515

BLANCHEFORT/ AGEE DE SOIX/ ANTE SEPT ANS/ DECEDEE LE/ XVII
JANVIER/ MDCOLXXXI/ REQUIES CATIN/ PACE

That Bigou was responsible for the wording of the headstone,
and the deliberate mistakes, is confirmed by Admiral Georges
Cagger's discovery that the name 'Bigou' is hidden in coded form
in the inscription – see the appendix to Jean Robin, *Le royaume
du graal*.

36 Gay Roberts, 'Jacques et le Bean Stalk: A Fairy Story', *Le Reflet
Newsletter in English*, no. 3.

37 · Alleged reproductions of the horizontal gravestone appear in the
Dossiers secrets in what is claimed to be an extract from a work
by the learned Eugène Stüblein (1832–1899), *Pierres gravées du
Languedoc*. These are the basis for all subsequent depictions
(although there are minor variations). However, no such work by
Stüblein can be traced, and the *Dossiers secrets* version, which
was deposited in the Bibliothèque Nationale in 1966, can easily
be shown to be a fabrication. But an engineer named Ernest Cros,
a friend of Saunière's, made a reconstruction of the inscriptions
in the 1920s. His notes record the main features of the 'Stüblein'
version, except for the *Et in Arcadia ego* motto.

38 The other two paintings were said to be *The Temptation of Saint
Anthony* by David Teniers – although which David Teniers
(father or son), or which of several versions of this theme painted
by both artists, is not known – and a portrait of the thirteenth-
century pope Celestine V.

39 De Sède, *Rennes-le-Château*, pp144–145.

40 Quoted in Robin, *Le royaume du graal*, p107. (Authors' translation.)

41 Migault, *Notre-Dame de Marceille, Limoux*, p5.

42 Deloux and Brétigny, p4.

43 Interview with Antoine and Claire Captier, Rennes-les-Bains, 25
May 1995.

44 Antoine Bruzeau, 'Marie-Madeleine: de la Bible à la legende, de
la legende à la tradition', in Rivière (ed.), *Lumières nouvelles sur
Rennes-le-Château*, p11.

45 Antoine Bruzeau, 'De Rennes-le-Château au Pilat', *Lumières nouvelles sur Rennes-le-Château*, p82.

46 Benoist Rivière, 'Bérenger Saunière à Lyon?', *Lumières nouvelles sur Rennes-le-Château*, p95.

47 *L'Indépendant*, 24 September 1987.

CHAPTER TEN: DIVINING THE UNDERGROUND
STREAM

1 Jean Robin, *Rennes-le-Château: la colline envoûtée*, p80, quoting from de Sède, *Les Templiers sont parmi nous*.

2 Baigent, Leigh and Lincoln, *The Holy Blood and the Holy Grail*, pp212–213.

3 Guy Patton, in *The Rennes-le-Château Observer*, no. 1.9 (December 1995), reports on information supplied to him by Roger-René Dagobert. Despite the evocative surname, Dagobert is a genuine descendant of a noble family from Normandy, whose forebears were closely involved in the Languedocian Masonic societies centred on the Marquis de Chefdebien and the Hautpoul family. According to this account, François Mitterand and Pierre Plantard (as he then was) were associates during the period of the Vichy regime in southern France.

4 See illustration.

5 Toscan du Plantier, *Dossiers secrets d'Henri Lobineau*. See also Baigent, Leigh and Lincoln, *The Holy Blood and the Holy Grail*, p170.

CHAPTER ELEVEN: GOSPEL UNTRUTHS

1 The discovery was unveiled in the BBC documentary 'The Body in Question', broadcast as part of the *Heart of the Matter* series on 7 April 1996 (produced and directed by Christopher Mann). See also Joan Bakewell, 'The Tomb that Dare not Speak its Name', *Sunday Times News Review*, 31 March 1996.

2 Vermes, *Jesus the Jew*, p114.

3 Golb, *Who Wrote the Dead Sea Scrolls?*

4 Knight and Lomas, p54.

5 The question of whether Jesus baptized has been a matter of debate since the earliest days of the Church. The only statements on the matter, which both appear in the Gospel of John, are contradictory. John 3:23 says that Jesus baptized, whereas 4:2 states that although his disciples baptized, Jesus himself did not. If the latter is true, this raises the question of who baptized the disciples.

6 This is recognized even by many Catholic theologians. For example, Father Philippe Devoucoux du Buyson, in 'Marie-Madeleine: témoin de la Passion-Résurrection', *Dieu est amour* (no. 115, May 1989) writes 'Mary Magdalene takes over from John the Baptist'.

7 Ricci, p172.

8 For example, Mark 2:18–22.

9 For example, Luke 7:18–23.

10 Luke 7:18, Matthew 11:11.

11 Vermes, pp32–33.

12 Smith, *Jesus the Magician*, p26.

13 St Victor, *Epiphany*, p81.

14 Eg Luke 5:7. (The King James Version has 'bottles', but the correct translation is 'skins'.)

15 See entry on 'Johannine Comma', in *The Encyclopedia of Religion* (ed. Mircea Eliade).

16 See Ian Wilson, *Are these the Words of Jesus?*, pp31–33. Some early New Testament manuscripts have this episode in Luke.

17 Vermes, p21.

18 Mark 6:3. Matthew, obviously aware of this problem, changes the words to '*son of* the carpenter', while the other Gospels omit the reference entirely.

19 A.N. Wilson, *Jesus*, p48.

20 The consensus is that Mark is the earliest, probably being
    written around 70 CE, and that Matthew and Luke were at least
    partially based on Mark and date from some time between the
    70s and 90s. Because of the very different character of John's
    Gospel, it is thought that this was the last Gospel to be written,
    some time around 100 CE. However, these dates are by no means
    unanimous: some still defend Matthew as the earliest, and even
    John has its supporters.

    These dates are based on deductions and conjectures that have
    to be made in the absence of any solid evidence. The oldest
    complete Gospel manuscripts date from the first half of the
    fourth century. There are fragments from the second century –
    the oldest fragment is, in fact, from *John's* Gospel, and has been
    dated to between 130 and 150.

    Recently, Carsten Peter Thiede has proposed that a tiny frag-
    ment of Matthew's Gospel – kept (ironically perhaps) in
    Magdalen College, Oxford – actually dates from the 40s of the
    first century, within ten years of the Crucifixion. If true, this
    would overturn almost all current thinking on the subject.
    However, Thiede's case is open to many criticisms, and it
    appears unlikely that he is correct. However, if further research
    does confirm his claims, there would be significant implications
    for our own hypothesis. The fragment contains parts of two
    familiar episodes, the anointing of Jesus by Mary of Bethany
    and the instigation of the eucharist at the Last Supper, both
    of which are important in our investigation, and such an early
    date would support the arguments put forward in Chapters
    Twelve and Thirteen. (See Thiede and d'Ancona, *The Jesus
    Papyrus*.)

21 See, for example, A.N. Wilson, chapter III.

22 For example, John A.T. Robinson, *The Priority of John*.

23 On the Council of Nicea, see Ayerst and Fisher, *Records of
    Christianity, Volume I: In the Roman Empire*, pp144–146.

24 Burton L. Mack, summarizing the current position of New
    Testament scholarship in *The Lost Gospel*, states that, of the just
    over 500 direct sayings attributed to Jesus, *at most* 10 per cent
    are regarded by scholars as having any claim to authenticity.

25 See Sanders, *Jesus and Judaism*, p15.

26 Crucifixion was a *Roman* penalty, used to punish civil crimes. If the Jews had executed Jesus for blasphemy, as the Gospels allege, then death would have been by stoning. In this event the Jewish leaders would not have had to involve the Roman governor.

27 Sanders, in *Jesus and Judaism*, gives a statement and analysis of the current position of New Testament scholarship, and deals in detail with many of the fundamental problems alluded to here. In fact, Sanders lists just eight 'indisputable facts' that are agreed about Jesus by scholars: (1) He was baptized by John; (2) He was a Galilean preacher and healer; (3) He had disciples; (4) His activity was confined to Palestine; (5) He was involved in a controversy concerning the Jerusalem Temple; (6) He was crucified by the Romans; (7) His movement continued after his death; (8) The new movement suffered persecution by at least some Jews. *Everything else* is disputed.

28 This statement will come as a shock to most readers, whether Christian or not. Yet it is a fact that nothing in the Gospels gives sufficient reason for Jesus' treatment. For a detailed discussion of this problem, see Sanders, *Jesus and Judaism*.

29 Schonfield, *The Passover Plot*, p109.

30 Jesus tells two of his disciples where they will find the ass tethered, and, if anybody asks what they are doing, to tell them that 'the Lord hath need of him', upon which they will be allowed to take it (Mark 11:2–7). (Ibid., p119.)

31 Ibid., pp138–139.

32 See Baigent, Leigh and Lincoln, *The Messianic Legacy*, p72.

33 Smith, *The Secret Gospel*. For reactions to Smith's discovery, see Shawn Eyer. 'The Strange Case of the Secret Gospel according to Mark', in *Alexandria 3*, p103.

34 Smith, *The Secret Gospel*, p17.

CHAPTER TWELVE: THE WOMAN WHOM
JESUS KISSED

1 Torjesen, pp9–10.

2 See Walker, p644.

3 Quoted in Newman, pp13–14.

4 Haskins, p40.

5 Our thanks to Keith Prince for researching this question for us.

6 Walker, pp613–616.

7 Starbird, *The Woman with the Alabaster Jar*, p50.

8 Vermes, p102.

9 Ibid.

10 Baigent, Leigh and Lincoln, *The Holy Blood and the Holy Grail*, pp348–349.

11 Phipps, *The Sexuality of Jesus*, p69.

12 Haskins, p18.

13 Phipps, *The Sexuality of Jesus*, p62.

14 See Schonfield, *The Passover Plot*, p156.

15 See Walker, pp501–508.

16 Qualls-Corbett, *The Sacred Prostitute*, p25.

17 For the many parallels between the Song of Songs and sacred marriage texts, see Pope, *Song of Songs*.

18 Starbird, p43, citing Bayley, *The Lost Language of Symbolism*.

19 Qualls-Corbett, pp102–104.

20 Baigent, Leigh and Lincoln, *The Holy Blood and the Holy Grail*, pp350–351.

21 Qualls-Corbett, pp104–105.

22 Pope, p192.

23 Redgrove, pp125–126.

24 Walker, p615.

25 Ibid., p614.

26 R. McL. Wilson, p21.

27 Both the quotes given from the Gospel of Philip concerning Mary
    Magdalene are in the context of discussions about the Holy
    Spirit/Sophia. See ibid., pp39 and 107.

28 Ibid., p50.

29 Schneemelcher, p93.

30 John 20:9.

CHAPTER THIRTEEN: SON OF THE GODDESS

1 Mack, p193.

2 Gasgoine, p12.

3 Quoted in Ayerst and Fisher, pp2–3.

4 Ibid., p11.

5 Ibid., pp14–16.

6 See Schonfield, *The Pentecost Revolution*, p34.

7 Ibid.

8 It is possible that the account of Jesus in the 'Slavonic Josephus'
   may contain a genuine reference to Jesus. This is a version of
   The Jewish War that was translated into Greek at an early
   date, and bypassed the editing process undergone in the West,
   remaining unknown in Europe until the late nineteenth century.
   It has been almost universally dismissed by scholars as in-
   authentic, but the picture that it gives of Jesus – as essentially a
   wonder-worker and rebel leader – is so unusual that it is hard
   to imagine it being fabricated by a Christian. As this depiction
   accords with more recent conclusions about Jesus – and
   those of this book – it would perhaps be timely for a re-
   appraisal of this text. (See Eisler, *The Messiah Jesus and John
   the Baptist*.)

9 Ashe, *The Virgin*, pp41–43.

10   Hector Hawton, Introduction to Robertson, *Pagan Christs*, p8.

11   Robertson, p52.

12   Ibid., p53.

13   Ibid., p68.

14   Ibid., p52.

15   Mack, p22.

16   Schonfield, *The Passover Plot*, p204.

17   Osman, *The House of the Messiah*.

18   Smith, *Jesus the Magician*, p147.

19   A.N. Wilson, p8.

20   Mack, p2.

21   Morton Smith devotes an appendix in *Jesus the Magician* to the evidence for this.

22   Smith, *Jesus the Magician*, p29.

23   Stewart, *The Foreigner*, p34.

24   Mack, p51.

25   Schonfield, *The Passover Plot*, p37.

26   Mack, p53.

27   Smith, *Jesus the Magician*, p68.

28   Mack, p59.

29   Ibid., p53.

30   Schonfield, *The Passover Plot*, p209.

31   Schonfield, *The Pentecost Revolution*, p278.

32   Keith Prince pointed out the parallel to us, which is an event recorded by three Roman writers, Dio Cassius, Suetonius and Pliny. In 66 CE Tiridates, King of Armenia, visited Nero in Rome, accompanied by the sons of three neighbouring rulers from Parthia, where Zoroastrianism – the religion of the magi – was strong. The purpose of the visit was to worship Nero as a god,

with Tiridates proclaiming: 'I have come to you my god to pay homage as I do to Mithras.' The account ends: 'The king did not return by the route he had followed in coming, but . . . by a different way' – just as in the Gospel story.

33   A.N. Wilson, p124.

34   Smith, *Jesus the Magician*, p147.

35   For example, Ian Wilson, *Are these the Words of Jesus?*, p20.

36   A.N. Wilson, p123.

37   For example, Stewart, p64.

38   Crossan, *Who Killed Jesus?*, p64.

39   Smith, *Jesus the Magician*, pp96–97.

40   Stewart, p61.

41   A.N. Wilson, p21.

42   Stewart, p119.

43   Ibid., p100.

44   Ibid., p133.

45   Schonfield, *The Passover Plot*, p219. See also Ayerst and Fisher, p32.

46   Schonfield, *The Passover Plot* (citing T.J. Meek).

47   Ibid., p227.

48   Ashe, p37.

49   Osman, p50.

50   Stewart, p77.

51   Mark 16:34–15 and Matthew 28:46–47.

52   Stewart, Appendix C, *The Foreigner*.

53   Ashe, p14.

54   Ibid., p39.

55   Walker, p454.

56   George Witterschein, Introduction to Gaus (trans.), *The Unvarnished New Testament*, pp15–16.

57   Gaus, p171.

58   On the Gnostics' association of Sophia and the Holy Spirit, see R.McL. Wilson, p14.

59   Luckert, p322.

60   See Morton Smith, *Jesus the Magician*, pp47–49.

61   Ibid., p94.

62   Ibid., p120.

63   Peter James, 'Birth of the Gods', *The Unexplained*, no. 154, p3063.

64   Smith, *Jesus the Magician*, p123.

65   Ibid., p33.

66   Ibid., p94. On the magical practices of early Egyptian Christians, see Meyer and Smith, *Ancient Christian Magic*.

67   Walker, p750

68   Wallis Budge (trans.), *The Book of the Dead*, p440.

69   Walker, pp748–749

70   Vermes, p114.

71   Schonfield, *The Passover Plot*, p177.

72   Luckert, pp320–322.

73   Walker, pp453–454.

74   Doresse, *The Secret Books of Egyptian Gnostics*, pp273–274.

75   Patai, *The Hebrew Goddess*, p53.

76   Luckert, p157.

77   See Ashe, p26.

78   Ibid., pp26–30.

79   Mack, p150.

80   See Heyob, *The Cult of Isis among Women in the Graeco-Roman*

World, p60, and Jones and Pennick, *A History of Pagan Europe*, chapter 4.

81 See Heyob, pp115–119.

82 R. Merkelbach, 'Isis', *Man, Myth and Magic*, no. 51, p1461.

83 Heyob, p60.

84 Merkelbach, 'Isis', p1463.

85 Ibid., p1461.

86 S.G.F. Brandon, 'Baptism', *Man, Myth and Magic*, no. 5, p217.

87 Ibid., citing Romans 6 as an example.

88 Jones and Pennick, p57.

89 Heyob, pp64–66.

90 S.G.F. Brandon, 'Dying God', *Man, Myth and Magic*, no. 26, p739.

91 Meyer (ed.), *The Ancient Mysteries*, p8.

92 S.G.F. Brandon, 'Osiris', *Man, Myth and Magic*, no. 74, p2088.

93 Luckert (p294) quotes Helmut Koester: 'It is . . . unthinkable that the Christian mission should have bypassed Alexandria for decades . . . The beginnings of Christianity in Egypt were "heretical", and therefore Christian writings composed in Egypt in this early period were not preserved.'

94 Doresse, pp138–139.

95 Eliade, vol. 1. p.85.

CHAPTER FOURTEEN: JOHN CHRIST

1 Luke 1:46–55.

2 The story of John the Baptist's execution is told in Matthew 14:3–12 and Mark 6:17–29. Luke tells only of his arrest, and John omits any mention of his fate.

3 The only alteration that may have been made is the addition of the epithet 'the Baptist', as it is debatable whether Josephus would have been familiar with the term.

4 Matthew's account (3:1–12) places John in Judaea, but on the eastern shore of the Jordan, which was actually in Peraea (the Jordan being the border).

5 Kraeling, *John the Baptist*, p7.

6 Ibid., pp10–11

7 *Antiquities of the Jews*, Book 18, quoted in Robert L. Webb, *John the Baptizer and Prophet*, p32.

8 Robert L. Webb, p36.

9 Schonfield, *The Passover Plot*, p72.

10 Kraeling, p87.

11 Ibid.

12 Luke 11:1

13 Wallis-Budge, *Egyptian Magic*, p116.

14 Vermes, p31.

15 Schonfield, *The Essene Odyssey*, p40.

16 Ibid., p58.

17 Knight and Lomas, chapter 11.

18 A.N. Wilson, p112.

19 Kraeling's article appeared in the *Journal of Biblical Literature*, LIX, 2 (1940).

20 Smith, *Jesus the Magician*, p34.

21 Kraeling, p160.

22 Smith, *Jesus the Magician*, p34.

23 Ibid., p97.

24 Ibid.

25 Eg Mark 12:27–33.

26 Book of James, 23:1–3. See James, *The Apocryphal New Testament*, p48. (Our thanks to Craig Oakley for bringing this episode to our attention.)

27   Kraeling, p16.

28   Ibid., pp169–170.

29   Luke 1:68–79.

30   Schonfield, *The Essene Odyssey*, p58.

31   *Clementine Recognitions*, I 60, quoted in Kraeling, p181.

32   Vermes, p95.

33   John 1:35–40

34   Yamauchi, *Pre-Christian Gnosticism*, p31.

35   Ibid., p25.

36   A.N. Wilson, p102.

37   Gasgoine, p24.

38   St Victor, p19.

39   G.R.S. Mead conveniently gathered together all the early references to Simon Magus in his *Simon Magus: An Essay*.

40   Luckert, p304. For parallels between Simon Magus' teachings and several of the Nag Hammadi texts, see Doresse, appendix I.

41   Schonfield, *The Essene Odyssey*, p165.

42   Luckert, pp302–305.

43   Ashe, p138.

44   The Acts of Peter, quoted in St Victor, p37.

45   Quoted in Mead, *Simon Magus*, p10.

46   Ibid., p26.

47   Ibid., p13.

48   Ibid., p24.

49   Ibid., p21.

50   Ibid., p28.

51   Ibid., p36.

52   Ibid., p19.

53 Luckert, p300.

54 Haskins, p41.

55 Romer, p194.

56 Luckert, p299.

57 Ibid., p305.

58 See Mead, *Simon Magus*, pp28ff.

59 Foerster, *Gnosis*, vol. 1, p32.

60 Eisler, p254.

CHAPTER FIFTEEN: FOLLOWERS OF THE KING OF LIGHT

1 The most extensive literature on the Mandaeans is in the German language. See the bibliography for English language works consulted. The most accessible recent work on the Mandaeans is Rudolph, *Mandaeism*.

2 Kurt Rudolph, 'Mandaean Sources', in Foester (ed.) *Gnosis*, vol. 2. Lady Drower, in *The Mandaeans of Iraq and Iran* (p14), obviously mindful of the sensibilities of her English readers, renders the opening words simply as 'When oppressed . . .'

3 We attempted to find out the Mandaeans' current situation through our friend Dominique Hyde, of the School of Middle Eastern Studies at London University. Due to the internal problems of today's Iraq, it is proving impossible to find out anything about the Mandaeans' plight.

4 Drower, p100.

5 Rudolph, *Mandaeism*, p3.

6 Schonfield, *The Pentecost Revolution*, p284.

7 Yamauchi, pp135–140.

8 Drower, p264.

9 Ibid., p3.

10 Only extracts from the *Sidra d'Yahya* are available in English

translation, in G.R.S. Mead, *The Gnostic John the Baptizer: Selections from the Mandaean John-Book*. This is based on the German translation of M. Lidzbarski, *Das Johannesbuch der Mandäer* (2 vols. Gießen, 1905 and 1915).

11 In a fourth-century Manichean hymn – see Haskins, p52.

12 Rudolph, 'Mandaean Sources', p398.

13 Quoted in Drower, p9.

14 Quoted in Rudolph, p299.

15 Quoted in ibid., p300.

16 Sections 33–35 of the *Sidra d'Yahya*.

17 See plate IV in Rudolph, *Mandaeism*.

18 Drower, p3; Yamauchi, p80.

19 Mead, *The Gnostic John the Baptizer*, p16.

20 Gaster, *The Dead Sea Scriptures*, pp21–22.

21 See: *Man, Myth and Magic*, no. 43, p1213; Riffard, *Dictionnaire de l'ésotérisme*, pp154 and 294.

22 Lindsay, p172.

23 Rudolph, 'Mandaean Sources', p126.

24 Yamauchi, p24.

25 Ibid., p126.

26 Quoted in ibid., p30.

27 Ibid., p35.

28 Ibid., p176.

29 Rudolph, *Mandaeism*, p3.

30 Schonfield, *The Passover Plot*, p208.

31 Yamauchi, p29.

32 Walter N. Birks, 'A Personal Reminiscence' (epilogue to Birks and Gilbert, *The Treasure of Montségur*).

33 Ibid., p154.

34   On the parallels between the Mandaean texts, Manicheanism, the
     Pistis Sophia (and other Nag Hammadi texts) and the doctrines
     of Simon Magus, see: Mead, *The Gnostic John the Baptizer* and
     Simon Magus; Yamauchi *Pre-Christian Gnosticism* and Doresse
     The Secret Books of the Egyptian Gnostics.

CHAPTER SIXTEEN: THE GREAT HERESY

1   Josephus, *The Jewish War*, p139.

2   The discrepancy between the number of followers given by
     Josephus and the Gospels is explained by Josephus' notorious
     penchant for exaggeration.

3   Robert L. Webb, p338.

4   Matthew 6:39–44.

5   Matthew 10:34.

6   Mark 7:9–10

7   Luke 14:26.

8   Schonfield, *The Passover Plot*, p81.

9   Mark 10:13–16.

10   Mark 9:42.

11   Gascoigne, p17.

12   John 6:26.

13   A.N. Wilson, p160.

14   Mark, the earliest of the Synoptic Gospels, mentions only 'five
     thousand men' (6:44), as does Luke (9:14). Matthew (14:21) has
     'five thousand men, besides women and children'. John is the
     most emphatic: 'So the men sat down, in number about five
     thousand' (6:10) and again, after the feeding, refers only to men
     being present (6:14) – there is no mention whatsoever of women
     or children.

15   A.N. Wilson, p161.

16   Thiering, *Jesus the Man*, pp84–85 and 390–391

17 Gospel of Thomas 61 (see Layton, p391).

18 Clement of Alexandria records this extract from the lost Gospel of the Egyptians in his *Stromateis*. See Ian Wilson, *Are these the Words of Jesus?*, pp153–154.

19 Luke 8:3.

CHAPTER SEVENTEEN: OUT OF EGYPT

1   Bauval and Gilbert, *The Orion Mystery*; Hancock, *Fingerprints of the Gods*; Hancock and Bauval, *Keeper of Genesis*.

2   Lurker, *An Illustrated Dictionary of the Gods and Symbols of Ancient Egypt*, p93.

3   M.L. West, 'Orpheus and Orphism', *Man, Myth and Magic*, no.74. p2082.

4   Baigent, Leigh and Lincoln, *The Messianic Legacy*, pp296–298.

5   'S. Roux', *L'affaire de Rennes-le-Château: réponse à Monsieur Lionel Burrus*. (See chapter 2, note 12.)

6   'Lionel Burrus', *Faisons le point* . . . (Supposed extract from the *Semaine catholique genevoise*, 22 October 1966). (See chapter 2, note 12.)

7   Ibid.

8   'Jean Delaude', *Le cercle d'Ulysse*. It is thought that the true author was Philippe de Chérisey.

9   Luckert, p29.

10 See, for example, Sanders, p8.

11 See Jones and Pennick.

APPENDIX I: CONTINENTAL OCCULT FREEMASONRY

1   Robert Amadou, 'Martinès de Pasqually et l'Ordre des élus Cohen', *L' Originel*, no. 2 (Autumn 1995).

APPENDIX II: RENNES-LE-CHÂTEAU AND THE 'TOMB OF GOD'

1 S.P. Simon, *L'Or du Temple et le tombeau du Christ,* quoted in Blum, p184–186.

2 Andrews and Schellenberger, *The Tomb of God,* p283.

3 Ibid., p295.

Select Bibliography

Addison, Charles Greenstreet, *The History of the Knights Templars, the Temple Church and the Temple,* Longman & Co., London, 1842.

Anand, Margo, *The Art of Sexual Ecstasy,* Aquarian Press, London, 1990.

Anderson, William, *Dante the Maker,* Routledge & Kegan Paul, London, 1980.

Ann, Martha and Dorothy Myers Imel, *Goddesses in World Mythology,* Oxford University Press, Oxford, 1993.

Ashe, Geoffrey, *The Virgin,* Arkana, London, 1976.

Ayerst, David and A.S.T. Fisher, *Records of Christianity, Volume I: In the Roman Empire,* Basil Blackwell, Oxford, 1971.

Baigent, Michael and Richard Leigh, *The Temple and the Lodge,* Jonathan Cape, London, 1989.

Baigent, Michael, Richard Leigh and Henry Lincoln, *The Holy Blood and the Holy Grail,* Jonathan Cape, London, 1982; revised edition: Arrow, London, 1996.

— *The Messianic Legacy,* Jonathan Cape, London, 1986.

Barber, Malcolm, *The New Knighthood: A History of the Order of the Temple,* Cambridge University Press, Cambridge, 1994.

— *The Trial of the Templars,* Cambridge University Press, Cambridge, 1978.

Bauval, Robert and Adrian Gilbert, *The Orion Mystery,* William Heinemann, London, 1994.

Bayley, Harold, *The Lost Language of Symbolism*, Williams & Norgate, London, 1912.

Begg, Ean, *The Cult of the Black Virgin*, Arkana, London, 1985; revised edition 1996.

Begg, Ean and Deike, *In Search of the Holy Grail and the Precious Blood*, Thorsons, London, 1995.

Beha, Ernest, *A Dictionary of Freemasonry*, Arco, London, 1962.

Bertaulet, Jos, *De Verloren Konig en de bronnen van de Graallegende*, Stichting Mens en Kultuur, Ghent, 1991.

Birks, Walter and R.A. Gilbert, *The Treasure of Montségur*, Crucible, London, 1987.

Black, Matthew, *The Scrolls and Christian Origins: Studies in the Jewish Background of the New Testament*, Thomas Nelson & Sons, London, 1961.

Blum, Jean, *Rennes-le-Château: wisigoths, cathares, templiers*, Éditions du Rocher, Monaco, 1994.

Boudet, Henri, *The vraie langue celtique et le Cromleck de Rennes-les-Bains*, Éditions Bélisane, Nice, 1984 (facsimile of original 1886 edition).

Bramly, Serge, *Leonardo: the Artist and the Man*, Michael Joseph, London, 1992; first published as *Léonard de Vinci*, Éditions Jean-Claude Lattés, Paris, 1988.

Budge, Sir E.A. Wallis, (trans.) *The Book of the Dead*, British Museum, London, 1899.

— *Egyptian Magic*, Dover Publications, New York, 1971.

Buenner, D., *Notre-Dame de la Mer et les Saintes-Maries*, Lescuyer, Lyons, n.d.

Calvé, Emma, *My Life*, D. Appleton & Co., London, 1922.

Captier, Antoine, Marcel Captier and Michel Marrot, *Rennes-le-Château: le secret de l'abbé Saunière*, Éditions Belisane, Nice, n.d.

Cavendish, Richard (ed.), *The Encyclopedia of the Unexplained*, Routledge & Kegan Paul, London, 1974.

— *The Magical Arts*, Arkana, London, 1984.

Chang, Jolan, *The Tao of Love and Sex*, Wildwood House, London, 1977.

Corbu, Claire and Antoine Captier, *L'Héritage de l'abbé Saunière*, Éditions Bélisane, Cazilhac, 1995.

Crossan, John Dominic, *Who Killed Jesus?*, HarperCollins, New York, 1995.

Daraul, Arkon, *Secret Societies*, Frederick Muller, London, 1961.

de Rosa, Peter, *Vicars of Christ: The Dark Side of the Papacy*, Bantam Press, London, 1988.

de Séde, Gérard, *Rennes-le-Château: le dossier, les impostures, les phantasmes, les hypothèses*, Robert Laffont, Paris, 1988.

— *Les Templiers sont parmi nois*, Julliard, Paris, 1963.

de Séde, Gérard and Sophie, *L'Or de Rennes, ou la vie insolite de Bérenger Saunière, curé de Rennes-le-Château*, Julliard, Paris, 1967.

de Voragine, Jacobus, T*he Golden Legend: Readings on the Saints*, trans. William Grayer Ryan, 2 volumes, Princeton University Press, 1993.

Delaude, Jean, *Le cercle d'Ulysse*, Éditions Dyroles, Toulouse, 1977.

Deloux, Jean-Pierre and Jacques Brétigny, *Rennes-le-Château: capitale secrète de l'histoire de France*, Éditions Atlas, Paris, 1982.

Descadaillas, René, *Mythologie du trésor de Rennes-le-Château*, Savary, Carcassonne, 1974.

— *Notice sur Rennes-le-Château et l'abbé Saunière*, Departmental Archives of the Aude, Carcassonne, 1962.

Dodd, C.H., *The Interpretation of the Fourth Gospel*, Cambridge University Press, Cambridge, 1953.

Doresse, Jean, *The Secret Books of the Egyptian Gnostics*, Hollis & Carter, London, 1960; first published as *Les livres secrets des Gnostiques d'Egypte*, Librairie Plon, Paris, 1953.

Douzet, André, *Elements du passé de Sainte-Croix-en-Jarez Chartreuse: pour servir à son histoire*, A. Douzet, Bages, 1994.

Drower, E.S., *The Mandaeans of Iraq and Iran: Their Cults, Customs, Magic, Legends and Folklore*, Clarendon Press, Oxford, 1937.

Eisler, Robert, *The Messiah Jesus and John the Baptist*, Methuen & Co., London, 1931.

Eliade, Mircea, *The Encyclopedia of Religion*, Macmillan, New York, 1987.

Fanthorpe, Lionel and Patricia, *Rennes-le-Château: Its Mysteries and Secrets*, Bellevue Books, Ashford, 1991.

Fideler, David (ed.), *Alexandria 3*, Phanes Press, Grand Rapids, 1995.

Findel, J.G., *The History of Freemasonry from its Origins down to the Present Day*, George Kenning, London, 1869.

Flowers, Stephen E., *Fire and Ice*, Llewellyn Publications, St. Paul, 1994.

Foerster, Werner (ed.), *Gnosis: A Selection of Gnostic Texts* (2 vols.), Clarendon Press, Oxford, 1972/74; first published as *Gnosis*, Artemis Verlags-AG, Zurich, 1969/71.

Fox, Robin Lane, *The Unauthorised Version*, Viking, London, 1991.

Gasgoine, Bamber, *The Christians*, Jonathan Cape, London, 1977.

Gaster, Theodore H., *The Dead Sea Scriptures*, Doubleday and Co., Garden City, 1956.

Gaus, Andy (trans. and ed.), *The Unvarnished New Testament*, Phanes Press, Grand Rapids, 1991.

Gilbert, R.A., *The Golden Dawn: Twilight of the Magicians*, Aquarian Press, Wellingborough, 1983.

Godwin, Joscelyn, *Robert Fludd: Hermetic Philosopher and Surveyor of Two Worlds*, Thames & Hudson, London, 1979.

Godwin, Malcolm, *The Holy Grail: Its Origins, Secrets and Meaning Revealed*, Bloomsbury, London, 1994.

Golb, Norman, *Who Wrote the Dead Sea Scrolls?*, Michael O'Mara, London, 1995.

Göte, Anton and Spatz, *Rennes-le-Château: clef du royaume des morts*, 4 volumes, Atelier Empreinte, Rennes-le-Château, 1984–1987.

Greer, Mary K., *Women of the Golden Dawn: Rebels and Priestesses*, Park Street Press, Rochester, 1995.

Grégoire, M., *Histoire de sectes religieuses* (6 vols.), Baudouin Frères, Paris 1828–29.

Griffiths, Richard, *The Reactionary Revolution*, Constable, London, 1966.

Guerber, H.A., *Legends of the Middle Ages*, American Book Co., New York, 1924.

Haeffner, Mark, *The Dictionary of Alchemy*, Aquarian Press, Wellingborough, 1991.

Hancock, Graham, *Fingerprints of the Gods*, William Heinemann, London, 1995.

— *The Sign and the Seal*, William Heinemann, London, 1992.

Hancock, Graham and Robert Bauval, *Keeper of Genesis*, William Heinemann, London, 1996.

Hancox, Joy, *The Byrom Collection*, Jonathan Cape, London, 1992.

Haskins, Susan, *Mary Magdalen*, HarperCollins, London, 1993.

Heyob, Sharon Kelly, *The Cult of Isis among Women in the Graeco-Roman World*, E.J. Brill, Leiden, 1975.

Hillgarth, J.N., *Lull and Lullism in Fourteenth Century France*, Clarendon Press, Oxford, 1971.

Holroyd, Stuart and Neil Powell, *Mysteries of Magic*, Bloomsbury Books, London, 1991.

James, M.R. (ed.), *The Apocryphal New Testament*, Clarendon Press, Oxford, 1953.

Jarnac, Pierre (ed.), *Les archives de l'abbé Saunière*, Pierre Jarnac, Sailles, 1995.

— *Les archives du trésor de Rennes-le-Château*, (2 vols.) Éditions Belisane, Nice, 1987/1988.

— *Histoire du trésor de Rennes-le-Château*, Éditions Bélisane, Nice, 1985.

— (ed.), *Les mystères de Rennes-le-Château: mélanges sulfureux* (3 vols), C.E.R.T., Couiza, 1994–1995.

Jones, Gwyn and Thomas Jones (trans. and ed.), *The Mabinogion*, J.M. Dent & Sons, London, 1974.

Jones, Prudence and Nigel Pennick, *A History of Pagan Europe*, Routledge, London, 1995.

Josephus, Flavius, *The Jewish War*, trans. G.A. Williamson, Penguin, London, 1970.

Jung, C.G., *Psychology and Alchemy*, Routledge & Kegan Paul, London, 1968.

King, Francis and Isabel Sutherland, *The Rebirth of Magic*, Corgi, London, 1982.

Knight, Christopher and Robert Lomas, *The Hiram Key*, Century, London, 1996.

Knight, Gareth, *Magic and the Western Mind*, Kahn & Averill, London, 1991.

— *The Rose Cross and the Goddess*, Aquarian Press, Wellingborough, 1985.

Kraeling, Carl H., *John the Baptist*, Charles Scribner's Sons, London, 1951.

Layton, Bentley, *The Gnostic Scriptures*, SCM Press, London, 1987.

Lévi, Éliphas, *The History of Magic*, trans. A.E. Waite, William Rider & Sons, London, 1913; first published as *Histoire de la Magie*, Germer Baillière, Paris, 1860.

Lincoln, Henry, *The Holy Place*, Jonathan Cape, London, 1991.

Lindsay, Jack, *The Origins of Alchemy in Graeco-Roman Egypt*, Frederick Muller, London, 1970.

Loomis, Roger S. and Laura H., *Medieval Romance*, Modern Library, New York, 1957.

Lucius Apuleius, *The Golden Ass*, trans. W. Adlington, Harvard University Press, London, 1989.

Luckert, Karl W., *Egyptian Light and Hebrew Fire*, State University of New York Press, New York, 1991.

Lurker, Manfred, *An Illustrated Dictionary of the Gods and Symbols of Ancient Egypt*, Thames & Hudson, London, 1980.

Mack, Burton L., *The Lost Gospel: The Book of Q and Christian Origins*, Element Books, Shaftesbury, 1994.

Malvern, Marjorie M., *Venus in Sackcloth: The Magdalen's Origins and Metamorphoses*, Southern Illinois University Press, Carbondale, 1975.

Mann, A. T. and Jane Lyle, *Sacred Sexuality*, Element Books, Shaftesbury, 1995.

Marie, Franck, *Alet-les-Bains: les portes du temps*, Franck Marie, Montrouge, 1984.

Marwick, Max (ed.), *Witchcraft and Sorcery: Selected Readings*, Penguin, London, 1970.

Mascetti, Manuela Dunn, *The Song of Eve: Mythology and Symbols of the Goddess*, Aurum Press, London, 1994.

Matarasso, Pauline (trans. and ed.), *The Cistercian World: Monastic Writings of the Twelfth Century*, Penguin, London, 1993.

Mead, G.R.S. (ed.), *The Gnostic John the Baptizer: Selections from the Mandaean John-Book*, John M. Watkins, London, 1924.

— *Simon Magus: An Essay*, Theosophical Publishing Society, London, 1892.

Meyer, Marvin W. (ed.), *The Ancient Mysteries: A Sourcebook*, HarperCollins, San Francisco, 1987.

Meyer, Marvin and Richard Smith (eds.), *Ancient Christian Magic: Coptic Texts of Ritual Power*, HarperCollins, San Francisco, 1994.

Montcault, Michel, *La basilique Sainte-Marie-Madeleine et le Couvent Royal*, Edisud, Aix-en-Provence, 1985.

Nataf, André, *The Occult*, W & R Chambers, Edinburgh, 1991; first published as *Les maîtres de l'occultisme*, Bordas, Paris, 1988.

Newman, Barbara, *From Virile Woman to WomanChrist: Studies in Medieval Religion and Literature*, University of Pennsylvania Press, Philadelphia, 1995.

Norvill, Roy, *Hermes Unveiled*, Ashgrove Press, Bath, 1986.

Oliver, Rev. George, *A Mirror for the Johannite Masons*, Richard Spencer, London, 1848.

Osman, Ahmed, *The House of the Messiah*, HarperCollins, London, 1992.

Pagels, Elaine, *The Gnostic Gospels*, Weidenfeld & Nicolson, London, 1980.

Partner, Peter, *The Murdered Magicians: The Templars and their Myth*, Oxford University Press, Oxford, 1981.

Patai, Raphael, *The Hebrew Goddess* (3rd ed.), Wayne State University Press, Detroit, 1990.

Pennick, Nigel, *Hitler's Secret Sciences*, Neville Spearmen, Sudbury, 1981.

Phipps, William E., *The Sexuality of Jesus*, Harper & Row, New York, 1973.

— *Was Jesus Married?*, Harper & Row, New York, 1970.

Picknett, Lynn and Clive Prince, *Turin Shroud: In Whose Image?*, Bloomsbury, London, 1994.

Pike, Albert, *Morals and Dogma of the Ancient and Accepted Scottish Rite of Freemasonry*, A∴M∴, Charleston, 1871.

Pope, Marvin H., *Song of Songs: A New Translation with Introduction and Commentary*, Doubleday, New York, 1983.

Qualls-Corbett, Nancy, *The Sacred Prostitute: Eternal Aspect of the Feminine*, Inner City Books, Toronto, 1988.

Rappoport, Angelo S., *Ancient Israel*, 3 volumes, Senate, London, 1995.

Redgrove, Peter, *The Black Goddess and the Sixth Sense*, Bloomsbury, London, 1987.

Reti, Ladislao (ed.), *The Unknown Leonardo*, McGraw-Hill, London, 1974.

Ricci, Carla, *Mary Magdalene and Many Others: Women who followed Jesus*, Burns & Oates, Tunbridge Wells, 1994; first published as *Maria di Magdala e le Molte Altre: Donne sul cammino di Gesù*, M. D'Auria Editore, Naples, 1991.

Riffard, Pierre, *Dictionnaire de l'ésotérisme*, Payot, Paris, 1983.

Rivière, Benoist (ed.), *Lumières nouvelles sur Rennes-le-Château*, Benoist Rivière, Lyons, 1995.

Roberts, Gay, *The Mystery of Rennes-le-Château: A Concise Guide*, Rennes-le-Château Research Group, Twylch, 1995.

Roberts, J.M., *The Mythology of the Secret Societies*, Secker & Warburg, London, 1972.

Robertson, J.M., *Pagan Christs*, Barnes & Noble, New York, 1993 (one-volume abridgement of 1903 work).

Robin, Jean, *Rennes-le-Château: la colline envoûtée*, Guy Trédaniel, Paris, 1982.

— *Le royaume du graal*, Guy Trédaniel, Paris, 1992.

Robinson, John A.T., *The Priority of John*, SCM Press, London, 1985.

Robinson, John J., *Born in Blood*, Century, London, 1990.

Romer, John, *Testament: The Bible and History*, Michael O'Mara, London, 1988.

Rudolph, Kurt *Mandaeism*, E.J. Brill, Leiden, 1978.

St Victor, Owen, *Epiphany*, Sancta Sophia, Leuvens, 1991.

Sanders, E.P., *Jesus and Judaism*, SCM Press, London, 1985.

Saul, John M. and Janice A. Glaholm, *Rennes-le-Château: A Bibliography*, Mercurius Press, London, 1985.

Schellenberger, Paul and Richard Andrews, *The Tomb of God: The Body of Jesus and the Solution to a 2,000-year-old Mystery*, Little, Brown & Co., 1996.

Schneemelcher, Wilhelm (ed.), *New Testament Apocrypha* (2 vols.), James Clarke & Co., Cambridge, 1991.

Schonfield, Hugh J., *The Essene Odyssey*, Element Books, Shaftesbury, 1984.

— *The Passover Plot*, Hutchinson, London, 1965.

— *The Pentecost Revolution*, Hutchinson, London, 1974.

Shu'al, Katan, *Sexual Magick*, Mandrake of Oxford, 1995.

Sinclair, Andrew, *The Sword and the Grail*, Century, London, 1992.

Sipra, Jean Alain, *L'architecture insolite de l'église de Rennes-le-Château*, Association Terre de Rhedae, Rennes-le-Château, 1992.

Smith, Morton, *Clement of Alexandria and a Secret Gospel of Mark*, Harvard University Press, Cambridge, Mass., 1973.

— *Jesus the Magician*, Victor Gollancz, London, 1978.

— *The Secret Gospel: The Discovery and Interpretation of the Secret Gospel according to Mark*, Gollancz, London, 1973.

Spence, Lewis, *An Encyclopaedia of Occultism*, G. Routledge & Sons, London, 1920.

Starbird, Margaret, *The Woman with the Alabaster Jar*, Bear & Co., Sante Fe, 1993.

Stewart, Desmond, *The Foreigner*, Hamish Hamilton, London, 1981.

Stoyanov, Yuri, *The Hidden Tradition in Europe*, Arkana, London, 1994.

Tarade, Guy and Jean-Marie Barani, *Les sites magiques de Provence*, Robert Laffont, Paris, 1990.

Thiede, Carsten Peter and Matthew d'Ancona, *The Jesus Papyrus*, Weidenfeld & Nicolson, London, 1996.

Tompkins, Peter, *The Magic of Obelisks*, Harper & Row, New York, 1981.

Torjeson, Karen Jo, *When Women were Priests*, HarperCollins, San Francisco, 1993.

Tyldesley, Joyce, *Daughters of Isis: Women of Ancient Egypt*, Viking, London, 1994.

U∴D∴, Frater, *Secrets of the German Sex Magicians*, Llewellyn, St Paul, 1991.

Upton, Nina, *The Valley of Pyrene*, Cassell & Co., London, 1955.

Ursin, Jean, *Création et histoire de Rite Écossais Rectifié*, Éditions Derry, Paris, 1993.

Vermes, Geza, *Jesus the Jew*, William Collins, London, 1973.

Waite, Arthur Edward, *The Hidden Church of the Holy Graal: Its Legends and Symbolism*, Rebman, London, 1909.

Walker, Barbara G., *The Woman's Encyclopedia of Myths and Secrets*, HarperCollins, San Francisco, 1983.

Wallace-Murphy, Tim, *The Templar Legacy and the Masonic Inheritance within Rosslyn Chapel*, Friends of Rosslyn, Roslin, 1994.

Webb, James, *The Occult Underground*, Open Court, La Salle, 1974.

Webb, Robert L., *John the Baptizer and Prophet*, Sheffield Academic Press, Sheffield, 1991.

Wilson, A.N., *Jesus*, Sinclair-Stevenson, London, 1992.

Wilson, Colin, *The Occult*, Hodder & Stoughton, London, 1971.

Wilson, Ian, *Are these the Words of Jesus?*, Lennard Publishing, Oxford, 1990.

— *Jesus: The Evidence*, Weidenfeld & Nicolson, London, 1984.

— *The Turin Shroud*, Penguin, London, 1979.

Wilson, R.McL., *The Gospel of Philip*, A.R. Mowbray & Co., London, 1962.

Witherington III, Ben, *Women and the Genesis of Christianity*, Cambridge University Press, 1990.

Wolff, Philippe (ed.), *Documents du l'histoire du Languedoc*, Édouard Privat, Toulouse, 1969.

Wolfram von Eschenbach, *Parzival*, (trans. A.T. Hatto), Penguin, London, 1980.

Wood, David, *Genisis: The First Book of Revelations*, Baton Press, London, 1985.

Woodford, Rev. A.F.A. (ed.), *Kenning's Masonic Cyclopaedia and Handbook of Masonic Archaeology, History and Biography*, George Kenning, London, 1878.

Yamauchi, Edwin, *Pre-Christian Gnosticism*, Tyndale Press, London, 1973.

Yates, Frances A., *The Art of Memory*, Routledge & Kegan Paul, London, 1966.

— *Giordano Bruno and the Hermetic Tradition*, Routledge & Kegan Paul, London, 1964.

— *The Occult Philosophy in the Elizabethan Age*, Routledge & Kegan Paul, London, 1979.

— *The Rosicrucian Enlightenment*, Routledge & Kegan Paul, London, 1972.

Index

Abraham 360

Abraham the Jew 230

Abraxas 135

Abydos 471

Acre 127

Acts of the Apostles 81, 326, 347, 417, 440, 446–447

Acts of Peter and Paul 421

Adam 176, 209, 430

Adamites 205

Adam Kasya 430

Adam Paghia 430

Adonis 301, 353, 354, 372

Adoration of the Magi (Leonardo) 32–33, 41, 46, 65, 158, 365, 471

Aesculapius 354

Against Heresy (Epiphanius) 419–420

Agostini, Bremna 278

Agrippa, Henry Cornelius 175, 218–219, 325, 480

Ahab, King 390

Aion 395–396

Alawites – see Nosairi

Albi 109–110, 184

Albigensian Crusade 109–110, 112–118, 133, 244, 260

alchemy, alchemists 40, 64, 106, 110, 148, 175, 202, 219, 230, 259, 282, 293, 397, 470

Freemasonry and 164–165, 170, 173

and Gothic cathedrals 147–148

in Grail romances 152–154, 157, 159–160

veneration of John the Baptist 150, 164

Knights Templar and 149–150, 161–164, 293, 467–468

Rosicrucians and 174, 181, 182–183 184–185, 216, 227

sexuality in 111–112, 148, 198–205, 207, 211–212, 218, 232, 237, 278, 282, 294, 342, 480

Alchemy (Fabricius) 198

Alet-les-Bains 110, 150, 164, 258–259, 260, 293

Alexander VI, Pope 177–178

Alexander the Great 352

Alexandria 204

alchemical, Gnostic and hermetic origins in 174–175, 202, 321, 397, 470

early Christianity in 397

and John the Baptist movement 417, 423–424, 440

Serapeum in 392–393, 397

Alpha-Galates, Ordre 53, 276

Amants, à Éléonore, Les (Labouise-Rochefort) 285

Amon 406, 451
Anand, Margot 210
Anath 111
Ancient and Accepted Scottish Rite
    of Freemasonry 192, 482
Ancient and Military Order of the
    Temple of Jerusalem 188–189
Ancient Mysteries, The (Meyer) 396
Anderson, William 214
Andraea, Johann Valentin 181–184,
    201
Andrews, Richard 240, 252, 485, 487,
    488
Anglican Church 77, 323, 325
Anhar 433
Anjou, Charles II d' 93–96, 287, 295
Anjou family 50, 96
Anjou, René d' 89, 90, 95–96, 170,
    225, 295
ankh 216, 397
Anne, St 33
Anthony of Padua, St 273, 288
Anthony the Hermit, St 243, 273,
    288
Anthroposophy 232
Antiquities of the Jews (Josephus)
    351, 403
Aphrodite, 148, 368
Apollo 218
Apollonius of Tyana 376
Apollos 417
Arabs 131, 148, 427, 428–429
Arachne 151
Aragon 137, 163
Arcadia 282–283
Arcana Arcanorum 231
Archelaus 362
Aretas, King 405
Ariège 108, 159
Aristides 386

Ark of the Covenant 130, 147, 184,
    240, 390, 472, 475
Arles 87, 282
Arques 257, 282–283
    'tomb' of 282, 283–285
Arthur, King 94, 153
Art of Sexual Ecstasy (Anand)
    210–211
Ashe, Geoffrey 352, 372, 373, 419
Asherah 390
Ashmolean Museum 166
Ashmole, Elias 166, 182
Asmodeus 270, 296
Astarte 368, 419
Atbash cipher 142
Athena 143, 201, 419
Attis 301, 340, 353, 354, 355, 373
Augustine Marie, Sister 258
Aurillac, Gerbert d' – see Pope
    Sylvester II
Aveyron 125, 230
Avignon 101

Babylon 169, 361
Bacon, Francis 181
Baigent, Michael 16, 47, 53, 54, 56,
    58, 59, 62–64, 101, 140, 147,
    155, 164, 167, 172, 188, 259,
    342
Baillard brothers 225
Balsamo, Giuseppe – see Cagliostro,
    Count Alessandro
Bannockburn, Battle of 167
Baphomet 128, 142–143, 158
baptism 345–346, 406
    of Jesus 35, 366–369, 408, 434
    John the Baptist's rite of 401–402
    in Mandaeism 428, 431
    in mystery cults 300, 354, 368,
        396

548

Baptistery, Florence 31, 400
Bar, Iolande de 225
Bauval, Robert 469
Beardsley, Aubrey 402
Becket, Thomas à 459
Bédarride brothers 231, 484
Begg, Deike 159
Begg, Ean 96–97, 101, 102, 103, 159, 222
Bell Laboratories 149
'Beloved disciple' – see John the Evangelist
Belvèze-du-Razès 257
Benedictus 413
Benjamin, tribe of 60, 61
Ben Stada 378
Bergson, Henri 234
Bernard of Clairvaux, St 116, 126, 139, 144–145, 147, 213, 292
Bertaulet, Jos 261, 262, 263
Bethany 243, 317, 319, 331–332, 333–334, 382, 387
Bethany across the Jordan 403
Bethel 279
Bethlehem 365, 371, 414
Béziers, massacre of 112–113, 117, 140, 292
Bibliothèque Nationale 54, 56
Bigou, Antoine 273, 280–281, 285
Billard, Felix-Arsène 245, 254, 261–263
Birks, Walter 119, 439
Birth of Venus (Botticelli) 207
Black Goddess, The (Redgrove) 343
Black Madonna, cult of 96–98, 103–104, 108, 161, 169, 227, 282
and Magdalene cult 96, 100–101, 106–107, 148, 282, 291–292, 323
and Isis 99–102, 103, 151, 292

and Knights Templar 106, 154–161
pagan associations of 97–100, 107, 147, 151, 161, 206, 211
and Priory of Sion 101–102, 103, 107, 225, 245, 250, 292, 341
and Song of Songs 102–103, 139, 221
and Sophia 342
Blanchefort, 'château' 273, 279
Blanchefort family 273
Blanche of Castille 118
Blois 101
Blue Penitents, Order of the 261
B'nai B'rith 276
Bogomils 120, 122, 123–124, 292
Bois, Jules 230, 233, 246
Book of Adam – see *Ginza*
Book of James 411
Book of John (Cathar) 124
Book of John (Mandaean) 429, 433
Book of Kings – see *Book of John* (Mandaean)
Book of the Dead 279, 388
Born in Blood (Robinson) 164
Botticelli 49, 206
Bouche, Madame 224
Boudet, Henri 254–255, 261, 263, 488
Bouillon, Godefroi de 69, 194
Boullan, Joseph 225–229
Bourbon, Henri de – see Chambord, Count de
Bourg de Bozas, Marquise de 275
Boyle, Robert 182, 183
Brandon, S.G.F. 396
Brethren of St John the Baptist 172, 482
Brétigny, Jacques 68–69, 285
British intelligence 4, 56

Brothers and Sisters of the Free
Spirit 205
Brothers of Christian Doctrine 225
Bruno, Giordano 39, 179, 217,
220–221, 468, 480
Brunswick, Duke of 186
Bruzeau, Antoine 288
Budapest 247
Budge, Sir E.A. Wallis 406
Bultmann, Rudolf 415, 437
Byrom, John 183
Bywaters, Charles 135–137, 140–142,
149–150, 263, 286

Cabala/cabalism 143, 153, 156, 177,
183, 187, 191, 202, 220, 235, 269
Cabala Club 183
Cabrières 230
Cagliostro, Count Alessandro 230, 483
Cagliostro, Serafina 231
Caligula 393–394
Calvé, Emma 125, 230, 236–237, 246,
248, 267–268, 276, 278, 296
Calvet, Melanie 224, 230, 269
Cana 311, 330, 365, 377
Capernaum 332
Captier, Antoine (elder) 245
Captier, Antoine (younger) 272–273,
281, 286
Captier, Claire 247, 249, 286
Captier, Marcel 281
caput 58 158
Carcassonne 110, 137, 241, 258, 266
carob tree 32, 41, 158, 471
Carpocratians 204, 318
Case, Paul Foster 234
Castille 163
Caterina 216
Cathars 15, 110, 123–124, 161, 184,
222, 223, 244, 252, 258,

260, 292–293, 294, 435, 439,
466, 473
beliefs 115–116, 119–120, 174, 418
Crusade against 109, 112–113,
116–118, 208, 450, 466
and Grail romances 155–158
view of John the Baptist 123–124
and Knights Templar 132–133,
135–136, 150, 156, 293
view of Mary Magdalene 121–122,
124, 292, 330, 466, 467
Treasure of 119, 265
Catherine, Sister – see Schwester
Katrei
Catholic Church 29, 38–39, 77, 84, 88,
148, 155, 171, 174, 175, 202,
208–211, 221–222, 228, 266, 269,
280, 289–290, 295, 313–314, 331,
341, 343, 369, 395, 441, 461–462,
474, 475
Celsus 378
Celtic Church 160
Celtic mythology/religion 152–153,
157, 161, 168, 471
Centre for Templar Studies and
Research (CERT) 134–135
Cep d'Or de Pyla 287
cercle d'Ulysse, Le 473
Chambord, Count de 245, 274
Chambord, Countess de 245, 274
Champagne, Count of 126, 153
Chartres Cathedral 45, 144, 147–149,
151, 206, 211
Châtillon 139
Chefdebien family 261, 275
Chefdebien, Marquis de 231–232, 274
Chemical Wedding of Christian
Rosenkreutz, The (Andraea)
181, 184, 201
Chevalier, Adèle 226, 230

Chevalier Bienfaisant de la Cité
Sainte 186, 274
Chinon 140
Chokmah (Wisdom) 142–143, 390,
418
Chrétien de Troyes 153–154
Christ/*Christos* 191, 336, 346, 372,
442
Christianity, 15, 16, 81, 146, 295,
311–312, 288, 462, 465,
475–479
early history 350, 356, 379
Egyptian roots of 388–389, 468,
473, 478–479
attitude to female sexuality 84,
100, 176, 330–331, 479
persecution of Jews 479
persecution of Mandaeans 428,
431, 440–441, 443
persecution of pagans 150, 479
mystery schools elements in rites
354–358, 364–365
role of women in early Church
80–81, 323–326, 330–331
Christians, The (Gascoigne) 451
Christmas 301, 364–365, 396
Church of Carmel 222, 224–227
Church of John – see Johannite
Tradition
Chuza 459
Circuit 52
Cistercian Order 126, 145, 155
Clarke, Lindsay 211
Claudius 394, 418
Clement V, Pope 128, 137, 140, 163
Clement VI, Pope 260
Clementine Recognitions 424
Clement of Alexandria 318–321
Cleopatra (alchemist) 203
Cleopatra (Queen of Egypt) 393, 445

Clermont-Ferrand 101
Clovis 62
Cocteau, Jean 43–47, 49, 52, 59–60,
65–67, 90, 105, 216, 268, 369,
471
College of Narbonne 260
Coming forth by Day – see *Book of
the Dead*
Compagnie du Saint-Sacrement 59,
246, 259
Confessio Fraternitatis 180
Confraternity of the Immaculate
Conception 34
Constant, Alphonse Louis – see
Eliphas Levi
Conte del Graal, Le (Chrétien de
Troyes) 153–154
Convocation of Venus 278
Coppens, Filip 263
Coptic Church 397
Corbin, Henry 215
Corbu, Noël 247–250, 265–267, 286
Corinth 408
Corpus Hermeticum 177, 218, 470
Couiza 239, 257, 272
Coustassa 256
Crossan, John Dominic 366
Crowley, Aleister 233, 276, 365
Crown of Nature, The 198
Cult of the Black Virgin, The (Begg)
96
*Cult of Isis among Women in the
Graeco-Roman World* (Heyob)
394
Cundrie 157
Cybele 79, 98, 102, 373

Dagobert II 50, 54, 55, 246, 459
Dali, Salvador 21
Dante Alighieri 213–215, 228

Dante the Maker (Anderson)
    214–215
David, King 62, 63, 147, 391, 445
David, Star of 234, 259
Dawe, Nicole 135–137, 140–141,
    149–150, 286, 287
Dead Sea Scrolls 130, 142, 300,
    302–303, 367, 435
Debussey, Claude 49, 229
de Chérisey, Philippe 252, 266
Dee, John 179, 183, 275
de Gaulle, Charles 53, 296
De gli eroici furori (Bruno) 217, 221
de Guaïta, Stanislas 228–229, 246
de Koker, Gaston 55
de Labouïse-Rochefort, Auguste 285
Delaude, Jean 473
Delos 372, 392
Deloux, Jean-Pierre 68–69, 285
Dénarnaud, Marie 244, 247–250, 253,
    267, 278, 487
Dendera 386
*De nobilitate et praecellentia foeminei
    sexus* (Agrippa) 218–220, 325
De occulta philosophia (Agrippa) 218
de Pasqually, Martinès 482
Descadeillas, René 247, 249
de Sède, Gérard 52, 55–56, 246, 250,
    251, 256, 265–266, 272–273
de Sède, Sophie 251
Diana 62, 87, 91, 98, 102, 111, 150,
    171, 292
Dionysus, Dionysianism 120, 218,
    301–302, 340, 354, 370, 373, 377,
    390, 393, 396
Divine Comedy (Dante) 214
Dodds, C.H. 407, 438
Dominican Order 85, 92, 93, 95, 116,
    260, 482
Domme 159

Doresse, Jean 388
Dositheus, Dositheans 424–425, 438,
    440–441, 466, 470
Dossiers secrets 54–62, 70, 172,
    181, 238, 240–241, 256, 265,
    279, 473
Douzet, André 253, 287
Drower, Lady 428, 432
Dylan, Bob 90

Eastern Orthodox Church 331,
    395–396
Eckhart, Meister 122
Eco, Umberto 125
Edward II 162–163
Egypt 144, 145, 178–179, 187, 190,
    327, 361, 367–368, 390, 419, 425,
    435, 446–447, 465–466, 468, 469,
    479, 483–484
  and alchemy 148, 175, 202–203
  early Christianity in 379, 397–398
  hermetic and gnostic origins in
    174–175, 178
  Mandaean origins in 432, 441
  religion of 178, 444–445
    influence on:
      Coptic church 397
      Gnostic Gospels 388
      gnosticism 440
      Christianity 379–380,
        476–477
      Judaism 423
      Mandaeans 431–433
      Simon Magus 421–422
      sacred sexuality in
        202–205, 340–341, 464,
        480
Egyptian Rite Freemasonry 187, 196,
    227, 231, 442, 483, 484

see also: Memphis, Rite of;
    Misraim, Rite of
Egyptian, the 446
Elect Cohens, Order of 482, 483
Elias 372, 403, 465
Elisabeth 401, 412–413, 433, 471
el Mejdel 326
Emerald Tablet 146, 178
Emmanuel Filibert, Duke of Savoy
    159
Emmaus 384
Encausse, Gerard – see Papus
Enishbai 433
Ennoia 419
Enoch 433, 434
Ephesus 408, 416, 417, 425
Epic of Gilgamesh 344
Epiphanius 419, 422
Epton, Nina 159
Eros 206
Erotic Papyrus of Turin 204
Essene Odyssey, The (Schonfield) 414
Essenes 15, 187, 302–304, 329,
    454–455, 488
Este, Isabella d' 216
Et in Arcadia ego 283, 285, 486
eucharist 22, 315, 345
    pagan parallels to 353, 377, 396
Eusebius 352
Eve 176, 210, 430
Ezekiel 327

Fabré-Palaprat, Bernard Raymond
    188–191
Fabricius, Johannes 198
Fama Fraternitatis 180
Farr, Florence 235–237
Fede Santa, La 214
Felix 446

Féral, Alain 60, 268, 273
Feugère, Pierre 55
Ficino, Marsilio 175–176, 218
fidele d'amore 214–215, 228
Fierefiz 155
Filipepi, Sandro – see Botticelli
Flamel, Nicolas 64, 148, 198, 230
Flamel, Perenelle 148, 198
Florence 31, 38, 41, 177, 400, 471
Flowers, Stephen E. 221
Fludd, Robert 49, 64, 175, 181–183,
    257
Fontaines 139
Foreigner, The (Stewart) 477
Fortune, Dion 234
Fouquet, Charles 284
Fouquet, Louis 283–284
Fouquet, Nicolas 283, 284
Francis I 48
Freemasonry 15, 49, 145, 184–185,
    270–273, 276, 370
    in England 164–166
    in France 173, 481–483
    and John the Baptist 165, 195–196,
        293–294, 400, 441–442
    and occult knowledge 165, 171,
        185, 186, 192, 470, 481–484
    origins 163–173, 192, 303, 484
    and Priory of Sion 58, 181–182
    and Rosicrucians 183–185
    women in 197, 230, 482, 484
    see also: Egyptian Rites of
        Freemasonry; Scottish Rites of
        Freemasonry; Strict Templar
        Observance
French intelligence services 57
French National Grand Lodge 482
French Revolution 222, 261, 280,
    474
furori, hermetic 217–218

Gabriel 401
Galaup, André 279
Galibert, Jean 284
Galilee 78, 326, 360–362, 365, 371, 378, 403
Gascoigne, Bamber 126, 359, 416, 451
Gau, Abbé 266
Gawain 154
Gélis, Antoine 255–256, 487
Genesis, Book of 242, 279
geometry, sacred 145, 146, 166, 168, 170, 179, 182, 183, 246, 467, 470, 486
Georgel, Anne-Marie de 110
Germaine, St 273, 288
Gethsemane 22, 253
Ghirlandaio 21
Gilbert, R.A. 119, 439
Ginza 427–428, 434, 437
Giordanisti 179
'Giovanni' 48–51, 67
Giscard 272
Gisors, Jean de 68
Gitta 418
Glastonbury 86, 94, 117, 154
Globe Theatre 179
Gnostic Gospels 81–83, 174, 313–314, 381, 388–389, 397, 440
    Mary Magdalene in 81–83, 114, 122, 205, 292, 295, 330–331, 345–348, 464, 466–467
Gnostics, gnosticism 110, 175–176, 178, 244, 251, 292–293, 429–430, 435, 440, 461, 470
    in John's Gospel 189, 311, 414–415, 427, 440
    John the Baptist as 441, 461
    Mandaeans 428–431
    and Sophia 142, 295, 345

    and sacred sexuality 203–204, 236, 422
    Simon Magus as 417
    in underground tradition 120, 157, 159–160, 174–176, 213–214, 215, 440–442, 468
Godwin, Malcolm 154, 156
Golb, Norman 302
Gold and Rosy Cross, Order of the 184, 233, 482
Golden Ass (Lucius Apuleis) 384
Golden Dawn, hermetic Order of 232–237
Golden Fleece, Order of the 170
Golden Legend 85, 159, 334
Golden Mean 145, 246
Golgotha 253
'Good Shepherd' 301, 327, 433, 437
Gospel of Mary 81, 82, 345
Gospel of Philip 191, 345, 346
Gospel of the Egyptians 458
Gospel of Thomas 82, 313, 345, 458
Gospels (canonical) 397, 454
    accuracy of 305–306, 310–311, 313–322, 331–332, 334, 449, 453–454
    dating and origins 309–313, 358–360, 437
    compared to Gnostic Gospels 83, 312–313, 388–390
Gothic architecture 45, 144–151, 183, 206–209, 211, 323, 467, 469
Gotthelf, Karl – see Hund, Baron von
Goult 101
Gozzoli 223
Grail romances 153–158, 160–161, 184, 211–212, 471
    Knights Templar in 154–157

and Johannite Tradition 160, 194
Grand Lodge of England 165, 183,
    481, 482
Grand Lodge of France 481, 483
Grand Orient 482, 484
Grat, St 106
'Great European Heresy' 257, 275,
    291–292, 293, 304
Great Questions of Mary 422
Great Revelation (Simon Magus) 421
Great Work 148–149, 198, 230, 278,
    282, 294, 342
Green Man 110, 149, 168
Greer, Mary K. 234
Guercino, Francesco 283
Guise, Charles, Duke of 257
Gulf War 428
Gumbach, Hugo of 163
Guzman, Dominic 116
gypsies 90, 169, 261

Habsburg family 50, 225
Habsburg, Johann Salvator von
    248
Hancock, Graham 16, 138, 142, 144,
    196, 469, 475
Hancox, Joy 183
Hannah 413
harmartolos 335
Harran 432, 436
Hasidim 316, 329
Haskins, Susan 77, 326
Hautpoul, Armand d' 274
Hautpoul family 280
Hautpoul, Jean-Marie-Alexandré d'
    274
Hawan Gawaita 429, 432, 434
Hawa Kasya 430–432
Hawa Paghia 430

Hebrew Goddess, The (Patai)
    389–390
Helen 419, 422–423, 461, 464
Helen of Troy 418
Helios 372, 410
Henry II 459
hermaphrodites 148–149, 421
Hermes 148, 168, 201
    Vessel of 201–202
Hermes Trismegistus 39, 146,
    175–178, 202, 218, 470
hermeticism 39, 59, 145–146, 160,
    168, 174–178, 213–214, 294, 397,
    419, 469–470
    and Freemasonry 166–167, 170
    and Gnosticism 174–176
    and Rosicrucianism 174, 181
    and sacred sexuality 215–221,
        232
    and Sabians of Harran 436
Herod Antipas 106, 111, 304–307,
    352, 362, 402–405, 408–409, 453,
    456–457, 459, 465
Herod family 86, 362, 459
Herodias 106, 111, 402, 456–457
Herod the Great 362, 375, 412, 440
Heyob, Sharon Kelly 394
*Hidden Church of the Holy Graal,
    The* (Waite) 160–161
Hidden Tradition in Europe, The
    (Stoyanov) 120
hierodule 339
Hieronymus 420–421
hieros gamos 339
Hildegard of Bingen, St 212–213
Hippolytus 420
Hiram Abiff 168, 173
Hiram Key, The (Knight & Lomas)
    16, 130–131, 303, 407
Hisler, Anne Léa 276

History of Magic (Levi) 192–193
Hiwel Ziwa 430
Hoffet, Émile 245, 247
Holy Blood and the Holy Grail, The
    (Baigent, Leigh & Lincoln) 15,
    47, 51, 52–53, 54, 56–57, 59,
    61–64, 68, 70, 84–85, 101, 187,
    239, 240, 252, 253, 266–267,
    327, 334
Holy Grail 152–153, 235, 240, 263,
    265, 439, 471, 472, 475
  and Priory of Sion 60, 61
  and Mary Magdalene 108
  and Cathars 119, 155–157
  and Knights Templars 158–161
  as symbol of bloodline 156
  – see also: Grail romances
Holy Grail, The (Godwin) 152
Holy Office 226
Holy Spirit 224, 225, 346, 376–377,
    418–420, 430, 469
Holy Vehm 276
horasis 339, 343, 422, 464
Horus 98, 190, 337, 354, 368, 369,
    395, 444
House of the Messiah (Osman) 355
Howells, Robert 271
Hugo, Victor 49
Hund, Baron von 172–173, 185–186,
    189, 230–233, 274, 481–482, 484
Hussein, Sadam 428, 439
Huysmans, J.K. 227, 246

Inexpliqué, L' 68–69
Inferno (Dante) 213
Innes, Brian 199
Innocent II, Pope 126
Innocent III, Pope 116

Innocent VIII, Pope 177
Inquisition 116, 117, 128, 135–136,
    171, 179, 208, 226, 231, 482
Invisible College 165, 182
Iohnists 196
Ireneus 413, 420, 425
Ishtar 431
Isis 68, 99–100, 119, 151, 168, 178,
    190, 202, 204, 216, 235, 292, 301,
    341, 354, 369, 385–386, 394, 419,
    423, 432, 444, 475, 478
  cult of 15, 87, 99–102, 150, 245, 282,
    292, 453
    as rival to Christianity
    385–386, 392–396
    Mary Magdalene and 373,
    380–381
  associated with Mary Magdalene
    61, 84, 101, 151, 236
  and Priory of Sion 61, 102–103,
    187, 236, 251, 292, 296, 341
  and Sophia 143, 158, 390, 419
  in Freemasonry 171–172, 186,
    231
Isis the Prophetess to her son Horus
    203
Islam 168, 209, 212, 439

Jacob 279
Jacques, Maître 173
James (apostle) 323
James the Just 356
James VI 164
Jarnac 296
Jennings, Hargrave 234
Jerusalem 126, 132, 159, 225, 254,
    279, 299, 318, 327, 333, 350, 356,
    362, 366, 375, 400, 434, 447, 475,
    488

Temple 303, 315, 356, 361, 404, 411,
425
Jesus' entry into 317, 391
Jerusalem Temple treasure 240
Jesuits 427, 431
Jesus 15, 28–29, 152, 194, 251, 295,
428, 438
aims 391–392, 397–398, 423,
445–446
anointing of 79, 251, 305–307,
331–334
baptism of 306, 337–339, 367–369,
402, 403, 408, 434
background and status 310, 365
birth stories 301–302, 412–413,
447
bloodline of 61–63, 67, 70, 85, 119,
155
body of 240, 299, 476, 485–489
Cathar view of 121
in Christian dogma 299–302, 450,
463, 476–477
Crucifixion of 62, 67, 78, 152, 353
as re-enactment of Osiris
myth 372–373, 380–384,
465
as Cynic 300, 358–360
divinity of 62, 299, 311, 314–315,
376–377, 463
parallels with dying-and-rising
gods 301, 344, 353–355, 359,
370–373
as Egyptian magician 375–379,
410, 476
and Egyptian religion 379–380,
384–385, 406, 465, 477
following:
group behind the scenes 316,
387–388, 458–460

inner and outer circles in 319,
387–388
women in 79–82
problem of historical identity
299–303, 314–317
historical existence of 349–353
as initiate of Isis/Osiris religion 85,
385–387, 391–392, 442, 448,
453, 465
and John the Baptist 306, 312,
410–411
as John's disciple 407, 433,
439–440, 448, 463
magical possession of John's
spirit 408–410, 466, 470,
471
rivalry with John 124, 305,
307–309, 405–408, 439, 448,
476
takes over John's movement
448, 453–460, 465
and John's death 455–460
and Judaism 311, 316, 357–363,
365–366
Mandaean view of 427, 430–431,
433–434, 441
marital/sexual status 84–85,
327–329
and Mary Magdalene 61–63,
70–71, 81–83, 291–292,
326–331
pagan mystery school elements in
story 357, 367–373
political aims/Messiahship
315–317, 444–445, 448–449
Resurrection 62, 78, 353, 384–385,
445
and sacred marriage 339–345, 348,
464

557

Jesus *(continued)*
  secret teachings of 318–319, 439
  survival of 381–382, 446
  in underground heretical tradition
      22–23, 28–31, 32–37, 65–66,
      122, 152–153, 190–192,
      242–243, 271–272, 294,
      441–442
Jesus (Wilson) 416
Jesus Christ Superstar (Rice & Lloyd
      Webber) 75
Jesus the Jew (Vermes) 316
Jesus the Magician (Smith) 376, 476
Jewish Revolt 302, 351, 356
Jewish War, The (Josephus) 446
Joanna 323, 459
Joan of Arc 49
Johannite Church 190
Johannite Freemasonry 195, 223, 439
Johannite Tradition 190, 214, 294,
      392, 439–442, 458, 460–461,
      468–469, 475
  and Freemasonry 192–196
  and Grail romances 160, 194
  and John the Baptist's Church 408,
      416–417, 425, 437–438,
      465–466
  and Knights Templar 69, 191,
      193–196, 467–468
  and Priory of Sion 69–71, 194,
      296
Johannites (nineteenth-century)
      222–223, 269
John, First Epistle of 310
'John gesture' 23, 31–34, 40–41, 158,
      471–472
John, Gospel of 311–312, 320–321,
      330, 332, 335, 344, 363–364,
      369, 401, 447–448, 455

Baptist source of 415–416,
      436–437, 440–441, 442–443
  dating of 312–313, 416
  gnosticism in 189, 311, 414–415,
      437, 440
  and *Levitikon* 189–191, 294
  parallels to Mandaean texts 437,
      441
  prologue to 374–375, 414–415, 437
  in underground heretical tradition
      124, 194–196, 228, 294, 439,
      442
John the Baptist 15, 116, 269, 296,
      326, 332, 346, 352, 355, 379, 447,
      463, 480
  alchemists' veneration of 150
  birth/infancy stories
      401–403, 411–413, 433, 440,
      447–448
  Cathar beliefs about 124–125
  Church of 407, 416–417, 425, 437,
      440, 442, 443
  death of 111, 304, 402–405,
      455–460, 461
  disciples of 367
  Egyptian influence on 464
  equated with Elias 372, 403, 465
  forefinger of 158, 471
  in Freemasonry 165, 171–172, 195,
      293–294, 400
  and French Johannites 222–223,
      226–227
  in Gospels 306–311, 312–313,
      336–337, 405, 417, 425–426
  as Gnostic 440
  in Grail romances 154, 158
  head of 106–107, 131–132, 158, 264,
      470, 471
  and Jesus:

baptises Jesus 305, 337, 368, 403, 408, 434

Jesus as disciple of 407–408, 444, 460, 464–465

as Jesus' forerunner 401–402, 425, 463

doubts Jesus' Messiahship 308, 408, 448

magical possession of spirit by Jesus 408–411, 465, 470

rivalry with Jesus 124–125, 307–309, 405–408, 425, 440, 476

in Johannite tradition 237, 257, 294–295, 304, 398–400, 441–442, 460, 464–465, 468, 489

confused with John the Evangelist 194–195, 293, 439, 442

and Judaism 425, 440

Knights Templar and 104, 107, 131, 150, 195, 293–294, 400

in Leonardo's works 30–38, 40–42, 67, 196, 400

Mandaean view of 428–434, 436–437

and Mary Magdalene 70–71, 304–306

as Messiah 406–407, 414, 426, 438

as miracle-worker 408

as Nazorean 439–440

popular following of 402–404, 411–412

political aims 444, 450, 453

Priory of Sion's veneration of 67–71, 131, 225, 291

'scriptures' of 412–413, 440

and Simon Magus 423–425

John the Evangelist 22–25, 65, 66, 68, 124–125, 311–312, 414–415, 417, 442

in Freemasonry 194–195, 294

in Johannite Tradition 160, 191, 194, 294

confused with John the Baptist 194–196, 293, 439–440, 442

John XXIII, Pope 49, 90, 266

Jordan 336, 401, 431, 434

Joseph (father of Jesus) 34, 299, 301, 375

Joseph (Old Testament) 371

Joseph of Arimathea 86, 152, 159, 317

Josephus, Flavius 111, 326, 352, 403, 446, 456–457

Josiah, King 390

Joyeuse family 257

Joyeuse, Henriette-Catherine de 257

Judaea 327, 361, 388, 423, 446

Judaism 209, 303, 316, 329, 362, 389, 390, 429, 435, 477

Jude, St 24, 33

Julian, Emperor 159, 425

Julius Caesar 393

Jung, C.G. 198

Justin Martyr 378, 396

Kabbalistique de la Rose-Croix, Ordre 228

karezza 211

Kellner, Karl 232

Kiess, Georges 135

King, Francis X. 236

King of Light 430, 460

King of the New Sion dethroned . . . 283

Kings College, Cambridge 183

Kloppenborg 359

Knight, Christopher 16, 131, 303, 407

Knights Hospitaller 103–104,
    163–164, 189
Knights of Christ 137
Knights of Malta 83, 104, 107, 230
Knights Templar 15, 44, 222, 466
  and alchemy 149–150, 161–164,
    293–294
  architecture 183–184, 400
  and Black Madonna cult 106, 139,
    161, 292
  and Cathars 132–133, 135–136,
    158, 292–293
  esoteric knowledge of 131, 134,
    136–138, 144, 161–164,
    182–183, 230–231, 292,
    436–437, 467–469
  and Gothic cathedrals 144–147,
    151
  and Grail 154–161, 293
  and Feminine Principle 139–140,
    143, 150, 212–216, 232, 292
  as antecedent of Freemasonry
    164–173, 185–187, 192–195,
    293–294, 484
  and Johannite Tradition 70, 160,
    190–195, 441–442, 467, 475
  veneration of John the Baptist
    104–105, 106, 125, 132,
    158–159, 164, 195, 293, 400,
    459–460, 465, 470, 471
  'inner circle' of 137–138, 142
  sites in Languedoc 112, 125,
    132, 134–135, 149–150,
    259–260
  and Mary Magdalene 139–140,
    161, 292–293
  origins 126–132, 153
  and Priory of Sion 49–50, 68–70,

    125, 130–131, 137, 194–195,
    215, 473–474
  sites in Provence 103–107, 159
  and Rosicrucians 174, 184–185,
    192–193, 294
  and Rosslyn Chapel 166–169
  and Sophia 143, 294–295, 341
  suppression 127–132, 137,
    141–142, 159, 162–163
  survival 137, 162–163, 167–168,
    189, 293
Koran 381, 428, 429
Kraeling, Carl 404, 409, 410, 413, 465
Kramer, Heinrich 208
Kundry 157
kyria 68, 419

Là-Bas (Huysmans) 227, 246
Labouré, Denis 202, 221
Lady Chatterley's Lover (Lawrence)
    85
'Lady M' 22–24, 65–66, 291
Lamb of God 131, 170
Languedoc 108–123, 130, 132,
    134–137, 149–150, 184, 238–239,
    244, 257, 259, 267, 272, 277, 288,
    293, 467
Lapasse, Vicomte de 228
Larmenius Charter 188–189, 196
Larmenius, Johannes Marcus 188
La Sagesse Lodge 228, 274
La Salette 223–224, 225, 230, 269
Last Supper 316, 333, 353, 370–371
  and Grail 152
Last Supper (Leonardo) 21–26,
    30–33, 45–46, 65–66, 152, 291,
    472
Last Temptation of Christ, The 76
Lawrence, D.H. 85

Lazarist Fathers 260
Lazarus 78, 86, 243, 278, 287, 321, 335
  raising of 311, 319, 331–332, 370, 381, 458
Le Clat 280
Leigh, Richard 16, 47, 53, 56, 58, 59, 61–63, 101, 140, 146, 155, 164, 167, 172
Leonardo da Vinci 15, 43, 45, 47, 107, 152, 228, 275, 334, 421, 480
  character and beliefs 26–27, 216
  and Christianity 25–26, 27–28, 38–39
  heretical symbolism in works 21–26, 29–38, 41–42, 59, 64–66, 149, 158, 291, 368, 471–473
  and John the Baptist 31–37, 40–41, 67, 69–70, 158–159, 195, 291, 400, 459–460, 470–472
  occult interests 38–40, 64, 145, 149, 177, 470–471
  and Priory of Sion 47–49, 53, 59–60, 63–67, 181, 207, 291
  as Rosicrucian 174, 181
  and Turin Shroud 28–31, 64, 381, 400, 471
Le Pilat 287–288
Lesbos 471
Lévi, Éliphas 191–193, 213, 228, 231
Levitikon 189–192, 294, 392, 423, 474
Libat 431
Liber Secretum – see *Book of John* (Cathar)
Lilith 111
Lincoln, Henry, 16, 47, 53, 54, 56, 58, 59, 61–63, 155, 172, 289
Lindsay, Jack 175, 204, 436
Lloyds Bank documents 56

Lloyd Webber, Andrew 75
Lodge of the Three Pillars 482
Logos 374, 414
Lomas, Robert 16, 130, 132, 303, 407
Lord's Prayer 406, 451
Lorraine 225
Lorraine, Cross of 159
Lost Gospel, The (Mack) 359
Louis IX 74, 94
Louis XIV 283
Louis XVI 222
Louis XVII 222
Lourdes 224, 269
Louvre 34, 36, 246
Lucifer 157
Lucius Apuleius 371, 384
Luckert, Karl W. 375, 385, 419, 422, 423, 477
Luculla 326
Luke, Gospel of
  dating of 311
Luke, St 273, 323
Lull, Ramon 132
Luther, Martin 179
Lyle, Jane 110, 200, 211, 212
Lyons 101, 227, 231, 287, 289–290, 483
  Convent of 186, 483

Ma'at 99, 390
Maccabean Revolt 390
Mack, Burton L. 349, 354, 359, 361, 362, 390, 477
Madone des Fenestres 106, 159
Maeterlinck, Maurice 229
Magdala 326–327
Magdolum 327
Magi 365, 377, 412
Magnificat 401, 413, 440
maithuna 205

Maledia 159
Malleus Maleficarum 208
Malleval 288
Malvern, Marjorie 122
Mandaeans 441, 466, 470
  baptism in 427, 431
  beliefs 428–431, 433–434, 441
  related to other Gnostic sects
    435–436, 439, 440
  history 427–430, 431–432, 436–437,
    440–441, 442–443
  view of Jesus 427, 433, 441–443,
    458, 460
  and John's Gospel 437, 440
  view of John the Baptist 427–434,
    436–437, 440, 453, 460
Manda-t-Haiy 433
Mani 435
Manicheans 435
Man, Myth and Magic 199, 393, 396
Mann, A.T. 110, 200, 211, 212
Man who Died, The (Lawrence) 85
Marconis de Nègre, Jacques-Étienne
  187, 232, 274, 484
Maria the Jewess 203
Marie, Franck 56, 259
Marie (Provence) 106
Mari-Ishtar 343
Mark Antony 393
Mark, Gospel of
  dating of 310–311
Mark, St 187, 318, 321
Mark, Secret Gospel of 318–321,
  331–332, 370, 458
marriage, sacred 338–344
Mar Saba 318
Martha 78, 86, 243, 278, 321, 332,
  335
Martinism 186, 227, 483
Martinist Order 484

Martin, Thomas 223
Mary Jacobi 86, 90
Mary Magdalen (Haskins) 77
Mary Magdalene 15, 216, 296, 299,
    321, 364, 433, 447, 463, 480
  as Apostle 78–79, 82, 88–91, 464
  body of 73–74, 91–93, 261,
    287–289, 306, 472
  Cathar teachings about 121,
    124–125, 466
  Catholic cult of 74, 102
  in France 61, 71–73, 85–96, 108,
    147, 151, 173, 289, 291, 334,
    446, 464
  in Gnostic Gospels 81–83, 114,
    122–123, 175, 345–347, 440
  in Gospels 77–81, 305–311, 405,
    417
  heretical cult of 202, 206, 373, 489
    and Black Madonna cult 96,
      101–103, 107, 282, 291–292
    and Holy Grail 157
    associated with Isis 61, 85, 151,
      236–237
    association with John the
      Baptist 103–107, 237, 257,
      295
    in Languedoc 108, 112–113,
      122–123, 212
    Priory of Sion's veneration of
      60–61, 71, 107, 291–292,
      341
    and Rennes-le-Château
      mystery 241–242, 248, 273,
      278
    and sacred sex tradition 237,
      282, 286, 291
  and Isis/Osiris cult 385–386, 465

and Jesus:
   anointing of Jesus 305,
      343–345
   role in Jesus movement 80–83,
      305–308, 326, 346–348
   role at Crucifixion and burial
      78–80, 306, 373, 380–382
   as wife of Jesus 61–63, 67, 70,
      156, 289–291, 327–328
   as sexual partner of Jesus
      83–85, 114, 121, 123, 292,
      330–331
   as Jesus' partner in sacred
      marriage 342–348, 422,
      463–464
   as Jesus' successor 464
identified with Mary of Bethany 63,
   78, 139, 305–306, 331–337,
   341–342
in Leonardo's *Last Supper* 22–23,
   65–66
name 81, 306, 326
as pagan priestess 63, 85, 291, 341,
   347–348
Peter's hostility towards 82, 105, 123,
   464
as prostitute 84, 335
in *Schwester Katrei* 205
and Song of Songs 102–103, 221, 291,
   343
and Sophia 143, 158, 418
traditional views of 74–77, 87–88,
   463
in underground heretical tradition
   257, 275, 290, 295, 304, 323,
   466–467
Mary of Bethany 243, 251, 321
   anoints Jesus 305, 333, 335–337
   identified with 'unnamed sinner'
      331–332

identified with Mary Magdalene
   63, 78, 139, 306–307, 333–334,
   341
as pagan priestess 335
Mary Salome 86, 89
Mary the Egyptian, St 87–88, 92
Mary, Virgin 32, 33, 65, 75, 77–78,
   81, 99–100, 140, 147, 151, 191,
   202, 206, 222–224, 229–301,
   321, 375, 386, 401, 412–413,
   440, 472, 476
   apparitions of 223, 269
Mas de la Madeleine 288
Maskim 344
Masters, R.E.L. 208
Mathers, Macgregor 233
Mathers, Moina 234
Matthew, Gospel of
   dating 311
Maximin, St 86
Mead, G.R.S. 420, 435
Medici, Cosimo de 177
Medici family 38
Medici, Lorenzo de 48, 177, 252
Memphis, Rite of 187, 231–233, 274,
   321, 484
   and Priory of Sion 187, 231
Memphis-Misraïm, Rite of 231–232
Meridiana 119, 203
Merkelbach, R. 393, 394
Merovée 62
Merovingians 50, 54–55, 60–64, 70,
   85, 102, 240, 246, 251
Mesmer, Franz Anton 184–185
Messianic Legacy, The (Baigent,
   Leigh & Lincoln) 56–57
Metz, Archbishop of 163
Meyer, Marvin W. 396
Micah, Book of 327
Migdol 327

Milan 21, 25, 34
Millau 230
Minerva 171, 221
Minne 122, 205
minnesingers 108, 122, 205–206
Mirandola, Pico della 177, 217
Miriai 434
Misraïm, Rite of 231–234, 274, 484
Mithras, mithraism 354, 396
Mitterand, François 296
Molay, Jacques de 128, 140, 172, 186, 188, 192, 193, 272, 474
Monaco 104
Mona Lisa (Leonardo) 31, 149
Montazels 239
Montbard, André de 126
Montfort, Simon de 117, 258
'Montgomery document' 63, 70–71, 334, 338
Montgomery family 50, 63
Monti, Georges 275–276
Mont Pilat 288–289
Montréal-de-Sos 159
Montsalvasch 156
Monts de la Madeleine 101
Montsegur 118–119, 124, 158, 260, 265
Monty Python's Life of Brian 75
Morals and Dogma of the Ancient and Accepted Scottish Rite of Freemasonry (Pike) 192–193
Moray, Sir Robert 182
Morgan, Lucien 278
Mormons 207
Moses 178, 360, 392
Mount Sion Abbey, Jerusalem 225
Mughtasilah 435

Nabataea 405, 432
naggar 310, 365

Nag Hammadi 81, 122, 123, 143, 175, 191, 300, 303, 313, 388, 397, 435, 458, 466, 467
Nantes Cathedral 149
Naomi 306
Napoleon 484
Narbonne 241, 260, 274, 287
Nataf, André 200
National Gallery 33–34, 37
Naündorff, Charles Guillaume 222–223, 269
Nazis 119, 265
Nazoreans 364
   John the Baptist as 438–440
   and Mandaeans 428, 438, 441
Nègre d'Ables, Marie de 273–274, 278
   grave of 248, 252, 273, 278–285, 487
Nègre family 280
Neo-platonism 219
Nepthys 98, 190
Nero 365
Newman, Prof. Barbara 123, 205, 219
New Testament, creation of 313, 319, 322, 349
Newton, Sir Isaac 49, 55, 64, 181–182, 196, 470
Nicaea, Council of 313, 322
Niven, David 104
Nodier, Charles 64, 274
Norwich Cathedral 110
Nosairi 439, 442
Nostradamus 49, 258
Notre Dame, César de 123
Notre-Dame de Confession 91
Notre-Dame de France, London 43–47, 65–66, 90, 105, 144, 151, 369
Notre-Dame de la Mer 89–90

Notre-Dame de la Paix 257
Notre-Dame de Lourdes 269
Notre-Dame de Lumières 101, 245
Notre-Dame de Marceille basilica
    259–264, 284
  underground vault at 261–264
Notre-Dame de Paris 128, 150, 296
Notre-Dame de Sion, Ordre de 225
Notre-Dame de Souterrain 151
Notre Dame, Michel de – see
    Nostradamus
Nostrim 364

Oeuvre de la Misericorde – see
    Church of Carmel
Olier, Jean-Jacques 259
Or de Rennes, L' (de Sede) 251
ordination of women 77, 219,
    324–325, 367
Origen 352, 424
Originel L' 202
*Origins of Alchemy in Graeco-
    Roman Egypt, The* (Lindsay)
    175, 436
Ormus 187, 194, 321
Orphée (Cocteau) 43, 471
Orpheus 471
Osiris 85, 98–99, 169, 190–191,
    203, 292, 340–341, 344, 377,
    393–395, 406, 433, 444–445,
    451, 469, 478
  cult of 15, 191, 442
  parallels to Jesus 302, 353–355,
    369–373, 379–381, 396
Osman, Ahmed 355–356, 387, 407
OTO – see Templars of the Orient,
    Order of
Otranto, Giorgio 324

Pagan Christs (Robertson) 353–354
Papus 230, 231, 246, 484
Parsifal (Wagner) 157
Parthians 432
Parzival (Wolfram) 155–158, 194, 211
Passover Plot, The (Schonfield) 316,
    355, 363, 382
Patai, Raphael 390
Paul, St 79, 81, 84, 191, 314, 350,
    353, 356, 358, 408, 416–417,
    446–447, 461
Pavillon, Nicolas 259
Payens, Hugues de 126, 130–131,
    167, 192, 228
Peasants' Revolt 164
Pech Cardou 485, 486
Péladan, Joséphin 228–229, 237, 246,
    273–274
Pennick, Nigel 184
Pentecost 347
Peraea 403, 404, 432
Peredur 153, 157
Perella, Ramon de 156
Perilla 156
Perlesvaus 154
Peste d'Azoth, La (Poussin) 472
Peter, St 26, 78, 81–82, 160, 190, 223,
    305, 323, 348, 353, 418, 421, 433
  hostility to Mary Magdalene 82,
    105, 123, 341, 345, 446, 464
Pharisees 360, 454–455
Philadelphes 232
Philadelphians 232, 274
Philip (apostle) 316, 365, 418
Philip (half-brother of Herod) 402,
    405
Philippe, Duke of Orleans 189
Philip the Fair 128, 137, 214
Phillippa 326
Philo of Alexandria 374

Philosopher's Stone 157
Phipps, William E. 333, 335
Phoenicia 418
photography 28–29, 40
Pike, Albert 192–194
Pilate, Pontius 328, 336, 351–352, 362, 377, 446, 463
Pinhas ben Yair 329
Pistis Sophia 82, 143, 175, 295, 346, 388, 419, 430, 435, 440, 459–460, 470
Pius X, Pope 261
Plantard de Saint-Clair, Pierre 53, 60, 62, 68–71, 102, 167, 196, 240, 251, 255–256, 265–267, 275, 283–284, 294, 460, 473
Plantard de Saint-Clair, Thomas 53
Plato, platonism 31–32, 146, 394
Pliny the Younger 351
Poher, Alain 296
Pope, Marvin H. 343
Poussin, Nicolas 21, 283–285, 472, 486
Prester John 155
Prieuré de Sion – see Priory of Sion
Prince, Clive 262
Prince, Keith 28, 262, 279
Priory of Sion 15, 48, 59–60, 89, 105, 155, 198, 207, 217, 225, 236, 246, 473–474
  aims 50, 54–55, 63–72, 240
  view of Jesus 67, 70, 294, 381
  and Black Madonnas 102–103, 107, 245–246, 250, 292, 341
  and Compagnie du Saint-Sacrement 246, 259
  and Isis 102, 187, 236, 250, 292, 294–295, 342
  and bloodline of Jesus 61, 63, 67, 85, 155

  and Johannite Tradition 70, 194–196, 296, 440, 441
  veneration of John the Baptist 67–71, 107, 132, 291, 293, 459–460, 475
  history 48–49, 58–60
  and Knights Templar 49, 69, 125–126, 130–131, 138–139, 173, 187, 196, 215–216, 474, 475
  and Mary Magdalene 60–61, 70–71, 74, 102, 105–106, 122–123, 237, 250, 291–292, 295, 307, 323, 341, 474–475
  modern existence 49–54, 266
  and occult 64, 148, 470
  and Ormus 187, 194, 232, 321
  paradoxical nature 55–58
  plans 69–70, 473–475
  political connections 295–296
  and Rennes-le-Château mystery 238, 240, 256, 265–266, 275
  and Rosicrucians 181–182
  and Strict Templar Observance 196
  titles and grades 67–68, 152, 293
prostitution, sacred 339, 343
Protestantism 39, 115, 349, 369
Protoevangelium 411
Proust, Marcel 229
Provence 86, 87, 89, 101, 103–108, 112, 122, 150–151, 155, 159, 212, 261, 287–288, 484
Provence, Count of 130
Provence, Kyot de 155
Proverbs, Book of 142
Provins, Guiot de 155
Ptah 204, 432
Ptahil 430, 432
Pythagoras 145

Q 359, 437
Qualls-Corbett, Nancy 341, 342
Queen of the South 111
Quested, Dr Digby 149
Queste del San Graal 155
Qumran 302–303

Ra 368
Rahn, Otto 265
Ramsay, Andrew Michael 171, 189
Raphael 31
Raymond VI, Count of Toulouse 116
Raymond Trencavel I 113
Rectified Scottish Rite of
    Freemasonry 173, 227, 261, 274,
    278
  creation of 187, 272–273, 483–484
  links with Egyptian Rites 187, 221,
    484
  and Bérenger Saunière 272–275
Redgrove, Peter 205–206, 343
Reformed Scottish Rite of
    Freemasonry 483
Reine Pedauque 119
Renaissance
  occult influence on 38, 143–144,
    176–179, 418
  Rosicrucianism and 173–174, 176
Rennes-le-Château 230, 260, 264, 285,
    287–289, 295, 296, 323
  mystery of 239–254, 255–258,
    265–266, 268–274, 278–281
  parchments of 240, 251–253,
    265–266, 279, 485–486
  and Priory of Sion 54, 60, 238,
    240–241, 278–279
  'treasure' of 239, 253–254, 284
  and 'tomb of Jesus' 485–489

*Rennes-le-Château: capitale secrète
    de l'histoire de France* (Deloux
    & Brétigny) 68–69, 285, 474
Rennes-les-Bains 135, 254, 255,
    256
Repanse de Schoye 155
Reuss, Theodore 232
Revelation, Book of 68, 386
Rex Mundi 251
Rhedae 241, 282
Rice, Tim 75
Richter, Sigmund 184
Riviera, Cesare della 202
Rivière, Polycarpe de la 288
Robertson, J.M. 353–354, 355
Robert the Bruce 167, 170
Robin, Jean 55, 138, 266, 272
Robinson, John J. 164, 166
Roché, Déodat 258
Roche, St 243
Romer, John 422–423
Roncalli, Angelo – see Pope John
    XXIII
Roquebillière 106
Rosamerta 225
Rose-Croix, du Temple et du Graal,
    Ordre de la 228, 273–274
Rosenkreutz, Christian 180, 182
Rose of Ruby and the Cross of Gold
    233
rose, symbolism of 151, 205–206, 211
rose windows 150–151, 206
'Rosicrucian Brothers of the East'
    186
Rosicrucianism 174–176, 180–185,
    193, 215–216, 227, 230–231, 270,
    484
  and Freemasonry 166, 183–185,
    187, 482

Rosicrucianism *(continued)*
   manifestos 64, 180–183
   and Priory of Sion 57–58, 63–64
Rosicrucians: Their Rites and
     Mysteries, The (Jennings) 234
Rospigliosi, Cardinal 283
Rosslyn Chapel 166–170
Rosslyn-Hay Manuscript 170
Roussillon 137, 288
Roussillon, Béatrix de 287
Roussillon, Gérard de 287
Roussillon, Guillaume de 287
Royal Society 165, 182, 183
Rudolph, Kurt 434, 436
Ruha 430, 434
Rustici, Giovan Francesco 31, 400
Ruth 306

Sabians
   Mandaeans 428–429
   of Harran 436
Sacred Prostitute, The (Qualls-
    Corbett) 341
Sacred Sexuality (Mann & Lyle) 200,
   211
St Andrew's church, Alet-les-Bains
   258
St Anne's church, Arques 257
Saint-Bertrand-de-Comminges 111
St Clair, Catherine 167
St Clair family – see Sinclair family
St Clair, Sir William (15th century)
   168, 169
St Clair, Sir William (14th century)
   168, 216
Saint-Dalmas 106
Sainte-Baume 87, 91–92, 173, 289
Sainte-Croix-en-Jarez 287–288

Sainte-Madaleine (Provence) 106
Sainte-Madeleine chapel, Le Pilat
   287–288
Sainte-Marie-Madeleine abbey,
   Vézelay 94
Sainte-Marie-Madeleine church, Aix-
   en-Provence 101
Sainte-Marie-Madeleine church,
   Azille 260–261
Sainte-Marie-Madeleine church,
   Rennes-le-Château 240–243,
   257, 268–273, 278–281, 289
Sainte-Marie-Madeleine church,
   Troyes 153
Saintes-Maries-de-la-Mer 86–87,
   89–90, 96, 100, 105, 282
St Hilaire, Abbey of 260
St Hospice Chapel 104
St-Jean-Cap-Ferrat 104–106
St Jean (Provence) 104
St John's Christians – see Mandaeans
St John of Malta, Aix-en-Provence
   103
St John's fort, Marseilles 91, 103
St John the Baptist church, Couiza
   257, 272
St John the Baptist church, Sion-
   Vaudémont 225
St John the Baptist (Leonardo) 31, 41
St Lazarus, Order of 171, 189
St-Martin-du-Vésubie 106, 159
Saint Martin, Louis-Claude de 186,
   228, 483
Saint-Maxent, Louis 55
Saint-Maximin-la-Sainte-Baume
   73–74, 87, 92–94, 261, 287–288
St Odile 225
St Omer, Godefroi de 131
St Omer, Lambert de 131
St Paul's Cathedral, London 169

St Paul's Churchyard 183
St Peter's Chapel, Villefranche-sur-
    Mer 105
St Saveur's church, Aix-en-Provence
    101
St Sulpice, Paris 150, 224, 246, 259
St Victor's abbey, Marseilles 91, 101
Sais 386
Salome (daughter of Herodias) 106,
    111, 402, 456–457
Salome (Jesus' disciple) 321, 323, 458
Salome (Strauss) 402
Salon of the Rose + Cross 41, 228,
    471
Samaria, Samaritans 361, 363, 391,
    418, 425, 440, 465
Sandri, Gino 71
sangraal 156
San Francesco Grand 34
San Leo 231
Santa Maria delle Grazie 21, 24
Sarah the Egyptian, St 86, 90
Sassanids 432
Saul, John 123
Saunière, Alfred 247–248, 275, 277
Saunière, Bérenger 230, 239–251,
    252–261, 264–272, 277–289,
    292, 295, 323, 485–489
  and Priory of Sion 256, 275
  and Rectified Scottish Rite 272
Saviours of Louis XVII 222–223
Schaeder, H.H. 437
Schellenberger, Paul 240, 252
Schmithals, W. 437
Schonfield, Hugh J. 158, 316, 317,
    333, 355, 366, 371–372, 382,
    384, 406, 414, 419, 438, 446,
    459
School of Athens (Raphael) 31
Schwartz, Lillian 149

Schweizer, E. 437
Schwester Katrei 122–123, 205, 292,
    146–147
Scorsese, Martin 76, 84
Scottish Rite Freemasonry 173, 192,
    196, 481–483
  – see also: Ancient and Accepted
    Scottish Rite; Rectified
    Scottish Rite: Reformed
    Scottish Rite
Secret Gospel, The (Smith) 458
Serapeum 392–393
Serapis 393
Serpent rouge, Le 55–56, 60, 236–237
Serres 285
Set 98, 190
sex magic 232, 278
sexuality, sacred 200, 210
  and alchemy 148–149, 198–205,
    207, 211, 219, 232, 237, 294,
    342, 480
  in ancient Egypt 204
  in Gnostic sects 205, 236, 318
  and Mary Magdalene 338–348
  and Simon Magus 420, 423
  in underground tradition 160–161,
    205, 211–237, 281–282,
    285–286, 293, 468–469
Shakespeare, William 179, 221
Shakti 346
Shaw, George Bernard 235
Sheba, Queen of 102, 149
Shepherds of Arcadia, The (Poussin)
    283–285, 485–486
Shu'al, Katan 233
Sicambrian Franks 61
sicarii 444

Sidra d'Yahya – see *Book of John* (Mandaean)

Sign and the Seal, The (Hancock) 16, 138, 142, 475

Simon Magus 376, 410, 417–419, 434, 438, 440–441, 461, 464, 470
   attacked by early Church 417–418, 419–421, 425
   influence of Egyptian religion on 422–423
   parallels to Jesus 420–423
   disciple of John the Baptist 424
   John's the Baptist's successor 444, 448, 459–460, 463, 465

Simon of Cyrene 381

Simon Peter – see Peter, St

Simon the Leper 322

Simon the Zealot 317, 454–455

Simpson, Elaine 235

Sinclair family 167, 169

Sinclair, Niven 143, 169

Sion 327

Sion, Switzerland 188

Sion-Vaudémont 101, 225

Sisters of the Sacred Heart 257, 264

Smith, Morton 318, 320, 321, 332, 360, 365, 368, 376, 379, 409, 410, 435, 458, 463, 465, 471, 478

Smith, Sir William Sydney 189

Societas Rosicruciana in Anglia 223

Société Angélique 288

Society for the Reparation of Souls 225

Solomon 147, 391

Solomon, Seal of 234

Solomon, Temple of 130, 143, 145, 147, 166, 173, 182, 184, 244, 271, 273, 390, 400, 445

Song of Songs 102–103, 139, 155, 221, 340, 343, 371

Son of the Widow 168, 187, 270

Sophia 210, 294–295, 340, 342, 374, 390, 419, 469–470
   and Knights Templar 142, 150, 158–159
   in Judaism 142
   and Mary Magdalene 143, 158, 295, 345–346
   and Isis 143, 158, 295
   in western esoteric tradition 186, 214–215, 220–221, 228

Soubirous, Bernadette 224

Soubise, Father 173

Spartacus 351

Spence, Lewis 182

spikenard 332, 335, 338, 340, 343, 381

Sprenger, Jakob 208

Starbird, Margaret 327, 340

Steiner, Rudolf 232

Stephenson, John 284, 285

Stewart, Desmond 368, 369, 370–371, 375, 477

Stevens, Ethel – see Drower, Lady

Stoker, Bram 232

stonemasons' guilds 144, 146, 166, 171–172, 173

Stoyanov, Yuri 120, 122

Strasbourg 122

Strauss, Richard 402

Strega, La (della Mirandola) 217

Strict Templar Observance 172–173, 186, 189–190, 196, 231–233, 481–483, 484
   becomes Rectified Scottish Rite 185–186, 484

Stuart, Charles Edward 481

Stuart dynasty 183, 481

Subbas 428

Suetonius 351–352
Sufism 212, 214, 435
Sulpice, St 246
Sun Club 183
Sydney, Sir Philip 179, 217
Sylvester II, Pope 111, 203

Tacitus 350
Ta'eb 363
Talmud 375–376, 377–378, 441, 460, 463
Tammuz 169, 301, 340, 343, 370, 371, 372, 433
Tantrism 199–202, 207–212, 231–232, 278, 294, 343–344
Taoism 199–202, 343
Tarot 156
Tempest, The (Shakespeare) 179
Templars of the Orient, Order of (OTO) 232, 276
Temple and the Lodge, The (Baigent & Leigh) 16, 140, 146, 164
Temple Bar 127
Temple Church, London 184
Temple Fortune 127
Temple Meads 127
Temple of Satan, The (de Gauïta & Wirth) 228
Templiers sont parmi nous, Les (de Sède) 52
Terribilis est locus iste 242, 268
Testament (Romer) 422
Teutonic Knights 163
Thaddeus, St 24, 33
Thecla, St 159
Theodora, Bishop 324
Theodore 318–319
Theodore bar Konai 438
Thiering, Barbara 457
Tiberius, Emperor 393

Tomb of God, The (Andrews & Shellenberger) 240, 485
Tompkins, Peter 234
Torjeson, Karen Jo 324
Tour Magdala 241–243, 268, 278, 296
Treasure of Montségur, The (Birks and Gilbert) 119, 439
Tristan 211
Tristan and Isolde 211
troubadours 108, 122, 151, 205–206, 211, 214, 236, 292
Troyes 153
   Council of 126
Troyes, Fulk de 129
Trypho 378
Turin Shroud 27–32, 40–41, 48–50, 59, 64–65, 70, 73–74, 381, 400, 471, 472, 475, 488
Tyre 86, 418

Unexplained, The 68, 101, 199
'unnamed sinner'
   identified with Mary of Bethany 331–337
   identified with Mary Magdalene 78, 334
Uriel 34, 36
Utelle 106, 150
Utriusque cosmi historia (Fludd) 182

Vaincre pour une jeune chevalerie 53
Valley of Pyrene, The 159
Vaudémont, Ferri de 225
Vaughan, Thomas 216, 220
Vaux-de-Cernat, Pierre des 112–113
Vella, Marcus – see Monti, Georges
Venanson 106

Venus 99, 151, 212, 218, 220, 235, 236, 278
Vermes, Geza 300, 309, 316, 328–329, 406, 414
Vézelay 94, 287
Vichy 101
Vielle Major cathedral, Marseilles 90
Vignère, Blaise de 252
Villa Bethania 241–243, 247–249, 258, 265, 275
Villefranche-sur-Mer 104–105
Vincent de Paul, St 259
Vintras, Eugène 222–224, 269
Virgin and Child with St Anne (Leonardo) 33, 472
Virgin of the Rocks (Leonardo) 34–37, 41, 368, 460
Visigoths 241, 248, 250
Vitruvian Man (Leonardo) 145
Voisins, Guillaume de 260
Voragine, Jacobus de 85, 159
Voyage à Rennes-les-Bains (Labouïse-Rochefort) 285
Vraie langue celtique et le cromleck de Rennes-les-Bains (Boudet) 254–255, 261, 263

Wagner, Richard 157
Waite, A.E. 160–161, 192–195
Walker, Barbara G. 111, 150, 201
Walker, Benjamin 199
Wallace-Murphy, Tim 168–169
Way, Captain 53
Webb, Robert L. 404
Westcott, W. Wynn 233
Westminster Abbey 367

When Women Were Priests (Torjeson) 324–325
whore wisdom 207, 282, 341–342, 419
Wilde, Constance 233
Wilde, Oscar 229, 233, 402
Wilhelmsbad, Convent of 186, 274
Willermoz, Jean-Baptiste 483
William of Tyre 130
Wilson, A.N. 310, 358, 365, 387, 416, 417
Wirth, Oswald 228–229
Wisdom – see Sophia
Wise Men – see Magi
Witchcraft Act 221
witch trials 110, 208, 220, 244–245, 450
Witterschein, George 324
Wolfram von Eschenbach 155–158, 194, 211
Woman with the Alabaster Jar, The (Starbird) 327

Yahweh 209–210, 366, 367, 378, 386, 389, 390, 480
Yamauchi, Edwin 415
Yates, Dame Frances 39, 174, 178, 180–181, 182, 217
Yeats, W.B. 229, 233, 235

Zacharias 401, 412, 433
Zakhria 433
Zechariah, Book of 317
Zen Buddhism 364
Zeus 99, 146
Zoroastrianism 120

THE PROPHECIES OF NOSTRADAMUS
by Erika Cheetham

Four hundred years ago Michel de Nostredame sat alone in a dark, secret room studying the forbidden books on the practices of witchcraft and the occult. By his side stood a brass tripod and placed on that was a simple bowl of water. But the water shimmered and grew cloudy and from within its depths came visions of the past and the future . . . visions which told of the Great Fire of London , the Second World War, air travel, and even the assassinations of John and Robert Kennedy.

0 552 09828 0

JESUS THE MAN
by Barbara Thiering

'The impact of *Jesus the Man* . . . may be as profound as that of Darwin's *Origin of the Species* on theories of human origins'
Focus

Jesus was the leader of a radical faction of Essene priests. He was not of virgin birth. He did not die on the Cross. He married Mary Magdalene, fathered a family, and later divorced.
    He died sometime after AD64.

This controversial version of Christ's life is not the product of a mind which wants to debunk Christianity. Barbara Thiering is a theologian and a biblical scholar. But after over twenty years of close study of the Dead Sea Scrolls and the Gospels she has developed a revolutionary new theory, which, while upholding the fundamental faith of Christianity, challenges many of its most ingrained supernaturalist beliefs.

Jesus the Man will undoubtedly upset and even outrage those for whom Christianity is immutable and unchallengeable. But for many who have found the rituals of the contemporary church too steeped in medieval thinking, it will provide new insights into Christianity in the context of the 1990s.

'[The] sensational nature [of the book's assertions] may disguise the strength of the research and scholarship which Thiering has displayed in the course of her narrative'
Peter Ackroyd, *The Times Saturday Review*

'Some will see her as an anti-Christ, a mischievous scholar determined to destroy Christianity. To others she will be a source of comfort and peace enabling them to live Christian lives without having to accept as fact Jesus's divinity, his miracles, the virgin birth and resurrection'
The Australian Magazine

0 552 13950 5

THE BOOK THAT JESUS WROTE
by Barbara Thiering

If Jesus did not die on the cross, as Dr Barbara Thiering has maintained in her two previous books, *Jesus the Man* and *Jesus of the Apocalypse*, what was his role in the years following 33 AD, and what part did he play in the religious movement we now call Christianity?

In *The Book that Jesus Wrote*, the author takes yet another bold, controversial step in her unravelling of the New Testament, suggesting that the Book of John was the work of Jesus himself, assisted by his Gentile friend Philip. His sense of humour, the recollection of his own life and his struggle to move away from strict Judaism and to open the door for a new religious philosophy and structure all emerge as clues in his writing.

The result is a clear and rational explanation of how Christianity came into being, and how Jesus himself was an active and inspirational figure behind its emergence both in the East and in Rome, and later in Western Europe.

0 552 14665 X

A SELECTION OF RELATED TITLES
AVAILABLE FROM CORGI BOOKS

THE PRICES SHOWN BELOW WERE CORRECT AT THE TIME OF GOING TO PRESS. HOWEVER TRANSWORLD PUBLISHERS RESERVE THE RIGHT TO SHOW NEW RETAIL PRICES ON COVERS WHICH MAY DIFFER FROM THOSE PREVIOUSLY ADVERTISED IN THE TEXT OR ELSEWHERE.

☐ 99065 5	THE PAST IS MYSELF	*Christabel Bielenberg*	£7.99
☐ 99469 3	THE ROAD AHEAD	*Christabel Bielenberg*	£7.99
☐ 99965 2	BLACK HAWK DOWN	*Mark Bowden*	£6.99
☐ 14493 2	THE JIGSAW MAN	*Paul Britton*	£6.99
☐ 09828 0	THE PROPHECIES OF NOSTRADAMUS	*Erika Cheetham*	£5.99
☐ 15027 4	THE GOD SQUAD	*Paddy Doyle*	£6.99
☐ 12833 3	THE HOUSE BY THE DVINA	*Eugenie Fraser*	£8.99
☐ 14164 X	EMPTY CRADLES	*Margaret Humphreys*	£8.99
☐ 14544 0	FAMILY LIFE	*Elisabeth Luard*	£7.99
☐ 14594 7	STILL LIFE	*Elisabeth Luard*	£6.99
☐ 13356 6	NOT WITHOUT MY DAUGHTER	*Betty Mahmoody*	£6.99
☐ 13953 X	SOME OTHER RAINBOW	*John McCarthy & Jill Morrell*	£6.99
☐ 14127 5	BRAVO TWO ZERO	*Andy McNab*	£6.99
☐ 14137 2	A KENTISH LAD	*Frank Muir*	£7.99
☐ 14288 3	BRIDGE ACROSS MY SORROWS	*Christina Noble*	£6.99
☐ 14632 3	MAMA TINA	*Christina Noble*	£5.99
☐ 14607 2	THE INFORMER	*Sean O'Callaghan*	£6.99
☐ 14303 0	THE HOT ZONE	*Richard Preston*	£5.99
☐ 14550 5	PURPLE SECRET	*John Röhl, Martin Warren & David Hunt*	£7.99
☐ 13378 7	MIND TO MIND	*Betty Shine*	£6.99
☐ 13671 9	MIND MAGIC	*Betty Shine*	£6.99
☐ 13998 X	MIND WAVES	*Betty Shine*	£5.99
☐ 13950 5	JESUS THE MAN	*Barbara Thiering*	£7.99
☐ 14665 X	THE BOOK THAT JESUS WROTE	*Barbara Thiering*	£6.99

All Transworld titles are available by post from:

Bookpost, P.O. Box 29, Douglas, Isle of Man IM99 1BQ

Credit cards accepted. Please telephone 01624 836000,
fax 01624 837033, Internet http://www.bookpost.co.uk or
e-mail: bookshop@enterprise.net for details.

Free postage and packing in the UK. Overseas customers allow
£1 per book (paperbacks) and £3 per book (hardbacks).